THE EMERGENT AMERICAN SOCIETY
LARGE-SCALE ORGANIZATIONS
VOLUME 1

Each volume in
The Emergent American Society
is complete in itself,

VOLUME 1

THE EMERGENT AMERICAN SOCIETY
Large-Scale Organizations

EDITOR W. Lloyd Warner
ASSISTANT EDITORS Darab B. Unwalla
John H. Trimm
AUTHORS June M. Collins
George D. Downing
Robert J. Havighurst
William E. Henry
Desmond D. Martin
Frank C. Nall, II
John H. Trimm
Darab B. Unwalla
W. Lloyd Warner
Gibson Winter

New Haven and London
Yale University Press
Nineteen sixty-seven

Published with assistance from the foundation established
in memory of James Wesley Cooper of the
Class of 1865, Yale College, and from the
Louis Stern Memorial Fund.

TO ALFRED L. SEELYE

PREFACE

Since its beginning the American society has grown and expanded enormously. More importantly, during this period the nature of the system has been transformed. A slowly changing traditional culture has become a rapidly changing system to the point that, paradoxically, to be what it is, our society is in continual process of becoming something different. In this process new social forms emerge, old ones modify their forms, change their traditional functions, and acquire new meanings. One of the more significant and important of these developments is the emergence of many varieties of large-scale organizations on which the society increasingly depends.

This volume, a collaboration of research experts and a product of their knowledge and present research, studies the several varieties of large-scale organizations. Its chapters present analyses of the evidence about types of great organizations and the changes that are modifying what these strucures are and what they do. The reader will immediately see that the book is not a collection of separate essays written by separate authors; rather it will be clear that all chapters are integral parts of the larger enterprise whose purpose is to understand such structures as big corporations, big government, big unions, religious, educational, and other large organizations, and also to see each of them as a part of the changing life of America. In brief, while each chapter is written by an individual author (or by coauthors), all chapters are also products of a common research collaboration.

The research and writing for this volume and the one that will follow (each complete in itself) could not have been undertaken without the generous financial support of the Carnegie Corporation. I wish to take this opportunity to thank them for their generosity and their staff for many valuable suggestions. I wish also to thank Michigan State University and the College of Business and Public Administration for their support, including such benefits as the salaries of research technicians and assistants. In particular I wish to thank my friend Dean Alfred L. Seelye, of the School of Business, for his strong and active interest in the work we are doing and for his constant encouragement. I have taken the liberty of dedicating this volume to him.

I am deeply indebted to the several collaborators and authors whose names appear on the title page and on the first page of each chapter. Each supplied an invaluable understanding of his subject

Preface

and contributed fresh research for his chapter. I think I should also say here publicly what I feel privately, that all of them performed their tasks so ably and willingly that few if any of the difficulties that usually arise in collaboration of many authors occurred in this study. As the work progressed, Dr. Darab Unwalla and Professor John Trimm assumed many functions and took on many activities that contributed substantially to the successful completion of the research. Their names accordingly appear as editors as well as authors.

. At the very beginning colleagues included Dr. Orvis Collins and Dr. Norman Martin; at a later period John Jackson made many valuable contributions to our research on national associations and was included as an assistant author of the chapter on these organizations.

A considerable number of professional and technical research assistants aided in various periods of the work. Among them were: Guvenc Alpander, John Barkham, Roger Benjamin, John Demaree, Michael Ferrari, Don Isaacson, William Kearney, David McCauley, Carolyn McManaman, John Maurer, Joyce Messenger, Thomas Natiello, Anant Negandhi, Ruth Robinson, James Shrier, Robert Trudeau, Morey Villareal, William Voiers, and Raymond Weinstein.

The authors are also indebted to the careful editing by Mildred Hall Warner and by the talented staff of Yale University Press.

All acknowledgments for help received, such as in this case, by their very nature are pale and inadequate. They can never tell fully how much was contributed not only by the people and institutions mentioned but by others who gave their understanding and their support to the achievement of the purposes of the work.

East Lansing, Michigan
April, 1967

W. Lloyd Warner,
Director

CONTENTS

Chapter 8

Chapter 13

Chapter 14

LIST OF CHARTS

LIST OF FIGURES

CHAPTER ONE

Introduction

THE EMERGENCE OF THE NATIONAL SOCIETY

In less than two hundred years the United States has changed from an awkward confederation of newly independent colonies, with a population of four million people spread thinly along one coastline, to a great continental community, approaching two hundred million in population and reaching across three thousand miles of land and water from the Atlantic to the Pacific Ocean. The original thirteen states have segmented, multiplied, and grown to fifty. The vast, amorphous wilderness of forests, prairies, and deserts that once extended from the eastern Appalachian frontier, across the Mississippi, over the Rockies to the Sierra Nevada and the Pacific has been transformed and domesticated. A folklike agricultural economy, 95 per cent rural in 1790, has become an urban, industrial community. A few little towns and two small cities have multiplied into thousands of urban communities, two dozen of them great metropolitan centers with a million or more inhabitants.

In the present volume, based largely on original research, we are concerned with the important varieties of large-scale organization that are part of the vast system of the contemporary national community—what is here called the emergent American society.[1] We will examine their size and condition and their emergent processes. We will analyze some complex corporations, the evolution of

This chapter is by W. Lloyd Warner. See Notes on Authors.

1. W. Lloyd Warner, *The Corporation in the Emergent American Society* (New York, Harper & Brothers, 1961). Some of the ideas and a few paragraphs that appear in this chapter were printed in this earlier volume. They were taken from an interim memorandum written to help guide the research on large-scale organizations and the emergent society. The earlier book came from three lectures I gave as Ford Distinguished Visiting Professor at the School of Commerce, Accounts and Finance, New York University.

1

dominant big government, and the powerful worlds of big education and other hierarchical organizations that are the "bony structure" of the great society that now exists. We will also describe the structural developments of organized religion—Protestant, Catholic, and Jewish—of trade and professional organizations, and of labor unions. These and other complex, hierarchically formed institutions are vital parts of the emergent processes and perform functions necessary for maintaining the integrity of the developing national community.

This volume is limited entirely to large organizations and their place in American society; a second volume will be concerned with more general social, economic, and technological processes that contribute to the developing society, such as the interdependent industrial-agricultural revolutions, the submersion of local communities into one national society, and the use of the traditional past by a society that increasingly innovates its future.

During the western migration of the American society thousands of local communities appeared and developed individual autonomies. Many have lost part of their full independence, but this loss is only one movement in a larger transition in which the more significant development is the coming into being of a primary national community. American society is rapidly growing into one great community, in which corporations, the state, and other structures play their significant roles. Change is built into the very nature of this social system, and in fact most innovations originate within it. To maintain order and still change, this society incorporates the persistent past into its moving future.

As part of this process the rationality of science and technology seeps through the values, beliefs, and practices of the national society. Meanwhile, opposing powerful, nonrational moral values also grow, strengthen, become public opinion, and find expression more and more firmly at the national level in Washington. There they are given ultimate legal sanction in the form of rapidly developing institutions that embody the understanding and opinion that make up our growing national life. There the secular part of the moral order, through the instruments of federal law and its agencies and through the reinforcements of national opinion, confronts the nonmoral demands of technology, science, and the marketplace.

Corporate hierarchies, most of which are located in a few large metropolitan economic centers, and big government, primarily centered in one political metropolis, along with other complex organizations, such as the churches, schools, unions, and trade associations, are themselves products of this same process. They are integral parts of the growing structure of the primary American community.[2]

The Growth of Cities

We can easily delineate some of the changes in the development of the American society. The human biological base has grown very rapidly—from about four million at the time of the first census in 1790 to some 190 million (180 million in 1960, the time of the last census), an increase of about forty-five times. The feeding base for the population has grown from 800,000 to three million square miles, an increase of three to four times. Twenty-four small towns and cities, most of which had fewer than five thousand population in 1790, have multiplied to over five thousand urban centers. Two hundred twelve of these are metropolitan regions, where the viable community extends far beyond the central incorporated city. Forty-six states have such regions. Ten regions have over two million and fourteen more over a million population; in their entirety such regions are home to more than one-third of the total population of this country.

From 1950 to 1960 the American population increased 18 per cent, but the population of the metropolitan regions increased 26 per cent; in fact, 84 per cent of the total population increase was in the standard metropolitan statistical areas (SMSA). Two-thirds of this metropolitan increase was around and just outside the central cities. The great city in America is no longer the simple hub of the wheel; it is also an aggregation of communities growing tightly together while spreading to ever-widening peripheries.

Three enormous polypolitan populations are now growing in the United States: one along the Atlantic coast, another on the Pacific, and a third on the shores of the Great Lakes. The Atlantic polyopolis extends from the Merrimack River southward to the Potomac and beyond and is contained partly by the Appalachian Mountains.

2. See Chapters 4 and 5.

Along the Great Lakes other populations spread and merge into what is becoming the central polyopolis—Milwaukee into Chicago, Chicago into Gary, and up the shore of Lake Michigan and past South Bend and eastward into Detroit, with gaps here and there, then Detroit sending its populations out, reaching closer and closer to Sandusky, Toledo, Cleveland, and ultimately to Buffalo. Still another, but a smaller, polyopolis spreads north and south from San Francisco, Los Angeles, and San Diego into the valleys and along the Pacific coast from Sacramento to below the Mexican border. Forty million people are concentrated in the Atlantic polyopolis, another twenty million are on the Great Lakes, and ten million are on the Pacific coast.

In these and other regions metropolitan communities merge and extend themselves, taking smaller cities with them into polypolitan aggregates, as the rural agricultural revolution and the urban industrial revolution depopulate the farms and bring multitudes into the cities and their satellites. Meanwhile, the citizens of the cities increase and move out toward distant peripheries. One may ask where the metropolis of Philadelphia ends and Newark and New York begin. Where does Baltimore start and Washington begin and end?

The Increasing Significance of the Large Organization

The growth of business, unions, government, and other large institutions is directly related to the development of the metropolitan regions. The headquarters of these national—often worldwide—empires are heavily concentrated in the three polyopolises.

Most of the hierarchies of the 500 largest industrial corporations listed each year by *Fortune* magazine extend to all parts of the United States and well beyond its borders. Although the organizations of some may be regionally bound, their business activities often extend from coast to coast and into other continents. The feeding field of a great corporation is not necessarily limited to its organizational territory.

While an astounding fifth of the American population is in the Atlantic polyopolis, the headquarters of an even larger portion— over half—of the 500 largest corporations in America are located there. A tenth of the American population is in the polyopolis of the Great Lakes region, but the central offices of more than a fourth of the 500 largest corporations (28 per cent) are located there. A smaller but very substantial number of the corporate headquarters of the 500 largest firms—over 6 per cent—are in the California region. In these three regions, which contain a third of the population, are the headquarters of 85 per cent of the 500 industrial empires of the country.

Although we shall concentrate our attention on each variety of large organization, we must remember that our nation contains many small groups.

Well over four million small profit-making enterprises are a significant part of our economic life; there are thousands of small local governments and, by estimate, possibly several million small social, civic, and other voluntary associations. Although the number of religious denominations with more than 10,000 members is probably less than two hundred, there are thousands of small sects, storefront churches, and separate rural and village churches that have important functions in urban and rural change. At the foundations of our institutional structure, millions of small family units live their separate autonomous existence; yet all are part of the web of kinship that spreads from coast to coast. Extended clusters of friends and cliques and other groups of informal relations also form an important microsocial tissue of the national moral order. However, the "bony structure" of the emerging society, which gives form and mobility to its evolvement, is the large-scale organization. Of the 4,700,000 private business and industrial enterprises in the United States, only 21,000, less than one-half of one per cent, have a net worth of over a million dollars. Yet this tiny fraction controls two-thirds of the national sales volume, employs four out of every ten workers, and pays half of all salaries and wages of private enterprise.

Since its beginning the federal government has grown enormously. In 1790 there were approximately 1,000 civilian employees, according to estimations for that time; by 1800 perhaps some 3,000 were employed; by 1860 this number had grown to 37,000, an increase of some thirty-seven times; and by 1960 the number had increased to 2,400,000. Comparisons of the rates of growth of big government and the American society are revealing. From 1860 to 1960 the United States population and its work force increased approximately six times as against over sixty times for federal civilian employees. The Washington government work force increased one hundred times during that period. Meanwhile, the Gross National Product (GNP) increased some seventy times from 1870 (when figures are available) to 1960, whereas federal expenses increased over two hundred times.

In brief, although our society has greatly expanded in population, in economic ability, and in capacity to use its natural environment and its technological base, the institutions of the federal government have increased in size and probably in strength far more rapidly. Government in America is by far the biggest hierarchical organization.

We will give attention to each of the major areas of modern organizational life—government, business, education, religion, and private association—and attempt to understand something more about their organization, function, and development. The national society in which they perform grows increasingly in the direction of complexity, diversity, and heterogeneity, but not in a simple linear development. The dynamics of emergent change are such that the movement toward heterogeneity, as expressed in many of the innovations of the present day, is held and modified by the tendencies toward homogeneity as they are expressed in the traditions and body of customs. Moreover, many of the innovative changes reinforce homogeneous tendencies and help consolidate some of the changes that have taken place. This is true at the technological level, as scientific experimentation becomes more organized. In social organization, as in all areas of our institutional life, simplification is bringing about more homogeneity. It is also true at the mental level, whether in the area of pure or applied science, of practical social experimentation, or of sacred thought and ecumenicism, that some aspects become less heterogeneous and more unified even as our thought differentiates. Paradoxically, homogeneous trends are necessary for heterogeneity's increase.

Other important directions of change are increasing rationality and increasing use of techniques for introducing change, rational or not, into this culture. With our industrial development, goods and services have grown enormously, and the distribution of goods and the standard of living have greatly increased. From 1940 to 1960 the GNP increased four times, from $125 to $504 billion. At the same time the processes of rational innovation, as expressed in research and development, took a larger and larger proportion of the GNP. In 1941 only 0.71 per cent of the GNP went to research and development; by 1961 this proportion had risen to 2.78 per cent, an absolute increase of some sixteen times. All of this was not merely in the universities or in industry, for the federal and other governments took increasing interest and spent more money in research. In 1941, 41 per cent of the expenditures for research were governmental, 57 per cent industrial, and 2 per cent were by nonprofit institutions. By 1961 the government proportion had risen to 66 per cent and industry had dropped to 32 per cent, while the nonprofit institutions, including large universities, had remained at 2 per cent.

From another point of view, one can also see the enormous expansion of the scientific activities that contribute to change in our social system. In 1900 there were some 42,000 scientists and engineers in our occupational system; by 1954 this number had increased many times to just under 700,000—men whose primary activity is to investigate the present and move toward change for the future. In 1945 there were slightly under 1,000 Ph.D. degrees granted in science and technology; by 1960 this number had multiplied six times. In 1920 there were only 300 industrial research laboratories with about 7,000 operating personnel; by 1950 this number had increased ten- or elevenfold to 3,300 laboratories and 111,000 operating personnel. Research and development itself has become big business—an important instrument of profit making and necessary to the competitive system.

The changing values of our social order and the characteristics of our organizations show quite clearly other directions of the emergent American society. Free capitalistic enterprise and free markets in America still exist, and it is generally believed that where they do not exist, they should. In fact, the ideal of free enterprise is only partly true, and profit making, as we all know, is the principal motivation of big and small business. Increasingly, under the legal and moral control of federal agencies and, to a lesser extent, of state and local agencies, free enterprise is limited and no longer recognizable in terms of the social Darwinism of Sumner or of the natural rights of Adam Smith. The economic rationality of laissez faire gives way to the moral and legal power of the national community. The free market is now crowded with other kinds of people; the unions, trade associations, and big government play their roles in limiting the freedom of action of the entrepreneur while he strives to make a profit. Furthermore, taxes are so arranged that the financial rewards of enterprise are greatly reduced and the income of government is greatly increased, particularly that of the federal government. The right of the people, through the instrument of their government, to take from private enterprise what it has earned is now so accepted that our moral system no longer permits us to believe that a man can keep for himself and his family all that he or his corporation has the power to accumulate. We now believe that the collectivity has the right to use part of this wealth for its own purposes.

Moreover, we also accept, not without some hesitation, that the federal government can use these funds for the support and nurture of the scores of bureaus and independent agencies that now organize and maintain the national community for those who comprise it. The crucial proof of what is happening to free enterprise is, of course, that the entrepreneur and corporation cannot charge, nor can they keep, what the marketplace or the profit motive would permit. The regulations of the Interstate Commerce Commission, the Food and Drug Administration, and scores of other independent agencies and bureaus, along with the laws and public opinion that lie back of them, make this impossible. Few Americans now approve of robber-baron tactics; they believe that if we are to increase our power and welfare as a nation, controls must be established and enforced. The federal regulation of buying and selling —for example, of agricultural products—regulation of the money supply, of wages and hours, and federal purchasing at the yearly rate of many billions of dollars are all part of the intervention of government in our economic life.

Meanwhile, scientific rationality and technology not only invade new areas of our lives by producing a greater variety of goods and wealth from the natural environment but also make the social and psychological sciences increasingly practical and effective. More and more we see ourselves as scientific objects, and we use the rationality of science to deal with the nonrational behavior of the individual and the society. At the same time there is increasing specialization related to scientific change and to changes in our moral order. There is also more fluidity in the occupational structure within the hierarchies that compose the great military and civilian organizations and among localities, as people live increasingly mobile lives, territorially and socially.

The primary family grows more autonomous and less involved in the extensions of kinship. Not that there is disregard for kindred, but their controls and demands outside the nuclear family grow less powerful in influencing the behavior of individual family members. With the lessening of local autonomy the many thousands of communities have become interrelated parts of the larger social system developing out of the interaction of the families and individuals who move from place to place. The national communication and transportation systems are now well used by most members of our society. Large-scale corporations, unions, trade associations, and federal government have greatly contributed to this loss of local autonomy; they are transforming us into one big society.

As our society becomes more diverse at all levels of behavior, as the number of products of the technology grow, as skills and technology increase in complexity, and as our biological base multiplies enormously, there is greater need for a secure yet flexible coordination of the various objects, people, and social groups and their activities to maintain order and hold the collective diversity in a cohesive whole. There can be no doubt that the appearance and development of the coordinating hierarchies are closely related to the need for maintaining order among the diverse parts. Moreover, as our society increases its control over the natural environment as well as over the human species, there is also the problem of placing and ordering the real power that comes from increased adaptation to, and control of, these natural worlds—atomic power is but one example—at both the national and the international levels. As a response to this and many other large-scale problems, big organizations play an ever more important and necessary role. These organizations are not "satellites of our society," as some people have called them, but fundamental and integral parts of the new kind of society and the one great national community that is rapidly developing.

THE NATURE OF LARGE-SCALE ORGANIZATIONS

The large-scale organization is a type of social system that has distinguishing characteristics and occupies a particular kind of place in the structure of any society in which it occurs. It performs coordinating and other functions necessary for the maintenance of the society itself. Its forms and functions may be viewed *internally* —what it is, how its parts fit and work together as one unit—or *externally*—how it fits into the structure of the larger social world and functions in the working processes of the whole. The term large-scale implies moderate measurement and at least some criteria for comparison with other social organizations.

The principal distinguishing characteristics of large organizations are their many statuses, the many and complex relations among the statuses, and the ordering of these complex relations and statuses into one or more hierarchies of ranked positions. These ranked statuses are coordinated into relations of superordination and subordination, of high and low prestige, of great and low power. When an organization is composed of several hierarchies, certain statuses within the subhierarchies are equated by those in and out of them as equal and coordinate. Again, in completely separate complex hierarchies quite different statuses are ranked by those in and out of them as coordinate and equal. The principal structural characteristic of large-scale organizations other than hierarchy is the coordination of complex statuses. The principal function of large-scale structures is to organize the numerous individuals with their technological, mental, and moral diversities to make better use of their powerful energies in performing the large collective tasks to achieve the goals of a vast society.

Complexity and Size

To categorize, measure, and compare large organizations, one must first ask about their *vertical extensions*. How many levels of ranked status compose an organization's extension from top to bottom? Two? Three? Many? In brief, is its vertical extension high, moderate, or low when compared with others of its kind—other big corporations, large government agencies, or education, church, and association hierarchies? Such an inquiry can be conducted by the scientific rules of field evidence, and measurements can be obtained with moderate accuracy. Moreover, the methods and results can be sufficiently free from the data to allow scientific comparisons among the hierarchies of diverse institutions. It is also possible to compare the large-scale organizations of one society with those of another.

All social organizations, simple or complex, small or large, are also *horizontally* extended. Provided close attention is given to the order of the facts being studied, this extension can be observed and measured. There are at least four kinds of lateral extension, usually closely interrelated although different, that are relevant here.

The *territorial* extension may be limited or very broad; it may be confined to one society or spread among several cultures. A corporate empire may extend all over the United States and beyond, or it may be large and confined to only one city. A hierarchy may extend widely in a tribe, a kingdom in Africa, in Micronesia, or the pre-Colombian Andes. When a hierarchy does spread widely in physical space, usually—but not always—the vertical extension is also great. The physical extension may be very limited yet the vertical extension quite high; a tiny monarchy may have an elaborate political hierarchy.

Among other orders of lateral extension, clear distinctions are necessary but are too rarely made when large organizations are observed. Each will now be briefly reviewed. At the demographic and biological levels the comparative number and extent of human beings that are part of the organization can be counted. How many men are members of a large organization? Are there 10,000 workers? A million federal employees? Several million church, school, or association members or only a few hundred? If we refer to this *biological* extension as volume, as some writers do, the consideration remains the same, and the problem and significance of size do not change since the number of people is, in fact, a part of the scale and lateral extension of any organization.

Closely allied to the latter is the *spread of social objects,* including economic and technical equipment and machinery, which are controlled by, or related to, many large-scale organizations. Are they in large numbers, only a few, or none at all? Are there many varieties of things? Among them is there multiplicity of kinds—apples and horses, shoes and sealing wax? Does the company or organization make but one part of a shoe or one small part of a stellar rocket? Is the involvement of the objects total and entire or highly limited to one moment in time and to one tiny aspect, such as a small company manufacturing one part of a complex space machine for the National Aeronautics and Space Administration, whose vast hierarchies are totally involved with a long-term national project?

In many ways the fourth kind of lateral extension is the most important and most difficult to study. It will be remembered that we are still asking what is meant by the term large-scale organization and, more specifically, by horizontal extension. If a social organization or society has many ranks and if each rank is differentiated into many roles, then this structural fact perforce means that the organization has a large horizontal extension. The order of facts that compose this *structural* lateral extension is the degree of complexity and amount of differentiation at any or all levels of organization. If a society is very simple and "primitive," as are the Australian aborigines and some of the mountain tribes of New Guinea, the degree of lateral differentiation, or vertical for that matter, is very low. On the other hand, the lateral extensions of large-scale American organization can be complex, diverse, and highly extended. A given corporation may have only one line of authority with very few and very simple statuses at each level of rank, or it may be complex and highly differentiated, with many lines of command and many segmental and diverse activities that spread enormously at the middle and lower levels, or sometimes at the higher levels, each subhierarchy being itself very complex, yet all converging and narrowing as they approach the top. The lateral extension of the second type of hierarchy will be greater, and measurably so, than the first.

Important probing questions about an organization's size are: Is an organization national, regional, or local in scope? Does it employ many or a few, 10,000 or 500 men? Does it produce several million objects (cars), govern a thousand people, or many, many less? Are its tasks highly differentiated? The answers to these questions give a measure of one or more kinds of size and a probable indication of the horizontal and vertical structural extensions of an organization. Sometimes studying them is all that is possible.

The several measures and scales of the size of organizations are usually in rough, and sometimes close, agreement, but at times they are not. Ordinarily a manufacturing corporation that is comparatively large by volume of sales or assets is also large in other ways, including number of men employed, and usually in the extended structure and the complexity of its spreading divisions and departments. Certain types of firms, however, such as financial ones, may do a large volume of business but be relatively small when ranked by number of employees. Yet all orders of size—volume of business, number of activities, number of employees or members—are broadly interrelated.

Within limits the correlations also hold among the activity types; corporations, government agencies, business enterprises, trade associations, schools, and churches vary greatly in terms of goals and activities but show strong resemblances among their measurements and extensions in men, money, or structure. There can, of course, be variations based on money spent or taken in, number of men, structural size and complexity, and so forth—usually within narrow limits—but it is more likely that the dimensions will correspond for each of the orders of size. Until extended systematic field studies are made of the interrelations of these several orders of size, only limited scientific conclusions about the interrelations can be positively stated. However, hypotheses based on evidence in hand can be offered to help us interpret the social meaning of bigness and the term large-scale, even if only partially.

Classification

A further analysis will help us in the study of the significance of large size. Each organization may be separately studied as an institutional type (corporation, association, church, school, government), as a social activity (economic, moral, relational), and as a social system (nature and degree of social stratification). Within each of these categories distinctions that differentiate the large from the small will become apparent.

Economic enterprises regulate technology and the facts and symbols of economic transaction. The churches, formal associations, and educational and political institutions are concerned with the moral order and arrange and regulate the energies, persons, and powers of the human biological base and partly transform that base and the individuals within it for social purposes. The educational institutions pass on not only traditional behavior patterns but the transforming ones of the changing, emergent society as well. They train the young to order their energies and to expend them in socially valued activities. They help prepare young people for personal maturity and for adaptation and contribution to a future society ever arriving. The churches and some other groups also help to relate men to each other and to the supernatural. For most men, they help reduce fear of the uncontrollable and the unknown, and they define and express the hopeful aspects of man's fate. They are the institutional senders and receivers of the symbols of man's outward communication with the Divine.

Activity type cuts across institutional type. Corporations exist as economic, social, moral, educational, and security-giving communities. For example, corporations deal not only with the facts, products, and skills of pragmatic and scientific rationality but also with the symbols and facts of material and nonmaterial wealth and the relations of managers and workers, not only with work and pay but also with the morality of right and wrong, of responsibility and obligation.

Our study of institutional and activity types is primarily intended to isolate their effects on large-scale hierarchical organization. Since hierarchies are intrinsic parts of the social structure of every large organization, an auxilary function of our study will be to distinguish this variety of social stratification from other varieties of rank to bring out the importance of the hierarchical phenomenon in our developing social system.

SIGNIFICANCE OF THE ENVIRONMENTS OF LARGE-SCALE ORGANIZATIONS

During the last fifty years big corporations, big government, and other large-scale organizations have proliferated in the United States and in European and other civilized countries, and their power and importance have become problems of conscious concern and debate. Since the rise is clearly associated with vast increases in population, technological advancement, and growing complexities of modern life, it is often assumed that these and other contemporary conditions are sufficient to explain and understand the nature of big organizations. In many respects this is too simple an assumption. It is sometimes far from the truth, although often it is part of it; but taken too literally it injures our scientific understanding of what these organizations are and what they do in this society. One needs to ask about the different kinds of demographic, economic, technological, and social worlds in which large-scale organizations exist. When and where do they not exist? Under what conditions do they flourish? When and why do they develop? We will briefly review the comparative evidence and apply the results of examination of other societies to our own.

Classification and Evolution of Human Societies

Simple typologies may be created in many ways to compare and contrast human societies, with each typology based ultimately on some division of social labor. From field evidence the range of complexity presented by the totality of all societies can be analyzed and determined for each typology and a taxonomy can be built within each typology employing a range running from very simple to very complex; any society, with a fair degree of accuracy, can be placed within each typology. For example, three types of adaptive systems might be distinguished, each with several possible degrees of complexity: the technology and economy, the social organization (moral order), and the sacred symbol systems. Each relates the society to a given environment. Confining our attention to the technological and organizational systems, we ask first what is the range of complexity and then where large-scale organizations appear or do not appear in these types of complexity. Finally we ask what kinds of large organizations are present in the various types of societies.

It is possible to conceive of a society so simple that it had no division of labor, no social differentiation, in which everyone was occupied with everything and all shared alike, and in which there were no suborganizations. But this is hypothetical, for there is no such

Introduction

society; even the infrahuman primate bands are internally organized. There are, however, human hunting and agricultural villages where there is little division of social and economic labor and almost all activities are organized by sex, age, family, and groupings based primarily upon biological differences. These people have small populations and are usually simple hunters and gatherers; the Australian aborigines and certain western American Indians are examples. It is unnecessary to state that with such low differentiation, technologically and organizationally, and with no formally organized government or economic system, none of these peoples has any kind of large organization.

Other somewhat more differentiated societies, including some with subsistence agriculture and pastoral technologies and formally recognized occupational classes, show few indications of the segmentary hierarchical orders of large-scale organizations. However, rudimentary forms of such organizations are found in some of these tribes. When the more complex among the nonliterate so-called primitive peoples and those outside the historical and neohistorical peoples are examined, clear evidence of the development of large organizations appears.

Hobhouse, Wheeler, and Ginsberg in their classic work [3] and other authors such as Bernhard Stern, who have made systematic studies of this very problem, divide the small societies of the world into three kinds of technology—hunters and gatherers, agriculturists, and pastoralists—and then divide each type into degrees of complexity. Accompanying the progression from the simplest hunters to the complex third level of agriculture where there is diversity of crops and several cultivating tools is a great advance in the percentage of tribes with government organizations hierarchically arranged from subjects to high chiefs and of tribes with a hierarchical system of high chief, district chiefs, and local ones. The same rise in percentages is apparent for systems of public justice with hierarchically arranged statuses. Moreover, in all three types of technology rank statuses, general statuses of nobility and slaves, and degrees of nobility as well as ranks of commoners, often associated with segmentary hierarchical systems, are frequently found

3. L. T. Hobhouse, G. C. Wheeler, and M. Ginsberg, *The Material Culture and Social Institutions of the Simpler Peoples* (London, Chapman and Hall, 1915).

when the social and technological system increases in complexity and the population grows more dense.

In the still more complex economies and social systems of early Europe, Polynesia, ancient Japan, China, and Africa the incidence of hierarchical systems is enormously increased. In this feudal type of system the population was numerous and dense; there were villages and towns, and the technology was tillage and herding. With a comparatively high division of labor, lords and nobles were managers of the workers and the ignoble, and families were stratified. The distribution of work and its products was unequal. There was no money payment, but goods and services were exchanged according to the rank system of general and segmentary statuses. In these more technologically and morally complex societies, hierarchical segmentary systems were universal; moreover, they tended to be more complex and more differentiated. The various kinds of functions were not carried out by one undifferentiated hierarchy; but rather the economic-political, ecclesiastical, and other activities of life were likely to be separated into different hierarchies and internally stratified. The observer concerned with the degrees and kinds of differentiation of segmentation and hierarchy can see that these large-scale systems clearly anticipate the highly complex type of contemporary national systems. That is to say, these several kinds of hierarchy were present, although the population base was not nearly so dense, the technology not very complex, and the social organization simple compared with contemporary society.

The United States—an extreme example of a modern and highly complex type of society—can be characterized within this range as having very elaborate economic and social division of labor with a high degree of economic differentiation and specialized occupations and with small, highly divided technological job units. The occupations are ranked, formally or informally, but the worker's position is not ignoble, as it was in the feudal systems. Wide markets with common transportation, common communications, and common exchange of products are based not on tradition but on the mathematics of a money economy. There is a large and dense population and a machine-power-driven, scientific technology. The social or moral system that organizes the behavior of its people is also exceedingly complex but flexible.

A principal characteristic of our moral order is the partial interrelation of the elaborate hierarchies of ranked status with the general social classes that arrange most people in orders of superiority and inferiority, in which social mobility is prized and is in the spirit of the system itself. Social differentiation has such flexibility that individual autonomy and free social movement of individuals in the general status system and within the various hierarchies are not only permitted but encouraged.

The Need for Coordination and Flexibility

The basic distinction between large-scale organizations in other societies—including less complex societies—and our own is not so much in their structures, since they are very similar in type, as in the high degree of differentiation and specialization and their very high number in our own society.

Despite their seeming rigidity, great organizations are probably far more flexible and more easily moved by the needs of the society than they appear to be. And despite the fact that they often seem conservative and their members reluctant to innovate as a social group, they respond adaptively to changes that occur in the larger social system. Their rapid development in all types of social activity in America is also related to the fact that this is an open system—open in the sense that no dominant political or other reigning sacred or absolute ideology reduces the creation of new organizations. Mergers, growth, and innovation bring new big corporations into being. Division, growth, and technological advancement are responsible for new government agencies. The organizing of new and specialized economic and social activity creates new professional and trade associations, new schisms, new mergers, and new hierarchies. In an emergent, open society such developments are necessary parts of the social system.

Given the nature of the evidence about human social life, it is not possible to state with complete security what factors operate to bring about the presence, absence, and flowering of large-scale organizations. However, by observing the several types of social systems from the simple hunting and gathering horde to the great electrical, machine, and scientific society, we can discern some environmental conditions and factors. In the simple societies extended organizations do not exist at all. In the somewhat more complex primitive ones a few appear, but they are undifferentiated. In the more complex literate societies still more appear; and in the neohistorical societies in which some social differentiation takes place, they seem to be more like our own. In our society they grow and expand luxuriantly in number, kind, and complexity.

With greater complexities in the biological, technological, and moral orders, increasing difficulty is experienced in interrelating each part to all others, both by individuals and groups, in maintaining internal cohesion, and in defining the multiplicity and variety of relations and statuses. Above all, there is greater need to solve the problem of coordinating the many relations and activities to allow men to work together for common purposes. This is achieved in part by the superimposition of general social goals over individual action. Superior statuses organize the multiple ones below them through their power and prestige. Thus, controlled by ranked statuses in a large hierarchy, the actions and power of many individuals and a large number of things can be harnessed for collective ends. The coordination of the increasingly diverse and more numerous social labor force is accomplished by the continuing development of the ranked hierarchies of the large-scale organizations and the reclassification of people in an open system where flexibility and mobility are stressed. Moreover, if innovations continue to move us toward more heterogeneity and greater manipulative control over our natural and biological environment—even the regulation of the human species—adequate systems of coordination to maintain the common enterprise must be developed. The hierarchies of large-scale organizations, which play such a major role today, can be redivided and changed, new hierarchies can be set up, and old developments modified so that they are amenable to both the changing and the traditional values of the emergent society.

The technological, economic, and moral problems encountered by a large society are much more difficult than those in a small one; to solve them the large society must call upon the skills and concerted collaboration of its larger population, more powerful technology, and more highly organized social system to maintain itself —and, with ongoing change, to contribute to its own advancement. While very small organizations may be important and necessary, they are not adequate for society's larger ends and more important tasks. They can be arranged in a collaborative order to achieve particular large goals in given periods of time, but their efforts are often highly inefficient and ineffective. The coordination part of the effort sometimes becomes permanently dominant, and from such informal collaboration among small organizations, large-scale organizations may be created. Many cooperative marketing institutions are examples of the formation of large-scale organizations from the temporary collaboration of smaller ones.

In a closed society, one highly extended and all-powerful complex hierarchy, authoritatively managed and dominated, has the power and the duty to assimilate new developments into old forms and to place them within the social system. This system sometimes performs very well, but it is often awkward and occasionally has disastrous results when scientific and biological changes progress rapidly. In our open society, fluid and in flux, wholly new organizations often come into being to arrange and order new technological developments and expansions; older economic and other social institutions modify their own structures and activities to fit the new. Thus a new invention may become the object of a new company or a division of a large corporation. It may also result in new professional and trade associations, new government agencies, or expansion of old bureaus and departments of an independent agency or department of the federal government.

As our national society becomes more and more a primary social and economic community, as space and time are less limiting in face-to-face interaction, and as simultaneity of coordinated action over great distances becomes more frequent and diverse, large organizations are increasingly used to order and maintain the national, primary action system. The telegraph, telephone, radio, television, and printing press facilitate communication and help determine and channel individual actions. Remote and isolated towns and villages become fewer; none is now outside the national network of communications and transportation or unreached by the mutual influences of direct interaction on a national scale.

All sizes and varieties of organizations exist and function successfully in this rapidly developing primary national community. Millions of small businesses, millions of families, hundreds of thousands of small associations, and many thousands of local schools, churches, and governments, with varying degrees of success, make up the small fiber of the life of 190 million Americans. Yet given the newly expanded territorial and biological basis of our society and its need for coordination of adaptive behavior; given the vast new elaborations of industry and the enormous growth in productivity; and given the increasing heterogeneity of ideas, beliefs, values, and behavior, the need for the small territorial units is decreasing, and more reliance is being placed on big, widely extended hierarchies.

States and communities willingly turn to the federal government to help solve their local problems. Meanwhile, the federal structure grows larger, and its activities advance in number, variety, and importance—from the care and control of the atomic bomb to the care and control of Navajo Indians and metropolitan affairs. Great universities, many of them bearing the names of the states that founded them, grow fearful of federal influence on their autonomy and their dependence on federal dollars. Even the ecumenical movement among the churches is, at the secular level, in part a response to the same factors and needs that are operating everywhere in the development of large-scale organizations.

CHAPTER TWO

The Big and Not So Big Corporations

TIME, SPACE, AND CORPORATE BIGNESS

Although big corporations are one of the several major types of complex organizations characteristic of contemporary American society, we still need to define what we mean by large-scale, corporate bigness, and degrees of bigness. The first purpose of this chapter is to distinguish among the kinds, degrees, and scales of corporate bigness and to determine the number and proportion of enterprises in each size. With the aid of research evidence and simple statistical measurement we will learn also about some of the other meanings of bigness among contemporary large-scale corporations.

The use in the literature of the terms for the various kinds of business enterprise are rarely, if ever, exact and probably cannot be. In general, the term *corporation* refers to enterprises that have been formed and incorporated under state laws, but this is not always true. The term *company* tends to be more inclusive as does the term *firm*. In general, here we use the term corporation most often for the large-scale enterprises that, usually, are truly incorporated. These include "the 500 largest" and many of the organizations of more than $1 million net worth. The terms firm and company also include such organizations as sole ownerships, partnerships, and so forth.

Certain questions must be answered. What is the comparative size of the several thousand big and little giants that exist among the many millions of smaller business enterprises in the United States of the 1960s? How big is big? Not so big? Big in what way—in men, money, organization, or perhaps all three? What is the relation of

This chapter is by W. Lloyd Warner and Darab B. Unwalla. See Notes on Authors.

22

the structural size of complex corporate hierarchies and the degrees of rank in big and small corporations to money and men? Where are the headquarters of the giant enterprises in the United States at the present time?

What happens if we ask these questions about an earlier period in this century and again about the last thirty years? Can we describe a process of change in relation to our corporate social system? What is the importance of interlocking directorates?

Statistical treatment of these questions will be followed by two chapters of a different sort, one analyzing and interpreting the personalities of managers in our evolving society and the other a detailed study of the processes of structural change at the management levels in one of the very largest corporations in this country, the General Electric Company.

HOW BIG IS BIG?

To establish the size of the very big and the moderately big contemporary corporations, we will first review the evidence for all enterprises of every size in the United States in 1960. The largest figure (published by the Internal Revenue Service [1]) includes all individually owned business firms and other forms of enterprise, including farms, ranches, and professional services, in which Americans earn a living. The inclusive extreme of economic activities amounted to more than eleven million enterprises in 1960; it obviously includes forms of economic and professional activities as well as business and industry. Only in the very broadest sense can all of them be called private enterprises; many are not strictly businesses.

The Office of Business Economics of the Internal Revenue Service supplies figures that exclude farms, professional services, and the like and include only business and industrial firms. It defines a business firm as a business organization under a single management that may include one or more plants or outlets; a firm doing busi-

1. U. S. Bureau of the Census, *Statistical Abstract of the United States, 1962* (83rd ed., Washington, D.C., 1962), p. 88, Table 646.

Big and Not So Big Corporations

ness in more than one industry is classified by industry according to the major activity of the firm as a whole. A self-employed person is considered a firm only if he has either one or more employees or an established place of business. The definition and count of firms differ from that of the Bureau of the Census, which counts establishments, e.g. manufacturing plants or retail stores larger than a minimum specified size.[2] The definition of the Office of Business Economics includes all varieties of business and industrial enterprise, including sole proprietorships, partnerships, and corporations; it is the definition used here and covers one of the kinds of business enterprise we are investigating. According to this count there were 4,658,000 such firms in the United States in 1960. This means that there were about thirty-nine Americans for each firm and about eleven households and sixteen men and women in the labor force for each business enterprise.

By this broad, inclusive reckoning, AT&T, General Motors, Sears, Roebuck, and other gigantic corporations are one with Smith's Grocery Store in Jonesville, Al's and Bill's Motel on State Route No. 9, and Joe's Cigar Store in Flatbush. How much business does a corporation have to have in order to be called big? What proportions of the sales do the big and little giants get? What are big and little giants? How many men do the big corporations and those that are not so big employ? How big are the big corporations of America?

Each year *Fortune* magazine lists the 500 largest industrial corporations by rank order of sales size; it supplements this list with 250 companies from other types of large business enterprise (financial, etc.). *Fortune's* excellent and important list tells us much about relative size among the 500 largest industrial corporations, including number of employees, but it does not give information about many very large corporations. For these purposes we turned to Dun and Bradstreet's *Million Dollar Directory* for 1960 (New York, 1961), which covers corporations with a net worth of $1 million or more and with a minimum of $1 million in yearly sales. There are 21,000 (actually 20,989, but for convenience we will use the round number) firms in this list. The information includes amount of sales, number of employees, type of business enterprise,

2. *Ibid.*, p. 485.

Table 1. Annual Sales of Large Firms

Size	Sales in millions of dollars	Firms in each category		Total sales for all firms 2nd millions of dollars	
		N	%		%
Very small	1	1,475	11.69	1,475	0.32
	2	1,143	9.06	2,286	0.50
	3	1,189	9.42	3,567	0.78
	4	990	7.85	3,960	0.87
Subtotal		4,797	38.02	11,288	2.47
Small	5- 10	3,087	24.47	19,852	4.35
	10- 15	1,317	10.44	14,829	3.26
Subtotal		4,404	34.91	34,681	7.61
Medium	15- 25	1,112	8.81	20,571	4.50
Large	25- 50	939	7.44	31,599	6.93
Very large	50- 100	611	4.84	40,520	8.89
Largest	100- 500	607	4.81	126,827	27.80
	500-1,000	88	0.70	58,574	12.84
	1,000- over	59	0.47	132,147	28.96
Subtotal		754	5.98	317,548	69.60
Grand total		12,617	100.00	456,207	100.00

and location of headquarters of firms ranging in sales from $1 million to more than $1 billion and in number of employed from less than a hundred to several hundred thousand.[3]

Only a very small proportion of the 21,000 big firms are very large. Table 1 tells most of the story. The very small firms ($1 to $4 million in sales) account for 38 per cent of all the firms, and the largest ($100 million and more) account for only 6 per cent. The combined sales of the very small to medium firms amount to only 15 per cent of total sales of the firms reporting sales figures (12,617). Only 88 corporations were in the $500 to $1,000 million rank, less than 1 per cent (0.70), yet they had 13 per cent of

3. A major portion of those not reporting sales were financial enterprises, whose source of income was not sales; there were 3,391, 94 per cent of all financial enterprises. The remaining 6 per cent were spread among the other types of business firms.

all sales; and only 59 had sales of more than $1 billion, comprising 29 per cent of all sales of the firms reporting.

As the category of yearly sales grows larger, the number of firms in each grows smaller, but the combined amount of sales rises enormously. Once again we ask, "How big is big?" but now we have our first empirical answer. For the present we will say that all firms (754) with more than $100 million in yearly sales are in the largest category; those with $50 to $100 million are very large (611); those with $25 to $50 million (939) are large; [4] those from $15 to $25 million (1,112) are medium; firms with less than $15 million but more than $5 million are small; and those with less than $5 but more than $1 million a year in sales are classed as very small. These 9,000 small and very small firms are still larger than the remaining several million private enterprises in the United States that depend on sales for income. Although they are at the lower end of sales among the big corporations, they are part of the less than half of one per cent of all American firms with sales and net worth of more than a million dollars.

Any distinctions and cutoff points on a range of bigness are obviously partly arbitrary and necessarily so, but somewhere in the spread from Mrs. Murphy's Boarding House to General Motors the designation of bigness is not arbitrary but real. The categories of degrees of bigness, as measured by sales, can vary according to analytical need, as they do here, at least as a beginning.

Let us now move from money to men and ask once again, "How big is big?" We have full information on the number of employees for 17,796 firms—85 per cent of the total of 21,000.

The range of the number of employees of these big corporations is very great, running from very small, 50 or fewer, to over 10,000. Some 1,500 (8.6 per cent) companies had fewer than 50 employees, and, at the other extreme, 14 had over 100,000. Broadly speaking, the very big firms are few in number, for only 2 per cent (345) employ 10,000 or more, less than 1 per cent (134) have more than 20,000, and 2 per cent are in the 5,000 to 10,000 class. Thus, only 4 per cent (708) employ more than 5,000 people. (See Table 2.) What is big when half of these giant firms employ less than 300 men and only 4 per cent more than 5,000?

4. The range of *Fortune's* list (1961) of 500 industrials goes from $13 billion down to $72,410,000 in annual sales.

Table 2. Big Corporations: Number of Employees

Size by number of employees	Firms in each category	
	N	%
Very small		
Less than 50	1,528	8.6
50 to 100	1,279	7.2
Subtotal	2,807	15.8
Small		
100 to 300	6,148	34.5
Large		
300 to 1,000	5,785	32.5
Very large		
1,000 to 5,000	2,347	13.2
Largest		
5,000 to 10,000	363	2.0
10,000 and more	345	2.0
Subtotal	708	4.0
Grand total	17,796	100.0

What is the nature and extent of the relationship between the two classifications of size, one based on number of employees and the other based on sales volume? What amounts and percentages of the aggregate sales of the 21,000 million-dollar companies are represented in each employee category? How do the percentages of sales and of companies accumulate as each larger employee category is added? What proportion of men and of companies is involved as employee size increases? Do increases in size in men and money correspond category after category and step by step?

We will use Tables 3 to 5 to learn about the relation of sales volume to number of employees in the big and not-so-big corporations. Each has to do with different aspects of the relative size and the relationship of the two orders. Since we first established the distribution of firms by size of sales, we will first ask questions anchored to this category. For example, 798,743, or 4.15 per cent of all employees in the sample, were in firms in the smallest sales category,

Big and Not So Big Corporations

Table 3. Employment by Sales Category

Sales in millions of dollars		Number of employees	Percentage of total employees	Accumulated percentage of employees	Accumulated percentage of firms
1 to	5	798,743	4.15	4.15	38.02
5 to	10	1,091,802	5.67	9.82	62.46
10 to	15	739,580	3.84	13.66	72.93
15 to	20	469,775	2.43	16.09	77.92
20 to	25	473,734	2.46	18.55	81.74
25 to	30	341,789	1.77	20.32	84.00
30 to	35	316,280	1.64	21.96	85.82
35 to	40	290,831	1.51	23.47	87.36
40 to	45	252,083	1.31	24.78	88.45
45 to	50	189,455	.98	25.76	89.18
50 to	60	572,603	2.97	28.73	91.01
60 to	70	355,019	1.85	30.58	92.04
70 to	80	360,777	1.87	32.45	92.99
80 to	90	275,742	1.43	33.88	93.61
90 to	100	196,300	1.02	34.90	94.02
100 to	200	2,155,724	11.19	46.09	96.75
200 to	300	1,495,721	7.77	53.86	97.85
300 to	400	1,128,494	5.86	59.72	98.44
400 to	500	967,693	5.02	64.74	98.83
500 to	600	663,517	3.45	68.19	99.12
600 to	700	324,977	1.69	69.88	99.25
700 to	800	650,023	3.37	73.25	99.39
800 to	900	413,900	2.15	75.40	99.47
900 to	1,000	356,800	1.85	77.25	99.53
1,000 to	2,000	1,933,137	10.04	87.29	99.83
2,000 and over		2,448,442	12.71	100.00	100.00
Total		19,262,941	100.00		12,617

but over a million were in the $5 to $10 million sales category, 5.67 per cent of the 19,260,000 employees in the 12,617 firms.

Clearly there is a close relation between the orders of men and money. For example, the tiny proportion of firms with over $1 billion in sales employ 23 per cent of the 19 million total work force; at the other extreme of size, $1 to $10 million, 63 per cent of the firms have only 10 per cent (9.82) of the total employees. The big

Table 4. Sales by Employment Category

Number of employees		Aggregate sales in millions of dollars	Percentage of total sales	Accumulated percentage of sales	Accumulated percentage of firms
1 to	50	5,588	1.28	1.28	8.59
50 to	100	3,352	.77	2.05	15.78
Over 100 but fewer than 1,000:					
100 to	200	15,549	3.58	5.63	37.74
200 to	300	10,554	2.43	8.06	50.33
300 to	400	12,091	2.78	10.84	60.87
400 to	500	8,451	1.94	12.78	67.71
500 to	600	7,782	1.79	14.57	73.29
600 to	700	6,472	1.49	16.06	76.69
700 to	800	4,770	1.10	17.16	79.27
800 to	900	4,769	1.10	18.26	81.53
900 to	1,000	3,780	.87	19.13	82.84
1,000 to	2,500	42,671	9.81	28.94	92.39
2,500 to	5,000	42,129	9.69	38.63	96.02
5,000 to	10,000	60,626	13.94	52.57	98.06
10,000 to	25,000	59,241	13.62	66.19	99.24
25,000 to	50,000	53,173	12.23	78.42	99.71
50,000 to	100,000	44,209	10.16	88.58	99.92
100,000 or	more	49,675	11.42	100.00	100.00
Total		434,882	100.00		

money firms are the big employee ones; those moderate in money are moderate in men; the small ones are small in men and money. The same relation could be deduced by studying aggregate sales by employment category (see Table 4).

The coherence and degree of relation between size of work force and sales, between men and money, can be examined profitably by asking whether the categories of sales and of the work force synchronically concentrate and spread together. Are the sales categories heavily concentrated, or do they spread evenly through many categories of men? We will examine Table 5, putting eighteen categories of work size on the left and spreading seventeen sales classes laterally. The totals at the bottom give the number of companies in each sales column; the totals at the right give the number of firms in

Table 5. Sequential Sizes of Firms: Sales and Employment

Number and percentage of firms by sales volume in millions of dollars per firm

Number of employees per firm	1		2		3		4		5		6		7		8		9		10	
	N	%	N	%	N	%	N	%	N	%	N	%	N	%	N	%	N	%	N	%
1–50	348	**58.4**	62	**10.4**	36	6.0	26	4.4	33	5.5	11	1.9	11	1.9	7	1.2	2	0.3	11	1.9
50–100	173	**28.5**	137	**22.6**	73	**12.0**	50	8.2	51	8.4	30	4.9	13	2.2	11	1.8	6	1.0	22	3.6
100–200	600	**22.9**	505	**19.3**	381	**14.5**	273	**10.4**	214	8.2	129	4.9	90	3.4	30	3.0	50	1.9	83	3.2
200–300	94	5.9	226	**14.1**	339	**21.2**	234	**14.6**	196	**12.2**	102	6.4	75	4.7	53	3.3	30	1.9	58	3.6
300–400	45	3.3	96	7.1	194	**14.3**	180	**13.3**	210	**15.6**	144	**10.6**	96	7.1	67	5.0	41	3.0	69	5.1
400–500	15	1.7	23	2.6	63	7.3	107	**12.3**	150	**17.3**	90	**10.4**	76	8.8	75	8.6	30	3.5	70	8.1
500–600	9	1.2	19	2.6	33	4.6	45	6.3	94	**13.0**	74	**10.3**	79	**11.0**	54	7.5	37	5.1	73	**10.1**
600–700	3	0.8	5	1.3	10	2.5	25	6.2	36	9.0	33	8.2	31	7.7	20	5.0	26	6.5	47	**11.7**
700–800	1	0.3	4	1.2	1	0.3	9	2.8	28	8.7	18	5.6	26	8.1	34	**10.6**	13	4.0	30	9.3
800–900	1	0.4	0	0	7	2.6	2	0.7	9	3.3	10	3.6	7	2.6	22	8.0	23	8.4	35	**12.8**
900–1,000	0	0	0	0	3	1.7	2	1.2	6	3.5	8	4.6	4	2.3	9	5.2	5	2.9	21	**12.1**
1,000–2,500	5	0.4	3	0.2	5	0.4	6	0.5	9	0.7	6	0.5	18	1.4	33	2.6	20	1.6	76	6.0
2,500–5,000	0	0	0	0	0	0	0	0	1	0.2	0	0	2	0.4	0	0	1	0.2	4	0.7
5,000–10,000	0	0	0	0	0	0	0	0	0	0	1	0.3	1	0.3	0	0	0	0	0	0
10,000–25,000	0	0	0	0	0	0	0	0	0	0	0	0	0	0	1	0.5	0	0	0	0
25,000–50,000	0	0	0	0	0	0	0	0	0	0	0	0	0	0	0	0	0	0	0	0
50,000–100,000	0	0	0	0	0	0	0	0	0	0	0	0	0	0	0	0	0	0	0	0
100,000+	0	0	0	0	0	0	0	0	0	0	0	0	0	0	0	0	0	0	0	0
Total	1,294		1,080		1,145		959		1,037		656		579		466		284		599	

Table 5. continued

Number of employees per firm	11–15 N	11–15 %	15–20 N	15–20 %	20–25 N	20–25 %	25–50 N	25–50 %	50–100 N	50–100 %	100–1000 N	100–1000 %	1000+ N	1000+ %	Total N	Total %	Number of columns containing over 10% of category
1–50	11	1.8	9	1.5	5	0.8	11	1.8	4	0.7	9	1.5	0	0	596	100	2
50–100	13	2.1	9	1.5	6	1.0	7	1.2	3	0.5	3	0.5	0	0	607	100	3
100–200	62	2.3	50	1.9	25	1.0	52	2.0	21	0.8	9	0.3	0	0	2,624	100	4
200–300	62	3.9	49	3.1	23	1.4	48	3.0	8	0.5	4	0.2	0	0	1,601	100	4
300–400	57	4.2	56	4.1	37	2.7	40	3.0	14	1.0	8	0.6	0	0	1,354	100	4
400–500	60	6.9	46	5.3	25	2.9	23	2.6	9	1.0	6	0.7	0	0	868	100	3
500–600	85	**11.8**	36	5.0	28	3.9	40	5.5	13	1.8	2	0.3	1	0.3	721	100	5
600–700	56	**14.0**	40	**10.0**	19	4.8	37	9.2	6	1.5	5	1.3	0	0	400	100	3
700–800	48	**14.9**	44	**13.7**	31	9.6	24	7.5	9	2.8	2	0.6	0	0	322	100	3
800–900	50	**18.2**	45	**16.4**	20	7.3	27	9.9	14	5.1	2	0.7	0	0	274	100	3
900–1,000	32	**18.5**	32	**18.5**	11	6.4	22	**12.7**	15	8.7	3	1.7	0	0	173	100	4
1,000–2,500	132	**10.4**	179	**14.1**	198	**15.6**	390	**30.5**	150	**11.8**	40	3.1	2	0.2	1,272	100	5
2,500–5,000	3	0.6	11	2.0	20	3.7	169	**31.1**	225	**41.4**	106	**19.5**	1	0.2	543	100	3
5,000–10,000	0	0	1	0.3	2	0.6	14	4.4	94	**29.5**	203	**63.6**	3	1.0	319	100	2
10,000–25,000	0	0	0	0	0	0	0	0	7	3.6	182	**93.3**	5	2.6	195	100	1
25,000–50,000	0	0	0	0	0	0	0	0	0	0	67	**84.8**	12	**15.2**	79	100	2
50,000–100,000	0	0	0	0	0	0	0	0	0	0	16	**44.4**	20	**55.6**	36	100	2
100,000+	0	0	0	0	0	0	0	0	0	0	1	7.1	13	**92.9**	14	100	1
Total	671		607		450		904		592		668		57		11,998	100	

that employment class; the percentages run laterally and give the proportion of firms within an employee size occurring in each sales size. In the column to the far right are tabulated the number of cells (cross-categories of men versus money) containing over 10 per cent of that row's sample. For reasons that will become apparent later, each of these 10 per cent cells has been underscored. Twelve of the 18 employment rows have three or fewer such cells; four have four; only two have five. Six, at the extremes of size, tend to have very high concentrations in one column, or in at most two; at the lower right of the table 93 per cent of all firms with over 100,000 employees have $1 billion or more in sales; 56 per cent of those with 50,000 to 100,000 employees are in this same sales category; 44 per cent are in the one to the left; at the other extreme (see upper left of table), 58 per cent of the firms with less than 50 employees are in the lowest sales category. Only three sequences are broken.

The table shows that:

1. In the great majority of the cases there is a steady unbroken progression of underscored cells running diagonally across the page, indicating that as the worker force grows progressively larger, the sales size steadily increases too; from the one million to the several billion categories, each grows with the other.

2. As we move across a row, it is evident that a concentration in one sales category of more than 10 per cent of the firms in an employment class will occur only three or four times and usually in an unbroken sequence of increasing sales volume.

3. The most concentrated sales category for a fixed employee class may also be the most concentrated for another employee class, in which case the classes will usually form an unbroken sequence of increasing employee size. For example, in the three smallest employee sizes, those up to 200 men, the highest concentration of firms for each was in the $1-million-sales class; of those with 300 to 500 men, the largest one was in the $5-million-sales class. There is a very heavy concentration and low spread of firms at the larger end of the ranges of men and money. In general, the concentration in a sales category of more than 10 per cent of the firms in an employee class is large enough, for the eighteen sizes of employees, so that the sum across a row of a sequence of three, four, or fewer

columns (of the seventeen sizes of sales) amounts to over half of all firms for any one of the worker categories.

Size and men and size and money, as measured by concentrations and dispersions of both, demonstrate that there is a close relationship and that this relationship is not spasmodic but runs serially and smoothly. Big and bigger corporations are big and bigger in both men and money; moderate and smaller ones are moderate and smaller in both categories. But the spread of sales in smaller and smaller proportions tells us that some corporations may sell more or less than their work force would indicate. No matter how these parts of the evidence are combined, men with money or money with men, bigness in business ordinarily means both men and money.

With this information about the sequential coherence of sizes in men and money, we can again ask the question, "How big is big?"

1. The *very small* firms among the big ones tend to be those with under a hundred employees and with $3 million or less in annual sales (others among them may have more income or more employees; see Table 5).

2. The *small* firms employ 100 to 300 men and have annual sales of $1 to $5 million (around them are others that spread in men and money).

3. The *large* firms employ 300 to 1,000 and spread from $3 to $50 million in annual sales and divide into two grades:

    1) 300 to 600 men and $3 to $15 million in sales

    2) 600 to 1,000 men and sales mostly $10 to $50 million

4. The *very large* firms employ 1,000 to 5,000 men and have sales of $11 to $1,000 million.

5. The largest employ 5,000 or more men, have sales of over $50 million, and divide into two grades:

    1) 5,000 to 10,000 men and $50 to $1,000 million

    2) 10,000 to 100,000 men and over and $100 to over $1,000 million

The problem now changes its direction. Having established by detailed evidence how the relative sizes of the orders of men and money are related among the firms for which we have evidence, we are ready to move forward to other questions about how big a big corporation is. We must now ask what the type of business activity has to do with size. What kinds of enterprises in mining, mer-

Table 6. Distribution of Firms by Standard Industrial Classification and by Employment Size

Number of employees

Type of operation	Fewer than 100			100–300			300–500			500–1,000		
	column %	N	row %	column %	N	row %	column %	N	row %	column %	N	row %
Agriculture	1.5	42	26.4	1.1	65	40.9	0.6	17	10.7	0.8	21	13.3
Mining	10.7	300	34.8	5.1	313	36.3	2.6	80	9.3	2.4	64	7.4
Contract construction	1.7	47	7.9	3.5	218	36.6	4.1	126	21.2	4.3	115	19.4
Manufacturing I (food, apparel, etc.)	3.5	97	4.5	9.9	609	29.6	15.1	467	22.2	17.0	459	21.9
Manufacturing II (paper, chemicals, etc.)	4.0	113	4.1	15.8	970	34.9	20.9	647	23.3	19.6	527	19.0
Manufacturing III (metal, machinery)	4.1	116	3.2	17.6	1,085	29.8	27.8	859	23.5	26.5	715	19.6
Transportation and utilities	8.8	247	18.5	5.7	349	25.9	5.4	167	12.4	6.8	183	13.6
Wholesale trade	17.8	500	23.6	19.1	1,171	55.3	8.3	255	12.1	4.6	124	5.8
Retail trade	7.9	222	12.7	11.7	717	41.1	8.2	253	14.5	9.2	248	14.2
Finance	38.1	1,071	52.8	8.4	517	25.4	4.3	132	6.5	6.0	162	8.0
Service	1.9	52	12.7	2.1	131	32.2	2.7	83	20.3	2.8	75	18.5
Grand total	100.0	2,807	15.8	100.0	6,145	34.5	100.0	3,091	17.3	100.0	2,693	15.2

Table 6 continued

Number of employees

Type of operation	1,000–5,000			5,000–10,000			10,000–1,000,000			Row totals		
	column %	N	row %	column %	N	row %	column %	N	row %	column %	N	row %
Agriculture	0.6	13	8.1	0.3	1	0.6	0.0	0	0.0	0.9	159	100.0
Mining	3.0	71	8.2	4.4	16	1.9	5.5	19	2.1	4.9	863	100.0
Contract construction	3.2	75	12.6	2.5	9	1.5	1.4	5	0.8	3.3	595	100.0
Manufacturing I (food, apparel, etc.)	15.7	368	17.6	14.9	54	2.4	11.9	41	1.8	11.8	2,095	100.0
Manufacturing II (paper, chemicals, etc.)	17.5	410	14.7	13.5	49	1.8	18.0	62	2.2	15.6	2,778	100.0
Manufacturing III (metal, machinery)	27.5	648	17.7	30.4	110	3.0	33.6	116	3.2	20.5	3,654	100.0
Transportation and utilities	12.5	293	21.8	14.6	53	3.9	15.4	53	3.9	7.6	1,345	100.0
Wholesale trade	2.6	60	2.8	1.1	4	0.2	0.6	2	0.2	11.9	2,116	100.0
Retail trade	10.2	239	13.7	10.2	37	2.1	8.7	30	1.7	9.8	1,746	100.0
Finance	4.9	115	5.6	6.3	23	1.1	3.5	12	0.6	11.4	2,032	100.0
Service	2.3	55	13.5	1.9	7	1.7	1.4	5	1.1	2.3	408	100.0
Grand total	100.0	2,347	13.2	100.0	363	2.0	100.0	345	2.0	100.0	17,791	100.0

Big and Not So Big Corporations

chandising, manufacturing, or finance tend to be very big and which relatively small? We will use as our definition of size the size of the work force rather than the volume of sales because this will permit us a sample of 17,796 firms. Only 12,617 reported sales figures (see Tables 1 and 3). The use of sales figures also might distort our picture of financial institutions (see footnote 3 above).

There are eleven types of business and industrial enterprise recognized in this part of our study of big corporations: five have more than two thousand firms, two have between one and two thousand, and two fewer than five hundred. The categories used conform to the Standard Industrial Classification (S.I.C.), under the sponsorship and supervision of the Office of Statistical Standards, Bureau of the Budget.

A very large number of subtypes and varieties of industry are collected under each of these major types. Let us briefly and broadly review what is found in each of them. Under agriculture there are large commercial farms, agricultural services, forestry (but not lumbering), and fisheries. The general category of mining includes metal, anthracite coal, and lignite mining, as well as crude petroleum, natural gas extraction, and quarrying of nonmetallic minerals. Contract construction includes general contractors, building construction, and special trade contractors. Manufacturing (I) includes food and kindred products as well as tobacco manufacturing; Manufacturing (II) includes lumber and wood products as well as chemicals, rubber products, and leather; and Manufacturing (III) includes metal and machinery and transportation equipment. In addition to local and interurban railways, bus lines, trucking, warehousing, water transportation, highway transportation, and air, rail, and pipeline, transportation expands into communications companies and other public utilities. Wholesale trade is self-explanatory. The retail trade again includes vending of all kinds of general merchandise to the consumer. Finance and real estate runs from banking and crediting agencies to insurance brokers and real estate. Services include a miscellaneous lot: hotels, camps, personal services, automobile repair, garage services, radio broadcasting, television, amusement, and recreation, and many others.[5]

We shall ask two kinds of questions about the kinds of enterprise

5. *Poor's Register of Directors and Executives, United States and Canada* (New York, Standard and Poor's Corporation, 1962), pp. 1–11.

related to size. How is each type distributed through the several sizes, and how does it compare with the others and with the results for all? What kinds of enterprise contribute most and least to the big and not-so-big work force sizes? We now know that about half the firms are in the two last categories—under 200 workers— that another third are in the next two categories—300 to 600—and that the remainder are in the categories of over 1,000 workers.

In Table 6, which covers close to 17,800 companies, we see that most types of business extend through all categories of size; some favor the small, some the large, but the largest percentage (47.7 per cent of all firms) is in the intermediate categories of 300 to 10,000 employees. How big is big among types of business? All kinds of manufacturing, transportation (and communications), and utilities are likely to be relatively big to very big; merchandising and finance corporations tend to be among the little giants. By consulting the percentages on the right in the first column, we see that five types [6] of business have a disproportionately high representation of firms in the under-100-employees class: finance, mining, agriculture, wholesale, and transportation and utilities. They are all above the general average of 15.8 per cent. Four are much below the general average: metal and machinery manufacturing, paper and chemical manufacturing, food and apparel manufacturing, and contract construction companies.

An overall view of Table 6 tells us that two-thirds of all agricultural firms are in the two lowest categories of size, those with less than 300 workers, and a large percentage of mining firms, wholesale companies, and finance enterprises are also small.[7]

MEN, MONEY, AND CORPORATE STRUCTURE

Despite a considerable spread of sales volume for each of the employee categories (Table 5), we observed earlier a close linear relation between sales volume and number of employees, between

6. Each firm is identified by its primary activity, so Sears is categorized as Merchandising, not Manufacturing.
7. See later chapters for problem of placing finance corporations.

Big and Not So Big Corporations

men and money. Corporations with the largest sales tend to be those with the largest number of men, and those with smaller sales are those with fewer men.

We now face the crucial question of how the categories of these closely connected two orderings are related to the structural sizes and extensions of big corporations. Are the relative sizes of the corporate social "anatomies," the structural compositions of big and not-so-big corporations, also related to the other two orders? Since very little has been systematically collected on structural size—only fragmentary surveys and independent corporate monographic studies and no compendia such as those for men and money (no Dun and Bradstreet, Moody, Standard and Poor's)—we must now change our procedure and turn to hypotheses and partial evidence to advance our knowledge. But, with luck, perhaps we can partly answer the really important sociological question about corporate size: What, if any, is the relation of corporate size in men and money to corporate structure?

Each large profit-making enterprise is a social system composed of positions (statuses) interconnected by social relations. The degrees of complexity and scale of any corporation, the extensions of its organization vertically in ranks and horizontally in complexity of status at the different levels of rank, are the major dimensions of its structural size. How many ranked statuses are in the line of command from top to bottom in a corporation's vertical dimension? How many positions, types of jobs, and how differentiated and complex are they at the different status levels of organization? The relative *structural* size of a big corporation can be stated only in such terms. It seems that size of assets, net worth, sales volume, size of earnings, and volume of products are all related to structural size. These measures tell about economic and social values attached to a company by the market and the society, but as such they are only *indicators* and *signs* of corporate organizational size, not the facts of organizational size. Sales volume and number of employees may be closely related to structural size. If we know them, we may possess knowledge about relative structural size, but these are not structural facts.

There have been many monographic studies of corporate organization and several small surveys, but the evidence about structural size is insufficient (or "not available") to provide measurements or even crude distinctions of relative size. We propose using the information we have to construct a model of probable corporate structural size and complexity, then testing the model against the monographic studies and corporation surveys. By so doing we will be able to relate the usual measures of size, such as men and money. Further testing from evidence not now available will still be needed. At this time our discussion cannot be based on hard deductive generalization from ample data; rather it is hypothesis and inference based on good but insufficient evidence and tested by too few and not always satisfactory cases.

If we find a possible high relation between the little-known structural sizes and those of the known number of men and amounts of money, we can then with relative safety assign appropriate structural size to corporations whose structural size and anatomy are not known and thus push our understanding of big corporations forward. By inspection of the present systematic listings (such as Dun and Bradstreet) of company payrolls, we can say that there are approximately X number of very large and not-so-large corporate structures with ten or more levels of command from top to bottom and with given degrees of complexity.

To achieve our ends and present models of relative corporate size for field testing, our procedures, documentation, and evidence will be somewhat arbitrary. But the model of structural size to be presented here is entirely subject to the control of future research evidence and probable modification. We will build on foundations of fact about the work forces of large-scale corporations and hypothetically relate the managerial hierarchy (coordinators) to theories.

Minimally the tasks of management positions in corporate organization coordinate the activities of those employed to produce a product or service for corporate gain. The lower, first-line management positions, such as straw bosses, and the topmost executives are included among "coordinator" statuses. To begin, let us arbitrarily assign two of the lowest coordinator statuses to every twenty-five workers, then assign one superior coordinating command status for each set of four coordinating statuses (some companies in fact will have more, some less). We will hold rigorously to these ratios for all work-force sizes, from 50 to 500,000.

We know that the two smallest categories of employment among

Figure 1.
Low Hierarchy, Small (100 Workers) Company

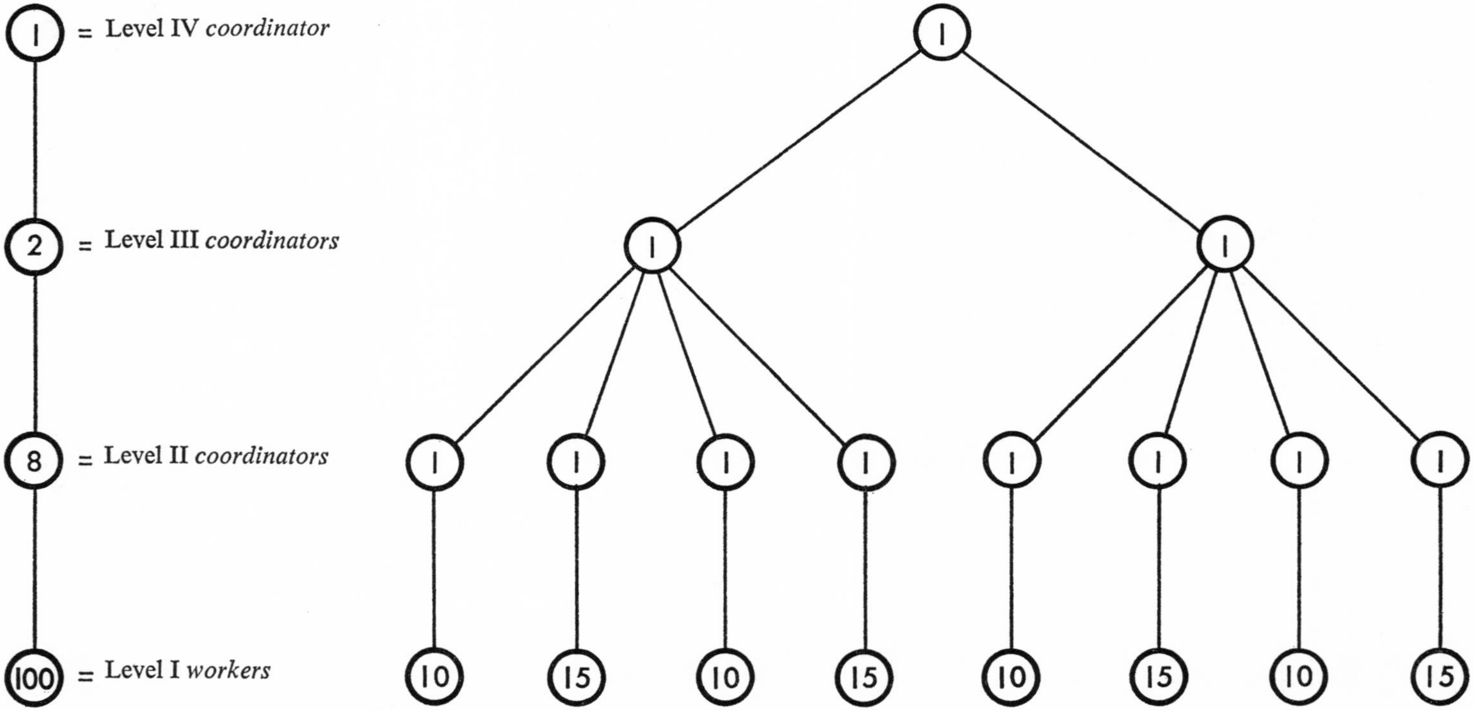

1 = Level IV *coordinator*
2 = Level III *coordinators*
8 = Level II *coordinators*
100 = Level I *workers*
1
1
1
1
1
1
1
1
1
1
1
10
15
10
15
10
15
10
15

the 21,000 large firms are those with fewer than 50 workers and those with 50 to 100. The combined application of these procedures on these two worker sizes produces four first-line coordinator statuses for 50 (two for each 25) and one superior coordinator status to command and close the first-line four. This produces a simple corporate hierarchy of three status levels: the worker, with 50 members; the first-line supervisor status, with four; and the top supervisor, with only one status.

The 100-worker size, of course, doubles the 50-worker size: eight first-line coordinators (two each for the four sets of 25 workers) and two coordinators for the first eight (one for each four). We now introduce the last principle: all top positions of two or more are closed by one command status, thus conforming to the empirical facts (president, general manager, etc.). This system of coordination and command produces, hypothetically, a corporate hierarchy of four. Figure 1 illustrates the structural differentiation and elaboration for the 100-worker size.

With these simple principles hypothetically established, let us move to some of the larger companies (see Figure 2). There we find a spread from the two lowest sizes for number of employees, through the less numerous firms that are larger, over to some of the very largest corporations in America.[8]

The four hypothetical types and eight subtypes can be structurally characterized and tentatively described. The small (with the subtypes of 50 and 100 workers) have three and four vertical levels of rank (see bottom left of Figure 2). The coordinating supervisory statuses double, from five for the 50 worker to eleven for the 100 worker size. In the large sizes (500 to 1,000 workers) the levels of rank increase to five, while workers advance ten times and the coordinator statuses are enlarged to 53 and 106. In the largest size (50,000 to 100,000 workers) the vertical levels move up to eight and nine, and the coordinator statuses grow to over five and ten thousand. At the fifth level of rank these very large hierarchies have more coordinator statuses than there are workers in the small firms; below this level are more than 10,000 coordinator statuses and above them forty more. Looking across Figure 2 on this same level (V), there is no one in the two subtypes of the small and only one

8. There are 14 firms with more than 100,000 workers in our sample; 36 with 50,000 to 100,000; about 1,000 in the 500 class; and 1,500 in the fewer-than-50 employee size.

Figure 2. Hierarchies: Workers, Coordinators and Levels

Number of levels		I Small		II Moderate		III Very large		IV Largest	
Coordinators	IX								1
Coordinators	VIII							1	4
Coordinators	VII						1	4	7
Coordinators	VI					1	3	15	30
Coordinators	V	1	1			6	12	60	120
Coordinators	IV		1	2	5	25	50	250	500
Coordinators	III	1	2	10	20	100	200	1,000	2,000
Coordinators	II	4	8	40	80	400	800	4,000	8,000
Workers	I	50(×2)	100(×10)	500(×2)	1,000(×10)	5,000(×2)	10,000(×10)	50,000(×2)	100,000
Levels		3	4	5	5	6	7	8	9
Total coordinators		5	11	53	106	532	1,066	5,330	10,662

Men, Money, and Corporate Structure

in the comparatively large firms of 500 to 1,000 workers. It is clear that with 120 coordinators at this fifth level of command and with four levels above and four below, the company has an exceedingly complex structure. Moreover, this vertical and lateral complexity becomes more apparent when it is seen that they, the 120, are relating to and directing 10,500 coordinators and 100,000 workers in the four ranks below them. In brief, structurally there has been not only an extension of the vertical structure from two to eight levels of command with a great social and status distance between the highest command and the worker, but also a great horizontal extension with increase in the status complexity of the coordinators.

Figure 3. Men, Money, and Structural Complexity

	I Smallest		II Moderate		III Large		IV Largest	
rkers	Under 50	50-100	500	1,000	5,000	10,000	50,000	100,000
centage of firms	8.6	7.2	5.6	9.6	2.0	1.2	0.21	0.08
egory of argest Sales %)	1 Million (58%)	1-2 Million (51%)	5-7,7-10 Million (56%)	25-50 Million (31%)	100 Million-1 Billion (64%)		Over 1 Billion (56%) (93%)	
tical evels	3	4	5	5	6	7	8	9
al of all oordinator ositions in ierarchy	5	11	53	106	532	1,066	5,330	10,662

If we divide the total number of coordinating statuses by the number of command levels (worker level not included) we get an index—perhaps an oversimplified one—of corporate hierarchical complexity. For example, for the 50-worker size there are two command levels and five statuses producing an index of complexity of 2.5. In the 100-worker size there are three coordinating levels and eleven coordinating statuses, giving an index of hierarchical complexity of 3.67. The index of complexity explodes to 1,333 for the very largest (see bottom of Figure 2, left to right).

Figure 3, adapted from Figure 2, relates the structural model to earlier information on the distribution of firms by employee size and the distribution of firms by sales volume for given em-

Big and Not So Big Corporations

ployee size. The top two rows of Figure 3 are based on the full count of firms by employee size (17,800); the fourth row is based on sales size (for 12,600 firms); and the last two rows are the estimates of Figure 2. From Column I we learn that the small-size corporations of 50 workers (8.6 per cent) hypothetically had three vertical levels and five coordinators. Moreover, we learn that the largest per cent of firms were in the category of sales of $1 million where the earnings of 58 per cent of all such firms were centered. At the other extreme of structural size and complexity (IV) there are only fourteen firms (0.08 per cent). They have, hypothetically, nine levels in the command ranks and a very elaborate lateral complexity with over 10,600 structural positions in the corporate organization. Their sales tend to be over $1 billion a year.

We must now ask a critical question of our general method and simple index: How accurately does it predict structural complexity and measure it with only an "arbitrary" use of employee size? A corporation is an economic action system socially organized to perform certain tasks in order to produce goods and services for profit. What is being coordinated is not merely the bodies of men but their most diverse occupational actions under conditions of corporate purpose subject to the multiple limitations and opportunities of a very complex, changing, open economy and society. A high degree of specialization of occupation and activity, a complex technological transformation of items of nonutility into those of salable utility, a great differentiation of function and structure all suggest that a simple, straightforward, mechanical procedure using only assumptions based on the coordination of "bodies" (individual employees) is likely to underpredict the structural (status and relation) size of a corporation.

We have suspected that men and money sizes of firms and structural size and length of the corporate hierarchies are closely interrelated. We must now inspect the insufficient available evidence about structural size and test the results of the hypothetical analysis. We will not pretend to test the hypothesis fully; if we could do so with ample evidence, this presentation would be quite different. Our efforts here are to see how far we can rely on the present procedure. If it is moderately exact, as we believe it to be, employment figures can be transformed with low chance of error into estimations of structural complexity, and further studies can test and improve the method and increase our insight into the factors that limit and expand size and complexity of corporate organization. With the use of empirical monographs, our own research, and a few surveys, we will proceed. Remember that we shall expect probable underprediction rather than exact or overestimation. We cannot hope to do any exact testing of the usefulness of our predicted number of coordinators as a measure of what we may call lateral complexity. Only estimations can be made. Of the studies of vertical levels in employee size, some are complete, but because the authors had other purposes and problems in mind, most are not. Let us turn to some of these studies for first test evidence.

We will select a few studies of individual corporate hierarchies and use some of the evidence from the surveys and evidence ranging from small to the largest corporations. We will know employee size and (with fair accuracy) the number of levels of company command.

Holden, Fish, and Smith [9] looked at the management hierarchies of thirty-one large companies with 30,000 to 50,000 workers. Inspection of their evidence indicates nine to eleven levels (our model would predict eight).

Forty companies and "several hundred organizational manuals and charts" were studied by Ernest Dale.[10] He examined the actual size of many companies ranging from less than 10 employees to approximately 500,000 employees. The very small (3 to 5 men) had two levels; those with 25 workers, four levels (our model predicts three); firms with 125 workers had four levels (the model predicts four). The evidence on levels for the other size firms is insufficient for our purposes; however, the largest size, just under 500,000 employees, had fourteen levels. The model predicts only ten. Sears, Roebuck, which we will examine in detail, with 150,000 workers at the time of study (1948), actually had eleven or twelve levels (the model predicts nine).

The model consistently underpredicts from small to large. But as the firms grow from fewer than a hundred to 50,000 and 100,000, the differences between the prediction and reality increase. By

9. P. E. Holden, L. S. Fish, and H. L. Smith, *Top Management Organization and Control* (Stanford, Stanford University Press, 1948).

10. Ernest Dale, *Planning and Developing the Company Organization Structure* (New York, American Management Association, 1952) Research Report No. 20.

Big and Not So Big Corporations

adding one level to the smaller firms up to 500, one to two for the 1,000 class, and at least two for the 50,000, and even as much as four for the 100,000 to 500,000 the prediction becomes more accurate. The increase in the number of ranks as the corporations increase in employee size from the model's theoretical prediction appears to be a result of the increasing amount and complexity of action at the top levels and the need to order this into rank statuses such as the reranking of vice-presidents into executive vice-presidents, group vice-presidents, and what may be called division managers. This explanation is somewhat oversimplified.

CASE STUDY: SEARS, ROEBUCK

The structure of the Sears, Roebuck organization has been well documented and extensively researched.[11] At the time (1948) Emmet and Jeuck wrote their book, *Catalogues and Counters,* Sears had 150,000 employees, 632 retail stores, 11 mail order plants, and 341 order offices; it was selling well over $2 billion worth of goods annually. It was "entirely decentralized," except for the buying function. The company, as all students know, is a classical example of a successful "flat" hierarchy, meaning that the vertical extension is deliberately and consciously limited and that command and decision are pushed as far down as possible, even to the lowest levels of authority.

In 1963 Sears' size had increased to 761 stores and 5.1 billion dollars a year in sales, three-fourths in stores and the remainder by catalogue. This vast organization still used centralized merchandising (buying, promotion, and advertising) and decentralized territorial control of daily and yearly operations. This means, as in 1948, that control of cost, quality, and quantity of each product and all merchandising decisions, big and little, of the fifty product category divisions took place at the highest levels of command in

11. Boris Emmet and John E. Jeuck, *Catalogues and Counters* (Chicago, University of Chicago Press, 1950).

the Chicago central offices.[12] Although Sears has grown by all measures—men, money, products, and territory—its basic organization remains very similar to what it was at the time of the 1948 study. We will use Emmet and Jeuck's description of the organizational structure.

Top management organization consists of a board of directors with a chairman and below him a president to whom five territorial vice-presidents report. The territorial headquarters are in New York City, Chicago, Los Angeles, Dallas, and Atlanta. The vice-president in charge of merchandising and four other vice-presidents also report to the president; they are all in the Chicago home office. A staff headed by the director of personnel, the assistant to the president for public relations, and the assistant to the president for operation are extensions of the presidential status and its activities. Each territorial vice-president supervises all mail order and retail store business in his province. As a territorial administrative officer, he is entirely responsible for his area and reports to the president; but for all merchandising decisions and communications he reports to the vice-president in charge of merchandising. In theory the vice-president in charge of merchandising may not have higher rank than the others, but in fact he does. His functions, responsibilities, and position in the central home office, where he controls buying for all provincial operations, put him on a higher level. The five territorial vice-presidents and the vice-president in charge of merchandising are the members of the committee on merchandising policy. It is significant that the vice-president in charge of merchandising is chairman of this committee.

Central buying has its own complex organization with six or seven levels of rank below the vice-president who runs it. Each territorial vice-president heads a vast organization—an extensive territorial, functional staff, rather highly differentiated. His territory and organization are first divided into "groups," each consisting of stores located near each other, usually in the same metropolis. The midwestern province had *eleven* in 1948. All were in major standard metropolitan statistical areas. Each group manager has a variety of managers who report to him from both "A" and "B" stores, including merchandising and sales promotion, personnel, and

12. John McDonald, "Sears Makes It Look Easy," *Fortune* (1964) pp. 120, 218.

Big and Not So Big Corporations

others. There are at least four levels in his apparatus. Some A store managers report directly to the territorial vice-president. In addition to the group in separate A store arrangements, there are the B store "zone" organization and the mail order structure. The midwestern zone, for example, has four territorial divisions, each with its separate stores and each with a zone manager with his own staff and field men. The managerial apparatus at this part of the organization has at least three or four status levels.

The A stores in Sears are the largest, do the most business, and offer the greatest variety of products; the several types of B stores are next; and the C stores are smallest. Some of the A stores are very large department stores with large staffs selling a great volume and variety of merchandise. Below the store manager are at least four levels—managers of different kinds of merchandise, operating superintendents, division managers, and sales people and clerks. The organizations of B and C stores are smaller and have less elaborate hierarchies as well as simpler types of organization at the several levels.

It is difficult to count the levels of command in a corporate structure; often it is necessary to go beyond company testimony and observe behavior. For example, is the vice-president in charge of merchandising at Sears above the other vice-presidents, or is he at the same command level? Are all the less formal levels of supervision, not easily identified and distinguished, to be counted? With some likelihood of small error the task can be accomplished. Despite the fact that Sears is a flat, decentralized organization, there appear to be at least eleven or twelve status levels, running from chairman of the board through president and vice-presidents and down to the clerks and sales people. There are five or six levels within the A stores, including the manager and the people at the sales counters. There are one or two above this in the group organization and possibly two more above them, vice-presidents included, in the territorial province. Above the vice-president level, at the home office, there are two and possibly three higher ranks, president and chairman of the board, and possibly a differentiated merchandising vice-president above the others. At the most, the number of ranks might reach a possible thirteen; some strict formalists would say no more than eleven.

Eleven or twelve ranks of this flat hierarchy are still extensive and necessarily elaborate for 1948 or for 1963. The model employee coordination predicts nine levels for the 150,000 workers. The strict body count that disregards other characteristics of organization and emphasizes coordinations of individuals, as we said, usually underpredicts. Before examining other corporate hierarchies to test predictions, let us review some of the factors that determine organizational complexity and hierarchical extensions of rank at Sears.

The rate of growth of the number of Sears retail stores has been extraordinary. There were eight in 1925, 192 in 1928, 482 in 1938, 632 in 1948, and by 1963 there were 761 stores. Meanwhile, after some experimentation, the status and organizational structure of Sears underwent drastic change to the present one of central control of merchandising with decentralized stores and provinces, each with its own vice-president. By 1948 Sears had stores in all but a very few states of the Union. The population had become not only urban but metropolitan with standard metropolitan statistical areas. The spread and concentration of the stores reflected not only population changes but also almost revolutionary technological and social changes. The five great territories, each with its vice-president, divided all of America and routed the Sears business from these provinces into the Chicago capital, the home of Sears, Roebuck. The group had organized the metropolitan clusters of stores within the provinces and had related Sears to the broad localities of the cities; the spreadout zones of the smaller stores also divided the five provinces. The managers of the groups and zones added a layer to the vertical extension of the hierarchies. Inside each of the worlds of the A, B, C, stores of the groups and zones was another small, highly contained kingdom run by a manager and his men, with their own local hierarchies and internal levels of command and rank. Not only did the stores grow more numerous, but many also grew larger in floor space, in volume of sales and variety of products sold, as well as in number of employees and complexity and differentiation of social structure. Within each store and between the statuses and ranks that hold and maintain the corporate empire, increasing diversity and volume of men, money, and merchandising are all factors that help increase the structural complexity of Sears and press against its formal management's efforts to keep a flat, decentralized enterprise system. The hard-nosed profes-

Big and Not So Big Corporations

sional policies of Sears, supported by its professional philosophy, have taught them to keep a simple hierarchy, low and limited, with standardized complexities. Yet, to do business and keep up with the rapidly emerging American culture, not only to hold its present growth but to get bigger and better, the ranks have expanded, and the levels have grown more complex.

A great variety of factors, all intertwined, are involved. We will examine a few. There has been not only a great increase in the dollar volume of sales but also a greater velocity of paper and money flow and the need to systematically handle this flow. There has been an enormous increase in the buying, vending, and sending of products, in the number and variety of products, and in the need for the kind of knowledge necessary to get and send the products to and from the stores, as well as to route them within the stores. This need is felt at all levels, from the counters to the committee on merchandising policy. There has been an increase in the number and size of the stores, in the number and kinds of customers, and in the amount of control and functional coordination necessary for the maintenance of these stores.

There has been an increase in the amount and kind of public and social interaction at the community and national level. There has been an increase in the number and variety of decisions and communications made by managers and in the amount and variety of data gathered and needed for the buying and selling of products and for the management of their increasingly diverse action system inside the Sears empire and outside as well. All these and more are parts of the growth of Sears as a social, corporate structure. The more it practices its philosophy of keeping its hierarchy flat and its structure simple, the more it is under the double fist of an expanding empire and an expanding American society. But still, the highly valued flat, vertical ranks contain the managers of individual stores, the group and zone managers, the territorial vice-presidents, and above them the president and chairman of the board in Chicago.

It seems probable that the single body-counting coordinator model we used, which only indirectly takes account of the coordination of the diversity of action in a corporate structure, is likely to underpredict rather than overpredict the rank levels in a complex hierarchy such as Sears. The fact that it predicts nine, rather than eleven or twelve, as the actual number in this organization, seems to demonstrate that the Sears philosophy of maintaining flat organization—and the efforts to enforce it—has not been so highly successful as the growth of Sears itself. To correct for the social differentiation and technological complexity that are part of this specialization at Sears and thereby to predict correctly the length of the hierarchy, it would be necessary to add at least two and possibly three more levels.

A few years ago Dr. Norman Martin, of New York University, studied the decision-making process of the managerial hierarchy of a large food manufacturing company of some 30,000 men.[13] From chairman of the board, through several levels of top command, down through the division superintendent, department and shift foremen, to the workers were nine levels of corporate rank. The employee model used here predicts only eight. In a shoe corporation studied by Warner and Low [14] there were 1,000 workers and seven levels: three were above plant manager—chairman of the board, president, and vice-president, and three were below, including the worker level. The employee model predicts only five levels of rank. Each of these smaller corporations—one of 30,000 and the other of 1,000—in fact has more levels than predicted by the coordinator model based only on size of employees. They conform to what we can now expect: the employee predictor is too parsimonious.

Whatever the underprediction of the model, the degrees of vertical and lateral extension advanced as would be expected in moving from the not-so-big to the very big. Within the model, as the size of the worker force moves from 100 or fewer to 500,000 or more and sales from $1 million to $1 billion and more, the number of levels goes from three to nine or more and the number of coordinating statuses from eleven for the firms with 100 men to 10,700 for the very large ones; the simple index of vertical-lateral complexity increases from a ratio of 3.67 to 1,333. We can now ask again what are big and not-so-big. Our present answer, of course, includes what was said in the previous several paragraphs, and we can continue by saying that firms with no rank are Pa and Ma stores (I), those with two to four levels and 100 employees are low in com-

13. Norman H. Martin, "Differential Decisions in the Management of An Industrial Plant," *Journal of Business*, 29:4 (1956), 249–60.
14. W. Lloyd Warner and J. O. Low, *The Social System of the Modern Factory* (New Haven, Yale University Press, 1947).

plexity and structurally small (II), those structures with five or six levels and 500 to 1,000 workers are comparatively large (III), and those with eight and nine levels and 50,000 to 100,000 employees are very complex structures and very large (IV), and those few with several hundred thousand men and ten to fifteen levels are the most complex and the largest. We can also say that our evidence is approximated by our model and that structural complexity, vertical extension, and lateral spread are closely related to the number of men employed and the volume of sales. One implies the other— men and money, and structure.

CHAPTER THREE

The Headquarters of Big Corporations

CONCENTRATIONS AND NATIONAL SPREAD

Headquarters is the place of ultimate corporate command. There at the top, where greatest power and highest prestige are hierarchically placed, legitimacy is given to all corporate decisions. To accent the great significance of headquarters and the importance of their location, many corporations place their highest administrative offices within the imposing reaches of a cloud-piercing skyscraper to which they give the corporate name. There, in the executive suites of top management, the chairman of the board, the president, many vice-presidents, and most of the other executives of high position perform their acts of utility and ceremony. On the floors below huge advisory, clerical, and supplementary staffs surround and support them. Up and down long chains of command, communications and decisions come and go to all regions of the vast empires—to the larger world of business, industry, and the general society. The significance and function of headquarters, their executive offices, and corporate elite are not those of command and utility only; they are symbols of corporate power and prestige. The physical location of headquarters is of great importance to everyone concerned with the well-being of an organization, for it is the capital city of a corporate enterprise.

Six questions guide this part of our inquiry about the 21,000 corporations studied in Chapter 2:

1. In which zones, regions, states and cities of the United States are their corporate headquarters located?

2. Are these headquarters spread throughout the country, or are they concentrated in certain patterns? How and why?

This Chapter is by W. Lloyd Warner and Darab B. Unwalla. See Notes on Authors.

Headquarters of Big Corporations

3. Do certain businesses and industries favor or avoid some regions or states? If so, why?

4. What cities are chosen for the location of the headquarters of big corporations? The new ones? The old ones? The very big, medium, or small cities? The eastern, central, or western cities?

5. What have size of corporation and size of city to do with location of headquarters? Do the very largest favor the large cities, the metropolises and polyopolises, and the small ones the smaller cities? Or is there no size relation?

6. During the last half century, have there been notable shifts in the concentrations of headquarters? With the development of one great American community closely tied together in space and time —partly by the structures of these same corporations and other giant organizations—do headquarters tend to appear throughout the national community area or to concentrate in one or more great commercial capital cities? Where are they now? Where were they thirty years ago?

To answer these six major questions we identified the 1960 locations of the headquarters of the 21,000 firms and categorized them by city, state, region, and zone. We also classified the states, cities, and regions by population size and by age and geographical position of headquarters and related them to corporate size and types of industry and business enterprise. To learn what changes, if any, have occurred in the last thirty years, we also followed these procedures for a 1930 sample of 3,055 companies. The 1930 sample was compiled from an initial random sample of 4,000 firms designed to give a final sample of 10 per cent of each type of firm in the 1931 Moody's manuals of industrials, railroads, public utilities and finance.[1] The data for assets, employment, operations, and geographical locations of the headquarters could be determined for 3,055 of the 4,000.

The 1930 data for headquarters are comparable to those for 1960 but with the following limitations. In 1960 cities were defined by the census in terms of standard metropolitan statistical areas (SMSA); in 1930 they were defined in terms of traditional metropolitan areas or cities. The difference will be discussed later in this chapter. Difficulties are also involved in comparing assets for the

1. New York, Moody's Investors Service, 1931.

two periods. The assets for 1960 firms varied from $1 million to more than $23 billion, whereas the assets for 1930 firms seldom exceeded $100 million. The latter difference was alleviated by scaling the assets of 1930 firms proportionately into five asset sizes based on the percentage-of-sales figures for 20,890 firms in 1960.

The concentration of headquarters follows most of the other tendencies of population growth and spread and the development of the various regions of the United States. Differences appear by type of business in how home office location responds to the larger developments of the society. The growth of the great cities and the spread and concentration of corporate headquarters are closely interconnected.

The emergent developments of American society increasingly redefine older economic and social functions and assign new ones. Clearly reflected in the current location of major company headquarters are the realignments of populations into urban agglomerations and the tightening of the great cities' interrelations with each other in time and in space. At least two fundamental processes of emergent change, each opposed to the other, can be discerned in the persistence and mobility of the location of headquarters of the approximately 21,000 large firms in our sample:

1. There is a general tendency now for corporate headquarters to be found throughout the United States, in all the nine major census regions, in every state, as well as in most of the large cities.

2. Despite this vast spread most corporate headquarters are concentrated in very narrowly confined territorial limits.

Although there are many thousands of urban communities, the headquarters of about 17,000 of the 21,000 large enterprises are concentrated in about 200 metropolitan cities. Moreover, the headquarters of other types of large-scale organizations are also clustered in a very few metropolitan centers. For example, the scores of agencies of the federal government as well as its executive, legislative, and judicial parts are all in one great center; the headquarters of large-scale civic and professional associations and trade associations are in a very few metropolitan communities, especially Washington, New York, and Chicago. Educational institutions, big unions, and the great church agencies show similar concentrations in a few large metropolitan centers.

American corporations, within limits, are often free to put their

Headquarters of Big Corporations

central offices anywhere they please and not necessarily where the productive work of the enterprise is carried out; they can be placed wherever seems wisest or most advantageous. Does the geographical location of a region, state, or city east of the Appalachians, north or south of the Ohio, or west of the Rockies, or the comparative age of a city, state, or region seem important?

First, a summary statement about the contemporary spread and concentration of population in the continental United States was prepared, for the purposes of this research, on a division of the forty-eight continental states into three geographical zones, corresponding to major topographical outlines and, roughly, chronology and development. The Eastern Zone spreads westward from the Atlantic to the Appalachian Mountains and southward from Canada to the Gulf of Mexico (see Figure 1). The Central Zone, bounded on the north by Canada and by Mexico and the Gulf on the south, on the east by the Appalachians and on the west by the eastern slopes of the Rocky Mountains, is in fact the great basin of the Mississippi River and its larger tributaries. The Western Zone spreads from the eastern slopes of the western mountains to the Pacific Ocean.

We have observed the nine major census divisions, here called regions for added clarity. New England, the Middle Atlantic, and the South Atlantic census regions are in the Eastern Zone. Four of the large census regions, the East and West North Central and the East and West South Central, comprise the great zone in the Mississippi Valley. The Western Zone is composed of the Mountain and the Pacific regions. The Eastern Zone roughly corresponds to the region of settlement during the colonial and early national period, and the East Central to the first half and the West Central to the latter half of the nineteenth century. The two tips, north and south, of the Eastern Zone developed somewhat later than the rest of the zone, and the Mountain states, generally speaking, grew after those on the Pacific.

Given the great differences in population and geography and the time of development of the country, particularly in relation to population and economics, how are the corporate headquarters distributed among the three zones or the nine regions? The relation of the proportion of population in the zones, regions, and states to the proportion of headquarters tells a significant story about the impor-

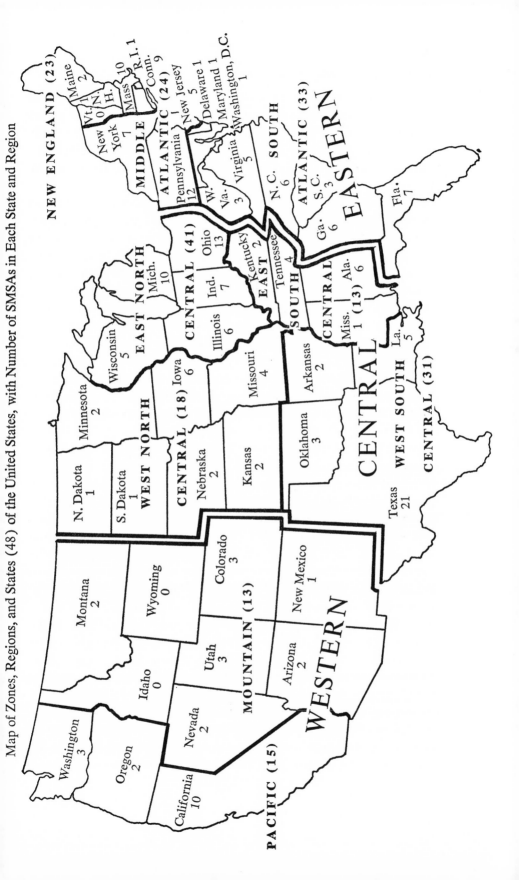

Map of Zones, Regions, and States (48) of the United States, with Number of SMSAs in Each State and Region

NEW ENGLAND (23)
Maine 2
Vt. 1
N.H. 1
Mass. 10
R.I. 1
Conn. 9

MIDDLE ATLANTIC (24)
New York 7
New Jersey 5
Pennsylvania 12

SOUTH ATLANTIC (33)
Delaware 1
Maryland 1
Washington, D.C. 1
Virginia 5
W. Va. 3
N.C. 6
S.C. 3
Ga. 6
Fla. 7

EASTERN

EAST NORTH CENTRAL (41)
Ohio 13
Mich. 10
Ind. 7
Illinois 6
Wisconsin 5

WEST NORTH CENTRAL (18)
N. Dakota 1
S. Dakota 1
Minnesota 2
Iowa 6
Nebraska 2
Kansas 2
Missouri 4

EAST SOUTH CENTRAL (13)
Kentucky 2
Tennessee 4
Miss. 1
Ala. 6

WEST SOUTH CENTRAL (31)
Arkansas 2
Oklahoma 3
La. 5
Texas 21

CENTRAL

MOUNTAIN (13)
Montana 2
Idaho 0
Wyoming 0
Nevada 2
Utah 3
Colorado 3
Arizona 2
New Mexico 1

PACIFIC (15)
Washington 3
Oregon 2
California 10

WESTERN

Headquarters of Big Corporations

tance of the various locations and the importance assigned to them by the corporate life of America. Generally speaking, there is strong correspondence between high or low percentages in population in each of the territorial units and high or low concentration of headquarters. The Central Zone has 45 per cent of the population and 46 per cent of all headquarters; the Eastern Zone has 39 per cent of the people and 42 per cent of all headquarters; 16 per cent of the population is in the Western Zone but only a little over 11 per cent of the corporate administrative centers (see Table 1). Headquarters in the two older zones are slightly above population size, and in the Pacific, the youngest, a little below. However, the Eastern Zone's proportion of headquarters is somewhat smaller than the comparatively more recent Central Zone.

Percentages for the regions partly verify the possible effects of comparative age of the society on the location of headquarters. For example, New England, one of the oldest, has 6 per cent of the United States population but over 8 per cent of headquarters, whereas the very young Pacific region has 12 per cent of the population but only 9 per cent of headquarters. Is this age factor true for all sizes of corporations? For example, the West South Central region (Texas, Oklahoma, etc.) has a relatively higher proportion of corporate headquarters (11 per cent) than population (9.5 per cent), yet it is one of the regions of very recent, rapid growth. Later analysis of size and type of business activities will tell us more about other forces operating in the location of corporate headquarters.

The Middle Atlantic region (23 per cent) leads in the Atlantic Zone. In the Central Zone, the East North Central region (those states along the Great Lakes) easily leads (24 per cent); and in the Western Zone the Pacific (9 per cent) is far ahead of the Mountain region. The concentration of headquarters still narrows.

In each region one state is usually the dominant and outstanding leader. Among the six states of New England, Massachusetts leads with 4.6 per cent of all corporate headquarters in the United States; New York state (13 per cent) is a strong first among the three in the Middle Atlantic; North Carolina (2.2 per cent) is almost tied by Florida and Georgia among the eight states of the South Atlantic. Illinois (7.5 per cent) is well ahead in the East North Central census region of the Central Zone. South and across the Mississippi, Missouri leads (2.8 per cent) all six states in its region; Texas (7.2

Table 1. Corporate Headquarters in the Zones and Regions of the United States and the Leading State in Each Region (1960)

Zones and regions	1960 population Number in millions	%	Firms in region Number	%	Leading state in region and % of headquarters in it State	%
Eastern Zone		39.4		42.2		
New England	10.5	5.9	1,748	8.4	Massachusetts	4.6
Middle Atlantic	34.1	19.0	4,856	23.3	New York	13.0
South Atlantic	26.0	14.5	2,194	10.5	N. Carolina	2.2
Central Zone		45.0		46.4		
East South Central	12.1	6.7	904	4.3	Tennessee	1.7
West South Central	17.0	9.5	2,220	10.6	Texas	7.2
East North Central	36.2	20.2	4,925	23.6	Illinois	7.5
West North Central	15.4	8.6	1,655	7.9	Missouri	2.8
Western Zone		15.6		11.4		
Mountain	6.9	3.8	529	2.5	Colorado	0.9
Pacific	21.2	11.8	1,864	8.9	California	6.7
Total	179.4	100.0	20,895	100.0		46.6

Headquarters of Big Corporations

per cent) is far ahead among the four states in the Southwest region; and Tennessee is ahead (1.7 per cent) in its region. In the Pacific region, California (6.7 per cent) far outstrips the other four (including Alaska and Hawaii for our purposes here). Colorado (0.9 per cent) is the leader among the eight Mountain states.

The statement that corporate headquarters are spread throughout the United States is demonstratively certain by the figures which we have examined; however, it is also clear that certain areas are very high and others low. Also, although corporate headquarters of large-scale organizations are not necessarily bound to regions of high population (since headquarters can be located away from the masses of employees), there is a relation between the number and proportion of headquarters and the size of the population in each area. However, it must be said that certain older areas, such as New England, rank higher for corporate headquarters than for size of population. On the other hand, certain newer regions, such as the West South Central, rank comparatively high for population and also for the percentage of firms located there. Overall, population size is directly related to the concentration of headquarters in any given locality.

Size of firm as measured by the number of employees (see Table 2) was divided into several categories from less than 100 to over 10,000. The distribution of company headquarters in each region according to size of firm has its own particular pattern. Two contiguous regions, the Middle Atlantic and the East North Central (Great Lakes), together have three-fourths of the headquarters of the biggest of all corporations, those with over 10,000 employees. They rank either first or second for every type of corporation; their combined total of 47 per cent of all the large corporations far surpasses all other regions for headquarters. The next two ranking regions, the South Atlantic (11 per cent) and the West South Central (10 per cent), fell far behind. The proportion of the Middle Atlantic, while high in all categories, drops step by step as the corporation types decrease in size, from 48.7 per cent to 17.2 per cent. New England is somewhat higher in medium-sized firms, those with 500 to 1,000 (9.9 per cent) and 1,000 to 5,000 employees (8.7 per cent), but has only 4.1 per cent of the very big and 9.0 per cent of the very small. The South Atlantic follows the New England pattern. The more rural states (Mississippi, Alabama, etc.) of the East South Central drop from their high of 5.7 per cent for the

Table 2. Corporate Size and Location of Headquarters by Percentage in Regions (1960)

Size of firms by number of employees

Region of headquarters	Under 100	100 to 300	300 to 500	500 to 1,000	1,000 to 5,000	5,000 to 10,000	10,000 and over	Total
New England	9.0	7.1	9.6	9.9	8.7	7.7	4.1	8.4
Middle Atlantic	17.2	20.1	22.4	23.5	26.7	36.0	48.7	22.3
South Atlantic	10.2	10.8	11.0	11.2	10.0	9.4	5.2	10.6
East South Central	5.7	4.2	4.8	4.1	3.6	2.5	0.3	4.4
West South Central	18.9	11.3	7.0	7.2	6.1	3.6	2.0	10.1
East North Central	18.0	25.0	25.8	26.7	26.8	25.1	26.4	24.6
West North Central	8.6	8.5	7.7	7.1	7.3	7.4	4.6	7.9
Mountain	3.8	3.0	1.8	1.7	1.8	1.1	0.6	2.4
Pacific	8.6	10.0	9.9	8.6	9.0	7.2	8.1	9.3
Total percentage	100.0	100.0	100.0	100.0	100.0	100.0	100.0	100.0
Total number	2,800	6,120	3,066	2,676	2,339	363	345	17,709*

* 84.3 per cent of our total sample of 20,989 firms, for which we have employment figures, and not including 87 firms with headquarters outside the continental United States.

Headquarters of Big Corporations

very small, step by step as the size of the corporation increases, to only 0.3 per cent for the very large. The rather rural regions, the West North Central and the Mountain, do likewise. The Pacific Coast percentages for all sizes hold close to their general average (9.3 per cent), as do those for the East North Central.

We demonstrated for all corporations that in most regions one state leads all others. Although a slightly modified picture emerges when corporate sizes are examined, the general tendency still holds. For example, in New England, Massachusetts leads for all seven categories of size, New York is far ahead for all sizes in the Middle Atlantic, Texas in the Southwest, Colorado in the Mountain region, California in the Pacific, and Missouri in the North Central. If the leading state's corporate percentages were removed from any major region, its score, in many cases, would fall far behind most other areas; for example, New England without Massachusetts would fall below all other regions except Mountain.

We next examined the spread and concentration of corporate capitals by activity type, such as finance, manufacturing, and retail trade (see Table 3). Businesses were categorized into nine types (Standard Industrial Classification).

To compare the New England region of the Eastern Zone with the Pacific of the Western Zone, it will be remembered that New England's average percentage for all United States headquarters was 8.4 and the Pacific's 8.9 (see Table 1). For financial corporations, one of the largest categories in our sample (3,600 companies), New England had more than double the concentration of the Pacific Coast (13.0 vs. 5.4). It also led the Pacific region, but only slightly, for the largest category, manufacturers (9.8 vs. 8.2), and was only slightly under for transportation (7.6 vs. 9.0). But in the six other categories of industry, the new West is far ahead of old New England. About a third of the agricultural (and fishing) corporations' headquarters are on the Pacific Coast and only 5 per cent in New England. Eleven per cent of the service enterprises are in the West and only 4 per cent in New England. In contract construction the Pacific is far ahead of New England, with 15 per cent to 4 per cent, and much ahead in mining, 6 per cent to less than 1 per cent. Moreover, the new West has more than double the concentration of New England in the third and fourth largest categories: wholesale trade, some 2,400 corporations, and retail trade, 1,900 corporations. The oldest large-scale industries, including

Table 3. Headquarters, Business Activity, and Region (1960)

Business activity by percentage in each region

Region of headquarters	Agriculture	Mining	Contract const.	Manufacturing	Transp. and utilities	Whole-sale trade	Retail trade	Finance and real estate	Services	Total
New England	5.3	0.8	3.9	9.8	7.6	5.2	5.1	13.0	4.2	8.4
Middle Atlantic	5.3	12.2	18.6	25.2	19.4	24.1	18.5	26.2	31.6	23.3
South Atlantic	17.6	5.0	13.2	9.8	11.9	10.3	12.1	11.8	11.0	10.5
East South Central	4.8	1.9	3.7	4.0	6.2	4.9	5.2	4.5	2.7	4.3
West South Central	16.5	55.5	12.0	4.7	10.5	9.8	13.8	9.6	10.7	10.6
East North Central	6.4	8.6	21.0	30.3	20.5	20.2	20.6	18.5	20.2	23.6
West North Central	6.9	4.9	8.6	6.8	11.0	9.4	10.1	8.4	5.5	7.9
Mountain	6.4	5.3	3.9	1.2	3.9	3.5	3.8	2.6	2.9	2.5
Pacific	30.8	5.8	15.1	8.2	9.0	12.6	10.8	5.4	11.2	8.9
Total percentage	100.0	100.0	100.0	100.0	100.0	100.0	100.0	100.0	100.0	100.0
Total number	188	1,131	720	8,950	1,558	2,360	1,909	3,599	475	20,890

Headquarters of Big Corporations

manufacturing and finance, are somewhat higher in older New England; the more recent, such as agriculture, service, and wholesale and retail chains, are well ahead in the newer West, which also passes New England in its share of transportation and utilities. Mining stays where the plants are.

Examination of the distribution of each type of enterprise among the nine regions modifies this simple polar analysis. We will be asking two questions to answer a third more important one. The first two are: What regions are very high and very low in number of headquarters for each of the general types of enterprise? What regions score well above or well below the general averages for all industries? Given this evidence, why are the corporate capitals concentrated and distributed in their present pattern?

The somewhat less than 200 firms in agriculture (and fishing) are very concentrated in the Pacific (31 per cent), the South Atlantic (18 per cent), and the West South Central (17 per cent). All other regions are less than 7 per cent. The West South Central, including Texas and Oklahoma, holds over half of the mining headquarters (petroleum included). Only the Middle Atlantic (12 per cent) among the other regions is above 10 per cent for mining. Two regions, the Middle Atlantic with 25 per cent and East North Central with 30 per cent, together have over half of manufacturing. Four regions, the Middle Atlantic, the East North Central, New England, and the South Atlantic, have 70 per cent of financial headquarters.

If our data are examined for regionally disproportionately high concentrations by type of industry, that is to say specialization in a particular class of home offices relative to the general concentration of home offices in that region, New England is above its general average only in manufacturing and finance and is low for all other types of enterprise. The Middle Atlantic is above its general average in services (32 per cent), finance (26 per cent), and manufacturing (25 per cent) and well below in agriculture and mining and below in retail trade. The West South Central is far ahead of its general average in mining (56 per cent) and far below in manufacturing (5 per cent). The Mountain states are well above their general average of 2.5 in agriculture (6 per cent), mining (5 per cent), and retail trade (4 per cent) but are below in manufacturing. The Pacific is well above in agriculture, contract construction, and wholesale trade but is below in finance and mining.

What does this analysis tell us about the activity types in which a region specializes? There is evidence that corporate headquarters of certain industries are still bound partly to their regions of production. This seems to be partially, but not entirely, true of agriculture and mining. The comparative age of a region and size of industry —the corporations large and the regions old—are interrelated. Big manufacturing in New England, in the Middle Atlantic, and in the East North Central, transportation in the Middle Atlantic and the East North Central, as well as finance in the Middle Atlantic, East North Central, and New England, all bear witness to this statement.

Now we can look at the data a little differently and ask what regions are above the average for all the United States for a particular industry. A table compiled by us but not presented here shows that although fewer than one-fifth of the corporations in the study were financial organizations, one-fourth of all corporations with New England headquarters were, making New England easily the leader over all other regions for this activity type. The East North Central, New England, and Mid-Atlantic led in manufacturing corporate headquarters. On the other hand, the Pacific led all other areas for the proportion of headquarters in agricultural enterprises. The Mountain and West South Central regions were far behind the nation in home offices of manufacturing corporations and far ahead in those of mining.

In most regions one state tends to be dominant not only for the general average of all corporate headquarters but for one or more types of enterprise. Table 4 shows the ten most populous states in 1960 and compares them with (a) the top ten states for all types of corporations grouped together and (b) the top ten within each of the nine activity types.

Nine of the ten most populous states are in the top ten states for all national headquarters. Florida, very recent in population growth, falls behind eleventh-place (in population) Indiana. It is also the state most likely to drop out of the individual ranking for the different types of industry. The most populous states also rank high for the different kinds of industry, except mining and agriculture.

In the Middle Atlantic region New York ranks first for six of the nine types of industry. Texas in the West South Central and Illinois in the East North Central are ahead of most other states. California shows up as either first or second for agriculture, contract construc-

Table 4. Top Ten States and Type of Enterprise by Percentage (1960)

Rank	Percentage of 1960 U.S. population	All types of industries	Agriculture	Mining	Contract construction	Manufacturing	Transportation	Wholesale	Retail	Finance	Service
1	N.Y. 9.4	N.Y. 13.0	Calif. 24.4	Texas 41.4	Calif. 12.2	N.Y. 13.3	N.Y. 10.0	N.Y. 15.9	N.Y. 11.5	N.Y. 14.6	N.Y. 22.2
2	Calif. 8.8	Ill. 7.5	Texas 13.3	Okla. 8.0	N.Y. 11.5	Ill. 9.2	Pa. 8.0	Calif. 9.2	Texas 8.8	Pa. 7.8	Calif. 10.1
3	Pa. 6.3	Texas 7.2	Fla. 9.0	N.Y. 6.0	Texas 9.0	Ohio 9.0	Texas 6.9	Ill. 6.8	Calif. 8.2	Mass. 7.2	Ill. 7.0
4	Ill. 5.6	Pa. 7.1	Mo. 4.2	Calif. 5.6*	Ill. 6.1	Pa. 8.0	Ohio 6.4	Texas 6.3	Ill. 7.5	Ill. 6.4	Texas 6.6
5	Ohio 5.4	Calif. 6.7*	Conn. 3.7*	Pa. 5.6*	Ohio 5.7	Calif. 6.0	Calif. 6.1	Pa. 6.0	Ohio 5.3	Texas 6.2	Pa. 5.9
6	Texas 5.3	Ohio 6.7*	Miss. 3.7*	La. 4.8	Pa. 5.3	Mich. 5.4	Ill. 5.5	Ohio 5.8	Pa. 5.1	Ohio 4.5	Ohio 5.5
7	Mich. 4.4	Mass. 4.6	Oreg. 3.7*	Ill. 3.4	Mich. 3.9	Mass. 5.2	Mass. 4.1	Mass. 3.8	Mich. 3.3*	Calif. 4.1	Mich. 4.3
8	N.J. 3.4	Mich. 4.0	N.Y. 2.7*	W. Va. 3.0	Ind. 3.5	N.J. 3.9*	Mo. 3.7	Mich. 3.4	Ind. 3.3*	N.J. 3.8	N.J. 3.6
9	Mass. 2.9	N.J. 3.0	Ill. 2.7* / Ohio 2.7*	Kan. 2.9	Mo. 2.8	Wis. 3.9*	Mich. 3.3	Mo. 3.3	Mass. 2.9	Mich. 2.9*	Fla. 3.2
10	Fla. 2.8	Ind. 2.8	Wash. 2.7* / Ariz. 2.7*	Ohio 2.6	Md. 2.4	N.C. 3.1	Ind. 3.1	Ind. 2.6	Mo. 2.8	Conn. 2.9*	Mass. 2.8

* States with equal percentages representing ties in rank have been listed in random sequence.

tion, wholesale, and services. Pennsylvania never appears as the first, and Ohio neither first nor second, for any type of industry. In New England, Massachusetts is among the top ten states for six different types of industry but, except in finance, is seldom among the top five states.

In brief, there is a very close relationship between population size of state and the location of corporate headquarters of all types. The top-ranking states for six of the nine types of business and industry also rank among the top ten most populous states. One industry, services, is in all ten of these most populous states; financial corporations are in nine; and retail, wholesale, transportation, and manufacturing are in eight. The states that tend to take the place of the most populous top ten are those next in size in population (less than one-half of one per cent below the top ten)—Indiana, eleventh in rank in population, North Carolina, twelfth, Missouri, thirteenth, and Wisconsin, fourteenth.

The story of the spread and concentration of corporate headquarters in the states and regions of the United States is a mixed one, but a few dominant tendencies stand out:

1. The most populous regions and states get more headquarters and an older region is likely to have an increased share.

2. The types of industry that developed their large-scale organization earlier are more likely to favor older regions.

3. The largest of the big corporations are most likely to be in the older states and regions.

Age, conservatism, and bigness seem to hold together and at the local level. To sharpen our focus still further, what is the relation between cities and other communities and the location of headquarters?

CITIES OF DECISION: 1960 HEADQUARTERS

The headquarters of big and not-so-big corporations are found in the big and not-so-big metropolises: 80 per cent of the 21,000 corporate giants are located in only 212 metropolitan cities in the

Headquarters of Big Corporations

United States, and the remainder are scattered through the other thousands of communities in the fifty states. This means that approximately 17,000 of the 21,000 firms limit the location of their headquarters to a very small number among the multitude of American communities. To make our analysis clear and the induction of conclusions valid and understandable, we will briefly review the evidence about the local communities in the United States and briefly define the principal term we use for them. According to the 1960 census there are 5,900 cities and 6,100 towns throughout the Union.[2] The rapid growth of population in the larger cities, its spread to the suburbs, and the growth of satellite communities around the cities, some of which were formerly independent and not satellites to the central city, have led demographers, the census bureau, and other government agencies to reclassify urban agglomerations to conform to the social and economic realities. These new and changing entities are called standard metropolitan statistical areas (SMSA). The incorporated central city and the towns about it no longer conform to the realities of city living and metropolitan organization. The larger area where thousands of people live, earn their living, go to church and school, subscribe to daily newspapers, and shop is often in several communities, all parts of one large, metropolitan, social, economic, and population complex.

Criteria for the inclusion and exclusion of given populations in any particular SMSA demand at least one city of over 50,000, at least 75 per cent of the labor force in nonagricultural occupations, and 50 per cent of the population in contiguous local civil divisions with at least 150 persons per square mile. The name of the metropolitan spread is taken from its largest city. The principal data used for determination are population, labor force, density, occupational facts, place of employment, commuting volume, volume of telephone communication, newspaper circulation, traffic volume, and public transportation.[3] SMSAs are important for the present analysis. To dispense with jargon, we will more often refer to them simply as metropolises.

2. U.S. Bureau of the Census, *United States Census of Population: 1960 U.S. Summary* (Washington, D.C., U.S. Government Printing Office, 1961), pp. 66–67.
3. Ibid., pp. 106–17. Also, *Structure of a Standard Metropolitan Statistical Area, Executive Offices of the President, Bureau of the Budget,* 1961; *Changing Metropolitan Markets 1950–1960* (Washington, D.C., U.S. Department of Commerce, 1961).

Table 5. Corporate Headquarters and Metropolitan Cities (212 SMSAs)

Population	Number of SMSA cities	Population	Percentage of U.S. population by SMSA size	Average number of firms for each SMSA	Number of firms	Percentage of firms
Over 2,000,000	10		24.3	676		32.2
1,000,000 to 2,000,000	14		10.0	205		13.7
500,000 to 1,000,000	29		10.7	86		11.8
300,000 to 500,000	28		5.8	57		7.7
200,000 to 300,000	41		5.7	35		6.8
100,000 to 200,000	68		5.5	19		6.2
50,000 to 100,000	22		1.0	14		1.5
Total for all SMSAs	212	112,885,178	63.0		16,766	79.9
Total for rest of U.S.A.		66,438,000	37.0		4,223	20.1
Grand total		179,323,178	100.0		20,989	100.0

Headquarters of Big Corporations

There are 212 SMSAs in the total United States; they are in every census region and in forty-six of the fifty states. They hold two-thirds (63 per cent) of our population—113 million people. Ten of these cities have over two million inhabitants, fourteen more have one to two million, and twenty-nine more have 500,000 to one million. Table 5 shows the population brackets.

About a fourth of our people are in the ten top cities, another 10 per cent are in the cities of one to two million, and 11 per cent are in those of 500,000 to one million. Although the percentage of the combined population for each of the next three brackets of city-size remains constant (just under 6 per cent for each), the number of SMSAs rises from 28 for those with 300,000 to 500,000, through 41 for those with 200,000 to 300,000, to 68 for those 100,000 to 200,000, then drops to 22 cities of 50,000 to 100,000 with a combined population of 1.0 per cent of the 179 million.

The ten cities of over two million population are fairly well scattered. Two are in California, in the Western Zone, three in the Central Zone, and five in the Eastern Zone. The fourteen cities of between one and two million are less well distributed. Five are in the East—Baltimore, Newark, Buffalo, the Paterson complex, and Atlanta; seven are in the Central Zone—Cleveland, Minneapolis, Houston, Milwaukee, Dallas, Cincinnati, and Kansas City; and two are in the Western Zone—Seattle and San Diego. It will be noted on Figure 1 that the Eastern Zone has 80 of the 212 SMSAs, the Central Zone 103, and the Western Zone only 28. (One is located outside the continental United States.) The East North Central region (the Great Lakes) has the largest number (41); and the Mountain Region and the East South Central, including Mississippi and Alabama, the smallest number (13 each).

The concentration of population in these two hundred-odd cities is very high—approximately two out of three of our people; but the concentration of corporate headquarters is still higher—eight out of ten. The strong attraction of the big corporate headquarters to big cities is even more dramatic. Only ten cities have over two million people each—one-fourth of the entire population—a very high proportion but much less than the one-third (32.2 per cent) of corporate headquarters located in these ten largest metropolises.

We have seen that the number of SMSAs tends to increase as the population decreases down to 100,000, and their combined percentage of the American population declines. The fourteen cities with one to two million have 10 per cent of our population but 14 per cent of corporate headquarters. Despite their disproportionately high share, the fourteen average 205 headquarters each, whereas each city of the top ten, those of two million or more, has an average of 676 headquarters. The twenty-nine cities of 500,000 to a million, with 11 per cent of the population, have 12 per cent of the corporate capitals. But big as they are, each of the twenty-nine drops to an average of eighty-six corporate headquarters. To go down a couple of brackets of size, each of the sixty-eight cities of between 100,000 and 200,000, has, on the average, only nineteen headquarters. As the cities decrease in size, their share of corporate headquarters drops precipitously.

The drop for each city from the two to one million size (676 to 205) is more than two-thirds; the next step, to 500,000 (205 to 86), is three-fifths. The combined populations of the cities in the 300,000 and those classed in the 200,000 and 100,000 brackets vary only a tiny fraction of a point. Yet the average of headquarters per city drops by size from fifty-seven through thirty-five to nineteen. There is a slight drop to fourteen for the 50,000 class. Bigness in population of the metropolis is heavily correlated with the number of headquarters.

When the two million category is opened and the individual cities are inspected, a similar story, but not quite the same, is told. Table 6, on corporate headquarters in the ten largest cities, tells the important points here. The ten largest SMSAs are ranked by population. The New York metropolis has by far the largest population, 11 million, about 6 per cent of all the people in the United States, but it has over 2,000 or about 10 per cent of all the corporate headquarters. At the other extreme (of the ten cities with over two million) are Pittsburgh, St. Louis, and Washington, each with a little over two million people in its SMSA. Yet each has but a little more or a little less in percentage of headquarters than its percentage of population. Washington, as a political and not an industrial capital, is a special case. Two other cities deviate. Although Los Angeles is second in population, it ranks well below Chicago in the number and percentage of headquarters; Chicago has 1,200 and Los Angeles only 695. Los Angeles and San Francisco are both growing, but the headquarters score for the very recent Los Angeles is

Headquarters of Big Corporations

well behind its population ranking. Boston is also of special interest. It is seventh in population, but it outranks Detroit and San
Francisco for headquarters; both are bigger in population but
smaller in the number of companies with headquarters located
there. Boston has held tightly to much of its economic power. Although its population and headquarters scores are tied, Detroit, as a
great city, falls from expectancy.

Table 6. Corporate Headquarters in the
Ten Largest Cities (SMSA) in 1960

City	Population in millions	Percentage of total population	Number of firms	Percentage of total firms
New York	10.7	6.0	2,089	9.9
Los Angeles	6.7	3.8	695	3.3
Chicago	6.2	3.5	1,200	5.7
Philadelphia	4.3	2.4	579	2.7
Detroit	3.8	2.1	438	2.1
San Francisco	2.8	1.6	403	1.9
Boston	2.6	1.4	539	2.6
Pittsburgh	2.4	1.3	307	1.5
St. Louis	2.1	1.1	352	1.7
Washington, D.C.	2.0	1.1	161	0.8
Total	43.6	24.3	6,763	32.2

The basic rule about the relation of the size of city to the size of
the corporation is that the big cities have the big ones, the small
cities, the small ones. The very big corporations tend to have their
centers of decision in the very largest cities; and although the lesser
ones also have their headquarters there, they do so in smaller proportions. As the size of the corporation declines, the proportion of
headquarters present in the smaller cities grows steadily larger.

The 1960 cities in the top ten, all those with more than two million people, have a third of all corporate headquarters, but the proportion for the very big corporations, those with more than 10,000
employees, in such cities goes up to 69 per cent. For the smaller

firms, those with up to 100 employees, the average drops to 21 per cent in the very big cities. As the size of the firm increases, from 100 employees through 300, to 5,000 and up to the huge 10,000 ones, there is a step by step increase in the proportion of headquarters located in the largest ten cities (see Table 7).

At the other extreme, the towns and cities not among the 212 metropolitan communities, an inverse relation exists: as the size of the firm increases, the percentage of corporate headquarters in such communities greatly decreases. Although only 20 per cent of headquarters are in these places, about a third (31 per cent) of the small corporations with less than 100 employees are in communities not in the 212. Only 2.9 per cent of corporations in the 10,000-employee class are located in such towns and cities; as the company's size decreases from the 10,000 class, there is a step by step increase in percentages.

As a further test of how corporate and city size affect location of headquarters we divided the headquarters of *Fortune* magazine's 500 largest industrials (1963) by the hundreds into five categories of size and related their corporate headquarters to the several categories of the 212 SMSAs. None of the headquarters of these big corporations was in the small metropolitan cities (SMSAs) of 50 to 100,000. The number of headquarters in the nonSMSA communities (less than 50,000) rose from one out of the hundred largest to 16 for the bottom hundred of the 500 largest industrials. On the other hand, 71 of the top 100 corporate headquarters were in the ten two-million cities, and only 49 of the last hundred were located there. New York City's own share dropped from 38 of the top 100 to 21 of the last 100. The cities of one to two million rose from 8 headquarters for the first hundred to 18 for the last. The smaller cities, those under 300,000, do not vary much with corporate size. Those of 500,000 to one million have more of the very big (still only 9) than they do for the headquarters of the last hundred (3). In general, the 500 largest industrial corporations listed by *Fortune* conform to the broader and more inclusive spread of the 21,000 big and not-so-big ones from Dun & Bradstreet that we have been studying.

In each region a leading state possesses one or more great metropolises. In those regions and states with small percentages of headquarters such metropolises are few or small. The presence of

Table 7. Metropolitan Headquarters (SMSA) of Large and Small Firms in 1960

Size of firms, by employees, with percentages in each SMSA size

Population	Under 100	100–300	300–500	500–1,000	1,000–5,000	5,000–10,000	10,000 and over	Total
Over 2,000,000	20.9	29.2	31.0	33.0	40.1	57.3	68.7	31.6
New York	6.2	7.0	6.8	9.0	13.6	23.4	35.4	8.9
Los Angeles	3.1	3.4	4.1	3.3	3.9	3.6	3.2	3.5
Chicago	2.9	5.6	5.6	6.9	7.9	10.4	10.4	5.9
Philadelphia	1.5	2.4	3.6	3.1	2.9	4.7	3.5	2.7
Detroit	1.4	2.5	2.3	2.3	2.3	2.2	3.8	2.3
San Francisco	1.0	2.0	2.0	2.0	2.5	2.5	3.8	1.9
Boston	2.4	2.4	2.9	2.5	2.7	3.9	1.7	2.5
Pittsburgh	0.6	1.5	1.4	1.6	2.0	1.9	4.9	1.5
St. Louis	1.2	1.6	1.8	1.9	1.7	3.3	2.0	1.7
Washington, D. C.	0.6	0.8	0.5	0.4	0.6	1.4	0.0	0.7
1,000,000 to 2,000,000	12.6	14.0	14.0	14.3	15.8	16.5	11.6	14.0
500,000 to 1,000,000	10.7	12.8	13.3	12.7	11.9	5.2	5.8	12.2
300,000 to 500,000	7.1	7.9	8.2	7.5	7.8	6.6	6.4	7.7
200,000 to 300,000	7.0	7.8	7.3	6.2	4.9	3.6	2.6	6.8
100,000 to 200,000	7.2	7.3	5.6	5.1	5.1	3.6	2.0	6.2
50,000 to 100,000	3.3	1.1	0.8	1.2	0.9	0.3	0.0	1.3
Total for 212 SMSAs	68.8	80.1	80.2	80.0	86.5	93.1	97.1	79.8
Number	1,932	4,922	2,482	2,154	2,031	338	335	14,194
Total for rest of U.S.	31.2	19.9	19.8	20.0	13.5	6.9	2.9	20.2
Number	875	1,226	611	539	316	25	10	3,602
Grand total	100.0	100.0	100.0	100.0	100.0	100.0	100.0	100.0
Number	2,807	6,148	3,093	2,693	2,347	363	345	17,796*

* Includes 87 firms with headquarters outside continental United States.

corporate headquarters in a zone or region is correlated not only with population but also with the number and size of metropolitan cities. It is conceivable that a large region with many small cities whose combined population outranks a smaller region with a few large metropolises might rank well below the latter for its percentage of headquarters. Corporate capitals are spread everywhere, but they concentrate in the biggest of the big cities, usually in a favored state in a favored region of each zone.

THE SPREAD OF HEADQUARTERS—1930

Where were corporate headquarters thirty years ago, before the great depression and World War II and the mass migrations that climaxed the slow western movement of the pioneers? Were they grouped in the same way and in the same constellation as in 1960? In the broadest terms, in the thirty years from 1930 to 1960 the Eastern Zone lost and the Central and Western Zones gained in national share of headquarters: the Eastern sustained a net loss of 15 percentage points, the Central gained 12 percentage points, and the Western, 3 percentage points.[4] Further inspection of these very broad territorial generalizations brings the picture of what happened to the locations of headquarters during this time into sharper view. Not all the regions of the Eastern Zone went down in terms of national share—one went up. The South Atlantic region (Maryland to Florida) gained 2 percentage points, New England lost 3 percentage points, and the Middle Atlantic went down 14 percentage points. This means, of course, that the far Northeast lost in national share while the Southeastern Atlantic states gained (see Table 8). Since all the other six regions advanced a little or a lot, this indicates that the South, the Southwest, the Middle Atlantic, and the Pacific states increased their shares as the nine states of the Northeast lost their high proportions. Of course, this does not mean

4. See p. 54 for description of the 1930 sample.

Headquarters of Big Corporations

that the latter suffered an absolute loss. Two facts should be re-marked about this loss:

1. In 1930, one half (49 per cent) of all headquarters were in these two Northeastern regions of the Eastern Zone, and even to-day almost one third (32 per cent) are in New England and the Middle Atlantic regions.

Table 8. Corporate Headquarters,
Region and Zone, in 1930 and 1960

	1930			1960		
Region and zone	Population* (in millions)	(%)	Firms (%)	Population* (in millions)	(%)	Firms (%)
New England	8.2	6.6	11.7	10.5	5.9	8.4
Middle Atlantic	26.3	21.3	37.4	34.1	19.0	23.3
South Atlantic	15.8	12.8	8.1	26.0	14.5	10.5
Eastern Zone	50.3	40.7	57.2	70.6	39.4	42.2
East South Central	9.9	8.0	2.6	12.1	6.7	4.3
West South Central	12.2	9.9	3.9	17.0	9.5	10.6
East North Central	25.3	20.5	20.7	36.2	20.2	23.6
West North Central	13.3	10.8	7.1	15.4	8.6	7.9
Central Zone	60.7	49.2	34.3	80.7	45.0	46.4
Mountain	3.7	3.0	2.2	6.9	3.8	2.5
Pacific	8.6	7.0	6.3	21.2	11.8	8.9
Western Zone	12.3	10.0	8.5	28.1	15.6	11.4
Total	123.2†	100.0†	100.0 (N 3,049)	179.4	100.0	100.0 (N 20,895)

* Source: U. S. Bureau of the Census, *U. S. Census of Population: 1960.*
† Difference in the row and column figures is caused by rounding off of figures in columns.

2. These figures do not mean absolute loss, only proportionate, and, in fact, in the thirty years these regions increased in actual number of headquarters.

The four regions of the Central Zone each increased their shares by 1 to 7 percentage points. The four states west of the Mississippi River (West South Central), Oklahoma, Arkansas, Texas, and Louisiana, went up seven percentage points, from 3.9 to 10.6. The seven West North Central states, including Missouri, Minnesota, and the Dakotas, rose the least in the Central Zone (7.1 to 7.9). The five Great Lakes states gained 3 percentage points; and the four south of the Ohio (East South Central), including Kentucky and Mississippi, went up 2 percentage points, about the same as the contiguous states previously mentioned in the South Atlantic. With the modest gain of the Great Lakes states and the considerable loss of the Middle Atlantic three, these two regions are now tied for first; in 1930 the Middle Atlantic was far ahead. The greatest gain in the Central and other zones was the Texas, Oklahoma, Louisiana region, the West South Central; their gain was more than double that of any other, including the Western Zone and the Pacific region. The Mountain region seems to have kept pace but gained very little, if any (2.2 to 2.5). On the other hand, the Pacific states, led by California, rose about three percentage points (6.3 to 8.9).

The American economy has grown enormously, and the number of big business enterprises has increased everywhere in the country but particularly in the Southwest, the South Atlantic, the Great Lakes region, and the Pacific Coast. All parts of the South, East, and West have gained in percentage of corporate headquarters. The Mountain states have held their own; the Northeastern have lost. The far eastern areas of continental America no longer control over half of all headquarters; rather the middle Atlantic, combined with the region of the Great Lakes in the Midwest, now have about half (47 per cent). Even here the dominance has lessened. In 1930 these two regions had 58 per cent of all headquarters and with New England had about 70 per cent. The spread of headquarters is far greater now from ocean to ocean and from north to south than it was in the thirties.

What does this mean? Did many of the 1930 firms move south and west to change their proportions and account for the Northeastern loss and the gains elsewhere? Did they stay in their own regions, and are the differences accounted for by the greater proportionate rise of business enterprise in the other regions of the United States? We do not have tables or an actual count of the firms of 1930 that stayed or moved during the thirty-year period, but from inspection of the corporate names and locations of headquarters it appears that the development of new big business enterprises throughout the United States is primarily responsible. For

Headquarters of Big Corporations

example, the growth of large enterprises in California, Texas, and elsewhere, rather than the transfer of headquarters from New York and Boston, contributed to the rising percentages of the West and the Southwest.

So far these broad zonal and regional comparisons for the periods disregard what we know to be important: the relation of the concentration and spread of headquarters to population. We have examined the 1960 figures and proportions of the leading states for each region and for the leaders among the forty-eight and fifty states. What were they in 1930? How was the population spread and concentrated then, and what are the differences in the percentages of corporate headquarters and the population in the two periods? We will compare regional population differences first.

While the U.S. population went from 123 to 179 million, each of the three zones and nine regions also increased but not proportionately (see Table 8). The Eastern Zone population rose from 50 to 71 million, but its proportion of the population dropped slightly; the Central Zone increased from 61 to 81 million, but it too lost slightly—4 percentage points of the U.S. total. The Western Zone went up from 12 to 28 million; its proportion of the total population increased 6 percentage points.

Comparisons of regional population and increases and decreases of headquarters in percentages reveal that they are not always covariant. In the Eastern Zone two of the three regions went down in percentage of population and in headquarters; one increased in population, as it did in percentage of headquarters. In the Central Zone, although the percentage of population for all of the four regions dropped a little, the proportions of headquarters of all four increased. The Western Zone population and headquarters covary; the Mountain region increased in percentage for population a little, but very little, as did its proportion of headquarters, and each rose (population and headquarters) considerably in the Pacific region.

For purposes of simplifying detail while bringing out the 1930–1960 changes in the concentrations of the headquarters of the various types of enterprise, we will compare only the eight largest types of enterprise (including mining, three different types of manufacturing, transportation and utility, wholesale and retail trade, and finance) for the four areas that showed the greatest changes. New England's proportion of food, textile, and apparel manufacturing dropped to half of what it was thirty years ago. The other two categories of manufacturing also fell considerably. Wholesale and retail business dropped, but the percentage for finance increased (9.6 to 13.0).

All the proportions of the eight most numerous types of enterprise, except wholesale (it gained slightly), went down in the Middle Atlantic states. On the other hand, all the same six rose in the Southwest Central regions, as did five in the Pacific. This spread of headquarters west and south seems general and not confined to a few industries.

The leading state in each region, despite absolute and relative changes in states and regions, remains fairly constant. For 1930 and for 1960 Massachusetts and New York lead in the two northeastern regions; Texas, Illinois, and Missouri lead in their respective regions in the Central Zone; and California leads in the Western Zone.

The study of the ten leading states in Table 9 shows that their rank and percentages changed considerably in the thirty years. New York, first in both periods, went down from 21 per cent to 13; Pennsylvania, second (11.4 per cent) in 1930, fell to fourth (7.1 per cent) in 1960; Illinois, despite a slight percentage point loss (8.4 to 7.5), rose to second; Massachusetts dropped from fourth (7.2) to seventh (4.6). Texas, not in the first ten in 1930, was third in 1960 (7.2). The range of percentages in 1930 among the ten was 19 points (21.3 to 2.3); in 1960 it had shortened some ten points (13.0 to 2.8). The eastern seaboard had five (see Table 9) in the top ten in the thirties and but four in 1960; Connecticut had dropped out and Indiana was in its place. In 1960 the Central Zone had five—Illinois, Ohio, Texas, Michigan, and Indiana; the Eastern four are New York, Pennsylvania, Massachusetts, and New Jersey; and the Western Zone has one—California.

Table 9 shows the states (with their respective zones) by rank according to both the 1930 and the 1960 population census. As many as seventeen states each had 2 per cent or more of the U.S. population, ranging from New York, with 9.4 per cent, to Tennessee with 2 per cent. Only two, Virginia and Georgia, are not in the top seventeen for percentage of headquarters. The ranking of two states in the top ten for headquarters falls considerably behind their population rank. California in 1960 ranked second with 8.9 per

Table 9. Distribution and Rank of Headquarters
Among States and Zones in 1930 and 1960

State	Zone	For 1930 Population* Per cent	Rank	For 1930 Headquarters Per cent	Rank among states	For 1960 Population* Per cent	Rank	For 1960 Headquarters Per cent	Rank among states
New York	Eastern	10.1	1	21.3	1	9.4	1	13.0	1
Pennsylvania	Eastern	7.7	2	11.4	2	6.3	3	7.1	4
Illinois	Central	6.1	3	8.4	3	5.6	4	7.5	2
Massachusetts	Eastern	3.4	8	7.2	4	2.9	9	4.6	7
Ohio	Central	5.4	4	5.8	5	5.4	5	6.7	5
New Jersey	Eastern	3.3	9	4.7	6	3.4	8	3.0	9
California	Western	4.6	6	4.5	7	8.9	2	6.7	5
Michigan	Central	3.9	7	3.4	8	4.4	7	4.0	8
Missouri	Central	2.9	10	3.2	9	2.4	13	2.8	10
Connecticut	Eastern	1.3	29	2.3	10	1.4	25	2.0	14
Texas	Central	4.7	5	2.1	11	5.3	6	7.2	3
Wisconsin	Central	2.4	13	1.7	12	2.2	15	2.6	12
Maryland	Eastern	1.3	28	1.6	13	1.7	21	1.3	23
Minnesota	Central	2.1	18	1.6	13	1.9	18	1.9	15
Indiana	Central	2.6	11	1.4	15	2.6	11	2.8	10
Virginia	Eastern	2.0	20	1.3	16	2.2	14	1.4	20
Georgia	Eastern	2.4	14	1.1	17	2.2	16	1.5	19
Delaware	Eastern	0.2	48	1.0	18	0.2	47	0.3	40
Kentucky	Central	2.1	17	1.0	18	1.7	22	1.1	25
Washington	Western	1.3	30	1.0	18	1.6	23	1.2	24
Maine	Eastern	0.6	35	0.9	21	0.5	36	0.4	37
Alabama	Central	2.1	15	0.8	22	1.8	19	1.1	25
Colorado	Western	0.8	33	0.8	22	1.0	33	0.9	29
Iowa	Central	2.0	19	0.8	22	1.5	24	1.4	20
Louisiana	Central	2.1	22	0.8	22	1.8	20	1.6	18
Oregon	Western	0.8	34	0.8	22	1.0	32	1.0	27
Kansas	Central	1.5	24	0.7	27	1.2	28	1.0	27

State	Region	%	Rank	%	Rank	%	Rank	%	Rank
Oklahoma	Central	1.9	21	0.7	27	1.3	27	1.4	20
Rhode Island	Eastern	0.6	37	0.7	27	0.5	39	0.7	32
Tennessee	Central	2.1	16	0.7	27	2.0	17	1.7	16
Utah	Western	0.4	40	0.7	27	0.5	38	0.4	37
Washington, D. C.	Eastern	0.4	41	0.7	27	0.4	40	0.6	34
Florida	Eastern	1.2	31	0.6	34	2.8	10	1.7	16
Nebraska	Central	1.1	32	0.6	34	0.8	34	0.7	32
South Carolina	Eastern	1.4	26	0.6	34	1.3	26	0.8	30
West Virginia	Eastern	1.4	27	0.5	37	1.0	30	0.8	30
Vermont	Eastern	0.3	47	0.4	38	0.2	48	0.2	45
Arizona	Western	0.4	44	0.3	39	0.7	35	0.3	40
Arkansas	Central	1.5	25	0.3	39	1.0	31	0.5	35
New Hampshire	Eastern	0.4	42	0.2	41	0.3	46	0.4	37
Idaho	Western	0.4	43	0.1	42	0.4	43	0.2	42
Mississippi	Central	1.6	23	0.1	42	1.2	29	0.5	35
Montana	Western	0.4	39	0.1	42	0.4	42	0.2	45
Nevada	Western	0.1	50	0.1	42	0.2	50	0.1	46
North Dakota	Central	0.6	38	0.1	42	0.4	45	0.1	46
South Dakota	Central	0.6	36	0.1	42	0.4	41	0.1	46
Wyoming	Western	0.2	49	0.1	42	0.2	49	0.1	46
New Mexico	Western	0.3	45	0.0	49	0.5	37	0.2	45
Alaska	Western	0.1	51	—	—	0.1	51	—	—
Hawaii	Western	0.3	46	—	—	0.4	44	—	—
Total		100.0		100.0		100.0		100.0	

* Percentages for population computed from the figures in statistical abstract of the United States, 1962; and rank assigned on the basis of figures and not rounded percentages.

Headquarters of Big Corporations

cent of the United States population but fifth for proportion of headquarters; Florida, tenth in population, was in sixteenth place for headquarters. Eight of the ten top states for headquarters are in earlier regions of settlement (only California and Texas are not), and this relation is largely true for the next ten. Generally, older states with large populations are most likely to be high in headquarters, and those more recently settled and with smaller populations tend to be low. For example, of the last ten in ranking for headquarters (all with 0.4 per cent or less of population and corporate headquarters), all but three—Vermont, New Hampshire, and Delaware, each with 0.3 per cent or less of the United States population—were recent in population growth.

With this evidence we will attempt to answer one of the major questions asked earlier: Has there been a notable shift in the location of headquarters among all kinds of corporations?

Detailed inspection of the internal configuration of each region by state and city [5] shows how corporate headquarters were geographically concentrated and spread in 1930. We shall examine the composition of each by the rank of the region. New York State, with 21 per cent of the 3,055, was dominant in the Middle Atlantic region, followed by Pennsylvania (11 per cent). New York City housed most of that state's headquarters—16 per cent of all firms in the total sample. Philadelphia (3.5 per cent) and Pittsburgh (2.2 per cent) were dominant in Pennsylvania. As in 1960, most regions had a dominant state, or sometimes two, and this leading state had a principal metropolis or two, which contained a large share of the state's, and sometimes the region's, headquarters. A further analysis of the data for 1930 and 1960 shows some of the emergent patterns in urban headquarters of corporations. For example, in 1930 as many as one out of every two U.S. corporations had its headquarters in the cities of 300,000 or less population compared with only 25 per cent in 1960. What happened to our cities in these thirty years? Only about one out of three corporate headquarters remained in smaller cities of less than 300,000; corporate headquarters increased to two out of three in the big cities, affected by urban development and redefined city limits, technically referred to as the standard metropolitan statistical areas. Does this evidence then sug-

5. The incorporated city, not SMSA, was used since no such urban entity was recognized for 1930.

gest that the big cities and big corporations have an affinity for each other? In 1930 Pittsburgh housed as few as one out of every five corporations in Pennsylvania; Cleveland and Los Angeles accounted for about one out of every three corporate headquarters in Ohio and California, respectively. However, outstanding among the top ten or twelve cities were New York, with seven out of every ten, and Baltimore and Chicago, each with eight out of every ten head-

Table 10. Comparison of Top Ten Cities' Percentage Share of Corporate Headquarters within Their Respective States, 1930 and 1960

1930 rank	1960 rank	Cities (1930) or SMSA (1960)	City's percentage share of the total number of firms in the state in 1930	in 1960	Gain (+) or loss (−) 1930–1960
1	1	New York (N.Y.)	68.2	76.5	+ 8.3
2	3	Chicago (Ill.)	80.9	76.9	− 4.0
3	4	Philadelphia (Pa.)	31.9	38.8	+ 6.9
4	5	Detroit (Mich.)	48.5	52.4	+ 3.9
5	2	Los Angeles (Calif.)	31.7	49.7	+18.0
6	12	Cleveland (Ohio)	27.5	25.8	− 1.7
7	9	St. Louis (Mo.)	54.5	60.9	+ 6.4
8	11	Baltimore (Md.)	80.0	70.7	− 9.3
9	7	Boston (Mass.)	47.2	56.1	+ 8.9
10	8	Pittsburgh (Pa.)	18.7	20.6	+ 1.9
11	6	San Francisco (Calif.)	45.3	28.8	−16.5
12	10	Washington (D.C.)*	100.0	100.0	—

Total percentage of corporate headquarters in the top ten cities of 1930			40.2	32.2	− 8.0
Total percentage of corporate headquarters in the nine states containing the top ten cities of 1930			66.8	53.4	−13.0

* The District of Columbia is treated as a state for 1930 and the Washington SMSA for 1960.

quarters in their respective states. Do these findings suggest that, just as in each region one state dominates, within a state one or two leading cities account for most of its corporate population? Again, is the hypothesis of the leading state and city true for 1930 and for 1960? To examine this hypothesis we will review Table 10 city by city. In 1960 seven of the top ten cities of 1930 had increased their share of corporate headquarters within their respective states. Among these cities, Los Angeles with its exceptional gain of 18 per cent ranked first followed by Boston with 8.9 per cent, New York

Headquarters of Big Corporations

with 8.3 per cent, and Philadelphia with 6.9 per cent. St. Louis, with 6.4 per cent, had gained fifth place. Detroit, the motor city, and Pittsburgh, the steel capital of the world, on the other hand, were comparatively slow in attracting U.S. corporations. Some of the big cities also lost some of their corporate headquarters to other cities in their state: Baltimore declined by 9.3 per cent, Chicago by 4.0 per cent, and Cleveland by 1.7 per cent.[6] The loss in percentage of corporate headquarters was most drastic for San Francisco, in contrast to its gain in population from eleventh place in 1930 to sixth in 1960. In 1930 it had 45.3 per cent of California's headquarters; in 1960 it had about 28.8 per cent.

An interesting fact is revealed if we study the change between 1930 and 1960 in the proportion of home offices located in the ten most populous cities of 1930 and in the nine states that contain those ten cities. The data for 1960 deal with the cities as SMSAs. In 1930 those nine states accounted for 67 per cent of the 3,055 corporations in our 1930 sample and the ten cities for 40 per cent; in 1960 the states accounted for 53 per cent of the 20,890 corporations in our 1960 sample and the cities (now SMSAs) for 32 per cent.

Comparison of the 1930 findings with 1960 data helps us conclude that, although the concentration of corporate headquarters has shifted southward and westward, headquarters continue to thrive in the comparatively large cities. In other words, although enormous changes took place in America and its business and industry from 1930 to 1960, the pattern of locating headquarters remained traditional and conservative. The location for some might change from north to south, from east to west, but the big city in a big state in a major region still was most favored. Inspection of age of company shows that most of the headquarters of the older corporations stayed in the very big cities of a few eastern and Great Lakes states. The proportion of headquarters did increase in the Far West, in the Southwest, and in the Eastern South, but those were generally younger corporations. They, too, sought out the rapidly growing metropolises of these regions to establish their places of ultimate decision. This affinity between big cities and big corporations is not strange. They are two parts of the many that compose the larger anatomy of the Great Society.

6. Baltimore and Cleveland, slipping from among the top ten in 1930 to eleventh and twelfth positions, yield their places to San Francisco and Washington, D.C., which were eleventh and fourteenth in 1930.

CHAPTER FOUR

The Expansion of Big Corporations

THE GROWTH OF BIG AND LITTLE ONES

Since our early history as a nation we have feared the power of big organizations and have been repelled by the centralized, aristocratic authority of large, extended hierarchies. Yet it seems fair to say that we have been attracted at the same time by their strength and their ability to get things moving "in a big way" while solving major problems that concern us. With the coming of the factory system and modern industry, we soon developed some of the most powerful, autocratic industrial empires in the world. Since the beginnings of big business, big corporations have grown even larger and have increased their economic if not their autocratic power. Thousands have grown into industrial giants. Millions still remain small, individually inconsequential, but collectively powerful and important.

This chapter is concerned with the growth of the corporate giants, the largest among the various types of business enterprise in the United States, how much bigger they have become from the beginning of the century to 1960, and what structural processes were involved in the expansion that moved them to the top ranks of size among American corporations.[1]

This Chapter is by W. Lloyd Warner and Darab B. Unwalla. See Notes on Authors.

1. Each year *Fortune* magazine publishes its very valuable directory of the 500 largest U.S. industrial corporations; it also lists the 50 largest of each of the following—commercial banks, merchandising, transportation, life insurance, and utility companies—making a grand total of 750 of the largest U.S. corporations ranked by sales for industrials and by assets for most of the nonindustrials. From the 1961 list we selected 362 industrial companies and 200 nonindustrials, a total of 562 firms. Primarily from *Moody's Manual of Investments* (New York, Moody's Investors Service), but assisted by other authoritative compilations on big business, such as *Dun & Bradstreet*, we traced their expansion.

Expansion of Big Corporations

Following the usual practice, all firms were classified by their major activity or Standard Industrial Classification and by the one in which they were placed by the *Fortune* listing. However, of the 562 firms there were seventeen in which *Moody's* manuals and the *Fortune* directory differed on the major division into industrial and nonindustrial. When we checked out these differences, by percentage in the tables that follow, we learned that the differences were neither large nor significant. We therefore held to the *Fortune* assignments of 362 industrials and 200 nonindustrials.

The number of standard industrial categories (SIC) for a company varied from only one SIC per company to seven and eight per company.

For a half century the assets of these great corporations grew enormously. Assets account for one kind of growth, but the growth of sales and other gross income and the growth in number of employees may tell a better story of the expansion of these giants. Therefore we ask: How much—and when—did the sales of the industrials and the other sources of income for the nonindustrials increase during the period of our study? How did the employee size increase during these decades? What differences in time and type of enterprise are present?

After we examine the growth of the sales, gross income, and number of employees, we will turn our attention to the structural processes of expansion. How often did these companies use outright purchases of other companies and how often mergers with them or consolidation of subsidiaries? What were the number of events occurring in the different kinds of structural growth and how many businesses followed a given pattern? Were the patterns different at different periods of time? Were there differences in patterns for industrial and nonindustrial enterprises?

First we need to know the general corporate environment in which our 562 giants functioned. For simplification we reworked the long, highly informative table supplied by *Historical Statistics* [2] and reduced it to two smaller tables. The first presents the number of corporations from very small to very large at approximately five-year intervals from the base year, 1931, to 1959. The second gives the "combined compiled receipts" of the several asset classes for

2. See "Source" at bottom of Tables 1 and 2.

each of these periods. Using 1931 as our base, we computed for each period the percentage change in the number of companies with a given level of assets and the percentage change in aggregate income for each asset class.

Table 1 allows us to ask and answer these questions: Did the big corporations grow more than the smaller ones, or did the small ones grow and multiply in number and expand their business with the expanding American technology? More technically, what was the comparative growth within each asset class? Let us look at the very small corporations with assets of less than $50,000 at the far left of the table. In 1931 there were 182,000; by 1959 their number had increased to 412,000, a percentage increase of +125.9 from our base year, or more than twice as many. However, this same column shows that there had been only a small increase in 1935 over 1931, that in 1940 there had been a small decrease from 1935, and in 1945 the number of small corporations had decreased below their number in 1931; the big jump ahead for the number of these small companies had been more than 100,000 at the end of the 1950s. To see what extreme size might indicate, let us look at the biggest ones in the column at the far right. In 1931 there were 632 corporations with $50 million or more in assets, and in 1959 there were 2,300—a percentage rate of increase of +266.9. They also experienced a sizable jump in the late 1950s. At no period did their number decline; but the great volume of increase was from 1945 to the 1960s.

This same simple overview of the other asset classes reveals that only the three largest classes, those with over $5 million in assets, had no period in which their number decreased below that of the base year, whereas even those in the $1 to $5 million categories had such a reverse in 1940. Such comparatively big categories as those ranging from $100,000 to $1 million had several periods below their 1931 base line. For example, the $500,000 to $1 million started with 19,000 corporations in 1931 and dropped below 18,000 in 1940 and again in 1945. Not until 1950 did its number grow beyond the base year. The two categories just below experienced similar periods of decline from the base year.

In 1950 the number of corporations in all categories of assets showed increases and did so again in 1955 and 1959. It is informative to see which enjoyed the greatest percentage increase over

Table 1. Number of Corporations with Different Sizes of Selected Corporate Assets, 1931 to 1959, with Per Cent Change Measured against 1931*

Assets

Year	Less than $50,000	$50,000 to $100,000	$100,000 to $250,000	$250,000 to $500,000	$500,000 to $1,000,000	$1,000,000 to $5,000,000	$5,000,000 to $10,000,000	$10,000,000 to $50,000,000	$50,000,000 and over
1959	412,100 +125.9	177,542 +190.4	212,573 +235.1	99,583 +220.7	52,048 +169.2	46,104 +151.3	8,022 +210.0	7,476 +253.1	2,319 +266.9
1955	299,564 + 64.2	131,510 +115.1	150,350 +137.0	70,483 +127.0	39,301 +103.3	40,853 +122.7	6,794 +162.5	6,246 +195.0	1,861 +194.5
1950	236,854 + 29.8	101,645 + 66.2	111,503 + 75.8	49,735 + 60.2	29,093 + 50.5	30,643 + 67.0	4,987 + 92.7	4,217 + 99.2	1,284 +103.2
1945	177,788 − 2.6	61,431 + 0.5	60,308 − 4.9	27,583 − 11.2	17,669 − 8.6	22,057 + 20.2	3,948 + 52.6	3,197 + 51.0	969 + 53.3
1940	225,000 + 23.3	61,053 − 0.1	59,059 − 6.9	27,832 − 10.4	17,505 − 9.5	17,627 − 3.9	2,603 + 0.6	2,266 + 7.0	771 + 22.0
1935	227,545 + 24.7	58,434 − 4.4	58,208 − 8.2	28,605 − 7.9	18,102 − 6.4	18,407 + 0.3	2,769 + 7.0	2,393 + 13.0	742 + 17.4
1931**	182,447	61,144	63,428	31,052	19,335	18,345	2,588	2,117	632

* Source: Historical Statistics, Vols. 113–27; for 1959, Statistical Abstracts No. 655.
** Base year.

1931. In 1950 the percentage increase in the number of the smallest corporations was only +29.8 over 1931; as one moves from these smaller businesses to the larger ones, there is a steady increase in the percentage growth over 1931, with the exception of three classes, until we reach a figure of 103.2 for the largest asset category. A similar relation is true for 1955. For the latest year in which we have information (1959) we learned that among the nine categories all except the smallest had an increase of more than 150 per cent over the base year and that five, including the three largest, increased more than 200 per cent.

The number of corporations in the three largest asset categories showed the largest percentage increase over 1931, and the largest category showed the greatest percentage increase of all. However, the number of two somewhat smaller categories, in the $100,000 to less than $500,000 classes, showed almost as large a percentage increase over 1931. Big, moderate, and little corporations all grew in number, but the big ones tended to grow steadily through all periods and to record the greatest percentage growth over the base year. The little companies were not being run out, but their breed was not multiplying as rapidly as the big ones. Some grew bigger and pushed over into larger categories of size. Some died. Others were absorbed in mergers or acquired by their powerful competitors.

So much for the absolute and comparative increase in the number of big and small corporations. We can now ask questions about what is probably an even more important measure, the compiled receipts. Did the combined incomes of each of these nine categories of assets demonstrate a similar differential growth? Did the total compiled receipts vary, and did the big corporations grow proportionately more than the smaller ones between 1931 and 1955? (Our figures for compiled receipts go only to 1955.) Table 2 tells this story. It will be noted that receipts are in millions of dollars and the percentages are increase or decrease from 1931.

Significantly, all sizes but one at every period, a total of forty-four out of forty-five instances, show an increase over 1931; except at one time for one size there is no period of decline from 1931 in receipts for any category. Interestingly, the only drop below the base year was in the largest class of assets, $50 million and more, and was for 1935. There aggregate income dropped 20.6 per cent be-

Table 2. Total Compiled Receipts of Corporations with Different Sizes of Selected Corporate Assets, 1931 to 1955, with Per Cent Changes in Receipts Measured against 1931*

Assets

Year	Less than $50,000	$50,000 to $100,000	$100,000 to $250,000	$250,000 to $500,000	$500,000 to $1,000,000	$1,000,000 to $5,000,000	$5,000,000 to $10,000,000	$10,000,000 to $50,000,000	$50,000,000 or more
	(Total compiled receipts in millions of dollars)								
1955	16,271 +134.0	19,811 +267.0	48,805 +454.4	48,144 +567.7	48,675 +587.6	97,583 +568.6	35,489 +535.1	77,254 +478.0	242,477 +569.0
1950	12,381 + 78.1	15,257 +182.6	35,585 +304.2	33,737 +367.9	34,453 +386.7	73,903 +406.4	28,430 +408.8	64,717 +384.2	154,061 +325.0
1945	9,031 + 29.9	8,651 + 60.3	16,660 + 89.3	15,829 +119.5	17,398 +145.8	42,251 +189.5	17,749 +217.6	39,917 +198.7	85,151 +134.9
1940	9,617 + 38.3	7,358 + 36.3	12,742 + 44.7	10,286 + 42.7	10,419 + 47.2	23,456 + 60.7	9,186 + 64.4	21,850 + 63.5	40,514 + 11.8
1935	9,364 + 34.7	6,089 + 12.8	9,668 + 9.8	7,888 + 9.4	8,014 + 13.2	18,446 + 26.4	7,434 + 33.0	16,386 + 22.6	28,790 − 20.6
1931**	6,952 100.0	5,398 100.0	8,803 100.0	7,210 100.0	7,079 100.0	14,595 100.0	5,588 100.0	13,365 100.0	36,247 100.0

* Source: *Historical Statistics*, Vols. 113–27.
** Base Year.

low 1931. Meanwhile, for this same period other asset classes showed increases of +9.4 to +34.7 in aggregate income over 1931, and, surprisingly, the percentage increase for the very smallest led all others for that year. Thereafter things changed. The increase over 1931 in total compiled receipts for the small corporations was by 1955 a modest +134.0 per cent, but for the very largest it was +569.0 per cent, an enormous quarter-century increase. All but the two smallest categories showed income increases of over 450 per cent, and the increases of five categories were over 500 per cent. Only the smallest class showed an increase of less than 200 per cent. Between 1931 and 1955 each asset category showed a greater percentage increase in receipts than it did in number of corporations. The percentage increase in the number of small corporations was less than that for large corporations; the smallest and largest asset classes showed growths of 64.2 per cent and 194.5 per cent, a ratio of 1 to 3. The difference in percentage increase in aggregate income was more marked: 134.0 per cent to 569.0 per cent, a ratio of 1 to 4.

How did the giants get big? Some grew internally and simply got bigger because they produced more and sold more; some bought outright, merged with, or absorbed their competitors or suppliers and grew big by structural use of their external environment. Such structural processes in growth are very old but, as Nelson declares in his excellent book:

> Mergers leading to enterprises of large size relative to national markets have become significant only since the Civil War. This process had to await the development of refinements necessary to a complex industrial system, and especially to the elaboration of the business corporation. The corporation, the basic instrument for mobilizing large amounts of capital with limited liability of the investors, and essential to the development of these large enterprises, has become important in the manufacturing and mining industries only in the last seventy-five years.[3]

3. Ralph L. Nelson, *Merger Movements in American Industry, 1895–1956* (Princeton, Princeton University Press, 1959), p. 3. Also see *Report on Corporate Mergers and Acquisitions,* Federal Trade Commission, May 1955, pp. 2–14.

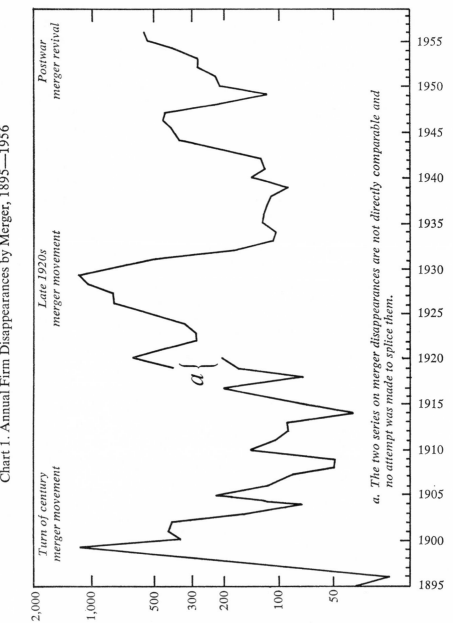

Chart 1. Annual Firm Disappearances by Merger, 1895—1956

Turn of century merger movement

Late 1920s merger movement

Postwar merger revival

a. The two series on merger disappearances are not directly comparable and no attempt was made to splice them.

Firm disappearances

2,000 · 1,000 · 500 · 300 · 200 · 100 · 50

1895 · 1900 · 1905 · 1910 · 1915 · 1920 · 1925 · 1930 · 1935 · 1940 · 1945 · 1950 · 1955

Source: Ralph L. Nelson, Merger Movements in American Industry, 1895—1956 (Princeton, Princeton University Press, 1959), p. 3.

The Old and the Young Giants

Nelson and others who have done the careful research on mergers, acquisitions, and other forms of combination that result in a single corporation where previously there were two or more show that there have been three great waves of mergers and other joinings since the turn of the century. The first was at the beginning of this century, the second in the 1920s, and the third began after the Second World War, declined somewhat in the later 1940s, and rose again in the middle 1950s. Chart 1 (adapted from page 3 of Nelson) illustrates the rhythm of structural change by showing graphically the rise and fall of the number of firms that disappeared each year from 1895 to 1956 due to merger. The annual rate of disappearance is marked on the left; the spread of time is given at five-year periods. It is composed of two series "not directly comparable" but sufficiently so to show the upward and downward ebb and flow of combination when firms disappear because "two or more previously independent enterprises" combined into a single one. It will be noted that before 1900 fewer than thirty disappearances were counted for those immediate years. Then, dramatically and suddenly, they climbed to more than a thousand in the 1895–1902 period, fell to fewer than fifty just before World War I (1915), and rose again to more than a thousand by 1930. During the depression and World War II they dropped to fewer than a hundred and rose to more than 500 in the middle 50s and almost to that immediately after the war.

With this background of structural combinations to help with our analysis of the external expansion of the very big firms, we must add another part to our understanding by examining the founding periods of these enterprises to find out how old they all are, to discover what differences are present among the industrials and nonindustrials, and to learn how time affects their growth.

THE OLD AND THE YOUNG GIANTS

To establish uniformity for determining the founding dates we used the date a given corporation was started or, if the present com-

Expansion of Big Corporations

pany is the product of a merger, the founding date of the oldest one in the merger. Finally, for the corporations with foreign beginnings, the date of establishment of the American branch was chosen.

Table 3 classifies our 562 firms into industrials and nonindustrials and by the decade in which they were established, going as far back as the beginning of the nineteenth century. Seven out of every ten firms in the study were established more than fifty years ago; many had survived dozens of management changeovers, weathered a number of recessions, and lived through three major wars and depressions. Among these, three financial companies—the Bank of

Table 3. Date of Founding of the Firms in the Sample, by Decade

Date of founding	Industrials		Nonindustrials		Total	
	N	Per cent	N	Per cent	N	Per cent
1800 & prior	0	0.0	3	1.5	3	0.5
1801–1810	3	0.8	1	0.5	4	0.7
1811–1820	0	0.0	2	1.0	2	0.4
1821–1830	1	0.3	2	1.0	3	0.5
1831–1840	1	0.3	7	3.5	8	1.4
1841–1850	11	3.0	17	8.5	28	5.0
1851–1860	15	4.1	15	7.5	30	5.3
1861–1870	24	6.6	25	12.5	49	8.7
1871–1880	14	3.9	12	6.0	26	4.6
1881–1890	46	12.7	19	9.5	65	11.6
1891–1900	71	19.6	15	7.5	86	15.3
1901–1910	64	17.7	28	14.0	92	16.4
1911–1920	40	11.1	14	7.0	54	9.6
1921–1930	48	13.3	25	12.5	73	13.0
1931–1940	18	5.0	7	3.5	25	4.5
1941–1950	3	0.8	8	4.0	11	2.0
1951–1960	3	0.8	0	0.0	3	0.5
Total	362	100.0	200	100.0	562	100.0

New York, the Chase Manhattan Bank, and the First National Bank of Boston—were started immediately after the War of Independence. How can the longevity and expansion of these corporations be explained? Is the maturity and expansion of our giant corporations only a function of time? If so, how can the establishment and development of the remaining 30 per cent of giant companies that were less than fifty years old be explained? It seems

The Old and the Young Giants

that the length of life of a firm, or longevity, is an important element but not the only decisive one. This is borne out in the case of fifty-four firms started in the decade 1911–20. In the comparatively short period of fifty years, these corporations had endured two world wars, the Korean conflict, and one of the severest depressions in the history of the United States. Another seventy-three firms started in the twenties, twenty-five around the depression of the thirties, eleven more around the second World War, and three during the war in Korea.

How do we explain the phenomenal growth of these 166 or 30 per cent of firms? Thirty-nine firms started or reorganized between 1931 and 1960: eight utilities, with average assets per firm of over $1 billion; seven food processing and food distribution firms with modest assets; and six aircraft manufacturing firms with assets of between $75 and $537 million. In addition there were four in electronics, four in general manufacturing, and three each in the chemical and lumber-furniture categories. Only two were banks, both reorganized, and the other two were transportation firms.

The above analysis of the lately started firms reflect three major advances of our society: electrification of our centers of population; revolution of the American kitchen and home from the innovations in food processing, storage, shipping, and organization of the channels of mass distribution of food products; and the phenomenal development of air travel, which facilitates movement of people and products through the length and breadth of the country.

Was the late birth of these firms a handicap? Eight out of twenty-four industrials had assets under $100 million and ranked between three hundred thirtieth and four hundred fifty-seventh in the *Fortune* ranking. Another thirteen, or 50 per cent of the twenty-six firms, had assets rank between the one hundred twelfth and three hundred thirtieth among the *Fortune's* 500. The remaining four industrial firms ranked still higher in the scale, between fifty-second and one hundred twelfth. So exactly half of the lately started firms obtained assets comparable to some of the oldest firms. Those with an average life span of thirty years or less did not rank among the top fifty industrials, but they did as well as, or better than, many others that started earlier; however, of the top ten industrials (ranked by assets) not one was started later than 1908; six were oil

Expansion of Big Corporations

firms, and as many as four of them were started long before the turn of the century.

In the case of nonindustrials, eight out of fifteen firms started after 1930 were utility companies. The contrast between the industrials and nonindustrials is apparent in size of assets. Four out of fifteen nonindustrials had assets well over $1 billion per firm; another seven had assets between $300 million and $1 billion; only five had assets under $300 million. Thus the assets of the nonindustrials far exceeded those of the industrials and ranked among the top fifteen in their respective categories. The assets' rank of some of the utilities were as high as fifth, eighth, and thirteenth. Of the two banks, the National Bank of Detroit, chartered in 1933, ranked fifteenth; and Manufacturers' National Bank, chartered in the same year and in the same city, was thirty-first by its assets.

This evidence strongly suggests that time is but one of the several important dimensions in the development of industrials and nonindustrials.

To answer the rest of the questions, we will follow Chart 2 and compare the industrials to the nonindustrials. By 1840, when less than 2 per cent of the industrial firms were established, almost 8 per cent of the nonindustrial firms were on the scene. Until 1860 the nonindustrial firms were established three to four times faster than the industrial firms. Not until the turn of the twentieth century did the proportion of industrial firms come anywhere near those of the nonindustrials; at the end of the first decade the difference between the two types had dwindled to a mere 4 per cent from as much as 23 per cent between 1871 and 1880. The percentage rate of establishment of industrials and nonindustrials has remained constant in the last fifty years.

The biggest proportions (11 per cent or more in any one decade) of the industrial firms were founded during the five decades between 1881 and 1930. Only three decades witness the establishment of more than 10 per cent of the nonindustrials and at three completely different time points—during the seventh decade of the nineteenth century and the first and third decades of the twentieth. The first and the third decades of the twentieth century saw the founding of an unusually large number of both industrial and nonindustrial enterprises.

Chart 2.

Cumulative Percentages of the Firms Founded, by Decade

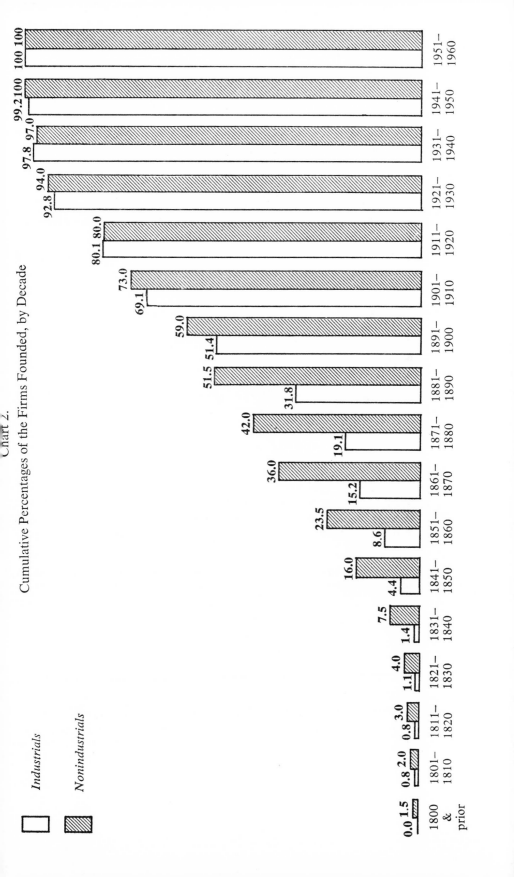

Industrials

Nonindustrials

Expansion of Big Corporations

SALES, ASSETS, AND EMPLOYMENT

As a group, the very large industrial firms in our sample expanded their sales by a considerable margin decade after decade. This is amply demonstrated in Table 4.

This table shows the numerical and percentage distribution of sales of industrial firms during the last three decades of the twenti-

Table 4. Distribution of Industrial Firms by
Their Sales during Last Three Decades

Sales		Decade ending 1940	Decade ending 1950	Decade ending 1960
Size I	N	190	67	0
Under $50,000,000	%	63.3	19.2	0.0
Size II	N	72	138	119
$50,000,000 to				
$150,000,000	%	24.0	39.5	32.9
Size III	N	38	144	243
Over $150,000,000	%	12.7	41.3	67.1
Totals	N	300	349	362
	%	100.0	100.0	100.0
Data not available		53	10	0
Firms not founded		8	3	0

eth century. For the purpose of this table the firms have been divided into three categories according to size of sales. The companies' sales were further subdivided by decade according to the information available for each period. In the decade ending 1940, six out of ten firms in our sample were comparatively small, with less than $50 million in sales. During the next decade the proportion of Size I companies dropped to 19 per cent, and in the decade ending 1960 no companies had sales under $50 million. During the same period the proportion of medium-sized companies (Size II) went up from 24 per cent in 1940 to about 33 per cent in 1960. The decade of 1950 seems to be the turning point in the sales history of the 362 largest industrials: Size II firms went from 13 per cent in 1940 to 41 per cent in 1950 and to 67 per cent in 1960.

When we direct our analysis to nonindustrials like commercial banks and insurance companies and study deposits and insurance in force instead of sales, we get a somewhat different picture. Sales, deposits, total operating revenues, or life insurance in force are the measures of business turnover peculiar to an industry. Assets, on the other hand, are a more enduring feature of a corporate establishment. The definition of the term, as used by the 1961 *Fortune* directory, is the "total assets employed in business at the year's end, less depreciation and depletion, but including government securities held as offsets against tax liabilities."

There is often a disparity in a firm's rank by its assets and by its sales, gross revenue, or deposits. For example, DuPont ranked eighth by its 1960 assets but thirteenth by sales; General Telephone and Electronics was thirteenth by assets and thirty-second by sales; and Aluminum Company of America was twenty-second by assets and fiftieth by sales.

The above differences in the sales and assets rank also reflect a changing ratio between sales and assets from one industry to another. Forty-eight of fifty merchandising companies had sales far in excess of assets. The Great Atlantic and Pacific Tea Company had sales of over $5 billion for about $700 million in assets; Sears, Roebuck sales were twice its assets. The forty-ninth- and fiftieth-ranked Pacific Gamble Robinson, of Seattle, and Lucky Stores, of San Leandro, California, each had assets under $36 million and sales of about $200 million.

This suggests that between industrials and nonindustrials there are two streams of assets orientation, comprising those with more assets than sales and others that maintain sales in excess of their assets. What could be the aggregate effect of these two trends on the total assets of our corporations?

Table 5 shows the distribution of firms by type and by assets at the close of the last three decades of this century. For the purpose of this table the companies were again divided by their assets into three size categories and further classified by decades.

As in the case of sales, the decreases for Size I industrial firms

Expansion of Big Corporations

(with assets under $50 million) were of dramatic proportions, dropping from 58 per cent in the 1940 decade to 2 per cent in 1960. The proportion of Size II industrial firms rose in the same period from 25 to 43 per cent. The number and proportion of largest industrials, with assets of over $150 million, increased in each period.

Table 5. Distribution of Industrial and Nonindustrial Firms by Their Assets, 1931 to 1960

Assets		Industrial			Nonindustrial		
		Decade ending 1940	Decade ending 1950	Decade ending 1960	Decade ending 1940	Decade ending 1950	Decade ending 1960
Size I	N	178	101	6	33	15	3
Under $50,000,000	%	58.0	29.7	1.7	17.3	7.6	1.5
Size II	N	78	137	155	38	22	18
$50,000,000 to $150,000,000	%	25.4	40.3	42.8	19.9	11.2	9.0
Size III	N	51	102	201	120	160	179
Over $150,000,000	%	16.6	30.0	55.5	62.8	81.2	89.5
Total	N	307	340	362	191	197	200
	%	100.0	100.0	100.0	100.0	100.0	100.0
Data not available		46	19	0	4	3	0
Firms not founded		9	3	0	5	0	0

The pattern for industrial firms seems to be different from that of nonindustrials. It was evident that in the decade ending 1940 a little less than one out of every five nonindustrials had assets under $50 million and an equal proportion had assets between $50 and $150 million each, while the other three out of five (63 per cent) had assets well over $150 million. By the decade ending 1950 these proportions had changed enormously, though in the same direction; only 8 per cent of the corporations were still in the Size I class, 11 per cent in Size II, and 81 per cent in Size III. At the end of the sixth decade (1960) nine out of ten nonindustrials had consolidated their assets and arrived in the Size III category; of the remaining 10 per cent, only three companies were still in the Size I category, and the eighteen firms accounting for Size II assets were utilities, transportation, or merchandising, and none was a bank or insurance company.

The contrast between the industrials and the nonindustrials is further brought into focus when we list the top twenty-five industrials and twenty-five nonindustrials by their assets and founding dates (see Table 6). Fifteen of these industrials were founded after 1900, while only three nonindustrials were founded in the same period. The range of assets of these fifty firms shows the even greater disparity between the two types: assets of the nonindustrials ranged from $2.4 million to $22.5 billion, and of the industrials, from $1.1 million to $10.1 billion.

Furthermore, of the top twenty-five industrials and nonindustrials in Table 6, eighteen are nonindustrials and only seven are industrials; eight of the same twenty-five firms started less than sixty years ago. Among all American firms of all types, none was so overpowering as American Telephone and Telegraph, with assets well over $22.5 billion. The next three firms in the list are also nonindustrials with considerably more resources than the first-ranked industrial: the Metropolitan Life Insurance Company with $18 billion, Prudential with $17 billion, and Bank of America with $12 billion led the first-place Standard Oil of New Jersey industrial.

The study of assets brings out two themes in the development of American firms:

1. Sales assets of all these American businesses continue to grow, but banks, insurance, and utilities grow faster than other nonindustrials, such as transportation or merchandising, and much faster than the industrials, such as auto manufacturing, oil refineries, and production of mechanical and electrical goods.

2. Within each subtype (industrial-nonindustrial) the growth pattern differs. Though older firms usually have larger assets, the incidence of younger industrials having large assets is significant.

The development of merchandising firms offers an example of what is happening in some of these areas. Thirty-two of the top fifty merchandising companies were founded in the twentieth century and seven more in the last decade of the nineteenth century. The creation and successful operation of these corporations suggest that they have ably served as channels of distribution and, more fundamentally, have had enough flow of consumer goods for continuous

Table 6. Firms by Their Year of Founding and by Assets

Assets in millions of dollars	Combined rank and year of founding		Rank Industrial	Rank Nonindustrial
22,558	1. Amer. Telephone & Telegraph	1885		1
17,941	2. Metropolitan Life Insurance	1866		2
16,551	3. Prudential Ins. of America	1873		3
11,942	4. Bank of America	1930		4
10,090	5. Standard Oil of New Jersey	1882	1	
10,040	6. Equitable Life Ass. Soc. U.S.	1841		5
9,260	7. Chase Manhattan Bank	1799		6
8,832	8. First Natl. City Bank of N.Y.	1812		7
8,553	9. General Motors	1908	2	
7,158	10. New York Life Insurance Co.	1841		8
6,127	11. John Hancock Mut. Life Ins.	1862		9
4,781	12. United States Steel	1901	3	
4,540	13. Chemical Bank Trust Co. N.Y.	1823		10
4,424	14. Morgan Guaranty Trust N.Y.	1864		11
4,198	15. North Western Mutual Life Ins.	1859		12
4,032	16. Ford Motor Co.	1903	4	
4,031	17. Aetna Life Insurance Co.	1883		13
3,974	18. Manufacturers & Traders Trust	1905		14
3,843	19. Gulf Oil Corporation	1901	5	
3,647	20. Texaco, Incorporated	1902	6	
3,594	21. Security 1st National Bank	1875		15
3,455	22. Socony Mobil Oil Company	1882	7	
3,430	23. Bankers Trust Company	1903		16
3,316	24. Travelers Insurance Co.	1863		17
3,136	25. 1st Natl. Bank of Chicago	1873		18
3,134	26. DuPont (E. I.) de Nemours	1903	8	
2,926	27. Standard Oil of Indiana	1889	9	
2,886	28. Continental Illinois Natl.	1857		19
2,873	29. Pennsylvania Railroad	1846		20
2,782	30. Standard Oil of California	1879	10	
2,762	31. Mutual of New York	1842		21
2,700	32. Wells Fargo Bank Amer. Trust	1854		22
2,551	33. General Electric Company	1892	11	
2,518	34. Southern Pacific Company	1884		23
2,512	35. New York Central Railroad	1826		24
2,440	36. Massachusetts Mutual	1851		25
2,275	37. Bethlehem Steel Company	1904	12	
2,205	38. General Telephone & Electric	1935	13	
1,885	39. Shell Oil Company	1911	14	
1,713	40. Union Carbide	1898	15	
1,665	41. Western Electric Company	1881	16	
1,647	42. Phillips Petroleum Company	1917	17	
1,624	43. I B M Corporation	1911	18	
1,521	44. Westinghouse Electric Corp.	1886	19	
1,487	45. Sinclair Oil Corporation	1916	20	
1,456	46. International Harvester	1902	21	
1,374	47. Aluminum Co. of America	1888	22	
1,369	48. Chrysler Corporation	1921	23	
1,343	49. Cities Service Company	1910	24	
1,139	50. Republic Steel Corporation	1899	25	

turnover. This is further borne out in the history and development of some of the largest. By the turn of the century establishments like the Great Atlantic and Pacific Tea Company of New York, J. C. Penney, F. W. Woolworth, Sears, Roebuck, and Montgomery Ward of Chicago, and Kroger of Cincinnati were already in business and doing well.

At the end of 1930 all the great merchandising companies had become bigger and expanded throughout the country, but none so spectacularly as A & P. The Great Atlantic and Pacific Tea Company, incorporated in 1901 and at that time small, was reorganized in 1925 by acquiring its own subsidiaries. In 1930 its sales soared to more than $1 billion. In 1940 the three grocery chains, A & P, Safeway Stores, and Kroger, experienced aftereffects of the depression and their sales declined, but Sears, Roebuck's and Montgomery Ward's did not. They succeeded in increasing their business by more than $200 million in 1940, the beginning of World War II. Since the end of the war the consumer has become more affluent, and these stores have steadily grown to their present size. By 1960 the top ten merchandising companies each had a business turnover of at least $1 billion. Kroger and Safeway had gone up to $2 billion, Sears to $4 billion, and the first-ranked Great Atlantic and Pacific Tea to well over $5 billion. Of the top ten, two, Federated Department and Safeway, started less than fifty years ago. In the course of thirty years the Federated Department Stores, of Cincinnati, had raised its sales from $117 million in 1930 to $785 million in 1960 and to the tenth rank among the top fifty merchandising companies. The Safeway Stores, of Oakland, California, founded about fourteen years earlier, in 1914, had also made spectacular progress. In 1920 its sales were around $219 million and in 1960 more than $2.5 billion. The same pattern holds for the other forty merchandising companies.

One can conclude from this that the merchandising corporations, by their recent emergence onto the American scene and by their aggressive role in capturing a large share of the American market, have become important ingredients in the emergent process.

While sales and assets of these 562 largest American corporations expanded, what happened to their employment? Are they also employing more men per company today than in the past? Or has automation shrunk employment size? Similarly, are there any

Expansion of Big Corporations

differences between business turnover and manpower of today and of a decade or two ago? If there are variations in employment size of firms at different time periods, do the patterns differ among similar industries like steel, automobile, and oil or among the more divergent types such as manufacturing, banks, insurance, merchandising, transportation, and utilities?

Let us begin with a basic industry like steel. In 1940 Bethlehem Steel had 118,000 employees and $602 million in sales; in 1950 employment increased to 136,000 and sales to about $1.5 billion; in 1960 employment reached 138,000 and sales $2.2 billion. When Inland Steel's employment more than tripled from 8,500 in 1930 to about 30,000 in 1960, sales moved up from $518 million to $747 million. But the biggest steel company, U.S. Steel, was different; in 1920 it had over $1.8 billion in sales and employment of about 267,000; at the end of 1930 and 1940 its sales had declined to about $1.2 billion, and employment ranged between 211,000 and 254,000. Ten years later, in 1950, when its sales had more than doubled, its employment had gone up by only a few percentage points. In 1960, when its sales reached $3.7 billion, its labor force dwindled to 225,000.

Between 1940 and 1960 American Motors raised its sales from $73 million to about $1 billion while doubling its labor force. On the other hand, Chrysler expanded its sales tenfold and its labor about fivefold from 22,000 in 1930 to 122,000 between 1930 and 1950. Ten years later, in 1960, the company grossed $3 billion with 17,000 fewer employees. Ford, the second largest automobile company, grossed $645 million with 75,000 employees in 1920, while in 1960, with more than twice as many men, sales were around $5 billion. The biggest company, General Motors, had about $1 billion in sales and 173,000 employees in 1930. In 1940 it doubled its sales and raised its labor force to 249,000 men. In 1950 its sales more than quadrupled, but its employment did not. Finally, in 1960, with over $12 billion in sales and 595,000 employees, General Motors increased its share of the total automobile market from 38.8 per cent in 1935 to 46.8 per cent in 1960 and was the largest industrial employer in the country.

The top ten oil corporations suggest another undercurrent. They all increased their sales dollars eight to tenfold but their work forces only twofold in the last forty years. Typically, when Standard Oil of New Jersey between 1940 and 1960 increased its sales from $822 million to $8 billion, its employment sluggishly moved from 120,-000 to 157,000.

Analogous patterns of economic growth and employment often blur the widely divergent trends from one industry to another. We will base our analysis on manpower, relating employment data for 200 nonindustrials in our study with sales and operating revenues for merchandising, transportation, and utility firms and with assets for eighty-six financial firms.

In the course of the last thirty years eight of the top ten banks for which data were available for 1930–1940 and for 1960 had their aggregate assets raised more than fourfold, from $10.4 billion to $44.2 billion, and their aggregate employment increased more than threefold, from 28,820 to 97,840. When the Bank of America's assets jumped tenfold, from $1.2 billion in 1930 to $11.9 billion in 1960, its employment changed only sixfold, from 5,000 to 27,900. Similarly, the Chemical Bank and New York Trust Company gained ninefold in its assets and only sixfold in its employment.

Some of the smaller and younger banks had a more dramatic growth. The National Bank of Detroit, reorganized in 1933, moved up about four times, from $627 million in assets and 1,050 employees in 1940 to $2.1 billion in assets and 4,100 employees in 1960. First City National Bank of Houston, started in 1919, raised its assets about thirty times and its employment about twelve times; the Republic National Bank of Dallas multiplied its assets nineteen times but its employment only six times. Finally, the Bank of California boosted its assets approximately thirteen times and its employment about five times.

In all the above instances two patterns are obvious. One, assets as well as employment for all the commercial banks have grown over a period of twenty to thirty years. Two, throughout, assets have gained in greater proportions than employment.

The aggressive pattern of growth of assets is nowhere more conspicuous than in the southwestern state of Texas and the Pacific state of California. Of the fifty largest banks listed in the *Fortune* Directory, as many as nine were located in California. Assets of eight of the nine banks for which information was available had gone up about eight times from $3.5 billion in 1930–40 to $27 billion in 1960 and their aggregate employment fivefold from 13,170 to 64,540 in the same period.

The assets and deposits of commercial banks have grown steadily

Expansion of Big Corporations

since World War II but not at so fast a rate as the Gross National Product. To offset the decline, especially in corporate deposits, banks have found it necessary to increase their volume of business through multiplication of savings accounts and suburban branches. Thus, though the actual number of commercial banks declined from 14,218 in 1946 to 13,439 in 1962, the number of bank branches rose from 4,063 to 12,491. It is estimated that in 1962, when there was one banking office for every 7,200 persons in the United States and much less than that in California, New York and Chicago had one banking office for every 11,800 and 47,300 persons respectively. In this regard, California is a pace setter. The Bank of California, for example, has expanded immensely in assets and employment since its reorganization in 1930. It operates all over California with 800 branch offices diligently catering to the needs of its customers and has succeeded in greatly raising its time and savings deposits.[4]

Like banks, life insurance firms have expanded their assets and employment considerably since 1940. The top twenty insurance firms in the *Fortune* list expanded their assets two to eleven times but kept their employment increase (available for only eleven firms) remarkably low—never more than three times. National Life and Accident increased its assets from $83 million in 1940 to $884 million in 1960 but increased its employment only from 4,500 to 9,040 in the same period. Similarly, Lincoln National had ninefold gains in its assets but only a threefold increase in its employment. Metropolitan, Prudential of America, Aetna, and Connecticut General also showed similar patterns over the last twenty or thirty years. Exceptional companies, like North Western Mutual and Mutual Benefit, have not enlarged their labor forces in the last three decades. With a threefold increase in its assets, North Western Mutual actually reduced its employment, and Mutual Benefit added only eighty employees after 1940.[5]

We could conclude from this that insurance firms, despite their huge assets, operate with relatively small labor forces.

4. Robert Sheehan, "What's Rocking Those Rocks, the Banks" *Fortune*, 68:4 (1963) 108–13, 242, 244–46.
5. The reader should make allowances for the practice of including or excluding certain categories of labor force such as field personnel, commission agents, etc. The type of insurance business and clientele should be considered here.

Some of the merchandising firms are the big employers in the country. Sears, Roebuck of Chicago employs close to 225,000 men in its 740 stores all over the United States. The Great Atlantic and Pacific Tea Company employs 145,000 persons in its seven divisions, supervising a total of thirty-seven units and 4,351 retail stores in most of the states and Canada. Six more chains each employ more than 50,000; and the rest each employ fewer than 50,000.

The growth of sales of merchandising firms is phenomenal. In 1940 the total sales of twenty-seven of the top thirty firms barely came to $5 billion; in 1960 the sales of A & P alone were $775 million in excess of the 1940 aggregate. To illustrate: the Great Atlantic and Pacific Tea Company rose to its present $5 billion sales level in 1960 from about $1 billion in 1940; Sears moved up from $617 million in 1940 to more than $4 billion in 1960, Safeway to $2.5 billion from $400 million, and Kroger to $1.9 billion from $258 million. More spectacular are the gains of some smaller firms, such as Foodfair Stores, which pushed its sales from $29 million in 1940 to $771 million in 1960 and Winn-Dixie, from about $2 million to $722 million. Grand Union, Jewel Tea, Arden, and A.C.F. Wrigley all expanded their sales eighteen to twenty times and their employment no more than four times.

In the transportation category there is a variety of firms—railroads, airlines, freight transport, and bus companies. The nation's largest railways—Pennsylvania and New York Central—have recently slashed their employment from more than 100,000 for each in 1940 to about 87,000 and 60,000 respectively and yet hope to double their revenues.

In contrast to the railways, eight leading airlines increased their employment forces about six times, from 2,700 employees per firm in 1940 to 14,940 per firm in 1960, and pushed up their sales nineteen times, from $20 million to about $375 million per firm in the same period.

In utilities employment has increased fairly slowly. In a decade or two a good many firms of the top fifty did not even double their labor force; American Telephone and Telegraph raised its labor force from 602,000 to 729,000 between 1950 and 1960 and quadrupled sales; Philadelphia Electric and Pacific Gas and Electric increased their sales six times but employment no more than 30 per

Table 7. Numerical and Percentage Distribution of Employment of Firms, Three Decades Ending 1960

Employment size of firm	Industrials						Nonindustrials					
	Decade ending 1940		Decade ending 1950		Decade ending 1960		Decade ending 1940		Decade ending 1950		Decade ending 1960	
	N	%	N	%	N	%	N	%	N	%	N	%
Under 1000	18	5.9	3	0.9	0	0	41	28.7	35	18.9	15	7.5
1000–5000	106	36.3	88	26.7	46	12.7	43	29.8	59	31.9	66	33.0
5000–10,000	77	26.4	102	31.1	121	33.4	18	12.5	31	16.8	45	22.5
10,000–25,000	58	19.8	80	24.3	107	29.6	26	18.0	33	17.8	50	25.0
25,000 and over	34	11.6	56	17.0	88	24.3	16	11.0	27	14.6	24	12.0
Totals *	293	100.0	329	100.0	362	100.0	144	100.0	185	100.0	200	100.0

* Where the totals for Industrials do not come up to 362 companies and nonindustrials to 200, either companies were not started or data were not available for the respective decade.

cent. Even among the recently started utilities these general patterns are apparent: Public Service of Indiana, Northern Natural Gas, Duquesne Light, and United Gas all made big gains in revenues with only moderate increase in total employment. Detroit Edison raised its revenues from $65 million in 1940 to $270 million in 1960 yet reduced its labor force by about a thousand.

To draw a composite picture from all this information about different types of firms we will now discuss employment alone for 362 industrials and 200 nonindustrials in our study. Table 7 confirms our observations that the industrials as well as the nonindustrials have been gaining employment at a rapid but different rate. Not one of the 362 industrials in our sample had employment below 1,000 in 1960. The two categories in which the gains and losses differ the most are 1,000 to 5,000 and 25,000-and-over employees. In the largest category, 25,000-or-more employees, the nonindustrials maintained an almost constant proportion of companies through the three decades, while industrials more than doubled their proportion within this category between 1940 and 1960.

The growth in terms of employment is in contrast to the pattern of development in the assets table. Employment figures show the industrials growing bigger and faster than the nonindustrials; the assets table shows the nonindustrials in the lead. The difference demonstrates a different ratio of employment to assets among industrials and nonindustrials.

MERGERS, ACQUISITIONS, AND CONSOLIDATIONS

Earlier we measured the corporate growth of the 562 companies in our sample in terms of sales and employment. Here we will discuss the expansion of American corporations in terms of structural changes—mergers, acquisitions, and the like. In the previous section we demonstrated an accelerated rate of growth among our big corporations. Here we will further analyze the growth as it refers to corporate structure. When the growth is structured, it has implica-

Expansion of Big Corporations

tions beyond the traditional frontiers of the corporate hierarchy, inasmuch as a management cannot merge, acquire, or consolidate without approval by the federal government. A significant part of our antitrust laws is intended to regulate the growth of corporate structure, of the large-scale corporations included in our sample. For example, DuPont could not continue to hold its major shares in General Motors; Ford was at first denied permission to conclude a transaction with Philco; the Pennsylvania and New York Central Railroads have had to prove their fair intentions. The government undertakes elaborate studies to determine the relationship between the parties to the transaction and to ascertain the impact of the proposed change on our competitive economy.

It is difficult to determine to what extent antitrust laws affect structural change except in actual instances. For example, in 1911 the United States Supreme Court sustained a lower court decision that Standard Oil of New Jersey was a combination in violation of the Sherman Antitrust Law and ordered it to distribute among its stockholders its shares in thirty-three companies. Despite this, in the area of structural change Standard Oil of New Jersey is a spectacular example. Since its inception in 1882 this firm has made structural changes that make impossible the identification of the present firm with the original one.

How did the company's assets grow to their present size? A few significant dates in the firm's last sixty years show the pattern of growth:

1882	Incorporated Standard Oil Trust in New Jersey
1892	Changed the name to Standard Oil Company
1911	Struck by dissolution decree passed by Supreme Court against the company
1922	Gained control of the West India Oil Refining Company
1924	Obtained joint ownership of Ethyl Gasoline with General Motors
1927	Divested itself of all physical property and became exclusively a holding company
1932	Contracted with Standard Oil Company of Indiana to purchase from the latter a big group of shares

1933   Transferred its entire interest in some three companies to Standard Vacuum Oil Company

1936   Liquidated Pan American Foreign Corporation and Mexican Petroleum Company, Ltd.

1937   Contracted for Venezuelan oil resources through a subsidiary of Standard Oil

1938   Expropriated some Mexican properties

1944   Acquired ocean-going tankers' ownership

1946   Sold out some major outstanding stocks entirely

1948   Started Domestic Coke Corp., a wholly owned subsidiary manufacturing coke

1948   Merged Stanco Inc. with Esso Standard Oil Company

1953   Sold interest in Interstate Natural Gas Company

1958   Acquired Lehigh Realty Company

1959   Formed Humble Oil and Refining Company

As a result of these and several other changes the company owns more than a hundred large and small subsidiaries in the United States and abroad.

Compared to that of industrials, growth of nonindustrials has been very high. How this happened can best be illustrated once again by the Bank of America.

The Bank of America National Trust and Savings Association raised itself from a position of $1¼ billion in assets in 1930 to close to $12 billion in 1960 through a series of structural changes.

In 1930 this bank was organized as a consolidation of the Bank of America of California and the Bank of Italy National Trust and Savings Association. At about the same time the Bank of America was formed to take over those branches not eligible to become branches of the consolidated bank under the McFadden Act. Subsequent to the consolidation the Bank of America merged a number of small banks, some of which had been affiliated. The Transamerica Corporation formerly owned almost the entire capital stock of the Bank of America National Trust and Savings Association; in the middle of 1937 more than half of the stock was distributed by Transamerica to its 155,000 stockholders, and the remaining half was disposed of in 1952.

The Bank of America also controls Merchants National Realty

Expansion of Big Corporations

Corporation, Small Business Enterprises, and the Bank of America (International New York). In 1955 it also organized the Continental Auxiliary Company to perform some of the functions previously performed by unaffiliated companies.

In looking for the success story of this institution, one has to look closely into its internal growth. The Bank operates through 800 branches in California and through overseas banking branches in Europe, the Far East, Middle East, and Latin America. In addition, it has forty military banking facilities in California and overseas.

The example of Standard Oil of New Jersey and the Bank of America are not intended to imply that only the old and established firms are affected by structural changes. Such a notion is not supported by what we find among some very recent independent firms, although the longevity of a firm may be a definite factor facilitating structural change. How do our corporations actually grow from year to year? Do the new ones grow through mass merchandising of products and services and the old ones through structural changes, or vice-versa?

The following illustration shows how some of our modern corporations develop in a short span of time.[6]

Control Data Corporation was incorporated in 1957. Since its incorporation the business has grown rapidly, and the scope of its operations has expanded both through the development of new products and market areas and through the acquisition of a number of businesses.

The company and its subsidiaries are primarily engaged in the development, design, manufacture, and marketing of advanced computing systems and related component and peripheral equipment. Other product lines include industrial and supervisory control systems, communications equipment, lasers, and electromechanical devices.

Between 1957 and now sales have increased from less than 30 million to more than 130 million dollars a year. A considerable part of its growth could be attributed to its structural development.

6. *Control Data Corporation, Prospectus,* May 18, 1965.

Mergers, Acquisitions, and Consolidations

Domestic Changes (the corporation expanded internationally too; for brevity, we exclude this)

1960   Organized Control Corporation as a wholly-owned subsidiary engaged in the design, manufacture, and sale of electronics.

1963   Organized Meiscon Corporation as a wholly-owned subsidiary engaged in the fields of civil and industial engineering consulting.

1964

1. Organized Rabinow Electronic, Inc., as a wholly-owned subsidiary; continued the development and manufacture of optical character and pattern recognition equipment.

2. Acquired Computer Laboratories, Inc. through an exchange of all its outstanding common stock for shares of common stock of Control Data; engaged primarily in the operation of data processing.

3. Acquired Adcomp Corporation through an exchange of all its outstanding capital stock for shares of common stock of Control Data; engaged in the development and manufacture of high-speed analog conversion equipment.

4. Acquired Holley Computer Products Company as a wholly-owned subsidiary; engaged in the development and production of peripheral equipment.

5. Organized TRG, Incorporated, as a wholly-owned subsidiary; continues the development and manufacture of lasers.

6. Acquired Macro Micro Corporation, Nugat Realty Corporation, and Rangot Corporation; all the outstanding capital stock of these corporations was included in the assets acquired by Control Data from TRG, Inc., now solely engaged in the ownership and management of real property and construction equipment, which they lease to TRG, Incorporated.

7. Organized Data Display, Inc., as a wholly-owned subsidiary; continued the development and manufacture of electronic digital display units.

8. Organized Datatrol Corporation as a wholly-owned subsidiary; continued to act as a consultant or advisor in matters pertaining to system analysis, computer programming, and computer processing.

9. Acquired Data Production, Inc., Marine Data, Inc., and Erickson Enterprises, Inc.; all of the outstanding stock of these corporations was included in the assets acquired by the company from Computech, Inc.; engaged in data processing services (as shown below).

Other Acquisitions
1963

1. Control Data acquired the business and principal assets of the Computer Division of The Bendix Corporation for a consideration consisting of shares of Control Data's common stock and cash payments to be made over a period of time. Engaged in the manufacture and sale or lease of digital computers and related equipment.

2. The assets of Beck's, Inc., were acquired by Control Data for shares of its common stock—makes a type of imbedded, insulated circuitry.

3. The Digigraphic System business and assets of Itek Corporation were purchased by Control Data for cash. Directly communicates with a computer by graphic means.

4. The business and assets of the Control Systems Division of Daystrom, Inc., were acquired by Control Data in exchange for shares of its common stock—engaged in the manufacture and installation of advanced solid-state digital computer control systems.

5. All of the outstanding stock of Bridge, Inc., was acquired by Control Data in exchange for shares of its common stock. The company liquidated Bridge, Inc., and its business is now being conducted as a division of the company engaged primarily in the design and manufacture of card punch and card reader systems.

1964   Control Data acquired the Data Systems Operation

assets of the Stromberg Division of General Time Corporation for a consideration consisting of shares of Control Data's common stock and cash. Manufactures and markets Transacter systems.

1965   Control Data acquired the business and assets of Computech, Inc., in exchange for shares of Control Data's common stock; engaged in the data processing service business.

Why does a company want to grow? There are many reasons; competition is one, and new market areas are another. A company such as Control Data faces the economic forces of competition from a number of corporations in the United States and abroad that make similar products and have similar scope as well as application in the same market areas. Moreover, its competitors include a number of companies, such as IBM, Honeywell, and Burroughs, that have greater financial resources and facilities.

Because of rapid technological advances in the industry as a whole, obsolescence of present computing equipment is always imminent. Only through continued emphasis on research and development and through structural changes can Control Data continue to develop products to maintain its position relative to competition and obsolescence.

How, despite competition, a company expands its business turnover is obvious from its emphasis on changing markets. A close inspection of its subsidiaries and the company's rationale for their acquisitions, available from one of their reports, shows how the company is maintaining an edge over its competitors by entering new areas before they do.

To understand and analyze growth in the 562 corporations in our sample we classify their structural changes into six different types—mergers, consolidations, acquisition, absorption, formation, and property or partial acquisition. The *Moody's* manuals of industry, finance, public utilities, and railroads have been the only source for data of this kind. An operational definition was worked out for each type of change in order to approximate the definitions used in other studies of corporate changes and make the maximum use of the data available to us.

With these guide lines, merger as a category is used interchangeably with amalgamation but distinct from consolidation, absorption, formation, or acquisition. Merger is often referred to as a form of transaction in which one corporation buys all the capital stock of one or more corporations and dissolves them. *Merger* here refers to that combination in which two corporations of about equal size compose themselves into a new, bigger firm. The process involves (a) the dissolution of two existing companies of about equal size, (b) the formation of a bigger company, and (c) complete merger of both ownership as well as control. It specifically refers to the joining of two firms and their unification into one as illustrated by the proposed merger of the Pennsylvania and New York Central Railroads.

Consolidation refers to the combination of more than two companies. This phenomenon implies that (a) more than two companies are combined, and (b) these combining companies may retain their separate legal entities and combine only their operations, or a new company may be formed and the existing companies dissolved.

Acquisition as a form of change is commonly used to indicate several different types of transaction. *Acquisition* refers to the process by which a bigger company purchases or obtains the control of a smaller one. It may be noted that (a) the prime mover is a bigger corporation, (b) the acquisition gives to the bigger corporation either ownership *or* merely control of the smaller corporation, and (c) only two corporations are involved in the process.

Absorption is a form of reorganization with special reference to a subsidiary's relation to the principal. *Absorption* refers to the merging of a subsidiary into the principal company. It will be noticed that (a) this phenomenon is confined to a principal and its subsidiary only, (b) the subsidiary ceases to exist after absorption, and (c) the subsidiary as a legal entity is dissolved.

Formation refers to creation of a new subsidiary of a major company.

Partial acquisition has reference to the purchase by one company of some assets of another company, such as land, equipment, and other property. This is a straight purchase transaction and does not necessarily mean the dissolution of the company whose assets have been purchased, though in practice this usually results. The point to be noted is that the name or goodwill of the vendor company is not purchased by the purchasing company.

Mergers, Acquisitions, and Consolidations

Our interest was in these *processes of structural change* and more particularly in the ways in which the very large corporations used their external environments to take over all or part of the structures and resources of some of the corporations around them for their own expansion. Since we wanted to learn how much each of the six processes was used at different periods of time to increase the size of these very large organizations, we identified and counted every instance (event) in which they bought or acquired through some other process other firms in their environment. When each event was noted it was then identified and classified by type of structural change. Was it a merger, an acquisition, or one of the other processes of structural change? In which of the three decades from 1930 to 1960 did this event occur?

More broadly, what were the corporate processes through which these giant corporations emerged to stand today as the largest of our corporate giants? Was the flow of change even throughout the thirty years or were there periods of relative quiet and then rapid activity? How many of the 562 firms studied were involved in a particular process in each decade?

Table 8 studies structural changes by classifying them by type and decade. We counted the firms in our sample and the number of structural events in which they were involved. (In this table only events are given; discussion of the number of firms is summarized in the text.) If General Motors had four mergers, three acquisitions, two absorptions, and one consolidation between 1931 and 1940, we record (through a multiple count) the one firm for each of these processes and the actual number of events, a total of ten changes. The totals for the events in each process and their grand total give the actual structural changes that occurred. (The totals for the firms in each process present the actual number of companies in that process.) This method of counting helps us analyze structural changes individually and collectively by disclosing the actual number of firms that made a particular type of change and the frequency with which all the events occurred.

In the course of thirty years 362 industrials made 5,136 structural changes, an average of fourteen changes per firm in thirty years. Fifty-seven per cent, or 2,943, of these changes were acquisitions, affecting on the average 219 firms during each decade. About 600 events of formations and absorptions each involved an average of ninety-five and ninety of the industrials per decade respectively.

Table 8. Types of Structural Change (Events) between 1931 and 1960

Type of structural change	Industrials					Nonindustrials				
	1931–40 events	1941–50 events	1951–60 events	Totals N	%	1931–40 events	1941–50 events	1951–60 events	Totals N	%
Formation	139	158	274	571	11	25	23	82	130	8
Merger	52	64	181	297	6	66	91	215	372	24
Acquisition	568	648	1,727	2,943	57	103	115	165	383	24
Absorption	173	154	273	600	12	43	46	20	109	7
Consolidation	217	64	219	500	10	189	159	182	530	34
Property and partial acquisition	70	74	81	225	4	11	17	21	49	3
Total number of events	1,219	1,162	2,755	5,136	100	437	451	685	1,573	100

Changes like absorptions, consolidations, and property or partial acquisitions accounted for a total of 1,325 events in thirty years and affected thirty-six to forty-nine firms on the average.

Among the nonindustrials the pattern of change was different. Since 1931 only 1,573 structural changes were recorded among the nonindustrials—less than eight per firm, compared to fourteen for each industrial. Nonindustrials also showed a more varied pattern of preference for change: 57 per cent of the industrials changed through acquisition, compared to only half that proportion of nonindustrials. On the other hand, one out of three nonindustrials changed through consolidation, and only one out of four through merger. Changes like formations, absorptions, and partial or property acquisitions occurred fewer than one out of ten times.

How many companies (nonindustrials), on the average, were affected by the changes? Our data show that in each decade about sixty-six firms were affected by acquisitions, thirty-seven by mergers, thirty by consolidation, nineteen by formation, thirteen by absorption, and eleven by property or partial acquisition.

More than five thousand changes over thirty years indicate an average of about 171 changes per year; one out of two industrials was affected by some type of change every year. Among nonindustrials change is much less frequent. Two hundred nonindustrials made an average total of fifty-two changes each year, which would affect only one out of every four nonindustrials per year. What are the types of changes that occur among these corporations? Does the incidence of any one or more types of change vary from decade to decade? Do we have more acquisitions in one decade and more absorptions and consolidations in another? Do industrials change mainly through acquisitions and nonindustrials through consolidation, or vice-versa?

Table 8 presents types of change as they occurred among different firms and also as separate events from decade to decade. According to this table, between 1931 and 1940, 1,219 changes occurred among fewer than 336 industrials founded before 1931. Less than half of these events were acquisitions, one-fifth were consolidations, and a little more than one-tenth were formations.

For industrials the decade of 1941–1950 was less eventful than the one before or after; only 1,162 changes were recorded, more than half of which were acquisitions. From among the rest a little more than one out of every eight events were formations, and the same ratio held for absorptions, with only a small number of events indicating consolidations, mergers, or partial acquisitions.

The decade 1951–1960, marked with 2,755 events, had more changes than the two previous decades combined. Once again more than 60 per cent of the changes were acquisitions, about 10 per cent formations, and 10 per cent absorptions, with mergers and consolidations far fewer.

Among the nonindustrials of the 1930s, acquisitions were not so common as consolidations; 189 out of 437 events were consolidations, and less than one-fourth were acquisitions.

Nonindustrials tended to change far more often through merger than did industrials. In the fifth decade the trends found in the 1930s became firmer; consolidations had lost some percentage points, acquisitions had moved up a little, and mergers up still further.

The last decade, with 215 mergers out of 685 events, marks the climax of mergers among nonindustrials.

The structural events of the decades of the 1930s and 1940s, it will be seen, remained constant; events in industrials and nonindustrials neither rose nor fell. But this period of comparative quiet radically altered in the 1950s for both groups; the rate of structural events doubled for industrials and increased half again for the nonindustrials.

More of the 362 industrial companies used more of the six processes in the 1950s than in the 1930s; for example, the number almost quadrupled for mergers. Among the nonindustrials the number of companies rose sharply for mergers, acquisitions, and formations and fell a very little for consolidations and absorptions.

It becomes apparent that the industrials and nonindustrials change differently and distinctly. Industrials concentrate on acquisitions in preference to all other forms of change. The nonindustrials show a number of preferences, among which consolidations, mergers, and acquisitions all rank high.

CHAPTER FIVE

The System of Interlocking Directorates

THE PROBLEM

The central fact of interlocking directorships is that one man often holds positions in two or more corporations. If it were impossible for the managers [1] of American corporations to be directors of companies outside their own, and if no nonmanager could hold more than one directorship, all corporate boards would be insulated and separate and the members of a board participants in only one corporation. There could be no interlocking corporate directorships. As the system now works, a manager may or may not hold a board position in his own corporation and at the same time may or may not be a director on other corporate boards. Also, of course, a man who is not a manager of a corporation may be on one or more corporate boards. Managers may be directors of other corporations in the same type of business in which they work or in other types.

Until now we have been concerned with individual corporations as separate units—their size, kinds of business activity, headquarters, and the structural processes of growth. Now we ask about *outside* interconnections of these great corporations. In terms of business status, what kinds of men are the directors of some of the largest corporations in America? How many are managers and how many outside "citizen-directors," i.e. nonmanagers? Where do these men come from—large, small, or very small companies? How much and in what way are the boards "interlocked," and how much are these boards connected with small and large American firms?

This Chapter is by W. Lloyd Warner and Darab B. Unwalla. See Notes on Authors.
1. Throughout this chapter the terms manager, officer, and executive will be used as inclusive designations of high officers of a corporation who participate in policy-making decisions.

121

The System of Interlocking Directorates

Since we are interested in large-scale, complex corporate enterprises, and, in this part of our study, in the "interlocked" directorates, we selected the boards of directors of 500 of the largest representative corporations in the United States. We will state the methods of our research more fully later. Briefly, we identified and counted the number of men who were directors of the chosen corporations and traced their interconnections with these corporations and with thousands of other companies in the United States. We learned whether they were managers in their own or in different firms or whether they had no managerial position. In tracing their connections, if any, with the boards of other corporations, we learned what kinds of firms were tied together.

The objects involved in the general exchange in this system are men, usually qualified by experience, age, and other criteria of fitness, significance, and importance to be directors and officers of corporations. An individual's membership on a corporate board is single, yet for any individual the directorial status may be multiple, for he can be a member of the boards of several corporations. Most of the men belong to two elite statuses, the boards of directors in their own or host companies and the top level of a company in which they are executives. There is a broad recognition of the principles of equivalence between the officers of the home company, which sends out one or more of its executives as directors, and the directors and officers of the host corporation, which receives these men. Given differences of size, power, and similar variations, this statement will be modified as we continue.

The interrelated boards of directors are parts of a larger system, but each is also a part of the corporate structure of each company; this statement views each corporation as a separate social entity and the corporate world as one social system. Although interlocking directorates have been the cause of considerable social and political distress and anger, at times rightfully, and of corporate debate about their usefulness, for the corporate system to exist in its present form, the interchange of officers and directors seems to be an essential part of the system. The exchange of officers and directors as members of boards sets up a social system of interconnected members in mutual influence that exists beyond the lifetime of individual members. We propose studying it, not "investigating" it. What is it as a social system? Is it one system or many? Is it one with many variations? Which characteristics persist and continue through time, and which change and possibly disappear? What is the meaning to corporate organization of this persistence in change? What is the meaning of these time processes of the interconnected corporate system as a significant part of the flow of the emergent American society?

Although the story we tell about the interlocking directorships among the largest corporations in the United States is a simple one, the phenomena involved are very complex. They include statistical facts about four kinds of things—corporations, directorships, managers, individuals—as well as the intricate relations established among all of them by the interlocked boards at the highest corporate level. Governing boards are interconnected (interlocked) only because most members are directors of more than one corporation. The firms are still more closely related by these multiple board members largely because most directors hold managerial positions in their parent firms as well as directorships in other corporations. Since the corporations interconnected by interlocked boards are of different sizes—some very big, some small or medium—and may be of different kinds, from manufacturing and mining to transportation and finance, and since their headquarters are scattered throughout the United States in great and small cities, the patterns of interconnection among them are complex, intricate, and at times difficult to trace and understand. Moreover, the variety of our discourse is not merely kinds of corporations but also kinds of directors; the multiple directorships and the patterns thus established among them are the central core of our inquiry. Since some directors are officers of firms and since some hold many board memberships and others single ones, and since they have other characteristics important for our inquiry, their story has its own complexities. We shall tell the story of interlocking boards in terms of the corporations, the directorships, the managers, and the individuals who hold these positions, but in particular in terms of the managers of large companies who serve as directors of other large companies.

The broad overall subject is not confined to the 500 corporations in our sample and their many thousands of directors but extends to thousands of other companies with which these directors may be involved as directors or managers. The boundaries of our research thus include all the several thousand directors of our 500 corpora-

The System of Interlocking Directorates

tions and all other American firms in which these men are directors or managers, but the research does not extend beyond the primary participation of the men who are directors of the 500 and who are directors or managers in other American firms.

We selected our sample of 500 of the largest representative corporations in the United States from *Fortune's* list of the 500 largest industrials, the magazine's supplementary lists for five other types of corporations (1961), and Dun and Bradstreet, and Moody. A sample for each type of enterprise was drawn. The number drawn for each activity type approximated the proportions for that activity type among the 21,000 firms of more than $1 million net worth used by us in Chapter 2. A little more than half (53 per cent) of these corporations, 265, are industrial, including mining, the different kinds of manufacturing, and contract construction; 100 are in merchandising, retail and wholesale; 65 are in finance; 20 each are in transportation, utilities, and life insurance; and 10 are in service enterprises. (Our sample of 500, of course, should not be confused with *Fortune's* famous "500.")

In size of assets our sample of 500 ranges from ninety-eight corporations with more than $1 billion to sixty-four with less than $100 million and in employee size from forty-seven with more than fifty thousand to twenty with less than a thousand. The headquarters' locations spread from New York (30.4 per cent), through Chicago (11.05 per cent), to San Francisco and Los Angeles, and, in decreasing numbers and proportions, down through communities with smaller populations. Only 2.4 per cent were not in a standard metropolitan statistical area (SMSA).

We identified all the thousands of men who were on the boards of directors. We determined which ones held single directorships, more than one, or very many among our 500 and other corporations. We learned whether they were managers. We counted the number of firms in which they were managers or directors and the total number of directorships they held. We identified the headquarters and the size and kind of business enterprise and computed the amount of connection among their interlocked directorships. From these computations we determined the system and subsystems of the interlocked boards of big business.

In our generalizations we do not treat each corporation or individual director separately, nor do we so intend. Ultimately speaking, the social system that continues through the generations is only momentarily concerned with any given individual. The personnel varies, individuals disappear, but the system persists or, modified, continues in new form. We concern ourselves with types of corporations and types of interconnections by directorial memberships that interrelate corporate structures. These are empirically derived interrelations we inducted to define the system or systems of memberships on boards and the interconnections of corporations.

For our purposes we use only three typologies: (a) the enterprise activity types, including the usual categories of the Standard Industrial Classification, finance, manufacturing and the like; (b) size, from our 500 largest to large (some of the 21,000 with assets more than $1 million), to small (all others); and (c) headquarters' locations by region and city of the interlocked boards.

We ask these questions about the types of corporations that interlock:

1. How do companies in the different cities and regions interconnect by membership on boards with those of other regions and cities? This question brings out the vast territorial system of real interconnectedness among the boards of the corporations, big and not so big, that are demonstratively interconnected.

2. How do the corporations of different sizes, the big, the medium and small, interconnect?

3. How do the different types of corporate enterprise actively interconnect?

We then arrive at a more technical question, but of great importance, in measuring the interconnection of different types of corporations. What are the numbers and proportions of the *outgoing* manager-held directorships from any given type to other types? And its companion question: What are the numbers and proportions of *incoming* manager-held directorships to any given type from each type? And then a final question: What are the measurable differences of outgoing and incoming connections between and among types? The answer to the last question gives the system or systems of corporate board interconnectedness and establishes the amount of relation and the kinds of relations among the several types. In the case of types of enterprise, an officer of a bank who was a member of the board of a manufacturing or transportation corporation would be an outgoing connection for the financial organization and at the same time an incoming member to the board of the manufacturing or transportation company. If the executive of a transportation company served as a director of the bank, he would be incoming to the bank, outgoing to the transportation company. In the case of size of city, an outgoing connection for the more-than-two-million class would be an officer from a corporation with headquarters located in the city of more than two million who was a member of the board of a corporation with headquarters located in a city of fewer than two million, and an incoming one would be an officer from a fewer-than-two-million city acting as a director in an over-two-million city.

We can recapitulate by saying that each manager may hold a directorial position in his own corporation or in another corporation within the category of his own corporation. If the position is outside the category of the corporation in which he is an executive, then it is counted as going out from that category to another, i.e. it is outgoing for the category containing the corporation in which the man is an executive. On the other hand, all directorships held within this category by managers of firms that belong to a different category are incoming. We will count from two points of view: the absolute number and distribution of directorships that come into a type and the absolute number and distribution that go out from it.

THE COMPONENTS OF THE SYSTEM

Before examining this system of interlocking, we will inspect and count the major parts of the interlocking organization, including the number of men who were directors, those who were also managers of corporations, the number and size of the corporations they manage, and the number of men who are directors of our 500, as well as other basic elements of the system. Our effort now is to dissect and count the parts of the system. This established, we will push our inquiry into how these parts are interrelated as functioning elements of the total system of interlocking directorates.

There were 5,776 men who were directors of one or more of our

500 largest corporations. They comprise the entire directorial staff, the complete personnel of the 500 boards, averaging about twelve directors for each company.

About three-fourths of the directors (4,374) were managers of corporations, and another fourth (1,402) were citizen-directors, holding no managerial position in our 500 or any other corporation (see Table 1).

If we now look at all corporations for whom these men serve as directors, the number of corporations expands enormously; the directorships held by these men amount to more than 20,000 (see later). More than a third of the individuals, almost 2,000, have but one directorship, necessarily one among our original 500 corporations. Such single directorship is more frequent among citizen-directors than among officer-directors. Twenty-eight per cent (1,224) of the managers were directors of but one corporation, again by definition one of our 500; more than half the officer-directors (2,418 or 55 per cent) were directors of no more than three companies of any size; and 9 per cent (375) of the approximately 4,400 directors who were also officers were directors of ten or more corporations. Over half (757 or 53 per cent) of the individuals who were citizen-directors held only one directorship; 83 per cent (1,175) held no more than three; and only a little over 1 per cent (18) held ten or more (see Table 1). Although the 757 are not managers of any firm, each is a director in one of the 500 in the original sample. The significant point in the expansion and multiplication of the directorships is that each of the 5,776 men was, of course, counted only once, but the directorships of each are multiplied from two to as many as twelve times. Thus, the 86 men who hold ten directorships might relate to as many as 860 corporations that are interlocked through their multiple directorial positions.

What kinds of positions and corporations are represented by the officer-directors? Three-fourths of them are presidents or vice-presidents (see Table 2), and another 18 per cent are chairmen of the board. The three positions represent more than nine out of every ten of the managers who were directors of at least one of the 500. Clearly, the exchange of officers as directors among these companies emphasizes the highest level of command. It seems more than probable, although we do not have an actual determination of

Table 1. Number of Directorships Held by Each Individual Citizen and Manager Director

		Number of directorships per individual												Total	
		One	Two	Three	Four	Five	Six	Seven	Eight	Nine	Ten	Eleven	Twelve or more	N	%
Number of Individuals		1,981	968	644	508	429	298	244	188	123	86	87	220	5,776	
Citizen-Directors	N	757	294	124	93	49	45	13	9	0	4	13	1	1,402	24.3
	%	53	21	9	7	4	3	1	1	0	0	1	0		100.0
Officer-Directors	N	1,224	674	520	415	380	253	231	179	123	82	74	219	4,374	75.7
	%	28	15	12	9	9	6	5	4	3	2	2	5		100.0

Table 2. Corporate Positions of Managers and Number of Directorships of Each

	One	Two	Three	Four	Five	Six	Seven	Eight	Nine	Ten	Eleven	Twelve	Total	Per cent of all officer-directors
Chairman	75	104	105	95	94	62	61	50	38	22	18	47	771	18
President	128	210	214	192	165	122	120	92	65	37	38	114	1,497	34
Vice-president	769	323	175	110	107	64	46	34	19	16	14	56	1,733	39
Secretary	29	13	12	5	2	1	3	3	0	3	1	1	73	2
Treasurer	24	10	4	1	1	0	0	0	0	1	2	1	44	1
Miscellaneous positions	199	14	10	12	11	4	1	0	1	3	1	0	256	6
												Total	4,374	100

their social rank as private citizens but only inspection of names and sporadic biographies, that these men also occupy high positions in the American community.

Significant differences in the proportions of single and multiple directorships exist between the different managerial levels; the higher managerial positions have more directorships. The number of individuals who were chairmen rises from 75 who were only single directors to around 100 for the two, three, four, and five multiple directorships (see Table 2). The number of men who hold multiple directorships who were presidents of companies is more than those who held a single one (128), up to five multiple directorships (165) and holds its own for six (122) and seven (120) multiple directorships. In sharp contrast, the figures for lower-ranked positions fall as directorships increase from single to double and triple. It seems probable that increasing height in the managerial hierarchy increases the likelihood of a man's taking on more directorships. Moreover, it seems probable that men who are successfully mobile to higher managerial positions become objects of higher attractiveness to other corporations because of reputed skill, power, and high status. It can be stated inferentially that these men are more likely to exercise their mobility motivations by becoming directors of more companies because greater accessibility to these positions exists for successfully mobile men.[2]

How many of these managers came from big corporations?

		(%)
Managers of our 500 firms (largest)	2,765	(63.2)
Managers of other firms of $1 million net (large)	931	(21.3)
Managers of firms with less than $1 million net (small)	678	(15.5)
	4,374	(100.0)

Most of the managers were of high position; most of those who held multiple directorships were the highest; and most managed large and very large-scale corporations. We already know that many were single directors of only the corporations of which they were managers, but how many and what proportion of these officer-directors of large corporations hold directorial positions with

2. See W. Lloyd Warner and James Abegglen, *Big Business Leaders in America* (New York, Harper, 1955).

The System of Interlocking Directorates

other large corporations? Table 3 shows that 3,696 (2,765+931) managers of large firms held a total of 6,280 directorships in big corporations and another 3,729 positions in small corporations, amounting to over 10,000 directorial positions held outside of their own firms by the managers of big firms.

In what numbers and in what proportions were the managers distributed in the different types of business enterprise? How many and what proportions of the managers of the different types of enterprise hold directorships outside their own firms? How many large and small ones? Table 3 shows the number and percentage of managers in each type of business enterprise (it will be recalled that our sample was first divided broadly into industrials, financials, and the like; here they are reclassified into the Standard Industrial Classification). All the managers in Table 3 are in large firms. The table on its right shows the number and per cent of the directorships in large and small corporations in which each type of manager holds outside directorial positions. The managers of certain types of firms tend to hold more directorships outside their firms than others. Some are lower, but most types have about the same percentage of outside directorships as their proportion among the managers would indicate. Let us briefly review the evidence, but before doing so we must caution the reader about the arrangement of Table 3. The figures and the percentages for the managers listed on the left are for the types of business enterprise they manage; the columns for the outside directorships on the right are for the sizes of the corporation in which they hold directorial positions. The table says, for example, that 6.1 per cent of the managers (228) were with mining corporations and that they held 6.9 per cent of the outside directorships in corporations of all sizes—9.9 per cent of the directorships of small corporations and 5.1 per cent of the large ones.

Which kinds of managers went over or under their proportions as outside directors? A few did, but most not very strongly. Finance rose from 13 per cent to 18 per cent and was particularly high among the big ones—up to 21 per cent. Transportation and utilities also rose, a few dropped, but generally, the differences in proportion are small.

Perhaps we should say here that there were 8,872 firms of all sizes interlocked by the directors and managers. How big were the firms themselves? They were the original 500 largest corporations

Table 3. Big Managers and Big Directorships

Types of large firms	Managers of large firms (classified by activity)		Outside directorships of managers of large firms					
			Firms with more than $1 million net assets		Firms with less than $1 million net assets		Firms of all sizes	
	N	%	N	%	N	%	N	%
Agriculture	6	0.2	22	0.4	10	0.3	32	0.3
Mining	228	6.1	322	5.1	369	9.9	691	6.9
Contract construction	37	1.0	78	1.2	73	2.0	151	1.5
Mfg. I food, tobacco, textile, etc.	414	11.2	511	8.1	348	9.3	859	8.6
Mfg. II lumber, furniture, paper	673	18.2	869	13.8	735	19.7	1,604	16.0
Mfg. III metal, machinery, etc.	762	20.6	1,273	20.3	795	21.3	2,068	20.7
Transportation and utilities	274	7.5	712	11.3	381	10.2	1,093	10.9
Wholesale trade	226	6.1	309	4.9	172	4.6	481	4.8
Retail trade	370	10.0	351	5.6	189	5.1	540	5.4
Life insurance, etc.	165	4.5	415	6.7	126	3.4	541	5.4
Finance, banks	479	12.9	1,329	21.2	431	11.5	1,760	17.6
Services	62	1.7	89	1.4	100	2.7	189	1.9
Total	3,696	100.0	6,280	100.0	3,729	100.0	10,009	100.0

The System of Interlocking Directorates

(5.6 per cent), another 3,625 (40.9 per cent) that were large, with over $1 million net worth, and 4,747 (53.5 per cent) small ones, of less than $1 million net worth.

We have been discussing the 10,000 outside directorships held in large and small corporations by the managers of large firms. We can now widen our inquiry and ask how many managers held directorships both inside and outside their own firms. How many held only an inside directorship in their parent corporation, and how many held no directorship in their own corporation but were directors in corporations other than their own? The simple tabulation below answers these questions. A very heavy percentage (70.5 per cent) of the managers were directors in their own and other corporations.

		(%)
Managers: both inside and outside	3,082	(70.5)
Managers: in own corporation only	1,224	(28.0)
Managers: outside only	68	(1.5)

Our attention has been largely concentrated on the managers and directors of large firms. We learned that these managers of large firms held 10,009 directorships in large and small corporations out of the total of 20,522 directorships of all kinds held by the men who were the directors of the 500 corporations. The other 10,500 directorships are also shown in the following tabulation. More than 3,000 were held by men who were managers of small firms, another 4,300 were directorships inside the parent corporation held by managers of large and small firms, and about 3,000 were held by citizen-directors.

Directorships Held by:		(%)
Managers of large firms in outside large corporations	6,280	(30.6)
Managers of large firms in outside small corporations	3,729	(18.2)
Managers of small firms in all outside corporations	3,241	(15.8)
Managers of large and small corporations in their own corporations	4,306	(21.0)
Citizen-directors, large and small corporations	2,966	(14.4)
	20,522	(100.0)

We can recast our figures and ask how many directorships were inside and how many outside the parent corporation. Since the citizen-directorship is held by an outsider, this type of directorship is, of course, an external one. Given this reckoning, 79 per cent of the directorships were external, and 21 per cent were internal.

When one asks what was the grand total of managerial and directorial positions involved in the system of interlocking directorships and managers and what proportion each had, the two add up to 24,896 of these elite statuses that were interconnected—18 per cent managerial and 82 per cent directorial.

Before leaving this section, which reports on these dissected dismembra of the system and on how the several parts expanded from 500 firms and the 5,776 individuals who were their directors, many readers may wish a retrospective summary to see how all the parts numerically relate to each other. Table 4 provides both a single reference for the dismembered parts and a preparation for the discussion and description of the parts as members of a social system of interlocking directorships and managers that will follow.

The table is divided into nine major topics. Beginning with the original sample of 500 corporations and their directors, it shows the amount of expansion in managers and directorships, the sizes of all interlocked firms, and the number and kinds of all the more than 20,000 directorships held in their own and other corporations by the men who direct the 500 largest corporations.

To recapitulate, we have now learned that the 5,776 men who were the directors of our representative 500 largest corporations were involved in approximately 25,000 managerial and directorial positions in about 9,000 companies. While a fourth held no managerial position, three-fourths were managers, and most of them were in high managerial positions in the 500. These are the parts and their amounts in the huge system of corporate power and prestige that interconnects the elite position of top managers and the directing boards of many thousands of American corporations to the 500 and to each other.

With this evidence we answer our most general and most important question: How and in what way are the 500 and other corporations interconnected through the interlocked memberships of their boards? Better put, what are the systems or subsystems of interrelated corporations established by their interlocked boards of directors? How narrowly or widely do they extend in American

Table 4. Directors, Managers, Directorships, and Corporations

1. Directors and corporations in the original sample
   Individuals who were directors of the
       largest corporations   5,776
   Number of the largest corporations   500
2. Total of positions held in all firms by the 5,776 directors
   Total of all managers (among directors)   4,374 (17.57%)
   Total of all directorships   20,522 (82.43%)
       Total of all interlocked positions   24,896 (100.00%)
3. Managers and size of their parent firms
   Managers in the 500   2,765 (63.21%)
   Managers in *other* firms of more than
       $1 million net worth   931 (21.29%)
   Managers of all firms of more than
       $1 million net worth   3,696 (84.50%)
   Managers of small firms (less than
       $1 million net worth)   678 (15.50%)
       Total of all managers   4,374 (100.00%)
4. Sizes of all firms
   Largest   500 (5.64%)
   Large (more than $1 million net worth)   3,625 (40.86%)
   Small (less than $1 million net worth)   4,747 (53.50%)
                          8,872 (100.00%)
5. Managers and directorships held in and outside
   their own firms
   Managers: directorship only in own corporation   1,224 (27.98%)
   Managers: both in and outside directorships   3,082 (70.46%)
   Managers: no directorships in own corporations,
       only outside   68 (1.56%)
                          4,374 (100.00%)
6. Kinds of directors in the 500 corporations
   Directors who were managers   4,374 (75.73%)
   Citizen-directors (no management position)   1,402 (24.27%)
                          5,776 (100.00%)
7. Directorships held by those inside and
   outside corporations
   External directorships   16,216 (79.02%)
   Internal directorships   4,306 (20.98%)
       Total directorships in all corporations   20,522 (100.00%)
8. Outside directorships held in large and small
   corporations, large firm managers
   Held by managers of large firms in outside
       large corporations   6,280 (62.74%)
   Held by managers of large firms in outside
       small corporations   3,729 (37.26%)
       Total outside directorships held by large
       firm managers   10,009 (100.00%)
9. All directorships: large and small corporations
   Held by managers of small firms in all
       outside corporations   3,241 (15.79%)
   Held by managers of large and small
       corporations in own corporations   4,306 (20.98%)
   Held by managers of large firms in outside
       corporations   10,009 (48.78%)
   Held by (outside) citizen-directors   2,966 (14.45%)
       Total directorships of all kinds   20,522 (100.00%)

corporate life? How closely, and to what degree, are these different kinds of corporations and other private enterprises thus interrelated, for example, finance with manufacturing, financial groups among themselves, and, since the exchange of directors may be a two-way street, manufacturing with finance? How many financial officers are directors of manufacturing corporations, and, in their turn, how many men in manufacturing are bank directors? What is the exchange among other varieties of boards and individuals of different firms—those among the largest, large, and small corporations? Or, to shift our attention to another system of interconnection among the corporations and their directors, what are the territorial arrangements and geographical systems among the interlocked corporations? How and to what degree is New York City related to San Francisco, to Boston, and to the other great and small cities of America, and, in turn, how are their boards and their managers related to the corporations in New York City? Are there more directors going out from New York to serve on the boards of corporations of other cities, or are there more coming into New York from the firms of other cities to serve as outside directors in New York? How do the results for New York compare with those of other great cities, for Chicago, Los Angeles, or Detroit, or for those cities in the 1,000,000 to 2,000,000 or 500,000 to 1,000,000 population classes?

Before proceeding to this task we must remind ourselves that we have already made a small beginning by counting the connections the managers of large corporations have with other corporations as directors of large and small companies, and we have learned something about the number of outside connections the managers of different types of enterprise have with other large and small companies. But this is only a very small beginning of the task that confronts us.

THE TERRITORIAL INTERCONNECTIONS

Our attention now shifts to the system of interconnection itself and to that system as it exists among the directorships of big corporations held by managers of big corporations. This means that not only the directors and managers of the 500 corporations originally selected are involved, but all (and only) those who are part of the system of corporations of more than $1 million net worth. This selection disregards all but the interlocked managers and directors of large-scale corporate enterprises—our 500 representative largest and all other enterprises of more than $1 million net worth. This universe, being concerned only with interlocking directorships held externally by managers of big corporations in other big corporations, excludes all directorships held by: (a) citizen-directors, for they are not in the system of manager-director exchange; (b) all directorships in small corporations; (c) all directorships of any kind held by managers of small corporations, for these small managers and small directorships are outside this system of exchange; and (d) the internal directorships held by the managers in their parent corporation, for they, by their nature, do not interlock corporations. The number of these external directorships in outside big corporations amounts to 6,280. The number of managerships is 3,696. The number of large corporations is 4,125. These corporations constitute a very large sample of those studied in the chapters on structures of large-scale corporations and the locations of headquarters.

The sharing of directorships on the boards of large corporations by managers of other large corporations sets up several networks of interconnection, including the territorial connections among the cities and towns and regions of the United States. The firms of the managers may be in New York, while their directorships may be in corporations whose headquarters are scattered from New York City through Chicago out to the West Coast; and officers of companies in San Francisco may hold directorships in Chicago, Los Angeles, New York, and elsewhere. The patterns of connection that exist in the interlocking positions among external directors and the headquarters of the parent and host corporations raise a whole series of important questions about the system of interlocking directorships among large-scale American corporations. Supplying evidence to answer some of these questions should give us new knowledge leading to further inquiry into understanding the social system of corporations and the exchange of elite directorial positions among the managers.

Before doing this we must again remind ourselves that when the kinds of directorships are restricted, dropping internal ones, citizen-directors, and those held by managers of small firms, the grand total of directors drops from 20,522 to 10,009 held by large company managers in all outside corporations; and when the 3,700 (3,729) outside directorships held in small corporations by large-corporation managers are excluded, the total drops to 6,280 external directorships held by managers of large-scale corporations in other large-scale enterprises. These are our present interests; we will first address our questions to the territorial system of interlocking directorships and marshall our evidence to answer the following questions.

Where are the headquarters of the parent and host corporations? How many of the outside directorships are in the same city as the headquarters of the managers' parent corporations and in what proportion? How many are in cities and regions beyond that city? Is there a relation between size of the city and the proportion of its interlocking directorships in and out of the city?

How are the ten cities (SMSAs) of more than two million ranked for the number of their interlocking directorates? Which size cities have their headquarters most closely interlocked with those firms within the city or within cities of the same size? Are the interlocking directorates more often within the city or spread else-where; for example, do more of Chicago's managers of big corporations direct other Chicago big corporations, or do more go to corporations elsewhere?

Well over half (3,789 of the 6,280) of the large-corporation directorates are held by managers of corporations with head-quarters located in one of the big ten cities—those of more than two million (Table 5). Among the ten cities, New York is far in the lead with 1,700 to Chicago's 469 and Phila-delphia's 290. The other SMSAs drop largely in order of size. The thousands of non-SMSAs combined have about as many (249) such directorates as does the one city of San Francisco (248). Of the total, more such directorates (53.9 per cent) are held inside their cities than outside. But this difference is true only for the cities of one-to-two and more than two million—60 per cent of such directorates in the former and 59 per cent in the lat-ter. All other sizes fall below 50 per cent. Among the big ten, New York is lowest (52 per cent) for such directorates internally

The System of Interlocking Directorates

locked within the city, and St. Louis is highest (with 73 per cent), which means that large size does not operate absolutely for determining the increase of directorates located within the city of the parent corporation of the manager. There is, of course, clearly a very definite relationship between size of the city and the

Table 5. Directorships Inside and Outside the City Headquarters of the Managers

Headquarters	Inside		Outside		Total	Total
	N	%	N	%	N	%
More than 2,000,000	2,134	58.9	1,655	41.1	3,789	100.0
New York	895	51.8	832	48.2	1,727	100.0
Los Angeles	128	58.7	90	41.3	218	100.0
Chicago	274	58.4	195	41.6	469	100.0
Philadelphia	171	59.0	119	41.0	290	100.0
Detroit	92	61.8	55	38.2	147	100.0
San Francisco	157	63.4	91	36.6	248	100.0
Boston	120	56.9	91	43.1	211	100.0
Pittsburgh	112	52.1	103	47.9	215	100.0
St. Louis	157	73.3	57	26.7	214	100.0
Washington, D.C.	28	56.0	22	44.0	50	100.0
1,000,000 to 2,000,000	600	60.4	394	39.6	994	100.0
500,000 to 1,000,000	265	47.6	291	52.4	556	100.0
300,000 to 500,000	166	43.7	214	56.3	380	100.0
200,000 to 300,000	52	35.9	93	64.1	145	100.0
100,000 to 200,000	72	47.4	80	52.6	152	100.0
50,000 to 100,000	5	33.3	10	66.7	15	100.0
Non SMSA	93	37.3	156	62.7	249	100.0
Total	3,387	53.9	2,893	46.1	6,280	100.0

amount of internal connection, but this is evidently not the only determining factor.

Two opposing factors seem to operate; territorial propinquities still function in a city of any SMSA category. The net effect is to pull the home city higher than the others, but as the city's population lessens and the corporations in each are fewer, there is less opportunity for intra-home-city interlocking. It is also possible that the pull and push of the other great cities may account for New York's somewhat smaller percentage of intracity couplings, and thus this figure may be related to the city's great claim to being the national headquarters for the United States. Corporations in other cities seek the managers of large New York based corporations as their directors; they take more than 800 such men into their boards, many times more than any other city sends or keeps. Despite the high participation by corporation managers on boards outside their cities where those headquarters cities are small, and despite the considerable demand for directorships to go to managers from corporations with headquarters in other cities, the factors pulling men to directorships in the home city still appear to be powerful.

How much are the headquarters of each of the ten cities interconnected among themselves and with the smaller metropolitan cities? How are the directorates of each city divided among the others in the largest ten and among the different sizes? In the column at the left of Table 6 are the locations of the managers' parent corporations, arranged by population. The columns that spread laterally list the same cities and categories of cities by size for the directorships held there by managers of corporations headquartered in cities listed in the left column. To the far right are the totals for directorships located inside and outside the cities in which the headquarters are located. The diagonal figures have two interpretations. For the ten named cities they give the proportion of interlocked directorships held by managers from the named city within their own city; for the size categories they give the proportion of interlocked directorships held by men from a city of that size, whether the same city or a different one. The other figures, all intercity, give the percentages of the directorates held in each of the big ten cities and in the other size categories by managers whose own firms have headquarters in other cities. For instance, the figure at the top left indicates that 51.8 per cent of 1,727 directorships of New York managers were in New York; in the next two columns, 2.1 per cent and 4.4 per cent of New York's total of interlocking directorships were held by New York men in Los Angeles and Chicago corporations. It will be noticed that every cell in the New York row has occupancy, indicating the wide territorial

Table 6. Location of Headquarters of Big Corporations with Interlocked Directorships

Location of headquarters of firms interlocked by directors

Location of headquarters of manager's parent firm	More than 2,000,000 population										1,000,000–2,000,000	500,000–1,000,000	300,000–500,000	200,000–300,000	100,000–200,000	50,000–100,000	Not SMSA	Totals N	Totals %
	N.Y.	L.A.	Chi.	Phil.	Det.	S.F.	Bost.	Pitt.	St. L.	D.C.									
1 New York	**51.8**	2.1	4.4	2.5	1.6	1.4	1.6	1.3	.6	.4	9.5	7.1	3.1	2.5	3.4	.3	6.4	1,727	100.0
2 Los Angeles	8.7	**58.7**	2.8	.9		6.0	.5	.5		.2	7.3	6.4	2.3	.9	.9	.4	4.1	218	100.0
3 Chicago	8.1	1.1	**58.4**	1.1	1.1	.9	.9	1.7	1.7		6.0	5.1	1.9	1.7	5.3		4.4	469	100.0
4 Philadelphia	12.1	.7	1.4	**59.0**	.7		.7	1.7	.3	.3	6.9	1.7	5.3	1.7	1.4	.4	5.8	290	100.0
5 Detroit	10.8	.7	.7	1.3	**61.8**			1.3			8.0	4.0	.7	4.7	1.3		4.7	147	100.0
6 San Francisco	12.5	8.9	.4	.4	.4	**63.4**		1.2	.4		2.8	2.8	2.8	1.2	.4	1.6	.8	248	100.0
7 Boston	10.4	.9	.9	.5	.9	.5	**56.9**	.9	.9		6.2	5.3	3.9	1.4	1.9	1.4	6.2	211	100.0
8 Pittsburgh	10.2		2.8	3.7	2.3		2.3	**52.1**	.9	.9	8.4	3.2	1.9	1.4	1.9		7.9	215	100.0
9 St. Louis	4.7	.9	2.3			1.4	.9	1.4	**73.3**	.5	5.6	1.9	1.9	1.9	.5	.9	4.3	214	100.0
10 Washington, D.C.	10.0		4.0				2.0			**56.0**	10.0	8.0	2.0	4.0	4.0			50	100.0
11–24 1,000,000–2,000,000	11.6	1.3	3.9	1.7	1.2	.8	1.0	.7	.9	.3	**60.4**	4.2	2.6	2.6	2.4	.1	4.3	994	100.0
25–53 500,000–1,000,000	11.7	1.8	3.2	1.8	.5	3.6	.9	1.3	.5	.5	12.6	**47.7**	3.8	1.4	2.7	.4	5.6	556	100.0
54–81 300,000–500,000	13.4	.8	2.9	1.6	2.6	.8	3.7	1.0	1.3		9.5	7.1	**43.7**	4.7	2.9	.3	3.7	380	100.0
82–122 200,000–300,000	14.5	1.4	6.2	2.1	2.1		.7	2.7		1.4	5.5	5.5	4.1	**35.9**	5.5	.7	11.7	145	100.0
123–190 100,000–200,000	5.3	.7	3.3	1.3	.7	1.3	.7	3.8	2.0	.7	10.5	9.9	1.3	3.8	**47.4**	.7	6.6	152	100.0
191–299 other SMSA	26.7						6.7	13.3	13.3			13.3	6.7			**33.3**		15	100.0
300–999 not SMSA	11.6	1.2	2.8	2.8	3.2	.8	2.4	3.6	.8		10.0	6.4	2.4	9.3	4.8	.4	**37.5**	249	100.0
Total number	1,386	230	465	279	171	238	200	196	206	49	1,050	580	335	210	245	29	411	6,280	

spread achieved by managers of New York based large corporations going out into the governing boards of large corporations in other large cities and also into some that are not in metropolitan areas at all. This continuous distribution accounts for the ranking of New York (which has by far the largest number of directorates among the big ten cities) in eleventh place for the proportion of its directors locally held. Chicago and Boston also have continuous spread in all other categories. All the other cities fail to be represented in one or more of the big ten cities or other categories.

The totals at the bottom of each column give the number of directorships that come into a city from all other places added to those held within the city itself by local managers. Thus New York has 1,386; cities of one to two million, 1,050; and those of 500,000 to a million, 580. The percentages given here show proportions for all the directorships held both inside and outside the city by big corporation managers in other big corporations.

Until now we have examined only the grand totals for inter- and intracity interlocking of those directorships outside the parent corporation. Moreover, we have examined only half of this, for we have inspected figures for directorships held by a manager within his city and other cities. Interlocking directorships are reciprocal. To complete our task we must ask, for example, how many directorships come from elsewhere into New York? Where do they come from and in what proportions? Where and in what proportions do New York's managers go as directors? The answers will establish the evidential interlocking of cities through their interconnected boards. To simplify our problem we will begin with the reciprocal interconnection of the boards in the ten great cities. We will ask how much each of the ten is connected with each of the other nine by its managers coming to and going out from them as directors.

What is the exchange of giving and receiving directors between pairs of cities? Between Boston and Chicago? Between San Francisco and Los Angeles? Between each pair of the others?

Table 7 answers these questions for all ten cities. To further simplify the communication about the evidence, only numbers are given. We start with New York, at the upper left. The arrow pointing from New York into the Los Angeles column indicates that thirty-six managers of large New York–based corporations sit as directors of large Los Angeles–based corporations; the lower arrow

Table 7. The Big Ten

Headquarters of parent firm (SMSA)	New York	Los Angeles	Chicago	Philadelphia	Detroit	San Francisco	Boston	Pittsburgh	St. Louis	Washington D.C.	Total
New York		↑36 ↓19	↑75 ↓38	↑44 ↓35	↑27 ↓16	↑25 ↓31	↑27 ↓22	↑23 ↓22	↑11 ↓10	↑7 ↓5	↑275 ↓198
Los Angeles	↑19 ↓36		↑6 ↓5	↑2 ↓2	↑0 ↓1	↑22 ↓13	↑1 ↓2	↑1 ↓0	↑0 ↓2	↑0 ↓0	↑42 ↓70
Chicago	↑38 ↓75	↑5 ↓6		↑5 ↓4	↑5 ↓1	↑4 ↓1	↑4 ↓2	↑8 ↓6	↑8 ↓5	↑2 ↓1	↑78 ↓102
Philadelphia	↑35 ↓44	↑2 ↓2	↑4 ↓5		↑2 ↓2	↑0 ↓1	↑2 ↓1	↑5 ↓8	↑1 ↓0	↑1 ↓0	↑52 ↓63
Detroit	↑16 ↓27	↑1 ↓0	↑1 ↓5	↑2 ↓2		↑0 ↓1	↑0 ↓2	↑2 ↓5	↑0 ↓0	↑0 ↓0	↑22 ↓42
San Francisco	↑31 ↓25	↑13 ↓22	↑1 ↓4	↑1 ↓0	↑1 ↓0		↑0 ↓1	↑0 ↓3	↑3 ↓1	↑0 ↓0	↑60 ↓46
Boston	↑22 ↓27	↑2 ↓1	↑2 ↓4	↑1 ↓2	↑2 ↓0	↑1 ↓0		↑5 ↓2	↑2 ↓2	↑2 ↓1	↑36 ↓42
Pittsburgh	↑22 ↓23	↑0 ↓1	↑6 ↓8	↑8 ↓5	↑5 ↓2	↑0 ↓3	↑5 ↓2		↑2 ↓3	↑1 ↓0	↑49 ↓47
St. Louis	↑10 ↓11	↑0 ↓2	↑5 ↓8	↑0 ↓1	↑0 ↓0	↑3 ↓1	↑2 ↓2	↑3 ↓2		↑0 ↓0	↑25 ↓25
Washington D.C.	↑5 ↓7	↑0 ↓0	↑2 ↓1	↑0 ↓1	↑0 ↓0	↑0 ↓0	↑1 ↓2	↑0 ↓1	↑0 ↓0		↑8 ↓12

pointing to New York from Los Angeles says nineteen directors of New York corporations come from Los Angeles. The next column is Chicago. The outer pointing arrow from New York indicates that seventy-five of its directors come from New York; the other arrow indicates that only thirty-eight New York directorships are held by managers of big Chicago corporations. In most cities with which New York is interlocked more directorships go to them from New York than go from them to New York—the difference between 275 and 198 (see far right column). It will be noted in the totals for some cities, including Los Angeles, Chicago, Philadelphia, Detroit, and Boston, that the exact opposite is true. Fewer directors are sent out to other cities than are received from them. Los Angeles, for example, receives a total of seventy and sends only forty-two.

San Francisco, the old financial and commercial capital of the West Coast, is more like New York. Its total of sixty directorships in other cities is higher than the forty-six it receives from the other nine. Why? It is the only city in the big ten that sends more directorships to New York than it receives. It sends twenty-two to Los Angeles and receives thirteen. These make up the major differences on the score for San Francisco. Moreover, almost all of San Francisco's reciprocal directorial relations with other cities are with New York and Los Angeles. Los Angeles has strong interconnections only with New York and San Francisco.

New York is the only city with strong relations out and in with all of the big ten. Chicago has moderate ones with Los Angeles, Philadelphia, Pittsburgh, and St. Louis. Philadelphia and Pittsburgh are moderately close. The one exception to all of this is Washington, which is low with all cities as well as for internal directorships. The city itself, of course, is not an industrial capital. New York, by these measures of importance, is easily the national corporate capital of the United States; no other city approaches it for the giving and getting of managers to be directors on the governing boards of corporations other than their own.

Table 8 measures the amount of interconnection among all sizes of American metropolises. It shows how much the cities of two million were connected with those of one million and the other sizes and, in turn, those of each size with all others. Or, more concretely and operationally, how many directorships managers with headquarters in the more-than-two-million cities had with those of the

Table 8. Outside Directorships of Managers of Large Firms in Other Large Firms with Headquarters in 212 SMSA and Other Areas, Classified by Population Movements among parent and non-parent firms

In each cell the first value (→) is the row percentage and the second value (↓) is the column percentage.

Headquarters of parent firm (SMSA)	Over 2,000,000	1,000,000 to 2,000,000	500,000 to 1,000,000	300,000 to 500,000	200,000 to 300,000	100,000 to 200,000	50,000 to 100,000	Non-SMSA	Total %	Total N
Over 2,000,000		→29.2 ↓59.1	→20.3 ↓49.3	→10.7 ↓50.0	→7.6 ↓48.4	→10.2 ↓37.6	→1.7 ↓70.0	→20.3 ↓46.8	100.0 =	1010 / 639
1,000,000 to 2,000,000	→59.1 ↓29.2		→10.7 ↓24.1	→6.3 ↓16.8	→6.6 ↓8.6	→6.1 ↓20.0	→0.3 ↓0.0	→10.9 ↓16.0	100.0 =	394 / 450
500,000 to 1,000,000	→49.3 ↓20.3	→24.1 ↓10.7		→7.2 ↓12.6	→2.8 ↓8.6	→5.2 ↓18.7	→0.7 ↓20.0	→10.7 ↓10.3	100.0 =	291 / 315
300,000 to 500,000	→50.0 ↓10.7	→16.8 ↓6.3	→12.6 ↓7.2		→8.4 ↓6.5	→5.1 ↓2.5	→0.5 ↓10.0	→6.6 ↓3.8	100.0 =	214 / 169
200,000 to 300,000	→48.4 ↓7.6	→8.6 ↓6.6	→8.6 ↓2.8	→6.5 ↓8.4		→8.6 ↓7.5	→1.1 ↓0.0	→18.2 ↓14.8	100.0 =	93 / 158
100,000 to 200,000	→37.6 ↓10.2	→20.0 ↓6.1	→18.7 ↓5.2	→2.5 ↓5.1	→7.5 ↓8.6		→1.3 ↓0.0	→12.5 ↓7.7	100.0 =	80 / 173
50,000 to 100,000	→70.0 ↓1.7	→0.0 ↓0.3	→20.0 ↓0.7	→10.0 ↓0.5	→0.0 ↓1.1	→0.0 ↓1.3		→0.0 ↓0.6	100.0 =	10 / 24
Non-SMSA	→46.8 ↓20.3	→16.0 ↓10.9	→10.3 ↓10.7	→3.8 ↓6.6	→14.8 ↓18.2	→7.7 ↓12.5	→0.6 ↓0.0		100.0 =	156 / 320
Total %	100.0	100.0	100.0	100.0	100.0	100.0	100.0	100.0	100.0 =	
Total N	1010 / 639	394 / 450	291 / 315	214 / 169	93 / 158	80 / 173	10 / 24	156 / 320		2248 / 2248

one-to-two-million cities and with those of decreasing sizes, down to SMSAs with 50,000 to 100,000. It also asks these questions for the managers in each of the other categories. Do the big cities tend to have more coming into them, or do they send more directorships out? Are there discernible patterns of giving and getting men of big business in the large corporate directorships? If so, what are they?

At the far left of Table 8 are listed, in descending order of size, the seven categories of SMSAs and a general category of those cities that are not SMSAs. Across the table are the same categories. The percentage of the total number of external directorships is given coming into a city size (←) and going out to others from it (→). The cities of more than two million population are related in each lateral cell to the right, first with the cities of one-to-two million population and, thereafter, those of decreasing size. In the one-to-two-million cell the outward pointing arrow (the one that points to the right) indicates that 29.2 per cent of all the outside directorships held by managers from cities of the more-than-two-million class on the boards of corporations located in smaller-classed cities are in the second-sized metropolises; the next column says 20.3 per cent of the outgoing directorships from the more-than-two-million class went to the 500,000-to-1,000,000-sized cities. As cities decrease in size, there is also a linear drop in incoming and outgoing directorships. The thousands of cities and towns not in SMSAs rise primarily because they have not been divided so rigorously as the SMSAs. The far right column shows that the total of extraclass directorships for the two-million class is 1,010 (100 per cent). The bottom row of figures in each cell, indicated by the left pointing arrows, gives the incoming connections, such as those directorships held in the more-than-two-million-class cities by the other sized cities. These percentages are the total for each of these sizes. To give examples, the arrow pointing left at the top of the one-to-two million column says that 59 per cent of their outside directorates out of 394 (see column 2, last row), are with the more-than-two-million cities. The next column, at the top left, says that 49 per cent of the outside directorates of the 500,000 to 1,000,000 class were with the over-two-million cities. The top figures in the far right column give the outward totals for the several sizes of cities. The lower figures show the totals of inward directorship for each size. For example, 639 of 2,248 total were those directorships going into

The System of Interlocking Directorates

the more-than-two-million size cities from all others. In the next cell down, 450 go into the one-to-two-million category from all others.

We have inspected some of the results. What are the significant facts of the overall system? In brief, there is a great territorial system of interlocking directorates. New York is the hub of this system, but all great cities have their own centers of power; the small cities are of very small importance and the totals show that the outgoing directorates of only cities of more than two million and of 300,000 to 500,000 are higher than the number that come into them.

WHAT TYPES OF BUSINESSES ARE INTERLOCKED?

Several studies have been made in the last few years of the amount of interlocking between the same and different types of business and industrial enterprise. Some were for purposes of governmental investigation, others for scientific reasons, and still others for business and market intelligence.[3] Our purpose here is, of course, to learn how these different types of enterprise interconnect and what the system of interlocking is that holds the managers and directors of the several kinds of big business in the larger social universe.

The territorial pattern is a giant national wheel of interlocking directorates with the New York hub dominating the many spokes that spread out from and back to it (North, South, East, and West) into and out of the other great cities of the country. The enterprise pattern is much more complicated.

With our evidence we can answer the following important questions about the kind and degree of enterprise interconnection the managers of large corporations create by holding outside directorships in the large corporations of other enterprise types. As outside

3. For example, see the report of the Free Trade Commission on Interlocking Directorship (1951) and the Survey of the National Industrial Conference Board (1961), etc.

directors of firms do they usually choose (or are they chosen by) companies of their own type, i.e. mining managers as directors of other mining companies, bank managers as directors of other banks? Or do they more often become directors of different types —bankers as directors of mining companies or managers of mining companies as directors of banks?

At the level of common experience we ask these questions about interlocking directorates: The men from what kinds of outside companies choose most often to serve on the boards of banks, manufacturing, mercantile, and other types of corporate enterprise? Conversely, in what proportions are the managers of other big companies present as directors on the boards of the companies of any one of the fourteen Standard Industrial Classifications? If one were a management consultant, for instance, and meeting with the members of the board of a large metal manufacturing firm or of a large New York bank, what might one expect as the representation of outside directors from other enterprises? What proportion of each type of enterprise?

At a more general and abstract level we can ask: What kind of all-embracing social system is established by this exchange of managers among the corporate boards, thus providing the interconnections which make up the parts of the entire interlocking system? Still using only deduction and not inference, we can learn how all the enterprise parts fit together in the exchange of managers as directors among them in the huge and powerful social system of interlocking directors. We will use Tables 9 and 10 to supply evidence and to answer these questions.

Table 9, on the interlocked directorships and managerial positions of fourteen types of business and industry, is arranged to show the proportion of each industry's outside directorships held within its own category and within each of the other categories. The type of corporation of the manager is listed in the column on the left, and the type of corporation in which the outside directorship is held is given in the columns to the right. On the far right are the totals for the directorships that the managers of each type of corporation hold in corporations beyond their own. Mining, it will be noted, has 322 directorships; food manufacturing (Mfg. I), 511; and finance, 1,329; all of them, with the others, amount to the grand total of 6,280 outside directorships held by managers of big

Table 9. Interlocked Directorships by Type of Parent Firm and Outside Firms in Which Manager Is a Director (Classified by SIC)

Type of parent firm of manager	Mining	Contract const.	Mfg. I	Mfg. II	Mfg. III	Railroads	Transp. (air, water, truck)	Utilities	Wholesale	Retail	Finance, banks	Life ins., etc.	Service	Agriculture	%	N
Mining	**17.1**	0.7	2.5	14.9	18.6	2.5	6.5	2.8	6.8	2.2	18.0	6.8	0.6	0.0	100.0	322
Contract const.	5.1	**0.0**	5.1	10.2	21.8	2.6	5.1	7.8	6.4	3.8	20.5	7.8	3.8	0.0	100.0	78
Mfg. I	2.4	0.0	**18.6**	9.6	10.6	4.9	3.9	2.9	3.5	5.3	24.3	12.3	1.3	0.4	100.0	511
Mfg. II	3.5	0.5	5.1	**22.0**	12.9	2.4	7.7	3.7	4.1	2.5	25.1	9.5	0.9	0.1	100.0	869
Mfg. III	3.9	0.7	2.8	9.8	**32.5**	1.9	5.9	3.3	2.4	2.0	24.0	9.1	1.7	0.0	100.0	1273
Railroads	3.6	0.0	0.9	1.8	4.9	**33.3**	9.3	2.2	2.7	1.3	16.9	23.1	0.0	0.0	100.0	225
Transportation	3.0	0.4	5.6	7.8	14.7	3.0	**17.8**	1.7	3.9	2.6	25.2	13.0	1.3	0.0	100.0	231
Utilities	7.0	0.4	1.2	9.0	10.5	5.5	3.5	**18.0**	2.3	1.2	24.2	15.2	2.0	0.0	100.0	256
Wholesale	2.9	0.6	13.9	14.3	10.0	1.9	4.5	2.9	**17.5**	6.2	19.1	4.9	1.0	0.3	100.0	309
Retail	1.1	0.6	6.8	4.6	9.4	1.4	6.6	3.4	5.7	**22.2**	25.1	10.2	2.9	0.0	100.0	351
Finance, banks	5.6	1.1	8.3	11.9	18.3	3.9	5.3	4.7	2.4	5.8	**10.0**	20.9	1.7	0.1	100.0	1329
Life ins, etc.	1.9	1.0	4.6	5.8	15.4	3.9	3.9	8.0	1.7	3.1	26.3	**22.8**	1.4	0.2	100.0	415
Service	11.3	0.0	7.9	10.1	14.7	2.2	3.4	16.8	1.1	1.1	16.8	6.7	**7.9**	0.0	100.0	89
Agriculture	4.5	0.0	27.3	4.5	9.2	4.5	0.0	4.5	0.0	4.5	22.8	13.7	0.0	**4.5**	100.0	22

Directorships by type of firm

What Types of Businesses Are Interlocked?

corporations of all types with other big corporations, the same total of outside directorships for the same managers we previously used for the territorial spread of directorships. The percentages are lateral and give for each activity type the proportion of its outside directorships in each activity type, including its own. Thus, 17 per cent of mining directorships in other corporations are with other mining corporations, and 19 per cent are with manufacturers of machinery and metal.

To answer the question we asked above about whether a manager favors his own type of enterprise, we will compare the percentages in the diagonals (boldface) of Table 9, giving interconnection of like with like, with the rest of the percentages in each row. For example, a third of the 225 outside directorships held by railroad managers are with other railroads; directorships in every other type are much lower, and among these life insurance (23.1 per cent) is the highest.

Other corporate enterprise types seldom select railroads. A glance down the column for railroads shows that no enterprise exceeds 6 per cent for directors serving on the boards of railroads (utilities, 5.5, is the highest). Railroad managers as directors appear to be closely tied to their own enterprise type and otherwise only interested in outside representation in banks (16.9 per cent) and life insurance companies (23.1 per cent).

Railroad managers' directorships are no more than moderate in total number (225). Let us examine two enterprise types having the largest number of directorships—metal manufacturing (1,273) and banks (1,329). Table 9 shows that a third (32.5 per cent) of the directorships held by managers of metal manufacturing companies (Mfg. III) are in their own type of enterprise. Except for banks (24.0 per cent), Manufacturing II (9.8), and insurance firms (9.1 per cent), they rarely choose to be directors in any other type. However, unlike the railroads, 9 per cent or more of the manager-directors of other types of enterprise regularly become their directors. Part of this larger apparent interest on the part of other activity types is, of course, due to the very large number of companies and therefore directorships available in Manufacturing III.

The directorships of bank managers display still another pattern of connection. Only 10 per cent of over 1,300 directorships are with other banks. About twice that number (20.9 per cent) are with life insurance companies, 18.3 per cent with metal manufacturing, and 11.9 per cent with lumber and chemical manufacturing firms. Moreover, the column for banks shows that all other managers favor banks more than bank managers do—most of them more than twice as much. The three types of manufacturing are all well over that percentage. The managers of eleven of the thirteen types of enterprise serve on the boards of banks more often than in their own types of enterprise. The proportion of managers of banks serving as directors of other banks is lower than that of any other type with its own type (with the exception of the three very small enterprise types).

If banks and their high proportions are eliminated from our immediate consideration, and agriculture because of its very small numbers is also taken out, comparison along the rows of boldface figures with the others for each type demonstrates that only three— service, contract construction, and mining—of the remaining twelve have a higher percentage of their outside directors with some other type than with their own.

Full inspection of each of the columns to learn if the managers of other types show greater preference for a given type than do that type's own managers shows that there are but two, contract construction and life insurance.

In brief, and very broadly, managers of big business of all types who are outside directors are most likely to choose to be on the boards of their own kind of enterprise and less likely to choose the boards of other types. There is, however, one major exception. The managers of banks less often choose to be directors of banks than do the managers of other types of enterprise. There is also a minor exception; managers of service enterprises choose relatively infrequently to become directors of service enterprise.

We must now view the question of interconnection from a different position. We have examined only how the directorships of managers of each type were distributed among all other companies; we have not learned the reciprocal representation of other directors on their boards. Put another way and metaphorically, we have learned how directorships are taken out of any given receptacle (category) and distributed among all of the other enterprise receptacles, and we have learned what the totals are for each of these; but we do not know the totals and proportions of directorships from the other enterprises in a particular receptacle (category). Table 10 helps perform this latter task and later allows us to compare the two processes, the taking out and distributing of directorships and the placement of them in a particular category of enterprise. These are the so called out-going and in-coming directorships.

To understand the structured interconnection of the interlocking directorships one must know for each activity type not only the distribution of the outside directorships held by managers of that activity type but also the distribution of managers from outside who sit as directors within the activity type.

Table 10 is set up to show both "in" and "out" connections of this two-way interchange of directorships by managers. The format of managers at the left and directorships spread right along the rows is the same as in Table 9. For purposes of precise comparison of inward and outward connections the outward interlockings shown in Table 9 have been repeated here. The proportion of the total outside directorships held on the boards of each type by managers of each type is shown in the lower figure of each pair of figures in the percentage column at the right (In ←); totals are at the far right. Thus we see again that mining had a total of 322 directorships held outside, and we learn that a total of 291 directorships on the boards of mining corporations were held by managers of outside firms. Stated differently, 5.1 per cent of all outside directorships were held by mining managers, and 4.6 per cent of all outside directorships were on the boards of mining corporations.

Down at the bottom of this column the grand totals for all the in and out totals are given (6,280 for each). All directorships held by managers in their own firms, to repeat, are excluded; only directorships of big corporation managers with other big corporations are included. The grand totals (6,280 directorships) for those going out to other companies and those coming in from others are necessarily the same, for both include only the outside directorships and both include all the outside directorships. The subtotals for Out → and In ← can be and are different (see columns at the far right for In and Out of Table 10).

Let us consider these similarities and differences by a brief inspection of them. The figures for the In and Out totals for the directorships show that the number of outside directorships (845)

Table 10. The Two-Way Interchange of Directorships by Managers

Type of parent corporation		Directorships by type of corporation														%	N
		Mining	Contract const.	Mfg. I	Mfg. II	Mfg. III	Rail-roads	Transp. (air, water, truck)	Util-ities	Whole-sale	Retail	Finance banks	Life ins., etc.	Service	Agricul-ture		
Mining																	
Out→		**17.1**	0.7	2.5	14.9	18.6	2.5	6.5	2.8	6.8	2.2	18.0	6.8	0.6	0.0	Out→ 5.1	322
In ↓		**18.9**	1.4	4.1	10.3	17.2	2.7	2.4	6.2	3.1	1.4	25.9	2.7	3.4	0.3	In ↓ 4.6	291
Contract const.																	
Out→		5.1	**0.0**	5.1	10.2	21.8	2.6	5.1	7.8	6.4	3.8	20.5	7.8	3.8	0.0	Out→ 1.2	78
In ↓		5.3	**0.0**	0.0	10.5	23.7	0.0	2.6	2.6	5.3	5.3	34.2	10.5	0.0	0.0	In ↓ 0.6	38
Mfg. I																	
Out→		2.4	0.0	**18.6**	9.6	10.6	4.9	3.9	2.9	3.5	5.3	24.3	12.3	1.3	0.4	Out→ 8.1	511
In ↓		1.9	1.0	**23.0**	10.7	8.5	0.5	3.1	0.7	10.4	5.8	26.6	4.6	1.7	1.5	In ↓ 6.6	413
Mfg. II																	
Out→		3.5	0.5	5.1	**22.0**	12.9	2.4	7.7	3.7	4.1	2.5	25.1	9.5	0.9	0.1	Out→ 13.8	869
In ↓		6.7	1.1	6.8	**26.7**	17.4	0.6	2.5	3.2	6.1	2.2	22.0	3.3	1.3	0.1	In ↓ 11.4	718
Mfg. III																	
Out→		3.9	0.7	2.8	9.8	**32.5**	1.9	5.9	3.3	2.4	2.0	24.0	9.1	1.7	0.0	Out→ 20.3	1,273
In ↓		5.4	1.5	4.8	10.0	**37.1**	1.0	3.0	2.4	2.8	3.0	21.9	5.7	1.2	0.2	In ↓ 17.8	1,116
Railroads																	
Out→		3.6	0.0	0.9	1.8	4.9	**33.3**	9.3	2.2	2.7	1.3	16.9	23.1	0.0	0.0	Out→ 3.6	225
In ↓		3.1	0.8	9.7	8.1	9.3	**29.1**	2.7	5.4	2.3	1.9	20.2	6.2	0.8	0.4	In ↓ 4.1	258

Industry		C1	C2	C3	C4	C5	C6	C7	C8	C9	C10	C11	C12	C13	C14		%	Total
Transportation	Out→	3.0	0.4	5.6	7.8	14.7	3.0	**17.8**	1.7	3.9	2.6	25.2	13.0	1.3	0.0	Out→	3.7	231
	In↓	5.5	1.0	5.2	17.5	19.6	5.5	**10.7**	2.3	3.7	6.0	18.0	4.2	0.8	0.0	In↓	6.1	383
Utilities	Out→	7.0	0.4	1.2	9.0	10.5	5.5	3.5	**18.0**	2.3	1.2	24.2	15.2	2.0	0.0	Out→	4.1	256
	In↓	3.1	2.1	5.1	11.0	14.4	1.7	1.4	**15.8**	3.1	4.1	21.5	11.3	5.1	0.3	In↓	4.6	292
Wholesale	Out→	2.9	0.6	13.9	14.3	10.0	1.9	4.5	2.9	**17.5**	6.2	19.1	4.9	1.0	0.3	Out→	4.9	309
	In↓	8.9	2.0	7.3	14.7	12.2	2.4	3.7	2.4	**22.1**	8.1	13.0	2.8	0.4	0.0	In↓	3.9	246
Retail	Out→	1.1	0.6	6.8	4.6	9.4	1.4	6.6	3.4	5.7	**22.2**	25.1	10.2	2.9	0.0	Out→	5.6	351
	In↓	2.4	1.0	9.5	7.7	9.2	1.0	2.1	1.0	6.6	**27.4**	27.0	4.5	0.3	0.3	In↓	4.6	286
Finance, banks	Out→	5.6	1.1	8.3	11.9	18.3	3.9	5.3	4.7	2.4	5.8	**10.0**	20.9	1.7	0.1	Out→	21.2	1,329
	In↓	4.5	1.2	9.6	16.9	23.7	3.0	4.5	4.8	4.6	6.8	**10.3**	8.5	1.2	0.4	In↓	20.5	1,288
Life ins., etc.	Out→	1.9	1.0	4.6	5.8	15.4	3.9	3.9	8.0	1.7	3.1	26.3	**22.8**	1.4	0.2	Out→	6.6	415
	In↓	2.6	0.7	7.5	9.8	13.7	6.2	3.6	4.6	1.8	4.3	32.9	**11.2**	0.7	0.4	In↓	13.5	845
Service	Out→	11.3	0.0	7.9	10.1	14.7	2.2	3.4	16.8	1.1	1.1	16.8	6.7	**7.9**	0.0	Out→	1.4	89
	In↓	2.0	3.0	7.1	8.1	22.2	0.0	3.0	5.1	3.0	10.1	23.2	6.1	**7.1**	0.0	In↓	1.6	99
Agriculture	Out→	4.5	0.0	27.3	4.5	9.2	4.5	0.0	4.5	0.0	4.5	22.8	13.7	0.0	**4.5**	Out→	0.4	22
	In↓	0.0	0.0	28.5	14.3	0.0	0.0	0.0	0.0	14.3	0.0	14.3	14.3	0.0	**14.3**	In↓	0.1	7
																Out→	100.0	6,280
																In←	100.0	6,280

The System of Interlocking Directorates

held inside the boards of life insurance companies was more than twice the number of outside directorships they held (415). On the other hand, the managers of Manufacturing I had 511 outside directorships, and only 413 directorships were held by others on the boards of corporations in Manufacturing I. Although a high proportion (18.6 per cent) of mining's outside directorships were with metal manufacturers, only 5.4 per cent of the outside directorships of Manufacturing III were in mining firms; and while 18 per cent of mining's outside connections were with finance, only 4.5 per cent of the directorships of banks were held by managers in the mining industry.

Inspection of the row and column for banks will bring out still other differences. The outward interlocking directorships of bank officers are only slightly more numerous than those coming into their boards from other corporations, but the relative contributions by type to the two totals are biased. For most types the percentage of their outgoing directorships held on the boards of banks is higher than the percentage of bank-manager-held directorships sent to them.

The number of directorships held by the managers of a given type of business with other companies of its type are always the same for both In and Out because the exchange is within the same category. If there are ten directorships held outside of a given type of firm by managers of the same type, necessarily the same ten counted on the boards of one type will be counted as ten coming from other firms of the same type. For example, there was an exchange of directorships among mining firms with other mining firms. The Out and In numbers are exactly the same (55). However, since there are more outside connections (322) than inside (291), the percentages are necessarily slightly different.

The percentages of the column totals at the far right of Table 10 give the proportions of outside directorships contributed to the grand total by the managers of each type. We learn, for example, that 322 directorships are 5.1 per cent of all (6,280) outside directorships and that the 291 total for directorships of mining come from other companies to serve on the boards of mining corporations and are 4.6 per cent of all directorships of the incoming type, which is once again 6,280. What outside connections among the

What Types of Businesses Are Interlocked?

firms are very much higher than this general average of 5.1 among the directorships of mining managers, and which are very low? We will consider the high ones double or more and the low ones half or less of this general average. This simple analysis gives us certain rough configurations among the directorships and managers of the enterprise types. The mining configuration is high with its own kind and with Manufacturing II and Manufacturing III and low with Manufacturing I, with railroads, and retail. We will eliminate for these purposes the three small enterprise types, contract construction, service, and agriculture, from the present analysis.

The configurations of the three types of manufacturing vary among themselves. Manufacturing I, which is food and apparel, is high only with others of its kind and with finance; Manufacturing II is high with none, including its own type, although finance is close to being twice as much as the average. None of Manufacturing III is high. The comparative place of the interlockings of Manufacturing II and III is partly due to their large size; but, given size, hypothetically Manufacturing II (lumber and chemicals), for example, could have been high with finance, and others of its kind and III might also have been high with finance, since these others we have mentioned have a high number of directorships.

Railroads, transportation, and utilities as public enterprises have many common characteristics. The percentages of their outside directorships here are also similar. Are the directional configurations also similar?

Each of these is high, as are all others, for their own kind. Railroads are also high with transportation, banks, and life insurance, and low with Manufacturing I and II and with retail stores. All three are low with retail stores, but so are most of the other types of enterprise. Both railroads and transportation are low with Manufacturing II. Utilities are high for their directorships in this type. Without further analysis one can say that the three are neither conspicuously alike nor too different from several others.

Inquiry about the two categories of merchandising, retail and wholesale firms, show them to be largely dissimilar; wholesale is high for all three types of manufacturing, retail is not. Both are high with banks and low with railroads, but so are many of the other forms of business enterprise. In brief, by this rough measure,

The System of Interlocking Directorates

although there are many similar paired preferences, there are no consistently larger parallel patterns of outward interlocking among the enterprise types.

In this overall view of the directorships held by managers the strong place of financial institutions needs discussion and analysis. Their managers have more outside directorships and more outsiders serve on the boards of banks than any other type. These facts, of course, influence the amount of banking interconnection with all types. The number of managers of big financial companies was third in order of size among those in our sample (behind those of Manufacturing III and II). Yet they led all others and these two in their outside directorships. Perhaps more surprising to some, the proportions of all other types of enterprise on the boards of banks are also high. The proportions of all directorships in banks from other enterprises is never less than 16 per cent of their total; many are more than one-fifth and some more than one-fourth of their entire outside directorships (contract construction, the three manufacturing types, utilities, merchandising, and life insurance). Given the all important position and power of money and credit in corporate activity, the high proportion of others on the boards of banks and of bankers on their boards is not only easy to understand but, it might be said, necessary.

There appears to be a reciprocal balance among the enterprise types of giving and getting managers as directors on the boards of the various corporations. Comparison of the totals (see numbers and percentage figures in the right hand column of Table 10) for the exchange of directors who are managers of big corporations shows that for most business types the outside directorships of managers of each type usually approximate the totals of inside directorships from others on their own boards. They come out more or less even. At the practical level, in most cases, the total number of directors of any given enterprise type from others approximates the total of its managers in these same enterprise types. In all fourteen cases the two, inside and outside directors, differ among the total scores of directorships held by the managers of each type. They are rather similar in size to the total held by all other managers on the boards of the first type. With two exceptions the percentages of the grand total (6,280) of directors, given and taken among the larger size types, are not too far apart.

What Types of Businesses Are Interlocked?

The world of interlocked big boards in this country is, paradoxically, very extensive and very widespread in the world of business from coast to coast and from enterprise to enterprise; on the other hand, it is tightly drawn territorially and in corporate life. All the big cities and many of the small ones contribute and are given shares of directors and managers; yet, overwhelmingly led by New York, managers that go to and from headquarters to be directors of interlocked big corporations are from a few great cities. All types of enterprises contribute; yet, less than 4,000 managers of large corporations hold the directorships that interconnect the elite classes of officers and managers of the major corporations that employ most of the workers and do most of the business in American life.

CHAPTER SIX

The Changing Structure of a Great Corporation

The General Electric Company is one of many very large-scale organizations that have been changing their internal structures to meet the demands of a rapidly changing society and technology. Many corporations have changed their management structure from a vertical hierarchy in which decisions were made at the top to several hierarchies, each involved with one product or group of products. In effect, portions of the organization and technological systems have been reassembled and decision making moved down in the organizational structure. The product departments in the new hierarchy are smaller profit-making business organizations but are still integral parts of the company. In Sears, Roebuck and other large merchandising corporations many decisions previously made at the top are now made by the manager of a local store or even by the head of a department in the store. This change is in part a reaction to the vast number and variety of activities, products, and people that have to be managed and to the changing competitive demands of a rapidly changing society. If decisions were to remain with top management alone, there would be misunderstanding, confusion, and slow and inefficient timing in relation to the demands of the competitive markets.

This story is pertinent here because it shows how a company has maintained a viable system of change within a larger system that is itself in continual flux. Along with changes in the technological environment great changes have evolved in the human environment of the larger society, social, political, and economic changes to which the entire electrical industry has had to adjust.

Probably no single industry more vitally and dynamically affects the economy and the welfare of the American society than does the electrical machinery industry. Born from the amalgam of technological inventiveness and entrepreneurial innovation, it has

This chapter is by George D. Downing. See Notes on Authors.

grown by feeding on the very technological innovations it creates. The industry has a history of vast proliferation. Its technological roots were in the development in the late 1870s and 1880s of arc and incandescent lighting and the power apparatus required to operate them.[1] It had to provide the marketing and financial innovations to finance, produce, and install lighting systems before the demand for them existed.[2] Hardly a product exists today, consumer or capital, that does not owe its present utility directly or indirectly to the technological and marketing achievements of the electrical industry.

Economically, this industry has permitted vast enlargements of the national productive capacity. By making greater tool power possible, it has significantly increased productivity per worker and national income. The industry provides the lifeblood of our complex industrial economy. Social contributions are also significant —higher living standards, reduction of drudgery in home and factory, increased leisure, convenience, and comfort, and higher real incomes in all social and economic segments of American society.[3]

THE PROCESS OF FORMAL ORGANIZATION CHANGE

Initially resulting directly from technological innovation, the electric machinery industry continues to create and absorb new technologies, not only providing a widening array of consumer products but also serving as the impetus and implementation of new engineered-product systems utilized by other industries. The electrical industry has always been a leader in research; in 1940 the industry's investment of 4.85 per cent of sales in research was almost twice that of the next largest industrial contributor. By 1957, sur-

1. Harold C. Passer, *The Electrical Manufacturers, 1875–1900* (Cambridge, Harvard University Press, 1953), pp. 1–13.
2. Edwin Vennard, *The Electrical Power Business* (New York, McGraw-Hill, 1962), pp. 4–10.
3. Jules Backman, *The Economics of the Electrical Machinery Industry* (New York, New York University Press, 1962), pp. 308–18.

passed only by the aircraft industry in actual dollars spent in research (as a direct result of the space program), the electrical industry spent twice as many dollars on research as the chemical industry, five times as many as the petroleum industry, five times as many as the telecommunications industry, and ten times as many as the primary metals industry.[4] Research, technological innovation, inventiveness—these have been the hallmarks of this industry and have established it as an institution, or collectivity of institutions, with unparalleled economic and social significance. One of the greatest enterprises in this complex of corporate enterprises, and a titan among all companies on any count, is the General Electric Company.

In the planning for the research we chose to give some of the intimate evidence of corporate structural change quantitatively presented in other chapters about all big American corporations. The research for this chapter is essentially a case study in depth. Four techniques and kinds of evidence were used:

1. Personal observation. The author was a member of the organization for twenty-three years and observed events reported. Prior to the field research he wrote a three-hundred-page "personal history" to put this experience in perspective.

2. Study of company documents. Internal company documents in his possession or on loan or examined in the company library provided historical data.

3. Study of other publications. Biographies, economic reports, the trade press, the news press, were secondary sources of data.

4. Field interviewing. A judgment sample of thirty executives was chosen for informal, open-ended personal interviews. Interviewees were guaranteed anonymity and should be regarded as informants rather than as respondents.

Technological Innovation, Entrepreneurial Ingenuity, and
Marketing Skills

The electrical industry sprang from the laboratories of such scientist-inventors as Edison, Brush, Sprague, and Thomson. The

4. Ibid., pp. 185–90.

development in the late 1800s of the electric-powered arc lamps for street lighting provided the initial stimulus to the formation of corporate enterprises—sometimes by the inventors themselves—to produce and market the new products. Power generating, regulating, and transmitting apparatus was also needed, as well as an entire new capital market to service it. In order to market lighting systems, syndicates formed independently owned lighting companies whose stock was accepted by manufacturers as part payment for equipment, thus developing the electric utility industry.

By 1900 a number of companies had been formed by inventor-entrepreneurs pursuing different technological paths. The Brush Company was producing and selling direct-current arc-lamp systems; the Thomson Houston Company was in direct competition; the Edison Electric Light Company was further developing the incandescent lighting system invented by Edison. A maze of patents both aided and hampered individual company growth, and mergers resulted;[5] the Thomson Houston Company, specializing in arc lamps, purchased a number of small companies and acquired the large Brush Company in 1889, and the Edison enterprise had purchased a number of smaller companies and by 1889 had been reformed into the Edison General Electric Company. These two major companies had begun to diversify into industrial power applications, particularly in the railway field, and both were committed to the use of direct-current power.

Meanwhile, in 1886, George Westinghouse formed the Westinghouse Electric Corporation from his Union Switch and Signal Company, which had served the railroad market notably with Westinghouse's invention of the air brake. Westinghouse entered the electrical market with alternating-current power, which ultimately extended the use of electric power into homes and factories by permitting transmission of power over relatively long distances.

Mergers and consolidations continued during the 1890s. The two major competitors, Thomson Houston and Edison General Electric, merged in 1892 to form the General Electric Company, with Charles Coffin as president. He was the entrepreneurial genius whose financial, organizational, and marketing expertise had guided Thomson Houston in its ten years to become a sizable cor-

5. Passer, pp. 352–53.

Changing Structure of a Great Corporation

poration by the standards of the era. Historians agree that this merger was a result of the complexities of interlocking patents, the heavy financial problems of license fees, and the difficulty of securing new capital.[6]

From the beginning General Electric, which continued as a balance of entrepreneurial talent and technological ability, faced organizational problems, which did not end as the company prospered and grew.[7] The merged companies' management had to be fused and duplicate manufacturing facilities reorganized. The company had a simple, centralized line and staff structure consisting of five departments: Manufacturing and Electrical, Selling, Accounting, Treasury, and Law.

Figure 1. Initial Organization Structure, 1892

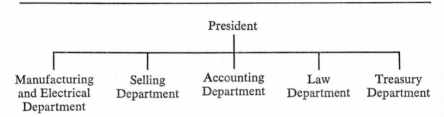

President

| Manufacturing and Electrical Department | Selling Department | Accounting Department | Law Department | Treasury Department |

Consolidation and Early Growth, 1892–1922

Before the newly formed General Electric had achieved a smooth-running, efficient organization, it was hit by the sharp depression of 1893, which necessitated the acceleration of efforts to consolidate and plan the growth of the merged manufacturing facilities. Particularly important was bringing the district sales offices, which had been operating with almost complete autonomy, under the direction of the centralized Selling Department.

By mid-1894 business had begun to improve, and General Electric began a long period of growth, stimulated by many technological innovations. The company's major marketing efforts had continued in the production and sale of lighting systems, although some

6. Backman, p. 106; Passer, pp. 324–26.
7. John W. Hammond, *Men and Volts, The Story of General Electric* (New York, Lippincott, 1941), pp. 192–212; also the source for early history in the rest of this section.

progress had been made in extending power equipment to other industrial applications. Untold credit in this field is due a genius of the age, Charles P. Steinmetz, who had come to G. E. via the Eickemeyer Company (purchased by General Electric in 1892) and had become head engineer in Schenectady. Steinmetz's mathematical genius overcame many obstacles to the use of alternating current and enabled the growing company to progress from the period of light to the period of light and power, paving the way for the use of electric power in factory and home.

Foreseeing rapid expansion of technology, the company recognized the necessity of training young engineers. Steinmetz personally instructed classes in the mathematics of electrical equipment design, the forerunner of a vast family of industrial training programs for which General Electric later became famous.

Many individual scientists and inventors of the predecessor companies remained with G. E., including Brush, Thomson, and Van Depoele, and so the aura of research and development persisted.

Steinmetz had been conducting research in a barn; but in 1899 a formal engineering department was established with a technical director. The research activity itself was formalized in 1900 with Willis Whitney, its first director, dividing his time between the new General Electric research laboratory and his professorial duties at the Massachusetts Institute of Technology. G. E.'s laboratory was the first established in industry for fundamental research rather than for product development and manufacturing techniques; it has an illustrious history of its own and ranks today as one of the world's greatest scientific laboratories.

Automatic lamp-making machinery had been developed outside G. E. (G. E. purchased rights to this equipment in 1917). To market the automatically produced lamps, many small lamp competitors of G. E. had "consolidated" into the National Electric Lamp Association, a collection of independently operated small "divisions" headquartered in Cleveland. Ostensibly the Association competed with G. E.'s lamp works, but it was in fact financed by General Electric. In 1911 the United States Government instituted an antitrust suit against General Electric and thirty-three of the "association" companies. General Electric submitted to a decree, and the National Electric Lamp Association was ordered dissolved. Even before the decree was issued, however, General Electric had

Changing Structure of a Great Corporation

exercised its option to purchase all stock in the Association and had become its sole owner. The affiliated lamp companies, known by the Association's initials as "Nela," were merged into General Electric; thus was born "Nela Park," the famous home of G. E.'s lamp division of today.

The young electrical industry was rapidly expanding into the fields of power machinery, developing applications in rail transportation (locomotives and street railways) and in industry (steel mill motors, elevator motors). Important inventions by General Electric's Alexanderson and Langmuir in the field of radio transmission put the company into radio research and development as early as 1906. By 1919 these G. E. scientists had developed equipment capable of transoceanic transmission. The company considered selling such equipment to the British Marconi Company, but the United States Government appealed to them not to do so. G. E. itself then entered the telecommunication industry by purchasing The American Marconi Company and established a new company to serve as selling agent for General Electric's newly developed radio products: the Radio Corporation of America.[8]

In 1913 Charles Coffin, after serving twenty-one years as president and chairman of the board, relinquished his duties as president and was succeeded by E. W. Rice, who had entered Thomson Houston thirty years earlier as a clerk. However, Coffin apparently did not relax his "keen supervision over the company's affairs."

Nine years later, in 1922, Coffin and Rice retired and the new executive team of Gerard Swope (president and chief executive) and Owen D. Young (chairman of the board) took command.

As the first executive generation left the active scene, it could look back upon remarkable growth in size, sales volume, diversification of product, entry into new domestic and foreign markets, and continued expansion of technology.

Despite its growth in many dimensions in its first thirty years, in 1912 the formal organization remained unchanged; it was still basically a simple, centralized, line and staff structure.

Of course, there had been some changes and additions. The research laboratory was added as a formal function in 1901; a

8. Ibid., pp. 376 and 424. By federal court decree in 1933 the common stock in RCA held by General Electric was to be distributed to G.E. stockholders as a dividend.

modicum of decentralization was accomplished by separating the lamp business around 1910, probably as a result of government action rather than for an organizational purpose; and staff functions were added periodically. The anatomy of the organization structure, however, had remained unchanged and was destined to remain essentially unchanged for nearly thirty more years.

Figure 2. Formal Organization Structure, Circa 1910

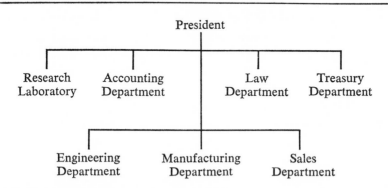

But between 1892 and 1922 great changes occurred in other dimensions. Although by 1920 the company's manufacturing facilities had not dispersed much geographically and still centered mainly in the northeastern section of the country, the number of plants had multiplied from three in 1892 to fifty-four in 1920 (Chart 2).

Equally dramatic is the company's growth in this period as recorded in Chart 3. Sales increased from $11 to $276 million, employees from 10,000 to 82,000, stockholders from 3,000 to 17,000, and number of product lines [9] from five to eighty-five. The growth in product lines was due to increasing technological innovation and the aggressive creation of new markets—capital goods markets for engineered, industrial-type products.

Note that this great growth was accommodated by the existing formal organization structure of the company. As new products

9. The term "product line" throughout this chapter is defined as a compatible group or "family" of products grouped together on one accounting basis. A product line includes a number of different individual products. For example, the product line "distribution transformers" (included as one product line in Chart 3) may include a hundred or more different models or types.

Chart 1. Formal Organization Structure (Management)

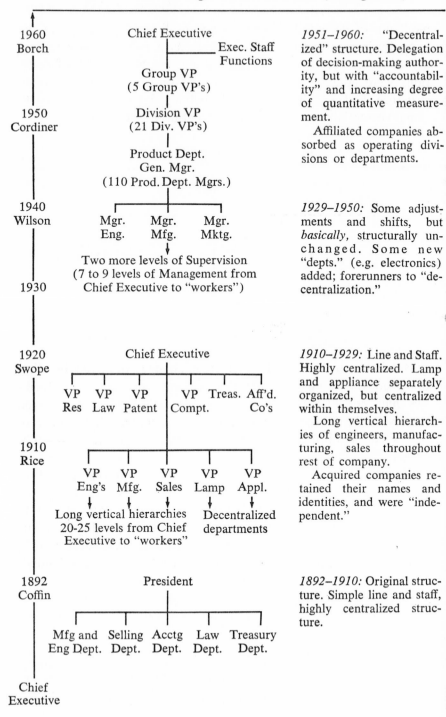

1960
Borch

1950
Cordiner

1940
Wilson

1930

Chief Executive
└── Exec. Staff
     Functions
Group VP
(5 Group VP's)

Division VP
(21 Div. VP's)

Product Dept.
Gen. Mgr.
(110 Prod. Dept. Mgrs.)

Mgr.   Mgr.   Mgr.
Eng.   Mfg.   Mktg.

Two more levels of Supervision
(7 to 9 levels of Management from
Chief Executive to "workers")

1951–1960: "Decentralized" structure. Delegation of decision-making authority, but with "accountability" and increasing degree of quantitative measurement.

Affiliated companies absorbed as operating divisions or departments.

1929–1950: Some adjustments and shifts, but *basically,* structurally unchanged. Some new "depts." (e.g. electronics) added; forerunners to "decentralization."

1920
Swope

1910
Rice

Chief Executive

VP   VP   VP   VP   Treas. Aff'd.
Res   Law   Patent Compt.   Co's

VP   VP   VP   VP   VP
Eng's Mfg.   Sales Lamp   Appl.

Long vertical hierarchies   Decentralized
20-25 levels from Chief   departments
Executive to "workers"

1910–1929: Line and Staff. Highly centralized. Lamp and appliance separately organized, but centralized within themselves.

Long vertical hierarchies of engineers, manufacturing, sales throughout rest of company.

Acquired companies retained their names and identities, and were "independent."

1892
Coffin

President

Mfg and   Selling   Acctg   Law   Treasury
Eng Dept. Dept.   Dept.   Dept.   Dept.

1892–1910: Original structure. Simple line and staff, highly centralized structure.

Chief
Executive

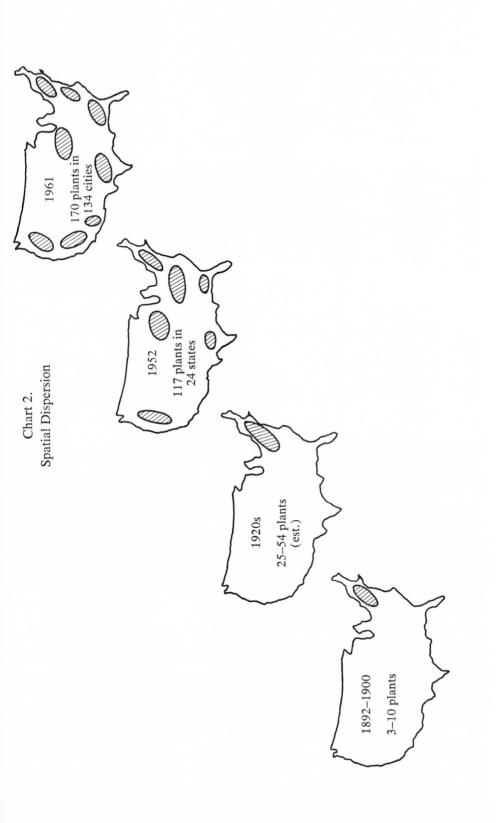

Chart 2.
Spatial Dispersion

1961
170 plants in
134 cities

1952
117 plants in
24 states

1920s
25–54 plants
(est.)

1892–1900
3–10 plants

Chart 3. Growth in Sales, Manpower, Product Lines, Etc.

	Sales in millions of dollars	Increase in sales from previous period in per cent	Number of employees	Number of stockholders	Number of plants	Number of product lines	Number of departments	Number of affiliated companies
1960	4,198	114%	251,000	417,000	168	400 (est.)	110	3
1950	1,960	330%	183,000	250,000	117	328	37	14
1940	456	21%	85,000	212,000	54	281		11
1930	376	36%	78,000	84,000	33	193		12
1920	276	289%	82,000	17,000	54	85		5
1910	71		36,200	9,000	13	30		1
1892	11		10,000	3,000	3	5		1

were developed and new markets created and exploited, the new engineering, manufacturing, and sales facilities were "hung on" the existing structure.

Structural Centralization and Concentration of Power

With the election of Gerard Swope as president and chief executive in 1922 General Electric passed from its pioneer period to one of growing industrial maturity. Although the formal management organization was to remain essentially unchanged during Swope's regime, his expressed philosophy and actions as president generated later structural change. Swope's early professional career had been with the Western Electric Company.[10] When he graduated from Massachusetts Institute of Technology in 1895, Swope was hired by Western Electric, which manufactured not only communication equipment, as it does today, but power apparatus as well, and was thus competing with General Electric and Westinghouse. During his twenty-four years there he was successively electrical engineer, salesman, sales manager, general manager of engineering, manufacturing, and sales of all machinery (including the large Hawthorne Works), and vice-president of International Western Electric.

Swope was an organizer and a systematizer. He became noted for reorganizing many operations, including sales, the Hawthorne Works itself, and Western Electric's foreign operations—all with notable success. General Electric became aware of Swope as negotiator for the sale of Western Electric's machinery business to General Electric when Western Electric left the field of power apparatus and General Electric agreed to leave the communications field. He was hired in 1919 to head up the International General Electric operations, where he embarked upon a vast program of reorganization that included setting up the International General Electric Company as an autonomous operation.

Early in his career he had formulated an approach to management that he called "analyze—organize—deputize—supervise," a

10. David Loth, *Swope of G.E.* (New York, Simon & Schuster, 1958) provides the source of much of the content of this section referring specifically to Gerard Swope.

phrase to be widely echoed throughout G. E. management. He practiced his formula diligently, although some of his critics maintained that he did not practice "deputize." He was a strong executive who made firm and prompt decisions and held very close control.

Swope's approach to executive management and his contribution to the changing orientation and activities of the company can be summed up in the following broad categories.

Changing Philosophy of Executive Responsibility

Swope viewed the corporation as a broader institution than merely a business enterprise. He felt, and his actions demonstrated, that the executive had an obligation to lead in the social responsibility of the corporation in enhancing the security and human rights of workers, management, and labor alike. In this he claimed no humanitarianism but stated publicly that it was "simply good business." Ahead of his time, he was viewed as a radical by many of his executive peers.

To prepare men in management and submanagement levels for greater responsibility, Swope held management seminars where groups of managers from diverse functions could gain the broad concept of the entire enterprise. He initiated an advisory committee of twenty-one top executives of the corporation who met monthly to discuss individual group and collective company problems, established a formal procedure of spotting talented young men within the company, and began the famous management meetings to advance his objective of viewing the company as a whole. All of this engendered an awareness of the personification of the growing company.

Development of Employee Benefit Programs

Swope consistently maintained that "men were more important than machines." Both his critics and his admirers agree that he was a pragmatist and not an idealist in this regard. He was a superior organizer and integrator and possessed optimum executive talent for marshalling and deploying all resources, human as well as physical and financial.

The emphasis on workers—and he always placed workers high

in the ranking of the various "publics" and late in his career was to place them in first position—resulted in a growing perception of the company among its own rank and file as a moral institution.

The emphasis on workers (management and labor alike) as a vitally important resource led to the implementation of a number of employee benefit programs. A pension plan had been initiated as early as 1915 and was greatly expanded in the 1920s; it covered all employees, and the company paid the entire cost. Numerous other programs involving insurance, health benefits, saving plans, employee training programs, and unemployment insurance for all employees were pioneered by General Electric. This must be viewed in the proper perspective; such programs, commonplace today, were perceived by many executives at that time as radical.

Closely allied to the importance attached to employee benefits was the philosophy of management's relations with trade unions developed by top executives. Swope believed in unions and accepted them as functional. This is not to say that there were not continual problems in negotiations; but G. E. executive management was not antiunion and, therefore, was regarded by many other industrial executives as being radically progressive.

Since the company was well known in the industrial and financial communities but little known to the public at large in the early 1920s, Swope and Young agreed that the name G. E. should be promoted broadly. About 1923 the General Electric monogram was put on millions of electric lamps that had formerly been "branded" with a wide variety of names. A well known advertising firm promoted the name of General Electric and the famous slogan, "More Goods for More People at Less Cost," in the newly entered consumer-goods market. The building of a highly respected public image had a twofold effect; it made the name General Electric synonymous in the minds of the general public with a strong, vast, and economically important institution and developed and reinforced an awareness of greatness in the company in the minds of company personnel.

Diversification and Expansion into Consumer Markets

By 1922, when Swope became president, General Electric had become the fourth largest industrial corporation in the country, significantly with many of its founding engineers and financial fathers still actively engaged in its management. Volume of sales was double that of its nearest competitor. The company centered primarily in the power industry, producing and marketing power generating apparatus for electric utilities and power utilization apparatus for industrial firms. The consumer market was limited to electric lamps. Many management people felt that future industrial growth would proceed at a slower rate; and many of the management within the company, having witnessed tremendous growth, felt that the company was as large as was physically possible.

But Swope saw new fields and made the decision to expand and diversify into consumer markets for electrical appliances. Again the company was to progress through marketing ingenuity as well as technological innovation. Early in the 1920s the company made the farsighted decision to diversify the company's business into about equal thirds—capital goods, industrial user goods, and consumer goods. The immediate decision to enter the electrical refrigerator market on a mass production basis was ultimately to make General Electric a household word.

The Formal Organization Structure, 1922–1940

The formal organization structure in 1922 (Figure 2 and Chart 1) remained basically unchanged throughout Swope's era. There were adjustments and modifications, of course. As the company entered the appliance business, the Appliance and Merchandise Department was created as a separate operating component with its own self-contained functions of engineering, manufacturing, and sales. Also, as the company acquired other electrical enterprises, including Telechron and Hotpoint, an executive policy decision was made permitting these companies to continue to operate quasiautonomously and under their own names. The Radio Department was added as a decentralized department. But the functional hierarchies within these departments—Appliance and Merchandise, Lamp, Radio—were highly centralized. For example, the manufacturing function of the Appliance and Merchandise Department consisted of a wide variety of separate production operations for a great diversity of products ranging from toasters to refrigerators, each reporting through a channel of manufacturing management, with no management tie at respective management levels with comparable engineering and sales operations. The organization structure even with these exceptions thus remained functionally oriented and highly centralized. From its beginnings in 1892 to the early 1940s the organization can be described as highly centralized and structured in vertical functional hierarchies.

The formal organization structure remained anatomically the same during this period of changing executive philosophy, changing market objectives, and changing market direction. But it is even more significant to view this organization's structural stability against the great changes in company productivity. Chart 3 shows that from 1920 (just prior to Swope's election as president) to 1940 sales rose from $276 million to $456 million, number of employees from 82,000 to 85,000,[11] number of stockholders from 17,000 to 212,000, number of plants remained 54,[12] number of product lines increased *significantly* from 85 to 281,[13] and number of affiliated companies increased from five to eleven.

The geographical dispersal of the company in the Swope period was still largely limited to the northeastern section of the country. Some of the acquired plants were in other locations (e.g. Hotpoint in Chicago), but the company had not yet begun to expand its manufacturing facilities broadly throughout the national community.

Many, many new product operations were "tacked on" the existing hierarchies of engineering, manufacturing, and sales, and each

11. These data are misleading. In the decade 1920–30, the number of employees fell from 82,000 to 78,000, the drop occurring in 1929 and 1930 because of the great depression. In fact, in the early years of the 1930s employment fell even below this. We have data only for 1930 and 1940 and do not know how far it fell below the 1930 figure. Thus, though the employment level at the end of the Swope era is only modestly over that of its beginning, great increases occurred in the period 1936–40.

12. This too is misleading. In 1930, midway in the Swope era, the number of plants had actually dropped to 33 primarily because of retrenchment due to the depression. In 1940 it had *risen* to 54 indicating significant growth in the period 1930–1940. And this did not mean that closed plants were all reopened; in some cases new plants were opened. We have no data on specific plants closed and/or opened; hence there is an element of conjecture in these statements. But the cyclical swings in employment of resources because of the great depression must be considered here.

13. Not all this increase came from entry into the appliance markets. New product lines in the industrial power apparatus and the electronics markets were also proceeding apace.

Changing Structure of a Great Corporation

hierarchy expanded vertically and horizontally striving to accommodate the "new."

Precursors to Organizational Change

In the late 1920s evidence of uneasiness about the organizational structure appeared in the minds of management. Around 1927 to 1928 the continued rapid growth of the company in sheer physical size, the tremendous diversification of products and markets, and the compounding of technology began to reveal to some managers evidence of an unwieldiness of organization. Executives at vice-presidential level, looking at the sprawling, parochial hierarchies below them, began to speak for reorganization. At a management meeting in 1929 a severe indictment of the centralized functional organization was formally voiced. Here then, in 1929, as some executives perceived the formal organization as cumbersome and limiting to growth opportunities, were the seeds of decentralization, which were to germinate for nearly twenty years before bearing fruit.

Another precursor of decentralization was the formation of management committees. New product lines had continued to be added, each, of course, requiring a group of design engineers, a manufacturing facility, and assimilation by the selling organization. In the early pioneer days of the company, about 1937, engineers, manufacturing people, and headquarters people were literally housed almost side by side; but with growth they became three work-function hierarchies physically separated and difficult or impossible to coordinate. To alleviate this difficulty, management committees, composed of representatives of engineering, manufacturing, and sales involved in a specific line of products, were established at various levels in the organization to coordinate their respective activities. Significantly, the various work functions often were housed in different plant cities.

The management committees had no integral managerial authority, per se. Unresolved problems still had to be passed upward through the respective hierarchies to a committee at a higher level. Even at a top level of the hierarchies, the vice-presidential level, a problem could still remain unsolved, in which case only the president could make an authoritative overriding decision.

The coming organization-structure change, indicated by these attitudes and makeshifts in the 1930s, was stopped by the great depression and World War II. From 1930 until about 1937 management turned its attention to the business of coping with the economic depression. From about 1940 to 1946 the company "went to war." From 1946 to about 1950 the company was accomplishing the gigantic feat of adapting engineering, manufacturing, and marketing to a vastly changed and changing social and economic world. Throughout the decades of 1930–50, therefore, a "moratorium" on organization-structure change was intentionally declared. We say intentionally because official company statements made at the outset of the great reorganization of the 1950s used that word.

A given formal organization structure can effectively accommodate physical growth, the development and assimilation of technology, and new programs of adjustment to external change only up to some optimum point. Beyond this point, existing structure can no longer accommodate such change effectively. Thus, pyramiding technology, the drive for physical growth, and the developing of new programs for market achievement are often essential ingredients in the process of organization-structure change.

DECENTRALIZATION OF DECISION-MAKING AUTHORITY

Swope retired in 1940, and Charles E. Wilson, former executive vice-president, was elected president and chief executive officer. Wilson had long been an outstanding advocate of organization-structure change and probably would have engineered change had it not been for the war effort. Immediately after his election to the presidency Wilson began to shape the company's productive facilities almost entirely to war production. For two years during the war he was tapped for governmental service on the War Production Board, and Swope returned from retirement to serve as president.

Changing Structure of a Great Corporation

As during the great depression, there was a moratorium on planned organization change.

Immediately after the war, in 1946, Wilson guided the company in its readjustment to the peacetime economy, focusing on expanding technology, adapting war-generated technology, and enlarging and refurbishing productive facilities. Chart 3 shows that during the decade 1940–50 (Wilson's term of office) sales increased from $456 million to $1,960 million, employees from 85,000 to 183,-000, number of plants from 54 to 117, and product lines from 281 to 328. Spatially, too, the company had expanded.[14] In the 1940–50 decade the familiar story of mushrooming technology, spiraling demand, increasing employment, increasing product development, and expanding productive facility, all "hung on" essentially the same basic formal organization structure that had existed for fifty years, continued.

But during this period Wilson, the advocate of organization change, prepared for change. In 1946 he charged Ralph Cordiner, first as an assistant to the president and later as executive vice-president, to formalize plans for vast reorganization. This was not a sudden executive move. During World War II officers of the company were predicting a future for the company of "almost explosive growth which caused its managers to question whether it might not be necessary to evolve new techniques of organizing and managing the company." [15] Near the end of the war company executives were forecasting a postwar opportunity for continuing and compounding demand for electrical and related products—a reflection not only of the general change in the economy and the society but also of the burgeoning technology, which had been further accelerated by technological innovations during the war era; by the end of the war in 1946 they predicted a doubling of the company's business in less than ten years—or a volume of $3 billion by the mid-1950s. It was stated repeatedly and publicly by company officers that a company with such growth characteristics and operating on such a scale required a different managerial approach than the company of the 1920s and 1930s.

14. Data on number of plants and locations are adjusted for 1950. By 1952 the number of plants has risen from 54 (in 1940) to 131, located in 98 cities in every section of the country.
15. R. J. Cordiner, *New Frontiers for Professional Managers* (New York, McGraw-Hill, 1956), p. 44.

Decentralization in General Electric was much beyond, and much deeper than, merely a reshuffling and reorganizing of facilities and organizational components, for underlying was a philosophy of the managerial process radically different from the one that had existed prior to decentralization. In his 1956 McKinsey Lectures at the Graduate School of Business, Columbia University, Cordiner said:

> Every company should be managed with some workable, ethical, responsible philosophy of management. That is, the managers of the company should be in general agreement on a set of underlying principles that will guide their work in providing leadership for the company. For some companies, the set of principles that guide managers may be tacitly understood without ever being presented systematically. This may be part of the company's tradition or it may even reflect the personal philosophy of the chief executive.[16]
>
> While General Electric's present philosophy of management has had a long evolution in company tradition and reflects the personalities of its great leaders in years gone by, considerable effort has been devoted in the past years to "thinking through" and presenting this managerial philosophy in a systematic way.[17]

This suggestion of a new scientific management at G. E., coupled with a damning by faint praise of management by personality, hints at the coming increase in rational and secular approaches.

Although it is true that there was a physical decentralization or rearranging of organizational units into smaller, more manageable pieces, and although decentralization was undertaken with respect to products, markets, geographical locations, and functional types of work, the real key to General Electric's concept lay in the decentralization of responsibility and authority for making business decisions.

The former vertical, functional hierarchies of engineering, manufacturing, and sales were dissolved, and the organization was reformed into a three-part structure, distinguishing between the

16. Here we conjecture that he is referring to General Electric's predecentralization.
17. Cordiner, pp. 40–41.

product departments (operating components), the services (company-wide staff), and the executive office. Following is a brief description of the organization structure of each of these components and their interrelationships.[18]

The Product Department: The Basic Building Block

The product department was more than simply a realigned structural arrangement. It was the formation of a distinct business enterprise engaging in an identifiable business on a profit and loss basis with a single product line (or "family" of highly compatible products) serving a very definitely identifiable market. To form the product department, horizontal slices were taken out of the former vertical functional hierarchies; engineering, manufacturing, and sales functions were assembled into an integrated business for a specific product line. To the management of this business were delegated operating authority and accountability for contributing to overall company growth and profitability. The criteria for the formation of this operating business were:

1. The department should represent a logical, identifiable, and complete product business entity.

2. It should be a business akin to a proprietorship, for which its executive manager can be held responsible and accountable for performance, achievement of required results, and achievement of profit in accord with measurable and assigned standards.

3. It must have an actual or potential sales volume enabling it to operate "on its own feet," quasiautonomously. (Average for department, about $25 million annual sales.)

4. It must possess all resources—human, physical, and financial —to perform its operation.

5. It must have its own distinct and identifiable market.

In essence then, the product department operated very much as an independent small company, with its general manager performing an executive role very similar to that of a president of a small company. Certain broad company policies, of course, were spelled out in the "charter" of the product department. For example:

1. Product scope was determined for the department; that is,

18. Ibid., pp. 57–58 for a more detailed description.

entry into new product fields as well as discontinuance of a product required executive approval (lest its discontinuance have unfavorable market impact on other departments).

2. Certain activities such as union negotiations and company-wide letting of contracts were reserved for high executive management.

3. Company-wide employee-relations policies, e.g. pension plans, had to be followed.

But except for the relatively few integrating policy requirements the general manager of a product department was given great freedom in operating decision-making:

1. In essence he rented building facilities from the company and proceeded to run his business.

2. He had authority to hire and fire, to purchase resources, to determine design of the product, to develop manufacturing techniques, to develop marketing strategy and programs, to price his products, to decide terms of sale, to establish service policies, and to train and develop personnel.

3. He had authority to make capital expenditure decisions of up to a half million dollars without approval from higher executive levels.

The position of the general manager in the product department was thus one of great authority and responsibility and demanded executive ability and performance of extremely high caliber.

The other side of the coin was his accountability. With his great decision-making authority he had a high degree of meticulously spelled out standards of accountability and was personally measured and evaluated by his department's performance and results in the following categories:

1. Profitability, short and long range, of each of the department's product lines, as measured by return on investment, net to sales, and total profits earned

2. Optimum sales volume, i.e. maximum long-range sales volume without sacrifice of optimum profits

3. Market position (the measure of his department's share versus competition's)

4. Productivity of his department

5. Technological leadership

Changing Structure of a Great Corporation

    6. Personnel development

    7. Employee attitudes

    8. Public and social responsibility

    9. Balance between short-range and long-range goals

Although dollar amounts or numbers assigned to these measurements varied from department to department, the standards themselves were uniform. A high degree of control of performance and results was achieved by setting a different kind of bounds on the general manager—prescribed measurable standards for the results —with the clearly published admonition that failure to achieve these predetermined results would subject him to removal from his position.

Figure 3. Product Department Organization Structure

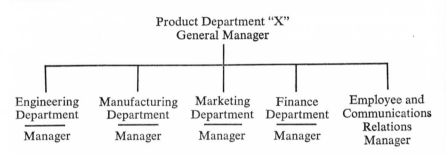

As the executive of a product business the product department's general manager was responsible for all the work functions required for that business. He was a coordinating executive for the functions of engineering, manufacturing, and marketing. Compared to the former organization structure, the decentralization "pushed" this coordinating level much farther down the hierarchical structure of the company.

Figure 3 shows that the organization of each product department was again a simple line and staff structure that had always been employed by the company as a whole; but now the sprawling organization was segmented into a large number of quasiautonomous individual line and staff organization structures. With the general manager in command the management team utilized and integrated the executive skills and the highly specialized work function management skills. Each of the functions of engineering, manufacturing, marketing had, of course, at least one and often two additional levels of management below it.

For the purpose of executive management [19] production departments were grouped into divisions, each of which might be described as a family of compatible businesses. The division general manager, a vice-president of the company, ostensibly had the role of long-range planning for his division and of periodic review of performance. Under the theoretical concept of decentralization he was directly in "line" chain of command between the executive office and the product department but delegated operating responsibility to the general managers of the departments.

Similarly at a higher level of management, the divisions were arranged in compatible "families" known as groups, each headed by a group executive designated as a member of the executive office.

The Services

With the company decentralized into a relatively large number of quasiautonomous businesses, the need for a strong company-wide staff service was accentuated. Staff groups, referred to as services, each headed by a vice-president designated as a service officer, were composed of individuals highly competent in various professional skills. The mission of the services was to carry on functional research in each of the functional fields (e.g. marketing) and to be available to the operating components to "teach, advise, and counsel."

The Over-All Management Structure

The management structure of the company after decentralization is shown schematically in Figure 4 and in Chart 1. Whereas under the former centralized structure the line of communication between an operating executive and individual workers was long and tenuous with a great multiplicity of management layers and the horizontal linkages between the long vertical functions were ac-

19. Ibid., p. 63.

Changing Structure of a Great Corporation

complished only by committees that possessed no decision-making authority, *after decentralization* the line of communication from chief executive to individual workers was greatly shortened to only seven levels (see Figure 4). In a few cases there was one additional level. Further, the functional work was horizontally linked or coordinated, with firm decision-making authority at the product

Figure 4. Management Organization Structure after Decentralization

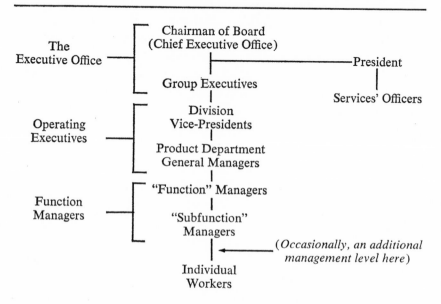

operating level. Thus, each of the product departments became a semiautonomous business with a simple line and staff structure but housed "under the same roof"—highly reminiscent of the total company in its early days.

Implementation of Decentralization

At the end of World War II there were no product departments in the organization structure. As decentralization began to be implemented, the growth in departments and divisions is shown in Figure 5. The great formative period was 1951–55, on which much of the discussion of this chapter is focused. At first glance it might appear that after decentralization the chief executive had

Decentralization of Decision-Making Authority

only a fraction of the real power formerly possessed by the chief executive in command of the highly centralized structure in which essential coordinating decisions could be made only by him. This is not the case, as is seen in the distribution of operating executive

Figure 5. Growth of Product Departments and Divisions, 1946–60

	Number of departments	Number of divisions
1946	16	6
1947	33	7
1948	33	9
1949	31	9
1950	37	9
1951	43	10
1952	62	20
1956	100	21
....		
....		
....		
1960	110	21

management by the end of 1961 (see Figure 6). In 1960 (Chart 3) the company had grown to sales of $4.2 billion; employment had risen from 183,000 in 1950 to 251,000, number of stockholders from 250,000 in 1950 to 417,000; number of plants [20] from

Figure 6. Operating Executives, 1961 *

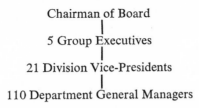

Chairman of Board
|
5 Group Executives
|
21 Division Vice-Presidents
|
110 Department General Managers

* *Annual Report, 1961*, p. 31.

20. We have no data for number of plant cities in 1960. However, in 1961 number of plants had risen to 170, located in 134 cities (Chart 2) and in every major geographic sector of the country.

Changing Structure of a Great Corporation

117 to 168, number of product lines from 328 to 400, and number of product departments from 37 to 110. This vast complex was managed and operated by a total of only 137 operating executives, and this management elite was organized as a pyramid with the chief executive in real control. We say "real control" on two counts:

1. The line of command in the operating structure had only five executives reporting to the chairman of the board; each of these five had approximately four division vice-presidents reporting to him; each of the division vice-presidents had only approximately five product department general managers reporting to him.

2. Further, and perhaps more significantly, the structuring, the assigned objectives, and the standards of measurement for each one of the 110 product department general managers were identical. Control was established by assigned standards of performance and quantitative measurement and complete coherence of management ideology.

Thus for the first time in the company's history the formal management organization structure had been truly, and drastically, changed. Even the "affiliated" companies that previously had been permitted to operate more or less on their own and with their own former company names were now included in the reorganization as divisions or product departments. For example, the former Hotpoint Company became the Hotpoint Division, and its office of president was replaced by that of vice-president (of General Electric) and general manager, Hotpoint Division.

The highly centralized functional structure that had served the company well in its pioneering and early growth days was recognized by management as becoming unyielding and limiting to continued growth as the company had expanded. As executives looked into the future, particularly during World War II, they perceived and correctly forecast greatly expanding technology, changing social and economic environments, and sharply increasing demands for electrical products in home, factory, and governmental defense operations. Correctly forecasting doubling company output in less than a decade, they deemed it imperative to realign the company's basic organization structure to provide for continued growth. This involved much more than a shuffling of resources, skills, and facilities; it required new concepts of management, new philosophies, new managerial attitudes, and new processes and programs.

The decentralized structure was not accomplished without mistakes, conflicts, and misunderstandings, which will be discussed next. The significant point is that this vast company did successfully, in the net, adjust to its changing external technological, economic, and social environments; and, in so doing, it initiated processes of change that even now continue to provide forces for further change, so that the company as a system and as a web of interrelated subsystems is in a continuing process of becoming something it is not.

THE APPARATUS BUSINESS

From its early days to the present time General Electric has devoted a large proportion of its resources and capacity to the production of capital goods. Even with the great growth of the appliance and other consumer goods business, which began about the middle 1920s, industrial machinery accounts for the major share of General Electric's sales. This is power apparatus, designed for and applied to industrial use, and includes power generating and transmission machinery, power distribution equipment, electrical measuring and metering devices, power control and switching devices, power utilization equipment including electric motors, and electrical heating equipment. Power equipment, or heavy and light capital goods, whether used directly by a purchaser (e.g. a motor to drive a steel mill roll-out table) or as a component in his marketed product (e.g. a motor purchased and installed on a lathe by a machine tool manufacturer), is subsumed under the generic industry category of apparatus.

The apparatus business is big. Even with the great growth of electrical consumer goods—refrigerators, ranges, washing machines, radios—the demand for apparatus applications in industry has continued to compound so that even today the apparatus busi-

Changing Structure of a Great Corporation

ness represents a major portion of output. General Electric's total sales of $4.5 billion in 1961, were: [21]

	%
Heavy capital goods	24
Components and light capital goods	27
Defense goods	24
Consumer goods	24

Even discounting "defense goods," which really are capital goods, and considering only sale of goods to industrial markets, about half, or over $2 billion, of G. E.'s output was in the apparatus category.

The apparatus segment of the electrical industry demands a high level of innovation in the application of electrical products and engineered systems to industrial customers' processes. For sixty years application engineers and systems-engineers have constantly analyzed industrial processes ranging from steel production to newspaper printing, asking: How can we do it better, more efficiently, more productively, more economically? The large electrical manufacturer (and this includes Westinghouse as well as General Electric) has thus been the innovative leader in a great many industries besides its own.

Structure Prior to Decentralization

Chart 1 shows the centralized, functional organization that existed until the late 1940s—the vertical parochial hierarchies of engineering, manufacturing, and sales. Our discussion will center primarily on sales in the predecentralization structure because the majority of the great advances in the innovative application of electrical products and engineered systems of products were made by the sales organization. Further, the feedback of information and analysis of industrial customer processes and problems, which set the stage for new product designs, were generated by this sales organization. Within the *engineering* hierarchy were industry-oriented and industry-assigned "application engineers" specializing in the innovative application of General Electric apparatus products and systems to various customer industries. These were market-

21. *General Electric Annual Report, 1961.*

oriented engineers in the engineering organization reporting upward through the engineering hierarchy. But within the sales organization itself prior to decentralization we note basically three distinguishable components, the general office product sales sec-

Figure 7. Apparatus Sales Structure Prior to Decentralization

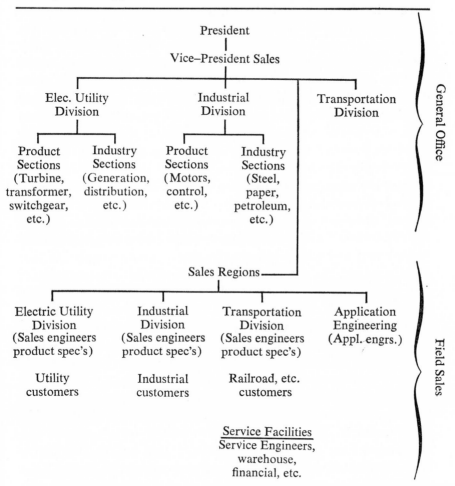

tions, the general office industry sections, and the field sales organization (see Figure 7).

Each line of products had a specialized sales group with the responsibility of providing product information to the field sales force, pricing the product, determining product sales policies, ex-

Changing Structure of a Great Corporation

ploring the need for new products, and maintaining liaison with engineering and manufacturing.[22]

For each customer industry a sales group in the general office specialized in the application of *all* apparatus products and the engineered-systems of products to the processes of that industry—a steel mill section, a paper industry section, a machine tool section —each headed by an industry sales manager and all grouped into an industrial division. Similarly, an electric utility division was composed of sections specializing in power generation, power distribution, and related fields. The responsibility of each of the industry sales sections was to become increasingly knowledgeable about its assigned customer industry, to understand the technological problems in that industry, to develop new applications of electrical apparatus to the processes of that industry, to make engineering and sales proposals for these new applications, and to assist the field sales force in sales negotiations.[23]

Even the companies that preceded G. E. had field selling organizations throughout the country. When General Electric was formed, those selling organizations were consolidated into a "selling department," which subsequently grew into a large technically trained and highly competent sales force known simply as "apparatus sales." The company had other field sales organizations, of course; for example, the lamp and appliance departments each had its own field sales organization. But for the apparatus-type products —industrial, electric utility, and transportation capital goods products—the apparatus sales organization was the field selling arm. It was organized in a number of sales regions (approximately fifteen), each headed by a commercial vice-president, with regional headquarters located in such major cities as New York, Boston, Chicago, and San Francisco, and branch offices in smaller cities. Each region's sales positions were staffed with college- and company-trained professional engineers; each region also had a corps of product specialists (field counterparts of the product sales

22. These are major functions and do not represent an exhaustive list. Looking ahead to decentralization it is clear that these sections were to be "pulled out" to form the core of the marketing sections of the new products departments.

23. It is clear that in decentralization these sections could not be spun off to individual product departments because they were industry-oriented and encompassed the application of many products and systems.

sections and headquarters) and applications engineers (field counterparts of the industry sales sections and headquarters); and each
region had its servicing facilities—order-service, financial, engineering service, warehouse.

The sales engineering positions (and the subregional management positions) were specialized to a degree in the larger urban
areas on an industry rather than a product basis. In the Chicago
office of the Central Region the commercial vice-president had
three division managers reporting to him—industrial, electric utility, and transportation—each of whom had a number of sales engineers. When the market potential warranted, an individual industrial sales engineer was assigned to customers in one industry only,
e.g. steel or petroleum, but in all cases the sales engineer sold *all*
apparatus products to his assigned customers, with the backup help
of product specialist in individual product and of applications engineers in engineered-systems of products. Ample evidence exists to
validate the claim that this large apparatus sales organization was
highly competent and commanded great respect in industrial circles, considerable envy among competitors, and great prestige
within the company itself.

As product departments were formed beginning in the very late
1940s and then proceeding at a more rapid rate in the early 1950s,
a number of organizational adjustments had to be made in the
apparatus segment of the company's business. As these product departments were formed, the appropriate elements of product engineering and manufacturing hierarchies were spun off, and the
appropriate *product* sales elements of the general office were spun
off and integrated into the new product department. Figure 7 shows
these as the "product sections" that were removed from apparatus
sales to become the nucleus of the marketing section of the new
product departments. This left the general office components of industry sales sections and the field sales force independent of the
product departments and their divisions. The *industry engineering*
sections of the former engineering general office organization were
then transferred to the apparatus sales general office organization.
This residue (which was, of course, the preponderant bulk of the
former sales hierarchy) was formed into the "apparatus sales division" and was given the complete responsibility for the field sales
function of all the apparatus-type product departments.

Changing Structure of a Great Corporation

Thus, as decentralization proceeded, the structural arrangement shown in Figure 8 evolved in the apparatus segment of the company's operation.

Although apparatus sales division provided the field sales function for a number of apparatus-type product departments, it was one organizational level above them; also, since it was assigned to one specific group executive, formal command and coordination existed only at the level of the president's office.

This, of course, is an organization dilemma, for it violates the principles of decentralization in separating an essential element of

Figure 8. Structural Relations, Apparatus Sales, and Product
Divisions and Departments

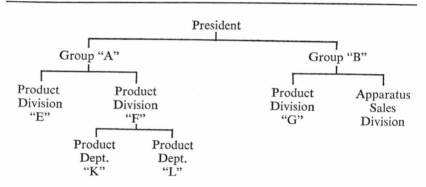

the product department—field sales—from its formal control. Why was this done? Because of market structures. Since the markets often required the engineered "put-together" into a system of the products of many product departments, there had to be some pooled sales function serving these markets. Further, strictly from a technological viewpoint, the future success and growth of the company lay not merely in continued product development but, more significantly, in the continued development of engineered-systems, such as completely automated steel mills and automated systems of material handling. This was the great technological backbone of the company marketwise, and the need was augmented by the greatly accelerating technology throughout all industry. Therefore, the ideals of decentralization were knowingly compromised in the apparatus portion of the company business, which, it will be recalled, represented approximately half the company's total sales. In a very real sense two major organization systems evolved as a result of the decentralization process: (a) the product departments, operating relatively autonomously as profit-centered business enterprises, and (b) the apparatus sales division, with authority to provide the sales function for the apparatus-type product departments.

After the spin-off of the product sales sections from the former sales organization and the absorption of the industry engineering

Figure 9. Apparatus Sales Division Organization Structure, 1951

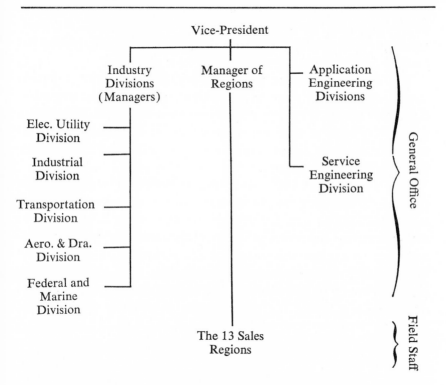

sections from the former engineering organization, the organizational structure of apparatus sales in the early years of rapid decentralization (1951–55) continued basically unchanged (see Figure 9). There were, of course, some adjustments; for example, a number of the larger regions were divided in order to better plan for, and operate in, the rapidly growing industrial markets, and the "manager of regions" position was divided between northern and southern areas.

Changing Structure of a Great Corporation

During the decentralization period (1951–55), while the sales structure remained relatively stable, the newly formed product departments were necessarily much involved with sheer organizational problems of welding together manufacturing, engineering, marketing, employee relations, finance, and other functional components into an integrated, going business enterprise with written charters for each position, objective setting, good deployment of people and physical facilities, and so forth. The "Services" from the executive office, with their wide variety of expertise in a score of specialized functions—organization planning, accounting and financial planning, as well as marketing, manufacturing, and engineering—were also involved with the process of decentralizing the product departments.

This did not all happen at once, of course; some product departments were formed early in the period, some reached organizational and management maturity earlier than others, and sometimes a relatively large product department was organized and later split into two or more departments—the latter process coming much more easily than the former.

Not until about 1955 were the majority of apparatus-type product departments "in place" with integrated, going managerial teams and looking outward to their markets rather than inward to their organizing processes. It was only then that the dynamic interaction of two major subsystems of the company—the apparatus-type product department and the apparatus sales division—each organizationally independent of, but interacting with and functionally dependent upon, the other, began to produce dysfunctional conflict.

Organization Structure Changes after Decentralization

In 1955 the vice-president of the apparatus sales division announced a major change in the organization structure, which had a twofold purpose: to better align the apparatus sales organization to the product departments it served and to provide more effective and economical distribution in the market place. The change was in two dimensions: (a) the separation throughout the entire structure of the selling functions from the various administrative and service functions, and (b) the decentralizing of the actual selling functions and their management into market-oriented suborganizations. Immediately below the level of vice-president and division manager of apparatus sales all administrative and service functions were "stripped out" through the entire organization, including the regional sales operations, and set up as self-contained departments:

1. Financial and Service Operations, responsible for all financial, order-service, and "housekeeping" operations, extending to the regions where a regional manager of financial and service operations was established, and reporting not to regional management but to the national manager of financial and service operations.

2. Installation and Service Engineering Department, providing engineering-service facilities to customers in installing or erecting and maintaining large apparatus and responsible not to the regional manager but to a national manager of installation and service engineering.

These two national suborganizations relieved the regional sales management of administrative and service responsibility, thus permitting it to devote its energies entirely to selling problems and planning. (This is not to imply that personnel administration within the sales units was removed.)

The remaining sales organization was then organized into three separate sales departments, each with a headquarters operation and a complete field organization. The separation was based on broad market or type-of-industry considerations:

1. The Users Industries Sales Department, responsible for the sale of all apparatus products and systems to customers purchasing for their own plant use and including such industries as electric utility, steel, automotive. The general manager of this department was located at division headquarters and reported to the division vice-president. The department had industry sales and application engineering functions as before and a regional sales organization.

2. The Components and Intermediate Distribution Department, responsible for the sale of all apparatus products and systems to customers purchasing apparatus not for their own use but for resale and including such industries as machine tool, pump and compressor, and to customers who were franchise distributors reselling apparatus to small industries, contractors, etc. The organization was similar to that of the "user" department with somewhat less emphasis on application engineering.

Figure 10, Apparatus Sales Division Organization Structure, 1955
(Staff Units and Positions Omitted)

3. The Aviation and Defense Industries Department, responsible for the sale of all apparatus products and systems to customers in the aviation, shipbuilding, and defense industries. Headquarters and regional organization were similar to the other sales departments.

This new apparatus sales division organization (see Figure 10) involved internal structural change but with the division remaining independent of the product department operations and reporting to a group executive.

In 1960 the Apparatus Sales Division again experienced drastic reorganization, this time destroying its identity as an organizational unit and as a social subsystem. This reorganization can be described as follows:

1. Product departments and divisions by 1960 had been realigned in quite compatible groupings. For example, the electric utility group consisted of divisions and product departments whose markets were in the electric utility industry. All organizational parts and functions of apparatus sales having to do with the electric utility market were thus split off through the division vice-presidential level and formed into a new sales division, the Electric Utility Sales Operation, and assigned to the electric utility group.

2. Since some of the product departments in this group produced for power generation and others for power distribution, within the newly formed electric utility sales organization further differentiation was made at the district manager and sales engineer levels, forming some field sales units selling only power generation products and other sales units selling only power distribution products.

3. Other product department groups also inherited their shares of "chunks" of the former sales division.

4. The breaking up of the sales division into parts assigned to, and in the sphere of, different product department groups resulted in a much higher degree of product specialization. Schematically, and oversimplified somewhat, the former structure appeared as illustrated at the top of Figure 11, and the new structure began as illustrated at the bottom.

This figure represents a new arrangement of interacting subsystems. While it still need not give each product department general manager formal and direct authority and control over the field sales

Changing Structure of a Great Corporation

function, it was a great step closer to that authority and control. Further, it greatly increased the dependency of the sales units on a few specific product departments. Additionally and significantly, each of the newly formed "fragments" of apparatus sales division was under the same group vice-president as the product divisions and departments to which it was assigned.

Figure 11. Product Departments and Apparatus Sales

Before apparatus sales reorganization

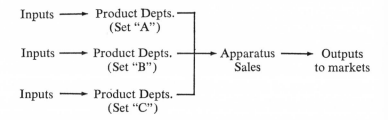

After apparatus sales reorganization

Inputs ⟶ Product Depts. ⟶ New Specialized ⟶ Markets
(Set "A")   Sales Unit "A"

Inputs ⟶ Product Depts. ⟶ New Specialized ⟶ Markets
(Set "B")   Sales Unit "B"

Inputs ⟶ Product Depts. ⟶ New Specialized ⟶ Markets
(Set "C")   Sales Unit "C"

Looking back at Figure 6, we see how the operating management authority in control of this giant corporation is vested in 137 individuals. Until the 1960 reorganization some thirty or forty of the product department general managers, accounting for $2 billion in sales, had no formal authority over a vital element of that operation—field sales. The reorganization of 1960 considerably enhanced the real authority of these 137 executives. More power was being centered in the management elite.

THE RATIONALITY OF CONTEMPORARY INNOVATION

The foregoing has described the General Electric Company's organizational change from a centralized functional management structure to a decentralized structure in order more readily to create and absorb new technology and to adapt to the changing external environment. This process was one of change in formal management organizational structure. But within this formal structure, what processes were there for enabling the individual, or groups of individuals, or systems of individuals to learn what the company meant, to come to understand what the individual work functions meant, to learn the do's and don'ts of managerial behavior, to learn how they were to be rewarded? All this, of course, was learned as it is in any social system, through the complex web of structure, norms of behavior, and social relationships, or in terms of a shared value system, shared sentiments, and shared corporate goals congruent with, and interacting with, personal goals. We shall attempt to describe and explain all this by examining a set of social structure variables both before and after the decentralization process. These variables were either knowingly or unknowingly, consciously or unconsciously under the control of management but—we hypothesize—influenced individuals' patterns of personality orientation and, interacting with certain purely organizational structural variables, thereby influenced patterns of managerial behavior. These variables are:
1. Entry
2. Early training
   a) "Test" program
   b) Business training course
   c) General course
   d) Functional courses
   e) Social influences
3. Job descriptions

Changing Structure of a Great Corporation

4. Individual performance ratings
5. Salary administration
6. Mobility
7. Later training
    a) Island Camps
    b) Elfun Society
    c) Advanced Management Institute

Entry into the Company

Generally the practice has been to recruit the technical and professional work force directly from colleges and then promote from within. For example, the 1961 Annual Report makes quite a point of the fact that the average age of officers and managers at the divisional general manager level and above was 52.5 years and the average length of service was 27.6 years. The company has maintained an active and formal recruiting program for professional employees for over forty years; in the early 1920s it was one of only a handful of industrial corporations recruiting engineering and business graduates at colleges throughout the country.

The criteria for hiring have always been highly demanding, including high scholastic achievement, outgoing personality, evidence of conceptual ability and problem-solving ability, technical competency, and a balanced interest in extracurricular activities.

Predecentralization

For thirty years prior to the decentralization of the early 1950s the company had recruited broadly in a geographic sense. The recruiting program was largely handled by two men, one recruiting engineers designated ultimately to fill technical and managerial positions in the functions of engineering, manufacturing, and sales and the other recruiting business and financial graduates designated to fill accounting and financial positions. Some universities provided many more graduates than others, and although there was no completely clear geographic pattern, the large state-supported universities of the Midwest had a high proportion relative to other sections of the country. By the mid-1930s Purdue University and Iowa State College, for example, ranked very high.

The Rationality of Contemporary Innovation

Because of the criteria for selection, these recruits had a number of characteristics in common. One manager of the company, thinking back about his early training days, remarked: [24]

> One thing that appealed to me in those early days was the fact that I was associated with young men who were very much like myself. I don't mean to imply any degree of conformity at all. As a matter of fact, I think that our particular group had quite a few non-conformists in it, such as [here, the informant named several individuals who later reached a high executive position in the company]. What I mean is that we all had ambition, a pretty high level of intelligence, the same basic technical background, and the same interests. It was a fine bunch of people.

The rate of hiring was fairly stable during the mid- to late 1920s, the Gerard Swope era. The people hired during this period were approximately fifty years old during the early stages of decentralization. Because of the great depression almost no new men were hired for about five years during the 1930s. In fact, during the period 1930–35, many of the younger men hired in the late 1920s were "furloughed"; most of these men later returned to the company, but not all, so this period shows a small net loss. Looking ahead briefly, we see that in the early days of decentralization, when the company was rapidly expanding, this resulted in a gap that created a sharply increased rate of upward mobility particularly after World War II. With the upturn of business in the mid-1930s the company again began hiring at a relatively high rate—about 400 engineers in 1936 and 500 in 1937. Throughout the period 1920–50 the young college graduates, both engineers and business graduates, reported for work at one of the major plant cities and were placed in a training pool, where they remained for approximately the first year.

Postdecentralization

Whether or not the company had decentralized, the recruiting process probably would have changed. The company had contin-

24. This and other quotations from company executives in the remainder of this chapter were made to the author in the course of his empirical research in 1961 for the purpose of preparing an unpublished doctoral dissertation.

ued to grow throughout the war years, and its technological processes were becoming increasingly complex. The many new technologies developed as a direct result of World War II demanded men with new skills. Recruiting itself, therefore, became somewhat decentralized, particularly in the technical area where the recruiting staff was enlarged from a handful of people to a large group of coordinators organized as recruiting teams to visit the technical universities. A typical recruiting team would include as many as five or six men specializing in such disciplines as nuclear physics, chemistry, engineering, mathematics. The important change here was that the college graduate was being interviewed not to come into the company's overall engineering training program, from which he would later progress to some specific functional area, but to enter the functional area itself.

Early Training

Predecentralization

All college graduates entering the company were placed in one of two initial training programs—engineers in the "test" program and business trainees in the "business training course," or "BTC." Each of these programs consisted of job rotational assignments together with formal classroom work.

The test program involved actual working assignments in the factory, testing large electrical apparatus, such as steam turbines, large motors and generators, large transformers. After such large machines or apparatus had been built, they were assembled and erected by factory personnel in a set of specified engineering tests by the young trainees, known as "test engineers," who had complete responsibility for determining whether the apparatus had been built to engineering specifications. Each individual had a test assignment for three months and was then moved to the testing department of another factory, sometimes in the same plant city and sometimes in another city, usually with a degree of choice. The majority of the assignments were in the company's largest plant city, Schenectady, New York, although there were also test assignments in such plant cities as Lynn and Pittsfield in Massachusetts, Philadelphia and Erie in Pennsylvania, and Fort Wayne, Indiana.

For the great majority of young engineers this was the first experience actually working in a factory. These were factory jobs; the test engineers punched a time clock, were paid on an hourly basis, carried their lunches. Yet they were clearly a group apart within the factory and so regarded themselves and were so regarded by factory personnel. These were responsible assignments and required the development of judgment on the part of the test engineer for the quality of performance of large complex apparatus.

A distinct camaraderie developed among test engineers, due partly to the relatively common backgrounds of the young trainees but also to the high status of the program within and outside the company. Essentially all of the technical people in the company, including those in management, had themselves been graduated in this program and regarded it with affection. To this day older men in the company speak nostalgically of their early "test" experience. As one vice-president of the company recently remarked:

> The test program certainly did something for people. It gave a background of technical experience, but more importantly was a common denominator for all people. It certainly made men feel much closer to one another. After all, when you gather young engineers from all parts of the country, from all schools, and put them in a common group in their first work experience, it was bound to develop a close and lasting relationship between these men.

One of the great advantages to the trainee of the test program was the opportunity to get a "feel" of the company and do some personal exploring during his first months on the program before he had to make a specific choice of a career assignment in manufacturing, engineering, or sales. All test engineers were hired only for the test program, with no specific designation of type of work they would do thereafter, which gave them the opportunity to change preconceived career ideas as they discovered more attractive avenues.

This exploration was made easy for the trainees. They were encouraged to interview managers in all functions in each of the plant cities in which they received assignments. Without exception those executives made themselves available for interviews. Of course, managers in each of the functions were anxious to "sell" their functions to the trainees, who represented the future manpower availability for their own specific work functions; in a sense, the functions were in competition for young engineers in the pool. But the important thing is that the young trainee quickly got a birdseye view of the apparatus component of the company, a feeling of camaraderie among his fellows, and, through intimate contact with management people, a feeling of being a junior member, but a member nonetheless, of a professional fraternity.

Normally, about six months after his entry the trainee made a decision on the functional career he wished to follow at the conclusion of his year's "test" assignment. He then applied for admission into the specialized program for that function.

The business and financial trainees embarked upon a rotational training program very similar to the test program except that their three month working assignments were in various accounting sections. Like the test engineers, they were given a relatively high degree of responsibility at the outset and performed working jobs in accounting or finance that required knowledge and judgment.

In the case of the business training course the end career had already been chosen, and trainees embarked immediately upon a functional training program in addition to the job assignments. They attended classes covering various phases of accounting and financial management.

Prior to career decisions all test engineers were required to enroll in the general course, a set of classes meeting twice a week, one meeting devoted to advance engineering application study and the other to a history of the company, a description by the respective managements of the various functions of the company (engineering, manufacturing, sales, accounting, etc.). These classes involved outside study for which the trainees frequently met together in groups, further reinforcing the camaraderie and also, significantly, reinforcing the shared perceptions of the various facets of the company.

Test engineers electing to continue design engineering as a career applied for entrance into the advanced engineering program. This highly competitive program selected candidates on the basis of written technical examinations. Upon acceptance, the trainee left the test program and again began a series of rotational assignments, this time of greater duration and in the design engineering departments. Concurrently, he was enrolled in courses of engineering and pure science given by outstanding technical men in the company. Trainees electing to follow commercial or sales engineering work as a career applied for the sales training program. This was also competitive, and selections were made after each candidate was interviewed by eight to ten high-level sales managers. After selection, the sales trainee continued his test assignments but began a program of course work under the administration of the sales training department. Courses included salesmanship, business letter writing, product application. Considerable ritual was connected with this program; announcements of acceptance into the program were made at dinner meetings held at local country clubs and attended by top executives of the sales organization; classrooms had the decor of a board room; classes were visited by sales executives; and instructors were well known sales managers. High esprit de corps quickly built up among the selected trainees. A sales executive of the company reminiscing about his first year in this program in the middle 1930s stated:

> The whole sales course was superbly presented and developed a very close personal relationship with associates. I remember we talked about very little over our cups of coffee and occasional beers other than the sales training program itself. . . . Some of my colleagues in this initial class were later to become product department marketing managers, general managers, regional sales managers, and division vice-presidents. Even to this day, to meet with one of these men over a martini is to signal a 'remember when' conversation.

Other social influences during the first couple of years of experience with the company further bound men to their respective groups. The living situations in the plant cities had a strong integrating influence. As recalled by one executive:

> In those days [the middle 1930s] a large percentage of the young men coming to work in Schenectady were not married. I should imagine that most of them spent six to nine months before marriage during which time many lived in a sort of cooperative arrangement, renting a house, hiring a housekeeper, and setting up shop much like a fraternity house on campus. These 'houses' had fascinating names such as the

Changing Structure of a Great Corporation

'Nudist Colony,' 'Testing House,' etc. They led a gay life. I can remember just the other day chuckling with one of my old friends about the day we had the big party in the 'Nudist Colony' when we made milk punch in the bathtub.

Close social friendships also developed among young married couples, often in the same functional training programs:

We all made about the same amount of money with nothing to spare at the end of the week for any entertaining other than dessert and bridge and an occasional bottle of beer. It was a most interesting group of people; there were competent young men and their inevitably attractive wives from all parts of the country dumped into a melting pot. My wife and I still trace some of our dearest friendships of the present back to those early days in Schenectady when we were making $30.00 a week on the old sales training program.

Postdecentralization

During the early years of decentralization, beginning about 1950, the initial training program in the country underwent a gradual change. With one exception the famous G. E. test program was gradually eliminated, and young men were recruited from the college campus for direct placement in manufacturing or engineering assignments of specific product departments.

The sales training program, however, has retained a number of test assignments. When a college graduate is hired by sales training recruiters, he enters the sales engineering career directly; but instead of going into the product section of one of the product departments or into the field sales force, he enters a one-year training program in which he is given three-month factory assignments on a rotational basis testing large apparatus. Thus, only for the engineering-sales trainees is there a training pool. Of course, the trainee has made the decision for a career in sales engineering, and his choice lies only between a product department marketing section and field sales.

Entering trainees in the financial function have chosen one career and, therefore, graduates of business and finance are recruited and assigned in much the same way as before decentralization.

The engineering training programs were largely eliminated. Prior to decentralization advanced engineering was taught by company engineers, but the pyramiding technology now makes this extremely difficult. In many cases now the company will send young engineers to engineering colleges for special programs.

The results of these changes in initial entry and early programs are:

1. Trainees no longer come into a common pool but are assigned directly to operating components of the company in specific functional assignments.

2. The common, shared experiences at work and in classes no longer exist.

3. The social camaraderie that developed as a result of these shared experiences is largely eliminated.

4. Whereas individuals quickly identify with specific operating components of the company, the identification with the total company is reduced.

5. Where the common, shared early training experiences do still exist, as in the business training course, a "family" camaraderie and a professional and almost "fraternal" identification still exist.

Job Descriptions

Predecentralization

Formal job descriptions were almost nonexistent in the centralized functional organization of the 1920s and 1930s. This is not to say that individuals did not understand what their jobs were or what performance was expected of them, but there was no formal mechanism explicitly spelling out the job. Role expectations were traditionally developed and passed on, as it were, from generation to generation. Through the symbol systems of the company and of each of the vertical hierarchies, understandings and perceptions of positions "came to be" in a number of ways. First, the individual observed his superior and how his superior functioned in his position.[25] Second, there was a very close manager-subordinate per-

---

25. We shall discuss mobility later. Here it is important to note that before decentralization mobility was almost entirely upward within the vertical hierarchies. Most mobility occurred when an individual "took over his boss's job," and thus reinforced the usual behavior of observing one's superior and how the superior functioned.

Changing Structure of a Great Corporation

sonal relationship. Traditionally, managers quite generally through-out the company regarded training and development of people—though not in a formal sense—as an important part of the managerial job. The general approach was in "giving the individual a full measure of responsibility and letting him develop himself in his job," and an example was the responsibility given to trainees in their early days. A vice-president referred to this in a speech given to The American Institute of Electrical Engineers at their annual meeting in 1942: [26]

> The engineering organization of a large industrial business is based on a number of principles:
> 1. Directness of action and freedom of action without conflict.
> 2. The engineering organization must be part of the total business.
> 3. *The form of the organization must be subordinate to its personnel and must shape to the qualifications of men.*
> 4. The organization needs a small central staff.
> 5. The organization needs supporting committees.
> 6. The organization needs manpower strength with runner-ups, with education, to cultivate and exemplify loyalty, spirit, and morale.
> 7. *The traditions of the engineering organization must act as a catalyst for such spirit and morale.*

The emphasis on shaping organization to the qualifications of men was typical of the managerial ideology in the company at that time, as was the emphasis on education to cultivate and exemplify loyalty and spirit. Other managers speak of the development and the understanding of the perception of jobs without formal job descriptions:

> I had over twenty years of experience in the company and a job paying over $25,000 a year before I ever had any written description of my job given me by a superior.

> We simply learn by experience. . . . There were certain traditions for certain types of jobs but they were informal in character. . . . I simply know that in a new job I would

26. Emphasis added. Note particularly the man-oriented sense of these statements.

The Rationality of Contemporary Innovation

more or less automatically come to know what was expected of me.

Postdecentralization

In contrast to the traditionally based understanding of jobs prior to decentralization, procedure after decentralization became highly objective. A written job description specifically outlining the duties of the job and accompanying authority and accountability was prepared for every position in the company, managerial and professional nonmanagerial—a written record against which performance in the position could be objectively measured.

The relation of one position to other positions was specified. Job descriptions were prepared for the position itself with no regard to present or potential incumbents. Under the concept of organizing principles candidates were selected who had behavioral traits, knowledge, and apparent skills for the spelled-out position. Individual performance and abilities were not subordinated, but the rational and objective description of positions became a highly important base point.

Furthermore, in the spelling out of job descriptions, and also in the spelling out of the "charters" of groups, complete uniformity prevailed. Before decentralization individual perceptions of management positions and the web of ideologies that grew up around different management positions were extremely diverse. After decentralization the position of a product department general manager, a product department marketing manager, or a division general manager was the same throughout the company. The individual job description of the general manager of product department A may have differed from that of the general manager of a product department B, but only in expected sales volume, dollar level of profitability, and other quantitative terms. The detailing of the position was identical.

Individual Performance Ratings

Predecentralization

Prior to decentralization there were methods for rating the performances of employees, but they varied widely from component to

Changing Structure of a Great Corporation

component even within the vertical functional hierarchies. An executive formerly with apparatus sales described the rating system within the component as follows:

There were really three ways in which we rated sales people. First was in the salary itself. If we could keep salary increases coming along fairly frequently, that in itself indicated to the individual that he was doing a good job. But then there was a formal rating system which consisted of a rating sheet on which the individual was rated in a number of categories, primarily personality trait kind of thing. For each of a number of traits he was rated on a scale from excellent to poor, and was given a final overall rating of effectiveness on the job and potential for advancement. Strictly speaking, each individual was supposed to be rated by this method once each year after being appointed to a new position for three years, and at least once every three years thereafter. The manager himself did not necessarily make the rating. Rating sheets were given to three individuals who knew the ratee and the manager was then supposed to discuss a composite of these three ratings with the ratee. I would say that only lip service was given to this rating method.[27]

Then there was another private and supposedly secret rating of individuals which the manager made but did not discuss with them. This took two forms. One was the submission to his higher headquarters of the list of younger men in the organization who had promise of growth . . . also, there was another form for each employee which was submitted to higher headquarters which rated each man on a number scale from 2 to 10, 10 being outstanding, on two points: present performance and potential for the future. This was an important rating because at times of salary reviews the "number" rating of the man often determined his eligibility for salary increase.

Although the individual did not often receive formal evaluations of his performance from his superior, he did perceive that he was

27. As late as the early 1950s an employee attitude survey conducted throughout the entire apparatus sales organization gave evidence that the great majority of professional people in this large organization had not received a formal discussion of performance evaluation from their superior in many years.

performing capably because he was in a position whose behavior patterns were set by tradition, and he was following the tradition. In fact, the very absence of a consistent formal performance rating system, coupled with the high esprit de corps that went with being a member of the corporation, was in itself a significant symbol in the web of symbol systems revolving about positions, man-to-man, and group-to-group relationships and behaviors.

Postdecentralization

Under the concepts of decentralization the delegation of authority for decision making carried with it an accountability for specific and objective measurements of performance. The concept of the manager's job clearly indicated the importance of his developing and expressing the factors, units, and systems used in measuring performance of individuals and work groups.

Every attempt was made to express rational and objective standards of performance in each job description under this rationale:

> Before decentralization there was really no pervasive and rational method of compensation and rating. Much was left to the discretion of the individual manager. You see, in those days the idea was we paid men. Now, of course, the idea is we do not pay men, but rather evaluate *jobs* and attempt to set limits on the value of that specific job to the company. The man is then paid somewhere in the range of the established value of the job. Thus, you see, formerly the appraisal of a man was based almost entirely on subjective factors and, of course, the subjective factors varied from manager to manager. Now all the emphasis is on the job itself; we have ample statistics on jobs now—past records of potential business from customers, actual received business from customers, the amount of influence the job has on business being placed elsewhere, etc.—therefore, we have a much more measurable approach to the job itself now than we ever had before. . . . To an extent at least it imposes a practical and rational approach to the worth of a job to the company. Formerly there was a tendency for apparatus sales management to rate all of their people rather uniformly 'excellent.' The rating systems didn't really mean very much. And as I said, there was a great

deal of variation in the individual bench marks used by individual managers.

The content and the value to the company of individual jobs varied, but the *structure* of the job description and the commensurate standards of performance were quite uniform.

As new organization components were formed and positions created, individual managers in these new positions readily accepted the rationale of definitive job descriptions and evaluation of performance. However, in those subsystems relatively unchanged by decentralization, where managers perceived no change in the methods or objectives of their work (as in the apparatus sales division), there was resistance not only to the formalized job descriptions but also to the imposition of specific quantitative bases of performance measurement. One regional sales executive, whose view was supported by other managers, stated:

They began to make their appraisals of the selling organization cold-bloodedly and over-emphasized measurement of performance. I have always insisted that one cannot adequately measure the performance of a creative selling organization in a technical business. There is absolutely no way to adequately quantify our performance in our activities today and the value of these activities for future business. But, unfortunately, the product department general management who were placed 'under risk' because of this concept of professional management turned out to be less managers than 'bean-counters.' What do I mean by 'bean counters?' Well, here is a division manager back East someplace, and looks at variations from budget, etc. He then bases opinions as well as his decisions on these figures. All he is doing is counting beans. He is not being really a creative manager . . . I think much of our management, particularly in the product departments, became 'measurement happy' with the end result of placing too much emphasis on figures and dollars and getting away from the importance of the human individual in the organization.

As decentralization proceeded, the product department management experienced increasing rationality with respect to jobs and performance measurement in those jobs, whereas traditionally oriented apparatus sales continued to resist.

Salary Administration

Predecentralization

Closely allied with the variables of job descriptions and performance ratings is the system of salary administration. Before decentralization there was no performance evaluation and no uniform salary administration plan. There were a few common ground rules, but each of the vertical functional hierarchies and components implemented salary administration quite differently. For example, throughout the sales organization managers periodically received instructions from higher headquarters for a "salary review." The ground rules for these reviews changed from time to time; one rule might state that only men with ratings 9.0 and above who had not had increases the year before would be eligible for salary increase, or only men in certain salary brackets would be eligible. Usually such ground rules completely tied managers' hands. Some may have felt that certain individuals not eligible for an increase had in fact earned one. Both the mechanics of the salary review and the philosophy underlying it therefore tended to "spread around" additional salary money when it became available. This was not discussed with individual professional employees, but the system was pretty well known. It was also quite well understood that if the requirements of the salary review were met, the discretion of the individual's manager was all important.

The idea was that the company paid *men.* Judgments on salary increases were subjectively made and varied from manager to manager. Executive decisions involved the quantitative amount of total salary increases and the ground rules for each salary review. Except for its tie to performance through specifications relative to the "secret managerial numerical rating of individuals," the integration of salary increases to job performance existed only subjectively in the minds of managers and thus varied greatly throughout the company.

Postdecentralization

A company-wide uniform salary administration plan was put into effect in the middle 1950s. This plan completely integrated job descriptions and requirements, personal performance in that job, and compensation. The emphasis was placed on the job not on the man. The value of the job to the company was determined, and all positions from chief executive down to individual worker were ranked in twenty-six levels, with numbers and a range of salary assigned to each. Each salary level had a minimum and maximum that did not vary throughout the company regardless of the type of work or organizational function. For the first time in company history a candidate could approach a new job knowing precisely what the job entailed, what was to be measured, and the "job level" (or the value to the company). He knew he would be paid at least the minimum salary for that level and never over the maximum.

Summary

In considering the variables of job description, personnel evaluation, and salary administration prior to decentralization, we conjectured that the traditionally based processes by which these variables evolved and were implemented resulted in the development of symbolic means wrapped around all of them, causing individuals to identify strongly with men rather than with managerial positions per se. After decentralization, with the advent of organization-structuring based on rational factors (that is, based on jobs and relationships with jobs rather than on people), the former symbols clustered about manager-worker relations became meaningless, and new symbol systems centered about positions rather than men—around rational, quantitatively measurable objectives rather than personal relations—evolved.

Mobility

Predecentralization

Prior to World War II and under the centralized functional organization structure, mobility was essentially entirely upward within the respective functional hierarchy. It was extremely rare for an individual to receive a promotion outside his hierarchy of engineering sales, or other function. Even within substructures of the several hierarchies mobility was upward through the specialized subcomponents; a motor-design engineer was promoted through the motor-designing function and an industrial engineer through the industrial subhierarchy.

The rate of mobility relative to that achieved after World War II was low. There was relatively little turnover in the higher management positions and an unusually low "quit-rate." It was not at all uncommon for an individual to be incumbent in a position for ten years or more.

All this, of course, reinforced the identification of individuals with their functions, that is, with the vertical hierarchy. Further, the relative stability of the organization reinforced the traditions and all the symbol systems evolving about positions, components, and functions.

During the twenties and thirties, as the number of product lines increased, new positions were created. As a new line of products was developed, engineering, manufacturing, and sales components were formed to design, produce, and market them. However, these were "horizontal" shifts, and although they did create new positions and hence provide a degree of mobility, the concepts of the positions were identical with those of analagous product lines. In the early thirties, moreover, the effects of the great depression reduced this relatively slow rate of mobility. Even when business picked up in the late thirties, mobility was affected more by retirement than by any other single factor. Thus the vertical hierarchies and the subcomponents within them were highly provincial and parochial in character; Fort Wayne engineers identified themselves as "Fort Wayne Engineers," Pittsfield engineers identified themselves as "Pittsfield Engineers," and regional sales people identified with their individual regions. In almost all cases there was a strong emotional attachment, intense pride, and sense of belonging to that vertical hierarchy and the subcomponent within it.

Postdecentralization

Great technological advances and continued growth in all markets after World War II would have resulted even without decen-

Changing Structure of a Great Corporation

tralization in company growth, limited of course, by the productive ability of the former centralized organization. But with decentralization and organization change into a large number of quasiautonomous departments, the number of management positions increased rapidly in the 1950s, and the rate of mobility increased tremendously.

In addition to the absolute increase of managerial and supervisory positions as a direct result of decentralization, another factor influenced the rate of mobility. As we saw previously, during the depression years of 1930–35, very few professional people entered the company. Sizable numbers were recruited in 1936 and 1937, but in the "recession" year of 1938 very few were hired. From 1941 to 1945, the years of World War II, the demands for technical personnel increased far beyond the company's ability to secure new men. From the end of World War II through 1950 the supply of graduating engineers was relatively limited, and competition from other industries increased. In none of these years did the company achieve anywhere near the number of technical men required. Hence, for a period of about twenty years, 1930 to about 1950, there were only three or four "good hiring" years. Large age gaps existed at the very time in the early 1950s when decentralization caused an even greater demand for men to fill newly created managerial positions. All this created rapid upward mobility for younger men in the company.

An even more striking change in the mobility pattern was the path of mobility. Whereas prior to decentralization mobility was essentially entirely upward within the individual's own professional component, after decentralization it rapidly became horizontal as well as vertical. It became common for a design engineer in one product department to be promoted to a managerial engineering post in another product department, perhaps be promoted again to a higher engineering position in another product department, and perhaps finally to attain the general managership in still another department. Managers whose previous experience had been entirely in the lamp department, for example, might be promoted to positions managing the appliance business or the power distribution business. This, of course, was particularly true in the early days of decentralization, when the need to fill general management positions was so great and when it was felt that there was a universality of professional managerial positions with unique, pervasive principles of management.

Significantly, during the early years of decentralization, 1951–55, the apparatus sales division was a prime source of managerial personnel for the marketing sections of the product departments. Apparatus sales regional operations contained many men highly trained in specific product lines—the product specialists who provided "back up" assistance. Many of these specialists were invited to transfer to product department marketing sections to assume such jobs as manager of product planning, sales, managers, and in some cases marketing managers. Thus, although there was a considerable amount of "cross breeding" in other parts of the company, apparatus sales managers continued to be appointed from apparatus sales ranks.

Increasing rationality also affected mobility. Down to a certain managerial level, for example, it was required that any manager considering candidates for a managerial position must consider at least three individuals outside his own component and present adequate evidence to higher headquarters that such consideration had been made—an intentional introduction of cross breeding. For the individual there was also increasing rationality. With the mobility pattern becoming so diverse, individuals were able to "get at" positions in other sectors, both geographically and organizationally, through the mechanism of what the company called "registers," which were maintained by certain of the staff groups at executive headquarters. These registers were essentially "employment agencies," which maintained complete dossiers of individuals who elected to utilize such service. If a manager desired to consider candidates outside his component, he could submit a set of specifications to one of the registers and receive a list of qualified candidates. This wide horizontal as well as vertical mobility fit the philosophy of executive management at that time, a philosophy wrapped around the concepts that management is a kind of "professional work" involving certain basic principles which, once mastered, enable a manager to perform efficiently in any kind of product business and technical milieu.

The range of this horizontal mobility began to decrease about the mid-1950s, however, for two reasons. First, it was found that it took more than a mastering of the so-called managerial principles

Changing Structure of a Great Corporation

to do an effective managerial job in many of the more technical aspects of the company's business. Second, by the middle 1950s the rate of formation of new product operations had decreased and with it the demand for new managerial personnel. Consequently, managerial promotions were made more and more from within the respective division and department. The rigid policy requiring consideration of outsiders was relaxed. As stated by a management consultant staff expert in 1961:

> Now it is generally accepted in the company that management requires more than the 'generic principles' of management; the manager must have insights into how to adapt to specific situations. . . . Much emphasis is being placed today on the technical know-how of the business and the demands that this technology places on the general manager of that business. This, of course, reinforces the behavioral reaction within the vertical chain more than in the horizontal chain. As individual managers now perceive the mobility as being somewhat more restricted to certain types of business, and probably the very wide mobility lies more closely within their particular organizational components. This means that the individual manager takes cues and signals from individual personalities in the hierarchy above him. This may explain some of the conflict observed between interdependent components of the company.

Summary

Prior to decentralization the "meanings" of things and the commonly shared beliefs and sentiments of people were all traditionally based and oriented. This system served well during the long period during which organization structure was relatively stable and mobility was largely limited to the parochial, traditionally oriented work components.

When the increasing technology was coupled with changes in the meanings of things—the meaning of managerial philosophy, of managerial positions, of work components—former traditions could not suffice. Through the media of job descriptions, focus on jobs rather than people, more quantitatively measured performance, establishment of a uniform salary administration plan, and the integrating of all these variables, meanings became more rational and more secular.

Later Training

Predecentralization

After early training there was little additional training. There were, of course, product and application engineering meetings and the like, but there was essentially no further formal training for management. However, two activities in the company deserve special attention because of their influence on the conception of managerial positions and their strong reinforcement of the traditionally based symbol system.

The company owned an island in Lake Ontario near the headwaters of the St. Lawrence River. It had been equipped as a summer meeting place and, beginning about the mid-1920s, was used each summer for the purpose of assembling managers above a certain level.

The facilities on the island were relatively simple. Tents on board flooring spread in a semicircle around a large parade ground on a central campus. Each tent housed two men, and there were facilities for approximately two hundred.

The island quickly became a most evocative symbol. Merely to be invited to attend an island meeting was equated with success. The meetings were conducted with great ceremony and ritual. Top executives of the company were always in attendance; ties and coats were forbidden, and everyone was on a first-name basis. When arriving attendees disembarked at the docks, they were met by a small band playing music composed for the island and a reception line of company executives; a holiday spirit prevailed. After sunset on the first night of each camp meeting a ceremony was held underneath a large elm tree, known throughout the management ranks simply as "The Elm"; the executives spoke to the newcomers to the island (always known as the "rookies"), speaking of the greatness of the company and charging the "rookie" managers with the responsibility of carrying on the great traditions of the company. All this was done with colored lights, background music, and

Changing Structure of a Great Corporation

always culminated with the appearance of an Indian in full battle regalia, who paddled a canoe to the shore of the island, disembarked, and made a sentiment-charged speech.

The island meetings lasted three days with business sessions in the morning and recreation in the afternoon. Normally there were short business meetings after dinner with guest speakers from outside the company, such as noted industrialists and university presidents. Usually there was one camp session during each summer known as "Camp General," which was attended by the top management of all functions. But most island meetings were held by work function and were oriented to the parochial vertical hierarchies.

To this day management in the company speak of the island with great sentiment. A vice-president of the company stated:

> The island was simply great. It provided tremendous appeal to management people. I think it was a mistake on the company's part to abandon it. The management meetings being held now are not substitutes for the old island. At the Island there was a feeling of esprit de corps. It gave management people an emotional feeling, a feeling of G.E.'s image and a feeling of G.E.'s greatness. Management's meetings today are held on some specific problem such as the profit situation, etc. The island, on the other hand, had its meetings focused on the traditions of the company themselves.

During an island meeting in 1929 the chief executive of the company proposed forming a group of management personnel destined to have great impact on managerial thinking for the next twenty years. The overt reason for the formation of this group or society was to provide a means for managers above a certain level to make investments on a personal basis through a trust fund to be administered at essentially no cost by company officials. The group was therefore called the Elfun Society, a contraction of the term "Electrical Fund." But this society quickly became something more than that, for the chief executive encouraged the development of this management group into a powerful informal management policy-making body and at one time called the Elfun Society "my informal board of directors." Perhaps a thousand managers throughout the company held the rank and stature for eligibility to the society. Local chapters were established at all plant cities and throughout the sales regions. The local chapters met monthly to discuss management problems within the company generally and developed projects for studies of management policy to be forwarded to the chief executive.

Powerful symbolic meaning built up around the Elfun Society. To be an Elfun meant status, recognition, and a feeling of participation in management policy making. Elfun did something more; it began to integrate management thinking across the functional vertical hierarchical barriers. The local monthly meetings of each chapter were attended by managers of all functions. The sales people usually had their cocktails with other sales people, of course, and there was a definite tendency for managers of like jobs to hang together. Nevertheless, the extracurricular projects of various Elfun chapters were carried on by study committees composed of managers from various functions.

Postdecentralization

With changing executive and managerial philosophy after decentralization, changes in organization structure, objectives, and role expectations and need for training throughout all age groups became acute. This was particularly true for the positions of operating general managers for product departments since those positions called for executive management blending of all aspects of business —technical, production, marketing, financial, etc. Except for a small handful of executives at the very top echelon of the former centralized functional organization, there were almost no men in the company with training and experience in more than a single function. At the outset of decentralization this was a most critical problem.

Recognizing the deficiency of broadly trained executive personnel, in 1949 the company initiated a program dubbed the "Crown Prince" by many because it involved the selection of functional managers generally in the age group thirty-five to forty who had demonstrated potential for general management. Each of these men was completely relieved of work assignments and given special assignments as assistants to top level managers in another function for a period of six months to one year. A sales manager in apparatus sales may have been appointed assistant to the comptroller for

Changing Structure of a Great Corporation

a period of six months and may then have been assigned as assistant to a top level engineering manager. It was hoped that within a year, or two at the most, such outstanding men would receive broad practical experience in many functions that would qualify them to assume in the future the exacting executive roles of general managers of product departments. This program was short-lived for several reasons. It was expensive because of the temporary waste of highly competent management manpower; the experience of the first few individuals demonstrated that the program did not provide adequate developmental training. The program was discontinued in 1950.

Meetings at the island in 1950, 1951, and 1952 served in a sense as managerial training media. They were not formal training programs, but they served a descriptive, analytical, and explanatory purpose. The meaning of, and reasons for, decentralization were thoroughly and analytically presented to approximately 3,000 managers who, through these meetings, began to perceive the company's new managerial philosophy.

After the Island Camp sessions in the first three years of the decentralization program were completed, the island was no longer used as a meeting place. It was finally dismantled and sold in 1956. Hence, a great old tradition in the company disappeared.

At the outset of decentralization the chief executive rejected the activities of the Elfun Society. Elfun activities attempting solutions of company problems and making recommendations to formal management were stopped. Elfun itself was not disbanded and continued to hold monthly meetings. But it was no longer "part of top management." Its meaning had changed.

In 1955 the company invested over $2 million in its well known Advanced Management Institute. An estate overlooking the Hudson River about five miles north of New York City was purchased; a number of facilities were added, including excellent living quarters and a classroom building. Removed from an urban atmosphere, the Advanced Management Institute had the environment of a college campus.

The Advanced Management Course began in 1956 as a "crash" program to train top level business managers. There were thirteen-week programs, and attending managers were temporarily relieved of all operating responsibilities and lived at the Institute. The program was aimed primarily at approximately 1,700 managers from the level of chief executive down through the functional managers reporting to the product department general managers. By March, 1961, the Advanced Management Course had 142 graduates, including 80 per cent of all the product department general managers, all but one division manager, and all five group executives. Directors of the program state that the objective was simply to improve the quality of managerial performance in present positions.

The first five or six sessions of the course, running through 1955 and part of 1956, centered primarily about the new managerial roles resulting from decentralization. Most general managers of newly formed product departments had had no experience in overall executive problems and decisions, and the program initially served as an important medium for inculcating in an individual manager's mind the basic principles of decentralization and the concept of the manager's job in the decentralized organization structure.

Reactions to the Advanced Management Course, its objectives, and its methods varied from enthusiastic acceptance to outright disdain. Possibly the most recurrent criticism was that the Advanced Management Course preached the doctrine of decentralization and the principles of management as dogma.

Regardless of criticism, however, many managers in the company did in fact approach the work of their positions using the so-called "managerial principles" emphasized during the early days of decentralization at the Advanced Management Course. Further, it developed a common language among division, department, and functional sectional managers throughout the company.

The Advanced Management Course was attended by executives and managers down to about the $20,000 per year level. A condensed version of it was prepared in a set of volumes covering such subjects as the concept of decentralization and the managerial principles of planning, organization, integrating, and measuring the work of the professional manager. A large group of conference leaders for this course were trained at the Advanced Management Institute and returned to their home components to present the program to a large number of individuals down to and including many selected nonmanagerial and professional employees. These programs were held throughout the company in about ten weekly sessions of approximately three hours each. By 1960 some 30,000 individuals had participated in this condensed version of the Advanced Management Course, widely disseminating the concepts and principles of decentralization, the present view or philosophy of executive management, and the concept and specific description of the professional manager's role in the company.

The Advanced Management Course and its condensed version were slanted toward the nonexecutive aspects of management. In addition to these programs, beginning about 1953 a number of functionally oriented programs were developed by the various staff or service components as advanced developmental training for functional managers who already had considerable experience in their work functions. Advanced marketing seminars, manufacturing management seminars, and so forth were given over two- to four-week periods, normally at the company's Advanced Management Institute. They were technical in content and highly specialized to the specific function involved. Almost without exception participants found them highly valuable in improving technical performance of their specific functions.

Later training ranging from the extremes of executive management to that of highly technical programs dealing with computer application and automation proliferated during the middle 1950s.

Summary

The underlying rationale of the decentralization process focused on the creation of a large number of quasiautonomous product operations, each functioning as a relatively independent business. Superficially it might appear that the organization's structural dividing of this multibillion dollar company into approximately one hundred quasiautonomous operating units was a fragmentation of structure, both technically and socially. This is far from fact.

The product department operations after decentralization have a number of important common aspects:

1. The philosophy, policy, and procedure of the delegation of decision-making authority to the general manager of the product department is congruous throughout the entire corporation.

2. The product department operation is "profit centered," and each department is established as a business with a high degree of

quantification of performance with regard to return on investment and sales.

3. The product departments had identical formal organization structure.

4. The product departments had a common set of performance standards.

5. The product departments had similar broad charters and similar roles in the corporate family.

6. The written "position guides" for product department general managers and their functional managers were identical for all product departments. In fact, the position guide of the product department general manager was widely disseminated throughout the entire company; it was discussed and exhibited at meetings during the early days of decentralization and was published in company journals and documents. The intended meaning of the position of the product department general manager was clear and definitive at the outset. Further, the definition of the job of product department general manager was established without regard to individual persons. That is, the job itself and its role expectations were highly specifically established. There was a commonness in this role expectation throughout the entire company.

7. In addition to these common strains, the concept of the "professional manager" provided a common linkage throughout the company. The principles of professional management proposed and advocated at an early island meeting and later in the Advanced Management Course provided a communality to the managerial position, ideologically speaking. Whether or not the Advanced Management Course preached dogma, it did accelerate a cluster of common conceptions about the general manager's job. The field counterpart of the Advanced Management Course further disseminated this concept throughout the entire company.

8. The definition of jobs on a rational basis, the establishment of a company-wide, uniform salary administration plan, and the increase of quantification of measurement of performance brought increasing rationality to the company.

The status system of the social structure, the formal organization structure, the expectation-sanction system, the communications system, and the decision-making system all changed and all became increasingly rational and secular.

CLINGING TO TRADITION

The discussion of changes in the formal organization structure over time described how the General Electric Company used the mechanics of decentralization to adapt its formal structure as the product departments were formed and as the tradition-based meanings became more rationally oriented. For market reasons the apparatus sales division had to be retained as the field selling arm of the apparatus type product departments, and it remained, in a sense, an island in a sea of organizational change. As the social system changes were activated and accelerated by executive action in much of the company, in the apparatus sales division the meanings of the company and the meanings of jobs remained traditionally based and strongly reinforced by symbolic meanings of rituals, practices, and procedures. Change was instituted deliberately in the product department subsystem but not within the apparatus sales subsystem; the apparatus sales subsystem resisted change, but change occurred nonetheless.

The apparatus sales division possessed at the time of decentralization a rich history of competency stemming from the early days when the men of the selling department were the appliers of the new electrical technology, literally creating a demand where there was none before. This innovative demand creation never stopped. Particularly from the mid-1920s until decentralization individuals in the division were highly capable. Almost all were college trained engineers; high standards of recruiting brought to the company outstanding technical men; the factory training, sales training, and additional training after transfer to a region increased individual technical capability.

The apparatus sales division enjoyed high prestige both in and out of the company. Individual apparatus sales managers and sales engineers were generally regarded with esteem, which was reflected in levels of compensation and such kudos as invitations to island meetings and the Elfun Society, which, although nominally restricted to management, were extended to a relatively large number of outstanding nonmanagerial and professional individuals in apparatus sales.

The individual sales engineer was regarded as an "executive type" in customer circles, where he had access to customer executive levels and, in a significant number of cases, became intimately acquainted socially with top management.

From the very start of the company the field sales organization was independently structured; in a sense, it had to be because of the continually growing complexity of engineered products and engineered systems applications with which it dealt. Even in the days of decentralization after World War II the main qualities of the complex industrial selling organization seemed to defy objective analysis through such techniques as operations research or the application of measurements.

This independence within the company was seen in a number of ways. Prior to decentralization, when product sales groups in the general office were part of the apparatus sales organization, it was normally the product sales manager who "ran the show" in unifying engineering and manufacturing efforts and integrating them with sales efforts. Within the sales organization itself the regional sales operations were quite independent and at least until the middle 1950s did "run their shows" quite independently. Apparatus sales management regarded individual sales engineers as executive businessmen and overtly recognized the sales engineer as the "manager" of his business and of his territory.

Thus, for many years a high value had been placed on individuality throughout this organization, and a considerable amount of freedom of operation and freedom to make decisions had been developed by all individuals. All this contributed to making a very proud organization, a social as well as organizational system with high esprit de corps, a very close "family" feeling, and intense loyalty to the company and to apparatus sales.

All this was reinforced by the nonrational aura of the selection and training of the members for this social subsystem. In selecting its trainees from the company pool of recently employed college graduates, apparatus sales management had a definite image of "the typical" apparatus sales person. In the initial sales training programs the lore of the division was internalized by the young trainee.

Changing Structure of a Great Corporation

Later, even after two to three years of general office training, he was required to "compete" for his ultimate job in regional sales. Regional managers or a manager of the regional staff periodically visited the various sales training locations at major plant cities and interviewed prospective candidates for regional jobs; sales trainees in turn had a choice of several regions and attempted to "sell" themselves to these regions. When a trainee accepted an offer to come to a region, he was "tagged" for that region until the conclusion of his training program. Great store was set on being "tagged."

In the region he often spent as much as two years as a sort of apprentice—answering telephone inquiries, handling quotation work for sales engineers—before being assigned to industrial customers as a full-fledged sales engineer.

Another significant tradition was the mobility pattern. Promotion came almost entirely from within; high-level management jobs at apparatus sales headquarters were filled with apparatus sales people; even within regions promotion was largely from within the region. The result was very little change in the social system relative to the function itself and in the perceptions by individuals of the meaning of apparatus sales as a social system. Technologies changed and technical knowledge increased, but the structure, management ideology, methods, the life itself were very much the same in apparatus sales from one generation to the next.

When decentralization brought drastic changes in the product department operations of the company, the function of apparatus sales remained essentially the same.

But by the middle 1950s the top executive management in apparatus sales foresaw change being forced on them. Vis-a-vis the new ebullient product department system, with no traditional past but with a high degree of emerging, rational structure and a new organization, new managerial ideology, and new techniques of business operations apparatus sales found its external environment (within the company) rapidly and radically changing. There were two independent but interdependent and interacting social systems: one traditionally oriented with a rich history, proud of the past, and in one sense living in the past but sensing the future moving in and the other born of dynamic change and accorded a high level of status and authority by the chief executive. The stage was set for ideological conflict.

Rationality Moving in on the Traditional

The following events occurred mostly in the period about 1955 to 1958 and are not described in chronological order. By the mid-1950s product department general managers had become the essential core of the entire company's executive operating management. There was a high degree of communality in all the product department general manager positions and a consistency of equated status, but many product department general managers had little or no personal contact with others. Yet in spite of this, common managerial behavior patterns with respect to apparatus sales evolved throughout all the apparatus type product departments to at least some extent. The interaction can be seen in the following statements; the first is from a high-level executive of the apparatus sales division who in 1962 (then recently retired) commented:

> The product departments were insisting on change. Yet they would not hold long enough for an adequate test period. The real way to examine the efficiency of an operation is to develop a theory, set up a model, apply the theory and test it. But the product department would not wait for the test. There were many things during those difficult days that I tried to do to eliminate criticisms of the product departments, but long before what we did could be proven right or wrong, the product departments were insisting on still further change. When Mr. Blank was apparatus sales division general manager, he took too long to make changes and was defensive, and tried to hold apparatus sales exactly as it was. I recognized that we had to make some changes and I attempted to do so. But I learned that it wasn't change that the product departments wanted, it was power and authority over us. The product department management and other executive management of the company were seeking change for the sake of change. Change itself became almost a fetish. It appeared to me that if an organization were in place and doing a good job, but had not made some kind of change during the last couple of years, eyebrows were raised, and it was assumed that the organization was less than completely competent. Change itself seemed to become an objective in the late 1950s.

Changing Structure of a Great Corporation

Contrast this with comments about the apparatus sales division of the mid-1950s made in 1962 by a group executive vice-president of the company:

> The 'old' apparatus sales division was an organization which had been so rooted in its own past that it never changed. This organization never replaced the manager except when incumbents became 65 years old and were required to retire. This simply doesn't make sense. There were management people in the 'old' apparatus sales division who simply could not understand or accept the changes in the present—could not realize that the whole nature of our business was changing—could not adjust themselves to it. Yet, this organization tried to keep itself fixed organizationally, and tried to keep its managerial individuals in their jobs indefinitely. Here is a case where I agree that change for the sake of change was probably a good thing.

The product department managers faced a serious personal dilemma stemming from the organizational dilemma previously discussed. In general, they were given great autonomy in decision making and in return were held highly accountable for results. They were not, however, given control over one critically important function: field sales.

Product department managements adopted several techniques to erode the authority of the apparatus sales department. The control of sales quotas and of the expense budgets of the sales department was taken over. The product managers threatened to appoint their own distribution agencies and underlined their threat by instituting formal studies of the organization required for such a move. That forced apparatus sales to institute their own organization studies, which then exposed them to criticism of their salary and level structures. The product managers showed personal favoritism toward sales personnel they thought shared their views. Often these sales personnel were specialists in a product line and were only loosely allied with the apparatus sales organization. As the culmination of the bid for supremacy the product departments formed an effective coalition and were able to exercise a veto in the selection of apparatus sales management personnel.

Sales Quotas and Expense Budgets

Each year in October the apparatus sales division prepared a forecast of orders for the following calendar year. Each sales engineer submitted to his manager a forecast of orders he expected, by customer and by product line; the reports were consolidated in the sales districts, further consolidated in each of the sales regions (with management adjustments being made at each level), and then aggregated at apparatus sales headquarters, again with adjustments based on market research studies and so forth. Each product department presented a forecast to its own divisional management and made periodic "business reviews" that proposed the potential of sales for the ensuing year. After receiving approval of their forecast, however, the product departments managements had to reconcile them with those of apparatus sales, which involved a negotiating process.

The product departments were legitimately aggressive. Each product department management understandably placed a strong "plus" factor on its new structure and tended to be on the optimistic side in forecasting. On the other hand, apparatus sales forecasting was traditionally conservative. In the negotiating process the product departments generally forced apparatus sales to accept a higher quota than had been submitted. When this quota was allocated to sales regions, the regional management frequently found the sales objectives materially higher than they felt could be attained. The percentage of quota achieved had become an important criterion, and the imposition of what was thought to be an unfairly high quota caused considerable concern for several reasons. Expense allotments were approved on the basis of quotas; if by midyear quotas were falling short of achievement, expense allotments were normally pared back, in some cases drastically affecting salary programs and forcing cutbacks in what apparatus sales management felt were necessary expenditures as investment for the future.

Further, failure to meet sales quotas was frequently cited by product department management as demonstrative of the inadequacy of the present apparatus sales organization, even though the quotas had been imposed by the product departments themselves.

Apparatus sales regional management began to feel that its own executive headquarters was losing its negotiating power with the product department operations.

The total selling expense of the entire apparatus sales organization was allocated to product departments essentially on the basis of time and effort spent on behalf of the various product departments. By the mid-1950s many product departments were objecting severely to these assessments because they were held accountable for profit but had no control over selling expenses—an untenable situation under the concept of decentralization. The product departments, therefore, forced negotiation for expenses as well as for orders. By demanding higher sales quotas and lower expense budgets the product departments succeeded in getting a large measure of control over the money by which the apparatus sales division lived.

Forced Reorganization Studies

Under the concept of decentralization each product department general manager theoretically had the freedom to choose his channels of distribution in the organization of his marketing effort. Although the apparatus sales division had been kept intact as a pooled selling organization, each product department general manager knew that if he wished, he could in fact withdraw from this arrangement and establish his own field selling organization. Ample evidence exists that most of them would have preferred to do this in order to secure complete control over their entire marketing and selling operations. Only the forces of the market prevented this.

Moves on the part of the product department management—some merely threats and others actual formal studies for an independent sales force—became apparent first to top management and then to all members of apparatus sales, causing resentment and, finally, fear and anxiety.

The formal studies by several product departments, and in some cases entire divisions, for setting up their own sales organizations had another effect: apparatus sales began studies of its own organization. One rather extensive study by an outside consulting firm showed that the current apparatus sales organization was highly desired by customers. A number of product department management people unofficially indicated that they felt this report was "rigged."

Other internal studies resulted in several previously described organizational changes. Each change was announced by apparatus sales executive management as "in tune with the times," adjusting the structure to fit the changing internal and external company environments. These self-studies were the beginning of a series of defensive maneuvers on the part of apparatus sales against the increasingly rational product department operations. None of these changes deterred the product departments in their continuing and increasing criticisms.

Attacks on Apparatus Sales Salary and Level Structures

As product departments were organized during the decentralization period and as the respective managerial positions were established, each position was assigned an appropriate "level number," as discussed under the salary administration plan of the company. Most product department general managers, for example, ranged from level 18 to 22, and their marketing managers were in levels 16 to 18. The level structure achieved by apparatus sales was relatively higher than this. Many regional managers, for example, were assigned levels and received compensation as high as some of the general managers of the smaller product departments. Similarly, one managerial step below regional manager, the district sales manager had levels equal to, and in some cases greater than, many of the marketing managers of product departments. This was a bone of contention. Perhaps even more serious was the fact that whereas all jobs, managerial and professional, in the product departments had specific level numbers beyond which the incumbents could not rise unless promoted to another job, the levels assigned to apparatus sales engineers and application engineers were flexible. A sales engineer could retain the same job and yet be progressively increased up to level 14 (which in 1960 carried a compensation of approximately $18,000 a year); professional men in apparatus sales were at a higher level (and had more opportunity to increase this level) than in a product department.

Of course, apparatus sales division management stoutly maintained that to the "executive type" sales engineers jobs could not be specifically pegged; that changing conditions in the marketplace, such as increased competition, changing customer practices, increasing complexity of technology, changed the characteristics of the selling job from year to year; and that by increased creative application and engineering ability a sales engineer in a specific job did have a potential to enlarge that job. Nevertheless, the power of the product departments prevailed, and by about 1959 or 1960 the apparatus sales division was required by executive management to restructure all its levels and completely change its managerial concept of levels. Each job in each of the regions was specifically pegged, that is, assigned value to the company and a specific, unchanging level.

Personal Favoritism

Perhaps more subtle behavior in securing greater control over apparatus sales came from some product department management's calculated favoritism (or conversely, lack of favoritism) for certain apparatus sales management and personnel. Such behavior was especially engaged in by those product departments most vociferous in overt and formal criticisms of apparatus sales. To understand this maneuver one must realize that much of the industrial capital type of business involved very large dollar volume orders; large steam turbines had a selling price of from $6 million to $12 million, and large power transformers sold for $50,000 to $500,000. Further, during the period we are examining—1955–60—prices were extremely competitive. On such large orders prices were usually negotiated; that is, a "normal" price was quoted to a customer, but very often the product department, with its complete control of pricing, extended to the sales engineer a certain leeway to try to secure the business. There were often other special concessions that product departments sometimes made to customers, through apparatus sales, in order to secure business.

But these price negotiations with their "leeway" and other concessions were not allowed "across the board," which would have been tantamount to a general overall lowering of the price structure in the entire industry. Hence, certain jobs were selected that the product department, for one reason or another, wanted very much to have; but they were often chosen on the basis of personal friendship or favoritism to selected apparatus sales management or professional personnel. The product department could use pricing to make certain apparatus sales personnel who they felt were "on the team" "look good" and others "look bad." This is a severe indictment, but there is validating evidence in numerous statements by informants in the company. When asked about organization conflict between product departments and apparatus sales, very specifically with reference to the seeking of power by product department management, a marketing manager of a large product department replied:

> Yes, there was a lot of conflict, in fact it was probably a lot worse than you might suspect. The product department management at that time, and I won't name any names, was certainly out to 'get' apparatus sales. Further, there were certain individuals in apparatus sales who were on the black list and they were particularly shot at. Further, our own departmental sales managers were told in no uncertain terms to approach apparatus sales with a chip on their shoulders. They were specifically told to be arrogant. I know I heard a lot of complaints from some of my friends in apparatus sales about the arrogancy of management—but you really mustn't blame the sales managers of our product departments—this was an edict from top management. It was part of an overall strategy to alienate apparatus sales, to pin it up against the wall, and finally to completely dissolve our division relationships with it.

Product Specialists

The product specialists in each of the apparatus sales regions, highly technically specialized in certain product lines, in a sense functioned as staff people under the administrative direction of the apparatus sales region but representing individual product departments. They were unofficially regarded as sales managers for their specific lines.

In about the middle 1950s the product specialists, assigned to various district managers in the field selling organization, were placed in a new regional organization structure known as "product sales" and directed by a regional product sales manager. In a sense they became regional staff people but with their own suborganization within the regional organization. This was done partly to alleviate some of the criticism by product departments of apparatus

Changing Structure of a Great Corporation

sales; but in one sense it boomeranged because the product departments unofficially began to regard product specialists in the field selling organization as "their own people." The product specialists —in their own "family" in the field selling structure—began to ally themselves conceptually with product departments and to divorce themselves conceptually from apparatus sales—a sort of "Trojan Horse."

That was not difficult to do because during decentralization in the early and even late 1950s many key openings in marketing managerial positions in the product departments were filled by product specialists, making cordial relations with the product departments they represented very important to them, especially to the younger ones.

One former apparatus sales product specialist, now a sales manager in a product department, commented on this process as follows:

> I was definitely aware, when I was a product specialist back in about 1956, that the product departments were not happy with the apparatus sales organization. . . . It didn't take long for me to realize that they regarded us, the specialists, as more or less their own people rather than as apparatus sales people . . . that apparatus sales was behind the times, and that it was just a matter of time before the product departments either took over the entire selling operations themselves, or there would be a drastic reorganization of apparatus sales . . . the product department people were antagonistic about our relatively high job level. . . . As a product specialist we used to attend specialist meetings back at the product department a couple of times a year. These meetings as you know were attended only by product department personnel and the product specialists from the field. There is no doubt that the product department used these meetings as a vehicle to stir up unrest among the product specialists. I admit that I myself began to question the apparatus sales division. Not only of the management specifically, but the system itself.

A regional product sales manager commented as follows, in regard to the product department relations with apparatus sales product specialists:

I know darned well that the product specialists, particularly the young ones, were playing the product department's game. . . . I do not really blame them for this—they were simply being opportunistic. If there is any blame, it is on the product department management, because I believe they were using our product department specialists to gain a foothold into apparatus sales and to enhance their criticism of apparatus sales.

Coalitions

Some of the tactics described above were initiated by separate product department management people, particularly by the product department marketing managers; but then they began to "get together" and coordinate their critical activities—according to informants—particularly exercising veto power.

Until the period 1955–58 apparatus sales held virtually complete authority for the selection of managerial and other key positions within its own structure. In appointing a new district manager the regional manager would select his candidate and ask approval from his own headquarters, which was almost always granted.

The power and high status of the product department marketing management system, however, began to erode this apparatus sales authority beginning about the middle 1950s. Aware of increasing criticism of apparatus sales by product department general management, apparatus sales executive management became acutely sensitive to personal relationships between its own management group at headquarters and in the field and the product department general managers and their marketing managers. Whether apparatus sales executive management was forced to begin submitting recommendations for managerial appointments within its own hierarchy to the product department management or whether it was done simply as a defensive measure is obscure; much evidence, however, indicates that beginning about the middle 1950s apparatus sales top management began to abdicate its authority on managerial appointments. Whenever a new regional manager, or even district managers and certain key sales engineers, was named, a list of candidates was submitted to relevant product department management for comments. For some time, even as late as 1959, apparatus

Changing Structure of a Great Corporation

sales executive management denied that the product departments had any direct influence on the selection of personnel within the apparatus sales organization and said they were merely being asked for advice. However, one high level apparatus sales executive flatly told this author:

> The reason that Mr. Blank did not get the position of ———— was that three important products departments blackballed him.

And here is a comment from a product department general manager.

> I think probably our dissatisfaction with apparatus sales started before we had any degree of say-so about apparatus sales personnel. But when apparatus sales finally did contemplate some degree of management specialization, we did have the opportunity to indicate our feelings about candidates for district sales manager positions. We would receive from apparatus sales headquarters a list of men being considered for sales positions in which we had interest, and we gave our comments on each.

When asked if this meant that he had the right to veto these candidates and a right to make additional suggestions for other candidates, this same product department general manager replied:

> The answer is yes to both questions, although in some cases it was done somewhat informally. But, yes, I would say we had a degree of power of selection of people in apparatus sales.

Another marketing manager of a product department stated:

> Well, I would say that if apparatus sales wanted to appoint a new regional manager or district manager, the product departments of our division would have a chance to look over a list of suggested names for this position as submitted to us by apparatus sales headquarters. If there was an apparatus sales individual on this list whom the product department general manager or his marketing manager did not like or did not feel was a "member of the team," that guy was dead.

Ample evidence from informants indicates considerable anxiety among apparatus sales personnel; some management embarked upon "programs" of improving personal relationships with various product departments management people; some, with faith in the traditional past, resolutely resisted what they called "politicking" with product department management; others adopted an anxious do-nothing attitude.

Ultimately, as presented in our description of the formal organization change, the proud, traditionally oriented apparatus sales division was reorganized drastically and fragmented into a number of more highly specialized work functions more directly in structural alignment with product department groupings.

CONCLUSIONS

This has been a brief description of the process of change over time in the General Electric Company along several structural dimensions and of changes in executive philosophy, in perceptions of, and attitudes to, managerial positions, in the web of symbols surrounding managerial life, and in certain managerial behavioral patterns. It has described how this great company, born of technology, continually creating new technology, and feeding on the very technology it created, grew in every respect—in sales, number of employees, physical size, geographical space, diversity of product lines, and diversity of markets. The company was able to generate and absorb new technologies with a relatively unchanging formal organization structure for nearly sixty years, but as its centralized and vertical hierarchies proliferated in depth and breadth, it was perceived to be becoming inefficient. Formal organization change was devised by company executives, in the form of decentralization, in order for the company to continue its growth and expansion through its continuing creation and absorption of new technology.

What is the meaning of all this, and what generalizations can we draw? Although it is dangerous to project from a single case study, we suggest that the following general observations can be made of the General Electric story and may be found in other large-scale organizations as new technology impinges upon them and as they

Changing Structure of a Great Corporation

grow and expand as the result of their use of the new technology.

1. *As new technology is created or absorbed, the corporation will initially accommodate it within its existing structure.* Certainly the General Electric case shows this to be true for the first thirty years of its growth. Even in the fortieth year of its life and with the addition of new products in the appliance field the basic organization structure of the company was anatomically unchanged.

2. *Continuing accommodation of new technology leads to increasing complexity of technical process, which leads in turn to physical growth in plant and people, and ultimately to spatial expansion geographically.* This is clearly shown in Charts 2 and 3.

3. *As new technology is adopted and as new processes and strategic programs are developed, they can be "tacked on" existing structure.* Chart 1 and the description of the organization change show that the vertical functional hierarchies of General Electric did adjust to such new technology and programs and grew in depth and breadth, hierarchically.

4. *Strategic programs to exploit the new technology (e.g. market-action programs) will also initially be accommodated within the existing structure.* The tremendous growth in technology both within the industry and within its customer industries from 1892 to the late 1950s was accommodated by the sales hierarchy of General Electric with little change in basic organizational structure and little change in management philosophy and ideology.

5. *As the hierarchical growth increases, coordination between work functions of the existing structure becomes more complex and more difficult.* As early as the late 1920s General Electric executives were voicing concern about the lack of adequate coordination as the work centers were becoming farther away organizationally and spatially from the coordinating executives.

6. *The hierarchical work functions will continue up to some point to adopt new technology but in a way unique to themselves.* The new technology is adopted, but it is also shaped and adapted by the work functions to their traditionally learned social organizations. There is no evidence of change in either the formal organization structure or the basic social structure of General Electric during its first thirty years or so. In the Swope era, however, in the 1920s, the company began to be something else as a social system. We hypothesize that this resulted from new technology interacting with

the traditions of the social system and acting, therefore, as an input of social system change. However, the more traditionally oriented the beliefs, the more commonly shared "the meanings" in the social organization; and the stronger the valence of these beliefs and meanings, the less readily will the social organization adjust to new technology, or accommodate new technology after some point. After the organization change the newly formed and rationally oriented product departments adapted readily to structural change, both formal organization structure and social structure. On the other hand, the traditionally oriented apparatus sales division, with strong traditions, rituals, and customs, tenaciously held on to these traditions and customs and resisted change.

7. *Changes in formal organization structure do not occur in isolation.* In the process of change of formal structure within General Electric many other social structure variables were changed, some intentionally and some unintentionally. "Old" ways of doing things changed; the symbolic meaning of various ritualistic and ceremonial processes changed. For almost a decade after 1950 all social structure elements of the company were in a process of mutual adjustment in seeking a new equilibrium.

8. *The more drastic and more rational an imposed organization structure change, the more readily will the other elements of the system adjust their social relations and modes of behavior.* This was clearly evident in the case of the product department operations. Here was an organization change imposed by executive order, with a new status system, a new expectation-sanction system, and highly rational and quantitative performance measurements. Product department management people readily adapted to this. Even apparatus sales personnel who transferred to product departments adapted their behavior patterns quite readily.

9. *Conversely, if formal organization structure is not imposed as new technology is absorbed, the resistance to social system change will be greater.* This is evident from the apparatus sales component of the company readily creating and adapting new technology but adjusting these technologies to the existing social organization.

10. *Given the lack of an imposed formal organization change, the stronger the traditional base for social structure and the stronger the symbol systems reinforcing shared sentiments, the greater will be the resistance to social system change.* The appa-

Changing Structure of a Great Corporation

ratus sales division resisted social system change until it was finally literally imposed upon them by executive order.

11. *The stronger the traditions and symbol systems, the greater will be the anxiety and conflict within the social system when its individuals perceive imminent imposed structure change.* This is evident from the expressed reaction of apparatus sales people in the mid-1950s as they perceived efforts from outside their own organization component to effect organization change.

12. *Once structure change is imposed, the stronger the traditions and symbol systems, the greater will be the lag in ultimate adjustment and equilibrium among all elements of the system and the longer and more dysfunctional will be the anxiety, frustration, and conflict.* The apparatus sales division personnel with its deeply rooted traditions and symbol systems experienced considerable anxiety, frustration, and conflict.

13. *Once a new equilibrium has been reached, however, the greater the rational base of the "new" structure, the more readily will all elements of the social system adjust to further change.* This is clear from the *relatively* greater ease of adaptation to the new organization structure by product department personnel as compared with apparatus sales division personnel.

14. *If in the process of social change time-honored symbol systems are threatened, altered, or destroyed, new symbol systems must emerge to keep pace with the social system change, and behavioral adaptation system change will vary directly with the speed of evolution and strength of such new symbols.* As the product departments were formed, individual management people experienced, of course, the deterioration or elimination of time-honored symbol systems from their old work hierarchies. On the other hand, through the management-development programs, the clear and definitive job descriptions, and group charters a new symbolic meaning of management within General Electric was rapidly developed. In the case of the product department changes, therefore, new symbol systems (although rational in character) did evolve rapidly and did assist the behavioral adaptation to change. On the other hand, in the apparatus sales division the time-honored symbol systems were altered, and individuals in that social subsystem did not perceive the emergence of new symbols keeping pace with social system changes rushing in upon them. This further caused a dysfunctional conflict.

CHAPTER SEVEN

Executive Personality

As corporation life grows increasingly complex in its interconnections, duties, and responsibilities, it will require as executives men and women able to provide their own internal autonomous stabilizing forces. Increasing corporate scale and complexity will lead to an increase in the range and variety of products and services, to a lack of geographic identity, and to the abandonment of traditional personal hierarchical controls. There will be an attendant diffusion of authority and the emergence of operating principles that are increasingly rational, abstract, and impersonal.

TOP EXECUTIVE FUNCTION

The demands of business in the past and, of course, in many sectors in the present have brought to the fore men who as executives have found particularly useful their abilities for immediate decision, assertive independence, and empathy with line authority. These men have operated in a company, large or small, organized as a hierarchical authority system in which rules of conduct have been personalized and to some degree have become traditionalized through the life histories and personal successes of known individuals and their symbolic residues in ritual and myth.

Within such personalized hierarchies with regularized, if only approximate, assignments of authority, the man who could resolve administrative predicaments with vigor and dispatch was highly valued. This was particularly true if such "decision-making" could be done within the organizational framework as already established and without disruption of the informal codes of interaction.

This Chapter is by William E. Henry. See Notes on Authors.

Executive Personality

The previous chapter, on the changing structure of General Electric and its executives, provided specific evidence about corporate organization that had been generally treated and quantitatively documented earlier. Here we shall discuss the same problem in terms of the persons who occupy high corporate positions and investigate their personalities.

No organization has ever been entirely a world unto itself operating free of outside influences. Nevertheless, many, particularly smaller companies in the past, have operated as though they were essentially independent units. Many executives in such companies worked in complete independence of influences from outside the company. Their decisions, apparently made up entirely out of their own heads and past experience, took on the character of sheer personal vigor and independent decisiveness. This image, a not entirely untrue one at any point, was nurtured in part by the symbolic figures of the "robber barons," whose extraordinary vigor, assertiveness, and almost willful independence appeared to represent the very model of the corporation executive.

But the task of the executive, conceivably excluding a few extremely independent persons, is more a social event than an individualistic act. The image of the executive "deciding" all day long in a series of quick transactions with subordinates is consonant with the idea of a lonely but powerful individual resolving dilemmas and initiating new events on his own through personal decisiveness and high energy. But the days of very few executives are so ordered. Far more commonly they are days of heavy interaction with a fairly wide range of persons, and only a few of these interactions result in "decisions."

The amount of time executives spend talking is a relevant factor here. Burns [1] reported that four executives in an English factory spent 80 per cent of their time "talking," while Carlson [2] notes twelve top German operating executives who spent 70 per cent of their time talking. In an American factory Ulrich, Booz, and Lawrence [3] estimate that 50 to 60 per cent of a department head's time is spent talking to men other than his immediate subor-

1. T. Burns, "The Direction of Activity and Communication in a Departmental Executive Group," *Human Relations, 8* (1954), 73–97.
2. S. Carlson, *Executive Behavior* (Stockholm, Stromborgs, 1951), p. 27.
3. D. N. Ulrich, D. R. Booz, and P. R. Lawrence, *Management Behavior and Foreman Attitude: A Case Study* (Cambridge, Harvard Graduate School of Business Administration, 1950).

dinates. The other side of this coin is noted by Carlson [4] in his observations on "aloneness." His data show that the average time the executive was by himself was only 14 minutes at a time for any given period—or only 8 minutes if interruptions by visitors and telephones are counted.

Within this framework of high verbal interaction the amount of time that does result in decisions is also low. In an excellent discussion of the studies of actual behavior of executives Dubin [5] summarizes other data from Carlson [6] and from Stogdill and Shartle.[7] Table 1 is presented slightly modified from Dubin.

Table 1. Percentage of Executives' Time Spent in
Areas of Functional Behavior

Area of functional behavior	*470 Navy officers*	*66 wholesale cooperative executives*	*Swedish managing directors, centralized organizations*	*Swedish managing directors, decentralized organizations*
Getting information	18	18	37.9	39.6
Advising and explaining	13	12	15.9	14.6
Making decisions	28	26	14.6	6.3
Giving orders	15	15	13.8	6.8
Others	26	29	17.8	32.7

As Dubin notes, the intriguing thing about these data is the small amount of time actively spent making decisions. It should be noted that the first two categories, Navy officers and wholesale executives, are based on self-reports. Even there only about one-fourth of the executive's time goes into decision making. In the latter two, from different settings but based on observations by others, decision-making time drops to between 6 and 14 per cent. The two sets of data may reflect truly different executive contexts, but it is tempting to suggest, as Dubin does, that there is some tendency toward

4. Carlson, pp. 72–73.
5. R. Dubin, "Business Behavior Behaviorally Viewed," *Social Science Approaches to Business Behavior* (Homewood, Ill., Irwin-Dorsey, 1962) p. 17.
6. Carlson, p. 27.
7. R. M. Stodgill and C. L. Shartle, *Methods in the Study of Administrative Leadership* (Columbus, Bureau of Business Research, Ohio State University, 1955).

inflation of the decision-making time by executives. It hints that the executive himself partakes of the myth of individualistic decision making as the central core of the executive task.

The principal point of these observations is that the executive spends most of his time in activities other than decision making. It is equally notable that the greater number of these nondecision events —advising, giving orders, getting information, explaining—all occur in interaction with others.

The situation in which decisions are made and the circumstances that necessitate them vary with the level of organization. At the higher executive levels one is only occasionally presented with a series of neat, prepackaged dilemmas requiring instant resolution. Far more characteristic is a kind of continual planning over a long period for events a long way off. Norman Martin's studies of business [8] have amply shown the continuous and anticipatory nature of the executive task. At the lower levels, including that of foreman, decision situations were characteristically short; 96 per cent required less than a week. At the highest level only 3 per cent of all decisions required so little time, whereas 35 per cent took over a month and 50 per cent took over a year to complete. At intermediate levels the ratios of short to long are in rough proportion to these extremes—a reduction in short-order decisions and an increase in longer-range planning in proportion to increase in level of organization.

Martin's work calls attention to a series of attributes important to our concern with the person able to function in an expanding and extending corporate complex. Executive decision situations are in themselves extensive; that is, they require focus upon a problem over a long period before a resolving action is determined. Further, such decisions are usually on matters of long-range import in which evidence of the soundness of the decisions is at best well in the future and may be entirely indeterminate. As one goes up the hierarchy, actions resulting in decisions are subject to fewer objective controls and thus involve more individual risk taking. As Martin has shown, a managerial decision is a present commitment to a particular line of action based upon anticipation of the future course of events. These decisions are thus subjective anticipations,

8. N. H. Martin, "Differential Decisions in the Management of an Industrial Plant," *The Journal of Business of the University of Chicago, 29* (1956), 249–60.

and therefore they have a future, seldom an immediate, referent. The executive initiates and modifies actions within a setting highly interactive socially and verbally. The actions taken are commonly long-range ones in which evidence of outcome is indeterminate and in which the evidence upon which initial actions are based contains many highly subjective and ambiguous elements. In such circumstances it becomes more relevant to see the executive as an implementor and a creator of values and aims rather than as a man of immediate firm decisiveness. The verbal and interactive setting in which this occurs is a small social system reflecting in its behavior the goals and values of the broader society of which it is a part as well as the values and common social practices of the subsystems within the company.

The high-level executive act is of the nature of an interactive social event. The personal orientations necessary to its satisfactory completion involve the abilities to sustain uncertainties and ambiguities, to take actions based primarily upon future anticipations, and to accept evidence of success based largely upon approximations to values and aims that in themselves alter with time and with the actions of others in the social interactive system of company and broader society.

THE CHANGING ROLE OF THE EXECUTIVE

As the tasks and organizing principles of business change, so do the demands on the men in charge. And as these demands—and possibilities for individuals—change, different kinds of men come to the fore. The men whose sheer personal vigor and direct ambition could create financial empires out of raw materials were men whose actions were greatly facilitated by a social and business atmosphere of individualistic philosophy and by company organizations based on the personal charisma of functional line authorities. As business has become more related to consumer preferences and to public reactions, men for whom the views of others are personally irrelevant become fewer in high executive positions, and men

Executive Personality

skilled to perceive and to influence the feelings of others are increasingly valued and more frequently promoted.

This volume is itself a record that the business scene is still changing. These changes are leading to an increasingly fluid and mobile society, larger and more complex in its internal nature and related in more, and in more intricate, ways to other social systems. As this occurs, the demands upon individual actors in this scene similarly become more complex, less fixed and predictable, and related in greater proportion to persons and events technically "outside" the corporation but increasingly considered "inside" in the sense of being able to take actions influencing the corporation.

The men who respond to this kind of emerging corporation complexity, who find themselves at home and able to work soundly within it, will be men of special character. In the sections that follow we will try to examine that character, to lay out some of its essential features, and to delineate some of its sources and the routes of its development. It will not be our proposal that these men are born rather than made. Examination of the contemporary operating personality features of some of these men and of some features of their early nonbusiness life suggests that significant modification in personality and character resulted from various late adolescent and early adult experiences. Such experiences include the training, both formal and informal, that occurs during the early adult years in business. Detailed studies of a longitudinal, developmental nature that would permit consideration of the influence of events during these middle years, however, are lacking. Before proceeding to this task we will try to describe those attributes of the emergent corporate society that seem to have relevance for personality and appear to require special personal orientation and abilities.

The Transferability of Person and Loyalty

The expanding complex of corporate structures demands of its executives an ability to see the "locale" of their operation as at least nationwide and, increasingly, as international. This requires not merely the development of an ability to manipulate paper with widely distributed postmarks but also the facility to think and to act in terms only of the business issue and without regard to immediate locus. At the most mundane level it means being at home with plane schedules; knowing where to get a quick cup of coffee on the way to the office in New York, Peoria, Paris, or Manchester; being at ease with the telephone when the operator says it is Istanbul; realizing that shirts really can be properly laundered away from "home"; and developing the same attitude toward going to the airport as toward driving to the office and making the trip with no more fuss and bother.

An equally important aspect of this feeling of easy movement, in a sense its psychic base, is the refusal to develop a personal identity that depends upon a particular place or, to phrase it more positively, to develop a sense of identity and work-purpose independent of residence or specific office. In mundane terms this means being able to consider a transfer, another job, a vacation in a place conveniently located relative to a business itinerary, without a sense of deserting the old places. It means that selling the present residence or moving the furniture is a realistic business matter only, not a matter of sentiment. The "bind" should be to the corporate purpose, not to the present residence. This implies a high sense of involvement in the business objectives, one that gives the individual a fairly full-ranged satisfaction, a sense that when at work one is always where one ought to be—rather than "always traveling" or "away from home" or "never settled down." In this sense one is always "at home" when pursuing the corporate purpose—and one's baggage will follow or, at the higher income levels, be sent on ahead.

Most people develop an identity with their place of origin. Strangers gain some sense of each other by asking, "What's your hometown? Where are you from?" This identity is deeper for the individual than mere regional accents or food preferences. The confidence of knowing who you are stems in some part from knowing that you are from a particular place and from knowing the topography, physical and social, of that place. At the least it can provide some ready-made viewpoints, perhaps an accent, and some topics of conversation that define you for yourself and for others. At the best it can give you a sense of confidence and personal identity that transcends and becomes independent of its source.

Social and occupational mobility within the confines of one's hometown is a good, if extreme, example of facilitation of identity and career through close association between a person and a known setting. The virtue of such a setting resides in the individual's prior knowledge of the pathways to success and the steadily decreasing need of the individual to prove his identity anew. From the individual's viewpoint a great deal is already known about the route to success. Specific figures are present to provide a guiding mythology, and their physical representatives can be seen and touched. The old—or new—mansion of the president of the town's biggest company exists as real and familiar proof that it can be done. The residential topography can be seen and visited. The native knows where the rich folks live and what their houses, cars, wives, and daughters look like. He also knows where they lived before they made it and what kind of cars they drove then and what bars and clubs they frequented.

In this sense it becomes easier to convince oneself and others of your career stage and of your next step when the physical evidence of various career stages is so evident and so abundant. Scrambling over the fence to the president's house as a child makes it easier to believe that you might one day live there and less anxiety-provoking later to walk through the front door as a junior executive. Movement upward within a single company, whether or not always in the same town, has many of these same properties. In such a setting the next steps are known, the necessary loyalties can be calculated, the next moves in the organization easily recognized. And the physical evidences of these are also known—the cars, the manner of dress, the clubs, the offices.

This small town "family" model of career mobility places a great premium on continuity of locus through time. It stresses the maintenance of specific loyalties and the development and rounding out of old associations. Unless the company itself changes at a very rapid rate, it is a model of the slowly modifying individual moving up through a familiar and essentially stable system in which experience in that system, seniority, and the patina of long established ties count mightily.

It is, however, a pattern that tends to bring with it a sense of loyalty and involvement with particular—and, in general, the same— people and places. In this sense one's feelings of stability and continuity tend to reside in the same people and places and to become fixed and bound to these same people and places. When these ties are severed through death or movement grief and loneliness occur, and one's sense of personal continuity suffers.

But for those men increasingly recruited into the higher echelons of the corporate complex such feelings of loss must be transitory and the sense of personal continuity unimpaired. They must be and must remain unbound in any emotional sense that might influence their behavior toward particular places and people. It is conceivable that personal life for the executive in the emergent corporate setting may be more callous, more impersonal. It certainly is if continued association with former friends and the "good old places" is the criterion. But this is not the only source of meaningful ties; nor is "impersonality" coupled with only a minimal degree of sustained personal loyalty to former associates identical with callousness.

Regardless of the possible implications for personal satisfaction, the crucial demand of the emergent corporate setting is for men of sufficient personal detachment to permit them to devote their energies to the corporate task without considering actions based on emotional ties to past associates and former circumstances.

The Increase in Subjective Influences

As business extends itself into broader scenes and as it decentralizes and compartmentalizes many of its functions, the range and complexity of the influences directing executive choice increase. And as the great corporate complexes relate themselves to more and more outside agencies (though not always by choice) and do business with the agencies and industries of other cultures, the active influences on the executive further extend themselves. At one level this is a matter of sheer numbers. More people in more units have more to say about a business already related in more diverse ways to more units, both inside and outside the organization. In this sense the volume of incoming information and stimulation has greatly increased. Although this is perhaps an oversimplification, the production-oriented factory of old did little to deter its top management from the aggressive conquering of more than its share of the market. Simplifying production procedures and costs, elaborating distribution facilities, and arranging the internal mechanics of company personnel fairly well encompassed the duties of top management. And their ideas and plans for those areas could be largely self-initiated and developed.

It was under those circumstances that the purely assertive and demanding executive rose to the top, finding little to interfere with or to modulate his ambition. Two essentially new sources of "outside" ideas and influences complicated the executive's task: the power of the labor unions and of consumer choice. He had more people to listen to; his purely self-initiated ideas and plans became attenuated by ideas initiated elsewhere.

These "outside" influences have long since become integral parts of business, developing their own procedures and codes, their own lobbies inside and outside the company, their own internal subdivisions. They have been joined by others, some broader and more amorphous in aim, such as public relations departments, and some more technical in aim, such as special laboratories and research departments. Each of these units is run by men attempting to be heard. And in one form or another and with varying degrees of interest the executive listens.

Each of these extensions and diversifications has brought not only more voices attempting to influence choice from within the organization but also more voices from outside the company—more voices speaking as though they had a right to influence executive action. In more recent times, and perhaps increasingly in the future, these outside voices represent the broad society. They do not say so much how the executive should run the company in order to maximize immediate business ends but rather how he should conduct himself to maximize the aims of the broader society. In this sense business has become a partner with society, not only in providing products and jobs useful to that society but also as a participant in documenting and maintaining its values and moral judgments.

In contrast to an earlier day, executives are now obliged to listen to more advice from more people. Their prerogative of purely self-initiated choice is reduced. Advice is also more complex in scope. On the one hand there is an increasing number of influences essentially objective and technical in nature, including findings and reports from specialized personnel and from internal and external laboratories and research units. The executive must find some way to cope with these influences and must develop a level of understanding sufficient to permit him to judge their relevance for executive action.

On the other hand there are a number of influences essentially subjective in nature. They are the moral judgments made from within and without about how the company should conduct itself. Is the company *fair* in its dealings with personnel? Is it too *callous* in the dismissal of junior and senior persons? Does it appear *generous* to the communty? Is it *unfair* in its dealings with competition —competitors who must increasingly become colleagues and quasi-partners? Does the company *participate* sufficiently in the community, and does it carry its *share* of the *moral burden* of welfare, urban improvement, education? For the large corporations operating on an international basis these issues are complicated by the necessity of dealing with the equally subjective judgments of men and organizations from cultures whose basic values and ways of conducting themselves differ considerably from ours. As the executive moves up in the organization, more and more of the influences bearing upon him will be of the subjective and evaluative sort.

Organizational Sensitivity

Men in large organizations have connections with, and in various ways are under pressure from, a goodly number of other persons. To some degree these pressures are from peers and coequals in the system. They tend to be pressures for conformity and apply both to the work scene and to off-work living. This is a kind of self-protective system, assuring in some degree that competitive peers are held to some common standards. It provides the mechanism for much of the dependence on organization that William H. Whyte has so succinctly documented.[9]

The advantage of such peer dependence is, of course, that it enables the newcomer to learn the system fairly easily and provides him with many ready-made solutions to common problems. The hazard to the potentially mobile man is that once he learns the system, he begins to live it. Once he does, he becomes one of the

9. W. H. Whyte, *The Organization Man* (New York, Simon & Schuster, 1956).

echelon of competent but indistinguishable men who move up to a degree more related to the general expansion of the business than to any individual merit or ambition. These are certainly the "organization men" of whom Whyte speaks.

To some degree the pressures in organization are provided by superiors. They can be of two kinds—pressures for work performance and pressures for attitudinal conformity. Undoubtedly, at lower levels in the organization and in any individual's first years in organization a recognizable degree of attitudinal sameness and a willingness to respond to work demands are advisable and probably characteristic. For the organization-dependent these two sources of pressures can become the guide lines to personal goals and aims. It makes a great deal of difference whether adherence to these pressures becomes central or whether knowledge of them comes to facilitate personal goals that are not identical with those pressures. The organization-dependent is a man whose sense of direction is provided by these pressures, by his perception of the dominant values of the system, by the observed habits of boss and peer. This does not mean that many of these organization men are not highly competent within this framework, nor that many do not rise to positions of dominance in corporations.

But there is another category of executive, conceivably indistinguishable in the early years, for whom sensitivity to system pressures serves other ends. They are men equally aware of boss and peer but with a strong sense of personal direction, which permits them to utilize system pressures without becoming consumed by them. The organization-sensitive has knowledge of organization pressures and realities and the ability to determine rationally their meaning and relevance. Their relevance for him resides in their relation to the pursuit of his own work goals. While their work goals will, as with the organization-dependent, tend to bear close relation to the goals of the company, they will always be distinguishable in the mind of this latter man.

In this sense the organization-sensitive man is less bound to the particular company, less personally tied to specific colleagues and superiors, more "movable" in that his awareness of organization provides him with knowledge helpful in refining his own goals and in calculating the next steps dictated by these personal goals. In contrast to the organization-dependent, this knowledge does not bind him further to the particular setting in which the knowledge was acquired.

The awareness of the organization-dependent is both more personal and less precise than that of the organization-sensitive. The former characteristically bases his perception of the system on personal relations—to boss and peer—and sees personal attributes and beliefs as highly important, whether they are about the protocol of personal dress or the purported intentions of government or a rival company. The crucial factor lies in the fact that some person has the relevant belief. In this context this man's perception of the system may be gross and imprecise, since in large part his beliefs are already an amalgamation of the beliefs of others. His interest is thus not a basic curiosity about all aspects of his personal and impersonal environment but a highly selective affinity for those personally communicated facts or attitudes that he prejudges to be conducive to his own peace of mind and normal progress in the company.

Another area in which these two kinds of men are in contrast—in part for the reasons suggested above—is in the realm of what Stanley Stark [10] has called creative temporal foresight. The essence of this attribute is "that intellectual activity which underlies the aborting of accessible hostile possibilities, the defense against those inaccessible—and, perhaps most important, the creation of a friendly future." In more mundane terms, this may reside in the creation of new alternatives, as pointed out by M. H. Jones. In discussing the inadequacy of merely reviewing the given, Jones notes that: [11]

> No middle level executive can expect to maintain his leadership and carry his part of the organization forward if he makes a practice of choosing between the alternatives offered for his consideration. The boss' job is to conceive better alternatives than those a subordinate originates . . . A good *chief* executive is also constantly called upon to create new alternatives.

10. S. Stark, *Executive Foresight: Definitions, Illustrations, Importance* (University of Illinois Bulletin, Institute of Labor and Industrial Relations, Reprint Series No. 96), p. 43.
11. M. H. Jones, *Executive Decision Making* (Homewood, Ill., Richard D. Irwin, Inc., 1957), quoted in Stark, n. 10, p. 43.

Executive Personality

The expanding organization, dealing with an extended network of relations to business, the consumer, government, and other agents of society, is in need of new alternatives. The men who can choose soundly between existing alternatives are probably less well represented among the men who will move to the top of the emergent corporation complex—though this very ability will make them valuable and assure them positions of merit. The men whose complex perceptions of the organization and of its extended environments enable them to imagine new futures and lead them to propose new routes are crucial to these extended complexes.

Important differences in these attributes may perhaps be found upon examination of executives in equally large-scale governmental organizations and of executives who have entered private entrepreneurship, whether by themselves or in combination with one or two colleagues. For the former another factor of organizational demand may alter the character of men desired and promoted. This is an almost philosophical element of social good and purpose, which forms the overall rationale of government organization and to which most government executives would subscribe, implicitly or explicitly. This setting is perhaps no less interactive than private business organizations, but is one in which the demands of cooperation and interdependence may be greater. In such a system the recognizable efforts at personal ambition and power must be attenuated, "cloaked as simple extensions of policy," as Warner et al. note in their study of federal executives.[12]

The private entrepreneur, in contrast, enters into a system in which a private and personal ambition may serve as the principal philosophical rationale and in which no prior organization exists.[13] He invents one to the end of productive business, but it is seldom one to which he himself must make major adjustments. Organizational dependence can perhaps develop more readily in the federal system, but organizational sensitiveness will be of equal value to the mobile man in either.

12. W. L. Warner, Paul P. Van Riper, Norman H. Martin, and Orvis F. Collins, *The American Federal Executive* (New Haven, Yale University Press, 1963).

13. Orvis F. Collins and David G. Moore, *The Enterprising Man* (East Lansing, Michigan State University Business Studies, Bureau of Business and Economic Research, Graduate School of Business Administration, 1964).

The Extension of Horizontal Relations

As businesses decentralize and as they deal increasingly with units not in direct subsidiary relations to them, it seems probable that more activities crucial to business conduct will take place among organization equals. Dealings with "opposite numbers," with peers, will become increasingly common and, further, will be more apt to result in direct action influencing the organizations represented. Melman's study [14] of the English automobile factory has already shown that with decentralization top management deals more with external problems of the business—with sales, with distribution and consumers, with public relations. Janowitz and Delaney [15] have shown that public agencies also spend an increased proportion of time in public relations and in maintaining contacts with other agencies. The men they deal with will most likely be men of comparable levels, "relieved" of some of their internal duties to the same end—maintenance of relations with the extended business environment. Some of these men will be purely messengers with no authority and from whom no crucial action is expected. Some will truly be emissaries, intended to further certain interests, to gather information of a vital nature, to do business in the usual sense.

The import of this for the person in these positions is the demand it makes upon him to deal with a peer, a colleague, a coequal about matters he usually deals with only with a superior or a subordinate. In the usual hierarchical line-authority system one learns how to manage—in effect, to take orders from a boss and give them to a subordinate—without losing dignity in either circumstance. One also learns how to influence the boss without antagonizing him and how to take "suggestions" from a subordinate without losing authority. These are ways of relating learned from the start of a business career, perhaps beginning on the groundwork of the concepts of authority learned in the family. But all these relationships have an essentially hierarchical principle as their base, perhaps even

---

14. S. Melman, *Decision Making and Productivity* (Oxford, Basil Blackwell, 1958).
15. M. R. Janowitz and W. Delaney, "The Bureaucrat and the Public: A Study of Informational Perspectives," *Administrative Science Quarterly,* 2 (1957), 141–62.

including deliberate and possibly overelaborate abandonment to the end of togetherness in "teamwork." The commonly noted peer relations in industry are generally managed with some such disguise. Their objective, genuine enough, is the joining of efforts or the pooling of information to some common end. They also frequently function as a training ground for nontogetherness, as a legitimate scene on which to best your colleagues as a way of bringing to the fore your genuinely competitive and individualistic properties. As such, of course, they are not peer events but ways in which to show others which of you is least equal. This may be in part because in the final analysis and in the day-to-day reckoning only one boss judges all of you. And, in principle, the boss is looking for the one who emerges victorious.

In systematic dealings between organization-equal (and commonly age-equal) peers from distinct settings, the rules are different and the goals are different. The effectiveness of each is being judged by different judges—the superiors of each in his own company or agency. In such contexts one loses the advantage of the protective screen of teamwork and gains less from the direct and personal competitiveness. In this context the peer is only so by accident, so to speak, by having the same stature at home, by being the same age. Each loses the ritualistic advantage of being either the superior or the subordinate, either the buyer or the seller.

We are, of course, accustomed to extensive peer relations in the same company teamwork sense mentioned just above and in the joint life-style sense of Whyte's discussion of Park Forest. But in the latter the emphasis is much less directly on work, and in the former the aims and goals are, if not identical, at least closely related. The peer dealings of the corporate complexes we are discussing here partake of a different character. They involve a dealing between equals from different settings, each with the goals of his company (or agency or bureau) in the foreground. They probably also partake of the quality of occasional relations. They are thus not the sustained clique-group relations in which the ground rules are worked out by frequent contact and experience. In this sense the executive must learn a method of relating to a new group of people in a manner that sustains the essentially equal nature of contact while still forwarding a set of goals recognizably different from those of the other. In this venture the more firmly in mind the executive holds his work-goals, the better; the less he is inclined to want to sustain a personal, as opposed to a work, tie, the better; and the easier it is for him to break and to easily reestablish these equalitarian ties, the better.

Personal Autonomy

The complex corporations in an open status system in a fluid society present their leaders with many problems not characteristic of the business lives of their fathers. While businessmen in the past developed many massive structures, they were commonly coherent, closely integrated, and tightly controlled. In form and principle they were strictly hierarchical in organization, with subordinate subsystems carefully limited in authority and closely checked by higher echelons. In these comparatively firmly structured organizations the logics of doing business were oriented primarily to issues of production and to the hard-headed tasks of making products available for sale at maximum profit. While this has never become an easy task, its background rationale was a comparatively simple one in terms of the kinds of factors that had to be considered and in terms of the success that could be achieved by sheer aggressive energy.

That same vigorous energy is undoubtedly still a vital factor in success at present, but the operating rationale has changed its nature. It may not be true that the executive task is now a harder one, but certainly the men who now find the task possible and rewarding are different kinds of men. They are different centrally in their ability to sustain the demands of contemporary corporate life through the development of a guiding set of abstractions—a new rationale integrating the heterogeneity of persons, issues, goals, and settings that now characterize corporate business. While the ultimate rationale may still be that of making a profit, the routes to that goal are many and devious and bear only the most indirect apparent relation to it. As the executive deals daily with this heterogeneity of factors, subjective in their nature and ambiguous in their meaning for profit, he must develop some set of principles to guide the choices he makes and the actions he initiates. To do this a man must be able to envision the possibilities and to resolve the dilemma of alternatives by personal choice.

Executive Personality

This means that he must have personal autonomy to a very considerable degree. The self-governing property is necessary for a man who is to provide direction and a consistent vigor toward business profit consistent with public policies and societal pressures. Autonomy is a personal attribute, coming from within the personality. As appropriate to the business scene or, in fact, any responsible adult venture, the self-determined choices of the autonomous men are related to, and broadly consistent with, the values and goals of the business community and of the broader society relevant to it. It involves both a practical and a moral component: the ability to determine the right and the wrong course and the courage to take action that is more commonly right than wrong—as judged by future events. It is not a subservience to pressures. It is a recognition of realities, influence, and pressure, a discrimination among pressures, and the decisiveness to choose.

It is thus our general proposition that the business scene of many sectors now and of many more sectors in the near future is of such a nature that men of particular character and abilities will be needed to manage their affairs. The crucial features of these structures will be their fluid and changing nature, their diffusion of authority and horizontality of interrelations, and their operation in a cultural environment of great heterogeneity of purpose. In addition, though perhaps not so marked a change from the past, they will demand great devotion and expenditure of energy.

The men who can meet these challenges will be men of personal detachment for whom the objectives of the complex business world will take priority over personal lives and family; they will be men with organizational sensitivity, able to sense a wide range of complex pressures and influences; they will be men of rational discrimination, able to give meaning to these pressures and to selectively utilize these judgments in pursuit of business goals. Above all, they will be men of high personal autonomy, able to withstand and ignore pressures when they so desire and able to choose for themselves the direction their business lives will take.

This type of man will be most prominent among the leaders of major corporate complexes, and his movement up from lower positions will be rapid to the extent that these dispositions show up early. Conversely, less frequent in the higher echelons will be men of less personal detachment, more dependent upon than sensitive to organizational pressures, and less able to act autonomously in complex and fluid circumstance. It also seems probable that in spite of their undoubted ability to learn from experience in their early business careers they will be men of a basic personality structure and a personal character that peculiarly suits them for this extraordinary way of life.

In the following section we will describe such limited evidence as exists on their personality structure and in so doing will present additional facets of the lives of men who appear to be or to be becoming executives of this character.

THE PERSONALITY OF THE EXECUTIVE

It seems clear that executive positions of this character require a great deal of the men who occupy them. While executive compensation has become practically an art in its own right, it is apparent that sheer monetary reward, in whatever manner received, is not sufficient to account for the long hours, the utter dedication, and the intense involvement of high-level executives in their careers. They are at one and the same time both intensely interested in their jobs and trapped by them. They complain mightily of the job demands that result in such long hours, but, in the final analysis, it is most commonly their own decisions that structure their work lives in this manner. They deeply regret that they have so little time for their family and friends, but they pay little attention to them when they do see them and leave again for work, in body or in spirit, at the faintest call of the office muse. They would love a few moments of peace and quiet, but they install radio-phones in their limousines, tell their secretaries and telephone answering services where they may be reached, and manage to play their golf or bridge or poker only with persons more likely than not to talk business. For many of these men the manicurist or the barber who comes to their office, the favorite waiter who brings their lunch, the chauffeur who keeps their limousine poised as though for atomic retaliation are among the few nonbusiness contacts they have for prolonged periods. It is little wonder that these persons become cherished and their tips so substantial.

We do not intend to suggest that these men have some kind of "make-work" policy or that some other hypothetical persons could accomplish the same in a regular forty-hour week. But executive work has a centrality for their lives that makes such constant occupation with it entirely fitting and proper for them. In a real sense work is the executive's life, and nonwork events are divisive and disruptive. They work in this fashion, they finish conversations on their limousine radio-phones on the way to a business lunch, just because of their very dedication to the complex, diffusely structured, and constantly present nature of their jobs.

For some people a job of this complexity, presenting daily such arrays of heterogeneous stimulation, the majority of which require some kind of response, would be frustrating, anxiety-producing, and ultimately destructive. And certainly some of these men also find it so. But more commonly than not they thrive on it and gain from the experience an ability to handle even more with confidence and dispatch. It will be suggested that the ability to sustain wide ranges of differing stimulation is a personality attribute of some stability, better described by the study of the life histories of these men than by knowledge of their immediate business careers. Evidence of this from studies of executives of this caliber is essentially nonexistent. But some clues to its genesis can be found and will be presented here.

First it is instructive to review a research by Professors Jacob W. Getzels and Philip W. Jackson reported in their book *Creativity and Intelligence*.[16] While initially it may seem somewhat far afield, its relevance will become apparent. Getzels and Jackson studied two groups of adolescents. One group was selected because of its preeminence in tests of intelligence but was below the top 20 per cent of its group in certain measures of creativity to be described shortly. The second group was preeminent in these measures of creativity but was below the top 20 per cent in measures of intelligence. Creativity was defined here as outstanding performance in several specific tests, high scores depending generally upon

16. J. W. Getzels and P. W. Jackson, *Creativity and Intelligence* (New York, John Wiley, 1961), pp. 13–76.

"the number, novelty, and variety of adaptive responses" to these tests. This is a special definition of creativity. It does not imply finished products in the "creative" fields of art, music, poetry, drama but is a cognitive property having to do with heterogeneity and lack of stereotypy in thinking. It also means "adaptive" responses, responses consistent with the stimulus and appropriately responsive to reality. It is just because of properties of this definition that for the moment we suggest some relevance for the executives who must respond with care, with adaptive relevance, to a business stimulation of high "numbers, novelty, and variety."

One of the first findings of interest to us here is that these two groups of students, differing in IQ (by 23 points) and in creativity, are equal in performance as defined by standard tests of achievement administered by the school. Both groups are special ones in the sense that they both exceed by significant amounts the achievement test scores of the school as a whole. But they do not differ from each other in such performance. The creative group, which is of interest here, is not a kooky group of wild-haired, imaginative, but sloppily performing adolescents. This group, able to cope successfully with ideas and concepts of high number and heterogeneity, also produces as well in the standard intellectual tasks required by achievement tests as the high-intelligence group.

The high-intelligence group member is essentially bound to the stimuli presented to him, while the creative group member is stimulus-free and has a self-determined perspective upon that stimulation. This is particularly true in test situations such as telling stories to pictures or making up pictures illustrating titles where the stimulation is notably ambiguous and subjective in nature. In such situations, as Getzels and Jackson say: [17]

> the high creatives tend to free themselves from the stimulus, using it largely as a point of departure for self-expression. The high IQ's tend to focus on the stimulus, using it as an invariant for communication. For the high IQ, the issue is essentially one of conserving what others give to him. . . . For the high creative, the issue is essentially one of constructing what he wants to give. [The stories] of the high creativity adolescents . . . seem more expressive of impulses from within. . . .

17. Getzels and Jackson, p. 42.

Executive Personality

> The high creativity adolescent has a more playful—or if you will, more experimental—attitude toward conventional ideas, objects, and qualities. *Rather than dealing only in predetermined categories, as the high IQ adolescent is likely to do, he tends to use categories that he himself originates* [italics added].

In this summary lie several of the abilities apparently crucial to confident performance in the emergent corporate complex—seeing stimulation but not being bound by it, an experimental attitude toward conventional explanations, an abstract guiding principle that permits one to decide what to do, and the ability to invent new categories to fit new circumstances.

We have, of course, no anticipation that the creative group will all become executives; the probabilities are that some of each group will. What is important for us is that a mental orientation, a cognitive style similar to what we proposed for the corporate executive, is identifiable as early as adolescence and even at that time distinguishes its holder from his associates. What seems probable—but this can be only a guess—is that the high creative who becomes an executive will at that later time conduct his business affairs in a manner similar to that in which he now conducts his school affairs. If so, he will differ notably from his high-IQ colleague, whose present style should predispose him to executive actions suggestive of the conventional explanations, predetermined categories, and flight from ambiguity and heterogeneity.

To trace backwards in time the factors responsible for this particular cognitive style is indeed a difficult task. However, Getzels and Jackson have some material about the parents of these two groups that has relevance for us. It gives some clue to the development of the less conventional mind and to the personal detachment and ease with horizontal-peer relations suggested as necessary for the corporate executive. They discovered, for example, that the mothers of the high-IQ group were much more given to noting unfavorable properties in their children and to making unfavorable comments about the ways the school was influencing the child. What is important in these data, Getzels and Jackson note,[18]

18. Getzels and Jackson, p. 69.

"is the greater 'vigilance' and 'critical' or at least 'less accepting' attitude of the high IQ mothers."

It seems not unreasonable to see in this greater vigilance also a greater tendency to bind the child to the mother, if only through the more constant and more critical attention the mother gives. In this sense the high creatives were less bound, less constantly reminded of the values and standards of the family. It should be remembered that the high-IQ group is notable for its conventionality and for its preference for known accepted standards and problem solutions.

An intriguing observation is also provided by the mothers' comments on the kind of friends they prefer their children to have—the training these two groups have had in horizontal-peer relations. The mothers of the high IQs desired in their children's friends— and presumably so guided their children—qualities and attributes of outward, socially valued conformity. They hoped for "good manners," "good families," "Sunday school children," thus predisposing their children further to conventional, predetermined categories and suggesting to them that they relate to peers in these formal terms. The mothers of the high creatives significantly more frequently preferred personal, internal attributes, such as "sense of values," "interest in something," "openness—not secretiveness." The high creatives were thus encouraged not only to seek relations to peers in terms of the actual personality attributes of those peers but also to consider important a sense of inner values.

When all factors differentiating parents of the two groups are considered, including some not reported here, "the overall impression of the high IQ family is that it is one in which individual divergence is limited and risks minimized, and the overall impression of the high creativity family is that it is one in which individual divergence is permitted and risks accepted." [19]

The subjects studied here are adolescents, not adult executives. Nor are the tasks and tests involved those of executive action. But the state of mind, the style of considering problems, and some of the freedom of action implied in personal detachment are here. We have seen some possible indicators of the social and instructional antecedents of that cognitive style. On the one hand, we see an openness to stimulation, an ability to consider new and less conven-

19. Getzels and Jackson, pp. 75–76.

tional solutions; we see a developing focus on an inner set of values and an awareness of dealing with peers in value terms and not formalistic terms. On the other hand, we see in the parental training the kind of encouragement for confidence necessary for easy movement in a fluid but demanding adult environment.

It can not be concluded that the difference between the two groups is that one is bright (high intelligence) and the other stupid but imaginative (high creative). The group of greater interest here performs equally well in achievement tasks, as already noted, and has an average IQ of 127, well above average and more than adequate for most life tasks.

Certain of the elements of this corporate constellation have been noted in other studies of men in business. In the earlier work of Henry [20] some attributes that appear to distinguish the mobile and successful from the less prominent are relevant. One of the attributes is the degree to which the successful men studied are work-oriented as opposed to symbol-oriented. This refers to a kind of devotion to, and enthusiasm for, work that makes the sheer accomplishment of tasks more rewarding than the prize that may come at the end.

Many men work for the symbolic end—the kind word, the promotion, the medal, the title on the door. The work-oriented executive is hardly immune to these symbolic reflections, nor displeased with them, but they are not the central reward; nor are they major indicators of the next tasks to be undertaken. This focus on work-task is unquestionably a vital element in an attitude that permits one to move rapidly through social space, seeing in it only cues to the next job and ignoring, except as occasional diversions, the resting spots and the symbolic accoutrements of past successes. It is also a central part of the tremendous energy that has been noted by all persons studying successful executives.

These men have also been found to view the authority system around them in an essentially benevolent fashion. In effect, they presume that the men in control are more apt to be sympathetic than not, more apt to be sound guides to action than not. These are not the men who scuffle with authority to convince themselves of their independence. They *are* independent, and they *work* to prove it. Nor are they the men whose assumption of the competence of

20. W. E. Henry, "The Business Executive: A Study in the Psychodynamics of a Social Role," *American Journal of Sociology, 54* (1949).

superiors encourages them to follow slavishly their leads and never to challenge their directives.

Most central to the development of autonomy of action and the personal detachment of easy social movement is the observation that successful executives have largely "left home." This implies that the deep emotional investments in their families, normally established during childhood, have been attenuated and that another set of loyalties has taken their place. This does not imply a disregard or bitter resentment of their parents, but it does mean that the involvement in their wishes and desires as they relate to the main adult decisions has been dissipated. They are thus less intermeshed with the demands of past tradition and can freely take personal action consonant only with their estimates of present circumstances and future probabilities. The fact that they have had a successful major life experience in breaking strong bonds without residual crippling resentment is most likely an important base for their doing so again in adult and less trying circumstances. They can, as Warner has said,[21] "break close ties with others; but they have the emotional capacity, as many able men do not, of maintaining feelings of warmth and closeness while keeping sufficiently detached so that, in the developing sequence of their careers, they can continue to relate themselves to other corporate men." The training the "creative" adolescents had in not having "vigilant" parents and the encouragement they received in setting their own limits and standards are undoubtedly important antecedents of the adult ability to retain some emotional closeness while not being bound by it.

Warner and Abegglen have studied a group of men at the top of current corporation life. In so doing they have distinguished those whose high position placed them in a social status essentially equal to that attained by their parents and those whose final positions were higher than those attained by their fathers. The latter, the mobile men of high corporate position, are probably most like, or in some cases actually are, the emergent corporate executives we are discussing.[22]

21. W. L. Warner and J. Abegglen, *Big Business Leaders in America* (New York, Harper, 1955), p. 52.
22. J. Abegglen, "Personality Correlates of Vertical Mobility" (Ph.D. Dissertation, Committee on Human Development, University of Chicago Library, Chicago, 1956); Warner et al., *The American Federal Executive,*

Executive Personality

Abegglen, in examining intimately the personality differences between these two groups, notes several very important characteristics of the mobile group. First, they are "separated" men. By this he means their avoidance of close emotional ties. Intimacy is shunned. Affect and feeling are not directed at people but "toward more general goals—independence, accurate observation, and effective goal achievement." [23]

Second, in accord with this reduced intimacy in personal contact, these men recall their parents and their childhood home essentially as a place they left. It is not, as with the nonmobile men, a place of fond, nostalgic memories. For the nonmobiles the mother is the central figure in this nostalgic drama, and they recall her with great fondness. The fathers are recalled very positively, especially as models for goals and values.

The mobile men, however, regard their mothers in more neutral terms. While they appear quite aware of the interest their mothers have in them, they leave home with ease and without regret. The father appears to have been a more complex figure, seen in part with some suspicious caution but also seen as an older male who is also a peer. This alliance of peers "is an uneasy and temporary one, however, with no obligations on the part of either person. Thus the mobile man in his relations with males would appear to accept a degree of cooperation and interaction . . . but he is ready at an instant to disengage himself. . . . The syndrome is distinctly consistent with the view that mobility requires accepting favors and aid from other men, while maintaining a readiness to break off the relationship at that point at which it proves unprofitable or a hindrance to one's self." [24]

Third, the contemporary family scene is one of realistic neutrality, but not one of high involvement. They see sexual enthusiasms as potentially distractive from their central work-task.

Fourth, they are self-contained men, confident of their goals and abilities. Abegglen reports: "They are men with considerable energy, capable of concentrating their energies and devoting them to the immediate task." [25]

The tasks of social and occupational mobility are ones for which

23. Abegglen, p. 71.
24. Ibid., pp. 73–74.
25. Ibid., p. 74.

these men are singularly equipped. They can focus and concentrate their energies; they are under some compulsion to break off social relations and move into new ones; they are not distracted by either marked unconventionality or intense investment in family or friends. Abegglen notes that the most common restraining tie for the socially mobile person is to his wife and children, but it is weak.[26]

Another interesting suggestion for this research stems from the comparatively low influence the mobile men's parents appear to have had on their goals and values. Although Abegglen has little directly relevant data, he suggests that, in contrast to the nonmobile men, this group has been singularly influenced in their childhood and early adult years by peers and other nonfamily persons. If this can be documented in other studies, it is an important confirmation of the suggestion that these men have developed special abilities to relate easily to peers and others who are related to them in horizontal as opposed to hierarchical authority relations. This becomes, then, a crucial base for skilled interaction in the fluid and diffuse organizational structure of the emergent corporate complex.

Two other crucial attributes are demonstrated by Abegglen in his quantitative analyses of test data from these two groups of men.[27] He developed a scoring system of Thematic Apperception Test data designed to bring out basic personality drives. He found that these men are not dissimilar in many respects, including their common interest in accomplishment and their ability to attack a problem vigorously, but they do vary significantly in three attributes predicted by him and suggested by our earlier proposals as to the necessary nature of corporate men. These are in the basic personality drives of dominance, autonomy, and exhibitionism. Dominance is defined here in terms of interest in controlling or influencing the environment by directing and guiding the behavior of others. Mobile men are notably higher than nonmobiles in this preoccupation. Autonomy, defined generally earlier, is more precisely seen here as an interest in avoiding the dominance of others, in being independent and free, in being unattached. In this the mobile men are notably high. Exhibitionism, for Abegglen's purposes here, sometimes includes a kind of childish desire to be seen and praised

26. Ibid., p. 75.
27. Ibid., pp. 77–99.

but centrally involves the desire for recognition and for personal satisfaction from accomplishment.

Of considerable importance is not only the fact that the mobile men are high on this last attribute but also the fact that the rewards and recognition are not sought from specific particularized figures (parents, bosses, wife, friends) but from impersonal and nonimmediate sources. As Abegglen notes,[28] this finding supports the view that an "internalized audience, distant and non-personal, provides a major source of satisfaction in the goal-oriented efforts of the mobile men." This would appear to be the basis of the strong need for some internal abstract guiding principles earlier suggested —an abstract "audience" independent of specific settings and persons.

SATISFACTIONS OF THE EXECUTIVE

The corporate executive in the emergent complex of fluid and diffuse structure is not necessarily a man on the run. Nor is he necessarily a happy man. He is unquestionably going places and in that process builds for himself few stable resources in personal affect or in interpersonal relations that will sustain him in nonwork periods or in retirement. But his relevant audience is an internal one, not in contemplative fantasy but in the personal satisfaction gained from successful work. This satisfaction does not hinge upon the specific approval of particular symbolic figures. Personal autonomy and the high energy and discriminatory power to gear it to reality are precious possessions. They may also be sufficient to sustain themselves and their possessor during crucial periods of nonaction. In this may lie an important key to the degree of total life satisfaction such a man possesses. His style is based on movement; his guide line is essentially internal. The hazard resides in whether during reverses or during retirement the active movement remains a necessity or whether the internal audience takes in sufficient body and

28. Ibid., p. 95.

richness to provide a convincing rationale. I have commented elsewhere [29] on the fear of failure not uncommonly experienced by obviously successful men during the latter parts of their careers. It stems, I believe, from the fact that as ceilings are reached in the industrial scene, the evidence of progress becomes less apparent. Unless a man can develop a convincing inner rationale at this point, anxiety mounts.

The corporate man we are discussing here is obviously from a subsample of the general executive population. He differs from the general group most probably in the very attributes that we have suggested make him successful—personal detachment, autonomy, sensitivity to systems, and discriminatory power. An accompaniment of personal detachment is indeed the absence of need for personal involvement of a particular and sustained nature. The assumption might be made that a substantial sense of personal worth can be obtained from the less intense, less inclusive, and less sustained interpersonal relations that this man does have. In that case we need not see his detachment as potentially distressful once the engaging hurly-burly of active corporate movement recedes.

It is probably also important that active hostility plays no central role in this man's life. The return of guilt during periods of inaction can be distressful, especially if there are no compensating positive distractions. But as Warner and Abegglen note, there is little evidence to sustain the myth of vicious hostile attacks on personal enemies among this level of executives. As they report, "these are not men who are distracted into personal duels, for they do not allow themselves to become so involved with others. At the same time, they are not men who know guilt. The distractions of consideration for others, of weighing the potential damage to others of a contemplated move, do not enter into their calculation." [30]

As the men review their lives with the aid of reminiscences, guilt does not arise to haunt them nor doubt to shatter their confidence. It might further be imagined that marked personal autonomy, once achieved, would not desert them and would provide the guiding rationale even when the need and opportunity for its exercise has reduced in scope.

Our principal effort here has been to propose what relevance the

29. W. E. Henry, "The Business Executive."
30. Warner, Van Riper, Martin, and Collins, p. 82.

changing demands of the corporate environment will have for executives and to suggest the kind of man most likely to find this work setting congenial. The man we envision is an unusual one, and we are not basically concerned with judging him in aspects other than his fitness for corporate life. It is, nevertheless, intriguing to wonder in what manner this life style can be satisfactory and in terms of what general model it is appropriate to consider this question. But it is certainly clear that the model of the home- and family-based man is not appropriate. By this we mean the model in which the principal life satisfactions are gained through a basic intimacy tie to the wife and secondary but crucial meanings for oneself garnered from children and their careers, all of this presuming a comparatively stable and positively cathectic locale. While these men generally have a residence—or several—and do have wives and children, and we presume they love them in a conventional manner, the central meaningful events in their lives do not reside there.

They are in this sense corporate men, not family men. Wives do not take precedence over work goals. Children are not precious objects. Wives must actively subordinate themselves to the husbands' work aims or, at the very least, not interfere with them. The key to an effective partnership, and we use this neutral word intentionally, would in fact be the degree to which the wife actively adopted the corporate goals and skillfully aided the husband in that direction. This makes of the wife a kind of high-class assistant, bound by marriage rather than salary but otherwise facilitating the work goals with the same sense of efficiency the husband would expect of his secretary and other office personnel. The all-embracing demands of corporate life do not permit distractions. The same relation undoubtedly holds for children, especially for the sons. While the father does not expect the same kind of direct aid from his son as from his wife, he probably expects him to keep out of the way. His attitude thus borders on indifference except insofar as the son begins to manifest work skills and interests analagous to those of his father.

There may be some logic in suggesting that this comparatively neutral, as opposed to affect-laden, relation to his family is a source of distress for the executive. But the study of the wives of the business leaders reported by Warner and Abegglen suggests the contrary.

Wives whose relationship to their husbands includes fairly active participation in their goals seem most common among their sample. Less common are the wives who focus almost entirely on their own interests, whether this means strict reliance on home and children or on independent careers of their own. In the modal case the wife's participation is as a hostess to business associates and as a community and philanthropic leader in areas apt to increase the status of the family and advance her husband's interests. This is the most adaptive pattern, the one most apt not only to advance the husband's career but also, by so facilitating his heavily invested interest, to bring the wife into close, if still work-oriented, contact with him. While many women will not care for this role or will not be able to sustain it, it does appear to be the most common one and to produce at least conventionally successful marriages. It may arouse in both partners a sense of dramatic joint venture, and this may well be as sustaining and personally rewarding as marriage based upon mutuality and the intimacy that can spring from a primary focus upon home and family. Given the limited sexual interests of these men—and conceivably of their wives—this form of interaction may indeed be the best base for marriage and may form, in fact, the soundest foundation for the long years after the honeymoon.

But if we presume that his affectively neutral family life actually facilitates certain of his goals while freeing him from some possible distractions, we must also presume that other facets of his work style are in themselves supporting. The corporate executive's ability to remain sensitive to wide ranges of stimulation from his organizational environment probably has an additional important feature. It is enjoyable and produces excitement. We have become prone to think of the happy man as the one whose work is done and whose problems are solved. That model may fit many people. But I doubt that it fits this man or a large number of men and women at the top of their respective professions whose roles are largely those of setting the pace, or inventing the new forms and ideas, or keeping open the channels of thought.

While the executive may differ in some respects from highly creative people in other areas, there are many similarities as well. Among them are probably a common sense of detachment, a highly developed degree of autonomy, and an active preference for the

Executive Personality

complex. MacKinnon[31] has reported on the study of highly creative architects, mathematicians, industrial scientists, artists, and many others. While these groups differ in various ways among themselves, MacKinnon comments that "all creative groups [studied] have shown a clear preference for the complex and asymmetrical, and in general the more creative a person is the stronger the preference . . . it is clear that creative persons are especially disposed to admit complexity and even disorder into their perceptions without being made anxious by the resulting chaos. It is not so much that they like disorder per se, but that they prefer the richness of the disordered to the stark barrenness of the simple."[32]

MacKinnon also comments on the high confidence level of his creative subjects and on their "sense of personal autonomy which was to develop to such a marked degree." He similarly notes a "lack of intense closeness with one or both of the parents" and that there "were not strong emotional ties of either a positive or a negative sort between parent and child, but neither was there the type of relationship that fosters overdependency nor the type that results in severe rejection."[33]

The similarities between the corporate man and the creative professional can be overstated, especially since the corporate man's focus in situations of complex stimulus may be more on resolution than invention. At the same time, the corporate man is obliged to invent new categories and new resolutions and to disregard useless shibboleths. And the creative men MacKinnon is talking about have demonstrated their creativity by solid and publicly recognized products over a period of time.

As with those men, I think it is apparent that the corporate executive manages fluid and diffuse systems with enthusiasm and skill. He does so because he prefers the complex to the simple, and his anxiety is not aroused by it. This preference, plus the autonomy to decide and act when he chooses, produces the confidence with which he goes about his job and makes his wholehearted devotion to it a pleasure and not a sacrifice.

This is in effect the burden of my earlier comment that "the more

31. D. W. MacKinnon, "The Nature and Nurture of Creative Talent," *American Psychologist, 17* (1962), 484–95.
32. MacKinnon, pp. 488–89.
33. MacKinnon, pp. 491–92.

complex the mind, the better the man." [34] And this is also the second major feature of the model by which the life styles of such men must be judged. The one is the personal life of low intimacy and high detachment, and the other is the positive investment in situations of active complexity.

THE IDEALISM AND SENSITIVITY OF THE EXECUTIVE

Whatever may be the degree of happiness achieved by these men or whatever they may find distressfully inadequate about their positions, self-doubt and hesitancy about the importance of their task are not the result. Nor are they necessarily genial heros, furthering the interest of corporate life with no damage to people they pass on the way. One feature of this highly focused, fast-moving existence is that the bumps are not noticed. This stems partly from the very impersonality of the task and partly from the fact that in almost all circumstances particular people are secondary to the work issue. The sensitivity to system earlier discussed should not be mistaken for sympathy or delicacy of feeling. Their awareness of the complex environment exists in terms of its relevance for the forward-moving corporate task. Issues judged irrelevant are forgotten.

The awareness of the environment may be a central dimension distinguishing the independent private entrepreneur, the corporate executive, and the executive in federal (or other bureaucratic) civil service.[35] For the federal executive the surrounding organization is more impelling. It is impelling in that it—meaning the other persons who are part of it and their guide lines in written standards and procedures—sets as part of its goals the maintenance and stabilization of the system itself. While highly skilled and fast-moving executives exist within the federal system, their progress is in part due to the degree to which they move without disturbing the central

34. W. E. Henry, "Age, Conflict, and the Executive," *Business Topics, 9* (East Lansing, Michigan State University, 1961), 15–25.
35. W. H. Whyte, *The Organization Man.*

system. These men are perhaps different from their colleagues in federal service in that they are intimately aware of the system but not impressed by it. Certainly more common, even at the higher ranks, are men whose awareness of the system binds them to it and whose attitudes of deference, caution, and protocol permit them to live comfortably within the system but not to modify or escape it. Within this framework many things of importance are accomplished, but the gains to the individual tend to be identical with benefit to the system and thus phrased in terms of duty and public service. The idealism of the federal man resides in this public service and takes its conditions from gains made within policy.

The idealism of the corporate man, and he has considerable, resides in devotion to tasks accomplished independently of the system or in the contribution of new organizational inventions aimed at facilitating a particular task. There will exist, of course, federal executives whose manner of operation more closely resembles that of the corporate man. They will be more common among the political appointees at high level and perhaps among the many professionals—lawyers, for example—whose future careers are not necessarily bound to federal service.

The private entrepreneur, at the other extreme, is one for whom large structures tend to be oppressive. Moving much closer to the direct work rather than accomplishing work through the manipulation of structure, the private entrepreneur sees even his administrative tasks as more of a craft than an intellectual endeavor. The private entrepreneurs who have developed large corporations either have varied skills or, more likely, have attracted high level subordinates who "administer" the necessary structure, leaving the big boss his independence.

The corporate executive is a special type, spawned on impersonality and hurried into the task of defending his individuality in the diffuse and open competition of nonfamily life. His energy to prove his competence again and again is extreme, and his need to recreate a safe and personalized nest is minimal. Equipped with adequate to high intelligence, his discriminations sharpened by heavy peer interaction and his ability to be dissatisfied with the given and at home with the disorderly, this man finds corporate life congenial and rewarding. The diffusion of authority, the lack of clarity in standards and procedures, and the freedom to imagine new solutions excite him and focus his energies. Undeterred by other than the purely conventional in personal life, he is able without sense of loss to devote his entire life to the executive task. It is on men such as these that the vast and amorphous corporate complexes must rely for their central direction. These men have the vitality necessary to the complexity of the task, the personal detachment vital to rapid movement and independent decision, and, above all, the personal autonomy to act consistently within the framework of the highly varied set of ambiguous environmental influences that characterize corporate life today.

CHAPTER EIGHT

National Associations

The present scene in America exhibits an astonishing number and variety of formal associations. Indeed, they so abound that they may be viewed as a form of social organization perculiarly characteristic of this country. Nothing could be more "natural" to an American than to join an association in the pursuit of interests shared by others; it does not matter whether the comembers be old acquaintances or largely strangers.

The data presented here were gathered through a questionnaire survey of national associations conducted in 1962. A sample of approximately one thousand associations was compiled primarily from Gale's Encyclopedia of American Associations and from several published lists available to the general public. The sampling strategy was shaped by three basic concerns. First, we wished to survey associations active in every social and cultural sphere. Second, we wished to cover the largest associations in each sphere. Third, we wished to include associations, regardless of size, when it seemed likely that they might play an especially important role in any given sphere. There can be little doubt that we achieved our objectives insofar as association size is concerned, measured in terms of members or income. We can only speculate, however, about whether we succeeded in including the really important smaller ones.

The overall response from associations was close to 72.5 per cent—an extraordinarily high percentage of returns for a mailed-questionnaire survey—and this percentage was approximately true for each sphere of activity. The survey yielded usable questionnaires from 793 national associations.

A few remarks are in order concerning our working definition of associations. In the generic sense both business firms and churches

This chapter is by Frank C. Nall II, with assistance of John Jackson. See Notes on Authors.

are true associations; they are not, however, what are conventionally conceived of as "associations" and, indeed, are sociologically different from organizations ordinarily referred to as associations. Business firms oriented to profit making and churches vested with religious authority are the basic organizational units in the respective institutional spheres of the economy and religion. Some organizations, even occasionally carrying the term association in their names, upon closer inspection turn out to be business firms. Moreover, certain kinds of associations, such as consumer cooperatives, are clearly intended to yield direct monetary benefits to their members. Labor unions also represent this type of association.

To qualify for our sample the association had to be a nonprofit organization and nonremunerative to its members in any direct way. In the area of religion we arbitrarily excluded known churches, denominations, and sects as not conforming to our definition of an association. In the political sphere political parties were eliminated. These are the areas in which the greatest difficulty arises.

It should be emphasized that the matter of differentiating associations from the basic organizational units in any sphere is essentially a marginal problem. It arose in relation to only a very small minority of organizations in our sample. Yet it points up that work is needed in organizational research in the study of the transition of simple associations into basic institutional organizations. Such transitions may be found in the historical development of churches, sects, denominations, business firms, labor unions, and political parties.

REQUIREMENTS FOR THE EXISTENCE
OF ASSOCIATIONS

What conditions are necessary for associations to appear? The most important social structural conditions seem to be: (a) a relatively high degree of differentiation and segregation of social relations; (b) a large plurality of "competing" social units; (c) the absence of broadly encompassing and highly diffuse collectivities;

National Associations

(d) the existence of a broad middle class; (e) the absence of a socially powerful, culturally exclusive, and inaccessible elite.

At the cultural level, the most critical conditions appear to be: (a) a relatively unified and standardized culture, widely shared but not universally shared in the same measure; (b) widespread public education and literacy; (c) the absence of values prescribing the ascendancy of any single institution or complex of institutions over all others.

The absence of collectivities is important because when a field is dominated by a single collectivity, the interests differentiated by the division of labor tend to become institutionalized as "administrative" problems of the organization rather than becoming foci for the development of associations. The reason for this lies in the "political" significance the development of such associations would have in terms of the internal management of the organization, especially in terms of the ordering of power.[1] It is this condition that accounts in some part for the relative absence of independent associations in totalitarian societies, such as the Soviet Union.

A broad middle class or its functional equivalent appears to be needed because such a class almost always has the differentiation of interests (especially economic) necessary for associations to develop and yet generally has a strong enough common culture to permit and encourage mutual identification and public interaction. The importance of this common culture is great and derives from the need to overcome the divisiveness inherent in a high differentiation of economic interests. Without a high degree of sharing of value orientations, belief systems, and cathectic interests, the chances of successful organization of stable associations are low. It appears to be more important that the middle class have a common culture than that there be a widespread sharing of culture across class lines. Nonetheless, it is helpful if the class system is not too sharply disjunctive at the point of separation of the elite from the middle class, or the latter will find it difficult to cloak its interest in the sacredness that only the charisma of the elite can provide.

1. Associations of employees of either the labor union type or mutual benefit type are overwhelming. One of the principal exceptions to this is the faculty organization of the modern university. The association of the faculty of a university is a clear case of the institutionalization of the interest of a class of roles as "administrative" concern of the collectivity in which the roles are integrated.

The need for the absence of values prescribing the ascendancy of any single institution or complex of institutions over all others may be inferred from the observation that the greater the cultural pluralism, the more favorable the grounds for the growth of associations appear to be.

At the highest level of generalization we may say that differentiation of social or cultural interests is a fundamental condition for the development of associations. A further condition seems to be the stabilization of these interests. Our own social structure fits these conditions in that it is highly differentiated and contains a proliferation of stabilized interests shared by many people yet not universally shared throughout the society.

ASSOCIATIONS AND DEMOCRACY

Three major themes appear explicitly or implicitly in the writings of social and political theorists on the relation of associations to the political order: the socialization function of associations, their insulating or buffering function, and the significance of their internal structure for the larger society. In addition, it is assumed by all writers that associations have a power function in providing their members with greater strength in the pursuit of interests than that which they would have as individuals acting alone. Among those touching on one or more of these themes are Alexis de Tocqueville, William Kornhauser, Robert Michels, Henry Kariel, and Max Weber.

De Tocqueville [2] believed that a functional relationship existed between the active associational life in this country and its democratic political order. He viewed associations, especially political ones, as an essential means of achieving the legitimate interests of a citizenry because of their latent functions for the formulation and expression of public opinion.

2. Alexis de Tocqueville, *Democracy in America* (New York and London, The Colonial Press, 1900). See especially Chapter XII.

National Associations

William Kornhhauser [3] has contributed an insightful study of the differing relation of "mass" and "pluralist" social structures to the maintenance of democratic political order. In his theory the involvement of a population in multiple group relationships describes a key part of the structure of pluralist society, which stands as the buttress of a stable democratic political order. Associations clearly constitute one primary, if not the only, type of independent group, which figures so centrally in this theory.

The third and final theme of this chapter is the significance of the internal structure of associations for the maintenance of democracy in the larger society—whether groups that support the democratic order of the larger society must themselves be democratically structured.[4]

It is generally assumed that there are thousands of voluntary associations in the United States today, but we can only speculate as to the exact number. Not even an approximately complete compilation of local and state associations exists; their number must greatly exceed 200,000, the majority purely local groups, few linked together by any formal ties, and most short-lived. For national associations there is no complete compilation, but a combination of several sources provides an approximate list of those with any appreciable number of members. We have counted 8,000 national associations but estimate the total to be about 12,000.

This study has grouped the associations according to the interests around which they are organized. The social class character of their membership, as determined primarily by occupational rank, has been examined to see whether our theoretical conceptions are supported by empirical reality and whether associations are largely a phenomenon of the middle classes in the United States.

The kinds of interests of national associations in the United States are patently generated by the differentiation and segregation of social relations in several major institutions. The economic sphere exhibits the highest degrees of differentiation and segrega-

3. William Kornhauser, *The Politics of Mass Society* (Glencoe, Illinois, The Free Press, 1959).
4. Among those who have addressed themselves to this general question are Robert Michels, in his *Political Parties* (Glencoe, Illinois, The Free Press, 1949; first published in 1915), Phillip Selznick, *TVA and the Grass Roots* (Berkeley, University of California Press, 1949), and Alvin Gouldner, *Patterns of Industrial Bureaucracy* (Glencoe, Illinois, The Free Press, 1954).

tion of social roles and activities, and it is there that the greatest number and variety of national associations are organized—around the broadly differentiating structural elements of ownership, management, production, and exchange. They are further differentiated into many structurally distinct subareas, such as agriculture, mining, construction, manufacturing, transportation, communications, utilities, wholesale and retail trade, finance, insurance, real estate, services, and locality interests.

Table 1. Number of National Associations in
Sample by Sphere of Interest

Sphere of interest	*Number*
Religion	30
Sociability	33
Government	39
Recreation	48
Education	81
Science and arts	114
Welfare	115
Economy	333
Total	793

Closely associated with, yet institutionally independent of, the economic sphere are the sciences and arts. National associations are organized around the physical, biological, social, and psychological sciences, engineering and the humanities, and education.

Large numbers of associations are found in the broad sphere of physical and social well being and its subareas—health, social welfare, and public affairs—and in the spheres of recreation and sociability and their subareas—avocations and hobbies, athletic and sedentary games, and fraternal and secret societies, including lodges and college fraternities.

Finally, a variety of national associations—but far fewer in number than those already mentioned—are formed in three institutional spheres: government, the military (obviously of tremendous importance to the society and of great complexity), and religion (not including religious groupings of sects, denominations, and churches). This finding is consistent with the hypothesis that relatively few autonomous associations emerge in a sphere in which the collectivities have diffuse interests.

Labor unions—one of the most important types of associations on the contemporary social scene in America and important in the emergent society—are treated separately in another chapter of this volume. Labor unions are the principal exception to our assertion that associations are a phenomenon of the middle classes.

Table 1 presents the number of national associations of each type on which data were gathered in the present research. The 793 organizations represented in our sample comprise most of the large national associations in the United States in each of the major and subareas of interest. They are the most important national associations, encompassing millions of members and organized around basic social and cultural interests. If associations do function as vehicles supporting a democratic order in the emergent American society, we should be able to discern this in the activities, social composition, and structure of this strategic sample.

SOCIAL CLASS AND ASSOCIATIONS

Social research, whether local or national surveys or studies of individual communities, has revealed that persons of all classes belong to associations in America with the proportion of at least one membership much greater among higher-status than among lower-status persons. Membership and participation in associations are both sharply differentiated by social class.[5] It is as important to

5. For a fairly comprehensive treatment of the subject, see: Wendell Bell and Maryanne T. Force, "Urban Neighborhood Types and Participation in Formal Associations," *American Sociological Review, 21*:1 (1956), 25–34; and "Social Structure and Participation in Different Types of Formal Associations," *Social Forces, 34*:4 (1955–56), 345–50. Floyd Dotson, "Patterns of Voluntary Association Among Urban Working-Class Families," *American Sociological Review, 16*:5 (1951), 687–93. John M. Foskett, "Social Structure and Social Participation," *American Sociological Review, 20*:4 (1955), 431–38. Murray Hausknecht, *The Joiners* (Potowa, New Jersey, Bedminster Press, 1960). Mirra Komarovsky, "A Comparative Study of Voluntary Organizations of Two Suburban Communities," *American Sociological Review,*

know the extent to which associations incorporate members from a few or from all strata as it is to know the extent to which persons in different strata belong to associations. Utilizing broad occupational categories as indices of social class, we examined in some detail the institutional spheres in which memberships in national associations are composed of either a narrow or a broad spectrum of the social classes. The occupational categories used in classifying member-ships, while admittedly very broad, provide a rough means of dis-cerning social-class differences. The original fifteen occupational categories [6] used in gathering the data were collapsed into six: managerial, professional, white-collar, blue-collar, farmers, and students. Table 2 presents the occupational composition of the membership of 688 national associations whose membership con-sists wholly or partly of individuals rather than of business firms, schools, and other organizations. Among the most interesting find-ings is the very high percentage of associations in several institu-tional spheres whose membership is composed exclusively of persons in management and the professions. Only in recreation and sociability is there a low percentage of associations having member-ships composed exclusively of management and professional groups.

The second column in Table 2 shows that only in the sphere of government is there a sizable percentage of associations whose membership is composed of a mixture of managerial, professional, and white-collar workers. The line between managerial and pro-fessional occupations on the one hand and white-collar workers on the other represents a significant status difference, and it is clear

---

27:2 (1962), 83–93. William G. Mather, "Income and Social Participation," *American Sociological Review,* 6:3 (1941), 380–83. John C. Scott, Jr., "Membership and Participation in Voluntary Associations," *American Soci-ological Review, 22*:3 (1957), 315–26. Charles R. Wright and Herbert H. Hyman, "Voluntary Association Memberships of American Adults: Evidence From National Sample Surveys," *American Sociological Review, 23*:3 (1958), 284–94.

6. The original fifteen occupational categories used in gathering data on the occupational composition of the membership are:
Business and Industry—owners and managers of small businesses, owners and managers of large businesses, white-collar (office workers, retail clerks, sales-men, etc.), blue-collar workers, professionals; *Government*—managerial and supervisory, white-collar workers; *Farming*—small farmers, large farmers and farm managers; *Other*—students, housewives, retired persons.

Table 2. Occupational Composition of the Membership of National Associations

Occupational Composition of Membership

Type of association	Managerial Professional	Managerial Professional White-collar	Managerial Professional White-collar Blue-collar Farmers Students	Other occupation combinations	Farmers	White-collar	Students	Number
Religion	22.8%	13.6%	50.0%	4.5%	0.0%	0.0%	9.1%	22
Sociability	7.1	3.6	25.0	0.0	0.0	0.0	64.3	28
Government	57.2	31.4	11.4	0.0	0.0	0.0	0.0	35
Recreation	8.1	16.2	75.7	0.0	0.0	0.0	0.0	37
Education	65.3	2.7	10.7	0.0	0.0	0.0	21.3	75
Science & arts	64.7	16.2	15.2	2.9	1.0	0.0	0.0	105
Welfare	41.2	6.2	43.3	6.2	2.1	0.0	1.0	97
Economy	61.4	7.8	8.9	11.5	7.4	2.6	0.4	269
Total	52.7	10.0	20.8	6.3	3.5	1.0	5.7	668

Figures indicate percentages of organizations within an institutional sphere having memberships composed exclusively of persons in a given occupational category.

from these data that status mixture at this level, while occurring in all institutional spheres in at least a few associations, is definitely infrequent. That the highest frequency of status mixture of this kind should occur in the sphere of government lends support to our earlier statement concerning the inhibitory effects of single large collectivities dominating an institutional sphere.

Only seven national associations in our sample are composed exclusively of white-collar workers, a surprisingly small number in terms of the size of this group in the labor force; all are in the general economic sphere. Farmers are not mixed with other occupational groups except in those associations in which all occupational categories are mixed. Consistent with the findings of other studies, this further justifies the treatment of farmers as an occupational category separate from business owners and managers.

In three institutional spheres—welfare, religion, and recreation —status mixture occurs with high frequency. They are in sharp contrast to the membership characteristics of associations in the economic, educational, science and arts, and governmental spheres.

None of the national associations in our sample reported a membership consisting exclusively of blue-collar workers. Indeed, the only associations reporting blue-collar workers had completely heterogeneous memberships, and they were in the spheres of welfare, religion, recreation, and sociability. Unfortunately, there are no data, from the present study or any other, on the proportion of blue-collar workers in the total membership of those associations having an occupationally heterogeneous membership; it seems highly likely that they do not predominate.

Persons of all classes belong to national associations, but the proportion of at least one membership is much greater among higher-status persons than among those of lower status; the several social classes are represented in the memberships of at least some in each of the major institutional spheres. In a majority of the associations in education, science and arts, the economy, and government the memberships are composed exclusively of persons of high social status. Welfare, religion, recreation, and sociability contain high percentages of status mixtures. They most closely approximate the stereotyped image of associational life in America; it is there that persons from all walks of life frequently share membership in the same association. Yet associations of that type constitute only a small minority of the national associations in the United States today—no more than 50 per cent even in those institutional spheres in which they are found most frequently, i.e. welfare, religion, recreation, and sociability. In general, the membership of the vast majority of national associations is composed of persons of middle-class status and above, while only a small minority include even a mixture of the several social classes. None of the national associations studied had a membership composed exclusively of lower-status persons. These findings strongly support our statement that a broad middle class is a necessary condition for the development of a great proliferation of associations.

EMERGENCE AND GROWTH OF ASSOCIATIONS

The emergence and growth of national associations in the United States has never been systematically studied; consequently, it has not been possible to grasp the dynamics of change in this dimension of the society. It seems to be generally accepted that a more or less continuous and great expansion of the number of associations has occurred. The data now available permit a degree of such analysis, and we can provide here a partial view of the dynamics of growth of national associations in the United States.

If it is true that a progressively greater proliferation of associations may be expected to accompany increasing structural differentiation in a society, we should find an overall increase in the number of national associations in the United States as the society has become structurally more complex. As a total social system the United States has undergone progressively greater structural differentiation since the turn of the century. Our findings show a very marked expansion in the number of associations founded after 1900; Table 3, shows that some 75 per cent of the associations in our sample were founded after that year.

A comparison of the patterns of emergence of associations shows considerable unevenness among the different spheres. While there are significant differences in percentages, a substantial percentage

Table 3. Percentage of National Associations by Date of Founding

Type of association	Founded 1900 or earlier	Founded 1900 to 1920	Founded 1920 to 1940	Founded 1940 or later	Number
Religion	34.6%	38.5%	7.7%	19.2%	26
Sociability	63.6	33.4	3.0	0.0	33
Government	21.6	21.7	35.1	21.6	37
Recreation	23.2	25.6	37.3	13.9	43
Education	25.3	43.0	19.0	12.7	79
Science and arts	28.9	26.2	17.8	27.1	107
Welfare	24.4	33.3	23.4	18.9	111
Economy	18.0	28.0	30.7	23.3	322
Total	24.3	30.2	25.2	20.3	758

National Associations

of associations had emerged in each sphere prior to the turn of the century. In each sphere there are a number of associations that can scarcely be considered new, in the American context, and the origins of a few can be traced to the early years of the nineteenth century and beyond; but there is a marked contrast between the relatively high percentages in some spheres and the relatively low percentages in others. For example, the differences between the spheres of education and welfare, on the one hand, and religion and sociability, on the other, are great.

Government and the economy were already characterized by large-scale, highly differentiated collectivities prior to the turn of the century, but both have undergone tremendous expansion and have become increasingly more differentiated since 1900. The very large percentages of associations appearing in these spheres since then reflect these changes. In general, the same relationship holds for education and welfare. On the other hand, nothing like these dynamic structural changes has occurred in the spheres of religion and sociability since 1900, even though very significant changes have taken place in the former. For example, although church membership in Protestant denominations has increased sharply and the number of local churches has expanded, this expansion has for the most part been fitted into existing organizational structures. The period since 1900 has not witnessed a tremendous increase in the number of denominations, nor has there occurred any very extensive elaboration of new roles within churches, in spite of very significant changes. The typical pattern within the sphere of religion has been the incorporation of new interests into existing associations by creating new departments, divisions, workshops, conferences devoted to these ends. This, of course, has not been entirely the case, but it is characteristic of the dynamics of this institutional sphere.

By 1920 substantially all the sociability associations had been founded, as well as a very large majority of the religious and educational associations. On the other hand, only slightly more than half of the science and arts associations had been founded by 1920, and less than 50 per cent of those in recreation, economy, and government existed. Thus, the growth of national associations had almost ceased in one sphere by 1920 and was nearing its upper limits in two others. In contrast, the growth of associations in those institu-

tional spheres experiencing continued structural change—
especially the sciences, the economy, and government—was in
1920 only about half of what it would be by 1961.

All of the sociability associations in our sample, as well as the
great majority of those in all other institutional spheres, had been
founded by 1940. The growth of associations in the sphere of
science and arts was still great after 1940, as it was in economic
and governmental associations. The changed position of religion
relative to economy and government represents a spurt in the
growth of associations in this sphere. While not shown in the table,
it might be noted that this growth occurred in the decade 1941–50,
when five new Protestant organizations were established.

The growth in membership of national associations is largely impossible to determine. It would be especially interesting to know,
for example, the membership size of all the associations shortly
after their founding and at the beginning of each decade thereafter.
Unfortunately, few national associations have maintained statistical
records. For example, nine religious associations were founded before the turn of the century, but only two could supply statistics on
their membership size in 1910. Of fifty-eight economic associations
founded by 1900, only twelve could supply statistical information
for 1910. The general pattern holds for associations in all other institutional spheres and for all succeeding decades.

It is possible to get some idea of current size of membership of
national associations, and these findings have considerable interest.
It is surprising that so many national associations are fairly small.
Table 4 shows the distribution of associations by size of membership. Almost one-third have fewer than 5,000; almost 50 per cent
have fewer than 10,000 members; and more than two-thirds have
fewer than 25,000. Almost 90 per cent of the associations have
memberships not exceeding 100,000 persons. Moreover, while the
figure of 100,000 is large, it can scarcely be considered large
enough to preclude effective integration of individuals into an
ordered and meaningful social system. Some of the basic professions in this society have associations whose memberships exceeds
this size. But whether one selects the figure of 100,000 or the lower
one of 50,000 as the probable upper limit of "effective" organizational size, the membership of the great majority of national associations in the United States will fall below such a limit.

National Associations

A very small percentage of associations do have large memberships: about 5 per cent exceed 500,000, and some 3 per cent exceed one million. It is highly doubtful, however, that those organizations claiming one million or more members in fact have anything like that number actually participating in the association other than through paying a fee or making a financial contribution. A very few associations, such as the American National Red Cross, do have several hundred thousand volunteers who regularly contribute their time to the association's activities. Those claiming one million or more members can usually be shown to be using either highly inflated figures or an exceedingly broad—and almost meaningless—conception of the term "member."

Table 4. Size of Membership of Those National Associations Having Individual Members, for 1961

Size of membership	Number of associations	Percentage	Cumulative percentage
1,000 to 5,000	177	32.6	
5,000 to 10,000	92	16.8	49.4
10,000 to 25,000	105	19.2	68.6
25,000 to 50,000	65	11.9	80.5
50,000 to 100,000	41	7.5	88.0
100,000 to 500,000	37	6.7	94.7
500,000 to 1,000,000	12	2.2	96.9
More than 1,000,000	17	3.1	100.0
Total	546	100.0	

The size of associations in the United States has often been pointed to as an indication of the increasing "massification" of life in this society. On the whole, our findings do not sustain such an image. Although a small percentage are, indeed, very large, the majority are not so large that even in the absence of local units it would be unreasonable to expect members to develop commitments to the complex of goals and cultural symbols embodied in the organization. We would infer that, as far as size is concerned, the great majority of national associations included in this research fall within the applicable scope of Kornhauser's conceptions of independent groups.

The aggregate total membership of the 547 national associations in this research is almost 160,000,000, an exceedingly large number that approaches a ratio of almost one member per each man, woman, and child, in the United States (see Table 5). However,

Table 5. Size of Membership (Individuals) of National
Associations, for 1961

Type of association	Number of individual members	Number of associations
Welfare	69,634,000	93
Economy	32,718,000	167
Recreation and sociability	19,836,000	66
Education	17,403,000	73
Religion	17,013,000	19
Science and arts	1,120,000	98
Government	745,000	31
Total	158,469,000	547

this figure includes many who are no more than anonymous financial contributors. Note the extraordinarily great number of members claimed by associations in the sphere of welfare.

A majority of the headquarters of national associations in most spheres are concentrated in three cities: New York, Washington, D.C., and Chicago. Only in the spheres of recreation and sociability are fewer than 50 per cent situated in these cities. Table 6 shows

Table 6. Locations of National Headquarters

Type of association	New York %	Washington D.C. %	Chicago %	Other %	Number
Religion	40.0	20.0	10.0	30.0	30
Sociability	6.2	3.0	27.2	63.6	33
Government	5.1	59.0	15.4	20.5	39
Recreation	20.8	8.3	4.2	66.7	48
Education	11.1	32.1	11.1	45.7	81
Science and arts	27.7	27.7	8.9	35.7	112
Welfare	40.9	14.8	17.4	26.9	115
Economy	24.3	24.8	19.8	31.1	334
Total	24.5	24.2	15.7	35.6	792

their percentage distribution among these metropolitan centers. New York and Washington, D.C., each with about 25 per cent, loom as somewhat more important than Chicago. As with other features of the emergent society, these three cities are also the principal focal points for administration of the majority of our national associations.

SIZE AND SOURCES OF INCOME

The size of income of national associations is extremely varied. In 1961, the year of our information, it ranged from the comparatively modest figure of less than $25,000 to more than $1,000,000. Table 7 shows that in the fields of religion, welfare, economy, sociability, and government the percentages of associations with incomes of $25,000 or less are very low and are noticeably larger, yet not high, in recreation and science and arts. Education is the only sphere in which about 20 per cent of the associations fall in the lowest income bracket. Significant percentages of associations in the spheres of education, the sciences and arts, and religion fall in the $25,000–$75,000 income bracket. In contrast, very high percentages of associations in the spheres of religion, economy, and welfare have incomes above $250,000; and high percentages of religious, welfare, and economic associations have incomes of more than $1,000,000. Indeed, there are very large percentages of associations in most spheres with incomes of more than $500,000.

It is obvious that there are great discrepancies in economic strength among the associations within each institutional sphere and between spheres as well. There are at least some associations in each sphere that are financially much more powerful than the rest, especially in religion, welfare, and the economy. However, since there are financially powerful associations in the other spheres as well, the associations covered in this research can scarcely be considered impoverished and without the financial means of promoting in significant measure the interests of their members. Aggregate total income of national associations gives another measure of their

Table 7. Relative Size of Income of National Associations in 1961

Type of association	Low $1,000 to $25,000 %	$25,000 to $75,000 %	$75,000 to $150,000 %	Medium $150,000 to $250,000 %	$250,000 to $500,000 %	High $500,000 to $1,000,000 %	Very high More than $1,000,000 %	Number
Religion	0.0	15.8	10.5	5.3	21.0	10.5	36.9	19
Sociability	0.0	13.6	40.9	13.6	18.3	4.5	9.1	22
Government	6.5	9.6	12.9	25.8	22.6	16.1	6.5	31
Recreation	14.7	11.8	26.5	14.7	5.8	11.8	14.7	34
Education	19.4	28.4	13.4	10.4	10.4	7.6	10.4	67
Science and arts	14.4	16.7	14.4	11.2	13.3	13.3	16.7	90
Welfare	3.2	9.5	8.4	14.7	15.8	15.8	32.6	95
Economy	3.0	9.1	16.6	13.6	21.9	15.4	20.4	265
							Total	623

financial power. Of the associations in our sample, 626, about 79 per cent, reported their 1961 incomes. The total approaches *one billion dollars*. The overwhelming amount of this income was concentrated in associations in the spheres of welfare and the economy. It must be emphasized that the $830,237,000 shown in Table 8 represents only current income for 1961 and does not reflect buildings and land, office equipment, securities, and other capital holdings.

Table 8 shows that $707,320,000 is concentrated in only 135 of the 626 associations reporting 1961 income, that is, less than 22 per cent of the associations account for over 85 per cent of the aggregate income. Moreover, 221 associations had incomes of more than $500,000 each in 1961, an aggregate $763,397,000; or about 35 per cent of the associations account for almost 92 per cent of the aggregate income.

The relative concentration of income in the spheres of welfare and the economy is very great. Thirty-four welfare associations, representing only about 5 per cent of the sample, each had an income of more than $1,000,000 in 1961, an aggregate of $367,456,-000, or 44 per cent of the total income of all associations reporting. Economic associations with incomes exceeding $1,000,000 represent about 9 per cent of the total sample and some 23 per cent of the aggregate income.

National associations vary not only in size of income but also in source of income. While in some spheres the overwhelming majority derive their income exclusively from their members, in others proceeds from sales and services, returns on investments, and appeals to the general public are the principal sources for a majority. The different sources of income have potential ramifications in the vigor with which associations may pursue their interests in the public arena. If we consider an association's autonomy, its potential for undertaking action toward the implementation of its members' interests, as in some part a function of the extent to which it is financially dependent on that membership, then Table 9 provides a good picture of the rank of the several institutional spheres.

Among science and arts, welfare, and religion considerably more than a majority of associations derive part of their incomes from sources other than membership. These are spheres in which most associations lack financial autonomy in the sense of having to de-

Table 8. Income of National Associations in 1961

Type of association	Total dollar income	Number of associations reporting	Total income of associations with income over $500,000	Number of associations reporting	Total income of associations with income over $1,000,000	Number of associations reporting	Number of associations in sample
Religion	$ 48,124,000	19	$ 46,519,000	10	$ 36,597,000	17	30
Sociability	7,244,000	22	4,196,000	3	3,611,000	2	33
Government	11,346,000	31	7,339,000	7	3,500,000	2	39
Recreation	31,103,000	34	28,378,000	9	25,770,000	5	48
Education	42,572,000	67	36,648,000	16	33,150,000	7	81
Science and arts	52,772,000	91	44,255,000	28	46,019,000	9	114
Welfare	385,664,000	96	376,726,000	48	367,456,000	34	115
Economy	251,412,000	266	219,336,000	100	191,217,000	59	333
Total	$830,237,000	626	$763,397,000	221	$707,320,000	135	793

National Associations

pend on transactions with nonmembers. In sharp contrast, in the fields of education, recreation, sociability, and the economy a very large majority of the associations depend exclusively on membership for financial support.

An approximately reverse order of financial autonomy is shown in the third column of Table 9. Large percentages of religious and welfare associations and a substantial percentage of science and arts associations derive their incomes from a great variety of sources, including, especially, the general public. In contrast, only small percentages of associations in other spheres seek funds from

Table 9. Sources of Income of National Associations in 1961

Type of association	Membership only %	Sales, services, investments, and membership %	Solicitation of general public, sales, services, investments, membership, and others %	Number
Religion	31.8	22.8	45.4	22
Sociability	79.1	20.9	...	24
Government	56.3	34.4	9.3	32
Recreation	70.6	14.7	14.7	34
Education	67.1	20.0	12.9	70
Science and arts	41.0	37.4	21.6	83
Welfare	38.6	25.0	36.4	88
Economy	73.0	25.0	2.0	263

the general public. Religion and welfare are spheres in which substantial percentages of associations have very high incomes; large percentages depend on the solicitation of funds from the general public and other sources. The economic sphere, on the other hand, also has a substantial percentage of associations with very high incomes of which almost none is derived from the general public.

This analysis of the sources of income of national associations leads to a further conceptualization of their sociological nature. It shows that there are basically two and possibly three types of associations. First, what might be termed "membership" associations, which derive their incomes exclusively from their members. They occur in all institutional spheres but with notably different frequencies. Second, there are what should probably be termed "public" associations. They may have regular memberships, just as the others do, which assist in financially supporting the organization, but they depend on the general public also for financial support. Finally, a third basic type of association should be distinguished; it derives its income in some measure from its membership but also obtains money from such sources as returns on sales, services, and investments. These associations are involved in processes of economic exchange with some sectors of the public, and their financial solvency is dependent in some measure on such exchange. The basis of their autonomy is somewhat different from that of those dependent only on their members. We shall refer to them as "semi-public" associations, placing emphasis on their dependence on the maintenance of (economic) relations with persons who are not members. Table 9 shows that there are significant percentages of associations of this type in all institutional spheres and that they are most frequent in science and arts and government.

THE GOVERNANCE OF ASSOCIATIONS

The governance of national associations is a complex subject. It is of interest in the present context because of the relationship between associations' governing bodies and the functions associations perform in the larger society. The present analysis is concerned largely with an examination of the sizes of governing bodies, the differing methods of selecting governing body members, and their lengths of tenure.

All governing bodies have in common certain functional responsibilities. They all, for example, have responsibilities in relation to organizational goals. Contrary to the views of one organizational theorist,[7] we urge that an association's goals are of prime importance to the general problem of maintaining its viability as a stable organization. Goals play a salient role in relation to the motivation

7. See Amatai Etzioni, *A Comparative Analysis of Complex Organizations* (Glencoe, Illinois, The Free Press, 1961).

of member-participants and outside facilitating publics. In one sense, the meaning of the organization for members as well as for the public resides in the definitions of organizational goals, and a principal function of governing bodies is to provide substantive definitions of goals through the setting and reiteration of policy. Obviously, policy-setting contributes to the ordering of many other organizational needs, in addition to performing this necessary motivational function. The acquisition and allocation of resources is crucially significant to the maintenance of all organizations and is an area of utmost importance for planning and policy-setting by governing bodies. For most associations the acquisition of resources poses substantially different problems from those faced by economic enterprises organized for the production and sale of goods or services. While some associations derive their incomes principally from sales and services, most are either exclusively dependent on their memberships for financial support or depend on a combination of contributions from the public, returns from sales and services, and membership (see Table 9). Insofar as associations are dependent on the maintenance of a nexus of facilitative relationships with the public, there follow fairly clear implications with respect to the size and composition of the governing body and the character of their goals. The more diverse the public supporting the association, the greater the need for the governing body to reflect this diversity in its membership and its policies. It seems most likely that the size of the governing body will be conditioned by its need to serve a representational function vis-a-vis the supporting public.

Fulfilling a representational function vis-a-vis the general membership is also, of course, a major aspect of the problem of securing internal democracy in associations, and this is associated with the size of the governing body. The more diverse the composition of the membership, the more necessary it is that this diversity be reflected in the governance of the association. Thus the size of the governing body is conditioned by both internal and external considerations having to do with the representation of differentiated interests. (See Table 10 for sizes of governing bodies by institutional spheres.) As stated earlier, however, although a diversity of interests may exist among the membership of associations, they generally cannot be expected to crystallize in the form of stable subgroupings except when based on geographical location. We believe that the size of the governing bodies of national associations is less likely to reflect internal than external representational needs. Nevertheless, size implies diversity, and so we should expect a rough positive relationship between the size of the general membership and the size of the governing body. Table 11 shows this relationship quite clearly.

Table 10. Size of Governing Body of National Associations

Type of association	Number of members of governing body				
	1 to 20 %	20 to 30 %	30 to 50 %	50 or more %	Number
Religion	23.3	10.0	13.3	53.4	30
Sociability	68.8	9.4	9.3	12.5	32
Government	42.1	15.8	15.8	26.3	38
Recreation	41.6	10.4	16.8	31.2	48
Education	69.1	9.9	7.4	13.6	81
Science and arts	56.2	24.1	10.7	9.0	112
Welfare	35.6	17.0	15.2	32.2	112
Economy	32.7	22.0	25.1	20.2	331

The maintenance of facilitative relationships with the public has an important bearing on the size of associations' governing bodies. Those associations dependent exclusively on their membership for financial support are least in need of governing bodies representative of the public. Their governing bodies, therefore, need be only

Table 11. Size of Governing Body by Number of Individual Members

Number of individual members	Size of governing body			
	1 to 20 %	20 to 30 %	30 or more %	Number
1,000 to 7,000	47.5	17.5	35.0	225
7,000 to 50,000	48.0	21.0	31.0	209
50,000 or more	35.2	13.3	51.5	105

large enough to permit the incorporation of some diversity of interests but not so large as to obviate more or less direct participation of members in the general processes of planning and policy setting, i.e. in the processes of governance. It seems likely that there would be no functional necessity for their exceeding fifteen or twenty

National Associations

members unless there are strong, multiple internal representational needs, e.g. state or regional interests. On the other hand, we should expect the size of governing bodies to vary directly with the extent to which associations are dependent on diverse outside publics for financial or other support. Associations dependent on financial support from "the-public-at-large" have the greatest need for representation of outside publics on their governing bodies. They might be expected then to be of considerable size. Table 12 shows that the

Table 12. Size of Governing Body by Source of Income

| Source of income | Size of governing body | | | Number |
	1 to 20 %	20 to 30 %	30 or more %	
Membership only	40.9	19.1	40.0	372
Sales, services, investments, and membership	47.1	18.3	34.6	159
Public fund raising, sales, services, investments, member- ship, and others	26.9	19.5	53.6	82

size of governing bodies is clearly related to their primary source of income. More than 50 per cent of the associations dependent on multiple outside income sources, including public fund raising, have governing bodies of more than thirty members, and only about 27 per cent have governing bodies of twenty or fewer members. Compare this with the distribution of associations deriving their income exclusively from their members and with those dependent on sales and services.

Although functional needs for representation of the public call for increased size of governing bodies, the exigencies of ordered, responsible policy setting demand a limitation of the numbers actively engaged in governance. In associations requiring such outside representation, there is always at least an incipient functional conflict between representational needs and those of ordered, responsible policy setting. To the extent that representational demands from many diverse internal aggregates or subgroups are permitted expression through additions to the governing body, this principle also holds true for associations financially dependent exclusively on their membership. Here, then, is a functional dilemma potentially facing all associations. It is likely to be both common and acute in those dependent on the maintenance of a nexus of facilitative relationships with the public, especially those involving financial dependency of the association on the public. We may assume its presence in a large proportion of associations regardless of sources of income.

The method of selecting the governing body of an association bears directly on the problem of internal democracy and focuses on representation from a different perspective. There are only three basic ways of selecting the governing bodies of completely autonomous associations: election by the general membership, election by representatives of the general membership, or election or appointment by incumbent members of the governing body. Any combination of these basic methods is possible and occurs among at least some associations in most institutional spheres. Certainly direct election by the general membership is the form that most closely embodies the concept of internal representative democracy. Except in associations of comparatively small size, however, direct election by the general membership is not very likely to conform closely to the ideal of knowledgeable participation by the electorate. In large associations selection of the governing body by this method tends to be both cumbersome and unresponsive to the representational needs of the membership. In such instances the crucial decisions are made by the nominating committee.

Election of the governing body by representatives of the general membership, although a less direct form of democratic participation, would seem to have some advantages over the direct election method, especially in the large association. It permits fewer members to participate directly, but it does encourage more knowledgeable participation and more authentically "political" behavior, e.g. bargaining, among the more limited electorate. There is also a higher potential for modifying the power of the nominating committee in this form of selection, particularly when the election takes place during an assemblage of the delegates.

Table 13 shows the percentages of associations in each institutional sphere that select their governing bodies by each of the three basic selection methods. A considerable majority of the science and arts, economic, and governmental associations utilize the method of

Table 13. Methods of Selecting Members of the Governing Body of National Associations

Type of association	Elected by general membership %	Elected by representatives of the general membership %	Elected or appointed by the incumbents %	Combined and other %	Number
Religion	30.0	40.0	10.0	20.0	30
Sociability	18.2	72.7	9.1	...	33
Government	59.0	15.4	10.2	15.4	39
Recreation	47.9	18.7	18.9	14.5	48
Education	40.8	30.9	6.1	22.2	81
Science and arts	63.7	12.4	9.7	14.2	113
Welfare	35.6	31.3	14.8	18.3	115
Economy	65.7	18.1	4.5	11.7	332

direct election by the general membership, and most of the remainder elect by this method or through representatives of the general membership. In contrast, only about one-third of the religious and welfare associations utilize direct election.

Table 14. Length of Term of Governing Body Members

Type of association	One year %	Length of term Two to three years %	Over three years %	Number
Religion	7.2	64.2	28.6	28
Sociability	15.6	53.1	31.3	32
Government	36.8	52.7	10.5	38
Recreation	30.4	49.9	19.7	46
Education	13.1	71.0	15.9	69
Science and arts	16.0	70.8	13.2	106
Welfare	19.4	60.2	20.4	108
Economy	26.6	66.2	7.2	331

Election or appointment of the governing body by incumbent members is farthest, of course, from a conception of representative democracy, and this form occurs among only a small percentage of associations but in all institutional spheres.

Table 15. Presence or Absence of Formal Limitations to the Number of Terms Governing Body Members May Hold Office

Type of association	No limitations %	Definite limitations %	Number
Religion	70.0	30.0	30
Sociability	51.5	48.5	33
Government	71.8	28.2	39
Recreation	70.8	29.2	48
Education	71.4	28.6	77
Science and arts	61.1	38.9	108
Welfare	62.8	37.2	113
Economy	67.4	32.6	328

The oligarchic tendencies of governing bodies, regardless of the organizations' commitment to democratic ends in the larger society, have concerned political and social scientists for a long time.

National Associations

Robert Michels' work still stands as a classic statement of the problem, even though his analyses are now seen to have lacked explanatory depth and a theory of organizational structure and dynamics. Alvin Gouldner, indeed, is apparently as ready to infer an "iron law of democracy" from the analysis of the governance of organization as Michels was to infer an "iron law of oligarchy." In fact, while a few studies of national organizations in the United States have focused on their internal politics, very little of a systematic nature is known about any considerable number in any institutional sphere. Our data show that, outwardly at least, the governance of most associations in all spheres conforms to the general cultural conception of democratic constitutionalism, with elections of most governing bodies either directly by the general membership or indirectly by representatives. The length of the term of office moreover, is generally quite short; for a majority of associations in all spheres, it is two to three years (see Table 14). Only in the spheres of religion and sociability are more lengthy terms of office fairly common. Although the term of office is generally short, most associations do not have formal limits to the number of terms a person may serve. This is so in all institutional spheres, as shown in Table 15. This could be an indication of a "loophole" for circumventing a circulation of offices among the general membership, but we are not inclined to infer this from the data of this or other studies, since the control of national associations today requires more subtlety than mere perpetuation in office of a cabal.

ADMINISTRATIVE STRUCTURES

Certain aspects of the administrative structures of national associations have fairly direct implications for the general problem of democracy in associations. Their size and degree of bureaucratization have a potentially significant bearing on the distribution of power within associations, on the availability of the means of articulating associations' ends, and on their stability as organizations. There seems to be confusion among many of the interested public concerning the size and degree of bureaucratization of associations' national administrative structures; they seem to be thought of as large, if not vast, bureaucracies that erode the ends of the associations, interpose themselves between members and the elected leaders, and envelope all in a pall of red tape. Some organizations, such as the American Red Cross, are singled out for especial abuse by a generally ill-informed public. Here we hope to bring at least a small measure of factual knowledge to this frequently confused and, insofar as internal democracy is concerned, very problematic aspect of national associations. Our discussion is limited largely to questions of the size and degree of bureaucratization and the extension of their administrative authority.

Contrary to popular conceptions, the administrative structures of national associations on the whole are actually strikingly small. Table 16 shows the number of paid full-time persons of all kinds

Table 16. Size of Employed Staff of National Headquarters

| Type of association | Number of employees | | | | | |
	None %	1 to 15 %	15 to 50 %	50 to 100 %	100 or more %	Number
Religion	6.7	33.3	20.0	10.0	30.0	30
Sociability		81.8	12.1		6.1	33
Government	8.1	46.0	37.8	5.4	2.7	37
Recreation	2.3	59.5	17.0	8.5	12.7	47
Education	22.2	52.0	16.0	4.9	4.9	81
Science and arts	13.5	45.1	25.2	8.1	8.1	111
Welfare	2.6	35.9	26.4	12.3	22.8	114
Economy	2.1	48.7	29.0	10.0	10.2	331

employed by national associations. Except for the spheres of religion and welfare, only small percentages employ more than 100 persons—scarcely an immense number—and most of those have fewer than 200. Only twenty-eight associations employ more than 200, and only seven more than 500. Table 16 shows that a majority in all spheres except welfare and religion have fewer than fifteen employees, and some have none at all.

Although the administrative structures of national associations are predominantly small, the degree of their bureaucratization is

National Associations

not so readily determined, because it does not directly follow size. A variety of elements, all of which are by no means completely agreed upon by social scientists, give an administrative structure its bureaucratic character and may be present in varying degrees. Important among these are: full-time employees, especially top officials, division of labor along lines of departmentalization, codification of procedures and the rights and duties of positions, codification of rules governing tenure and promotion, and fixing of monetary remuneration according to a formal schedule.

Table 17 shows the classification of associations according to the

Table 17. Degree of Bureaucratization of Administrative
Structures of National Associations

Type of association	Degree of bureaucratization			Number
	Low %	Medium %	High %	
Religion	50.0	17.9	32.1	28
Sociability	94.0		6.0	33
Government	79.5	17.6	2.9	34
Recreation	71.7	15.2	13.1	46
Education	77.7	15.9	6.4	63
Science and arts	70.8	19.8	9.4	96
Welfare	50.5	26.1	23.4	111
Economy	67.9	21.6	10.5	324

degree of bureaucratization of their administrative structures. Those classified as "low" exhibit no more than three of the elements just referred to; those classified as "medium" exhibit four to six; those classified as "high," seven or more. The data in Table 17 reveal that high degrees of bureaucratization are rare in the administrative structures of national associations; there is some in all spheres, but only in religion and welfare are noticeably large percentages of associations highly bureaucratized, and all spheres do not even show a "medium" level of bureaucratization. In fact, so simple are the headquarters of most national associations that— rather than concern with the specter of entrenched bureaucracies —questions as to the effectiveness of such small and loosely organized administrative structures might be more in order.

Central to the problem of democracy in national associations with a dispersed membership organized into local units is the degree of power exercised by the national headquarters over the local units. We examined the downward extension of formal administrative authority from the national headquarters to the employees of local units. About 50 per cent of our sample (some 394 associations) have organized local units, but only a little more than half of them have employees working at the local unit level. Of the 169 associations with at least some employees in local units, the headquarters of 122 had no records indicating their number—an obvious indication of the absence of downward extension of strict administrative authority from the national headquarters to the local units. Only seven national associations pay the salaries of local units' employees; only twenty-two replied affirmatively to the question, "Are the paid officials in the local units subject to the direct administrative authority of the national association?" Thus, regardless of whether associations are organized as national federations or as corporate units with local branches, the downward extension of strong and direct administrative authority is exceedingly rare.

SOME RELATIONS WITH GOVERNMENT

The ties linking national associations and the several levels of government in the United States are many and varied. All associations do not have regular or involved links with local, state, or federal government, but sizable percentages in most institutional spheres do. For example, the responsibilities of the principal officers of slightly more than 40 per cent of the national associations in our sample require them to be in regular contact with federal government officials; and the national officers of about 25 per cent have regular and necessary contacts with state government officials. In sharp contrast, yet not surprisingly, the national officers of only 15 per cent of the associations are in regular contact with local government officials. Regular contact with federal officials does not imply anything more than information channels to federal agencies; it clearly points to a widespread need among national associations to maintain close contacts with the government.

Table 18 shows that in all spheres except sociability very large

Table 18. National Associations Having Activities with Federal Agencies

Type of association	Cooperative activities		Formal working agreements	
	Number	%	Number	%
Religion	28	35.7	29	17.2
Sociability	31	6.5	32	
Government	38	57.9	39	20.5
Recreation	42	28.6	45	6.7
Education	76	40.8	77	14.3
Science and arts	99	53.5	104	22.1
Welfare	103	64.1	109	20.2
Economy	300	50.0	321	11.5
Total	717		756	

percentages of associations are engaged in cooperative activities with federal agencies and that a considerably smaller, but nonetheless significant, percentage also have formal working agreements with federal agencies.

Table 19. Number of National Associations Carrying on Cooperative Activities with Federal Government Departments and Specific Subdepartments or Independent Agencies

Government department or agency	Number of associations
Health, Education and Welfare	115
Commerce	77
Defense	68
State	57
Agriculture	56
Labor	29
National Science Foundation	28
Interior	25
Treasury	23
Veterans Administration	14
U.S. Information Agency	13
Housing and Home Agency	13
Executive Office of the President	11
Small Business Administration	11
Justice	10
Atomic Energy Commission	10

Cooperative activities with the federal government are dispersed throughout all the federal departments and a great variety of sub-departmental and independent agencies. Table 19 lists only those federal departments and specific agencies with which ten or more national associations carry on cooperative activities. The Department of Health, Education and Welfare is the focus of the largest cluster of associations, most of which are, of course, themselves in the general field of welfare. In descending number national associations are also linked to the Departments of Commerce, Defense, State, Labor, Interior, and the Treasury.

These widespread linkages between federal agencies and national associations are not merely of a simple informational character, permitting associations to keep abreast of current practices and policies of federal agencies in areas of special interest to the associations. They also involve cooperative undertakings that are presumably mutually beneficial. These findings confirm the fact of widespread ties of more than an ephemeral nature linking a great many national associations (in all institutional spheres) with agencies of the federal government. There can be little doubt that linkages of this kind produce mutual influences and accommodations, and it would be reasonable to suppose that they indicate an important locus of associations' pressures on the government.

INFLUENCING PEOPLE AND ISSUES

The thesis that independent groups buffer their members from the pressures of elites through the stabilization of members' commitments to the group interests and serve as vehicles for the expression of those interests in the larger society contains several implications for national associations if they are to be adjudged as actually fulfilling the functions imputed to them by this thesis. Most of the implications of this thesis have been discussed already. But there remain two particularly important aspects of national associations— the associations' efforts to influence the cognitive and affective orientations of their members on the one hand and of outside publics on the other. If associations do buffer their members from elite pressures by fostering the formation of opinions and cognitive awareness, there must be some evidence. This is especially important in relation to national associations because we cannot assume that the social processes occurring as a matter of course in the small, face-to-face group are also at work in these numerically large and spatially separated collectivities. These factors preclude treating national associations as collectivities whose members are engaged in relatively high rates of interaction and thereby obviate the assumption—however valid in the small-group context—that a coalescence of affective and cognitive orientations will flow "naturally" from membership in a national association.

Educational programs, however narrow or broad, represent a principal mechanism of this type of formation of awareness and cognitive opinions. A great many associations do carry on educational programs for their members.

The functions of independent groups as mechanisms for the expression of interests in the larger arena of social power and competition must also be examined, and this will round out our analysis of the applicability of the Kornhauser thesis to national associations in the United States. There are two basic questions. First, how and to what extent do they attempt to propagate their interests in the larger society? Second, to what extent do they involve themselves in public issues that transcend the interests of their membership alone, and how do they seek to implement their positions on such issues?

In the matter of influencing members' affective and cognitive orientations, substantially all the associations maintain one or more formal communications media addressed to their members; about 60 per cent publish an official journal on a regular basis, approximately the same percentage publish a bulletin or "memo," and 65 per cent circulate a newsletter. The need for one or more such communication mechanisms is obvious where members are widely dispersed throughout the country. In fact, without a mechanism of this sort it is questionable whether they could be considered true social organizations. Such communications, of course, vary considerably in content, from the scientific journal to the chatty newsletter; but, regardless of content, they provide common objects of affective and cognitive orientation for members.

Almost 85 per cent of the associations also carry on internal educational programs. There is very little difference in this respect among associations in the several institutional spheres. Indeed, science and arts is the only sphere in which as many as 20 per cent of the associations do not carry on educational programs of some kind for their members; the great majority of associations do devote attention to molding their members' opinions and cognitions. What is more, most of this activity occurs on a face-to-face basis. Conferences are the most frequent form utilized by associations, as shown in Table 20, with talks, lectures, workshops, and seminars figuring very importantly, but with relatively few organized classes.

Table 20. Number and Percentage of National Associations Utilizing Different Forms of Internal Educational Programs

Form of program	Per cent	Number
Conference	83.7	552
Talks, lectures	66.0	440
Workshops	53.8	353
Seminars	45.6	301
Demonstrations	25.0	164
Classes	21.0	139

Far fewer associations direct programs to the general public. Nevertheless, the figure is close to one-half of the associations in our sample and is evidence of considerable effort to influence the public. The only numerically significant means utilized to reach the public were talks, lectures, publications, conferences, and the mass media. The programs of 80 per cent of these associations consisted of talks, lectures, and the dissemination of published materials; 38 per cent of those having such programs held conferences; 34 per cent used one or another of the mass media; and only small percentages used other means.

What is the involvement of national associations in public issues that transcend the interests of their members? In exploring this very sensitive area, we asked their professional staffs the following questions: "During the past three years, has the association taken an official stand on any public issues?" Forty-nine per cent of the officers replying indicated that their associations had taken an official stand on a public issue in the past three years—quite evidently very widespread involvement in public events. However, the proportions

National Associations

of associations involved varied with the institutional sphere (see Table 21). Almost 70 per cent of the religious and government associations took an official stand, but only about 30 per cent of those in education, science and arts, and sociability did. Moreover,

Table 21. Number and Percentage of National Associations Taking an Official Stand on Public Issues

Institutional sphere	Per cent	Number
Religion	67.9	19
Sociability	28.1	9
Government	66.7	22
Recreation	42.3	19
Education	32.1	25
Science and arts	28.4	31
Welfare	48.6	53
Economy	58.4	178

not only did a firm majority of associations in the economic sphere take an official stand, but their absolute number is large.

A great variety of issues and events are represented, some of very narrow scope and of slight general social significance and others of broad societal interest. In order to bring some measure of coherence to this diversity, ten broad classes of issues were developed

Table 22. Number and Percentage of Associations Taking Public Stands on Issues, by Types of Issues

Type of issue	Number	Per cent of associations taking a public stand (N = 347)	Per cent of associations in the sample (N = 793)
General legislation	133	38.3	16.8
Taxation, fiscal policy	118	34.0	14.9
Health, welfare	106	30.5	13.4
Labor relations	57	16.4	7.2
Public resources, transportation	52	15.0	6.6
Foreign affairs	49	14.1	6.2
Education	46	13.3	5.8
Civil liberties	35	10.1	4.4
Agriculture	32	9.2	4.0
Military affairs	19	5.5	2.4

from the data: general legislation, taxation and fiscal policy, health and welfare, labor relations, public resources and transportation, foreign affairs, education, civil liberties, agriculture, military affairs. Table 22 shows the number of associations in each of these issues areas and the percentages these numbers represent of (a) all the associations taking stands and (b) all the associations in the sample. These comparisons give greater perspective.

It is apparent that no single issue or group of issues attracted overwhelming or even widespread attention among the 347 associations taking public stands. While some 38 per cent reported taking a public stand on a piece of general legislation, the diversity of specific matters was very great. Those issues classed as Taxation and Fiscal Policy represent as great a focus of specific attention as any. But even there only 34 per cent of the associations taking a stand focused attention in that area. Health and Welfare issues attracted the attention of about 30 per cent of those taking stands. No other broad class of issues attracted the attention of more than 17 per cent of the associations. Finally, the last column in Table 22 shows that not one of the general classes of issues was an area of interest to a sizable portion of the total sample of 793 associations.

The interpretation of these findings must be approached with some caution. First, the issues reported by associations cannot be interpreted as representing all the issues on which public stands were taken by associations. Our data, we suspect, reflect a considerable underreporting of the issues on which these associations took public stands. Second, the necessary codification (under ten rubrics) of the great diversity of issues reported obscures the wide range of concerns. Thus, while about 50 per cent of the associations in our sample reported taking no public stand, it seems plausible to conclude that a fair portion of them probably take if not a formal, then an informal, position on public issues and events.

The very diversity of the issues reported is itself a datum of considerable interest. There is certainly little evidence of widespread mobilization of associations around a single or even a few issues. In this respect the findings are consonant with Kornhauser's theses concerning the functions of independent groups in pluralist societies. It is difficult to conceive of mobilizing any great number of these national associations in a concerted action of a public character.

CHAPTER NINE

Big Trade and Business Associations

THE COOPERATIVE GROUPS OF COMPETITORS

The big trade association is a form of large-scale organization that grows luxuriantly in America. Such organizations are large in number of members, income, structure, hierarchical extension, and territory. Many are very large and powerful because they reorder and express the interests and purposes of some of the largest and most powerful corporations in America; their size and influence must be measured not simply in terms of themselves but also in terms of the organized power of great private enterprise. There is no segment of the American economy in which they do not play an important role; there is no part of this country's life—political, educational, religious, or social—on which they do not exert influence. Their power is felt in the halls and committee rooms of Congress, in state legislatures, and in city councils. They are active in local civic affairs, and their influence on the moral and ethical life of the national community is always felt. This chapter reports on a nationwide study of trade and business associations that was conducted as part of a larger research project on all types of large-scale formal associations (Chapter 8).

The trade association is only one variety of the formal associations that penetrate every aspect and activity of American life. It is a nonprofit institution that operates cooperatively for and among the competitive profit-making corporations. Its larger purposes are to promote and foster free enterprise as a system, but it often functions to reduce the free, competitive practices of members who might injure or violate the legal and ethical rules of the business enterprise. As agents of free enterprise these organizations operate in

This chapter is by W. Lloyd Warner and Desmond D. Martin. See Notes on Authors.

the marketplace to advance the competitive advantages of their own against the interests of others or combine with them for the well being of the larger industry.

The fact that trade associations are cooperative in nature for their members does not mean that they are not in conflict with other groups in the American society. The well known opposition and open conflict between big unions and big trade associations are seen constantly on many battle fronts, including state legislatures and the national Congress, local, state, and national elections in and between the two parties, and in public relations and for public opinion. "For every new car manufactured each member of the United Automobile Workers (UAW–CIO) pays $10 from his wages to fight for legislation and for working conditions (as well as wages) that he wants," warns the brochure of an automobile dealers' association. "The UAW–CIO has both a defensive and an offensive fund. Both are in the millions! Rest assured that the unions are going to keep working. . . . Franchised new car and new truck dealers need a strong arm to fight for what is best for the general public welfare and the country as a whole. . . . They have it when every franchised dealer is a member of the American Car Sellers' Association!"

From this same publication: "The Teamster's Union is spending a million and half dollars right now to mastermind the unionization of automobile dealerships. . . . Their membership is not based on a 'crisis' in the industry. Their dues go on and on, every month, in good as well as in bad times."

Each of the many specializations and divisions of American technological and economic life has its own trade association; hundreds and sometimes thousands spread through manufacturing, banks, merchandising, and other types of enterprise. These separate, more specialized trade associations often combine into larger groupings such as the National Association of Manufacturers, the U.S. Chamber of Commerce, and other general groupings that represent and help order the larger business world.

Trade associations are not in themselves profit making, but they advance the profit making of each member and benefit his industry and business. As such they are one kind of economic organization, and at the same time, by all criteria, they are formal, voluntary associations with formal rules of entrance, exit, and occupancy in

Big Trade and Business Associations

which each member as an insider has rights, duties, obligations, and privileges, usually in writing and formally agreed to, that determine how he can and cannot act and that make him different from those who do not belong. Because they function as economic institutions and help integrate and bring coherence to many cooperative corporate activities and because they are structurally an important and numerous variety of the American formal association, they are described and examined here as parts of the apparatus of business organization and are reexamined as parts of the larger report on all the varieties of American large-scale formal associations.

All the trade and business associations studied here are large scale; they also represent the spread and variety of enterprise activity in the United States. The principal purpose of the activities of all of them is to support and advance the interests of production, ownership, management, distribution, and exchange in the American economy and the American society. The sample was drawn from several sources, but primarily from Gale's *Encyclopedia of American Associations* (see Chapter 8). Several criteria for inclusion in the sample were set up, including number of individual members, number and size of member organizations, territorial spread, and the size of the organization's administrative staff. Satisfaction of any one of the criteria was sufficient to make an association a candidate for the sample.

An eight-page questionnaire was sent to slightly more than a thousand large-scale associations initially selected for the sample, of which trade and business associations were one of the several activity types. The return was high: 72.5 per cent of all associations and 75.6 per cent (334) of the trade and business associations returned usable questionnaires.

To determine how representative the actual sample of respondent trade associations was, each organization was categorized by use of the Standard Industrial Classification into six types according to the primary industrial interest it supported with an additional category for the more general business associations, such as Rotary and Kiwanis clubs and the U. S. Chamber of Commerce.

Table 1 gives the numbers and percentages for the seven categories of enterprise types. All except national business associations are broad forms of the Standard Industrial Classification used in other chapters.

Growth and Development of Trade Associations

We will limit our examination of these several varieties of trade and business associations to their place in the organization of business enterprises and leave their significance as a variety of American association to the chapter on large-scale associations.

Table 1. Number and Percentage of Trade Associations
by Enterprise Types

	Number	Per cent
Transportation, communications, utilities	28	8.4
Finance, insurance, real estate	31	9.3
National business associations	34	10.2
Agriculture	40	12.0
Wholesale, retail trade	47	14.1
Services	62	18.5
Manufacturing	92	27.5
Total	334	100.0

We shall first examine the growth and expansion of trade associations and then report on the characteristics of the organizations that serve the different types of business and industry. Later in this chapter we will discuss their size and complexity, relating structural variability to the several types of business enterprise, and will conclude with an analysis of their relations to government and their efforts to influence public opinion.

GROWTH AND DEVELOPMENT OF TRADE ASSOCIATIONS

The merchant guilds of an earlier economy and simpler society represented many of the same interests and performed some of the same functions that many modern trade associations do. However, the early merchant guilds were concerned with monopolistic control of their respective trades; as the economic forces generated by the introduction of new industries and the more modern factory system caused companies gradually to lose control over the regulation of industry, the purposes of the guilds became incompatible with the new world of free competition.

In their fight for survival the entire nature of these guilds was changed. Their activities were expanded to provide opportunities to pool the interests and knowledge of individuals or enterprises in order to assist each other in dealing with mutual business problems, such as relations with employees, competing enterprises, and the general public.

The oldest national trade associations in the United States, those formed between 1861 and 1865, were characterized by this pooling of knowledge and promotion of the general welfare of the respective industries. Among the earliest trade associations were the Writing Paper Manufacturers Association, organized in 1861; the United States Brewers Association, 1862; the American Iron and Steel Association and the National Association of Wool Manufacturers, 1864. While there were many local associations in the late eighteenth and early nineteenth century, these four associations organized before 1865 are generally believed to be among the oldest national associations in this country. The Writing Paper Manufacturers Association claims supporting evidence to prove it is the oldest of the national associations, and the U. S. Department of Commerce does not dispute this claim.

There were also a great many employers' associations in the early nineteenth century with rather different characteristics, since their principal objective was dealing with employees. Regulation of hours, work, wages for different types of skilled jobs, and length of employment were among the basic decisions, supposedly resolved to the mutual advantage of employee and employer. Thus, some of the organizations, such as the Master Plasterers, had objectives similar to those of our trade and business associations while many functioned as company unions. The latter group of employers' associations was an outgrowth of the early craft guild, which differed from the merchant guild and was more like a labor union than a trade association.

As this organizational state of the American economy progressed, there was also multiplication of the number of methods employed to reduce conflicts arising between individuals, groups, and organizations. Although these methods developed rapidly, there was a parallel development of a wider range of conflicts resulting from demographic, economic, and social forces. In short, the vast and multiple changes of an emerging society affected the business environment by favoring new organizational development to deal with these new and challenging economic conditions. It is important to trace the development of these forces and to identify their nature and extent.

During the latter part of the nineteenth century, when big business began to flourish, when mergers were numerous and industrial capacity greatly increased, when large markets and market centers arose to handle the greater amounts of goods that flowed from the growing industries, many trade and business associations were founded, and some of them became national organizations.

Many of the small firms of the time began to be replaced by larger ones dominating certain fields of production. For example, a large part of steel and petroleum as well as other markets fell under the control of a few firms in each industry. The public became concerned, as did its lawmakers. They made their feelings known through individual and group action and through such legislation as the Sherman Antitrust Act of 1890, and, still later, through other acts designed for similar purposes. Conversely, industries and specific firms within these industries wanted to assure their own competitive places in the changing industrial society. The smaller firms were in a fight for survival, while the position of the larger firms was constantly challenged by public opinion and the passage of regulatory measures.

Many of the modern trade associations arose from the attempts to deal with this new range of problems. Probably the most important single factor leading to an association of firms and individuals concerned with trade was the changing competitive environment in the late 1800s and early 1900s. The existing economic power of large-scale enterprise of this period created threatening self-interest through attempts to gain greater shares of the market or greater control of the marketplace. As large corporate structures developed, goods tended to be distributed in wider geographical areas; in contrast to earlier smaller enterprises, these large-scale business organizations were dealing with mass markets about which relatively little was known. Many of the early trade associations were designed to meet the resulting need for information about the channels of distribution and the nature of the marketplace in the ex-

Big Trade and Business Associations

panding regions. There was also the increasing fear of regulatory legislation.

Modern trade associations are in part outgrowths of attempts to satisfy the crucial need for knowledge about competitors in the marketplace—a need that had become apparent to competitors by the turn of the twentieth century. Some writers refer to the period 1890–1911 as the formative stage of trade associations; our analysis suggests that the attending problems of the merging economy produced this formative stage. Businessmen desired to adjust their activities more intelligently and accurately on the basis of the best technical practice and actual market conditions in this very extended economy.[1] The so-called "open price" trade associations distributed exchange-price information among their competitor members, and a large group of closely related trade associations dispersed a wide range of trade statistics but excluded prices. Essentially, it was the complexities of bigness that generated a common interest sufficiently enduring to sustain collective action. Particularly, this common interest arose from the prevailing competitive situation; and competitive influences shaped the trade association function.

At the beginning of World War I the basic framework of the trade association and many of its functions had been built by American industry with an increasing awareness of the significance and importance of collective industrial action. The war was a fertile period for trade and business associations. According to the U. S. Department of Commerce, the number of trade associations increased rapidly between 1914 and 1919, from about 800 to 2,000.[2] This increase can be partially accounted for by wartime production problems and the establishment of the War Industries Board, which desired to deal with industries in organized groups. During periods of great crisis, including wars and deep depressions, governmental organizations arise and cause—even if unintentionally —the pulling together of competitive corporations and companies into larger industrial cooperative institutions, which, when formally organized, often become trade associations. Mobilization and pro-

1. J. G. Glover, W. B. Cornell, and J. T. Madden, *The Development of American Industries* (New York, Prentice-Hall, 1932), p. 872.
2. L. E. Warford and Richard A. May, *Trade Association Activities* (Washington, D.C., U.S. Department of Commerce, Government Printing Office, 1923), p. 304.

duction for war, unification of industrial production, and more efficient distribution were basic factors that stimulated trade association growth and the formation of new organizations. Emphasis was shifted from competitive problems within the industry to production problems as an extension of the unified efforts of the society to organize through the federal government and the use of the military.

Many new techniques for coping with previous problems emerged during this period. There was a rise in the use and practical application of statistical information. The need to coordinate production quotas coupled with the urgent need to allocate resources in the most efficient way encouraged cooperative use of statistics. This intellectual tool also expresses and emphasizes the generalities and commonalities rather than the specifics.

Wartime shortages and production problems and controls brought many associations into close contact with government officials for the first time. This was encouraged by formal agencies, such as the War Industries Board, because close contact between government and business was necessary to produce the needed goods. Many existing associations resulted from the need for organization of their industries in the first World War. Since then the government's role has become increasingly important, both in its interest in trade and business associations and in these associations' interest in government. Many trade associations, if not most of them, frequently serve as mediators between the private and public sectors of our national life. It is true that these associations had an earlier interest in government and in early trade legislation, but the closer contact with government due to the war strengthened this relationship.

At the close of World War I trade and business associations had assumed many of the characteristics that are typical today. The competitive aspects began in the late 1800s, but statistical interest and political and governmental relations became prominent during the war years. While many of the large national trade associations were formed after 1920, the basic stimulus to their formation was in the society by 1920.

The great depression of the 1930s caused a new crisis in our social and economic life, and once again the federal government intervened. Many agencies began that now regulate and support

Big Trade and Business Associations

American industry and the relations of some of those closely associated with it. The depression years and their problems had a decisive influence on American trade and business associations. Because of the basic threat to our economic system and to the society itself industry saw the need to restrict competition and to erect safeguards against price cutting. Concern among businessmen about general market conditions overshadowed prior emphasis on intraindustry competition, and with this came a recognized need to learn more about the marketplace in order to develop ways to increase sales and survive. Trade associations were faced with a distinct challenge if they were to serve their respective industries. The mass promotional campaigns of the 1920s were reexamined with a new emphasis on market research. The preliminary report made by the trade association department of the U. S. Chamber of Commerce indicated that more than 200 trade associations increased cooperative advertising in the 1930s at a cost of several million dollars and that 143 associations adopted specific programs of market research. Trade and business associations had been forced to realize the urgent need to gain a greater understanding of all the factors entering into the market environment.

The short-lived National Industrial Recovery Act of 1933 put new life into the trade and business association function, serving in the same way that various organizations had served during World War I. This act put many trade associations into key positions by recognizing them as having central authority for their industries. The act provided for these associations to draw up a code of fair competition for their respective industries and then to take an active part in developing and enforcing its practices. The N.I.R.A. established the trade association as an instrument of industrial control, and although its effectiveness in this area was questioned, the act certainly helped to secure an established position for trade associations in the modern industrial setting. There was an apparent trend toward closer internal regulation in industry, and trade associations continued an active role in this area throughout the 1930s. While their effectiveness during the depression has sometimes been challenged, the N.I.R.A. strengthened their position and possibly avoided a substantial decline in their growth.

Moreover, the development of many of the administrative and regulatory agencies that started to put government in a more active position in the economic life of the country during the New Deal acted as a great stimulus to the growth of trade associations and to their significance in handling industrial affairs, particularly with the central government.

The outbreak of World War II interrupted the move toward closer internal regulation of industry but greatly stimulated activities of associations by bringing them once more into close and continuous touch with the government. They participated with varying degrees of responsibility in the allocation of materials to manufacturers, played a critical role in providing statistical information about their industries for national defense purposes, and in other ways facilitating relations between government and industry. As previously mentioned, the exchange of statistical information among association members and the government grew out of problems created by the earlier war, but World War II expanded this function. Partially as a result of these wartime influences, trade associations emerged from the second World War as strong and influential forces in our economy. Many experienced their greatest gains in membership during this period.

Increases in productivity put the informational function in a permanent high position among large-scale national trade and business associations. The governmental relationship, particularly involving actual and potential legislation that might affect specific industries, was given renewed emphasis. Many trade and business associations increased their lobbying activities, and many maintained legal counsel and offices in Washington, D.C. The cooperative promotional activities characteristic of the 1920s were given renewed status, and many associations originated advertising and promotional departments and used market research as a tool to determine the extent and effectiveness of their promotional appeal. Interest in research extended into the social and psychological sciences to the point where many used research to understand the relation of public opinion to the interests of their industry.

A major influence started after World War II added an additional function to trade and business association activity. The emergence of large-scale production and attendant service industries directed attention to the need for establishing and maintaining good public relations. In response to this need many of the large associations not only established public relations departments but also

Big Trade and Business Associations

effectively used consulting research organizations to understand problems having to do with public opinion. These departments were, for the most part, designed to stimulate national interest in behalf of the major activities that were represented.

The growth and expansion of trade associations is clearly related to many of the basic changes that are part of our emergent society and the changes that have occurred in our technology, our economy, and the development of big government. There has been a whole realignment of public opinion about the place of business and business enterprise in our economic system. There have been radical changes in corporate enterprise itself. Furthermore, the very rapid, not to say explosive, development of our scientific technology has produced whole new technologies and whole new industries to organize the production, distribution, and consumption of their products. Moreover, our local economic and social systems have increasingly been more fully incorporated into the national economy and the national society, with the result that the national trade association has new strength and new reasons for being.

In broad overview, the several periods when trade associations originated and grew luxuriously are those of rapid change and crisis in the economy or crisis of the United States in the world society. There was the earlier strong push toward industrialization and the revolutionary beginnings of many of the new manufacturing enterprises. This was followed by the crisis of the first World War, when government entered the economic arena. The crisis of the depression followed, when government came in again with a preliminary period of adjustment to the new situation with the N.I.R.A. and a later apparatus of regulatory agencies; again trade associations grew, prospered, and performed important services previously not so much needed by the corporate competitors. Finally, World War II again brought our society into crisis and conflict, and once more the central tendencies in our society asserted themselves, and local and private tendencies were partly reorganized into public cooperative ones, some of which took the form of trade associations.

At the present time we seem to be in a new period that is not so much an aftermath of World War II as one in which the national society continues to develop and restructure itself and the federal government takes an increasingly important role. More and more trade associations help regulate and discipline the members of an industry, increase their profit-making effectiveness and their technological skills, and handle the relations of all competitors through cooperative efforts in the trade association. They influence public opinion, which generates the legislation that expands or limits the federal regulatory agencies. One can predict that the power and functions of the national trade associations will grow rather than diminish.

THE STRUCTURE OF SIMPLE AND COMPLEX ASSOCIATIONS

Compared to most of the many thousands of associations that organize the cooperative activities of our economic life, all the associations in this study are large-scale and likely to be structurally complex; this statement holds true for all the enterprise types that compose our sample. There are tendencies among them, however, that bring together elements of complexity and size or of simplicity, which make certain kinds of associations complex and others comparatively simple. We will examine the simple and complex configurations, inspect how each of the structural elements is distributed among the enterprise types, assemble them into a rough typology, and at the conclusion of this section place them in a range of structural complexity and draw interpretive inferences.

There are several structural elements on which we have evidence whose presence marks or contributes to the simplicity or complexity of the structure of any given trade association. The presence of affiliate organizations structurally related to the organization extends it laterally, spreads its effective relations into other parts of the industry and society, may add greatly to its complexity, and possibly contributes to the levels in its vertical hierarchy.

The memberships of some associations are entirely composed of organizations, which means that the association not only helps order their behavior as members but through them also extends into their corporate hierarchies and thus spreads both laterally and vertically. Since many of these organization members are large scale in their own right—some of them among the largest corporations in America with elaborate, complex hierarchies—the extensions of the trade association, vertically and horizontally, are often very great. On the other hand, a considerable number of associations have memberships composed entirely of individuals. In one sense these individuals represent only themselves: structurally they bring no extension beyond themselves; their effect on the structure is to limit and simplify rather than to extend and complicate. Still another type of association is composed of both individual and organizational members. These three types are differentially distributed among the enterprise types and are important for understanding the nature of the different kinds of economic groupings of associations.

Our evidence also shows that the structure of trade associations varies considerably in the number of departments that organize their activities and divide the labor of those who manage affairs. High and low departmentalizations are related to other elements of simplicity and complexity.

Some of the associations have quite large, others very small, paid staffs. Although the number of paid staff members is, of course, related to the degree of departmentalization, this is not always true; sometimes low departmentalization is associated with large paid staffs, and large departmental complexity is associated with small staffs. High and low numbers of staff are therefore a separate and independent factor.

The incomes of some trade associations run into the millions; others are relatively small, some no more than a few thousand dollars.

There is at least one other element that at first seems strange in this configuration of complexity—the location of headquarters. Certain kinds of associations locate their headquarters overwhelmingly in three great metropolises—New York, Washington, and Chicago; about half of those have their headquarters in the first two. Still others are more likely to spread their headquarters among other American cities. This difference in placement is related to the other elements in the complexity configuration. By inference we will attempt to show why this is so and, hypothetically, why these differences are likely to add to or to reduce the complexity of trade association activities.

The number of members varies from the hundreds into the millions. Presumably size of membership could be related to the complexity of trade associations. The average number of members for those where we have data was 43,000. The difficulty in discussing size of all varieties of associations by membership is that in some the members pay nominal annual dues and participate in no other way while in others the members pay large dues, appear regularly at meetings, take responsibility for the maintenance of a solid organization, and are in fact participating members. This question is of less importance in trade associations, however, because most, if not all, have members who are, in the true sense of the word, members of the organization.

Annual Incomes

When attempting to get solid estimations and conclusions about size of trade associations, the size of the annual income is in many ways a better general measure than membership because of the differences in the kinds of members—organizational and individual. Table 2 shows the annual incomes according to type of enterprise. Over a third of the trade associations had annual incomes over $500,000. The associations of certain types of enterprise outranked all others for the proportion of those with high incomes, more than $2 million. These were transportation, communications and utilities (16 per cent), finance (14 per cent), and manufacturing (13 per cent). Two of these, finance (32 per cent) and manufacturing (14 per cent), also led in the million-dollar class, and two, manufacturing (21 per cent) and transportation (21 per cent), in the $500,000-to-$1-million income category. Most of the trade associations were in the middle bracket, $75,000 to $500,-000.

That two-thirds of trade associations report annual incomes of less than $500,000 a year rather than figures at least twice that size will be surprising to many. It must be remembered that a good third of them, and about half of the manufacturing and financial associations, are in the higher brackets, but even so the very largest incomes of these cooperative trade associations only match the lowest levels of the annual sales and income figures for the big private competitive, profit-making corporations.

Table 2. Size of Annual Income by Enterprise Type

	$1,000 to $75,000			$75,000 to $500,000			$500,000 to $1,000,000			$1,000,000 to $2,000,000			$2,000,000 or more			Total	
	N	%	Rank	N	%	Rank	N	%	Rank	N	%	Rank	N	%	Rank	N	%
Transportation, communications, utilities	1	5.3	(6)	11	57.9	(4)	4	21.0	(1)	0	0.0	(7)	3	15.8	(1)	19	100
Manufacturing	5	6.9	(5)	33	45.8	(5)	15	20.9	(2)	10	13.9	(2)	9	12.5	(3)	22	100
Agriculture	8	28.6	(1)	12	42.9	(6)	2	7.1	(6)	3	10.7	(3)	3	10.7	(4)	28	100
Finance, insurance, real estate	2	7.1	(4)	10	35.7	(7)	3	10.7	(5)	9	32.2	(1)	4	14.3	(2)	28	100
National business associations	7	23.3	(2)	18	60.0	(2)	2	6.7	(7)	1	3.3	(6)	2	6.7	(5)	30	100
Wholesale, retail trade	2	5.3	(6)	25	65.7	(1)	6	15.8	(4)	3	7.9	(4)	2	5.3	(7)	38	100
Services	7	14.0	(3)	29	58.0	(3)	9	18.0	(3)	2	4.0	(5)	3	6.0	(6)	50	100
Total	32	12.1		138	52.1		41	15.4		28	10.6		26	9.8		265	100

Table 3. Type of Membership by Enterprise Type

	Individual members only			Organization members only			Combined				
	N	%	Rank	N	%	Rank	N	%	Rank	N	%
Transportation, communications, utilities	8	32.0	(3)	13	52.0	(3)	4	16.0	(6)	25	100
Finance, insurance, real estate	5	18.5	(6)	16	59.3	(2)	6	22.2	(5)	27	100
National business associations	8	27.6	(4)	3	10.3	(7)	18	62.1	(1)	29	100
Agriculture	13	40.6	(1)	6	18.8	(6)	13	40.6	(2)	32	100
Wholesale, retail trade	11	27.5	(5)	19	47.5	(4)	10	25.0	(4)	40	100
Services	20	36.3	(2)	21	38.2	(5)	14	25.5	(3)	55	100
Manufacturing	15	14.1	(7)	59	75.6	(1)	11	10.3	(7)	85	100
Total	80	27.3		137	46.8		76	25.9		293	100

Big Trade and Business Associations

Unlike certain other types of associations in America, most of these organizations get their money from their membership. This means that for those who have organizational members only, income is not from individuals but from corporations and sometimes from other large trade organizations. The incomes of about three-fourths (73 per cent) are only from their membership, and 98 per cent of these associations report their incomes as only from private sources. Very, very few reported additional income from public sources such as foundations.

Table 3 shows the membership make-up of the various kinds of associations. Since most of the organization members are corporations, the strength of the association is often enormous. This becomes evident when it is remembered that these are national associations covering the entire country and that their members are national and international corporations.

There is a considerable difference in the proportions of the kinds of memberships among the enterprise types.

Affiliation

Affiliation with other trade associations is popular among all kinds of trade associations. Seventy per cent of all associations have at least one affiliate, about 30 per cent have none, and 13 per cent have five or more. Agricultural, with 46.2 per cent reporting no affiliates, and financial associations, with 42 per cent, are the low ones for this kind of organization. Wholesale and retail trade associations rank quite high, with 84 per cent having affiliations, but none reported as many as five affiliates. National business associations also have a significant (65.6 per cent) number of affiliates, but again only 3 per cent had more than five affiliates. Large national manufacturing trade associations report over 21 per cent with more than five affiliates. The functional nature of the manufacturing activity types seems to call for a larger number of affiliates. This finding can be partially explained by common problems that face many industries, such as labor relations, governmental legislation, and cooperative promotional activities. It can be concluded that the manufacturing activity type is also more likely to be structurally cohesive, given the extent of the affiliation among its associations. One of the most prominent cases of this type is, of course, the National Association of Manufacturers, which solidifies the entire manufacturing activity type through its ties with a very large number of affiliated associations.

The merchandising associations are particularly given to affiliation, but they do so with only a few affiliates per association, suggesting that this type of activity is not nearly so cohesive as manufacturing, although certain problems faced and functions performed do call for between one and five affiliates for most of their associations.

The functions of national business associations (many in this type, it will be recalled, are semiautonomous state and regional organizations) are shown in their affiliation patterns. Since, by their very nature, many of these associations are state and regionally oriented, it is not surprising to find that they rank next to the bottom, with only 3 per cent reporting more than five national affiliates. However, the American Farm Bureau Federation and others play a crucial role in bringing together the divergent locations, backgrounds, and interests of American farm families, and the cohesiveness of the agricultural type is certainly strengthened by their dominant parent organizations.

Size of Staff

For our purposes a high degree of departmental differentiation is defined as four or more distinct administrative departments in an association. An average of 47 per cent of all the associations in the sample report this high departmentalization; finance (67 per cent) and manufacturing (54 per cent) are well above this general average; wholesale and retail trade (43 per cent), and transportation, communications, and utilities (38 per cent) fall significantly below. Agricultural associations have the least degree of departmentalization; only 27.5 per cent have four or more administrative departments. The functional activities of both finance and manufacturing associations develop departmental organization most frequently, while those of agricultural associations seem not to produce this effect.

About a third (31.4 per cent) of all trade associations had staffs

Big Trade and Business Associations

of more than thirty employees; 10 per cent had more than a hundred, and 18 per cent from sixteen to thirty. Staff size, of course, is an important indicator of how the association functions with its members and with its activities and obligations. A staff of less than fifteen was reported by 48.6 per cent of the sample. Small staffs are characteristic of the associations in wholesale and retail trade, and in agriculture.

Finance, insurance, and real estate; transportation, communications, and utilities; and manufacturing enterprise types reported the largest percentage of staffs of more than a hundred people. These same three activity types reported the largest percentage of organizational members. These and other findings suggest a distinct relationship between type of membership and size of staff. Enterprise types reporting a relatively larger average number of individual membership associations—agriculture and the merchandising trades—also report smaller staffs; and those with a relatively larger number of organizational members—transportation, communication and utilities, and manufacturing—report relatively larger staffs. The first conclusion to be drawn is that the functional nature of associations with greater percentages of organizational members supports a larger staff; and the opposite is true for associations with greater percentages of individual members. These findings also support the earlier statement that, at least for certain purposes, the organizational membership extends the trade association vertically out into the hierarchies of these other corporations and that their influences are likely to contribute to vertical expansion and to departmentalization of the trade association itself.

Very few (2.1 per cent) large-scale trade and business associations have no paid staff; these associations probably utilize volunteer workers. The national business association type had the largest percentage (8.8 per cent) reporting no paid staff. A simple *chi* square measurement of the relation between the size of the paid staff and the extent of departmentalization shows a significant relation between the two.

Associations can be placed in a range running from complex to simple and from large to small. The components of size include those that represent broad, wide interests and spread over the total activities of one or several industries; or they may be broad and have very general interests that spread across everything that the in-

Table 4. Components and Ranks of Complex and Simple Organizations

Components	High	Medium	Low
Departmental differentiation	Finance Manufacturing	Business Services Merchandising	Transportation Agriculture
Organizational members	Finance Manufacturing Transportation	Merchandising	Agriculture Business Services
Affiliation complexity	Manufacturing Merchandising Business	Services Transportation	Agriculture Finance
Size of staff	Finance Manufacturing	Services Agriculture Transportation	Business Merchandising
Income	Finance Manufacturing	Transportation Merchandising	Business Agriculture Services
Number of members (all kinds)	Agriculture Business	Finance Merchandising	Manufacturing Services Transportation
Location of headquarters in big three cities	Transportation Services Merchandising Manufacturing Finance		Business Agriculture

Big Trade and Business Associations

dustry does; or they may be highly specialized and limited to one part of an industry or to one kind of activity, such as technical rather than managerial. They may be big in terms of income and, of course, in terms of number of members.

In terms of complexity the spread is both lateral and vertical: in number of affiliations, in type of membership, in degree of departmentalization, and in size of staff. Table 4 shows the degree of complexity of each type of organization according to these criteria and to location of headquarters, overall number of members, and income. Income correlates to the degrees of complexity in size more than does the number of members, primarily of course, because the members being counted are of a different character—one being individual and the other organizational.

The Big Three Headquarters

Three cities—Washington, New York, and Chicago—contain the overwhelming majority (69 per cent) of the headquarters of all trade and business associations (see Table 5). Washington falls far below the other metropolises of more than two million population for headquarters of corporations, running a very poor last; yet it is at the top of the headquarter cities for trade and business associations. There are indications that it is slightly increasing its proportions of trade association headquarters, not among the old so much as among the more recently established organizations.

The headquarters of the trade associations not located in the big three are scattered everywhere in large American cities, but mostly in the East and Midwest. The drop in number of headquarters from the big three is very great; each of the next eleven cities had between 1 and 2 per cent of headquarters, but only one reached 2 per cent. Philadelphia and Boston in the East, St. Louis and Detroit in the Midwest, and Los Angeles in the West were among those at this weak second level.

Three-fourths of the financial, insurance and real estate headquarters are in the big three cities, as well as three-fourths of the headquarters of the manufacturing associations and four out of five of the merchandising trade associations and those associations that organize and support service enterprises. Topping them all are the

Table 5. Location of Headquarters by Enterprise Types

	Chicago			New York			Washington D.C.			Other			Total	
	N	%	Rank	N	%	Rank	N	%	Rank	N	%	Rank	N	%
Services	11	17.7	(5)	22	35.5	(1)	11	17.7	(5)	18	29.1	(6)	62	100
Transportation, com-munications, utilities	5	17.9	(4)	3	10.7	(4)	20	71.4	(1)	0	0.0	(7)	28	100
Finance, insurance, real estate	8	25.8	(1)	11	35.5	(1)	4	12.9	(7)	8	25.8	(3)	31	100
National business associations	5	14.7	(6)	2	5.9	(5)	5	14.7	(6)	22	64.7	(1)	34	100
Agriculture	4	10.0	(7)	1	2.5	(6)	10	25.0	(3)	25	62.5	(2)	40	100
Wholesale, retail trade	11	23.4	(3)	13	27.7	(3)	13	27.7	(2)	10	21.2	(5)	47	100
Manufacturing	22	23.9	(2)	29	31.6	(2)	20	21.7	(4)	21	22.8	(4)	92	100
Total	66	19.8		81	24.3		83	24.8		104	31.1		334	100

associations that service transportation, communications, and utilities: all of the headquarters in our sample are in the big three. Only agricultural trade associations (37.5 per cent) and the business associations (35.3 per cent) are below the general average.

Since these three metropolises are the centers of many of the major large-scale activities in this country—two for big business and one for big government—it is not surprising to learn that large-scale trade associations locate their headquarters there. Table 5 suggests an apparent relationship between the enterprise type of an association and its headquarters' location. New York and Chicago attract more than 60 per cent of the headquarters of the financial, insurance, and real estate associations. A closer examination of the individual associations within this large, general enterprise type reveals other important information. For the most part, the banking associations are heavily concentrated in New York with some in Chicago; the insurance associations are also concentrated in New York, with a few in Washington; the real estate associations most frequently choose Chicago for their national headquarters. Services and manufacturing are often concentrated in New York. New York and Washington attract more than half of the mercantile headquarters. Associations with headquarters in cities other than these three tend to locate in those identified with their industries; some national insurance associations are in Hartford and Philadelphia.

The manufacturing activity type contains a unique pattern of headquarters' location, with almost a third in New York. The larger associations representing the more general aspects of a particular industry also have headquarters in New York, including The National Association of Manufacturers, the most general for manufacturing representation, and The United States Brewers Association, which promotes the entire brewery industry. While Chicago attracts some of the more general representative organizations, it tends to have many of the more narrowly defined enterprise types, such as those representing only farm equipment or only mobile homes. Washington attracts both broad and narrow interest associations in manufacturing, but to a lesser extent. Those associations located outside these three cities consist primarily of manufacturing associations that are near the centers of their respective industries. For example, many of the national associations for iron and steel are in Pittsburgh and Cleveland, for automobiles in Detroit, for petroleum in Texas and Oklahoma, and for lumber in the Northwest.

The service enterprise type, which ranks high in percentage of New York headquarters, contains service associations in many fields. Those associations primarily concerned with industry services, such as management and advertising, tend to locate in New York. Those dealing with credit management and accounting services are rather evenly distributed among New York, Washington, and Chicago. Twenty-nine per cent of those with headquarters located elsewhere are, for the most part, those offering more special services, such as hotels.

The wholesale and retail enterprise type, with national headquarters fairly evenly distributed among the three big cities, contains other patterns. New York attracts a great majority of the merchandising trade associations directly concerned with industrial products, such as trademarks and standards, as well as particular industries, such as the shoe business. Chicago has the great majority of national trade associations in food distribution, such as the National Association of Retail Grocers, which claims to be the largest trade association in the United States. Washington, D.C., is used by a variety of wholesale and retail trade associations; it is difficult to determine a definite trend here beyond a basic interest in the legislative aspects of the distribution process. That this city is the most frequent location of headquarters of all trade and business associations shows, of course, a strong relationship between big government and big trade. Over 70 per cent of the transportation, communications, and utilities associations in our sample are located in Washington. Agricultural and business associations also have higher percentages in Washington than in New York. The close relationship between agricultural problems and federal legislation and the functioning of national business associations in the activities of government are well known.

Although Chicago has a high representation of headquarters from each enterprise type, in spite of its midwestern location it attracts only 10 per cent of the agricultural associations, much less than its representation for the other types. Both the national business and agricultural associations in our sample locate their headquarters primarily outside the three big centers.

Inspection of the particular associations in these categories explains this. Business associations lead all activity types with twenty-two associations (65 per cent) locating their headquarters outside the big three cities; but most of these associations are very large,

Big Trade and Business Associations

populous state chambers of commerce and the like, with their head-quarters located in their respective states. If only national business associations are counted, virtually all of them are in the three cities. There is variation in this type because large, complex business organizations that conform to the criteria for inclusion are in the sample even though they are not national but state and regional organizations. The large national chambers of commerce, such as the United States Chamber of Commerce and the Council of State Chambers of Commerce, are in Washington, and the International Chamber is in New York. The remainder of the national business association category is composed primarily of national service clubs, such as Lions and Kiwanis. They tend to locate their national headquarters in Chicago. Since the activities of these service organizations are widely dispersed geographically, it is not surprising that they choose Chicago's central location for their headquarters.

The agricultural type, which ranks a close second to the business associations for locating headquarters outside the three major cities, is quite different. An analysis of the individual associations in this category indicates that they are specialized crop and cattle associations that stay near the areas where these commodities are produced. Most of the national cattle and wheat associations are in the middle and western states; their headquarters are more likely to be in Texas, Nebraska, Kansas, Missouri, or Iowa. National to-bacco, fruit, and vegetable associations are also near their growing areas—North Carolina for tobacco, California and Florida for citrus fruits. Agricultural associations concerned with a wider variety of products over wider areas of production tend to follow the general trends and locate in Washington and Chicago. A prime example is The American Farm Bureau Federation, whose head-quarters is in Chicago. Many of the national agricultural associations most directly concerned with governmental legislation are in Washington. Forestry and wildlife management organizations with widely dispersed geographical interests are also in this latter group.

The transportation, communications, and utilities enterprise type, with no associations outside the major three cities, is heavily concentrated in Washington, D.C. Inspection of the individual associations of this enterprise type indicates that most of the public power and transportation control associations are in Washington, but a few of the more technical ones are in Chicago and New York.

Examples of these are the American Railway Engineering Association in Chicago and the Edison Electrical Institute in New York. Government and industry control and regulation seem to account for the Washington location; those associations in the other two cities are more likely to have more specialized and technical interests.

Generally speaking, headquarters in the three major metropolises provide protection and an opportunity for promotion of interests.

Washington, the smallest of the ten cities of more than two million population, has a very small number of corporate headquarters but is tied for trade association headquarters with New York City, by far the most populous metropolis in the United States and the queen city for corporate headquarters (and for the managers of interlocking directorates); this is more than a symbol of the public and representative role of these cooperative business organizations. The factors operating to bring the big trade associations to Washington and to New York are strong ones and undoubtedly pull the associations there for good reasons. However, this attraction also expresses and symbolizes other processes in contemporary American society. The great attraction of New York for trade associations is of course related to the heavy concentration of industries located in the mass of that great metropolis. The increasing strength of the central tendencies in the national society with big government and its powerful agencies structuring the emerging processes of this society are reflected in Washington's highly preferred position. It raises the question of what the activities are between the big trade associations and the big agencies of the federal government.

PUBLIC INFLUENCES OF TRADE ASSOCIATIONS

Every day decisions are made in Washington [declares a brochure sent to the members of the American Car Sellers' Association] which affect you, your profits and your future.

Congress is constantly considering legislation which could increase your costs of doing business. Surely new labor legislation, tax reforms (good and bad), commerce controls, and bills which will, if enacted, further rob your profits and make your business difficult to operate, will be considered.

Dealers need a strong voice, not only before Congress but before every federal governmental agency. They have this voice in ACSA.

Scores of agencies in Washington administer laws which affect your cash register and your future. With these, like with Congress, dealers have a strong and unified voice through their American Car Sellers' Association.

The trade associations of all enterprise types, including car sellers, are active with the federal, state, and local governments. Everyone knows that their influence on government is great, that lobbying is a necessary part of some of their activities, and that efforts to influence public opinion, to foster or prevent legislation and at times executive action are great. But not all of them are directly involved with federal affairs. To find out more about their relations with the several levels of government, we asked a number of questions, particularly: Do the responsibilities of the association's principal (voluntary or paid) officers require them to be in more or less regular contact with federal, state, or local government officials?

We did not expect uninhibited replies, yet most of the literature that accompanied the returned questionnaires, apparently addressed to the members, readily spoke of the problems of business and industry, making sure that the influence of others, notably labor unions and an uninformed public and Congress, would not interfere with the well being of the industry represented by a particular trade association. They are interest groups and they strive to serve the interests they represent. Since the giant professional, religious, and philanthropic associations as well as the unions present and serve their own ends by the same procedures, this activity, although often viewed with suspicion by many Americans, is increasingly accepted as normal and even necessary.

How did the different enterprise types respond to questions having to do with their activities in relation to the federal and other governments and to influencing public opinion? Slightly more than half (52 per cent) declared that their officers' responsibilities required them to be in regular contact with one or several government levels; more than two-thirds (70 per cent) of the agricultural associations, somewhat more than half the merchandising (55 per cent) and business associations (53 per cent), about half the finance (52 per cent) associations, and 41 per cent of service so reported.

To learn where and at what levels they contributed their attention, the replies were divided among these categories: only federal government; only federal and state; the combination of federal, state, and local; and none. Three types led all others for activities with only the federal government—merchandising (38 per cent), transportation, communications, utilities (32 per cent), and agriculture (30 per cent). The average for all types of trade and business associations was 23 per cent. Fourteen per cent of the trade associations worked at federal and state levels only. Finance (26 per cent), agriculture (23 per cent), and business (21 per cent) led all others in the federal and state category. Business (21 per cent), services (20 per cent), and agriculture (18 per cent) were above the 15 per cent average for contact with all three government levels.

Only 12 per cent of the trade associations had written, working agreements with any agency of the federal government, but a third (34 per cent) of all the agricultural associations did. Less than 15 per cent of all the rest had such agreements. Questions broadly formed and requiring an easier answer about *informal* cooperation with federal agencies solicited a larger response. Fifty per cent of all of them said they did have such informal relations with one or more federal agencies. The finance, insurance, and real estate people led all others (69 per cent), followed by agriculture (56 per cent), merchandising (51 per cent), and manufacturing (49 per cent). Business organizations (45 per cent), transportation (48 per cent), and services (41 per cent) were at the bottom.

Agricultural associations have the most frequent and closest ties with the government. General farm legislation, price support programs, and crop restrictions now help to account for this, and historically the government has played a definite role in organizing and controlling food production in the United States. This has been of such importance that agriculture has rated a cabinet position in the federal government since 1889. Agricultural associations are an excellent example of the usefulness and power of trade associations for influencing government decisions. Through them the farmers and their organizations are able to express their own interests and to adapt those interests to the society. Often the interests of society as set forth in proposals for legislation do not mesh with the interests of a tightly knit membership-oriented association. If membership needs are to be fulfilled, some compromise must be reached between the interests of agriculture and those of other groups in the society. Legislation and federal action such as price supports and crop-control programs are products of the emergent forces of this society. United, collective action through formal associations is necessary to achieve congruence of rural and urban competitive positions and the general welfare of each individual farmer. By acting as an individual the latter is not likely to be effective in promoting his own interests. It is through the collective action of his formal association that his interests are given sufficient organization and strength to influence legislation.

Agriculture has served here as a solid example of the relations between government and trade and business associations, but the same statements are applicable to the other six enterprise types. They do not necessarily hold the same official status that agriculture occupies in government, but the importance of the relation is apparent, largely through the governmental activities these associations use to influence the society in general. Government in our democracy represents the interests of the people in the total society; trade and business associations represent the general and special interests of their respective industries and the individual memberships in a specific sense, and the promotion of either obviously produces effects on both. The promotion of trade associations' interests in government may produce an alteration of the total society's position regarding the specific interests involved; and conversely, the promotion of the general society's interests can easily result in an alteration of the trade association's position regarding a specific interest.

This interrelationship between government and trade associations results partly in the proliferation of associations' activities throughout the society and conflict or congruency with the society's emergent processes. A major national trade association may wish a high tariff levied on imported goods its industry produces. Through congressional lobbying it actively campaigns for the tariff. Its passage may raise the price of those goods to American consumers, who make known their opposition to the proposed legislation, and a compromise may result. The compromise, or conflict, or defeat represents an adaptation of interests in which the trade association membership, the association itself, and the society have all shared.

Fifty-eight per cent of all trade and business associations take active public stands on economic, political, and social issues: three-fourths (77 per cent) of the business associations, 73 per cent of merchandising, 71 per cent of agriculture, two-thirds (67 per cent) of finance, and 63 per cent of transportation. Only among manufacturing (46 per cent) and service (39 per cent) associations do fewer than 50 per cent assume public stands on public policy.

The issues on which they state positions and work to influence political and public policy vary greatly. They range through domestic and foreign affairs from fiscal and taxation questions and labor relations to agricultural policies and public resources. Half (51 per cent) of all those who take public positions are concerned about taxation and fiscal matters, by far the most contested issue; more than a third (37 per cent) speak out on general and various legislation, about a fourth (24 per cent) on health and welfare, and 23 per cent on labor relations.

The special interests of each industry are evident in the issues on which its trade associations take stands. Eighty-seven per cent of the transportation, communications, and utilities trade groups spoke out on issues involving public resources, far more than the proportion reported for any other type of association. Half the finance, insurance, and real estate associations were interested in questions of health and welfare, and 75 per cent spoke out on the most popular issue of all, taxation and fiscal policy.

Most concerned with foreign affairs were the manufacturing associations (32 per cent), closely followed by agriculture (26 per cent), with the general average for such issues 16 per cent. Only agricultural associations showed high interest (56 per cent) in the problems of agriculture. Fewer than 10 per cent of each of the others were interested in such issues, and the average was only 13 per cent.

In ten categories of issues trade and business associations took

Big Trade and Business Associations

positions. All but three—education (6 per cent), military matters (2 per cent), and civil rights (2 per cent)—have been referred to here. On these three issues as well as on agricultural issues either only a few or almost all associations within a given category showed both public interest and political activity. Since any association could take a stand on any issue, the percentages do not necessarily add to 100 per cent.

Slightly less than half (47 per cent) also have programs to influence general public opinion, for which, of course, they have their own internal policies of education and information. This effort to influence public opinion (propaganda to some) is most readily stated by the agricultural groups (68 per cent) and by the manufacturers (53 per cent), followed by the financial groups (48 per cent). All the others run slightly below average, with 46 per cent of business associations and 33 per cent of merchandising associations admitting to their efforts.

The complex relations to the federal government involving national as well as local opinion, when viewed broadly, quickly tell us more about how the enterprise types fit into the larger world of influencing public opinion by stating their positions on social and economic issues and acting on them in relation to the federal government. Three—agriculture, followed by finance and merchandising—rank highest for such activities; manufacturing, transportation, communications, utilities, and business associations are intermediate; and service associations rank lowest. Agriculture is unique—it ranks high in all activities. The service associations are generally low. To better understand this ranking of the public and governmental behavior of trade and business associations, we need to think about the types just mentioned together with that we have called simple and complex varieties of associations.

Although it is clear that there are strong relations between the size and degree of complexity of types of associations and the likelihood of their headquarters being in one of the big three cities because of either the high decisions being made in corporate headquarters in New York and Chicago or the political ones in Washington, there seems to be no clear relationship between the simplicity and complexity of enterprise types of association and their political and governmental activity. We will briefly review this evidence to bring out certain concluding points. Agriculture, most active in all relations with the government, is also the largest in size of membership, but these are individual, not organizational members. We know that it is low in headquarters in the big three, but this is because the big industrial centers of New York and Chicago are not favored; one-fourth of its associations are in Washington. Inspection of them indicates that those associations with limited purposes (one crop, one breed of cattle) stay in the local regions where their economies are but that those with broader, more comprehensive purposes tend to go to Washington. Those are the farm and ranch associations, which are most likely to take stands to influence political and public opinion. They are also likely to have close relations with the federal agencies and with the members of Congress as well as with the Cabinet and executive offices.

The associations that organize service enterprises are at the other end of the scale and make the fewest attempts to influence opinion or to act informally or formally with government agencies. But, like agricultural groups, they rank high for the number of their individual members and low for organizational ones. They tend to have small staffs as well; although they have a high percentage of headquarters in the big three cities, they have few in Washington but have as many as finance in New York City.

Finance and merchandising rank high in political and governmental activities, along with agriculture. But the highest proportion of financial associations are not located in Washington but in New York City. And the wholesale and retail associations' headquarters are fairly equally spread among the three big cities.

The enterprise types of trade and business associations differ in the relationship between associations' headquarters and structural complexity, government activity, and efforts to influence public opinion. They do not fit a neat configuration. The big pools of industry and business in New York and Chicago take many of the finance and manufacturing headquarters to New York and spread merchandising associations between Chicago and New York; but the high-level political decisions and decision-makers in Washington bring a huge proportion of transportation, communications, and utilities and a sizable percentage of merchandising associations to Washington. We cannot give the statistical counts, but reinspection of the associations in each enterprise type with regard to the kinds of simplicity and complexity shows us that those national

Big Trade and Business Associations

associations that function for an entire industry rather than those that are specialized for a particular part of an industry or for a small division of the industry are most likely to locate in Washington and secondarily in New York or Chicago—in other words, in the big three. However, since more than two-thirds of all the trade and business associations are in the big three rather than generally spread throughout other big cities, one can assume that the corporate and government headquarters located there bring all kinds to these places; the many supplementary offices in either or both of the other big three or other major cities express in fact and in symbol the spread of interests, obligation, and responsibility felt by these organizations for their members and their industries. But, increasingly, in order to act as the cooperator of competitors in doing business for the profit-making individuals and organizations who compose their membership, they have business with the national government.

CHAPTER TEN

Labor Unions

Labor unions today are an important type of large organization in American society, although they have only recently achieved their current scale. During the three hundred years of their existence in this country they have grown in size, in geographical distribution, in complexity of structure, and in number and type of functions performed.

In their beginnings unions were limited to the town or region; now the great majority of members belong to national and international unions. From dealings with a few owners of workshops unions have progressed to negotiations with management at the apex of great national corporations. The growth and increasing ramifications of big business have been matched, with rough equivalence, in big unions. Along with the same trend, the level of government concern with unions has shifted from local and state to federal. Because the decisions of these great organizations affect the entire nation, the President of the United States may intervene in union-management disputes. The request of the United Steelworkers for an increase in pay or of the United Auto Workers for a flexible work week is now viewed as a matter of national interest.

From a kind of union organization totaling fifteen or twenty men in which a few officers set forth the items they hoped to obtain in their contract, the structure has changed to one in which these matters receive attention from a number of staff members of the International Union, including scientific experts on the cost of living and pension plans. The importance of the international staff has increased; regional or district offices have grown up as intermediate structures between the local and the international.

The concern with the well being of the whole man as contrasted with that solely of the worker on his job is old in the union move-

This chapter is by June M. Collins. See Notes on Authors.

ment. Today this concern takes planned, precise, complex forms requiring careful thought and considerable financing. Providing sickness benefits in the form of money and through clinics, such as those of the International Ladies' Garment Workers, is an example. This union shows expansion of function also not only by making vacation time possible for the worker but by maintaining vacation resorts as well. A policy of care for the retired is expressed today in the Auto Workers' recreational centers for retired men as well as in pension plans.

Instead of grappling only with local problems, such as the price of bread in New York City, union officials now think ahead in their programs to developments that affect the entire western world, such as increases in automation. They make recommendations for legislation in areas of federal taxation, public works, and education, which do not directly involve their own workers on their jobs.

This study is presented in three parts. The first is devoted to the history of American unions; the second to the types, characteristics, structures, and belief systems of unions; and the third to one union, the United Automobile, Aerospace and Agriculture Implement Workers of America (hereafter abbreviated UAW), used as the example of contemporary unions.

The first two sections are based largely on library research. Helpful here in addition to the library of Wayne State University was the library of the UAW International, which has an extensive collection of books on labor as well as documents, such as constitutions and annual reports, issued by many unions. The section on the UAW is the result of work done periodically over four years, 1961–65, at Solidarity House, the headquarters of the UAW International in Detroit. Interviews with officers and staff members of the Union provided abundant material. Unpublished documentary data in the files of the International, such as letters, contracts, reports and public addresses of the officers, were very helpful in preparing this section.

ORIGINS AND GROWTH OF THE LABOR MOVEMENT

Sometimes the impression is given that unions are a recent phenomenon lacking in respectable antiquity, but the roots of labor unions in the United States extend well back into colonial times.[1] Authorities differ on the date of the first association of tradesmen and of the first strike. Before the Revolution in 1776 several groups of tradesmen are credited with organizing or with strikes. The house carpenters of Philadelphia, according to John R. Commons, had the first authenticated organization of the building trades in 1724.[2] That organization probably consisted of master carpenters; owner, master, and worker were often combined in the same person at this period, so the early associations were not of employees as we think of them today. The date often given for the first strike is 1741, when New York bakers are alleged to have struck against city authorities, who set the price of bread.[3]

The first union organizations in the United States were locals, limited to one craft and to one city. The shoemakers of Philadelphia organized in 1792, the first society for the purpose of maintaining and raising wages, but this association lasted less than a

1. The following sources on labor history are recommended: John R. Commons et al., *History of Labour in the United States* 4 vols. New York, Macmillan, 1961. Lloyd Ullman, *The Rise of the National Trade Union,* Cambridge, Harvard University Press, 1955. Charles O. Gregory, *Labor and the Law,* 2nd rev. ed. with supplement, New York, Norton, 1961, is an excellent history of labor in relation to the laws and court decisions. Gregory begins with the position of labor in English common law and carries through the early years of unions in the United States to 1961. Comparatively brief histories of the labor movement include: Mary Beard, *A Short History of the American Labor Movement,* New York, Macmillan, 1924. Foster R. Dulles, *Labor in America,* New York, Crowell, 1959. Selig Perlman, *History of Trade Unionism in the United States,* New York, Macmillan, 1937.
2. Commons, I, 68. This union, called The Carpenters' Company of the City and County of Philadelphia, was not incorporated until 1792.
3. Ibid., I, 53, 54 expresses some doubt about this event, although he says it is certain "that even after the adoption of the constitution the master bakers in New York refused to bake because the assize [price established by the local authorities] was too stringent."

year; the Federal Society of Journeymen Cordwainers, founded in 1794, lasted until 1806; the printers of New York began the Typographical Society in 1794, which lasted three years.

The jurisdiction of these early unions was purely local. Each was independent in its trade, and the relations among "locals" extended only to feeble attempts to ward off personal competition. Occasionally members of different locals corresponded on trade matters, notifying each other of their purpose and the nature of their demands, or expressing fraternal greetings. The Philadelphia Typographical Society gave financial aid to the Franklin Typographical Society of New York to the extent of $83.50 for the relief of members who had become ill during an epidemic.[4]

The early unions were mainly benevolent societies organized to give members and their families help during sickness, unemployment, and death. This limitation was sometimes but not always due to the desires of the members; the attitude of the courts and of legislatures was not favorable toward organizations of working men. In the eighteenth century, before the Revolution, English courts had already given unfavorable decisions in cases of workmen who organized to improve conditions of their employment. English judges treated these cases, including strikes of workers, as criminal conspiracy. Charles Gregory explains these decisions of the judges as the result of their beliefs "that the use of the economic power made possible by combination and the concerted action of working people was bad for the economy of England. Since individual refusals of wage earners to work under conditions not acceptable to them had no discernible effect on the national economy, the vice was combination and concerted action." [5]

American courts and legislatures used the same approach in the early nineteenth century. For example, state legislatures refused to permit workmen to put the word "protective" in their articles of incorporation. In 1818 the New York Typographical Society was permitted to incorporate only when it struck the word "protective" from its articles and inserted a statement that it should not "at any time pass any law or regulation respecting the price or wages of labour or workmen, or any other articles, or relating to the business

4. Ibid., I, 113.
5. Gregory.

which the members thereof practise or follow for a livelihood." [6]

Acts incorporating journeymen societies included a clause to the effect that "the legal existence of the society ceases automatically if the funds of the society are misappropriated or if the organization is convicted of an attempt to fix scales of wages." [7]

These regulations probably grew out of reactions to workmen's attempts to regulate wages. The chief purpose of correspondence among typographical societies in different cities was to keep neighbors informed of improved working conditions, especially increases in wages. In 1809 the New York printers wrote members of other typographical organizations about their new price list, and in 1810 the Philadelphia society sent a copy of its price list to the New York society. The latter organization called a special meeting, at which they approved these demands and pledged themselves not to "take any situation vacated by any of our brethren in Philadelphia under the present circumstances"—an early expression of worker solidarity.[8]

The concept of the union's role in validation of the skill and ability of its members is shown in an 1814 resolution by the Pittsburgh cordwainers, "to write to societies in Baltimore and Philadelphia, and to agree with them not to receive any members of their societies unless they produced certificates of belonging to their societies, and then if he came to the place without one, they would not work with him!" [9]

The year 1827 is important for several reasons. Growing out of a strike of carpenters for a ten hour workday, the first association of unions within one city was formed in Philadelphia. This grouping of a type, later called the "city central" and still present today (for example, among the building trades), was named the Mechanics' Union of Trade Associations. In addition to carpenters it included bricklayers, painters, glaziers, cordwainers, and hatters. This early

---

6. Commons, I, 186, quoting McMaster, *History of the People of the United States*, III, 511.

7. Ibid., I, 86, quoting New York, *Laws,* 1807–1809, act incorporating New York Society of Journeymen Shipwrights.

8. Ibid., I, 113, quoting Stewart, *Documentary History of Early Organizations of Printers,* p. 876, New York Typographical Society, Minutes (Mss.), Sept. 24, 1810.

9. Ibid., I, 114, quoting John R. Commons, *Documentary History of American Industrial Society,* IV, 31.

tendency to unite at the city level was to expand into regional, national, and international organizations, culminating in the AFL–CIO federation in 1955.

In 1828 the Philadelphia Mechanics Union of Trade Associations gave birth to the Working Men's Party, a political organization of craftsmen, other wage earners, and farmers. A counterpart in New York was soon established. This party had among its planks universal education, abolition of the militia system, a less expensive law system, all officers to be elected directly by the people, a lien law for laborers, no legislation on religion.[10] The theme of concern with broad, national policies as apart from wages and hours is shown here at an early date. Attempts at political action on the part of labor are traditional in the United States.

A new type of labor organization, part work-oriented and part political, came into being in 1831 and lasted until 1834. It was called the New England Association of Farmers, Mechanics, and Other Working Men and included farmers, mechanics, workingmen, and factory operatives. (Delegates to a meeting of this Association in 1832 came from Connecticut, Rhode Island, New Hampshire, Maine, and Massachusetts.) Its origins lay in the movement for the ten-hour day. When this goal did not seem practical, the members turned to political issues of a broad nature. Here we see a combination of goals such as characterizes the AFL–CIO today. When they have felt themselves blocked on job-related issues, labor unions down to the present have shifted to national or state legislative programs.

The structure of the New England Association was not too different from contemporary unions in that its constitution provided for auxiliary branches in each town and manufacturing village where there were fifteen members. It had a war chest into which each member paid an annual tax of fifty-five cents. Each local branch was to appoint a committee that could obtain funds from the general treasurer to help a member who lost his job through his membership.

The second convention, in 1832, paved the way for later national conventions of unions by proposing that a general committee of the association be established in each state (including states out-

10. Ibid., I, 217, 218.

side of New England) and that a national convention be held on this basis. Evidence of interest beyond the New England states is shown by the presence of John Farrel from Pennsylvania at the 1833 Convention.

The first unions, partly for traditional reasons and partly because of the requirements of legislatures, were, for the most part, benevolent societies. In the 1830s new organizations began to form, often within a trade that had a benevolent association. For example, in 1831 the printers began the New York Typographical Association, whose aim was "to elevate the character and advance the interest of the profession, by maintaining a just and uniform scale of prices for their labour"; [11] and the Philadelphia Typographical Association appeared in 1833. In both New York and Philadelphia the old typographical societies continued but only as benevolent societies.

During the 1830s different unions within a single city began to work together on occasion, although they were not necessarily united in a formal organization. In 1833, when the carpenters in New York struck, fifteen trades within the city met separately and promised financial help. In Baltimore in the same year a number of trades joined in opposition to hatters who were employers and who were trying to lower the wages of their own journeymen.

During this period in the early 1800s, as industry flourished, eastern cities grew in size and number. Trades unions or city centrals (associations of unions in one community) were formed to protect the increasing number of workmen. The first such city central appeared in New York City in 1833; three years later similar trades unions appeared in Baltimore, Washington, Boston, New Brunswick, Newark, Albany, Troy, Schenectady, Philadelphia, Pittsburgh, Cincinnati, and Louisville.

In 1834 the National Trades Union was organized in New York City. Followed by many later attempts, this was the first attempt to unite labor unions nationally. The main structure of the union was a convention that met annually for five years. Despite the national intent, delegates were sent by city centrals located for the most part in the eastern states. The organization attempted to promote trade unionism, to publish and spread information useful to workers, and

11. Ibid., I, 336, quoting Stewart, *A Documentary History of the Early Organizations of Printers,* in U.S. Department of Labor, *Bulletin No. XI,* pp. 894–900 and Appendix I, No. 5.

Labor Unions

"to unite and harmonize the efforts of all the productive classes of the country." [12] Among the subjects considered by the conventions were the factory system, the labor of women and children, prison labor, education, the ten-hour day, tariffs, the use of public domain, and cooperation among unions—another example of national unions extending their interest far beyond employment alone.

The First National Unions

The first national unions appeared in the 1830s, the earliest being the Cordwainers (the National Cooperative Association of Journeymen Cordwainers) in 1836. Although national in scope, the Cordwainers had delegates at their first meeting from eastern states only—New York, Connecticut, New Jersey, Pennsylvania, and Delaware. Other national unions that followed rapidly were the printers, combmakers, carpenters, and hand-loom weavers.

Workmen who formed organizations for the betterment of working conditions or who struck were from time to time convicted as criminals by American courts, following the precedents established by English courts. In 1842 a new precedent was established. Chief Justice of the Massachusetts Courts Lemuel Shaw (1781–1861) had to decide whether or not to uphold the lower courts in a decision against seven journeymen bootmakers who had struck against their employer in Boston. Shaw, who was not an advocate of labor, nevertheless decided that organizing in itself even to obtain power was not bad. The court would not assume that the purposes or goals were evil or harmful—it would have to be proven. Shaw did not deny the idea of criminal conspiracy but said in effect that the mere organizing of workmen could not be automatically regarded as criminal. This interpretation meant that while charges of criminal conspiracy could continue, as in fact they occasionally did, they could not be depended upon for convictions without evidence of harmful results.

The Shaw decision was followed by considerable union activity both in industrial congresses and in organizing. The industrial

12. Ibid., I, 425, quoting *Constitution* adopted August 28, 1834; *The Man*, Sept. 2, 1834; John R. Commons, *Documentary History of American Industrial Society*, VI, 221.

congresses from 1845 to 1856 are important as the forerunners of the later national labor unions. One of the first of these attempts at national organization was the National Reform Association. It met in May 1845 in New York City; like the other national meetings of the day, it is probable that the Northeast and Central Atlantic States supplied most of the members. Among others, representatives of the New England Working Men's association attended. In this association as well as similar ones, unions, mechanics, or workers were not the only groups represented. Agrarian reformers, advocates of cooperatives (including the famous Robert Owen), antirenters, and others were present. It is interesting in terms of present-day labor-management negotiations that well over a hundred years ago Horace Greeley, editor of the New York *Tribune,* hoped for "a congress of employers and wage earners, equal in numbers, which would determine, by voluntary agreement, uniform conditions of labour for the entire union, so that a ten-hour day 'might be adopted without injury to any and with signal benefit to all.' " [13] Greeley's wishes were not realized; although workers attended, employers did not go to the congress. At the annual meeting of the congress the following year in Boston, in order to be eligible for membership persons had to pledge their support for a ten-hour day in public works and establishments authorized by law.[14] After the 1846 meeting the membership of all but the agrarians fell off greatly, although the annual meetings of the congress continued until 1856. An important point to note is that trade unionists worked together and found common cause with Americans of other economic origins and interests.

During the decade after 1849 state and city gatherings were also held. The latter, tending to focus more directly on labor, were sometimes called in the face of threats to specific workers. The workingmen's congress in Pittsburgh in December 1849 was requested by a group of trades when the wages of certain ironworkers were cut by the manufacturers. State industrial congresses were held in the East and as far west as Illinois; the city congresses attended sometimes by the members of many different trades were also held in the Midwest as well as the East.

One of the goals of these congresses was to obtain aid for men on

13. Ibid., I, 548, quoting *New York Tribune,* Sept. 30, 1845.
14. Ibid., I, 550.

the job, such as the ten-hour day, through legislative action. At least partly as the result of the first of these conventions and the attendant publicity, as well as of the New England State Working Men's Association, individual states began to pass laws stipulating the ten-hour day. New Hampshire was first, in 1847. The next year Pennsylvania enacted a similar law, except that it was limited to employees in textile and paper factories; Maine followed in the same year with a law requiring a ten-hour day for all workers except those in agriculture. Here we see early precedent for legislative action as a means of reaching labor's goals.

A number of laws either requiring the ten-hour day or extending it to minors were passed in the 1850s. In 1855 Connecticut established a ten-hour day for mechanical and factory labor; Pennsylvania extended the ten-hour day of 1848 to include minors in the textile and paper factories.

In the 1850s the first national unions of specific trades that have survived to the present appeared. The International Typographical Union, the earliest, was formed in 1852; others, such as the Iron Molders (Molders International Union) followed despite the blow to unionism during the depression of 1854–55.

The period immediately after the Civil War saw great economic development—in coal mining and in the spread of the railroads west. The workers in the extractive and building industries proved ripe for organizing into unions.

The National Trades Union, formed in 1834, set a precedent for the National Labor Union of 1866–72. This association first met in Baltimore with representatives from only thirteen States and the District of Columbia. These states were in the Northeast, Middle Atlantic, and the Midwest as far as Illinois, Iowa, and Missouri; as the Midwest and West became settled and industrialized, delegates came from these areas.

Most of the delegates in 1866 were sent by trade unions limited to single cities; the others represented joint bodies such as trades assemblies.

Like many other union organizations, the National Labor Union held annual conventions. Its structure was largely limited to these meetings, to which each national and international union could send one delegate and each combined organization, such as a trades union, one delegate for the first 500 members and one for each additional 500 or fraction thereof. This principle of proportional representation in conventions remains today in individual unions and in the AFL–CIO. As a major plank the National Labor Union supported the eight-hour day in 1866 and the economic policy of Greenbackism in 1867. The question of the extent to which labor unions should engage in politics, an issue continuing to the present, led to the weakening and eventual disappearance of the National Labor Union.

The pressure of labor groups for the eight-hour day had some success. In 1868 the United States Congress passed the first federal law to declare an eight-hour day, but it applied only to federal employees.

In Europe the International Workingmen's Association was established in 1864 to help trade unions in different countries by controlling migration of workers to those countries during strikes. In 1866 the National Labor Union invited the International Workingmen's Association to send a delegate to their next convention in Chicago. Relations have continued, in varying degrees, between American and European labor leaders, even though the labor movement in this country has differed considerably from that abroad.

"The Knights of Labor"

The success of labor led to extreme countermeasures by management—the formation of company police and the breaking of strikes by force. During the severe depression from 1873 to 1879 employers used lockouts, blacklists, and legal prosecution, when possible, to discourage union activity. In order to protect their members against the acts of employers, labor organizations began to be secret, the most famous example being the Noble and Holy Order of Knights of Labor, founded in 1869 (although it did not become active until 1873).[15] In the 1870s the Knights supported

15. For sources on the Knights of Labor, see: Norman Ware, *The Labor Movement in the United States, 1860–1895,* New York, Appleton, 1929. Terence V. Powderly, *Thirty Years of Labor, 1859–1889,* Columbus, Ohio, Excelsior Publishing House, 1890, and *The Path I Trod,* New York, Columbia University Press, 1940. Foster R. Dulles, *Labor in America: A History,* 2nd rev. ed., New York, Crowell, 1960. Henry J. Browne, *The Catholic Church and the Knights of Labor,* Washington, D.C., 1949.

the Greenback party, which had a program of broad social reform based on the Greenbackism philosophy of currency inflation. A specific work-oriented goal stressed by the Knights, particularly in organizing, was the eight-hour day.

The Knights of Labor differed from the national trade unions in that they included all workers in the United States rather than those of a specific trade. Despite this inclusive nature and the emphasis on secrecy, especially in the early days, the Knights were much like the present-day national unions in structure. At the apex was the general assembly, with a general executive board governing between sessions. The country was apportioned into districts on a territorial basis, each with its own assembly, and below the districts were the local assemblies, made up of ten or more members. At least three-fourths of these local members had to be wage earners.[16] At the height of its strength in 1886 the Knights had 5,892 assemblies and 702,924 members. While the greatest strength of the Knights lay east of the Mississippi (nearly half of the members were in New York State, Pennsylvania, Massachusetts, and Illinois), they had members in almost every state and sufficient membership in Southwest District Assembly 101 to strike against the Texas and Pacific railroad in 1886 and to have a sympathy strike against the Missouri-Pacific supported by workers in Missouri, Kansas, Arkansas, Indian Territory, and Nebraska.[17] Strikes and the boycott were the two principal weapons used by the Knights to gain their goals.

The willingness of the Knights to accept all workers led to difficulties. Artisans, with their concepts of trade organizations firmly grounded in the crafts unions, wanted to dissociate themselves from unskilled workers and to retain some autonomy as members of individual crafts. The leaders of the Knights successfully fought this tendency, but in so doing they encouraged dissatisfied craftsmen to look elsewhere for association.

They did not have far to look. The forerunner of the present American Federation of Labor was organized in 1881: the Federation of Organized Trades and Labor Unions.

The federal government's growing concern with labor matters was

16. Perlman.
17. Commons, II, 383.

shown in 1884 in the formation of the Bureau of Labor, at first part of the Department of Interior.

During the latter part of the last century workers continued to use the strike in the hopes of raising their pay and reducing their hours of work. The presence of the national organizations, such as the Knights of Labor and the national trade unions, made possible the general strike, a very powerful weapon. One of the most famous of these was the general strike for the eight-hour day in 1866, carried on simultaneously in Chicago, New York, Cincinnati, Baltimore, Milwaukee, Boston, Pittsburgh, Detroit, St. Louis, Washington, and other cities. The leaders of the Knights were opposed to this strike, but many members nevertheless took part.

In Chicago members of the "Black Internationale," formed in Pittsburgh in 1883 (nickname for the International Working People's Association, because of its left-wing and "anarchist" members), took part in the strike. Trade unions, especially the building trades, furniture workers, and cigarmakers, were much more active in the Chicago strike than the Knights. Chicago participation in this strike became famous because of the Haymarket Riot. On May 3, in a fight between police and workers, a policeman who had been hit with stones shot and killed four workers and wounded others. On May 4 in Haymarket Square one of the anarchists killed a policeman with a bomb. In reaction against this violence the public turned against the Knights, although the latter had not officially taken part in the strike. Membership in the Knights began to drop; by 1893 it had fallen to 74,635 from 700,000 before the Haymarket Riot. Despite their loss in strength, their cooperative ventures in the manufacture of shoes and in coal mining continued for a time. Although they never recovered their earlier power, the organization continued until 1917, when it ended formally. Unionists had turned to a new organization.

The AFL

The American Federation of Labor grew out of a committee of the Federation of Organized Trades and Labor Unions. This committee, devoted to legislative matters, reported to a conference of trade unions officials in Columbus, Ohio, at a meeting in 1886. The delegates, who represented twenty-five trades organizations claiming 316,469 members [18] declared this meeting to be the first annual meeting of the American Federation of Labor and began to draft a constitution. Later in 1886 the older union formally merged with the new American Federation of Labor. The AFL remained the principal association of unions in this country and set the direction of the labor movement until the middle 1930s. As an organization it stayed independent until 1955, when it merged with the Congress of Industrial Organizations.

In the organization of the old union, each state had its own Federation of Trades and Labor Unions, which sent delegates to the national conventions. The structure of the new AFL recognized the desire for organization identity and autonomy among crafts and trades—for independence and representation on the basis of kind of work. National and international unions were the basic units; their delegates had voting power at the conventions in proportion to the number of union members they represented. The only local unions represented at the conventions were those that did not belong to a national or international union. This representation of the individual national unions, each with considerable autonomy, seems responsible for both the strength of the AFL and its weakness. The satisfaction of the member crafts and trades unions with their importance in the structure surely accounts in considerable part for the enduring quality of the organization as compared with the short-term previous attempts at national associations of unions. The weakness lay in nonrepresentation or weak representation of unskilled and semiskilled workers. In the twentieth century, as the assembly line developed in the automobile industry and spread to other manufacture, the proportion of semiskilled workers increased greatly in the labor market but not in representational strength in the AFL.

Toward the end of the last century the federal government showed increasing involvement with labor-management relations through the passage of the first federal labor relations law in 1888. This law was designed only for the railroads, but it did establish a continuing pattern for the federal government of participation in arbitration between management and labor.

18. Ibid., II, 410.

In 1890 Congress passed a law that was construed by the courts in some cases as applying to labor unions. This was the Sherman Act, which congressmen meant to apply to business corporations. The sections of the act that later came to be important to labor were:

1. "Every contract, combination in the form of trust or otherwise, or conspiracy, in restraint of trade or commerce among the several States, or with foreign nations, is hereby declared to be illegal."

2. "Every person who shall monopolize, or attempt to monopolize, or combine or conspire with any other person or persons, to monopolize any part of the trade or commerce among the several States, or with foreign nations, shall be deemed guilty of a misdemeanor." [19]

The lower courts were divided as to whether labor unions qualified as combinations in restraint of trade or commerce, an idea that had roots in England. In 1908 the Supreme Court ruled that secondary boycotts by a union were actions in restraint of trade and therefore were illegal under the Sherman Act.

During the period from 1900 until World War I the dominant American Federation of Labor followed a policy different from that of the Knights of Labor in the 1870s and 1880s. Instead of developing a labor party in politics or giving all its support to one of the already established parties, the AFL adopted a bipartisan plan, sponsoring planks favorable to labor in the platform of each party and assisting candidates who promised most help to labor. The AFL placed emphasis on legislation as a means of improving labor's position. To a limited extent this goal was realized, although federal and state legislation to improve working conditions or union strength was usually declared unconstitutional by the Supreme Court. Nevertheless, legislators continued to pass bills helping labor.

An example of the effect of the Supreme Court on labor legislation is the Clayton Act, passed by Congress in 1914 to expand and clarify the Sherman Act of 1890. Section 20 of the Clayton Act was written to deny management the injunction, a powerful weapon in struggles with labor, and this section was received with great enthu-

19. Gregory, p. 201.

siasm by union leaders. But in 1921 the Supreme Court decided (in the Case of Duplex Printing Press v. Deering) that Section 20 applied only in cases of striking employees and their immediate employers and then only to action that was already acceptable under common law. Using the secondary labor boycott to force workers to organize was an issue in this case. The Supreme Court took the position that this was still illegal. In other words, despite the intent of Congress, the net effect of the Clayton bill for labor was to legalize peaceful picketing of employers by striking workers.

Laws to assist workers continued to be passed. In 1915 conditions of employment for maritime workers were set forth in the LaFollette Seamen's Act. The following year the Federal Child Labor Law limited child labor and estabished a minimum wage for workers. This law was declared unconstitutional and was followed by a similar law, also pronounced unconstitutional. In 1924 Congress approved a resolution proposing a child labor amendment to the Constitution. The need for this amendment (which did not become part of the Constitution) disappeared when the Fair Labor Standards Act was passed by Congress in 1938. This act established a minimum age of sixteen for those engaged in producing goods for interstate or foreign commerce and of eighteen for particularly hazardous occupations. An amendment to the Act, effective in 1950, prohibited the employment of children under sixteen years in agriculture during school hours but did not include children working for their parents or those in intrastate agriculture.

Workers continued to strike during disputes in the 1900–17 period. A notable means of settlement was reached after a two-month strike of the International Ladies' Garment Workers' Union in 1910; the resulting agreement between labor and management contained a clause for preferential union hiring, a board of grievances, and a board of arbitration. This agreement was followed by an increase in arbitration, which had been initiated by the federal government in the railway labor law of 1888.

The rather slow, cautious approach of the AFL through support of labor legislation did not satisfy all within the labor movement. As early as 1905 dissidents formed the Industrial Workers of the World, known as the IWW or the Wobblies. Rather than working to bring about change within the existing structure, the IWW sought to do away with the wage system entirely.

A great part of the appeal of the IWW lay in its willingness to include unskilled workers. The AFL had given little attention to the great mass of unskilled laborers, and the IWW moved in to organize them and with considerable success, especially in the coal fields, wheat farms of the West, and lumber camps. Because of the growing membership of the IWW and the realization that here might be a successful rival, the AFL gave organization of the unskilled a high place on the agenda of its 1912 convention. The AFL miners' union took as members many anthracite workers in Pennsylvania who might otherwise have joined the IWW. In other industries and areas of the country the AFL either did not attempt or was not successful in competitive organization. However, despite its temporary success after 1913, the IWW rapidly lost ground after sponsoring a series of unsuccessful strikes in the textile industry.

A theme of unresolved conflict within the labor movement is the extent to which labor should support the existing system and the extent to which it should propose change. The AFL traditionally, the present-day AFL–CIO, and union leaders generally support and work within the present governmental system.

As periods of full employment are likely to do, World War I brought gains for unions. The National War Labor Board was established in 1917 to mediate in labor disputes and to promote good relations between labor and management. This government board was significant, for it was formal, public recognition of the importance and value of unions. The board encouraged workers to bargain with management through their union representatives, expressing the belief held by government and later by business corporations that industrial peace and cooperation can best be obtained through the existence of labor organizations with responsible leadership. During World War I representatives of labor were made members of a number of federal boards and committees where they could voice complaints for labor in groups where action might be taken. Union membership increased in many industries, including some unskilled and semiskilled kinds of work.

The period between 1918 and 1929, the beginning of the depression, is sometimes called "the open-shop decade." After the dissolution of the War Labor Board and termination of wartime contracts, employers in some cases refused to recognize unions. Despite strikes and other efforts, unions lost membership in the early twenties and later in the thirties as the growing numbers of unemployed during the depression allowed corporations greater control. The unemployed demanded governmental assistance. Franklin D. Roosevelt became president in 1932, and between then and 1952 many laws and practices that directly and indirectly assisted labor unions were instituted under the aegis of the Democratic Party. One of these was the Norris–La Guardia Act of 1932, which prohibited federal injunctions in labor disputes except as specified and outlawed so-called "yellow-dog" contracts, that is, agreements signed by the worker as a condition of his employment forbidding him to join a union.

The National Industry Recovery Act (NIRA) of 1933 stated that "every NRA [National Recovery Act] should guarantee the right of employees to organize and bargain collectively through their representatives without interference, restraint, or coercion by employers." [20] Title I of the NIRA was declared unconstitutional in 1935. In the same year the National Labor Relations Act—also known as the Wagner Act—protected for the first time on a national basis the right of the worker to organize and to elect representatives for collective bargaining.

The CIO

In the early thirties, growing out of dissatisfaction with economic conditions in the country on the one hand and with the AFL on the other, a new and important association of unions, the Committee for Industrial Organization, came into being,[21] headed by John L. Lewis, president of the United Mine Workers. The name of the Committee was changed in 1938 to the Congress of Industrial Organizations—CIO.

CIO unions were not organized, as most AFL unions were, on the basis of trades or crafts; they encompassed an entire industry, taking all or nearly all the workers in steel or rubber or automobile

20. *Brief History of the American Labor Movement,* U.S. Department of Labor, Bureau of Labor Statistics, Bulletin No. 1000 (Washington, D.C., U.S. Government Printing Office), 195.

21. For sources on the CIO see Edward Levinson, *Labor on the March* (New York, Harper, 1938) and *CIO, 1935–1955* (Washington, Congress of Industrial Organizations, 1955).

companies. The need of unskilled and semiskilled workers for adequate union representation found expression here. The unions that first made up the Committee for Industrial Organization were the United Mine Workers, Amalgamated Clothing Workers, International Ladies' Garment Workers' Union (which did not affiliate and returned to the AFL in 1938), United Textile Workers, International Union of Mine, Mill and Smelter Workers, and International Association of Oil Field, Gas Well, and Refinery Workers. Four unions soon joined: International Union of United Automobile Workers, United Rubber Workers, Amalgamated Association of Iron, Steel, and Tin Workers, and Federation of Flat Glass Workers.

As these names suggest, the CIO was successful in organizing in a number of industries. A technique of getting recognition from management for which the CIO was noted during this early period was the "sit-down strike," in which workers sat at their benches and places of work day and night until agreements were reached.

In 1938 Congress passed the Fair Labor Standards Act establishing minimum wages (40 cents an hour) and overtime (time and a half) for hours over forty a week and regulated child labor in interstate commerce or in production of goods for interstate commerce —explicit recognition of the right of the federal government to concern itself with wages.

In 1940, in the case of Apex Hosiery Company v. Leader, the sit-down strike was judged, in the absence of intent to impose market controls, not to be an illegal restraint of commerce under the Sherman Act. The sit-down strike as a technique in gaining recognition of unions was thereby given further impetus, but it was curtailed by the start of World War II.

Shortly before the United States entered the war the UAW was recognized by Ford Motor Company after a strike of ten days. The agreement between the UAW and Ford Motor Company stipulating a union shop was the first such agreement with an auto manufacturer.

As in the first World War, labor was subject to a number of restrictions, but it also received governmental protection and approval. Late in 1941 the AFL and the CIO voluntarily restricted their own activities by agreeing not to strike (the so-called no-strike pact) until the end of the war.

Labor Unions

In 1942, after the United States entered the war, President Roosevelt instituted the National War Labor Board, organized on a regional as well as national basis, to bring about agreements in disputes between labor and management. Its members represented labor (equal numbers from the AFL and the CIO), management, and the public.

Freezing wages was one of the restrictions on labor's objectives during the war, but there was also the idea that wages should to some extent reflect changes in the cost in living. The "Little Steel" formula permitted increase in wages to meet a 15 per cent rise in living costs from January 1, 1941, to May 1, 1942, but it also set limits to wages.

After the end of the war there were, of course, many disruptions in industry. Contracts for the manufacture of arms and other articles for wartime consumption were canceled. Many men were thrown out of work at the same time that demobilization returned thousands of men to the labor force. During the war unions had become increasingly restive under the restrictions on wages but were bound by their no-strike agreement. Once the war ended, workers' dissatisfaction with wages and working conditions were expressed in a series of strikes, especially in the automobile, coal, oil, and steel industries. From August 1945 to June 1946 forty-two major strikes occurred. The strike of the United Steelworkers (CIO) in 1945 ended after one month, resulting in a negotiated wage increase of 18½ cents an hour. This sum served as a pattern for other industries; the idea that wage increases in one industry be introduced into others rapidly gained acceptance.

In the UAW strike against General Motors Corporation in 1946 a fact-finding board appointed by President Truman recommended an increase of 19½ cents per hour. The UAW and General Motors Corporation, after the strike had lasted three and a half months, negotiated an agreement that gave the auto workers a raise of 18½ cents an hour, following the pattern set by the steelworkers.

Most of the laws dealing with labor between 1900 and 1947—except the restrictive wartime laws—assisted labor in reaching its objectives. Some laws, such as the child labor laws of 1916 and 1919 respectively, were declared unconstitutional by the Supreme Court, and other decisions of the courts were often unfavorable; but legislation was clearly in the direction of expanding the legal rights of unions. This trend in legislation received a check in 1947 with the passage of the Labor-Management Relations Act, known as the Taft-Hartley Act. Passed over the veto of President Truman, this act provided a number of restrictions on labor: the closed shop was banned; regulations were listed for the union shop concerning check-off (a procedure by which the corporation deducts union dues from the worker's pay check), welfare funds, and grievance procedure; illegal labor practices were listed, including the secondary boycott; rules were given to enforce time lapses before strikes could begin.

Because of the importance to unions of the strike as a technique the rules governing it in the Taft-Hartley Act are significant. In conflicts between labor and management that imperil the national health or safety, the President of the United States may appoint a board of inquiry to examine the situation, and he can ask the courts for an injunction to forbid a strike or to stop the strike for eighty days. During this eighty-day "cooling-off period" efforts are made to reach a satisfactory agreement. If the union and management do not reach an agreement within sixty days, the employees vote by secret ballot on whether or not to accept the latest offer of the employer. If they reject the offer, the injunction is dissolved, and the union members are free to strike if they wish. The idea of the cooling-off period is partly that settlement may be reached during this time without the disruption of work. This concept of the regulation of time is also found in individual contracts between unions and corporations; periods of time are allotted for the various steps in grievance procedure, the regulation of time allowing an opportunity to make mutually satisfying decisions and at the same time establishing limits so that negotiations cannot be prolonged indefinitely.

While the Taft-Hartley Act restrains unions in the measures they may take, it does not deny them the right to strike. Labor union spokesmen maintain that this right, in the sense of quitting one's job, is upheld by a statement in the United States Constitution forbidding involuntary servitude.

The Taft-Hartley Act has not always been interpreted as restrictive to labor rather than management. In 1949 in the case of Inland Steel Company v. United Steelworkers of America (CIO) the Supreme Court upheld a decision of a lower court that the Taft-

Labor Unions

Hartley Act or Labor Management Relations Act *requires* employers to bargain with unions on retirement plans. This court decision encouraged the burgeoning of pension plans in labor-management agreements during the 1950s.

Some support for labor unions in the United States has always come from left-wing groups. This has been particularly true in CIO unions, since they have been regarded as more progressive politically than AFL. After World War II, when there was concern about American Communists in several spheres of national life, the CIO examined its own member unions. The CIO convention of 1949 passed an amendment to the constitution denying office in the national CIO to any individual "who is a member of the Communist Party, any fascist organization, or other totalitarian movement" or who "consistently pursues policies and activities" followed by such organizations. During this convention two unions, the United Farm Equipment and Metal Workers and the United Electrical, Radio and Machine Workers, were tried for violations of this amendment and expelled; during 1950 nine other unions were removed for similar reasons.

In the decade following 1950 attempts to unite the CIO and the AFL into one association were successful. The process of banding together of unions, which had been going on since the early 1800s, reached a new high level with the federation of the AFL–CIO in 1955. While the overwhelming majority of union members in the United States belong to this federation, there are still 1,200 or so small independent unions.

In 1959 Congress passed the Labor-Management Reporting and Disclosure Act (LMRDA), also known as the Landrum-Griffin Act,[22] revising part of the National Labor Relations Act of 1947. The Landrum-Griffin Act seems in part to be a response to the investigations of the McClellan Committee during the 1950s, which revealed corruption in several large unions. This act has many provisions, most of which regulate internal behavior of unions. According to Title I the union must engage in democratic voting procedures and must use the secret ballot, must permit individual members to bring suit against the union and its officers after having exhausted the union's own procedures for justice, and must see that

22. For this discussion of the Landrum-Griffin Act the writer has relied heavily on Gregory.

every member receives a copy of the current contract with management. Under Title II each labor union must have a constitution and bylaws and must file copies of them with the Secretary of Labor. He must also be given much additional information concerning the amount and use of funds owned by the union. The subsection of the Taft-Hartley Act that required union officials to take an oath that they did not belong to the Communist Party was repealed. Union officials are required by this Title to report stocks and bonds they own and all receipts coming from work in labor relations. Employers must report payments and loans to union officers or their agents; they must also state expenditures to restrain or coerce employees in connection with union activities and give details of arrangements made with labor consultants.

Title III of the Act provides for trusteeships in which the national or international union may take over a local and administer its affairs for a time. The legitimate reasons for such trusteeships are spelled out so that they cannot be used to interrupt the democratic process in a local.

Title IV states the procedures required for honest elections within unions and empowers the Secretary of Labor to investigate departures from the rules upon complaints from union members.

Title V is devoted to the restrictions on handling of finances by the union officials. Union officials must be bonded according to a rather elaborate procedure (bonding of the financial officers is commonly required by constitutions of unions). Unions may not lend officials more than $2000. Communists and exconvicts of certain types may not hold office in unions or act as consultants until after a specified period of years.

Title VI is designed to do away with extortionate picketing and to insure that criminal sanctions of the statute do not interfere with the enforcement of criminal laws of the states. It also establishes as a crime the use of violence, threats, or coercion while a union member is exercising his rights under the Taft-Hartley law.

In the final part of the Act, Title VII, there are a number of miscellaneous amendments to the Taft-Hartley Act. One is the removal of the "no-man's land" between the jurisdiction of the states and that of the National Labor Relations Board. Cases that had fallen into this no-man's land were beyond the scope of the individual state but could not be heard by the National Labor Relations Board because of the small volume of business done by the employer. The National Labor Relations Board is also permitted by the Act to give its regional directors more powers to deal with representation matters.

A major effect of the Landrum-Griffin act is to interrelate American labor unions more closely with the federal government and to grant the government increasing responsibility for their supervision. This tendency is paralleled, although not in exactly the same ways, in the relationship between government and business. It is perhaps inevitable that large-scale national organizations, being in many respects beyond the scope of individual states, become subject to the regulation of the federal government, acting for all citizens.

CHARACTERISTICS OF UNIONS

What can we learn about unions from number of members, wealth, and influence? In 1960, 184 unions with United States membership of more than 18 million [23] accounted for approximately 97 per cent of all union members in this country.

A fourth of the nation's total labor force and about a third of the employees in nonfarm establishments belonged to labor unions.[24]

Unions are divided into three categories on the basis of affiliation, number of employers, or geographical distribution. One group is formed by the 134 unions affiliated with the American Federation of Labor–Congress of Industrial Organizations (referred to hereafter as AFL–CIO or as affiliated). These 134 unions had about 83 per cent of union members in 1960. A second group is made up of the fifty unions called national that are not affiliated with the AFL–CIO, but that (except for unions of government employees, which have agreements with only one employer—the

23. *Directory of National and International Labor Unions in the United States, 1961,* Bureau of Labor Statistics, U.S. Department of Labor, Bulletin No. 1320, March, 1962, p. 46. Note that the international unions among these 184 have 1,112,000 members outside the United States, principally in Canada.

24. *Union Membership, 1960,* Preliminary Release, Bureau of Labor Statistics, U.S. Department of Labor, November, 1961, p. 1.

United States government) have contracts with more than one employer or extend into more than one state.[25] The term national does not mean limited to the United States; most, like the affiliated unions, are international. National is used to emphasize the extensive breadth and scope of most of these unions as compared to the intrastate and single-employer category.

The third type includes unions referred to here as localized; they bargain with only a single employer or are confined to one state. The term localized seems appropriate since many of these unions are limited to a single area, and the great majority have only one local. (The term localized should not be confused with the term local, referring to a unit or chapter of a national or affiliated union.) The first thorough study of localized unions reported 1,277 in the United States.[26] Their large number was offset by their small membership; in 1962 they totaled 452,463, 2.6 per cent of all union membership.

Industrial distribution of union members according to type of work showed almost half (8.6 million) of the 18 million affiliated and national union members in manufacturing, a little less (8.4 million) in nonmanufacturing outside of government service, and a small remainder (1.1 million) in federal, state, or local government service. One group of localized unions, the single-employer, had nearly three-fourths (72.1 per cent) in manufacturing and a little over one-fourth (27.7 per cent) in nonmanufacturing. The other category of localized unions, the intrastate, had almost the exact opposite, with nearly two-thirds (63.1 per cent) in nonmanufacturing and a little over one-third (35.6 per cent) in manufacturing.

Within manufacturing the largest numbers of all union members were employed in electrical machinery, other machinery, transportation equipment, and chemicals and allied industries. The affiliated and national unions contributed most heavily to this distribution. Of localized unions, single-employer unions were almost identical, with a few more members in chemicals and allied industries than in transportation. The intrastate localized unions again showed marked differences in manufacturing with leather and

25. *Directory of National and International Labor Unions*, p. 45.
26. Unless otherwise specified, the data for the unaffiliated unions confined to a single employer or a single state are taken from Harry P. Cohany and James Neary, "Unaffiliated Local and Single-Employer Unions in the United States, 1961," *Monthly Labor Review, 85* (1962), 975–82.

leather products the largest, electrical machinery next, and transportation a low third. Nonmanufacturing work, services, and retail trade accounted for more than half the members.

Blue-collar workers still predominated in labor unions. One out of eight members of the affiliated and national unions were white-collar employees as compared to one out of four of the localized unions. This should not be taken to mean that white-collar workers were joining localized unions in large numbers, for although the proportions were high, the number of white-collar members in these unions was small (113,029) compared to the number (2.2 million) in affiliated and national unions.

In comparing the distribution of affiliated and national union members on the one hand with the localized on the other Cohany and Neary conclude that the latter "do not appear to be serious competitors" with the former "in particular industries." [27] All three types are about equally unsuccessful in organizing certain industries—agriculture, finance, and insurance.

The tendency to large-scale organization is shown by the concentration of union members in six large unions, which together had more than one-third (6.2 million) of all union members. Each of these six unions had more than 700,000 members, while the other unions individually had fewer than 100,000.[28] All but one of these six belong to the AFL–CIO; the remaining one, the Teamsters, is a national union. By contrast, about one-third of localized unions, comprising the largest single grouping, had fewer than 50 members; fewer than one-tenth had more than 1,000. A few localized unions

27. It should be noted that the 1,277 unions are not all the unions in this category, although Cohany and Neary believe they comprise the great majority. Since many small, one-local unions are short-lived, it is difficult to discover the exact numbers at any one time, Cohany and Neary obtained their information about these unions from mailed questionnaires. While the response rate was high (1,545 returned out of 1,805 sent), 268 of those returned were not usable. The largest single number (154) of the 268 were unused because they were "no longer functioning or were no longer unaffiliated." The remainder either had no agreements with the management at the time, submitted incomplete statements, or claimed to be national unions.

28. *Directory of National and International Labor Unions,* p. 49. The six unions had the following memberships: International Brotherhood of Teamsters, Chauffeurs, Warehousemen and Helpers of America, 1,484,433; United Steelworkers of America, 1,152,000; International Union, United Automobile, Aircraft and Agricultural Implement Workers of America, 1,136,140; International Association of Machinists, 898,139; United Brotherhood of Carpenters and Joiners of America, 800,000; and International Brotherhood of Electrical Workers, 771,000.

(200 out of 1,277) belonged to associations of independents, and the largest of them, the Confederated Unions of America, had 12,000 members.

Union members relate to one another first at the local level. In 1960, 181 unions (including affiliated and national) had 77,010 locals, with an average of about 425 locals per union. Thirty per cent of those unions had more than one local.[29] The localized unions again stand out from the others in the number of locals. Only 6 per cent had more than one local; the intrastate rather than the single-employer type were likely to be multilocal.

In American union tradition membership is disproportionately male, with men outnumbering women by six to one in the AFL–CIO and the national unions, although their proportion is only three to one in the labor force.[30] A greater percentage of women members (30 per cent, or twice that in the AFL–CIO and national unions) characterize the localized unions; often these unions have a majority of women members (70 per cent or more). Localized unions are organized in hospitals and related occupations, the telephone industry, electrical machinery, leather products, and retail trade, which supply the largest numbers of women workers to unions.

Union members were still concentrated in certain regions of the United States in 1960; more than half (55 per cent) of all members lived in the northeastern and central sections, that is, the three Middle Atlantic states (New York, Pennsylvania, and New Jersey) and the five East North Central states (Illinois, Ohio, Michigan, Wisconsin, and Indiana). In geographical distribution the localized unions were really similar to the affiliated and national unions, with more than half of all their members in the heavily industrialized Middle Atlantic and North Central states. As in the case of industries, states in which national and affiliated unions have not gained a strong foothold, including states with "right-to-work laws," have low numbers of independent members belonging to localized unions.

29. Ibid., p. 54. The figure of 181 is used instead of 184 as the combined total of affiliated and national unions because the U.S. Bureau of Labor Statistics did not have data on the number of locals for three unions. Only locals within the United States are included in the number of 77,010, although many unions have locals in Canada.
30. Ibid., p. 38.

Labor Unions

The headquarters of unions reflect the membership distribution. Washington, D.C., has the national office of the AFL–CIO and nearly one-third (53) of the headquarters for the 184 unions. Well over half of union headquarters are in six cities: Washington, New York, Chicago, Cincinnati, St. Louis, and Philadelphia.[31] The regional distribution of union headquarters outside of Washington in 1961 was: East North Central states, 45; Middle Atlantic, 43; Pacific, 12; New England, 10; West North Central, 10; South Atlantic, 5; Mountain, 4; East South Central, 1; and West South Central, 1. Areas where industries first developed or flourished are overrepresented in national headquarters.

Comparable data are not available for localized unions, but since the great majority have only one local and do not belong to any federation or other organization of unions, the headquarters and the local are often the same. Since the philosophy of these unions stresses local autonomy at the expense of national control, one might expect to find greater proportions of the localized unions in the southern states, in which states' rights are emphasized. The geographical distribution of the localized unions, however, like that of the AFL–CIO, showed fewer members in the South than in the North.

By 1960 union wealth had become substantial, although it did not compare with that of business corporations. According to a news release by Secretary of Labor Arthur Goldberg, the total assets of all American unions in 1960 or 1961 (depending on the end of their fiscal year) were $1.5 billion; two unions, the International Brotherhood of Electrical Workers and the United Mine Workers of America, reported assets over $100 million each, eight others reported over $21 million, and seven over $12 million; sixty-five national and AFL–CIO unions each possessed assets of more than $1 million.[32] Moreover, "one of every four national [referring to both AFL–CIO and national unions as the terms are used here] unions took in more than $1 million a year in dues and other revenue, and one out of ten had annual receipts in excess of $5 million."

31. Cohany and Neary, p. 56.
32. News Release by Arthur Goldberg, *Detroit Daily News,* June 14, 1962. Although welfare and pension funds form part of union assets, they are not included in these figures since the great majority of such funds are administered by the company rather than by the union.

Union receipts for the fiscal year ending in 1959 or 1960 ranged from a high of $65,344,000 for the International Brotherhood of Electrical Workers (AFL–CIO) to a reported low of none for the International Allied and Chemical Workers of America.[33] According to figures for 41,796 union locals, only 4 per cent had receipts of more than $100,000. The median union had receipts of $3,600; it paid its officers an average of $767 and had a net worth at the end of the year of $2,276. In a study of forty single-firm unions (one of the categories of localized unions) in 1960–61 Arthur B. Shostak found that thirty unions, or 75 per cent of the sample, collected dues of less than $3.00 a month. He speaks of the financial situation of what he calls "a typical weak union," meaning a weak, single-firm, unaffiliated union, and quotes the leader of the union: "We used to charge 25 cents dues a member a month. But nobody was really interested, so we had no money in the treasury from the start in 1938 up until the present." [34]

Unions and Their Technological Base

Unions may be placed along an axis moving from those most closely associated with a single craft to those most inclusive in terms of varied work done by members. The widely used example of a model craft union is the Patternmakers League of North America. A characteristic that would place this union at one end of the axis is its emphasis on formal apprenticeship (five years) as the criterion for acceptance into the League. The laws of the Patternmakers do admit an alternate route "where the applicant has been found upon investigation to be a competent workman and able to command the current rate of wages." [35] The National Labor Relations Board described the union in this way: "Unlike most other craft organizations, the P.M.L. [Patternmakers League] has rigidly adhered to its traditional craft lines. It does not admit to member-

33. News release by Arthur Goldberg headed "Net Union Assets Put at $3 Billion," *New York Times,* June 6, 1962.
34. Arthur B. Shostak, *America's Forgotten Labor Organization* (Princeton, Princeton University Press, Industrial Relations Section, 1962), p. 24.
35. *Laws of the Pattern Makers' League of North America* (adopted Madison, Wisconsin, June, 1962), p. 24.

ship, nor seek to represent, employees who have not met the strict qualifications of the craft." [36]

Other unions toward the craft end of the continuum admit members who perform more than one type of work, such as the Plumbers and Pipe Fitters (United Association of Journeymen and Apprentices of the Plumbing and Pipe Fitting Industry) and the Carpenters and Joiners (United Brotherhood of Carpenters and Joiners of America), which, as the titles indicate, are composed of two crafts. Sometimes such unions are called trades unions because they embrace more than one craft.

Historically, the early unions were craftlike and gave a character to the union movement that has been altered only in the last thirty years. The nature of the craftlike work is such that its members need not be based in a factory and may even work alone or be self-employed. The likelihood of craftsmen being distributed over a geographic area has led to differences in union structure and procedure from the factory-based industrial union. The possibility of these craftsmen being proprietors of their own shops has allegedly led to a tendency on their part to identify with businessmen, a tendency not so likely to be found in factory workers.

At the opposite end of the continuum from the craft ideal is the industrial union, which takes in members who do widely diversified kinds of work. The Auto Workers and the Steelworkers are examples. Auto Workers members include unskilled, semiskilled, and skilled blue-collar workers and both clerical and technical white-collar personnel. They work in several industries—automobile, aerospace, and agricultural implements. Sometimes the term multi-industrial is applied to such a union.

The difference in technological base from the craftlike union has several consequences. The members cannot, for the most part, on the basis of their skills, set themselves up in business; they are dependent upon the technology of the factory for their livelihood; being plant-based, the unit of organization is often the company or the factory. For example, in the UAW (Auto Workers) one hears references to Ford River Rouge Local 600, meaning the local at the River Rouge plant of Ford Motor Company. The plant and the industry rather than the kind of work being the origin of structure

36. Jack Barbash, *The Practice of Unionism* (New York, Harper, 1956), p. 90.

means that in industrial-type unions many members work together in one industry but at different kinds of jobs.

The basis for membership in industrial unions is employment within a factory rather than education, moral character, or skill. The level of formal education may vary widely, with more members who have not completed grammar school or high school than in the craftlike unions, which often have graduation from high school as a prerequisite for apprenticeship. As the assembly-line system and partial automation came into being, semiskilled or unskilled workers were needed. Negroes as well as whites and recent ethnic groups in the United States who might not have been accepted in the skilled trades were employed for this work. Industrial unions are likely, therefore, to have more Negroes and descendants of new immigrant groups than the craft unions. Also, industrial unions, in origin, are identified with a liberal political ideology.

The great growth in partial automation and of the factory system has meant the increase in membership of industrial-type unions at the expense of the craftlike.

Changes in Unions and Technological Changes, 1900–60

Union membership more than doubled between 1900 and 1960. This is not surprising in view of the growth of industry during the same period. Unions not only kept pace with the increasing proportion of the American working force drawn into nonagricultural employment but went beyond. Data are not available for 1900, but between 1930 and 1960 the percentage of nonagricultural workers who were union members increased nearly three times.

From 1900 to 1960 the number of individual unions also more than doubled. This steady increase cannot be projected because of the trend toward amalgamation or combining of unions and the growth of multicraft organizations.[37]

The significant factor is increase and decrease in types of unions. Since 1915 craft unions have been declining in number as industrial unions have increased. This trend began before the

37. Mark L. Kahn, "Contemporary Structural Changes in Organized Labor," *Proceedings of the Tenth Annual Meeting Industrial Relations Research Association, Institute of Labor and Industrial Relations* (Detroit, University of Michigan, Wayne State University, 1957).

present century; in 1921 it was observed that industrial unions had "increased greatly since 1894." [38]

Since unions are based in the working force, it is enlightening to compare membership in unions with concentration of workers in industry. The six largest unions in 1960 did not match exactly the largest concentrations of workers in industry, but they were closely related. The industries in 1960 that accounted for the largest percentages of employed people were wholesale and retail trade (18.2 per cent), durable goods manufacturing (15.2 per cent), nondurable goods manufacturing (11.9 per cent), professional and related services (11.7 per cent), transportation, communications, and other public utilities (16.9 per cent), agriculture, forestry, and fisheries (6.7 per cent), personal services (6.0 per cent), and construction (5.9 per cent).

The second largest category, durable goods manufacturing, accounts for four of the largest unions—the United Steelworkers, the United Auto Workers, the International Association of Machinists, and the International Brotherhood of Electrical Workers. The fifth largest—transportation, communications, and other public utilities —accounts for the International Brotherhood of Teamsters, the single largest union in 1960.

Attempts to relate the largest unions and the industries with most workers show not only some coincidence but also discrepancies. One of the six largest unions is the Brotherhood of Carpenters and Joiners of America; yet only 5.9 per cent of all American workers are engaged in construction. The size of this union's membership is due to the early and continuing efforts of carpenters to unionize and remain active in their unions. The number of workers engaged in construction increased little between 1930 (3,030,000) and 1960 (3,815,937).

In 1960 wholesale and retail trades had the single largest group of employees, but only a little more than one-third belonged to the two unions, Retail Clerks International Association or Retail, Wholesale, and Department Store Union. Many of these workers would be classified as white-collar workers, which are slow to

38. Theodore W. Glocker, "Amalgamation of Related Trades in American Unions," *Trade Unionism and Labor Problems,* 2nd series, John R. Commons, ed. (Boston, Ginn & Co., 1921), pp. 362–85.

organize as compared with employees engaged directly in manufacturing, for example.

At the end of the 1950s unions had slowed in growth, and in some cases membership had dropped slightly, probably due to the disproportionate increase of white-collar workers and technicians in relation to skilled, semiskilled, or unskilled workers. The number of union members can continue to grow only through spread of unionization into fields in which it has in the past been relatively insignificant.

Union Structure

The lowest level of formal structure in a union is the local.[39] It most often has an industry-factory combination or a craft-area as a basis. It has a constitution and elected officers, usually a president, vice-president, and secretary-treasurer; they may do the union work after hours for no pay, or they may receive a salary from the local for full or part-time work. Most unions have an elected executive board.

Locals not associated with a single plant usually employ a full-time business agent who is either elected by the membership (most common procedure) or appointed by the officers. He handles grievances the stewards cannot settle, takes part in collective bargaining, acts as an employment officer (he tells employers of available workers and workers about jobs), sees that members of his union do not suffer in jurisdictional disputes, and often represents his union in various labor organizations, such as a central labor body in a city. In some locals the business agent may appear to the members to be a more important man than the president. He has his office in the headquarters of the local outside the plant.

In plant-based locals that do not have a business agent these duties are parceled out among several people, including the presi-

39. A number of good sources devoted either in whole or in part to the local are used in this chapter and will not be cited separately: Jack Barbash, *Labor's Grass Roots,* New York, Harper, 1961. William M. Leiserson, *American Trade Democracy,* New York, Columbia University Press, 1959. Leonard R. Sayles and George Strauss, *The Local Union: Its Place in the Industrial Plant,* New York, Harper, 1953. Arnold S. Tannenbaum and Robert L. Kahn, *Participation in Union Locals,* Evanston, Row, Peterson, 1958.

dent, the chairman, and the members of the Bargaining Committee. If such a local has one full-time union officer, it will be the secretary-treasurer. The factory local does not usually play a part in hiring; it is likely to have less autonomy and more assistance in bargaining since its contract may be included in the agreements of its International with the corporation.

In both types of locals representatives of the union are stationed in the plant or work force or move from one work site to another as needed. These stewards, or committeemen, or chairladies (in the case of garment workers) are either elected or appointed. A worker contacts them first about a grievance or complaint. The steward or committeeman then takes the matter to the lead man or to the foreman, usually a man in the lowest level of the plant management. If the foreman and steward do not reach a satisfactory arrangement, the steward may take the grievance to the next level within the union, perhaps the business agent. The routes and personnel involved, for both the union and management, are usually spelled out in the contract. If the entire procedure is exhausted without satisfactory agreement, the local may decide to strike. Usually a meeting, discussion, and vote of the members are necessary for a strike. In some unions a local may not strike without the permission of the International acting through its executive board or other assemblage. In other cases the local has this autonomy.

The powers in the local of an affiliated or national union may be summarized as follows:

1. The governing of the local, including election of its officials, collection and allocation of dues.

2. Participation in collective bargaining.

3. Discussions and decisions concerning strikes.

4. Employment service.

5. Communication between the members of the local on the one hand and the International and other labor bodies on the other.

6. Social services for members, such as credit unions, housing cooperatives, scholarships for members' children, and medical clinics.

7. Educational and recreational programs for members.

8. Community activities, such as participation in the United Fund drive.

9. Political responsibilities, i.e. encouraging members to vote and drawing their attention to pertinent legislation.

While these functions are found in many unions, all locals do not carry on all of them.

Member attendance at the usual local monthly meeting is customarily low, not necessarily because of indifference but probably because of the tendency in American associations for a relatively small group to take care of the routine business. When an issue is at stake, however, whether it is voting for officials in a closely contested election, the drafting of an agreement for collective bargaining, or a decision about striking, attendance increases to 30 to 60 per cent of the members.

Intermediate Structure

Affiliated and national unions divide the United States (and often Canada) into sections, each having a regional headquarters —an intermediate structure between the local and International levels. The UAW, for example, has sixteen regions, some with subdivisions according to the number of members. Areas where the automobile industry is old have more subdivisions and smaller geographical units than regions where it is newer. Michigan, for example, the center of the automobile industry, is one region divided into four parts; region 2 includes Ohio, Pennsylvania, and West Virginia; and region 6 is Washington, Oregon, California, Idaho, Nevada, Utah, Arizona, Alaska, and Hawaii.

In the UAW the director in charge of each region is elected during the biennial national convention by delegates from locals within the region at a meeting of their own. Some regions, such as 1, have two codirectors and are further subdivided on a geographical basis, with one or more subregional directors in each of the subsections. For example, region 4 (Illinois, Iowa, and Nebraska) has a regional director and assistant director with headquarters in Chicago and five subregional directors with offices in Illinois at Rockford, East Moline, and Peoria, and in Iowa at Des Moines and Waterloo. Regions are subdivided into new regions or subregions by the Executive Board of the International. Because the regional director is elected by delegates from his own region and is therefore a man with political strength who has a following, the Executive Board is not likely to subdivide a region or divide it in two until the director leaves his job. Regional directors in UAW tend to hold their jobs for some years. The position is regarded as a difficult one and anxiety-producing. If this is so, the reason may lie in the dual nature of the position: the regional director represents his region on the International Executive Board and may submit proposals to the Board that come to him from the locals within his region; he is also an official representative of the International within his region and should implement the policies of the International and carry out the instructions of the Board within his region.

In the UAW the regional director must, according to the constitution, "examine all contracts." As evidence of International support and as another link binding him to the International, the director is assigned two union representatives by the Executive Board to assist him in his work.

The regional director may spend most of his time organizing locals and then delegate work to subordinates, or he may engage in collective bargaining for new contracts or act as a general troubleshooter in the region for any difficult problems concerning internal union affairs or any problems between locals and employers. His functions may also include those of chief advisor and consultant for local union officers, supervisor of the regional staff, leader of regional political action, chief public relations man for the region, office manager, and many other lesser ones.

Unions show some variation in their intermediate structure. Instead of a regional director there may be a district council, district councils subsumed under a state council, regional councils, or joint boards. Members of these councils or boards, like the UAW regional directors, are usually elected by the locals within the territorial unit.

The International Staff

At the apex of an affiliated or national union (which, like the local, is governed by a constitution) are officers usually elected by delegates from the locals at the national conventions: president, several vice-presidents, a secretary-treasurer or a financial and a recording secretary, and an executive board. The length of office varies; common periods are two and four years.

The president is the supreme executive and administrative officer. He usually plays an important part in the formation of policy and in the appointment of personnel; he chairs the national convention, and he may have several other specific jobs within the organization.

The president is the chief spokesman for the outside, and if his union is large and powerful, he is likely to be a public figure. His image is associated with that of the union.

The president of the UAW has considerable power to initiate action, although most of his acts must receive the formal approval of the Executive Board. He administers union affairs between meetings of the Executive Board, presides at meetings of the latter and of the conventions of the International, calls regular and special sessions of the Executive Board, assigns officers of the UAW to particular tasks, and appoints staff members. He may withdraw a field assignment from an officer when "he becomes convinced that the officer has been derelict in his duty or been guilty of a dishonest act." He decides disputes in controversies, including "all questions involving the interpretation of this Constitution." These decisions not only are subject to the approval of the Executive Board, as are the preceding, but may also be challenged in an appeal by members first to the Executive Board and then to the delegates in the convention. The president may call special meetings of councils or local unions and he may grant to locals "dispensations relating to initiation fees, per capita tax, and/or Strike Insurance Fund dues." The president is required to make a report of his activities to the locals and the membership, to the Executive Board, and to the convention.[40]

In the Patternmakers, a craftlike union in contrast to the multi-industrial UAW, the powers of the president are similar. However, the Patternmakers president collects dues and authorizes expenditures, a job that the secretary-treasurer carries out in the UAW; he does not specifically have the right to assign officers duties or re-

40. Constitution of the International Union, United Automobile, Aerospace and Agricultural Implement Workers of America, UAW (adopted at Atlantic City, New Jersey, May, 1962), p. 12.

move them from appointments, and he cannot initiate acts subject to the approval of the Executive Board.

The secretary-treasurer of the UAW keeps records, collects dues, handles reimbursements, and acts as president in the latter's absence. In some unions, as in the Patternmakers, the president may have the responsibility for dues and care of funds while the specific work involved is apportioned between the financial secretary and the treasurer. The Patternmakers also have a recording secretary.

The vice-presidents of the International usually have special duties. In the UAW, which bargains with many employers, each vice-president is assigned several corporations and departments. Many other unions also have an administrative board similar to the International Executive Board of the UAW, sometimes called a council or board of trustees; and some unions have both an executive board and board of trustees, who are usually elected. In the UAW the executive board comprises three categories of persons: the officers—president, vice-presidents, and secretary-treasurer; the three executive board members-at-large; and board members, one for each of the nine regions within the United States and one from Canada. (These ten regions do not include the subdivisions, such as Region 1A or 1B. For this reason not all regional directors are Executive Board members.)

For the UAW, then, the Executive Board functions to relate leaders from different sections of the country to the International officers who have been elected by delegates from locals throughout the country together at the biennial conventions. With its broad powers the Executive Board of the UAW acts as the governing instrument of the union between the international conventions. It must give its approval to acts of the president and initiate action, such as deciding whether to add new departments and whether to enlarge or curtail certain activities. The Board acts as a judicial body in receiving appeals from the locals about the internal administration of their affairs or from any member about the decisions of the president. Staff members at UAW headquarters often refer to the Board in explaining or justifying the existence of a department or activity.

The General Executive Board of the Patternmakers' League operates in a similar way. It is responsible for the bonding of the International financial and district officers. It interprets the laws of the League, passes on preambles and bylaws, hears appeals, and is subject only to a referendum of the members and to the Convention.

The structure so far described is common among American organizations formed for many different purposes. One outstanding aspect of union organization is the lack of honorary positions with few, if any, duties; there is close approximation between an office and meaningful functions.

The staff of the International also includes persons appointed or hired by the officers or the Executive Board—specialists such as attorneys, industrial engineers, economists, journalists, social workers, and experts on contracts and welfare plans.[41] The staff may include physicians and nurses in clinic or health-care programs, economists and educators to teach in union training programs, career union experts who may have worked for a number of unions, and Washington lobbyists. Regarding the extent of influence and power of these specialists, Wilensky concludes: "It is clear that the union staff expert is used, has influence, and in very rare cases may exercise power." [42]

The UAW employs personnel for the legal department, research and engineering, special projects and economic analysis, and others. Union members are hired, when possible, for all positions.

An important part of the structure in labor unions is the International Convention, the highest body in most unions. Delegates to the convention are usually elected by the locals according to size. Bylaws are instituted by vote of the convention; appeals from decisions of the local, the president, or the Executive Board may often be made at the convention; and officers are elected. It serves in both legislative and judicial capacities.

In the UAW the regular meetings of the International Convention are held every two years. The convention has the power to amend the constitution, to pass resolutions, and to hear appeals from decisions of the president and the Executive Board. Special meetings of the convention may be called by a two-thirds vote of

41. For a lengthy discussion of these specialists see Harold L. Wilensky, *Intellectuals in Labor Unions* (Glencoe, Illinois, The Free Press, 1956).
42. Ibid., p. 179.

the Executive Board or by a referendum vote of at least 20 per cent of the membership representing a minimum of five different states or provinces.

Each local union in the UAW has one delegate for up to 200 members, one delegate for the next 300, and one delegate for each additional 800. In voting, each local has one vote for the first 100 or fewer members and one vote for each additional 100 members. No delegation may have more than eight votes. (There are exceptions for amalgamated local unions, both in the number of delegates and in votes.) [43]

The Convention of the Patternmakers is held every five years. Like the Convention of the UAW, it is a law-making body, may amend the constitution, and, on a referendum of its members, can hear appeals from decisions of the General Executive Board. One delegate appears for each unit of twenty-five to fifty members and has one vote for each additional fifty. Because there are many small associations (the group corresponding to the local), those having fewer than twenty-five members may combine and be represented by one delegate.

The convention serves as a check on the officers and the executive board and is a meeting place for delegates from widely dispersed locals and officers and staff of the International. The importance of the convention to communications can hardly be overestimated.[44]

In addition to the International Executive Board, many unions also have a board of trustees. This board usually has the function of auditing the books and reporting on finances to officers and members. The UAW has a three-man Board of Trustees, elected at the International Convention.

Unions provide their own system of checks on honesty and devotion to duty of officers. Much publicity has been given to corrupt practices. The International Labor Office sent a mission to this country in 1959, which inquired specifically into this matter. The investigators concluded:

43. Constitution of the UAW, pp. 16, 17.
44. For a study of a convention, see George Won, "Democratic Sentiments in Unionism: A Case Study of the UAW Convention," Unpublished Ph.D. thesis, Department of Sociology and Anthropology, Michigan State University, 1962.

The striking fact is that proof of lawlessness and dishonesty has only been established in a minute number of cases— although this does not stop sweeping conclusions from being drawn. . . . After many years of investigation by Congress and bodies armed with subpoena powers and by the AFL– CIO itself, only a handful of union officials, belonging to a small number of unions, have been shown to have used their positions dishonestly for personal gain. In a movement embracing some 18 million members and having several thousand elected officers, it would not have been surprising if the extent of the corruption had been greater. The mission had the impression that much of the publicity given to examples of corrupt practices in the labor movement was being used to discredit the labor movement as such.[45]

Unions affiliated with the AFL–CIO have, in addition to their individual structure, a place in the greater organization. The AFL–CIO is organized on an international level, on a statewide level, and on a city level. Both state and city organizations have officers, an executive board, and conventions or meetings, and they acquaint members of locals with AFL–CIO policies and encourage them to take initiative in legislative matters and to assist, if necessary, in collective bargaining and jurisdictional disputes. Some union locals are affiliated directly with the AFL–CIO and do not belong to a national or international union. The AFL–CIO is by far the largest association of unions, but there are others, such as the Confederated Unions of America.

Affiliated or unaffiliated locals may also belong to city or regional groupings, such as the town building trades council, which is made up of the various unions involved in construction work, or the hotel trades councils, which include unions that bargain with hotel managements.

Belief Systems of Unions

Unions in the AFL–CIO subscribe to four constitutions. The most inclusive is the constitution of the AFL–CIO; each depart-

45. International Labor Office Report on U.S. Trade Unions, *Monthly Labor Review, 84* (1961), 278, 279.

ment in the AFL–CIO, such as the Building and Construction Trades Department, the Food and Beverage Trades Department, the Industrial Union Department, has its own constitution, and each international or national union and each local has a constitution.

National unions that do not belong to the AFL–CIO have two constitutions, the national and the local. Localized unions belonging to an association of independents also have more than one.

The AFL–CIO constitution governs 83 per cent of American union members. Its Objects and Principles speaks of aiding "workers in securing improved wages, hours and working conditions with due regard for the autonomy, integrity and jurisdiction of afflilated unions."[46] These goals directly related to the work situation are characteristic of the American labor union and are firmly imbedded in tradition. Another principle is "legislation which will safeguard and promote the principle of free collective bargaining, the rights of workers, farmers and consumers, and the security and welfare of all the people and to oppose legislation inimical to these objectives"; such expression of broad concern with social objectives that benefit all citizens are also an old theme in the American labor movement.

Emphasis is placed on reaching goals through legislation. The preamble of the AFL–CIO constitution explicitly states as means:

> democratic processes within the framework of our constitutional government and consistent with our institutions and traditions . . . at the collective bargaining table, in the community, in the exercise of the rights and responsibilities of citizenship, we shall responsibly serve the interests of all the American people.

In the first two pages of the constitution the two main procedures —collective bargaining and legislation—are stated.

For the legislative program the AFL–CIO has a Committee on Political Education (COPE), which gives workers information about election issues and candidates. The national committee is assisted by state locals of COPE.

46. All quotations here are from the AFL–CIO Constitution, as amended by the Fourth Constitutional Convention of the AFL–CIO, December 7–13, 1961, Washington, D.C., American Federation of Labor and Congress of Industrial Organizations, January, 1962.

The UAW, as an example of an affiliated union, has a COPE in each local. Along with their monthly dues UAW members may contribute $1.00 to COPE, but it is not compulsory, and members may designate this sum to be paid to a charity.

In accepting collective bargaining as a method of achieving goals, the Auto Workers say: "The organized worker seeks a place at the conference table, together with the management, when decisions are made which affect the amount of food he, his wife and family shall consume; the extent of education his children may have; the kind and amount of clothing they may wear; and their very existence." [47] Here the rationale for collective bargaining is put clearly and precisely in terms of income and its uses for the workers. The constitution of the Tobacco Workers states that their union is formed in part "to promote the acceptance of mutual working agreements between the employer and the employees and the settlement of disputes by arbitration." [48]

The emphasis on legislation in the AFL–CIO does not appear in the constitutions of all the affiliated unions. But the Auto Workers state as their function:

> to vote and work for the election of candidates and the passage of improved legislation in the interest of all labor. To enforce existing laws to work for the repeal of those which are unjust to labor . . . To engage in legislative, political, educational, civic, welfare and other activities, which further, directly or indirectly, the joint interests of the membership of this organization in the improvement of general economic and social conditions in the United States of America, Canada, and generally in the nations of the world.[49]

The Doll and Toy Workers state as an object "to further legislative protection for all working people in their rights to organize for their mutual protection and improvement." [50]

Whether or not affiliated unions have such statements supporting

47. Constitution of the UAW, p. 4.
48. Constitution of the Tobacco Workers, International Union, AFL–CIO (September 19–23, 1960), p. 3.
49. Constitution of the UAW, p. 5.
50. Constitution of the International Union of Doll & Toy Workers of the United States & Canada, AFL–CIO (revised May 27, 1960), p. 3.

Labor Unions

legislative programs for all citizens, by accepting the AFL–CIO constitution they have pledged themselves to this goal.

In contrast to the affiliated unions, the localized unions give little or no attention to matters beyond their immediate work situation. Shostak says that the single-firm independent union is "inclined to lag rather than lead in the area of ideas and action. It is not particularly imaginative or daring. The union's plant-orientation also helps here by screening out unsettling ideas developed elsewhere." [51] Presumably, then, if concepts of broad legislative programs or even of new types of workers' compensations, such as the UAW Supplementary Unemployment Benefits (SUB), trickle into a localized union, they might be eliminated. Shostak continues, "Survival is thought sufficient, particularly by the older members who predominate in the common, small workshop . . . Pioneering or even progressive behavior involves risk-taking that frightens and alienates many members."

Localized unions, however, use collective bargaining, the other major method of the large unions, but not in concerted action, which the AFL–CIO and national unions believe is essential. Before combining in 1955 the American Federation of Labor and the Congress of Industrial Organizations emphasized the help unions could give one another by working together—an old and dominant theme in labor history. Since they are not affiliated, the localized unions obviously do not accept this idea. (A small number of these unions—fewer than 200 out of the 1,277—have joined associations of various kinds, but not, of course, the AFL–CIO.) [52] Their rationale is, not too surprisingly, like that of small businessmen. Shostak gives three related beliefs for localized unions:

1. The American way is best exemplified by the small enterprise, union or business.
2. The small enterprise is the victim of a joint conspiracy of Big Government, Big Business, and Big Labor.
3. The small enterprise could flourish if not for this little-published but very effective conspiracy.[53]

51. Shostak, pp. 13, 14.
52. Cohany and Neary, p. 7.
53. Shostak, pp. 14, 15.

These beliefs are opposed to the concepts that led to the great union federation and to the large national unions, which may be summarized:

1. Joining together is the heart of the union movement. Uniting gives strength.
2. The person who belongs to a large-scale organization through its strength has freedom which he could not achieve by himself.
3. Large-scale organization and resources are necessary in order to achieve the goals of job-related improvements for the worker and the well-being of all citizens.

How do the affiliated and national unions compare with the localized unions in collective bargaining, a method shared by both groups? The benefits of uniting are clearly shown. In the preliminary stages of bargaining some single-firm unions "make little effort to compare their contracts with those at other plants or with contract conditions in the area or industry." [54] Further, they have no assistance in checking on what management tells them about the financial condition of the company. "The weak single-firm union depends heavily in bargaining on the knowledge the employee-members have of the employer's business record. Pertinent studies suggest that this is an unreliable source of data." [55] Members of such a union do not have the help of staff members in collecting information about wages and hours in the industry and economic data such as the cost of living, on which they might base arguments for increases in wages.

Affiliated unions, apart from the parent AFL–CIO, and national unions have their own resources for investigating these matters. For example, the UAW has a research department that collects needed data on work-related subjects or broader concerns; within this department is a Contracts Office, whose function is to prepare contracts. The Special Projects Department gathers and organizes information on economic trends. Localized unions must bargain without such resources, although in some cases they may be helped by a governmental price-fixing board or a neighboring local of an affiliated or national union.

54. Ibid., p. 12.
55. Ibid., p. 41.

Labor Unions

When the resulting contracts are compared, the localized unions come off poorly compared with the affiliated and national unions, who seek to introduce major changes in their agreements while the localized unions tend to cling to the past and seem afraid to introduce even ideas initiated elsewhere. Their contracts—average at best—are probably aided by the indirect effect of affiliated and national unions, which, in raising standards in many different industries, provide a climate in which all unions function. So-called "strong" localized unions further use the possibility of affiliation with the AFL–CIO or a national union as a threat in bargaining.[56]

The AFL–CIO constitution includes provisions for examining and expelling (by a two-thirds vote) any member union dominated by the "Communist Party, any fascist organization, or other totalitarian party," and any member union proven of corruption. The AFL–CIO has expelled member unions for being controlled by Communists and for corruption, and the International Labor Office reports on these actions:

> The more responsible unions have not hesitated to tackle the problem of corruption. The AFL–CIO has taken energetic action to demonstrate its conviction that 'free, democratic trade unionism must be clear, honest trade unionism.' Its Ethical Practices Committee, which started work in 1956, has drawn up codes of ethical practices which were approved by stages in 1956 and 1957. Investigations were also started in some cases before the McClellan Committee began work, into the position in some unions where the situation seemed to call for intervention 'to achieve the correction of abuses and to help the members of unions having dishonest leadership.' The unions against which these charges were levelled were asked to take the necessary action. The AFL–CIO did not hesitate to take the most drastic step of all in order to keep the movement on the right path by ordering the expulsion of several unions including the powerful Teamsters union in December 1957.[57]

Jurisdictional disputes, that is, conflict over which union should take a given group of workers as members, have been a source of

56. Ibid., pp. 36, 48.
57. ILO *Monthly Lab. Rev.*, *84*, 278–79.

difficulty in the union movement. One of the major contributions of the AFL–CIO to the labor movement is its no-raiding policy, which is stated as an objective in its constitution.

THE UAW

No single union is typical of all. In discussion of the UAW as a large-scale, complex union, there is no implication that other unions resemble it exactly. One reason for selecting the UAW [58] is that it carries on both of the major traditions of American unionism —broad social objectives and work-centered goals. A second reason is in the multi-industrial character of the UAW: it is inclusive rather than exclusive in its membership. In this respect it is part of the trend to accept workers who are excluded by the nature of the work they perform from the craft- or trades-type unions. The rapid replacement of men by machines involves an accompanying change in the character of work done by men; automation means a steadily higher proportion of white-collar and technical work. The flexibility of the industrial union in accepting *any* employee as a member may enable it to maintain its membership while unions with narrowly defined memberships may disappear. A third reason for selecting the UAW is that its leadership is believed by many to be responsible and capable of looking ahead in planning for the well being of workers.

In 1960, with a membership of 1,136,140, the UAW was the

58. For good sources on the UAW, see: Sidney Fine, "The Origins of the United Automobile Workers, 1933–1935," *Journal of Economic History* (Sept. 1958), the University of Michigan-Wayne State University, Institute of Labor and Industrial Relations, Reprint Series, 5. Clayton W. Fountain, *Union Guy*, New York, The Viking Press, 1949. Walter Galenson, *The CIO Challenge to the AFL, A History of the American Labor Movement 1935–41*, Cambridge, Harvard University Press, 1960, Ch. 3. Irving Howe and B. J. Widick, *The UAW and Walter Reuther*, New York, Random House, 1949. Edward Levinson, *Labor on the March*, New York, University Books, 1956, Ch. 7. Rose Pesotta, *Bread Upon the Waters*, New York, Dodd, Mead, 1944. Jack Skeels, "The Development of Political Stability within the United Auto Workers Union," unpublished doctoral dissertation, Department of Economics, University of Wisconsin, 1957. Jack Stieber, *Governing the UAW*, New York, John Wiley, 1962.

third largest union in the country, represented in all but ten states and in Canada, Puerto Rico, and the Canal Zone. Only a small proportion of the membership was white-collar.[59]

The history of the UAW is, of course, closely related to that of automobile production. The automobile industry originated in the early years of the twentieth century. Henry Ford is credited with introducing the assembly line on a large scale to American manufacture; the assembly line had particular importance to the American labor movement because it meant hiring large numbers of semiskilled workers.

In the auto industry in the 1920s, it was difficult or impossible for the workers to bargain successfully with their employers because they belonged to many different unions. Also, many were ineligible for the crafts-type unions and so were not represented at all. Union membership was largely limited to patternmakers, molders, and metal polishers. In the early 1900s some auto workers belonged to The Carriage and Wagon Workers' International Union, formed in 1891. Because it was involved in many jurisdictional disputes, this union was expelled from the AFL in 1918; it became the United Automobile, Aircraft and Vehicle Workers of America, which disappeared in the 1920s. Some of the members then joined the Auto Workers Union, a small, left-wing union that should not be confused with the UAW.

The open-shop policy of the 1920s and the depression of the 1930s militated against unionism in the automobile industry. It was not until the National Industry Recovery Act with its clause granting workers the right to organize that William Green, president of the AFL, became actively engaged in organizing automobile workers. Green's idea was not that a single national auto workers' union be established but that each auto plant have its own local, a so-called Federal Union, chartered directly by the AFL.

In 1933 Green sent William Collins to organize auto workers in Detroit, but he was not successful; in 1934 the Detroit Federation of Labor asked that Collins be removed. Green then sent Francis Dillon, who had had experience with the Patternmakers' League but not with semiskilled or unskilled industrial workers.[60]

These internal difficulties, together with the competition of com-

59. Stieber, p. 105.
60. Fine, p. 258.

pany unions, which were established by all automobile corporations except Ford, made progress slow. Auto workers were paid low wages and had little security.

Meanwhile, employees in mining, steel, rubber, textiles, garment manufacture, and oil had joined the push for industrial unions, with John L. Lewis, president of the United Mine Workers, spearheading the movement.

Lewis, Sidney Hillman, president of the Amalgamated Clothing Workers Union, and others who wanted industrial unions first tried to work within the AFL framework. In 1934 at the national convention of the AFL the delegates unanimously accepted a report of the resolutions committee directing the Executive Council "to issue charters to national and international unions in the automotive, cement, aluminum, and such other mass-production and miscellaneous industries." [61] This report represented the recognition at an intellectual level of the needs of the unskilled industrial worker; it also protected the existing structure by providing for the "jurisdictional rights of existing unions." Members of any existing structure resist widespread change, and the social structure of the AFL as it was then constituted could not quickly adapt to the incorporation of industrial unions. At one level the vested interest of the already existing unions would be threatened by loss of possible members to the industrial union, and at the topmost level the old power group would be threatened by the entrance of great new unions that could give their leaders the backing of millions of members. Even where the industrial-type union, such as the United Mine Workers, had grown up within the AFL, little formal recognition of the large numbers of Mine Workers was shown. Lewis did not hold national office within the AFL and was not even the chairman of a committee.

At the AFL convention of 1935 a minority report of the resolutions committee calling for "unrestricted charters" to industrial unions was rejected by the delegates. Unrestricted charters meant that charters could go to groups of workers, including some who might be eligible for AFL craft unions. The defeat of this resolution is an important symbol in the schism. Shortly after the convention

61. *Brief History of the American Labor Movement*, U.S. Department of Labor, Bureau of Labor Statistics, Bulletin No. 1000 (Washington, D.C., U.S. Government Printing Office, 1950).

the eight unions formed the Congress for Industrial Organization.

The UAW was formed in 1935 under AFL auspices, although disapproved of by AFL leaders. Green appointed Francis Dillon as president. The following year the UAW joined the recently organized CIO. Homer Martin was elected president. Of the officers at that time, only one, Walter Reuther, a member of the Executive Board and president of a west side UAW local in Detroit, was still an officer in 1965.

Although membership in the UAW grew rapidly, automobile companies were not prepared to recognize the union as a bargaining agent. A series of sitdown strikes, which had begun in Akron, Ohio, in the rubber industry, spread to automobile factories. Some of the most famous were the strikes in General Motors plants in Flint, Michigan, early in 1937; a court injunction, the usual recourse of management, was issued ordering the workers to leave the General Motors factories under "threat of imprisonment and $15,000,000 fines." [62] The strikers submitted a statement to Governor Murphy of Michigan that they would not leave the plants and were willing to face death.

In terms of common law and of statutory law strikes were legal if they satisfied certain requirements. No rulings existed for the sitdown strike, which probably in part explains the hesitation of Governor Murphy during this period. He vacillated about calling out the state militia to enforce the court injunction by removing the strikers forcibly. Instead, he insisted that William Knudsen, president of General Motors, negotiate with John L. Lewis of the CIO, but the meeting was indecisive. There was ample precedent for the President of the United States to intervene personally in a strike, and President Roosevelt wired General Motors asking members of management to meet with labor. The result was the first UAW agreements with General Motors.

Contracts with General Motors

This contract, dated February 11, 1937, had two major features. First, it recognized the right of the union to bargain but for its members only. Later the union was permitted by law exclusive bar-

62. Howe and Widick, p. 60.

gaining rights.[63] Second, the union **and** the corporation agreed to begin collective bargaining negotiations, opening the way for bargaining in the immediate future. These two provisions may not seem like great advances, but they were essential to the survival and success of the union.

A second, related agreement [64] between the UAW and General Motors Corporation, signed on March 12, 1937, gave the details of the first contract: grievance procedure; rules governing lay-off or temporary discharge of employees, transfer from one department to another, and rehiring; rights of senior over junior employees and of men with dependents were included. "Timing Operations" dealt with a major problem for the union—"speed-up." It is possible to move conveyor belts so rapidly that men can hardly keep up with the work and may labor at a speed injurious to themselves. The agreement stated that "reasonable working capacities of normal operators" be considered in time studies.

The length of working hours, a traditional focal point for American labor was established as an "eight-hour day and a forty-hour week with time and one-half for all overtime after eight hours per day or forty hours per week."

The large body of unemployed and the consequent competition for jobs in the 1930s meant that workers active in labor movements were particularly vulnerable. Despite the guarantee of the Wagner Act they might be discharged—although not ostensibly because of union activity—and their names placed on blacklists that would bar them from employment elsewhere. This early UAW contract provided that workers claiming to have been discharged for union activities (discriminatory discharge) could present grievances within three days of the discharge, which the local plant management had to review and decide upon within five days thereafter.

No wage scale was specified. That was to be determined by "the

63. Document entitled *General Motors Agreement (With International Union, U.A.W.)*, dated February 11, 1937, signed by William S. Knudsen, J. T. Smith, and D. Brown for General Motors Corporation and by Wyndham Mortimer, First Vice President, Lee Pressman, General Counsel, John L. Lewis, Chairman, CIO; Frank Murphy and James F. Dewey.

64. *Agreement entered into this 12th day of March, 1937*, between the General Motors Corporation (hereinafter referred to as the Corporation and the International Union, United Automobile Workers of America, (hereinafter referred to as the Union) is supplemental to and a part of the agreement dated February 11, 1937, between the parties.

local plant management for each plant," although the corporation prefaced this statement by saying, "General Motors believes in high wages and will continue to pay high wages in the future as it has in the past."

A third contract,[65] still supplemental to the February one and issued in March, included additional decisions about grievance procedure, including the size of the Shop Committee and Bargaining Committee, and stating that "the Company agrees to pay each Committee member while attending his duties as Shop Committeeman for the time spent . . . on the basis of not more than 4 hours each during their regular shift."

There is no mention of vacations, medical care, compensation for disability, pensions, or profit-sharing plans.

In 1938 a request was made by the UAW that vacations with pay be given all employees covered by contract.[66] At that time the UAW was still affiliated with the AFL but was expelled from the AFL later that year; from then until the merger of the AFL with the CIO in 1955 it remained a CIO union.

Fringe benefits were gradually accumulated in succeeding contracts. In the 1940 contract [67] between General Motors Corporation and the UAW vacation is first mentioned: "In lieu of vacation with pay for the year 1940, forty (40) hours' pay at each employee's rate of pay on July 1, 1940, not including overtime and night shift premiums, will be paid each factory employee." In that contract the union also obtained sick leave for "any employee, who is known to be ill, supported by satisfactory evidence, not to exceed ninety days." This principle of pay for vacation if the vacation itself were not granted continued until 1961. Because of the seasonal cycle of the automobile industry, especially around changeover to

65. *Supplemental Agreement, effective April 12, 1937.*

66. Letter by Homer Martin, International President, U.A.W. to C. E. Wilson, Vice President, General Motors Corporation, dated October 21, 1938, from files in Research Department, International Union, UAW, Solidarity House, Detroit, Michigan.

67. *Agreement between General Motors Corporation and the International Union, U.A.W.,* dated June 24, 1940, signed by R. J. Thomas, President of the International, George J. Addes, Secretary-Treasurer, Walter P. Reuther, Vice President and Director of the General Motors Department of the UAW, and William Stevenson, President of the UAW Local 157 and Chairman of General Motors Negotiations Committee, for the union and by F. O. Tanner, H. W. Anderson, B. Coen, and S. M. DuBrul for General Motors.

new models, periods of lay-off are likely and can serve as vacations. Model changes formerly took place in the winter, an undesirable vacation time for workers with children in school. Now some model changes are introduced in the summer, providing opportunity for vacations then. Company policy in 1960, although not stipulated by contract, permitted workers to arrange vacation periods with their foremen or other immediate supervisors, and grievances are heard on the scheduling of vacations.

Through the 1930s a company could summon large numbers of men to work, have them wait, and then tell them they were not needed. The Call-in Pay clause of the 1940 contract guaranteed pay for the employee reporting for work when the company had no work for him:

> Any employee called to work or permitted to come to work without having been properly notified that there will be no work shall receive a minimum of two hours' pay at the regular hourly rate, except in case of labor disputes, or other conditions beyond the control of the local Management.

In comparing the contracts of 1962 with early ones we find improvement in the original items as well as added fringe benefits. Sometimes it is said that labor today is no longer interested in increasing wages or improving other basic items but is concerned only with benefits. UAW contracts show both increases in pay and improved benefits. The following items are taken from a statement, "What's in a Typical UAW Contract," prepared by the Research and Engineering Department, International UAW in January, 1962. Wages are dealt with in the contract. An average hourly rate is $2.85 and fringe benefits give 40 cents more; time-and-a-half for Saturday work and double time for overtime and pay for six full holidays and two half-holidays a year are included. A cost-of-living clause means that each year the UAW member receives 6 cents more an hour or 2½ per cent of his basic wage, whichever is greater. After working fifteen years the worker receives three weeks of paid vacation. His usual pension when he reaches 65 is $2.80 a month for each year of service in addition to his social security benefits. An average worker covered by a UAW contract today who retires with thirty years' seniority will be paid $84.00 monthly from a pension financed entirely by the company (in addition, of course, to social security). When the worker dies after retirement, his widow, if she is the same age as her husband, receives 45 per cent of her husband's basic benefit. The permanently disabled worker is paid $5.60 a month for each year of service.

Further, the average auto worker today has a life insurance policy of $6,500. For himself and his dependents he has hospital-surgical-medical insurance financed by the corporation giving him 365 days of hospital care for each hospitalization and covering most of the items for which he may be charged, including room and board, drugs and medicines, and anesthesia.

When an employee is discharged through no fault of his own, he receives severance pay; if he is transferred to another plant of the same company more than fifty miles away, he is given a moving allowance of up to $580.

In 1961 the UAW initiated profit sharing with a major automobile company, American Motors Corporation. Profit-sharing by management and labor is not new in American industry, but before this time it had not been instituted with a large automobile concern. According to this plan the corporation pays a stipulated amount (in the form of common capital stock of the company) into each of two funds: A, which is to be used for pensions and Supplementary Unemployment Benefits payments, and B, which is to be issued annually to employees. Accounts equal to all cash stock dividends are payable on these shares annually to employees. The way in which these assets are distributed to employees is determined by a joint committee, three members of which are appointed by the union and three by the company. This plan was considerably modified in the contract of 1964 between the UAW and American Motors Corporation. At the time of this writing the future of this program with American Motors seemed uncertain; it is dependent on a number of variables, including the extent of the corporation's production and profits, the reactions of employees covered by the plan, and the decisions of negotiators in future bargaining sessions. The history of the program at American Motors does not necessarily provide us with a measure of the possible success or failure of such a plan with other corporations or industries. However, if profit sharing should be instituted on a large-scale basis in this country, it will pose a whole series of new questions that will have to be faced by both management and labor. The resolution of these questions would mean the establishment of new ground rules for management and labor in areas not as yet clearly defined.

Major Achievements of UAW

The major achievements of the UAW that have benefited the labor movement generally include the Public Review Board and Supplementary Unemployment Benefits (SUB), a plan by which workers are guaranteed an income during layoffs from a fund established by the company. Clauses concerning SUB in the agreement between General Motors Corporation and the UAW of October 5, 1964, can be used as an example. When added to state unemployment compensation, these benefits will yield the employee 62 per cent of his gross wages plus $1.50 for each dependent (up to four), with a maximum of $50 to $56 weekly, the variation being due to the number of dependents. A short-work-week benefit of 50 to 75 per cent of the hourly pay is available for employees who work less than forty hours a week. The greater percentage is paid if the short work week is scheduled by the corporation as part of its planning. If, however, the short work week occurs as a result of causes beyond the corporation's control, such as power failure or unavoidable delay in delivery of parts needed for work, then the smaller percentage is paid the employee.

Even though there may be differences in the level of unemployment benefits in various states, the total SUB would be the same for General Motors workers drawing the same hourly rate. In 1965 the average UAW member with a wife and three children received about $81 a week when out of work and for as long as a year; further, he continued to be covered during this time of unemployment by hospital-surgical-medical insurance financed by the corporation. In 1965 about a million automobile workers were covered by SUB. UAW contracts with all the great automobile companies contain clauses establishing SUB.

These agreements have proved most successful. In those cases of a one-industry community payments from SUB funds have mitigated the economic distress to the total community caused by an extended layoff of auto workers. During the 1958 recession, a period of considerable unemployment in the automobile industry, funds for SUB, in spite of very heavy drains, were more than sufficient.

Other unions in this country and abroad have followed the pattern set by the UAW with SUB. For example, in 1958 "a supplemental unemployment benefit plan covering an estimated five million workers was negotiated in France by the non-communist unions and the national association of employers." [68]

The Public Review Board, a second major achievement of the UAW, was instituted in 1957 at the sixteenth Convention [69] to receive appeals directly from UAW members. (The earlier right of appeal of any member to the convention remained as an alternative choice.) This problem of recourse for an individual dissatisfied with his treatment within the hierarchy faces all large-scale organizations with democratic ideals. When a UAW member has exhausted all means of redress within the union, he may turn to the Public Review Board, an outside but related structure. The Board is also responsible for enforcing the ethical practice codes of the AFL–CIO and of the UAW. Its seven members are appointed and approved by the UAW International Board and approved by the convention; none are union members; they are men of stature drawn from religious circles, academic life, and the courts. During the 1957–58 period the Public Review Board heard twenty-four cases—eleven from the International Executive Board at the latter's request and thirteen appeals by members from decisions of the International Executive Board. The Board wrote decisions in sixteen of the twenty-four cases, dismissed five for jurisdictional reasons or abandonment by the appellant, and left three to decide during the next period. [70]

Major Concerns and the Future

These accomplishments lead to the question of the nature of UAW rationale or the system of social logics that underlies its plans and actions. The two major principles are those we have seen ap-

68. Report of UAW President Walter P. Reuther to the 17th Constitutional Convention, Atlantic City, N.J., Oct. 9–16, 1959, p. 64.

69. Jack Stieber, Walter E. Oberer, and Michael Harrington, *Democracy and Public Review* (Santa Barbara, Calif., Center for the Study of Democratic Institutions, The Fund for the Republic, 1960) gives a thorough report on the Public Review Board.

70. Reuther, p. 280.

pear and reappear throughout the history of American unionism. One is concern with objectives related directly to the job; wages, hours, seniority, and fringe benefits are the major examples. Increase in pay, reduction of hours, and increase in benefits, such as pensions, receive constant attention not only in contracts with individual companies but also in terms of what should be established in American industry generally. The underlying assumption here, as in the case of profit sharing, is that the American system of business enterprise will and should continue but that the employee should increasingly receive a larger share of the proceeds as well as job security and provision for those periods when through sickness or old age he is unemployable. There is an expression here of treating industry as a corporate venture in which both management and labor have vested interest. UAW spokesmen, for example, have repeatedly said that if a manufacturing concern is considering going out of business or relocating, say, from Michigan to the South, UAW officials will consult with management and possibly give assistance—not, of course, at the expense of the workers. UAW officials insist that their members will not subsidize inefficient management by accepting a lower wage, for example. This willingness to find common cause with corporations has been the subject of criticism within the labor movement. Paul Jacobs says: "What has happened is that the union has become almost indistinguishable *in its own eyes* from the corporation. We see the phenomenon today of unions and corporations *jointly* lobbying." [71] However, unions and corporations are both part of the same society and, further, are drawn especially close because both tend to be dependent for their survival, at least in their present forms, and their well being on the same kinds of work or industries. If a given type of work or industry, such as the manufacture of carriages, disappears, both the corporations and the unions may disappear with it. It does not seem strange, therefore, that they find grounds for common, cooperative action.

Among the major principles of the UAW is the traditional belief that unions should have broad social objectives that affect not only workers but all Americans. The achievements of work-oriented

71. Paul Jacobs, *Labor Looks at Labor* (Santa Barbara, Calif., Center for the Study of Democratic Institutions, The Fund for the Republic, 1963), p. 13.

404

Labor Unions

goals have sometimes led us to overlook the importance that ideals about the rights of all men have played in the American labor movement. Some of these ideals, which led to the American Revolution, were reflected before and after in various labor movements and have continued to the present day. In giving these ideals current interpretation, UAW leaders examine social trends and present proposals for the future.

The UAW view of the American economy is that it is capable of unlimited abundance. Lack of purchasing power on the part of American consumers is the limiting factor, not production capacity. Irving Bluestone, administrative assistant to Walter P. Reuther, in an interview with the author on July 1, 1963, stated:

> For a long-range policy, we advocate a National Planning Agency. . . . We do not suggest how or where this might be structured into government . . . This National Planning Agency would determine economic needs and resources, collect data, and establish practices with regard to the use of these resources and the meeting of these needs, and to develop and recommend programs to meet these needs.

Many specific policy recommendations of UAW leaders come back to the necessity of planning on a national basis. They point to unemployment throughout the nation and in regionally depressed areas as a condition that can be remedied effectively only with the assistance of the federal government. Walter Reuther recommends that the federal government carefully consider the economic need of communities in awarding defense contracts and adds that the price differential of the product manufactured should not be the only consideration in giving a contract. He suggests that the federal government issue licenses to corporations for building new plants and consider, in giving these, the availability of workers in the proposed area and other needs as well.[72] The British Government under Tory leaders instituted similar licensing of new plants. Reuther also recommends a system of investment in distressed areas. Sweden has tried out such a plan and found it successful. In

72. Walter P. Reuther, Statement before the Subcommittee on Employment and Manpower Presented on behalf of the American Federation of Labor and Congress of Industrial Organizations, unpublished, May, 23, 1963.

addition to the National Planning Agency the UAW asks for a National Manpower Agency and a Technological Clearing House.

One of the major concerns is the rapid displacement of men by machines, now often called automation; neither the term nor the process of displacement is new. The UAW recognized the value of the Manpower Development and Training Act in retraining workers thrown out of jobs. According to UAW leaders, this act, or programs sponsored by other legislation, must provide for the "hardcore" unemployed, that is, those who are older, unskilled, or members of minority groups. Thinking of the annual crop of high school "dropouts," UAW leaders recommend legislative programs to reduce the "economic pressures that drive youth prematurely into the labor market." [73] Specifically, they ask for a Federal Youth Opportunities Agency that would hire students from needy families on a part-time basis, a kind of latter-day National Youth Administration such as existed during the 1930s and early 1940s. For those who remain in school and who do not plan to attend college, the UAW finds the vocational training inadequate and asks that it be revised in terms of the kinds of jobs likely to be available in the future. Because of the increasing demand for college graduates, UAW leaders urge federal assistance to needy college students so that those with ability do not have to forego college because of the expense.

Although these proposals formed only part of UAW recommendations in 1963, they can be examined for deeply imbedded assumptions. One such assumption is that the procedure by which change is to be brought about is legislative and within the present

73. *Workers' Problems are Democracy's Problems,* UAW Special Collective Bargaining Convention, April 27, 28, 29, 1961, Detroit, Michigan, p. 100.

The author wishes to thank the following members of the UAW International staff: Irving Bluestone, Administrative Assistant to Walter Reuther; Woodrow Ginsburg, Research Director; and the following members of the Research Department: Richard J. Laufle, Librarian; Luther Slinkard, Leonard Klue, and George Schwartz, Contracts Office. These men were unfailingly helpful in arranging interviews with the appropriate persons in the UAW, in providing data on the Union, and in contributing their own knowledge and experience. The author would also like to thank Nat Weinberg, Director, Special Projects and Economic Analysis Department and Anthony W. Connole, Administrative Assistant to Douglas Fraser, Board Member-at-Large and Director of American Motors Department for their assistance, as well as all of the many staff members and office personnel who opened their Departments and gave generously of their time.

governmental structure. There is no suggestion that our form of government itself requires drastic change but rather that by taking political action—supporting candidates for office and voting—citizens can bring about legislation they desire. This rationale became well established in the American Federation of Labor during the early years of this century. However, not all critics of labor or of the UAW are satisfied with this assumption.

Looking to the future, UAW leaders believed in 1963 that legislation rather than collective bargaining would be the major means of working toward their goals. It is one matter to recommend legislation and another to bring it about. The format in which most of the proposals have been presented shows one way—an advisory capacity. Walter Reuther, as vice-president of the AFL–CIO, chairman of the AFL–CIO Economic Policy Committee, and president of the UAW, incorporated the ideas in a statement before the Subcommittee on Employment and Manpower of the House of Representatives and in a statement on the President's Economic Report.

A second means of implementation is through the support of political candidates and parties. Everyone does not agree that labor unions should properly be concerned with politics, and the leaders of American unions have differed in their views on this subject. The UAW takes the position that union members as citizens have a responsibility to be active in politics. The UAW supports candidates of the Democratic Party at both state and national levels. This does not mean that all UAW members vote as a political unit. During the 1962 gubernatorial campaign in Michigan, while the International staff worked for Swainson, the Democratic candidate, the president of at least one UAW local publicly announced his stand for Romney, the Republican candidate, who was elected.

The concern of UAW officials is not with the choice of party but with the political apathy union members share with many other Americans. Quoting again from the interview with Mr. Bluestone: "Our members do not understand [the importance of voting.] I would say we [the UAW] have the best Education Department of any union, the most effective. Yet we are not doing enough in this respect."

Of all the structures of society, American labor unions are most closely interrelated with business corporations and with government. Government has established itself as regulatory of both unions and corporations and as an intermediary between them.

Unions have continued as powerful organizations because, except for brief setbacks, they have steadily increased in membership and improved in administrative skills. Their strength in the future will depend on their ability to incorporate white-collar and technical workers and to present programs that will give them the attention and political support of their members and like-minded citizens.

CHAPTER ELEVEN

Religious Organizations

Religion has emerged in the United States as a major organizational enterprise, although its scope and complexity may seem rather insignificant in comparison with industrial and governmental organizations. The numerical change in religious membership gives some hint of this organizational revolution. In 1890 the membership of the twenty principal religious bodies represented 94 per cent of the country's religious membership; these twenty bodies organized the activities of 20.5 million members. In addition to these major bodies there were 533 congregations of Jewish affiliation and 123 other small religious groups. The membership of the twenty principal bodies of 1960 represented 88 per cent of the nation's religious membership; these twenty bodies organized the religious activities of 114 million members. At that time there were also 4,079 congregations of Jewish affiliation and 239 other small religious groups.[1]

To speak of religious organization over this seventy-year period is at least to reckon with a membership explosion of major proportions, correlated, to be sure, with growth of population. In this same period there has been a shift from a rural to an increasingly urban constituency. Expansion and change characterize this period of religious life in the United States, whether one investigates membership, expenditure for buildings, missions, benevolence, federation, or merger.[2]

What pattern, if any, can be discerned in this expanding religious activity? Is a profile discernible in the way the religious bodies have organized this massive membership? Certainly there has been or-

This chapter is by Gibson Winter. See Notes on Authors.

1. Sources for these comparisons are the *United States Census, 1890; Statistics of the Churches*, p. xxiv, and *The Yearbook of American Churches, 1960;* no brief is held for the accuracy of religious statistics, which are notoriously unstable, but the comparison is not out of line with specific observations.

2. An analysis of the transformations in membership from 1870 to 1950 is given in the author's book, *The Suburban Captivity of the Churches* (Garden City, L.I., Doubleday, 1960).

ganizational growth, but it remains to be seen whether this organizational development is out of proportion to the increase in size of membership. Are we merely dealing with an increase in the scope of organization to handle larger numbers, or can we detect a qualitative change in the character of the organization of religious activities? In brief, are we dealing with expansion or revolution?

EXPANSION OR REVOLUTION?

The evidence thus far suggests an organizational revolution that is far from complete. Here we shall attempt to describe and document that revolution, identifying the common elements in Protestant, Catholic, and Jewish developments while giving due recognition to differences. That there would be common elements could perhaps be predicted from the general acceptance in American religious life of what Sidney Mead has called the voluntary principle, that is, the use of special associations and agencies to carry out limited mandates. Though originally described by Mead because of its importance in American Christianity, it has certainly been equally characteristic of the Jewish congregations and of American social and political movements as well.[3] The voluntary principle achieved expression in religious life under varying restraints. Some religious communities, such as the Roman Catholic, demanded orthodoxy in hierarchical and institutional forms as well as in the forms of worship. The principle did influence, however, to a greater or lesser degree all of these institutions, just as the emerging social and cultural situation set them common problems. Indeed, voluntarism constitutes the prime example of the pragmatic tradition in American social and political philosophy—it worked.

The result for religious organizations was the development of the agency and its attendant bureaucracy. We shall have occasion to examine this device in some detail. Agencies here mean the task forces, voluntary associations, boards, and committees developed to cope with emerging problems. The proliferation of agencies posed a

3. Sidney E. Mead, "Denominationalism: The Shape of Protestantism in America," in *Church History, 23* (1954) 291–320.

Religious Organizations

serious problem of unity of command within the religious organizations, for agency bureaucracy grew up before a corresponding ideology or ecclesiology was developed for their control. That an organizational problem of such a simple, everyday character should arise is not surprising, particularly in terms of Daniel Boorstin's interpretation of American political development, although it is somewhat unexpected in the religious field, in which careful appeal to, and elaboration of, doctrine is normally regarded as crucial.[4]

The theological problem of organization goes back to the beginnings of Christianity (and to the Old Testament for the Jewish community). Some American denominations, such as the American Baptist Convention and the Disciples of Christ, anchor their organizational position in the primitive, relatively undeveloped stage of church organization. The difficulty of coming to terms with organizational elaboration is much greater for such bodies than, for example, for the Episcopal Church, the Presbyterian Church, the Lutheran bodies, or the Roman Catholic Church, all of which provide for some type of development in ecclesiastical structure.

Several consequences followed from these ambiguities in ecclesiological formulation:

1. The problem of church unity of command was aggravated by differing perspectives on the validity of given forms of organization, particularly when mergers brought together conflicting traditions of organization.

2. The goals of an organized activity could easily become divorced from the organization's original theological task because there was no clear articulation of the relationship between that task and the administrative form utilized to achieve it.

3. The parent religious organization was often denied effective participation in the decision making of an agency as a result of the church's failure to become organizationally sophisticated.

Such problems form underlying themes in the history of religious institutions; as problems they become much more pressing in a period of organizational revolution.

The term *organized* is usually applied to churches in a pejorative way, particularly with reference to activities peripheral to "religious" matters. This fact calls for some clarification. Organization is the application of rational processes of coordination and commu-

4. Daniel Boorstin, *The Genius of American Politics* (Chicago, University of Chicago Press, 1958), especially Chapter I.

nication with a view to achieving clearly defined goals or objectives. In this sense almost any human activity is amenable to some degree of organization; in fact, one way we distinguish the commonsense world of everyday life from dreaming, fantasy, and esthetic enjoyment is by the degree of organization expected in our activities and responses. We do not expect dreams to manifest their contents in highly organized forms; in fact, many dreams seem to reorder haphazardly the basic themes of everyday life. Organization means a rational ordering in which various elements and phases are directed toward the effective realization of an anticipated state of affairs.[5]

This is the meaning of the term organization as we apply it to the various religious faiths. When we speak of organization in the field of religion, we refer primarily to the coordination of activities, the introduction of rational systems of accounting, the use of functionally specialized staffs, the application of objective criteria to gauge performance, and the designation of specific goals to be served by functional units within the enterprise. Our principal task will be to give an account of the extent and character of elaboration of organization within the religious bodies. After this task is accomplished, it will be possible to consider the functional problems arising from this elaboration and the direction in which resolution of these problems is being sought.

How can one hope to speak coherently of such a vast organizational development in such short compass and on the basis of the limited research available? One can hope only to establish the profiles of these religious organizations at this time. The complex problems of informal organization require investigation of the "hard" data of interpersonal communication in these organizations, and only a limited amount of such data, including that developed by the present research, is available. One of the major results of this research is the pointing out of the research needed in this organizational revolution.

Paul Harrison's study of the American Baptist Convention blazed the way for the study of religious organization in the Protestant tradition.[6] Without his study this essay would not have been

5. Alfred Schutz, *Collected Papers, Vol. I: The Problem of Social Reality* (The Hague, Martinus Nijhoff, 1962), especially the essay "On Multiple Realities."

6. Paul M. Harrison, *Authority and Power in the Free Church Tradition* (Princeton, Princeton University Press, 1959); in addition, many historical texts contributed substantially to the data and theory.

possible, not only because some very important data were uncovered in his research but also because the major lines of organizational development were already detected in his study. It is a basic study of a Protestant denomination—the American Baptist Convention—whose theological understanding anchors religious authority in the individual believer and at most in a congregation of believers.

We have established a study parallel to Harrison's in an examination of the historical records of the organizational development of the Disciples of Christ, whose ecclesiology is somewhat comparable; the study traces the lines of organizational elaboration. A somewhat complementary study was done of Methodist organization in order to contrast a much larger organization and because this denomination developed from a preachers' church governed by the ordained.[7] In contrast to the two studies of lay Christianity (Baptist and Disciples) and the study of the preachers' church (Methodism), an examination of the organizational development of three Lutheran denominations on a regional level provides some picture of organization in more confessional and liturgical traditions.[8] We also had available the work of Valorous Clear, who carried out research on the transition of the Church of God from a sectarian, informal structure to a formal organization.[9] This careful study provides illuminating insight into the dynamics of the organizational process because it concentrates in a short time a process that took many years in most of the more formal denominations.

In addition to these denominational studies we have investigated a federation of churches in a major metropolitan area. This distinctively Protestant form of religious organization mirrors the major lines of denominational organization since a council or federation

7. The studies of the Disciples of Christ and the Methodist Church were done in collaboration with John Paynter; this research would not have been possible without his thorough investigation of these denominations. These were historical investigations of journals and records, later checked with several authorities in the Methodist tradition to verify interpretations.

8. The Lutheran studies were done in collaboration with Robert Benne; his creative approach to this research contributed data and theoretical formulation to the total project. This study included a review of records and interviews with the regional executives of the three major Lutheran bodies including interviews of executives.

9. Valorous Clear, "The Church of God: A Study in Social Adaptation," Dissertation in Partial Fulfillment of Requirement for Ph.D., University of Chicago, 1953, unpublished.

manifests the coordinated organizational thrusts of various religious groups.[10] Here too some "hard" data were available for consultation and reference; they provided extremely interesting clues to the problems of the denominations, because an organizational study of the National Council of the Churches of Christ in America had just been completed and was of great importance in discerning trends, even though only those sections that had been openly discussed in meetings of the Council could be made public.[11]

Finally, a study was made of the pattern of organization of the evangelistic movements as represented by Billy Sunday and Billy Graham.[12]

Sufficient data are thus available for drawing an initial profile of the organizational revolution in Protestantism. The adequacy of the data will, of course, be indicated at each stage in the presentation. There is no question that much further research is needed; indeed, generalizations about the Protestant profile have to be made with reservations, but the general picture is reasonably clear. The most serious gap in this presentation of Protestantism is the pattern of organization in the Negro Protestant churches.[13] Investigation now underway discloses the complexity and special character of this

10. Research on the Church Federation of Greater Chicago was contributed by Stanley Hallett and helped to broaden the perspective on the denominational development; the author is also indebted to Mr. Hallett for his theoretical contributions. This study was done from the inside including a study of records and examination of personnel and policies and discussion with staff.

11. The study of the National Council of Churches of Christ in the U.S.A. is being carried through by Booz, Allen and Hamilton, Management Consultants; this is a confidential study, as indicated, but the problems and insights in the study were illuminating on the total spectrum of Protestant development. The basic insights of this study were borne out by our own research on a regional level.

12. This investigation was made by Robert Bates, and, although much of the data could not be incorporated into this essay, the larger perspective on religious oganization was strengthened by the research; revivalism, as Sidney Mead has noted, is one of the distinguishing marks of Protestantism in the United States and no study of organization can afford to omit it. In addition to historical study, an interview study of the Billy Graham Chicago Crusade—35 counselors and participants—shed light on organizational aspects of revivalism.

13. The Protestant denominations have approached such homogeneity that Gerhard Lenski found it difficult to discriminate among them with reference to the many variables he had explored; on the other hand, Negro Protestants showed up in the Detroit Area data as markedly different from White Protestants on many points. See Gerhard Lenski, *The Religious Factor* (Garden City, N.Y., Doubleday, 1961); J. R. Washington, Jr., *Black Religion* (Boston, Beacon Printers, 1964); and the author's discussion in *The Suburban Captivity of the Churches.*

Religious Organizations

problem. The interweaving of religious and racial themes in more than thirty organizations will have to be explicated before any clear picture of this problem can be drawn.

Generalizations about the profile of such a complex phenomenon as American Judaism could not be attempted without the excellent studies by Marshall Sklare, Nathan Glazer, Robert MacIver, and many others.[14] MacIver's study of the Jewish Community Relations Agencies is most illuminating, although it provoked considerable controversy at the time of its submission. This controversy disclosed some of the trends in the Jewish organization, trends that have significant counterparts in Protestantism. Such comparisons need to be made with reserve; however, we are inclined to overlook the commonalities in the emerging pattern of American society, and we need to strike some kind of balance between a proper concern for differences and an honest acknowledgement of the common patterns of organization that have arisen in relation to very similar problems.

In some ways our picture of the Roman Catholic organization is most adequate and clearcut.[15] The Roman Catholic faith manifests itself through a much more clearly defined institutional structure than the other faiths on the American scene. To this extent the lines of its organizational patterning are more definite; in fact, those lines are rather precisely specified in Canon Law. However, organizational development has also come about through Catholic voluntary associations; those agencies are linked to the hierarchy and yet are somewhat free to pursue their functional tasks. We have investigated the organizational growth of Catholic administration and voluntary agencies. A profile of Catholic organizational development emerges from these investigations when they are set against some of the historical studies that have been done by Catholic authors.

14. For references to these works, see the text. The author is especially indebted to Abbott Rosen of the Anti-Defamation League of B'nai B'rith for access to the MacIver Report and for counsel on the Jewish profile; needless to say, Mr. Rosen is in no way responsible for any opinions expressed in this essay.

15. Research by Michael Schiltz made possible the analysis of Roman Catholic organization; the author is doubly indebted to Mr. Schiltz for the clarity of his understanding of the emerging organizational problems in this vast, religious structure; this research was based on existing records in the religious body and some of the fine historical studies that are extant.

However, we need much more internal data on the development of power between administrative and parochial units, on the adequacy of the overloaded diocesan machinery in the huge urban areas, on the allocation of resources in a rapidly changing metropolitan area, and, perhaps most importantly, on the informal exercise of influence between voluntary associations and hierarchical authorities. Such internal information will be difficult to obtain, partly because it impinges on the traditional authority of the bishop. Nevertheless, such information is needed for an adequate profile of the direction in which Catholic organization is moving and would consequently be of great importance to the hierarchy of American Catholicism. Meanwhile, we can make certain general statements about the lines of force that seem to be emerging; these statements are made with reserve, but they may prove fruitful in suggesting significant lines for further research.

The justification for drawing profiles of religious organization at this stage in research is that we have enough data to see our way, and until this data can be expressed clearly, we shall probably not direct further research in the most profitable paths. One would never confuse a profile with a detail map, and one would not confuse a profile with a dynamic analysis of operative forces in their consistent patterning. We therefore set about the task of sketching profiles without the illusion that more is possible at the present time.

THE PROTESTANT DEVELOPMENT

The phenomenon of organizational growth can be measured by growth of administrative staff relative to local units and by centralized expenditure relative to budgeting for local needs. These indices convey some measure of degree of centralization. The first step in shaping a profile of Protestant organization is to assess the degree of administrative centralization that has occurred. We consider this process first in the Disciples of Christ and the Methodist Church.

Growth of Administrative Staff

The Disciples of Christ formed in the mid-nineteenth century as one of the movements for restoration of New Testament Christianity under the leadership of Alexander Campbell; it created a "General Convention of the Christian Churches of the United States of America" in 1849.[16] Prior to this meeting societies of individuals and congregations had gathered in various regions, and even the apparently formal meeting of 1849 represented a collectivity whose principle of organization was individual and at most congregational. Missionary societies formed within the community of Disciples as voluntary associations, but tensions existed through the latter half of the nineteenth century over the assimilation of such boards to a certified body. The basic problems confronting home and foreign mission boards involved those of regularizing collections from congregations rather than operating on individual subscriptions. By 1892 some regularized collections had been established; hence, this date gives a baseline for estimating changes in administrative staff.

Table 1 provides the raw figures for sample years from 1892 to 1962; the number of staff can be seen in relation to nonnational ministers, meaning those not on national agencies, and in relation to churches as well as members. The Disciples did not achieve formal support for development of full-time paid staff until revision of the constitution in 1939. Despite this delay in formalization, staff developed through the earlier period; the gradual growth of social welfare activities, Bible School department, and missions activity led to increasing centralization of program.

These figures reflect a process of urbanization in recent decades

16. General historical information on the Disciples of Christ is drawn from W. E. Garrison and A. T. DeGroot, *The Disciples of Christ, A History* (St. Louis, Christian Board of Publication, 1948); Yearbook data for the Disciples will be classified as *Yearbook* for the appropriate year, although the yearbooks follow different nomenclature and sponsorship in different periods; 1892 and 1895, Christian Publishing Company; *American Home Missionary,* Yearbook issue for 1897, 1903–1918; American Christian Missionary Society, 1920; the United Christian Missionary Society, 1921–35; Yearbook Publication Committee, 1936–46; International Convention of Disciples of Christ, 1947–62. (Data on charts and for tables will simply be listed as *Yearbook* for convenience, but reference should be made to the proper publication for a particular year.)

and consequently an increasing size of congregation, accounting in part for the gradual growth in membership and decline in number of churches. The significant figures for centralization, however, are the proportionate increase in administrative staff relative to nonnational ministry and to churches since 1940. These are the decades of formalization in the denomination and are marked by a doubling in central staff. We can note, moreover, that this occurred without

Table 1. Disciples of Christ: National Staff, Churches, and Members, 1892–1962

Year	Number of national staff*	Number of "non-national" ministers†	Number of churches	Number of members
1892	10	3,897	7,850	700,630
1900	16	6,197	10,401	1,141,600
1908	21	6,662	11,307	1,285,123
1916	26	6,001	9,415	1,142,206
1924	46	6,383	8,877	1,359,884
1932	59	7,212	8,220	1,572,732
1940	68	7,448	8,070	1,669,222
1948	92	8,089	7,877	1,724,905
1956	131	7,498	8,062	1,930,760
1962	162	8,434	8,058	1,749,539

* These figures include technical staff members but exclude office secretaries; see *Yearbook* for appropriate years as indicated in footnote 16.

† Not holding office in a national agency.

appreciable increase in membership. In fact, the central staff increased by ten times since 1900 in sharp contrast to the increase in membership over the same period by little more than half.

Before considering comparable figures for administrative development in Methodism, it may be helpful to indicate the rather complex process of Methodist development.[17] The "Christmas Confer-

17. Several secondary sources provide information on the historical development of Methodism in the United States; R. W. Goodloe, "The Office of Bishop in the Methodist Church," Ph.D. Dissertation, University of Chicago, 1929, unpublished; N. B. Harmon, *The Organization of the Methodist Church* (New York, Abingdon-Cokesbury Press, 1948); J. L. Peters, *Christian Perfection and American Methodism* (New York, Abingdon Press, 1956); W. W. Sweet, *Methodism in American History* (New York, The Methodist Book Concern, 1933).

Religious Organizations

ence" of Methodists in 1784 is usually taken as the date of establishment of the Methodist Episcopal Church as an independent body, although Methodist preachers had been meeting annually in America since 1773. From this starting point two lines of organizational development concern us: (1) development of subgeneral or subnational units of organization below this General Conference level; (2) the formation of task-oriented boards or agencies.

Initially the bishops, elders (preachers set aside for supervisory work), and preachers formed the Conference and administrative structure. By 1792 the elders had become presiding elders (called district superintendants) and by 1820 were responsible for the quarterly conference (meeting of the circuit-unit) and the district conference. Thus the General Conference and lower-level quarterly and district conferences were operative in the early period of the westward expansion. Several other administrative units were necessary between these top and bottom levels, particularly since territories were vast in this period and occasions for coordination essential. The Annual Conference was established in 1792 as the basic administrative unit of Methodism, although the General Conference retained legislative responsibility and met guadrennially. The Annual Conference elected delegates who in turn comprised the legislative body of the General Conference. The relative influence of various conference levels is not significant to our immediate concerns, but certainly by the 1870s the Annual Conference and its Board structures had become pivotal in the administration of Methodist activities. The Board, commission, and committee structures that were developing in Methodism during the nineteenth century were later reproduced on the district conference level so that an extensive administrative machinery was being elaborated on each of these conference levels.

The Episcopal area developed simultaneously since bishops originally traveled throughout the entire Methodist community and were only gradually urged to define particular territories of responsibility. By 1872 the General Conference expressed its desire for stable residence of bishops by areas, and by 1924 this definition of responsibility was clarified. The bishops developed principal organizational ties to the Annual Conference, and with the merger in 1939 of the Methodist Episcopal, the Methodist Episcopal South, and the Methodist Protestant Churches, six jurisdictional confer-

ences were established with meetings set quadrennially.[18] This
complex picture of conference levels and episcopal areas can be

18. The Methodist Church was constituted in 1939 by the merger of the
Methodist Episcopal, the Methodist Episcopal, South, and the Methodist Protestant Churches. In order to get a full view of the Methodist Church, one
would need to examine each of its constituent strands. Such an approach has
not been employed here primarily because of the unavailability of sources on
the Methodist Episcopal, South, and the Methodist Protestant Churches. The
General Conference Journals of the former were available but contain no
systematic or thorough presentation of reports on the various General agencies. The Annual Conference minutes of the Church, South, were also available and the relevant statistics from that source are included. No primary
sources whatsoever were available on the Methodist Protestant Church.

In the face of these handicaps only one alternative remained: to examine
the development of the Methodist Episcopal Church up to the time of the
merger and then to concentrate on the Methodist Church since 1939. This
"last resort" is not, however, without internal justification. Quantitatively, the
Methodist Episcopal Church constituted the largest of the three uniting bodies.
In 1932 it recorded 3,908,262 members, 12,699 effective preachers, and 24,-
801 churches. The Methodist Episcopal Church, South, recorded 2,645,142
members, 6,610 effective preachers, 16,188 churches. The Methodist Protestant Church, according to the 1936 U.S. Census of Religious Bodies, recorded
148,288 members and 1,498 churches (no ministerial figures available).

Even more important than this quantitative consideration, however, is the
high degree of continuity between the modes of organization in the Methodist
Episcopal Church and the modes of organization in the Methodist Church.
Not surprisingly, the largest of the three churches seems to have played the
dominant role in the determination of the shape of the new church. This fact
is the more understandable when it is realized that the Methodist Episcopal
Church, South, according to both Sweet and Goodloe, followed a pattern of
development very similar to that in the Methodist Episcopal Church.

The following sources were used to compile the charts and tables on Methodist organization; reference will be made simply to the Minutes of the Annual Conference or the Discipline or the Journal, but according to the year
and the branch of Methodism, the actual publication can be checked.

The Methodist Yearbook
    (1869–1933)   The Methodist Episcopal Church
The Methodist Factbook
    1954   The Methodist Church
    1957   "   "   "
    1960–62   "   "   "
Handbook of Quadrennial Reports
    1940–1960   The Methodist Church
Annual Report, Woman's Foreign Missionary Society
    1884–1939   The Methodist Episcopal Church
Annual Report, Woman's Home Missionary Society
    1884-1932   The Methodist Episcopal Church
Annual Report, Board of Foreign Missions
    1939   The Methodist Episcopal Church
Annual Report, Board of Home Missions and Church Extension
    1939   The Methodist Episcopal Church
Annual Report, Board of Missions
    1940–1960   The Methodist Church
Annual Report, Commission on World Service and Finance
    1941–1960   The Methodist Church

seen schematically in Chart 1 as two lines of administrative responsibility interconnected at crucial points: the Episcopacy links to the General Conference with its commissions and committees, to the jurisdictional conference at the second level, and to the Annual Conference; the Episcopacy is also related through the Board of Managers to the board structure, which is reproduced at each level; moreover, the district conference and quarterly conference levels operate under episcopal direction though not under direct supervision.

Chart 1. Simplified Schema of Organization of the Methodist Church*

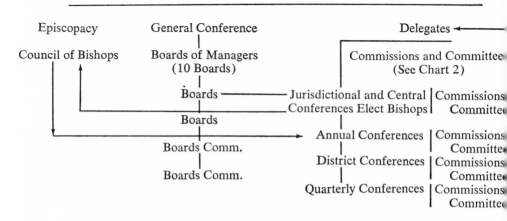

* For recent definitions of Conference responsibility and Board structure, see *Discipline, 1960.*

The board or agency structure can best be considered as a parallel and interrelated organization that stands in some tension with the conference line of organization. One can oversimplify the nature of the development of boards without damage to the complex process of historical development by seeing the boards as an outgrowth of voluntary societies formed to meet special tasks and largely dominated by laymen, who were excluded from the conference structure until 1872. Actually, the societies or boards developed with many ties to conference and episcopal administration, and they were gradually incorporated by legislation under the *Discipline;* but the board structure has never lost its relative autonomy as a task-oriented structure paralleling the conference structure.

The boards originated in agencies such as the Methodist Book

Concern (1789), the Missionary and Bible Society (1819), the Methodist Sunday School Union (1827), the Methodist Church Extension Society (1864), and the Methodist Freedman's Aid Society (1866). By 1876 the General Conference had brought the Missionary and Bible Society under the *Discipline*. By 1872 the Church Extension Society became the Board of Church Extension and in 1876 was defined more precisely in the *Discipline*.

The structure of the Boards was stabilized in relation to the conference structure by 1939 with the merger. The Board of Managers was constituted of all effective United States bishops (with vote) and members elected quadrennially by the jurisdictional conferences (ratio of one minister and three laymen for every *n* number of members in the jurisdiction), and its duty was to fix the staff and salaries, review staff work, and provide plans for auxiliary boards. The General Executive Committee was chosen by the Board of Managers and exercised its powers ad interim. The Executive Staff was elected by the Managers and made responsible for development and execution of program. The Auxiliary Boards, which are corresponding organizations in every annual, district and quarterly conference, were made subject to the parent board.

In his study of the Office of Bishop in Methodism Robert Goodloe has given a concise statement of the significance of this parallel board structure that can clarify much of this organizational picture:

> Bishops are "itinerant general superintendents"; Board Secretaries are localized managers of specific interests. Each Board is incorporated under the laws of the state in which it maintains its headquarters and gives itself exclusively to the forwarding of the cause for which it was organized. These Secretaries are elected by the General Conference, are directed in their work by the Board which they represent, and are responsible to the General Conference, not to the Bishops. In fact, then, since 1860 there is a group of "general managers" in the Methodist Church, and also a body of "special managers"; and the general managers have no direct oversight of the special managers. And, what might be very correctly observed, as the work of the special managers increases, the general managers of the Church find their field correspondingly narrowed.[19]

19. Goodloe, p. 178.

Chart 2. General Conference Commissions of the Methodist Church*

1940

1. Joint Committee on Religious Education in Foreign Fields
2. Interboard Committee on Missionary Education
3. Commission on Records, Forms, and Statistical Blanks
4. Curriculum Committee
5. Interboard Committee on Cooperation and Counsel on Negro Education
6. Joint Committee on Cooperation and Counsel
7. Interboard Committee on Education and Lay Activities
8. Joint Committee on Architecture
9. Interboard Committee on Town and Country Work

1948

1. Joint Committee on Architecture
2. Interagency Commission on Audio-Visual Materials
3. Interboard Committee on Christian Vocations
4. Committee on Cooperation and Counsel
5. Joint Commission on Cooperation and Counsel
6. Interdivision Committee on Foreign Work
7. Interdivision Committee on Work in Home Fields
8. Joint Committee on Materials for Training for Church Membership
9. Interboard Committee on Missionary Education
10. Joint Committee on Missionary Personnel
11. Joint Committee on Religious Education in Foreign Fields
12. Interagency Committee on Social Issues
13. Joint Committee on Temperance Education
14. Interboard Committee on Town and Country Work
15. Church Survey Commission
16. Committee to Study the Relation of the Editorial Division of the Board of Education to the Board of Publications
17. Commission to Study the Advisability of Establishing a Methodist Headquarters

1956

1. Coordinating Council
2. Interboard Commission on the Local Church
3. Joint Committee on Christian Education in Foreign Fields
4. Interboard Committee on Missionary Education
5. Interboard Committee on Town and Country Work
6. Interboard Committee on Ministry to Neglected Areas
7. Interboard Committee on Christian Vocations
8. Committee on Family Life
9. Curriculum Committee
10. Interboard Commission on Christian Social Relations
11. Interagency Commission on Cultivation, Promotion, and Publication
12. Commission on Promotion and Cultivation
13. Television, Radio and Film Commission

* See *Discipline* for appropriate years.

Chart 3. Formal Organization of the Disciples of Christ (1956)*

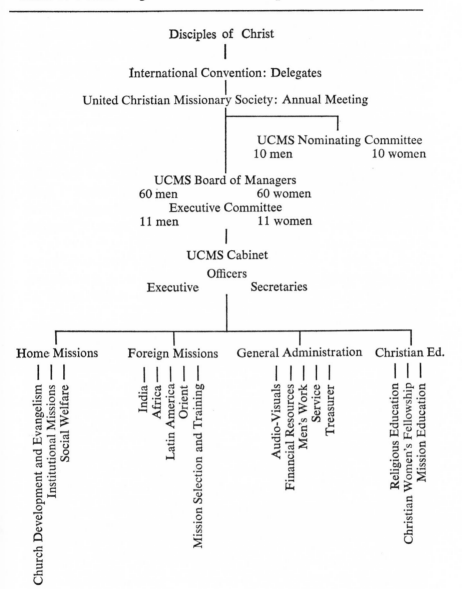

* See *Year Book* of International Convention, 1956.

Religious Organizations

A final stage in this organizational development illuminates the complexity into which these parallel structures had moved. By 1916 the General Conference undertook to coordinate the work of the boards with respect to budgeting and allocation of resources on an equitable basis through a commission on finance. Such commissions or quasiboards serving a coordinating function expanded rapidly and stabilized somewhat by 1956 (see Chart 2). The joint committees and interboard commissions attempted to coordinate boards that the bishops could not direct and also to meet needs that did not fall under the responsibility of particular boards. Consequently Methodism exhibits an organizational development starting from what might be called a "preachers' church" through the lines of organizational structure—conference (preachers) and board (lay)—leading to parallel organizations. The General Conference admitted lay delegates by 1872, and the boards were never simply lay enterprises, but the parallel structure does reflect these two sources.

The comparison of the Disciples and Methodist organizations can be seen in simplified expressions of their organizational patterns in Charts 1 and 3. The significant difference is the parallel board structure in the Methodist pattern, although Methodist bishops chair policy-making committees and keep some control. The common element is the structure of task-oriented boards, commissions, committees, and agencies. Chart 1 would be too cumbersome if the commissions, committees and various boards were itemized; consequently, the real complexity of this organization is somewhat concealed. Some of this complication emerges in the consideration of the centralization of finance.

Centralization of Budget

Control of budget is a sensitive index of centralization. Table 2 presents budget figures from 1916 to 1962 for the Disciples of Christ as seen from the perspective of the local church, and Table 3 gives comparable figures for expenditures of national agencies (1868—1962). Several changes in the distribution indicate administrative centralization. From 1916 to 1962 there was a 5 per cent drop in the proportion of money raised by local churches and expended by the local churches. The proportion of the money sent to

Table 2. Disciples of Christ: Budget for Local Churches*

Year	(1) Total amount raised by local churches	(2) Amount of (1) devoted to local church expenses	(3) Amount of (1) sent beyond local church	(4) Amount of (3) to state and local causes	(5) Amount of (4) directly to state society	(6) Amount of (3) to national level	(7) Amount of (6) to national unified promotion	(8) Amount of (6) to nonunified promotion causes
1916	$ 6,590,960	$ 5,843,481	$ 747,479	$ 90,847	$ 90,847	$ 656,632		
1924	14,071,049	11,055,156	3,015,893	1,083,737	314,125	1,932,156	$1,884,996†	$ 47,160
1932	13,316,189	11,217,169	2,099,020	733,019	192,620	1,366,000	1,105,452†	260,548
1940	12,805,545	11,065,287	1,740,258	763,274	16,777	976,983	938,229	38,754
1948	34,720,511	28,092,774	6,627,737	2,707,060	42,561	3,920,677	2,079,161	1,841,516
1956	70,968,597	60,546,264	10,422,333	4,292,847	76,586	6,129,486	4,420,224	1,709,262
1962	89,097,370	74,673,718	14,423,652	4,785,545	7,658	9,638,107	7,820,693	1,817,414

* Compiled from *Year Books*; see footnote 16 for titles by year.
† United Christian Missionary Society (Unified Promotion created in 1934).

Religious Organizations

the national level from local churches that was allocated to administration of National Brotherhood (all denominational agencies recognized by the Convention) almost doubled between 1924 and 1960; Table 4 shows ratios. This represents a coordination of funds

Table 3. Disciples of Christ: Budget for National Agencies*

Year	(1) Total amount expended at national level	(2) Amount expended on administration of national unified promotion causes	(3) Amount expended on administration of national nonunified promotion causes	(4) Total amount expended on national brotherhood administration
1868	$ 7,569	no figures	no figures	no figures
1876	5,841	"	"	"
1884	52,637	"	"	"
1892	168,187	"	"	"
1900	425,581	"	"	"
1908	846,452	"	"	"
1916	1,288,770	"	"	"
1924	2,565,670	$ 504,362†	$ 50,471	$ 554,833
1932	2,816,925	505,212†	363,856	869,068
1940	2,825,628	543,730	57,464	601,193
1948	8,961,748	1,004,482	458,833	1,463,315
1956	18,205,553	1,777,081	1,191,053	2,968,134
1962	30,809,078	3,212,548	1,893,783	5,106,331

* Compiled from *Year Books*; see footnote 16 for titles by year.
† United Christian Missionary Society (United Promotion created in 1934).

and expenditures through the national offices. At the same time, moreover, the total budget on the national level was increasingly drawn from other sources (compare Table 2, column 6 with Table 3, column 1). This meant that funds were being raised from private gifts, foundations, and so on, thereby freeing national agencies for a role in creation of program without dependence on the local units. Another indication of the process of central coordination was the creation of National Unified Promotion in 1924 to unify fund raising and develop an equitable allocation of resources. The effectiveness of this process can be seen from the decreasing proportion of funds expended at the national level on administration of National Unified Promotion (Table 3); between 1924 and 1962 the cost of administration dropped from 20 per cent to 10 per cent of total expenditure. Thus we see in the budget allocations of the Disciples of Christ a full confirmation of the centralization of administration that is outlined in Chart 3.

Local churches of the Methodist Episcopal Church (as the principal partner in the 1939 merger) and the Methodist Church after 1940 contributed increasing proportions to episcopacy and conference; between 1884 and 1960 this proportion increased from 11 per cent to 20 per cent. This is an appreciable increase in dollars since the local church fund in 1960 exceeded $550 million. Centralization of funds and control of budget are even more clear in Table 5, where the costs of the major administrative structures can be in-

Table 4. Comparison of National Agency and Local Church Budgets*

Year	(4 Nat'l) / (6 Local) Ratio of amount expended on National Brotherhood Administration† to amount of local church budget sent to national level	(6 Local) / (1 Nat'l) Ratio of amount of local church budget sent to national level to total amount expended at national level
1916		.50950
1924	.28716	.75308
1932	.63621	.48493
1940	.61536	.34576
1948	.37323	.43749
1956	.48424	.33668
1962	.52981	.31283

* Ratios drawn from comparison of Tables 2 (local) and 3 (national).
† Brotherhood Administration—all denominational agencies acknowledged by the Convention.

spected. The increased cost of Mission Administration in the national office from 3 per cent to almost 14 per cent of the total mission budget signifies a growing complexity of the task, improvements in training, allowances, and so forth; but above all it represents an increasing staff and activity on the national level.

Several other figures are suggestive. The increasing importance

Table 5. The Methodist Church: Numerical Basis for Ratios on Administrative Costs *

Year	(1) Cost of the episcopacy	(2) Cost of the general conference	(3) Cost of missions	(4) Cost of mission administration	(5) Cost of missions with share of cost of central treasury	(6) Cost of mission administration with share of cost of central treasury
1868	(no figure)	(no figure)	$ 1,030,978	$ 35,000		
1876	$ 98,021	$ 4,482	957,645	62,657		
1884	54,047	29,086	1,179,363	69,321		
1892	92,361	39,832	1,863,313	105,805		
1900	88,597	79,127	1,911,752	124,286		
1908	94,614	15,991	3,720,147	256,913		
1916	206,009	152,631	4,067,976	248,011		
1924	(no figure)	(no figure)	14,791,713	818,875	$15,333,109	$1,360,271
1932	429,162	486,781	6,965,572	710,180	7,021,355	765,963
1939	398,075	(no figure)	3,238,727	353,106†	(no figure)	(no figure)
1941	482,680	136,522	4,233,918	433,295	4,257,449	456,826
1948	678,049	273,808	10,925,953	1,224,307	11,069,921	1,368,275
1956	1,099,944	1,031,828	25,490,587	3,133,156	25,843,282	3,485,851
1960	1,326,114	1,263,957	22,995,083	3,188,885	23,348,133	3,541,935

* Compiled from *Journals* and *Annual Reports*; see footnote 18 for titles by year.
† Excludes W.H. M.S.—no figure.

of commissions and committees of the General Conference as compared to cost of the Episcopacy is evident in Table 5 from the ratio of column 2 to column 1 (see Table 6, for ratios); furthermore, the establishment of unified promotion through a central Treasury in 1924 did not result in reduced costs, as in the Disciples of Christ, but actually showed an increase in costs (see Table 6). This problem

Table 6. The Methodist Church: Ratios on Administrative Costs*

Year	(2)/(1)	(4)/(1)	(6)/(1)	(4)/(3)	(6)/(5)
1868	(no figure)	(no figure)		.03395	
1876	.04572	.63922		.06543	
1884	.53816	1.28261		.05878	
1892	.43126	1.14556		.05678	
1900	.89311	1.40282		.06501	
1908	.16901	2.71538		.06906	
1916	.74089	1.20388		.06097	
1924	(no figure)	(no figure)	(no figure)	.05536	.08871
1932	1.13426	1.65481	1.78479	.10196	.10909
1939	(no figure)	.88703	(no figure)	.10903	(no figure)
1941	.28284	.89769	.94644	.10234	.10730
1948	.40382	1.80563	2.01796	.11205	.12360
1956	.93807	2.84847	3.16912	.12291	.13488
1960	.95313	2.40468	2.67091	.13868	.15170

* See Table 5 for designations of numbers in parentheses.

has to be considered in another context, but it reflects the addition of promotional coordination without eliminating other promotional units that simply compound costs. In general, we see broad trends to centralized programming and expenditure, which bears out the picture already drawn of the elaboration of administrative units.

Two further aspects of the Methodist structure are illuminated by the allocation of money. Since the merger in 1939 there has been a marked trend toward increase of contributions from local church budget to subgeneral conferences as compared to the General Conference; these contributions are largely directed to Annual Conference level, where the board structure has developed considerable staff and responsibility. Although such contributions were about equally distributed between subgeneral conferences and General Conference in 1940, by 1960 local church budgets con-

Religious Organizations

tributed over $73 million to subgeneral conferences and $37 million to General Conference (see Table 7).

Another significant shift in allocation of funds occurred in the

Table 7. The Methodist Church: Contributions from Local Churches
to Subgeneral and General Conferences*

Year	Amount to subgeneral conferences	Amount to general conference
1940	$ 8,303,163	$ 8,377,736
1948	24,046,680	14,674,888
1960	73,179,445	36,955,779

* Compiled from *Journal*; see footnote 18 for titles.

distribution of money between General Conference and Episcopacy; although General Conference received only one-third of the amount allocated to Episcopacy in 1941 (see Table 5), by 1960 the allocations were approximately equal. This is actually an index

Table 8. Benevolence per Member for Regional and National Purposes
in the Lutheran Church of America, Missouri Synod,
and American Lutheran Church*

Year	L.C.A.		M.S.		A.L.C.	
	Synod	National	District	National	District	National
1920	$ .80	$1.02	$ 1.10	$ .90		
1930	.97	1.73	2.00	1.81		
1940	.38	.76				
1950	1.67	2.68				
1955	2.89	3.40				
1958	5.30	4.71				
1961			10.00	10.50	$.32	$6.20
1963	4.64	7.14			.36	7.96

* L.C.A. and A.L.C. figures are compiled from regional annual reports for appropriate years (see footnotes 20 and 23); M.S. statistics are compiled from 1920 and 1961 *Statistical Yearbooks*.

of the attempt to achieve coordination of boards through quasi-boards and interboards in view of the failure of the Episcopacy to coordinate the board structure.

The Protestant Pattern of Organization

Three basic trends characterize the Protestant denominations in their organizational growth: (1) elaboration of administrative staff; (2) centralized control of fund-raising and budgeting; (3) functional specialization through agencies and boards. We have traced these trends intensively in the Disciples and Methodist development. This general pattern holds for the rest of the sample with some variations; in fact, the range of patterning is rather well exemplified by the three Lutheran organizations. A brief consideration of these variants will make it possible to consider some general characteristics of this pattern.

The three Lutheran denominations on our sample were examined primarily on a regional or synodical level; budgeting, agency development, and staff relationships were considered on this middle level between the national organization and the local units. The Lutheran Church in America, the result of the 1962 merger of four Lutheran bodies, conforms reasonably well to the pattern shown by the Methodist Church but with a much less complicated organization, partially as a consequence of organizational streamlining effected at the time of the merger.[20] However, the board structure tends to parallel the line organization of committees, posing the problems of collaboration and unified action. The centralization of board and agency work has developed to the point where many national representatives bypass the synodical or middle level and deal directly with local congregations. This power in the central agency is largely a consequence of centralized control of funds for mission development.

The Missouri Synod is a Lutheran denomination that originated with the Stephenites from Germany between 1837 and 1847.[21]

---

20. Statistics for the Illinois Synod, Lutheran Church in America, were drawn from the *Minutes of the Annual Convention of the Illinois Synod of the United Lutheran Church in America*—years 1920, 1930, 1940, 1950, 1955, 1958, 1960; the 1962 figures of the merged church, Illinois Synod, Lutheran Church in America, were from the *1963 Yearbook of the Lutheran Church in America* (Philadelphia Board of Publication of the Lutheran Church in America, 1962), pp. 210, 250, 277.

21. Statistics for the Northern Illinois District, Missouri Synod were drawn from *Report to the Church—Proceedings of the Northern Illinois District, The Lutheran Church—Missouri Synod*, years 1920, 1930, 1955, 1960. The 1962 figure is estimated on the basis of *The Statistical Yearbook* (St. Louis, Mo., Concordia Publishing House, 1961), p. 174.

Religious Organizations

The Missouri Synod is still an intensely German, ethnic communion, although a rising middle class and intellectual elite are posing serious problems to this traditional orientation. The Missouri Synod is a doctrinal or confessional body held in line by its directors and president in each synodical area. This doctrinal framework and ethnic base give the Missouri Synod a much more coherent religious patterning than other Protestant denominations. The agencies or functional structures are voluntary associations; unlike other denominations these agencies have remained independent of the pastoral organization. Thus the pastoral direction and agency bureaucracy develop in association, so that agency development does not subvert the authority of the pastoral and teaching office. (This pattern has parallels in the Roman Catholic structure.) Moreover, the district or regional level retains considerable autonomy so agencies on the national level cannot encroach on local authority. The Missouri Synod deviates markedly from the modal pattern of Protestant organization; it is more doctrinally controlled, and it maintains communications through an ethnic communal network rather than through a national bureau of promotion.[22]

The American Lutheran Church resulted from a merger in 1960 of Norwegian and German branches of Lutheranism.[23] The ALC combined the strong central authority of the Norwegian branch with the more balanced structure of the German branch with a consequent impoverishment of local authority. The constitution and development of the ALC has subsequently intensified centralization and control almost to the dissolution of all intermediate levels of responsibility. A highly rationalized structure of committees (boards and agencies as we have been analyzing them) operates through regional directors paralleling the pastoral and representative structure of the region and controlling local activities. The net effect is to take over control of budget and program on the national level

22. This ethnic patterning gives the ordained ministry of the Missouri Synod a familiar character, as indicated in research by Ross P. Scherer, "Career Patterns in the Ministry: The Lutheran Church—Missouri Synod," paper read at American Sociological Association, Annual Meeting, Aug. 30, 1962.
23. Statistics for the Illinois District, American Lutheran Church, were drawn from *The Convention Report of the Illinois District, The American Lutheran Church, 1961*, pp. 56–58; the 1962 figures were from the *1963 Yearbook of the American Lutheran Church* (Minneapolis, Augsberg Publishing House, 1962), p. 229.

and to implement national programs on the regional and congregational level. This ALC pattern is one of the most highly centralized organizations in Protestantism and probably represents a temporary aberration in the unstable period of organizational revaluation. By contrast, the Missouri Synod retains a pastoral structure and voluntary associations in the nineteenth-century style.

The degrees of centralization, although not the forms of agency control that have been described, can best be seen through a comparison of local and national benevolences in the three Lutheran bodies. The figures in Table 8 indicate the distribution of control of funds between district (or Synod) and national level. The Missouri Synod has maintained about the same ratio since 1920; the LCA has approached a 1:2 ratio in a moderate centralization; the new ALC structure is almost completely centralized. Investigation indicates that the LCA is carrying considerable mission obligation toward inner-city churches in changing areas, whereas the more rural and ethnic Missouri Synod is spending its national funds for missions only in areas where the Synod has little strength.[24] The ALC has little work in home missions on a district level, and, indeed, the regional director covering several districts in mid-America handled a budget of $1,400,000 in 1962–63. The difference between these denominations should not be exaggerated, but there is evidence that centralization of activities is in part related to loss of local and ethnic ties. In general, the development of national and agency structures is borne out in the Lutheran sample, but the doctrinal and communal base of the Missouri Synod retains much more autonomy on the middle levels of organization and protects the pastoral structure by confining the agency growth to voluntary associations. Data on the voluntary societies of the Missouri Synod would balance the picture somewhat, since these societies are the long-range source of bureaucratic centralization in Protestantism.

With this broad confirmation of the emerging Protestant profile of organization, we can now turn briefly to several additional characteristics and problems in this new organizational style. Data from other samplings in this investigation bear out the broad trends but also highlight certain aspects of this organizational profile.

24. Interpretations are drawn largely from interviews with district level executives of the three branches of Lutheranism.

Organizational development

The organizational development of Protestantism has been largely a pragmatic, rational process. Paul Harrison's study of the American Baptist Convention documents this generalization for that
denomination, and the present study bears out his findings.[25] Paul
Harrison has noted the lack of ecclesiology in the development of
the American Baptist Convention. This is another way of designat-
ing the pragmatic character of the development for, whatever the
ecclesiological base, the various denominations have followed a
roughly comparable pattern of large-scale bureaucratic organization. In the Lutheran mergers, efficiency of organization won out
despite traditional differences. Deficiency in a theology of organization, so characteristic of the Protestant tradition, has allowed for
flexibility and pragmatic norms in the development of organization.
On the other side, emerging problems of unity and coherence in organization create a need for a theology of organization. The controversy over the Faith and Order Working Paper, "The Ecclesiological Significance of Councils of Churches," and the intense de-
bates at Montreal in the summer of 1963 over the ecclesiastical
status of the World Council are further indications of this question
of the theological significance of religious organization.[26]

The process of adaptation according to the criterion of efficiency
is exemplified further in Valorous Clear's study of the Church of
God. The Church of God moved out of sectarian simplicity into a
formalized denominational pattern; Clear's organizational study of
this process is particularly dramatic. We see in the splintering and
change encountered by the Church of God an intensified expression
of the development many denominations experienced in the nineteenth century. Although the whole of this study has bearing on the
Protestant profile, the following quotation summarizes the pragmatic character of this development:

25. Harrison, p. 209ff.
26. For the discussion of these questions, see *Faith and Order Trends,*
March 1963, Vol. 3, No. 2, "Churches, Councils and Unity?"; see also the
working paper, "The Ecclesiological Significance of Councils of Churches"
(The National Council of Churches, 1963); the meeting in Montreal, 1963,
was the Fourth World Conference on Faith and Order of the World Council
of Churches.

Perhaps the most striking change has been in the area of formal control. Born in a setting of anti-organization, the movement in seventy-five years has developed to the point where the most recent *Yearbook* lists over two hundred names of persons holding office in the national organization of the group. Most of the first thirty-eight pages are devoted to describing activities of the various national and regional organizations.

This tightening of lines of control has tended to discourage deviant thought. The publishing of one's name in the *Yearbook* has assumed tremendous significance; it is a type of *nihil obstat.* If his name does not appear in the *Yearbook,* a minister experiences great difficulty in gaining an audience if he should desire to make contact in another state, and his colleagues in his home state hold him in question until he makes satisfactory explanation.

An additional factor in strengthening the lines of orthodoxy, a factor not yet fully appreciated by most of the Church of God ministers, is the recently instituted ministerial pension plan. A minister pays a portion of the premium; his congregation pays part. As long as he remains in fellowship his account is credited with both amounts; but should he be disfellowshipped he loses all the funds which were contributed to his retirement plan by a church. As time goes on, as men grow older, as the sums grow larger, this financial penalty on needy older ministers will probably be increasingly effective as a deterrent to deviant thought. And it is among the older ministers that the most stress falls in a religious group with a pattern of rapid change such as the Church of God has had.

However, changes in the area of organization have also served to give definition to the group. Homogeneity is more easily achieved or maintained when a committee is established to judge whether a candidate meets the qualifications established by the larger group. Although in the early years homogeneity was maintained through the close communication made possible by the smallness of the group, as the body increased in size and in geographic distribution the types of persons entering the group were broadened. This meant a diversification which has been partly brought under control by the formal organization, and particularly by the state and sectional registration committees which certify ministers' names for inclusion in the *Yearbook*.[27]

This pragmatic type of development is also evident in the large-scale organization of evangelism. Evangelism would seem to lose its authentic flavor when it becomes formalized through a bureaucratic structure. In order to test the extent to which organization is a rather universal phenomenon in the religious life of the United States, a study was made of the organizational forms employed by Billy Sunday and Billy Graham. Such organizational development is restricted by the central place of the Evangelist himself; that is, the organization is built around a figure whose gifts and image are to be accentuated and whose deficiencies are to be minimized. Hence, the organization of the evangelistic enterprise takes a different direction from the functional and task-oriented organizations which we have been considering. Nevertheless, centralized control of finance, accounting, development of highly specialized staff, recruitment and organization of volunteers, and expert utilization of communications techniques are incorporated into the large-scale evangelistic campaigns of our day.

In general, the application of organizational techniques occurred under Billy Sunday and has been developed by Billy Graham. This transition to organization came at the turn of the century, as Bernard Weisberger has shown, and marks a transition to a new era in evangelism and perhaps reflects a much broader transformation in American religion.[28] To be sure, there are differences, for Billy Graham has access to mass media and can cultivate a national clientele, partly through the Crusades but largely through the intensive follow-up and promotional work of the Billy Graham Evangelistic Association. These are differences of degree; however, the similarity of style must be stressed. In both cases we meet a pragmatic application of organizational techniques to increase the number of "trailhitters" or "inquirers."

Despite the refinements in organization, the revival seems to become more costly; inflation, as well as the competition of other in-

27. Clear, p. 361f.
28. Bernard A. Weisberger, *They Gathered at the River* (Toronto, Little, Brown & Co., 1958), p. 270f.

terests and opportunities, aggravates this situation. Table 9 gives a comparison of the receipts for the two evangelists in their New York and Chicago campaigns and the number of decisions in each campaign. The decisions can be reckoned as the productivity of the campaigns and the receipts as the costs to the cities for these decisions. The average cost per decision in the Billy Sunday campaigns

Table 9. Receipts and Decisions in the New York and Chicago
Evangelistic Campaigns of Billy Sunday and Billy Graham

| | Billy Sunday | | Billy Graham | |
	Receipts	Decisions	Receipts	Decisions
New York	$320,669[a]	98,264[c]	$2,500,000[e]	56,767[g]
Chicago	191,000[b]	49,165[d]	783,219[f]	16,451[h]
Total	$511,669	147,429	$3,283,219	73,218
Average cost to cities per decision	$3.47		$44.84	

a. William G. McLoughlin, Jr., *Billy Sunday Was His Real Name* (Chicago University Press, Chicago, 1955), pp. 109, 174.

b. *Ibid.*, pp. 109, 115.

c. *Ibid.*, p. 103.

d. *Ibid.*, p. 103.

e. William G. McLoughlin, *Billy Graham, Revivalist in a Secular Age* (New York, Ronald Press, 1960), p. 149.

f. Official Report on Billy Graham Greater Chicago Crusade.

g. McLoughlin, p. 149.

h. Official Report on Billy Graham Greater Chicago Crusade.

of New York and Chicago was $3.47. The cost in the comparable Billy Graham campaigns was $44.84. It could be argued, of course, that Billy Graham's improved techniques are a greater help in fund-raising than in producing decisions, but from the point of view of the central goal of the campaigns, one has to acknowledge the greater efficiency of the Billy Sunday organization.

These figures do not suggest a greater effectiveness in Billy Sunday's work since Billy Graham may well be conducting crusades under more difficult conditions—competing with TV, encountering a more secular mood, facing a rising social and economic level of the White Protestant constituencies. Two important considerations

Religious Organizations

appear in this comparison. Billy Sunday had already developed a very effective organization; from this perspective, the continuity in Billy Graham's approach is very marked. Furthermore, the scope of the financial operation in Billy Graham's activities puts his enterprise in the field of large organization. To this extent, the most informal and personal religious activities have become a field of major organizational development in these decades of urbanized life and mass media.

Managerial personnel

Protestant organization has brought professional, managerial personnel into the religious bureaucracy. This further characterization of the organization of Protestant denominations is not meant pejoratively. Large-scale, highly rationalized bureaucracies cannot operate on a familistic basis. They require skilled managerial personnel who can decide on objective criteria about programs and advancement. This creates a conflict between the "organization men" and the constituency; promotion becomes one way of overcoming this tension. Nevertheless, the emergency of managerial personnel needs further research since it touches a wide range of conflicts in religious organization. Pastors experience this conflict in the tension between career and calling; the exercise of a calling requires some organizational structure, but large organizations transform callings into careers.[29] Organizational staff encounter this strain in local churches as the tension between cosmopolitan and local interests. Organization of religious activities on a centralized basis favors a cosmopolitan type who can move from one organization to another; his skills are detachable; they can be used in any comparable organization with minor adjustment.[30] Local congregations are interested in a man with local pastoral concern; the large organization turns the pastor's attention to the organizational demands—increased membership and fund-raising. The conflict between institutional structure and local values is accentuated with every step toward the development of large organization. Robert

29. Scherer notes that even the use of the term *calling* is weakened with the developing sense of organizational career.
30. The study of personnel in the Church Federation of Greater Chicago indicated the high mobility and specialized skills which characterize this group; no member of the staff had been resident in Illinois when hired.

Rankin found evidence of intense feeling over this conflict of interests in a Methodist District in California.[31]

The Protestant Profile: Pastorate Agency Bureaucracy

The Protestant organization combines a pastoral structure with an agency bureaucracy. The pastoral structure is concerned with proclamation and teaching within the believing fellowships. The agencies have developed to maintain and extend the pastorate in a changing social situation; arising largely from lay, voluntary societies, they were gradually incorporated into the denominational structure. These agencies specialized in tasks such as church extension, education, fund-raising, and promotion. The pastorate is responsible for faith and discipline in the confessing communities, while the agencies are preoccupied with the institutional development and maintenance of these communities. The work of pastorate and agency should be complementary, but much of the time they are at cross purposes or are unrelated to one another.

The complementarity between pastoral direction and agency bureaucracy can break down in several ways: 1. The pastorate can hold its traditional authority so rigidly that agency development remains extraneous. This is the problem implicit in the Missouri Synod situation.

2. Pastoral direction and agencies can follow separate lines, thus running the risk of a dual organization and competing powers. This is the problem confronting the Methodist structure.

3. The agency structure, preoccupied with organizational extension and promotion, can take over the whole religious enterprise, directing all units toward institutional interests. This is the danger present in the American Lutheran Church and confronting most of the Protestant denominations.

The idea of complementarity between pastorate and agency assumes that there is a reflective task of grounding action in faith (the work of pastorate) and a task of communicating faith within

---

31. Robert P. Rankin, "The Professionalization of the Calling: Functional Implications," paper read at American Sociological Association, Annual Meeting, Aug. 30, 1962; the materials for this paper were drawn from research incorporated in Robert Rankin's Ph.D. dissertation, "Religious Ideas and Church Administration: A Sociological Study of Methodism," University of California at Berkeley, 1958, unpublished.

Religious Organizations

the structures of a changing society (the work of agencies). In a static society the task of communication through agencies would be quite secondary. In a rapidly changing society agencies of communication can easily supplant pastoral direction. This is undoubtedly the principal difficulty confronting the Protestant denominations, the third situation described above, in which the religious enterprise is transmuted into promotion and organizational extension. Agency domination is a particular threat to Protestant denominations because they lack a principle of authority for the pastorate. Protestant strength lies in its concern to redeem culture without giving ultimate status to any cultural forms, biblical or otherwise; in line with its genius, Protestant organization needs to sustain its agencies as missionary expressions within the twentieth-century society. Freedom to live in the contemporary society with flexible organization should typify Protestant life.

In the nineteenth century agencies were very real vehicles of pastoral concern. The missionary orientation of that century saw the total enterprise as winning souls for Christ, and the agencies were implementing the essential task of the religious enterprise. This missionary understanding has disappeared, as Sidney Mead has noted, and the agencies are left with their own perpetuation as a major endeavor. The fulfillment of the complementary task of these structures will come, therefore, when mission and ministry are interpreted in terms appropriate to the twentieth century. This is the work with which the leading forces of Protestantism are now preoccupied, and only such a complete renewal of vision can preserve Protestantism from domination by an agency bureaucracy or degradation to a struggle for power among the agencies.[32]

Agency domination can be seen even more clearly in the interdenominational organizations. The lines of communications in Protestantism are increasingly horizontal—from agency to agency; the home-missions' specialists communicate across denominational lines, as do foreign-missions specialists and other agency personnel

32. The meeting of the World Council of Churches at New Delhi called for an investigation of the Missionary Structure of the Congregation as part of its report on Evangelism; this study continued during 1962–64 with widespread interest in Europe, North America, and Asia; the problem of missionary structure is acknowledged to be one of the most critical questions confronting Protestantism and bears directly on the problem of religious organization.

in the fields of education, publicity, and social action. Development of program and allocation of funds for particular projects are effected between these various bureaus and institutionalized through corresponding bureaus in the federated structure. Hence centralized policy making and budget formation become almost impossible; policy and budget allocations become purely formal activities; the operative processes occur within and between agencies. The source of this agency power is often in the large endowment income that they control. Furthermore, specialists within a particular federated bureau gain support for their programs from their denominational agency, which designates its funds to the federation for specific agency purposes. This process should not be exaggerated since the denominations carry a limited amount of the total federation budget in most cases (22 per cent in the Chicago Federation in 1962), but appointments of personnel and allocation of the important funds above basic maintenance will tend to originate in the bureaus rather than in the executive offices of the denominations. Lay representation in decision making, except through agency boards, becomes very difficult under these circumstances.

Attempts at reorganization within denominations and especially within the National Council of the Churches of Christ demonstrate the dual character of Protestant organization. The National Council is a particularly sensitive mirror of this effect of agency bureaucracy since it was a formation of independent agencies that retained agency autonomy within the body of the Council. Planning and budget were largely controlled in the bureaus, a predicament aggravated by the role of denominational boards and agencies. The Council of Churches became, therefore, a cluster of competing bureaus. Bureau executives operate within two frameworks of authority and communication; they participate in the formal organization of the Council but retain effective power only through the informal lines of power radiating from the denominational agencies and boards. Coherent development of policy and program is, of course, almost impossible under such conditions; even personnel appointments operate from bureaus rather than from denominational authority.

The National Council of Churches reorganized its structure as of January 1, 1965, in order to achieve more centralized direction without losing the strengths that come from agency cooperation

Religious Organizations

The Proposed Revised Constitution approved by the General Assembly in December of 1963 in Philadelphia reflects the attempt of Booz, Allen and Hamilton, Management Consultants, to guide the organization toward a more centralized structure. The executives of the member denominations hope to achieve more coherent planning within their own denominations through a similar process of centralization of authority and budget; they hope that the National Council will set a pattern. Whatever is achieved in the way of formal simplification, agency bureaucracy will not be transformed into a representative organization until and unless centralized financial planning can replace unilateral budgeting under agency control.

The organizational problem of Protestantism should not be exaggerated. Administrative staffs and general operations are relatively efficient, at least as far as this regional sample could detect. Even the National Council study was concerned with greater efficiency rather than with total ineffectiveness. The major difficulty arises from the irrelevance of much agency activity in the tasks confronting Protestantism in urban America. The clarification of goals will not be possible, however, until the denominations achieve clarification of their basic views of church structure.

THE CATHOLIC DEVELOPMENT

The development of a Catholic profile is somewhat simpler than the construction of the trends in the Protestant development; on the other hand, an intensive study of the informal organization of Catholicism might be far more difficult to execute. Our present concern with profile in organizational elaboration makes it possible, however, to assess the overall pattern of Catholic development.

The central fact in this organization is the diocese whose head, the bishop, exercises responsibility in all clerical affairs within the defined ecclesiastical jurisdiction.[33] The bishop has two adminis-

33. Two general works provide basic information and interpretation of Catholicism in America: Louis J. Putz, C.S.C., editor, *The Catholic Church, U.S.A.* (Chicago, Fides, 1956) and John Tracy Ellis, *American Catholicism*

trative lines through which he exercises his authority. One line is made up of chancery officials—the vicar-general, chancellor and auxiliary bishops—who advise and exercise within a framework of legally defined duties; the other line comprises activities and organizations such as charities, schools, hospitals, cemeteries, administered largely by clerical functionaries and related to the bishop's office through priest-directors or chaplains. Organizational elaboration has occurred primarily in the associations and activities, although the chancery bureaucracy has also expanded. We can discriminate two lines of development, chancery and agency. The former is hierarchical and the latter is voluntary; at least, the more the activity is removed from the bishop, the more likely it is to follow a voluntary association pattern. These are dual developments with varying types of interrelation. We cannot untangle the informal lines of influence within the dual organization since budget data are not available to give some indication of sources of power; but only research on the informal structure of power would disclose the lines of policy that are actually operative. For the purposes of a profile, two kinds of data have been used: (a) a statistical study of the growth of the organization, employing indices of key officials in both administrative lines—chancery and agency; (b) the agency or associational development is considered separately as an indication of the pattern of growth. The data on association are drawn primarily from the development of the National Catholic Welfare Conference, the closest thing to a national organization of the Catholic Church in the United States.

The Growth of Catholic Organization

In order to provide a workable index by which to identify dioceses along the urban-rural continuum and an index that, at the same time, could be derived from available data over the entire 1900–60 study period, a simple "density ratio" was computed for

(Chicago, University of Chicago Press, 1955); for a brief but valuable interpretation see Will Herberg, *Protestant, Catholic, Jew* (Garden City, L.I., Doubleday, 1955), Ch. 7 , "Catholicism in America." The statistics on membership and functionaries are drawn from *The Official Catholic Directory* (New York, P. J. Kenedy & Sons, by years); reference is made to this as *Kenedy*.

Religious Organizations

every diocese in 1960 by dividing the square miles of territory of the diocese by the number of parishes within the diocese which were listed as having resident pastors. Thus the *Density Ratio* represents the average number of square miles served by each parish within the diocese.

At the same time the number of parishes for each diocese in 1960 was computed, arrayed, and quintiles assigned. All the

Table 10. Density Ratios* of Sample Dioceses at
Beginning and End of Study

| | *Urban sample* | | *Rural sample* | | |
	1900	1960			1960
Boston	15	0	Amarillo (1930)	3,300	1,001
Brooklyn	7	0.8	Atlanta (1960)	850	760
Chicago	46	3.7	Baker (1910)	4,700	2,300
Cleveland	75	15	Boise (1910)	3,500	1,550
Detroit	142	17	Charleston (1900)	3,300	500
Hartford	37	12	Cheyenne (1900)	8,100	2,640
Milwaukee	60	18	El Paso (1920)	1,950	1,030
Newark	14		Gallup (1940)	4,400	2,440
New York	17	12	Grand Island (1920)	920	740
Philadelphia	23	2.2	Great Falls (1910)	4,300	1,430
Pittsburgh	58	13	Helena (1900)	4,800	940
Providence	27	7	Nashville (1900)	1,900	564
St. Louis	181	25	Pueblo (1950)	1,200	865
St. Paul	100	29	Rapid City (1940)	530	642
Trenton	70	21	Reno (1940)	6,400	3,250
			Salt Lake City (1900)	17,000	2,500
			Savannah (1900)	4,800	1,040
			Tucson (1900)	8,200	620
			Yakima (1960)	660	650

* The density ratio represents the average number of square miles served by each parish within the diocese.

dioceses which fell into the most dense quintile and the quintile with the most parishes per diocese were then identified as the urban sample. All the dioceses which fell into the least dense quintile and the quintile with the least number of parishes were identified as the rural sample. Because two quintile criteria were used for identifying each sample, the resulting number of dioceses in each sample is not the same; that is, fewer dioceses in the urban sample qualified under both the density and number of parishes criteria than in the rural sample.

As it happened, the urban dioceses that were selected from the 1960 evaluation all were in existence at the beginning of the study period—1900. This was not true of the rural dioceses. Nevertheless, about half the urban dioceses underwent division and resulting shrinkage in area, during the sixty-year period. Consequently, it was necessary to compare the 1960 density ratios with those in 1900 or at the point when the diocese first entered the sample (that is, the census year after its erection).

Table 11. Summary of Parish-Diocesan Growth Pattern, 1900–60*

	1900	1920	1940	1960
Number of dioceses	82	100	112	139
Total N of parishes	6,530	10,192	13,094	16,778
Median N of parishes per diocese	66	85	90	105
Average N of parishes per diocese	79.6	101.9	116.9	120.7
Median size of parishes (sq. mi.)	257	233	120	108
Average size of parishes (sq. mi.)	540	345	275	216

* Kenedy, 1901, 1920, 1940, 1961, *passim.*

Table 10 identifies all the dioceses used in each sample and displays the two density ratios. The parentheses after the dioceses in the rural sample indicate the census year in which the diocese first entered the sample and consequently the year for which the first of the two density ratios is computed.

It will be noticed that the highest density ratio in the urban sample is 181, for St. Louis in 1900; the lowest density ratio in the rural sample is 530, for Rapid City in 1940. This indicates that the division on the urban–rural continuum made on the basis of the 1960 figures is valid throughout the study period.

The growth of dioceses is given in Table 11. The notable changes in the period from 1900 to 1960 are in the increase in the median

Religious Organizations

number of parishes per diocese and the decrease in the median size of each in square miles. Although the number of dioceses increased by 70 per cent, the bishop of the median diocese still was responsible for 60 per cent more parishes by the end of this period. Hence the "span of control" between bishop and pastors increased through

Table 12. Pattern of Diocesan Growth by Number of Parishes in Diocese, 1900–60*

Number of parishes in diocese	Number of dioceses			
	1900	1920	1940	1960
Under 50	30	25	19	13
50 to 100	27	36	44	52
100 to 150	15	19	21	44
150 to 200	5	8	9	11
200 and over	5	12	19	19

* Kenedy, 1901, 1921, 1940, 1961, *passim*.

this period. This "span of control" is seen more clearly in Tables 12 and 13, which shows decrease in number of smaller dioceses and increase in number of larger ones.

Table 13. Percentage Distribution of Dioceses by Number of Parishes in Diocese, 1900–60*

Number of parishes in diocese	Percentage of total dioceses			
	1900	1920	1940	1960
Under 50	36.6	25.0	17.0	9.4
50 to 100	32.9	36.0	39.3	37.4
100 to 150	18.3	19.0	18.7	31.6
150 to 200	6.1	8.0	8.0	7.9
200 and over	6.1	12.0	17.0	13.7

* Kenedy, 1901, 1920, 1940, 1961, *passim*.

The problems of complex organization are perhaps even more dramatically evident in the emergence by 1960 of massive dioceses such as the following:

The Catholic Development

archdiocese/diocese	number of parishes
Chicago	437
New York	402
Boston	400
Pittsburgh	312
Detroit	309
Los Angeles	297
Philadelphia	290
Buffalo	267

There were in 1900 only five dioceses that had as many as 200 parishes.[34]

The average number of square miles per parish gives some estimate of urbanization of diocese, although some dioceses include a hinterland joined to an urban center, which can make the figures

Table 14. Pattern of Diocesan Growth by Average Square Miles
per Parish in Each Diocese*

Average square miles per parish	Number of dioceses			
	1900	*1920*	*1940*	*1960*
Under 20	3	4	8	19
20 to 100	18	10	28	44
100 to 200	15	37	23	18
200 to 300	7	14	15	16
300 to 500	5	11	14	14
500 to 1,000	4	17	17	15
1,000 and over	30	7	7	13

* Kenedy, 1901, 1920, 1940, 1961, *passim.*

deceptive. As a general measure, the figures in Table 14 reflect an increasing urbanization. There is, of course, a considerable range; for example, in 1960 the Diocese of Brooklyn averaged 0.8 square miles per parish and the Diocese of Reno averaged 5,250 square miles per parish. In 1901 the two dioceses of highest density were Newark (14.9 square miles per parish) and Boston (15.9 square miles per parish); the following figures for 1960 indicate this increasing urbanization in relation to these two dioceses:

34. Kenedy, 1900 and 1960.

Religious Organizations

diocese/archdiocese	square miles per parish
Brooklyn	0.8
Newark	2.2
Chicago	3.7
Boston	6.2
Providence	7.1
Philadelphia	7.5
Bridgeport	8.3

Our data on bureaucratic growth need to be evaluated in relation to urbanization since it could well be a simple function of overall growth. In order to test the relationship of bureaucratic develop-

Table 15. Priests, Parishes, and Population: Urban and Rural Groups, 1900–60*

	1900	1910	1920	1930	1940	1950	1960
Urban							
Total priests							
per parish[a]	2.08	2.15	2.38	2.68	3.24	4.10	4.61
Diocesan priests							
per parish[b]	1.59	1.60	1.78	1.88	2.38	2.46	2.54
Catholic pop.							
per parish	2,680	2,400	2,570	2,480	3,390	2,960	3,820
Catholic pop.							
per priest[a]	1,280	1,130	1,080	925	854	720	830
Catholic pop. per							
diocesan priest[b]	1,680	1,490	1,440	1,320	1,160	1,200	1,510
Rural							
Total priests							
per parish[a]	1.78	2.06	1.68	1.83	1.83	2.10	2.30
Diocesan priests							
per parish[b]	1.24	1.36	1.10	1.17	1.25	1.19	1.26
Catholic pop.							
per parish	1,460	1,040	1,105	1,080	1,000	1,150	1,540
Catholic pop.							
per priest[a]	820	510	652	625	527	546	670
Catholic pop. per							
diocesan priest[b]	1,175	770	1,000	910	802	965	1,220

* Kenedy, 1901, 1910, 1920, 1930, 1940, 1950, 1960, *passim*.
a. This figure includes all priests, secular (diocesan) and religious orders, and includes priests associated with colleges, universities, seminaries, high schools, and other non-parochial functions.
b. This figure includes only secular (diocesan) priests, although it includes those secular priests associated with non-diocesan functions. It does not include religious order priests.

ment to urbanization a rural and urban sample of dioceses was isolated by means of a density ratio (see last section of this chapter). In addition, certain bureaucratic offices were identified to serve as an index of growth. The number of parishes, estimated total Catholic population, and number of diocesan priests active in the diocese were used as controls to stabilize the diocesan samples. Figures on Catholic population in the Kenedy directory are not considered very accurate, but they provide an approximate measure of change at ten-year intervals.

Table 16. Number of Primary Bureaucratic Functionaries per Diocese, Urban and Rural, 1900–60*

	1900	*1910*	*1920*	*1930*	*1940*	*1950*	*1960*
All functionaries[a]							
Urban	2.7	3.3	5.0	8.1	11.6	15.9	23.2
Rural	1.1	1.3	2.5	3.0	4.3	8.1	8.7
Chancel functionaries[b]							
Urban	2.7	3.1	4.5	7.3	9.2	11.6	15.5
Rural	1.1	1.3	1.7	2.3	2.7	4.4	5.1
Agency functionaries[c]							
Urban	0	0.2	0.5	0.8	2.4	4.3	7.7
Rural	0	0	0.8	0.7	1.6	3.8	3.6

* Kenedy, 1901, 1910, 1920, 1930, 1940, 1950, 1960, *passim.*
a. Sum of functionaries included in notes (b) and (c).
b. Sum of vicars-general, chancellors, vice-chancellors, assistant chancellors, auxiliary bishops, and the diocesan directors and assistant directors of Catholic charities, hospitals, schools, and cemeteries.
c. Sum of diocesan directors and assistant directors of Confraternity of Christian Doctrine, Catholic Youth Organizations, or similar organizations, CANA, Family Life groups, Councils of Catholic Men, Councils of Catholic Women, Catholic Action Federations, Rural Life Conference, Legion of Mary.

The general figures for the urban-rural analysis are presented in Table 15. These figures give an overall impression of an increasingly complex pastoral and administrative development in the urban diocese in terms of increasing ratio of priests to parish and population per parish. This impression is borne out by Tables 16 and 17, where chancel and agency functionaries are compared for urban and rural dioceses. The notable increase of the agency functionaries in the urban diocese as compared to rural is most marked in Table 17, where it is evident that chancel functionaries were in-

Religious Organizations

creasing at approximately the same rate in rural and urban dioceses from 1900 to 1960.

In order to control for size in view of the difference between

Table 17. Change in Primary Bureaucratic Functionaries
per Diocese, Urban and Rural, 1900–60

	1900	1910	1920	1930	1940	1950	1960
All functionaries							
(100:1900)							
Urban	100	122	186	296	432	590	860
Rural	100	118	164	209	390	735	790
Chancel functionaries							
(100:1900)							
Urban	100	122	167	270	341	430	575
Rural	100	143	187	254	298	485	560
Agency functionaries							
(100:1920)							
Urban	0	40	100	160	480	860	1,540
Rural	0	0	100	87	200	475	450

urban and rural dioceses, Tables 18 and 19 present the number of chancel functionaries in terms of parishes, population, and secular priests per diocese. Here we get some understanding of the relationship of bureaucratization within the chancel line in the urban and

Table 18. Relationship of Chancel Functionaries to Total Parishes,
Catholic Population, and Secular Priests, in Urban and Rural Dioceses

	1900	1910	1920	1930	1940	1950	1960
Parishes per							
functionary							
Urban	12.8	13.7	18.2	14.8	13.3	9.7	9.7
Rural	60.0	67.0	51.4	37.4	26.8	24.2	18.0
Population in							
thousands per							
functionary							
Urban	20.1	13.8	20.0	16.0	13.3	11.4	14.3
Rural	159.0	160.0	133.0	76.4	61.4	70.6	56.5
Secular priests							
per functionary							
Urban	17.2	18.3	20.0	17.5	16.4	11.7	11.7
Rural	95.0	114.0	91.5	69.7	53.0	59.5	45.0

rural dioceses. The intensive development of chancel bureaucracy from 1900 to 1960 is quite evident and far more marked for the urban than for the rural diocese; nevertheless, the two groups begin

Table 19. Change in Relationship of Chancel Functionaries to Total Parishes, Catholic Population, and Secular Priests, in Urban and Rural Dioceses

	1900	1910	1920	1930	1940	1950	1960
Parishes per functionary							
Urban	100	107	143	115	104	76	76
Rural	100	112	86	62	45	40	30
Population in thousands per functionary							
Urban	100	69	99	80	66	57	71
Rural	100	100	83	47	39	45	35
Secular priests per functionary							
Urban	100	106	117	102	96	68	68
Rural	100	120	97	73	56	63	47

to approach one another by 1960. However, the change is striking in the increase in agency functionaries in the rural diocese (see Table 20). The sudden change in these relations in 1930–40 is

Table 20. Relationship of Lay-Organization Functionaries to Total Parishes, Catholic Population, and Secular Priests, in Urban and Rural Dioceses*

	1900	1910	1920	1930	1940	1950	1960
Parishes per functionary							
Urban	0	1,040	431	338	102	63	35
Rural	0	0	360	433	23	12	13
Population in thousands per functionary							
Urban	0	2,500	1,120	835	284	192	135
Rural	0	0	397	468	23	13	20
Secular priests per functionary							
Urban	0	1,675	765	635	244	159	90
Rural	0	0	399	514	24	14	16

* For sources and definitions, see Table 15.

partly a function of the large increase in staff when a centralized office is established in relation to a relatively small population, number of parishes, and number of secular priests. Nevertheless, the increase in agency functionaries for the rural diocese is striking throughout the sample period. This period of rapid increase may well reflect a development of lay organizations moving out from the large urban centers.

The bureaucratic development of the Catholic organization is demonstrated with reasonable validity by these data, but more striking even than the relationship to urbanization is the intensive increase in agency functionaries, which we considered in the Protestant growth in terms of agencies and boards. These task-oriented groups are related to the chancel bureaucracy, as the indices of functionaries indicate, but the two bureaucracies are in a certain sense insulated from one another and form separate lines of organizational growth. Coordination becomes an increasing problem with this pattern of bureaucratization, but there is no danger of the assimilation of chancel or pastoral direction to the agency bureaucracy. Some further clues to this dualistic structure are provided by a more careful examination of the development of the agency line.

The Agency Development

In considering the emergence of the agency bureaucracy it is essential to recognize the role of the chancery bureaucracy in the Catholic pattern of organization. The most crucial struggle in the victory of the chancery was undoubtedly the "trustee" conflict in the 1830s.[35] The issue arose over the role of the trustees who assumed ownership of property under the common-law arrangements of various states. Two types of problems emerged with the attempt to fit Catholic control of property into the common-law tradition: 1) questions of inheritance had to be settled when property was held by bishops or priests; 2) questions of discipline and control developed when priests or laymen assumed authority on the basis of their control of property. In brief, the congregational or

35. Henry J. Brown, "A History of the Church in the United States" in Putz, pp. 27 and 30; Harry J. Byrne, "The Financial Structure of the Church in the United States" in Putz, p. 103f.

parochial autonomy of the Protestant tradition or perhaps even the general practice of local autonomy and a voluntary conception of organization were infiltrating Catholic organization. The question of title to property focused this struggle, although a similar localism emerged in the Kehensly struggle for ethnic Catholicism versus the universal character of the Catholic religious organization. The parish corporation method, especially as patterned on the New York law that allowed the archbishop to veto any act of the corporation, resolved the "trustee" controversy, and this pattern was instituted with minor variations throughout the church in the United States.

We have already suggested that the issue of chancery control can be generalized to the struggle against local identity, e.g. ethnicity, by the more universal structure of the diocese. This issue was not one of lay, voluntary control versus chancery and hierarchical authority, but it reflected the American stress on voluntary association, which played into the ethnic issue. The ethnic issue was resolved by compromise; nationality parishes were to develop alongside the territorial structures.

A related, though somewhat different, aspect of the struggle for control by chancery arose in the question of Americanization and the problem of an American Catholicism. As long as the bishop in his diocese formed the fundamental unit of authority and organization, all bishops were in principle directly related to the Holy See, and no American Church as such could emerge.[36] The history of Catholicism in America is in many ways a story of compromise between the hierarchical principle of direct line organization between the Holy See and the diocesan chancery on the one hand and on the other the formation of a conference of American bishops with a somewhat voluntary character. We cannot enter into this long and fascinating story of competing ethnic groups, strong episcopal leaders, struggles with American situations so alien to past experiences of the Catholic church in a time of poor communication, and so on. The hierarchical chancery line seems to have won the day in a formal sense, and canonically there is no question about this line of authority. The American bishops did, to be sure, meet in plenary conference to clarify issues, make recommendations for appoint-

36. Edward A. Ryan, S. J., "The Holy See and the Church in the United States" in Putz.

Religious Organizations

ments of bishops, and develop uniformities of practice in administration, but during the years until 1908 the American Church was
administered by Propaganda or Propagation of the Faith under the
Sacred Congregation as a missionary area. The bishops were meeting annually from 1889 to 1918, but their decisions were guiding
rather than authoritative and had to be cleared at Rome. Needless
to say, practice and appointments were developed in these assemblies, but they rested upon approval in Rome. Papal representation
has been formally maintained since 1893, when the Apostolic Delegation to Washington, D. C., was appointed by Pope Leo XIII, and
has worked closely with the American bishops.

The hierarchical line of authority should be neither overstated
nor underestimated in this American development; papacy to
chancery remains the formal line of authority and is clearly formulated in the code of Canon Law of 1918; [37] nevertheless, by 1919
the annual assembly of bishops had become the originating structure and continuing source of direction for the National Catholic
Welfare Council, remaining to this day the voluntary association of
American bishops and the source of a growing agency bureaucracy
through which national and functional problems have been handled.[38] Thus chancery and agency bureaucracies have emerged with
more balance than the formal structure would suggest. Moreover, the national bureaus and agencies are reinforced with other
voluntary associations that extend beyond the centralized National
Agency. The proliferation of agency functionaries on the diocesan
level has its source in a horizontal functional bureaucracy that
moves across diocesan lines and creates an upward flowing process
of communications even within the chancery structure of the
diocese. The Catholic organization has, therefore, two principles of
development and communication. We readily see the importance of
the agency bureaucracy when we consider its development and
elaboration in recent years.

In general, one can say that national functional problems such as

37. T. Lincoln Bouscaren, S. J. and Adam C. Ellis, S. J., *Canon Law: A
Text and Commentary* (Milwaukee, Bruce, 1946).
38. On the emergence of the National Catholic Welfare Conference from
the plenary meeting of bishops and the National Catholic War Council, see
John Tracy Ellis, *The Life of James Cardinal Gibbons* (Chicago, University
of Chicago Press, 1952), two volumes; Francis L. Broderick, *Right Reverend
New Dealer: John A. Ryan* (New York, Macmillan, 1963); and C. Joseph
Nuesee "The National Catholic Welfare Conference" in Putz.

education, publicity, and rural life have been handled through voluntary agencies within the Catholic organization. These voluntary associations have been related to the chancery through episcopal and clerical direction, but the associations have taken a relatively advanced, innovating role in the total development of Catholic life. Typical of such developments is the emergence of the National Catholic Educational Association in 1904 as the project of all those concerned with the welfare of Catholic education. Its advisory role was later closely coordinated with the National Catholic Welfare Conference through interlocking chairmanships and executive direction, but NCEA continues to play a significant role in the total educational program of the dioceses.[39]

One gains a picture of the complexity and scope of Catholic education and the formidable problems of organization it has encountered from a brief review of the educational statistics.[40] By 1954 the total enterprise included more than four million students and more than 130 thousand teachers. Between 1920 and 1954 the elementary school pupils increased in number by more than 40 per cent, and the secondary school enrollment increased by about five times. The schools are operated largely within the parochial or diocesan structure, although some are affiliated with orders or private associations. The NCEA and the Department of Education of NCWC have no executive authority in relation to the school system. On the other hand, development of national policy on schools, the problem of state aid to parochial schools, practice in pursuit of Catholic values in educational materials, and other general concerns that cut across local authorities have been explored through these national agencies.

The bureaucratic development of the National Catholic Welfare Conference is the most significant form of centralization in American Catholicism. At its inception in 1919–22 objections of some of the American bishops to a threat to their jurisdictional authority struck a sympathetic chord in the Holy See, where uneasiness has always existed over "Americanism" and an "American Church."

39. Kenedy, 1960, p. 820; *National Catholic Education Association Bulletin, passim.*
40. Frederick G. Wochwalt, "The Catholic School System in the United States" in Putz, and note that Rt. Rev. Msgr. Frederick G. Wochwalt held the post of director of the Education Department of NCWC and that of president-general of the National Catholic Education Association in 1960.

Religious Organizations

The net effect was the near dissolution of the whole structure in 1921, but, through the good offices of leading American prelates, an approval of the Consistorial Congregation was finally won in 1922.[41] In giving approval, however, the Congregation was very explicit about the voluntary character of the association, instructing that all minutes be reviewed by the Holy See, that even the troublesome term "council" be eliminated, and finally that the "agents" of the organization hold office only from meeting to meeting in order to prevent the development of a permanent bureaucracy.[42] Thus Cardinal Gibbons' hope for a "representative" and "authoritative" council of American bishops was disappointed, although the NCWC has in fact largely fulfilled this purpose despite the formal limits imposed by the Consistorial Congregation.

Chart 4 provides a rough schematization of the organization of the NCWC, indicating the bureaus and offices that have emerged within and alongside the departments.[43] In many cases a bureau develops in the secretariat for handling a special problem and then grows to such proportions that it emerges as a separate department, for example, Immigration, which handled more than 50,000 cases by 1954. The elective source of the administrative board, as is seen in Chart 4, is the annual meeting of the bishops. The Episcopal chairmen of the board are rotating offices, thus providing a distribution of responsibility. The administrative chairmen under the bishops generally provide the basic continuity of policy and procedure. As schematic and simplified as this presentation is, some sense of the scope and elaboration of this agency bureaucracy can be gained by noting some of the fields of interest of the various departments. Table 21 summarizes the development of departments in relation to bureaus and offices, suggesting the significant growth of the secretariat.

Chart 4 does not indicate the scope and variety of Episcopal committees emerging within the Administrative Board. These com-

41. John Tracy Ellis, "The Founding of the National Catholic Welfare Conference and Its Final Approval by the Holy See, May 1, 1919–July 4, 1922" in *Documents of American Catholic History* (Milwaukee, Bruce, 1955), p. 630.
42. Ibid., p. 634f; for a discussion of the diverse sources of opposition to the Conference, see Aaron I. Abell, *American Catholicism and Social Action* (Garden City, N.Y., Hanover House, 1960).
43. C. Joseph Nuesse; see also John F. Cronin, S.S., *Catholic Social Action* (Milwaukee, Bruce, 1948); also Kenedy for appropriate years.

Chart 4. Organization of the National Catholic Welfare Conference
(1954–55)

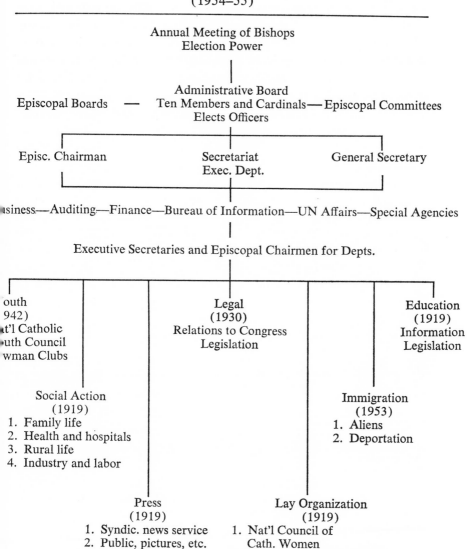

Annual Meeting of Bishops
Election Power

Administrative Board
Episcopal Boards — Ten Members and Cardinals — Episcopal Committees
Elects Officers

Episc. Chairman   Secretariat   General Secretary
                       Exec. Dept.

isiness—Auditing—Finance—Bureau of Information—UN Affairs—Special Agencies

Executive Secretaries and Episcopal Chairmen for Depts.

outh
942)
t'l Catholic
uth Council
wman Clubs

Legal
(1930)
Relations to Congress
Legislation

Education
(1919)
Information
Legislation

Social Action
(1919)
1. Family life
2. Health and hospitals
3. Rural life
4. Industry and labor

Immigration
(1953)
1. Aliens
2. Deportation

Press
(1919)
1. Syndic. news service
2. Public, pictures, etc.

Lay Organization
(1919)
1. Nat'l Council of
   Cath. Women
2. Nat'l Council of Cath. Men
3. The Catholic Hour (1930)

Religious Organizations

mittees, twelve in 1950 and nineteen in 1960,[44] include such activities as the American Board of Catholic Missions and the Committee on Motion Pictures. This phenomenon, even more than the administrative bureaucracy of NCWC, indicates the national interests and tasks that bring the Episcopal forces together across chancery lines and turn attention to the American situation. An urbanized society of large-scale organizations develops problems and

Table 21. National Catholic Welfare Conference; Increase in Bureaus,
Offices, and Departments, 1930–60

	1930	1940	1950	1960
Departments	6	6	6	7
Bureaus and offices	6	10	11	12
Total	12	16	17	19

correlated channels of communication that can be approached only on transregional and transdiocesan lines. The development of the NCWC is a realistic recognition of these facts. The increasing scope of committee structure within the administrative board likewise reflects the struggle to cope with an increasingly complex, national and even international web of interests.

The Administrative Board, at least between 1947 and 1959, has

Table 22. Urban–Rural Representation on Administrative Board,
NCWC, 1947–59, in Percentages

	Rural–Urban					
	1	2	3	4	5	Total
All members*	3.4	5.7	6.1	37.1	47.7	100.0
Elected members	4.4	7.8	8.6	46.4	32.8	100.0

* The category "all members" includes the American cardinals who are ex-officio members of the administrative boards; see notes on validation at close of chapter.

been drawn largely from the densest urban areas. Table 22 summarizes these figures within the quintile groupings developed in the note at the end of this chapter. The excessive representation of the large urban areas, even though the distribution of bishops extends

44. Kenedy, 1950, p. 74 and 1960, p. 852f.

over all dioceses and actually overrepresents the rural prelates relative to actual memberships, suggests the dominant role of urban areas in the problems that have given rise to the agency bureaucracy. The secret ballot used in the election of the Administrative Board prevents it from becoming a self-perpetuating, permanent bureaucracy, and one can only assume that activity, attention, concern, involvement, and some informed influence enter into this close correlation of intense urbanization and the development of agency bureaucracy.

Despite limits imposed by the Consistorial Congregation the NCWC has exerted an influence on the development of American Catholicism far beyond the potential of an informal secretariat. This is not a lay organization in the Protestant understanding, although laymen are more and more active as professional staff. The agencies have served an important innovating function and in this sense have carried a liberalizing role in Catholic development.[45] There has been a development of skilled staff who enjoy sponsorship from members of the hierarchy and exercise considerable influence in the development of national programs and even policy. Such staff members were well sponsored and exercised due caution, because no overt displacement of staff has occurred since the inception of NCWC.[46]

A fair appraisal of the role of NCWC should include the recognition that this agency bureaucracy has also provided a medium for transmission of papal ideas across diocesan lines. The process seems to be one of sponsorship of such ideas by one or several leaders, often bishops, who develop an idea by gaining support of the Holy See and implement it through NCWC or who further an idea that has long been encouraged by the Holy See. The Confraternity of Christian Doctrine is a case in point since its development into a major instrument for the instruction of nonparochial Catholic children came many years after command by the Holy See (Acerbo Nimis, 1905) and primarily through the work of Bishop Edwin Vincent O'Hara.[47] This is an interesting story of the rapid spread

45. Francis L. Broderick, p. 236.
46. Ibid., pp. 137, 155–59.
47. On the development of the Confraternity of Christian Doctrine, see "Archbishop Edwin V. O'Hara, D.D., L.L.D.; A Biographical Survey" in *The Confraternity Comes of Age* (Paterson, Confraternity Publications, 1956); also Miriam Marks, "Teaching Christ in America" in Leo R. Ward, editor, *The American Apostolate* (Westminster, Md., Newman, 1952).

of an agency structure through diocesan organizations after many years of work and primarily through the National Catholic Rural Life Conference. The papal-chancery line could not promote this program by mere fiat. Thus the NCWC represents not only a national agency structure for the American Church but also a channel of development from the Holy See to the national activities of American Catholicism. Development of program requires testing and propagating useful instruments horizontally through the church. The NCWC has proved extremely effective in this task. Here the vertical structure is sustained by the complementary work of a horizontal structure.

The Catholic Profile: Hierarchy–Agency Bureaucracy

The dualistic character of Catholic organization in America can best be expressed in the couplet hierarchy-agency. We have seen that the National Catholic Welfare Conference and other structures of agency bureaucracy are not radically separate from the hierarchical diocesan line of authority; indeed, the governing board of agencies in one way or another stands in close relationship to the authority of the bishops. Nevertheless, we have also noted that the agency structure has a voluntary, coordinating character that crosses the hierarchical line of authority.

The hierarchy-agency structure derives from separate principles of development held in tension through the episcopal office. The hierarchical principle represents the cultic line of development; thus the line of authority from Holy See to diocese, explicitly formulated in Canon Law, preserves the integrity of the Catholic faith as a sacramental system. This line of administrative authority and organization has developed into a diocesan bureaucracy in the emerging urbanization of American life. The agency line develops in terms of functional problems in an increasingly complex national society; this functional principle produces a bureaucratic development that cuts across the diocesan-territorial structures and yet depends on the authority of the bishops.

The problems within this dualistic structure deserve much more intensive investigation than has been possible in this research; such research would require access to confidence that might be possible only within the Catholic organization itself. Much could be learned from a study of this complex and in some ways remarkable combination of organizational structures; for example, studies of financial allocations and program development both within dioceses and on a national level might indicate the difficulties and advantages of this dualistic principle of organization.

Problems emerging from lack of centralized authority in the American Church may be offset by gains in stability in the ecclesiastical structure. Gains in efficiency within the national structure of Catholicism have to be balanced against dangers arising from too nationalistic an orientation for the American Church. The universal frame of reference provides a broader framework within which to evaluate gains and losses from the dual structure of Catholic organization. For this reason simple criteria of efficiency or adaptive flexibility, which might favor increasing the coordinating role of the NCWC, must be counterbalanced with universal concerns for the unity of a world Church. These are the principles explicitly acknowledged in the Catholic organization.

In analyzing the organizational development of American Catholicism Will Herberg laid considerable stress on the role of Americanization through an Irish hierarchy. This emphasis is to some extent borne out in the present study since NCWC is a distinctively American type of development within Catholicism. In some ways such an agency bureaucracy on a voluntary basis could develop only in an American atmosphere, for it presumes an acceptance of pragmatic criteria for organizational development and a voluntary principle in meeting problems. Gustave Weigel has remarked on this pragmatic, activistic, and adaptive character of American Catholicism,[48] noting that the pragmatic emphasis on action has always been closely correlated with a marked piety and dependence on priestly leadership. His characterization of American Catholicism is borne out by the dual and yet interdependent patterns of organizational development. The recognition of the American character of Catholic organization has to be kept closely in balance with the consistent centering of Catholic authority in the papal-diocesan line of organization. This is an authoritative and yet voluntaristic structure—an American Catholicism.

A decentralization of papal authority under the Ecumenical

48. Gustave Weigel, S. J., "An Introduction to American Catholicism" in Putz.

Religious Organizations

Council may transform the American situation by increasing the authority of national churches. The American hierarchy has already developed an agency bureaucracy through which such a decentralization could be effected. In fact, the balance between diocesan and agency bureaucracy that has emerged in the United States may well provide a prototype of decentralization for the Catholic Church. Moreover, the potentiality of the agency bureaucracy in American Catholicism will remain unrealized until the Catholic Church recognizes the national and functional character of the problems confronting the churches. Such a recognition implies a degree of reorganization that even the liberal wing of the Ecumenical Council may not yet envision. Until that time, however, the compromise between diocese and agency in American Catholicism seems to be workable.

THE JEWISH DEVELOPMENT

Understanding the organization of the Jewish community as a community of faith presents almost intractable problems to both insider and outsider. Here we are pressed even more self-consciously to speak only of profiles. Nathan Glazer expresses this enigmatic character of the Jewish community: "A social group, with clearly marked boundaries, exists, but the source of the energies that hold this group separate and of the ties that bind it together has become completely mysterious." [49] We shall attempt to penetrate certain aspects of this mystery but without pretending to unveil it.

The mystery of Jewish identity lies in its destiny and place in the American and world communities. The Jewish community has not been assimilated into American culture, whatever that may be; studies by numerous sociologists concur at this point.[50] Accultura-

49. Nathan Glazer, "What Sociology Knows About American Jews," in *Judaism, 3* (1950), 284.
50. One distinct advantage for this investigation has been the selfconscious study of the Jewish community by Jewish social critics and social scientists; this was particularly important since the present investigation had to depend upon prior research of Jewish organization. In addition to specific references

tion has occurred, if by this one means the discarding of ethnic styles and linguistic patterns for an Americanized style of life and worship. But assimilation implies more than acculturation; it is a transformation of the substance of Jewish life, a dissolution of the distinct calling, a loss or transmutation of the ethos and historical memory, a substitution of American memory for the recollection of "the people." Assimilation in this sense has occurred on the borders of the community, although the extent and rate would be hard to estimate.[51] Certainly the Jewish population level has remained fairly stable since the end of the major immigrations, and in view of the relatively low birth rate in the Jewish population within the United States one can infer a slow rate of what Catholic sociologists would call "leakage." Acculturation without assimilation is the situation of Jewish communal identity in the United States.[52] Jewish communal identity is preserved and communicated through a complex structure of voluntary associations and agencies; at the same time it is sustained and expressed through a sacred structure of symbolic acts and communal involvements. There may well be a unifying principle underlying both of these expressions of Jewish communal identity in the United States, but that principle has no unifying organizatonal expression at the moment and is actually rejected on the ideological level by many of the most influential structures of the Jewish community. Unlike American Catholicism, Jewish communal existence in America has no single voice or representative agency.

---

in the text, the following works have been particularly helpful in giving different perspectives on the development of the Jewish faith in the United States: *American Jewish Year Book* (New York, The American Jewish Committee, Annual), which contains excellent demographic and sociological materials according to general research and current problems; Jacob Bernard Agus, *Guideposts in Modern Judaism* (New York, Bloch Publishing Co., 1954); *The American Jew: A Composite Portrait,* ed. by Oscar I. Janowsky (New York, Harper, 1942); *The Jews: Their History, Culture, and Religion,* ed. by Louis Finkelstein, 4 vols. (Philadelphia, The Jewish Publ. Soc. of Am., 1949), esp. v. 4 in the concerns of this essay; Nathan Glazer, *American Judaism* (Chicago, Univ. of Chicago Press, 1957); Oscar Handlin, *Adventure in Freedom: Three Hundred Years of Jewish Life in America* (New York, McGraw-Hill, 1954); Will Herberg, especially Chapter 8; Marshal Sklare, *Conservative Judaism: An American Religious Movement* (Glencoe Ill., The Free Press, 1955).

51. Mention should be made in this connection of the searching study of this problem published by Louis Wirth, *The Ghetto* (Chicago, Univ. of Chicago Press).

52. Nathan Glazer, "Social Characteristics of American Jews, 1654–1954," American Jewish Year Book, *56* (1955), 11.

Religious Organizations

The problem of the unifying principle of Jewish identity is not merely a matter of inconvenience to sociologists or theologians. This problem troubles the leadership of fund-raising campaigns, the welfare agencies, some defense agencies, and most religious associations. Who speaks for the Jewish community? Who carries the ethos of Jewish life? What structures are pivotal in the coherence of Jewish identity? How does the Jewish community give voice to its political concerns when its status in the American community is threatened or when issues of Church and State impinge upon its life? These and innumerable other questions arise for the Jewish community and lie just below the surface of every fund-raising program.

This problem is familiar in the Protestant community; perhaps we can gain some clue to the best method to arrive at a profile of Jewish organization by recollecting certain features of Protestant life. The complexity of Protestant organization and the ambiguity of an agency that purports to speak for Protestantism arise from the voluntarism and pluralism within Protestant religious life. This is also true of the Jewish community. To say Protestant or Jewish community is to project a fuller unity and coherence than is warranted by the actuality of either of these communities. Jewish life, even more than its Protestant counterpart, is thoroughly imbued with an ethos of voluntary association and local initiative. These are characteristics we associate with middle-class style in the United States; the Jewish people are, in this respect, more middle-class and more American than any other American group.[53]

Whatever the roots of this middle-class style within the Jewish community—and some obvious sources come to mind, such as orientation to law and norm, emphasis on literacy, intensive experience of communication, and stress on verbal skill—the pluralism and voluntarism inherent in this style of life set major obstacles to centralization on a national basis. When Abraham Duker laments the impressionistic understanding of Jewish organization and the lack of rigorous studies of this phenomenon, he could as well

53. Ibid., p. 35; however, even such generalizations about the middle-class character of the "average" American Jewish person must be hedged with qualification; note, for example, the liberal political views and voting behavior of the American Jewish Community—a troubling anomaly in Gerhard Lenski's attempts to categorize this community (pp. 319–21).

lament the lack of clear subject matter for such a study.[54] There are no neat hierarchies; indeed, there are no comprehensive organizations whatsoever, and the resistance to their formation runs very deep within the American Jewish community. American Jews came to espouse the cause of Israel in the 1940s, but few could submit their own lives to such a nationally organized community. Hence, the enigma of a Jewish communal identity with a pluralistic structure of voluntary associations will circumscribe our efforts at a profile.

Another distinction must be made in the phenomenon of Jewish organization. There is no neat discrimination of religious organization from the totality of Jewish life in the United States or anywhere else for that matter. This is in the nature of the case because the Jewish faith reflects a calling that embraces the totality of the historical life of this people. We shall see in our consideration of Jewish religious life that the insulation of religious symbols from the public life of the people in society presents one of the most disturbing problems to Jewish culture in America, but in principle the faith of the people has meaning only within the totality of its historical life.[55] Particular cultural and social forms preempted a chosen place within this historical process, either the forms of inter-testamental Judaism or the Yiddish culture of Eastern Europe; as long as the faith found expression in historical, cultural forms, any particular form might pretend to ultimate significance. However, the historicity of Jewish faith also involves the relativity of the forms in which it finds expression—not an historical and social relativity but a relativity in terms of the sovereignty of the One whose

54. Abraham G. Duker has made an important contribution to the analysis of Jewish organization; see his "Structure of the Jewish Community" in O. I. Janowsky, and *Jewish Community Relations: An Analysis of the MacIver Report* (New York, Jewish Reconstructionist Foundation, Inc., 1952).

55. Louis Finkelstein expresses this understanding clearly as follows: "Judaism is a way of life that endeavors to transform virtually every human action into a means of communion with God." See his chapter, "The Jewish Religion: Its Beliefs and Practices," in Finkelstein, *The Jews*, 4, 1327. Even this seemingly clear perspective within Jewish faith would not be uncontested; in fact, it is somewhat undercut by the distinction between vertical loyalty to values and horizontal loyalties to nation and community which is proposed by Jacob B. Ague in "Assimilation, Integration, Segregation—The Road to the Future," in *Guideposts, 3* (1954) 498–510; here again the issue would not be one of principle since loyalty to the substance of Jewish faith would be unquestioned and the only problem will be method of sustaining that loyalty under changing social and cultural conditions.

Religious Organizations

will demands obedience in every historical time and place. Consequently, acculturation can occur in Jewish communal life only as long as this does not abrogate the substance of the Jewish faith. However, the one thing that cannot happen is the dissociation of faith from the historical life and obedience of the people.

The definition of Jewish faith in terms of the whole scope of Jewish life complicates the question of Jewish organization. One cannot offer a profile of formal religious organization that discloses the organization of Jewish life in either an historical or a religious sense. Jewish faith manifests itself in both the religious and the cultural expressions of Jewish community life. Of course, we cannot hope to glimpse the structure of the total life of the Jewish community, but we can recognize the major agencies that express its ethos and sustain its common life. To this extent we remain within the framework defined by Jewish faith, the only framework by which its own communal organization can be properly understood. In fact, this very definition of faith as embracing the total life of a community creates the problem of Jewish identity within middle-class American culture; the Jewish community is at the very least a subculture with a sense of historical identity and calling—no less American than any other of the myriad subcultures within the society and yet religiously qualified in a distinctive way.

We shall confine ourselves primarily to the Jewish development in the period since World War I. Several factors warrant such an arbitrary starting point; immigration slowed to a trickle after World War I, and the Jewish population began to stabilize; whereas the Jewish people comprised only 0.6 per cent of the total population of the United States in 1880, they reached 3.5 per cent by 1917 and have remained at approximately that point to this day; the major waves of immigration came between 1880 and 1917, but by the 1920s a native-born, second-generation leadership had begun to take over the agency structure of the Jewish community. By the 1920s all the elements were present for the shaping of the Jewish community; the ethnic institutions were rapidly losing their prominence, the agency bureaucracies were multiplying and expanding, the charitable enterprises were assuming major proportions both locally and internationally, and the new ethos of religious life was slowly making itself felt. Deep within this process one could trace the role of the Sephardic aristocracy and the German Jewish oligarchy, but the astonishing upward mobility of the second-generation Jews from Eastern Europe soon placed them in a competitive position within the agency structure. We miss much by starting so late in the Jewish pattern of development, but we can pick up most of the threads in these crucial years. The new Jewish community, replacing the rapidly disappearing Yiddish culture, came into being in the period between the great wars and that immediately following the founding of the State of Israel in 1948.[56]

Our procedure in discerning the pattern of development will be to go from the fund-raising structure to the defense agencies and then to the formal religious structure. Many important facets of Jewish life and culture are missed in such a procedure, but these three organizational patterns are crucial to understanding the character of Jewish communal and religious life. The term agency is used very broadly since we use it to refer to the complex associational life and the emerging national bureaucracies. However, we do miss the role of art in defining the Jewish communal identity, and we necessarily miss the very significant contributions of the social criticism developed by social scientists and historians.

The Pattern of Agency Development

The character of agency activity shifted markedly with the Americanization of the Jewish community. The fraternal orders and benefit societies began to disappear and change functions in the 1920s and were replaced by community centers with social and recreational activities. In 1913 the fraternal orders achieved a peak membership of more than half a million members; after that they dropped in number and membership steadily (by 1940, 345,000 members in thirteen orders).[57] Some, such as B'nai B'rith, shifted their direction, taking on new functions and continuing to expand their local memberships and influence. The development of community centers had begun early with the Reform synagogue movment as part of the Americanized program of Jewish life. These centers carried on social and recreational programs for the young under the direction of professional workers. In 1921 there were

56. For the full sweep of these events, see Handlin, especially for an understanding of the role of Yiddish culture in the process of Jewish immigration and Americanization.
57. Duker, p. 146ff.

Religious Organizations

forty-seven such centers with 100,000 members, and by 1941 there were 234 with 435,000 members. These centers were serviced by the National Jewish Welfare Board and are indicative of a widespread development of professional services.

The Jewish community organized and supported numerous welfare institutions from its earliest period of immigration, but these agencies expanded rapidly after World War I; professional social work skills and techniques became prominent in the agencies. This expansion of social work agencies (using the term broadly) and the corresponding professionalization of personnel removed the social work development from the central development of Jewish communal identity.[58] The indirect role of welfare agencies in shaping Jewish communal organization gives some warrant for focusing on the fund-raising and defense-agency structures rather than on welfare activities.[59]

The federating of Jewish welfare funds is perhaps the most comprehensive expression of the unity of Jewish life in America. Charity and philanthropy are characteristic of Jewish religious and communal life, perhaps more characteristic than any other feature of the Jewish ethos. The ethnic diversification of Jewish communities during the great immigrations and the increasing diversity of local and overseas needs for help, further complicated by the Zionist movement and the multiplicity of associations that emerged around one or another ideological aspect of this movement, all contributed to a proliferation of diverse fund-raising programs in the Jewish communities of America. This pluralism has not been completely overcome, as we shall see subsequently with reference to the defense agencies; nevertheless, beginning with a federation in Boston in 1895, the process of federating welfare funds spread rapidly to most of the Jewish communities of the United States. By 1915, forty-six cities had federated their giving, leading to a development of community councils to coordinate and allocate these

58. This pertains only to the major thrust of this profession and not to their concern; Samuel C. Kohs in "The Jewish Community," Finkelstein, 4, 1306 draws attention to this problem; on the other hand the centrality of concern with Jewish communal life is quite evident in *The Jewish Social Service Quarterly,* *17*:1 (1940); for a balanced presentation see Herman D. Stein, "Jewish Social Work in the United States: 1920–1955," in *The Jews: Social Patterns of an American Group,* edited by Marshall Sklare (Glencoe, The Free Press, 1958), pp. 173–204.

59. For a discussion of these agencies and associations, see Kohs.

funds; by 1941, 266 urban centers had such federations. Two coordinating agencies emerged as a consequence of this process: the Council of Jewish Federations and Welfare Funds (1932), which has already been noted, and the Large City Budgeting Conferences. These national organizations were to become major factors in the pressure toward a national coordination of the activities of the various agencies and associations acting on behalf of the Jewish community.[60]

The need for centralized budgeting became acute with the growth of overseas relief. The period after World War I was marked by a sharp rise in antisemitic feelings and propaganda, culminating in the tragedy of Hitler Germany. With each passing year needs for overseas relief increased, further complicated by the Palestine question. Several factors contributed to the development of a united front of American Jewish people with respect to needs overseas. The Joint Distribution Committee (1914) intensified its activities during this period; by 1936 the major movements in support of Zionism joined in the United Palestine Appeal; by 1938 both of these groups joined forces in their national campaign under the United Jewish Appeal. By 1948 giving to all the charitable and philanthropic funds had reached a peak of over $200 million. After this point contributions dropped off, but to some extent needs abroad had also diminished.[61]

Before turning to defense agencies attention should be drawn to the crucial role of the federated welfare funds and the United Jewish Appeal in symbolizing the identity of the American Jewish community. Participation in welfare is widespread in the Jewish community, extending far beyond any organizational or formal religious memberships. Jewish identity comes to focus each year in these campaigns; through a contribution one can express one's membership in Jewish life. Moreover, the overseas giving symbolizes the universal aspects of Jewish identity, reaching not only beyond ethnic and communal groupings but also far beyond American identity. Such symbolization is very difficult to categorize, yet one can see the role of these campaigns in bringing coherence to American Jewish life. Samuel Kohs writes with strong misgivings

60. Abraham G. Duker in Janowsky, p. 153f.
61. Samuel C. Kohs in Finkelstein, pp. 1316–21; for summary figures on the annual level of charitable giving, see *American Jewish Year Book, 63* (1962) 248, Table 1.

about the centrality of fund raising in the Jewish communities of America, but his very concern reflects the importance of this process in the coherence of this community.

One can easily exaggerate the unity of this philanthropy, however; the defense or community-relations agencies serve to complicate this picture of Jewish organization. The most powerful of the defense agencies, the Anti-Defamation League (1915) and the American Jewish Committee (1906), carried on their own campaign under the Joint Defense Appeal until 1963, when they launched independent campaigns. These agencies, along with the Jewish War Veterans, the Jewish Labor Committee (1934), the American Jewish Congress (1917, 1922, and 1938), and the Union of American Hebrew congregations (Reform), engage in various kinds of research, litigation, and educational work on behalf of the Jewish community. With the increasing antisemitic propaganda after World War I the activities and budgets of these agencies grew rapidly.

The defense agencies played an increasing part after World War I in clarifying the position of the Jewish community in the United States and the world. Between 1935 and 1944 allocations to national agencies went from 2.3 per cent to 6.1 per cent of total charitable expenditure; when one realizes that the total amount expended on charity almost tripled during these years, the increase is considerable.[62] The American Jewish community was dispersing rapidly into various regions of the United States, and American life was becoming much more complex. This was particularly true with respect to the task of transmitting an understanding of Jewish life to a second and third generation without the benefit of a close ethnic community. Publications, educational materials, defense propaganda, and extensive fund raising became more prominent features of Jewish organization with each new decade. Some sense of this proliferation of national agencies is given in the following figures: there were 26 such agencies in 1935, 50 by 1940, and 268 by 1946–47, of which 15 were founded before 1900 and 47 after 1940.[63] Needless to say, efforts toward centralized budgeting and controlled fund raising met major obstacles in this rapid expansion of agencies. Moreover, some of the major defense agencies had

62. Samuel C. Kohs in Finkelstein, Table 2, p. 1288.
63. Ibid., p. 1295.

large local constituencies and rejected supervision by budgeting agencies.

One structure attempted centralization of finance; pressed by the Large City Budgeting Conference, the American Jewish Assembly was called in 1942 to bring various agencies together to work toward central planning. This group finally met when it changed its name to the American Jewish Conference, but attempts to make the conference a planning and coordinating agency caused the defection of B'nai B'rith, which realized that its autonomy would be jeopardized by such a scheme; finally the Conference dissolved in 1949. This was one of a series of abortive attempts to coordinate Jewish community-relations work.[64]

Under similar pressures and also out of a desire for a more adequate strategy, a movement toward centralization developed within the community-relations agencies themselves. Many of these movements toward unification of Jewish agencies and activities developed during the war years, and such a coordinating agency—the National Community Relations Advisory Council—emerged in the community relations field in 1944. Under pressure from the Large City Budgeting Conference the NCRAC agreed to a fact-finding survey on the activities and expenditures of the agencies. In 1946 a survey had already been made, which led to much conflict and discussion, so the attempt was made in 1950 to obtain a neutral study under the technical direction of Robert MacIver.[65] The study report recommended specialization by agencies on limited activities in order to avoid duplication, coordination of budget and planning, centralized control of strategy under NCRAC, and increase in local responsibility through the Community Relations Councils in various communities. After several years of controversy the Anti-Defamation League and the American Jewish Committee withdrew from the NCRAC in protest against implementing the recommendations.

64. Ibid., p. 1302ff.
65. The original study was done by Martin Kohn and Arnold Gurin, *A Study of National Civic Protective Agencies* (New York, Council of Jewish Federations and Welfare Funds, 1945), mimeographed; the second major report by R. M. MacIver, *Report on the Jewish Community Relations Agencies* (New York, National Community Relations Advisory Council, 1951), offset; critique of the MacIver report by Abraham G. Duker, and an objective review of the total controversy by Selma Hirsch, "Jewish Community Relations" in *American Jewish Year Book, 54* (1953).

Religious Organizations

In terms of the organization of Jewish communal and religious identity in the United States the failure to achieve centralized co-ordination of agency activities on a national level has very important implications. The pluralism of Jewish communal life was reinforced by the failure to coordinate the agencies; these national agencies balance and supplement one another in their different perspectives on the crucial issues confronting the Jewish community. Professional domination of the structure of Jewish communal life required a centralized, coordinating bureaucracy. Whatever the rabbinate may have anticipated from such coordination, it never would have come except through the power of the major agencies, and this in turn would have assured the decisive voice of these agencies in the American Jewish community. The present situation may be less efficient, but it assures a certain balance of power between agencies and welfare funds, between rabbinate and agency professionals.

The Formal Religious Structures

When we turn from welfare and community-relations activity to the formal religious sphere, we are struck by the surface simplicity of the religious organization. This appearance is illusory, however, since the organization of Jewish religious activity is in many ways as enigmatic as the network of agencies and bureaus. Judaism in America exists in a kind of tripartite structure of roughly equal elements—Reform, Conservative, and Orthodox.[66] The Sephardic Jews of the earliest settlement align themselves to this day with the Orthodox tradition insofar as they preserve distinctive congregations. In general, Reform Judaism represents the most liberal transformation in observance and interpretation while the Conservative movement stands as the mediating position in the adaptation of orthodox observance to an American setting.

A brief historical picture of the emergence of formal organization in American Judaism suggests the relative position of each organization in the structure of Jewish life. The Jewish community is very old on the American scene, going back to a seventeenth cen-

66. The author is particularly indebted to Will Herberg and Marshall Sklare for this brief characterization of the Jewish religious organizations; see also Samuel G. Kohs in Finkelstein, v. 4.

tury Sephardic settlement, and in every phase of settlement, from Sephardic aristocrat to East European, the Jewish community found religious expression through synagogue prayer and communal life. The synagogue as a house of prayer was not, however, a formal organization with professional leadership but rather a communal organization under lay leadership and managed by a sexton. Rabbinic leadership was brought to America for its customary role of interpreting the Law in the life of the community; the rabbi participated in the synagogue prayers as any other man of the community. Thus Jewish religious life centered in the community and its common struggle; the synagogue reflected the depths of that life but did not itself form its center.

Formalization of synagogue and rabbinic association is a sign that the communal bonds in Jewish life are weakening and formal structures are arising as substitutes. Since there can be no substitute for communal life in Jewish faith, these formal structures remain ambiguous. Will Herberg describes this process as transition from ethnicity to religiousness in Jewish identity in America. Another writer sees it as transition from Jews in America to Jewish Americans.[67] This is the import of Will Herberg's stress on the struggle for Jewish self-identification in the larger American community. Religious forms, national agencies, and fund-raising campaigns contribute to the maintenance of Jewish identity. This total complex of differentiated structures unfolded from the Jewish community with its house of prayer, fraternal order, burial society, and Torah talmud or communal school. As the communities of first settlement (to use Marshall Sklare's formulation) made their adaptations to American life and effected transitions to communities of second and third settlement, these communal activities were translated into associations and agencies. The fiber of the community weakened in the second generation; ethnicity dissolved as a bearer of identity; formal structures attempted to sustain Jewish identity in a complex, pluralistic situation. The key problem is whether an authentic Jewish identity can be sustained through formal associations and agencies.

The first major adaptation to American life came with the Reform movement under the inspired leadership of Rabbi Isaac Mayer Wise. He developed a prayer book according to American

67. Agus, especially p. 503f.

Religious Organizations

custom, promoted the formation of the Union of American Hebrew Congregations in 1873, established the Hebrew Union College for theological training in Cincinnati in 1875, and helped to bring together the rabbinical association of Reformed leaders in the Central Conference of American Rabbis.

This movement received doctrinal expression in the Pittsburgh Platform of 1885 adopted by some Reform rabbis—an extremely liberal statement within the tradition of German idealism. The movement toward a moderate position after World War I led to a modification of the Pittsburgh position in the Columbus Platform of 1932; this brought the Reform movement closer to the central position of American Judaism. Rabbinic and congregational associations were only consultative; authority remained with the congregation. This is no centralized bureaucracy with agencies, propaganda machinery, and coordinated budgets. This is the voluntary association *par excellence;* it opened communications within Reform Judaism through its seminary associations, scholarly writings and publications; in an increasingly complex, urban world, a network of communications was forged.

The Conservative movement came into its own after World War I, although its groundwork had been laid with the reorganization of the Jewish Theological Seminary in New York. The Seminary was founded in 1886 to counteract the effects of the Reform college in Cincinnati but had little appeal as an orthodox training ground and reached the verge of bankruptcy at the turn of the century. Under the combined influence of lay concern and the genius of Solomon Schechter, the Jewish Theological seminary undertook the task of training rabbis for the new waves of immigrants—a rabbinate that could help in the transition from Yiddish culture to American Jewish life. This was the second-generation movement in vision and style, a movement that was to prove remarkably effective in areas of second and third settlement. The focus of studies and program developed around historical Judaism; English and Hebrew ranked together in this historical appropriation. The continuity of Judaism during American adaptations became the central task of the Conservative movement. With this inspiration the Rabbinical Assembly (1900) gained momentum, and somewhat later the federation of Conservative synagogues was achieved through the United Synagogue (1913).

Marshall Sklare's analysis of the Conservative movement has demonstrated its appeal to second- and third-generation Jewish people. When the Jewish community moved out of ethnic culture into some kind of accommodation to the American environment, the Reform program still seemed much too radical; the Conservative program was both familiar and accommodated. Sensitivity to historical Judaism and concern for the second generation of immigrants led also to the Reconstructionist movement under the leadership of Mordecai M. Kaplan. This movement within the Conservative tradition attempted to link concern for historic Judaic civilization with a naturalistic philosophy. The added stimulus of Reconstructionism and the rapid upward mobility of the Jewish immigrants after World War I launched the Conservative movement into a ranking position in American Judaism; at the present time it rivals the other main traditions in Judaism and may well outstrip them during the next decade. A strategy and voice of American Judaism may well come through this center position; certainly Reform and Orthodox Judaism modify their own traditions toward the center as the dual forces of accommodation and formalization put an increasing burden on religious symbols to sustain Jewish identity.

Orthodoxy, as one would anticipate by its deep roots in traditional communal Jewish life, moved toward formalization much later in the period of Americanization. Between the world wars and after the restriction of immigration several branches of Orthodoxy formed associations and achieved a certain coherence. The struggle of the Sephardic Jewish community to create an organization in New York resulted in a Union of Sephardic Congregations. During the 1920s the Yeshiva College (later University) undertook the training of an American rabbinate; their alumni, along with the growing body of graduates of the Hebrew Theological College in Chicago, developed an American Orthodox rabbinate. The Rabbinical Council of America and the Union of Orthodox Jewish Congregations represent a final stage in the process of formalization of American Judaism. The complex variety within Orthodoxy need not concern us here; nevertheless, this simplified schema of development should not be allowed to conceal the congregationalism and diversity within Orthodoxy.

The Jewish religious associations came together in the Synagogue Council of America in 1926, affiliating rabbis and congregations from the various branches of American Judaism. The task of providing chaplains for the armed forces in wartime and communicating on the problems confronting American Judaism have strengthened this association, yet it speaks for Judaism only on points of unanimity. Rabbis and congregations have maintained association by protecting the autonomy of the local congregation and limiting the growth of a central organization. American Judaism has no counterpart to Protestant or Catholic organization on a national level. American Judaism has proved intractably local in organization. This is in itself remarkable in an age of organization, and it indicates the special role of a total, communal life in embodying Jewish faith.

Educational development is a mark of the changed function of the synagogue. In the immigrant period, as indicated earlier, the Talmud Torah fulfilled a teaching function under the auspices of the community. By 1955 a survey of schools in the urban centers indicated that 90 per cent of the children were receiving instruction under congregational auspices.[68] All through the period following World War I educational facilities and programs were being expanded. National agencies for education, surveys, and elaboration of programs reflected the struggle to cope with second- and third-generation phenomena in American Judaism. This activity came to focus in the elaboration of synagogue education. The basic increase in educational enrollment from 1900 to 1960 expresses this concern with formal training in the Jewish tradition; where Jewish population increased by a multiple of five during this period, school enrollment increased by a multiple of twelve; moreover, the weekday schools (meeting several times a week and teaching Hebrew as well as Jewish history and Bible) increased much more rapidly than

68. Uriah Zevi Engelman, "Jewish School Enrollment," *American Jewish Year Book*, 56 (1955) 250. See Engelman's brief monograph *Hebrew Education in America: Problems and Solutions* (New York, J.T.S.P. University Press, 1947) for a discussion of the inadequacy of the congregational school which is criticized primarily as an inadequate, foreshortened version of the Talmud Torah with a serious attempt to establish Jewish education on modern terms (especially Chapter IV, "The Sodom Bed of Jewish Education"); congregational schools have continued to grow, as noted above, and concern for the quality of these schools has exercised both educational and rabbinical associations; see Sklare, *Conservative Judaism*, pp. 145–58, and especially the discussion of conflict between interest and building synagogue institutions and needs for general, Jewish education in the total community.

the Sunday Schools or one-day-a-week educational programs. The growth of weekday schools is a good index of development of the Conservative movement as well, since Conservative synagogues developed weekday schools, while the Sabbath School of one day is more generally a Reform program. From 1948 to 1958 the weekday schools grew by 156.5 per cent as compared to Sabbath schools, which increased by 106.5 per cent.[69]

Parental and leader expectations of synagogue schools bear out this interpretation of their function in Jewish life. Both parents and leaders saw the function of the schools as primarily giving knowledge of Jewish life and culture.[70] Their responses to a survey of attitudes undoubtedly reflect the value given to knowledge in Jewish culture, but they also indicate the concern of parents that their children not lose touch with their Jewish identity and tradition. How effectively the schools are fulfilling these expectations cannot be properly assessed for several generations, because even immediate effects are not always helpful indices of religious education; but the parents and synagogues have invested more and more of their time and effort in this enterprise.

One other aspect of synagogue life illuminates the function of religious activity in the total spectrum of Jewish organization. The communal-center movement developed in the area of second settlement to provide activities for the young as well as social and recreational activities for adults. The center program was originally directed to the immense task of Americanization, but by 1945 this program had been redirected to the task of enrichment in Jewish life and culture. Such a transition seems very natural in view of the changed situation of the immigrant groups after one or more generations. However, the interesting development in this redirection was the fusion of the communal center and the synagogue into one common enterprise of education and cultural activity. Thus the synagogue becomes more and more central in the social and recreational life of the community, assuming many of the functions of the ethnic community. This concentration of activity and influence in the synagogue has stirred resentment among agency professionals, especially in smaller communities, but to some extent the fusion of

69. Uriah Z. Engelman, "Jewish Education," *American Jewish Year Book, 61* (1960) 128 and 129, Table 1.
70. Ibid., Table 12, p. 142.

Religious Organizations

religious and educational tasks in the synagogue seems inevitable with the attenuation of Jewish communal life.[71]

The period after World War II has also been marked by suburbanization of the Jewish population in major metropolitan areas such as New York; this process involves the dissolution of the multiplicity of agencies and centers that had provided services in the second settlement areas and opens the way for the concentration of social, educational, and religious activities under the common roof of the suburban synagogue. To this extent the development of the synagogue center corresponds with comparable developments in Protestant and Catholic religious organizations.[72]

The role of the rabbi, as Marshall Sklare has made very clear, undergoes radical transformation with the new function of the synagogue. In the "organization" synagogue with its educational, social, and recreational functions, the rabbi becomes a professional leader of worship and a professional director of a complex organizational enterprise.[73] He becomes pastor and professional friend, fund raiser and administrator, director of a large staff of specialists, organizer of a school, symbol of the continuity of Jewish faith. This new role, still under the rubric of rabbinate, contrasts markedly with the traditional role of rabbi and fits poorly with the role for which the rabbi is trained in theological school.

71. The growth of the Jewish Center was notable between the World Wars—from 47 centers in 1921 to 234 by 1941; this corresponds to the second and third settlement process which we have been tracing—see Duker, p. 148. The fusion of center and synagogue, to the extent that it has occurred, is a more recent phenomenon and stirs resentment in smaller Jewish communities which depend upon the center for activities; see Max Arzt, "The Synagogue and the Center in Contemporary Jewish Life," *Judaism, 3* (1954).

72. The social and recreational role of the synagogue is linked with the second and third generation phenomenon; Marshall Sklare has noted the lack of conflict with community centers because synagogues of the second settlement offered similar kinds of programs for their constituents, p. 138f; the fusion of recreation and synagogue seems to be intensified with suburbanizations, see *American Jewish Year Book, 54* (1953) 98 and *61* (1960) 52, and Judith R. Kramer and Seymour Leventman, *Children of the Gilded Ghetto* (New Haven, Yale University Press, 1961) especially p. 46f; for difficulties in estimating suburban population in the New York area, see *American Jewish Year Book, 62* (1961) 53ff.

73. Sklare, *Conservative Judaism*, Chapter 6, "The Conservative Rabbi," which is an excellent analysis of general problems in the rabbinic role; the diversity of rabbinic types is well developed by Jerome E. Carlin and Saul H. Mendlovitz, "The American Rabbi: A Religious Specialist Responds to Loss of Authority," in Sklare (ed.), *The Jews*, pp. 377–414.

The rabbi in Jewish tradition is interpreter of the law, the code by which life is organized and directed to its preservation and fulfillment within the Covenant. He is not leader of worship but participant with the men in prayer. He is not director of education and communal activity, although he is traditionally learned and called upon to teach. His expertise and influence derive from his knowledge of the Law and his capacity to interpret that Law in the complexities of daily life. Whether supported by a trade or the community or a patron or a wife, his learning and discernment enrich the community and keep its direction within the saving form of Torah.

The "organization" synagogue and the new role of the rabbi insulate him from the daily world of the Jewish laity and consequently from the task of interpretation of daily life for which he has been trained. The traditional understanding of the role calls for full attention to the Law in communal life; the rabbi actually has little access to the occupational and political world in which the Law needs interpretation; he lives in the private world of residential activities and feminine interests. Many rabbis do maintain contact with public life and exercise a very significant role in the larger community, but this task puts endless burdens on their time; the successful rabbi finds his attention drawn to the complex administrative and pastoral tasks of the synagogue. He finds himself in the synagogue rather than in the community. He is isolated to an increasing degree from the public and occupational sphere in which Jewish men live and through which the destiny of Jewish people is shaped.[74]

The center of gravity of Jewish religious life is local and private in the most extreme sense; it is local, autonomous, voluntary and to a large extent private in scope of concern. Religious symbolism maintains the memory of the Jewish people, keeping a sense of the past through which its identity is nurtured. The synagogue thus becomes the carrier of the tradition that had previously been borne in

74. The general acknowledgment of loss of influence by the rabbis reflects their circumscription by the private interests of residential communities in which they are trying to make the synagogue central; see Jerome E. Carlin and Saul H. Mendlovitz in Sklare, and note that their optimistic conclusion that the rabbi may be a specialist in a community "built up around the Law" presumes an access to the public community of Jewish life which the rabbi has forsaken on behalf of the residential synagogue; in this connection, they might have pursued somewhat more carefully the special type which they call the Social Reform Rabbi.

the common life of the Jewish community. If the full burden of Jewish identity rested on such formal religious association, the Jewish community of the United States would be weak indeed. We have seen, however, that Jewish identity is sustained by a configuration of agencies—philanthropic and religious associations—forming a network of communications and meaning, which defies simple delineation.

The Jewish Profile: Community–Agency Association

A profile of American Jewish organization emerges from this consideration of the national agencies, the federation of charitable work, and the new role of rabbi and synagogue. Jewish organization has its national networks of communications and strategy; it develops its own bureaucracies for defense and fund raising; it creates a variety of associations and bureaus for education and propaganda. American Jewish identity is sustained by these various forms; it is pluralistic in structure and more adequately described as a democratic association of various functions than as a bureaucratic organization. Three major structures organize American Jewish identity: propaganda agencies, promotional funds, and religious associations. However, this identity transcends these structures, informing the agencies with a concern for human rights, directing the funds to human need, and pointing the religious constituencies toward a universal hope.

The *national agencies* grew out of particular needs of the Jewish community within American society. These needs gave rise to diverse educational, publishing, welfare, religious, occupational, and defense activities. The agency was a product of particular interests and has become a source of interests, educational activity, promotion, and propaganda. This is said without pejorative implication since this is the function of professional leadership; indeed, a similar interpretation could be given for the role of a political representative in relation to his constituency—he is elected to represent, yet he cannot lead in representing without guiding his constituency to a vision of what is in its best interests.

The agency bureaucracies thus assumed the ideological role for the American Jewish community—interpreting the changing historical situation in the light of Jewish struggle for identity and engaging in research on particular needs of the community. The ideological role is, of course, crucial to the continued existence of any community since the understanding of the present situation orients the community to its historic past and guides it toward the future. The ideological task was assumed by the national agencies as heirs of the fraternal orders and local institutions. The resistance of these agencies to centralization therefore reflects more than resistance to change; the agencies arise from the diverse interests and perspectives of the Jewish community; they will centralize their activities only when the Jewish community approaches unanimity on interests they can represent. In this sense religious centralization would be easier to accomplish than coordination of the ideological work of the national agencies.

The most important function of the agency bureaucracy is the maintenance of communications among Jewish leaders with respect to communal interests. This network functions both within the Jewish community and between Jewish leaders and the other major communities of American life. Such a network is, of course, crucial to the effectiveness of ideological self-definition, but it also provides the materials with which the ideological task is performed.

The agency structure of activity and communications, as we have seen in the Protestant and Catholic developments, is quite closely correlated with the functional diversification of activities and interests in the American community.

The structures of a complex society are too diverse to be handled by one agency This need for functional pluralism expresses itself in the diversity of Jewish agencies. In the long run such diversity may be useful in strengthening communications within the Jewish community. The biggest handicap in the present structure, however, is the rivalry and competition on the local level between the agency memberships. A study of fund raising in St. Louis indicated that such rivalry was very damaging to campaigns in the city, largely because it "jammed" communications and confused local givers. Whatever the final pattern of agency organization may be, its significance lies in its ideological self-definition of American Jewish life and the development of communications on a national level; its major contribution on the American scene, however, has been its continuous effort on behalf of human rights.

The other pair in the Community-Agency Association is the

communal structure of Jewish faith in America. This structure has two functional aspects: charity provides a secular focus, and the synagogue offers a sacred focus. Charity and philanthropy provide a secular focus for the total Jewish community regardless of levels of religious commitment or observance. We can call this secular, although charitable works are if anything more central to religion in Jewish life than the more formalized activities of the modern synagogue. The United Jewish Appeal and the federated campaigns provide a unifying focus for the Jewish community that could not be achieved through formal religious structures or agency propaganda. Works of mercy in American Jewish life bring together local and national concerns, uniting the Jewish community in responsibility. The universal, world identity of Jewish faith is thus kept before the American community. The national scope of this fundraising and the network of communications through which it is accomplished provide a second major organizational aspect of Jewish life in America.

The sacred focus of Jewish life is maintained through the new role of rabbi and synagogue; the house of prayer has become more and more a substitute for Jewish communal life in transmitting the tradition to the young; the rabbi has become less a scholar interpreting the Law for the community and more the director of a religious institution. This problem of Jewish community—and it is a problem to sustain the integrity of such a community in America —has emerged out of the very openness of American society to Jewish participation in economic and public life. The loosening of Jewish communal life has placed an increasing burden on the synagogue, the Hebrew school, and the ritual forms of Jewish religious observance. As the rabbi finds himself standing more and more at the center of this religious institution, he is increasingly isolated from the public involvement of the Jewish community; his scope of activity is narrowed to the private concerns with nurture within the residential community; the expectations of his scholarly activity diminish with each passing decade.

The task of the synagogue in the new Judaism has brought about a reversal of roles between the rabbis and the agency professionals. The rabbinate is confined largely to the institutional operation of the synagogue and becomes a managerial role. The agency professional becomes ever more deeply implicated in the public life of the

Jewish community, interpreting its place in the American community and effecting a self-interpretation for the Jewish people. Thus the ideological task falls to the agency professional, while the task of sustaining the Jewish communal network falls to the rabbi. These are both important tasks, but they reverse the traditional understanding of the interpretive and ideological work of the rabbi. This situation may well account for the increasing tension between rabbis and agency professionals. Only the pluralism of associational life and the failure to achieve centralization sustain an equilibrium between these conflicting interests, enabling each to fulfill his task.

This profile of the organization of Jewish life is misunderstood if *religious* is interpreted to mean what happens in the synagogue or what is done by the rabbi and people assembled for worship. Religion within the Jewish tradition is all that bears on the life of the people, its faithfulness in commitment and action, its self-understanding, and its contribution to the world. In this sense the Jewish faith is entirely secular and temporal in a way that Protestantism and Catholicism are not; at the same time the Jewish faith and community are much more holy and religious than either Protestant or Catholic communities. Thus the profile of Jewish organization—a configuration of agency bureaucracies, philanthropic endeavors, and synagogue activities—can be understood as providing a vehicle of Jewish identity. The center of gravity is now as always to be found in the Jewish *community* as a people with a holy past and a promised future. Whatever forces may emerge in the next decades of this "Adventure in Freedom," to use Oscar Handlin's telling phrase, Jewish organization is proving remarkably effective in sustaining Jewish identity through a very difficult process of acculturation.

DIFFERENCES IN DEVELOPMENT OF THE THREE FAITHS

Whatever the basis of organization in the three faiths, certain common situations have confronted the religious communities and produced similar responses. However, the net effect on each faith

Religious Organizations

has been different: a tendency to agency control appeared in Protestantism; a cleavage between formal diocesan authority and operative agencies is evident in Catholicism; a tension between synagogue and agency developed within Judaism. We can comprehend these emerging problems more adequately when we grasp the different principles from which the three faiths proceed in their organizational development.

The Protestant understanding of faith is founded in the hearing of the Word in the congregation. Whatever the variations on this theme in the Protestant tradition, the gathering, hearing, and believing congregation forms the center of Protestant life. The proclamation of the Word is *the* source of life in Protestant Christianity. The pastoral structure of Protestantism receives its mandate from the Word in the congregation. Voluntary societies, agencies, boards, and committees have the task of maintaining, extending, and strengthening these congregational fellowships. Protestantism takes an utterly pragmatic view of organization; as long as agencies contribute to the preaching of the Word, the administration of the sacraments, and the maintenance of pure teaching, they are justified.

The crucial significance of promotion in Protestantism arises from this congregational understanding of the structure of faith. For one thing, the congregation is a voluntary unit and can be maintained only by promoting support from the membership. Even more important, however, is the dependence of all organizational structure upon the authority vested in the congregational units; Protestant traditions vary in their interpretation of organizational authority, of course—Methodists originally vested authority in the preachers and Baptists in the baptized individuals. Nevertheless, the mainstream of Protestantism operates its organizations from delegated assemblies or conventions to which both pastoral and agency bureaucracies are ultimately accountable—for funds if not for validation. Consequently, the bureaucracies are forced to propagandize the congregations for support. These promotional efforts readily become the preoccupying activity of all Protestant agencies. Thus the congregational principle of authority—the Word heard and received in the congregation—readily leads to organizational superstructures preoccupied with promotion.[75]

75. Protestant denominations vary in their interpretation of authority for

Differences in Development of the Three Faiths

The Catholic church has a different principle of organizational development. Catholic organization exists to maintain and extend the institution as a cultic body and a set of cultic activities. Diocesan and agency functionaries justify their existence by preserving and extending the sway of these cultic forms. In contrast to Protestantism, the cultic activity of the local congregation derives its real authority and validation from the bishop's office; priestly authority is in this sense delegated from the pastoral authority of the bishop, and even the papal authority has its source in its role as first bishop in the See of Peter. This means that the authority of the organizational superstructure is quite clear; in fact, it is canonically so well established that a real question hovers over any other center of authority, such as a parish or an agency bureaucracy. The hierarchy thus preserves the institutional form within which authority is exercised and serves as final referent for any activity that purports to express that plenary power. The actual situation is exactly the reverse of Protestantism since Protestant organization falls into promotion in order to sustain congregational support, whereas Catholic agencies depend upon sponsorhip, propaganda, and influence in order to maintain hierarchical approval. Protestantism finds it difficult to validate any organization beyond the congregation. Catholicism finds it difficult to condone any activity not directed by the diocesan authority.

The Jewish principle of organization is different again from the Protestant and Catholic because the Jewish faith pragmatically validates any organization that nurtures, preserves, and enhances the Jewish community and its integrity. The proliferation of associations in American Jewish life has the Jewish community as its common source and ultimate point of accountability. Whatever arguments and tensions may arise among rabbis, agency professionals, social workers, fund raisers and teachers, the final arbiter will be the Jewish community, which will give or withhold support. Studies of the attitudes of rabbis indicate that they evaluate themselves and their position largely on the basis of their influence in the

organization, and these variations create serious problems in church union. These problems are further complicated by historic conditions; for example, organizational problems in Methodism arise largely because it was meant to be an evangelical order within the framework of Anglicanism—see Albert C. Outler, "Do Methodists Have A Doctrine of the Church?" in *The Doctrine of the Church,* ed. by Dow Kirkpatrick (New York and Nashville, Abingdon Press, 1964), p. 12f.

Religious Organizations

Jewish community; even the synagogue is a secondary point of reference for the rabbi since his success with synagogue activities must ultimately be evaluated within the Jewish community.

The communal principle of authority in the Jewish faith leads to the wide range of activities and associations that comprise what we have called Jewish organization; we find that community-relations agencies, social work, welfare activities, united appeals, educational work, and synagogue activities all contribute to the creation of a network of communications and propaganda through which the integrity of the Jewish community is maintained. In contrast to Catholicism, the Jewish community has refused to institute any central authority to coordinate Jewish propaganda and centralize an organizational strategy. Whereas Protestantism struggles to keep its organization accountable to local congregations, the Jewish community vests increasing responsibility in rabbi and synagogue but gives them relatively little voice on behalf of the total Jewish community. The community is the ultimate bearer of faith for the Jewish people; agencies and instrumentalities that contribute to the defense and enrichment of that community can win support and honor, while those that fail to justify such support through their contributions to Jewish community soon wither and disappear.[76]

Despite the striking differences in principle from which organization gains its authority and validation, the three faiths have developed rather similar bureaucratic structures. We have expressed this similarity in the dual structure of each faith group: pastorate-agency bureaucracy for the Protestants; hierarchy-agency bureaucracy for the Catholics; community-agency association for the Jewish faith. This broad similarity of organization has its source in the forces at work in American life. The internal force is the voluntarism of religious association in the United States. This fact has been repeatedly noted in our analyses of religious organization, it provides a common pattern of religious formation despite differences in religious principle. The voluntary aspect forces increasing

76. Seymour M. Lipset attributes the pluralistic structure of the Jewish community largely to the value emphasis of American culture; despite the interesting hypothesis in this article, the pluralism seems quite clearly a manifestation of the religious principle of Jewish identity—the community—in a complex, pluralistic culture; see S. M. Lipset, "The Study of Jewish Communities in a Comparative Context," Institute of International Studies, General Series, Reprint No. 130.

Differences in Development of the Three Faiths

emphasis on promotion within the religious organization. This common feature, long ago noted by Sydney Mead in his discussion of American Protestantism, sets up strong forces toward centralization of the pastoral structures. As we have seen, only the Jewish community has resisted the full force of this tendency to centralization in promotion and finance; even within the Jewish community, moreover, united fund-raising has fulfilled this function of unified promotion.

Common features of the American situation have provided an external principle for this organizational development of the faiths. Rapid urbanization introduced complex problems of planning and communications. The diversification of educational, welfare, occupational, and residential spheres of activity called for a considerable diversification within the religious organizations. Although each faith community shaped its own pattern of organization according to the dominant principle of its own ethos—congregational, cultic, or communal—the emerging bureaucratic structures were very similar. This is the most striking feature in the organizational development of the major faiths in the United States. Similarity of situational demands and corresponding similarities of organizational development indicate a large degree of commonality among these faiths, at least on the structural level.

The common structural elements among the faiths should not obscure the differences in their organizational development. Those differences can be expressed most sharply in a few remarks on the significance of these faiths in the public arena of American life. Talcott Parsons in an essay, "Christianity and Modern Industrial Society," has argued cogently that the emergence of denominational pluralism in the United States represents a further differentiation of religious and secular spheres on the formal level and a deeper penetration of religious values on the informal level. American religious life is voluntary, pluralistic, and broadly accepted. Much like the family, and he means this in a very positive sense, the religious faiths operate through personal values and support an extension of spiritual values already grounded in the culture; they strengthen personal integrity and lend support to the rising moral expectations and individual responsibility that characterize American development. This interpretation suggests that secularization represents a deepening of religious faith and values rather than a

Religious Organizations

degeneration of faith and morality in an orgy of materialism. Secularization represents the endorsement of personal and social responsibility in the public spheres of life and the encouragement of voluntary, personal faith associations and activities in the private spheres. The broad principle is that specialization of activities can enrich social and cultural development when they occur in a context of broadened social integration of values and norms.

In this sense the three major faiths represent denominations of faith in the single, cultural context of American life. These are great, denominational bodies with varying degrees of internal coordination. This study indicates that the similarities among them are striking, and Parsons' stress on the denominational form seems to be borne out. The Catholic denomination is the most unified, as we have seen, although there is far more structural diversity than is generally assumed. The Protestant faith has a diverse congeries of subdenominations within the total configuration. Robert Lee has argued in *The Social Sources of Church Unity* that the increasing number of mergers in Protestantism reflects an increasing homogeneity of Protestant faiths in correlation with growing unity of social and cultural patterning of American life. Gerhard Lenski found homogeneity among the Protestant groups in his study, *The Religious Factor*. The notion of a Protestant faith as a great, denominational body is not out of line. The diversities within the Protestant formation may be serious and in the long run of some significance—for example, the special character of Negro Protestantism has already been noted, though this seems to be a transitional, cultural, and social phenomenon rather than a fundamental difference in faith. The Jewish faith is far more diversified in internal structure but also represents a broadly homogeneous structure in its organizational expression. We could argue for a fourth major force in American life—secularism—but its lack of organizational form and its shifting interests make the concept somewhat ambiguous. Hence the study of religious organization corresponds to a notion of a tri-faith denominationalism with organizational similarities.

However, Parsons' argument also makes value judgments about the deepening penetration of American life by the religious values of these faiths and the broader institutionalization of the fundamental religious ethos within the secular spheres of American life.

Differences in Development of the Three Faiths

These are broad judgments about the quality of American life and cannot be evaluated from this organizational study; indeed, there is deep difference of opinion on this issue within the faiths. However, the stress on informal, denominational, and voluntary penetration of American life needs to be balanced with an appreciation of the scope and significance of the organizational enterprises these great denominations are producing. Two aspects of this organizational development need to be stressed in order to balance our assessment of the religious situation in the United States.

The maintenance of the sacred or pastoral aspect of faith requires increasing organizational strength in a complex society with pluralistic and voluntary structures. The organizational development of the major denominations—Protestant, Catholic, and Jewish—is integral to their task of maintaining proclamation, worship, and religious celebration in the diverse private contexts of a pluralistic culture. Hence it is not merely the organizational complexity of American life that has generated such large organizations of religious life but also the task of promoting religious faith on a voluntary basis. Here the internal diversity of the three faiths is very important, and internal diversities within Protestantism may become very significant. Organizations for the promulgation of faith have to be evaluated in terms of their adequacy to extend the faith without substituting their organizational activities for the central task.

The Catholic hierarchical structure seems most adequate to keep its organizational elaboration in line with the task of faith. Whether this is a viable alternative in the American context, even for Catholicism, seems uncertain, and there is some evidence that it is not so hierarchical as the formal organization would suggest. The Protestant subdenominations are having considerable difficulty in coordinating their agencies to the task of proclamation. The difficulty seems to lie in the lack of an ecclesiology to interpret organization in relation to faith and legitimize adequate structures of representation, decision-making, and goal-setting. For many subdenominations of Protestantism organization is a contradiction in terms, since they anchored their position in primitive notions of the Church prior to its full organizational formation. Here the diversity in Protestantism becomes very important because some of these groups have a strong ecclesiological ground that can provide a pat-

Religious Organizations

tern for Protestant development. The present talks among six of the major subdenominations become extremely important from this perspective since they may provide a way toward a more coherent ecclesiology that would bring the organizational elaboration into line with the task of proclamation.

The Jewish faith has the least organizational development on its sacral side, a fact that corresponds to the place of worship in the total context of the Jewish understanding of faith and community. Nevertheless, the strains experienced in the rabbinate and the organizational growth of local units would indicate a general need for a much more coherent development of national organization on the pastoral side. This may become possible only if the religious diversity of expression within Judaism decreases. In general, the informal penetration of American life by religious faith on a voluntary basis has called forth an enormous organizational apparatus in all denominations, though to varying degrees.

The maintenance of the secular impact of faith on public structures has also evoked an organizational development—the agency structures. This organizational elaboration is only now ramifying on a broad scale and raises some basic questions about Talcott Parsons' interpretation of religious life. Again we cannot evaluate the quality of American life. Such an evaluation requires the founding of a set of evaluative norms, which is outside the scope of this chapter. Nevertheless, the three great denominations have developed very complex agency bureaucracies in order to articulate their faith commitments in the arena of American life. Agencies have emerged and are being developed with reference to human rights, economic life, political development, international concerns, welfare structures, educational activities, and mass media. The growing complexity of American society has required an internal differentiation of agency structures within the denominations. These agencies exist in part because the faith communities question many of the values and norms that inform the American development. The faiths attempt to influence and direct the course of American development along lines congruent with the values supported by these faiths. Parsons' optimism about the course of American development is therefore not borne out in the organizational elaboration to which the faiths have been pressed in coping with a pluralistic culture.

This is not to say that these faiths are in fundamental disagreement with the American development but only that they are creating organizational structures to certify that the course meets their own understanding. If, for example, urban development seemed adequate, they would not need new agencies. The striking example of agency development is the organizational support of the civil rights movement by the three faiths from 1963 to 1965. For the first time the three faiths in concert have thrown their weight behind an issue of public justice through demonstration and informal pressure. The issue for the denominations with respect to agency structures comes down to coordination of agency interests with the broader tasks of religious and moral concern.

The agency bureaucracies are anomalies in all three denominations to differing degrees, as we have seen. The three faiths can express their moral and public concerns for the course of American life and its international impact only through agency structures that can work directly with the diverse structures of a complex society. In this sense secularism created a new milieu for faith. The impact of these faiths on the American scene will depend, therefore, on the degree to which they can coordinate the work of the agencies with the central concerns of the faith communities. The fulfillment of Talcott Parsons' optimism depends, in other words, on the organizational achievements of these great faiths.

CHAPTER TWELVE

Social Change and Education

It has never been clear to what extent education is an agent for social change and to what extent it is a product of such change. The economic and political leaders of the United States have generally seen education as an agent for social change and have used it accordingly, at least since 1862, when the land-grant colleges were established to upgrade agricultural and industrial occupations.

Education has facilitated social change by training people and through research. Money from the states has been supplemented by money from the federal government to train the people needed by an expanding economy, ranging from milk-testers to space scientists. The research function has been most highly developed in fields useful to an expanding technology as well as in the field of health. Private industry has used education to develop men needed for leadership in business and to develop the materials and processes that create profits.

SOCIAL FUNCTION OF EDUCATION

Education has been an instrument of statesmen to help realize the promise of American life. This was demonstrated in Wisconsin when the state university was put to work to improve the life of the common man during the early years of the century. Senator Robert Marion LaFollette, the leader in this movement, said in 1904, "The state welcomes the ever-increasing tendency to make the University minister in a direct and practical way to the material interests of the state."

This chapter is by Robert J. Havighurst. See Notes on Authors.

492

Figure 1.

Types of Growth in Education

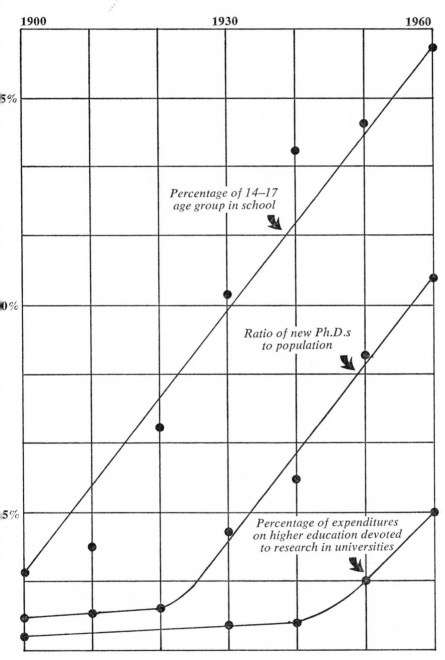

Social Change and Education

Whenever the way to improvement is clear and education clearly has a function, the educational system has been made to serve that function. However, in areas of deep and complex problems for the society, the solutions are not at all clear. One such area is urban renewal, the remaking of the great cities to solve the problems of urban blight and poverty in the midst of economic affluence. Here educators have not been told what to do, and they are uncertain how to act to improve the life of the city. While some bold and imaginative innovations have been tried, much of present educational practices in the big city may impede urban renewal rather than help it.

Figure 2.

Percentage of Various Age Groups Attending Educational Institutions

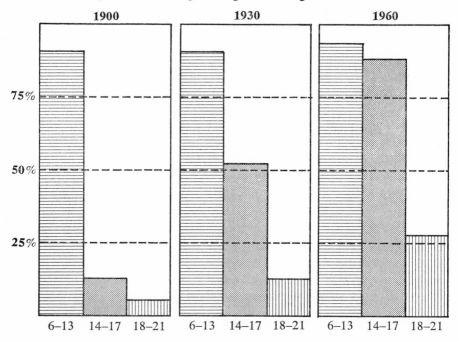

More sure and positive has been the educational response to the trend toward internationalism. At the college and university level, centers have been established for research and training in international relations, and the college curriculum has been vastly expanded by the introduction of courses on the Far East, for example, and in all the major foreign languages, in addition to the Germanic and Romance languages that prevailed during the prewar period. University attendance of foreign students in the United States and attendance of United States students in foreign institutions is far greater than one could have predicted from the trends up to 1940. The Peace Corps is essentially an experiment in education for international good will.

The adaptations of education to the social situations are illustrated in Figures 1 and 2. One response is sheer growth, as is illustrated by the curve in Figure 1, which shows the percentages of youths between 14 and 17 in school. Another is a change of emphasis, a qualitative change, to meet new demands. In Figure 1 we see that the proportion of newly created Ph.D.s to the total population was constant during the first two decades of the century and then increased rapidly. A second example of qualitative change is the curve showing the percentage of the funds for higher education spent on research in universities and colleges. This percentage rose very slowly during the first forty years of this century and then shot up rapidly.

MAJOR CHANGES IN SOCIETY
REFLECTED IN EDUCATION

The major social changes of the current century have all had repercussions in education. Without great detail, several of these change areas will be mentioned as illustrations of this proposition.

It is generally accepted that the proportion of people in the middle classes of American society has increased remarkably during the present century, as indeed it has in most of the countries which have gone from an agricultural to an industrial economy during this period. This is illustrated for the United States by Table 1, which shows the changing occupational distribution in the period from 1910 to 1960, with a projection to 1980. The first three occupational classes consist of people usually considered members of the upper-middle and upper classes, with some lower-middle-class peo-

Table 1. Occupational Distribution in the United States, 1910–80 (projected)*

Occupational class	Percentage of males					Percentage of females			
	1910	1930	1950	1960	1980	1910	1930	1950	1980
1. Architects, physicians, lawyers, etc.	1.2	1.5	1.4	1.5	1.5	0.2	0.4	0.3	0.4
2. Proprietors, officials, and managers in manufacturing; bankers, stockbrokers, engineers, scientists, clergymen, college teachers, state & federal gov't officials, etc.	2.4	2.7	4.8	6.5	9.0	0.9	1.6	1.9	2.0
3. School teachers, musicians, other professions, trained nurses, real estate and insurance agents, retail merchants, salesmen, city & county officials, other proprietors & managers, semi-professional occupations, owners of large farms, etc.	11.9	11.5	17.4	19.0	23.0	13.1	16.8	15.1	15.0
Subtotal of classes 1, 2, 3	15.5	15.7	23.6	27.0	33.5	14.2	18.8	17.3	17.4
4. Clerks & salespeople in offices & stores, stenographers, foremen, locomotive engineers, restaurant & tavern owners, owners of medium-sized farms, etc.	17.2	19.4	15.8	15.0	14.5	16.9	31.5	35.1	35.1
5. Skilled workers, policemen, firemen, mail clerks & carriers, delivery men, cooks, farmers with mortgages, small farm owners, tenant farmers, etc.	25.2	25.5	24.7	23.5	19.5	18.3	11.7	7.3	7.0
6. Semiskilled workers, factory operatives, truck drivers, miners, etc.	18.0	18.8	29.4	28.5	27.5	15.7	18.6	30.5	30.5
7. Unskilled laborers, farm laborers, domestic workers, etc.	24.1	20.6	6.5	6.0	5.0	34.9	19.4	9.8	10.0

* This table represents ages 21–44 for 1910 and ages 25–34 for the later years. It is based on analysis of census data and on projections of the labor force published by the U.S. Bureau of Labor Statistics. Source: Robert J. Havighurst, *American Higher Education in the 1960s* (Columbus, Ohio

ple. Class 4 consists mainly of lower-middle-class men. The percentages for the men show the proportions in the first four classes rising from 33 per cent in 1910 to 42 per cent in 1960, while the proportions in the first three classes almost double in this period of time.

The ratio of white collar to blue-collar workers has increased and probably will continue to increase throughout this century. For example, it is common to hear labor force experts say that factory workers will be as scarce in the year 2000 as farm workers are today, as a result of automation.

It appears probable also that the social distance between the better-paid and more skilled manual workers and the lower-level white-collar workers has decreased during this century. This means that the social and economic differences between the upper-lower class and the lower-middle class have decreased and are decreasing.

Education has been a means of bringing about these changes, though it is hardly a cause of them. That is, the educational system has provided secondary education for all, or almost all, young people and higher education for a growing proportion, thus giving them a general education as well as a specific vocational education which together transmit the basis for middle-class attitudes and middle-class occupational careers.

Business and industry are now heavily involved in the process of education, which was far outside their province in 1900. The greatest development is the educational procedure of *training within industry,* in which employees are trained for specific jobs and tasks. This involves the training of new employees for a great variety of positions, ranging from the simplest and lowest in the job hierarchy to those of middle-level complexity. It also involves the retraining of employees as the nature of the job changes. Some technical operations in such industries as petroleum change so frequently that retraining is required as often as once a year.

With the coming of automation many of the simpler jobs are disappearing, and learning new ones may become the worker's responsibility, in which case he must seek training in vocational schools or with new employers. Or retraining may be regarded as the employer's responsibility. Employers as well as schools and colleges are using a variety of teaching devices to improve the performance of adults at work: teaching machines, films, film-strips, etc. Nearly every large corporation now has a program for selection and training of personnel which justifies its being called an educational institution.

The relation between the employer, the employee, and the formal educational system has changed greatly from 1900, when there was nothing but a casual connection. Employers hired people for manual work with little or no interest in their education except where evidence of skill was required. When looking for middle-level positions the prospective employee didn't expect his school or college to help him beyond supplying information or letters of recommendation when these were specifically requested. In the professions the young person just out of law school, medical school, or divinity school might get informal assistance at times from some of his professors.

By 1930 a relationship was apparent between educational institutions and employers. Schools and colleges were just beginning to provide machinery for the guidance and placement of their graduates. Employers were beginning to send scouts to the universities and colleges in the spring of the year to look for likely prospects. For example, the Eastman Kodak Company as early as 1920 was sending a man to visit the major university departments of chemistry to discuss employment possibilities with graduating chemists. Soon afterward came the establishment of graduate and undergraduate schools of business administration, whose students would be recruited by business and industry for careers in management.

After World War II the business of recruiting college graduates became highly competitive because of the shortage of young people ready to enter careers in a booming economy. Even the major school systems sent out representatives to liberal arts and teachers colleges to recruit new teachers. By 1960 there was not a college or university that did not regard itself as responsible for the occupational placement of its students, and all large employers had people specialized in recruiting and hiring college graduates.

Meanwhile another relationship was developing between industry and the institutions of formal education. The idea of *research and development,* so familiar to business and industry in 1960, was an unknown concept in 1900. A few industries—especially the electric, the communications, and the chemical industries—were dependent for the growth of profits on the process of discovery and invention, which at first meant finding and using men like Thomas Edison, Henry Ford, Louis Pasteur, Luther Burbank, Babcock, Baekeland, mechanically-minded geniuses, chemists, or experimental biologists. Then came General Electric, Eastman Kodak, Goodyear, Standard Oil, DuPont, Consolidation Coal, U.S. Steel, Bell Telephone, Western Electric, with industrial research laboratories that worked closely with university research laboratories, exchanging men and ideas. This process was already well established in 1930 but did not become fully recognized until after World War II, when "research and development" became known as the key to profitable growth, and industry began to invest in research with the expectation of greater returns than an investment simply in physical plant.

By 1960 the universities could not get along without industry, and industry could not get along without the universities; each had a major interest in the training of highly skilled men and women and in employing them in research and development. Hiring practices had become far different from those of 1900. Except for the family farm and small business, few employers would hire a youth below the age of sixteen, and most large employers required high school graduation. Juvenile jobs were disappearing. In a labor market that always had a substantial group of adult job-seekers, most employers gave preference to adult applicants. The large number of part-time jobs still available to young people were mainly in service occupations and gave little or no advantage for later employment in a full-time job.

The economy of 1960 employed a working force with a far higher proportion of jobs requiring special training than did the economy of 1900. The educational system prepared people either through a general education that helped them to learn their jobs or by training them specifically for certain types of work. A large number of twentieth-century careers that had never existed before were invented or discovered—reseach scientist, automobile mechanic, television mechanic, electronic engineer, clinical psychologist, dental technician, radiologist, sales engineer, teacher for exceptional children, industrial sociologist, market research specialist.

The national government itself has contributed to the development of some of these new twentieth-century careers by spending large sums for the training of highly selected students for new kinds of positions needed in the national defense and for the development of new processes required by our economy for military and scientific development. (See pp. 552–53 for the role of the National Aeronautics and Space Administration in 1962 in training graduate students.)

Along with these changes in the structure of the labor force and the nature of jobs went changes in the meaning and accessibility of work. At the beginning of the century it was common for a boy or girl to quit school at fourteen and go to work. For a boy this was the beginning of manhood. For a girl this might be the beginning of a career but more often was an apprenticeship to a housewife or a brief interlude before marriage and a lifetime as wife and mother.

By 1930 the pattern had not changed much, though boys and girls stayed a few years longer in school before going to work. But the depression and the changing technology thereafter transformed the nature of adolescence for the vast majority. Instead of quitting school for work or marriage, a large number found themselves going through a period of unemployment and aimlessness. When this phenomenon became evident during the depression, steps were taken both through the schools and through government-supported work projects to keep these young people occupied profitably for themselves and for society. Thus the schools for the first time took on the custodial function of caring for youth, as distinct from educating them.

This was not to be a temporary phenomenon. In spite of the economic boom after the war there persisted a serious problem of unemployment of youth. During the 1950s the rate of unemployment among young people aged sixteen to twenty was about twice as high as the general rate of unemployment. The proportion of unskilled jobs in the labor force was decreasing. For example, it is estimated that during four years of the 1950 decade the number of jobs as elevator operator decreased by 30,000 in New York City.

The schools, then, were called upon to find ways of keeping nonacademic boys and girls in school and constructively occupied even though they were not doing the kind of academic or vocational work usually expected of sixteen to eighteen-year-olds. They were to be aided by the schools to find a pathway of growth to adulthood, since prewar alternatives of quitting school and going to work were less and less accessible to them.

EDUCATION FOR THE SOLUTION OF
SOCIAL PROBLEMS

The process of urbanization is full of paradoxes. It has resulted in the actual loss of population between 1950 and 1960 by more than half the counties of the United States—and by eleven of the twelve largest cities. However, the urban part of the population increased by 30 per cent between 1950 and 1960, while the rural population decreased by one per cent. The urban population—those who live in communities of 2,500 or more—increased from 64 to 70 per cent of the total. Nearly 113 million people, 63 per cent of the total, lived in 212 "standard metropolitan statistical areas" (any central city with 50,000 or more inhabitants together with the countryside in which it is located and such contiguous counties as are economically and socially oriented to the central city).

The population growth for 1950–60 was largely in the suburbs, which are a twentieth-century phenomenon. During the first four decades of this century the suburbs absorbed less than one-third of the total population increase while the central cities were doing most of the growing; from 1940 to 1950 the suburbs provided half the population increase; and from 1950 to 1960, two-thirds.

Urbanization, American style, since 1940 has consisted of the growth of suburbs around the central cities and a stratification of the population in economic, racial, and ethnic terms, making the central cities more and more solidly lower-class while the suburbs are largely middle-class. The central cities have always had their slums and have always had social and economic stratification and segregation. In 1900 and 1910 it was the Italians, Poles, and Hungarians who lived quasi-segregated in city slums. But the slums were smaller then, since the cities were smaller, and there was relatively more mixing of classes in school and other public institutions than there is today.

Social Change and Education

As the Italians, Hungarians, and Poles have moved up the social scale and out from the central slum areas, their places have been taken largely by southern Negroes, southern whites, and Puerto Ricans. As recently as 1910 more than 90 per cent of the country's Negro population lived in the South. In 1960 that figure had fallen to 60 per cent, with 34 per cent living in the Northeast and North Central regions. The number of Negroes in the North increased 50 per cent from 1950 to 1960, while the number on the West Coast doubled. The Negro population of the twenty-five largest SMSAs ranged from less than 3 per cent of the total (Minneapolis-St. Paul) to 54 per cent of the total (Washington). Negroes made up 14 per cent of the central city in New York, 23 per cent in Chicago, 26 per cent in Philadelphia, 29 per cent in Detroit, and 13 per cent in Los Angeles.

In the course of these social changes, a number of social problems have nearly disappeared, such as the problems of grinding poverty and child labor, but in their places have arisen other problems that are being treated at least partly by educational means. Among the major domestic social problems of this kind is cultural deprivation. In the slums of the great cities and in depressed rural areas are many families that do not give their children adequate intellectual stimulation and training to prepare them for a competent life in modern society. To meet this problem a number of school systems have developed a program of "compensatory education," designed to make up for deprivation in the home and the local neighborhood. The program may start at the kindergarten-primary level or at about the level of the third grade. It is supposed that many of these children under ordinary school conditions fail to master the task of reading and stumble along for the first years of school, after which they become confirmed non-learners and tend to be social misfits in the schools during their adolescence. By putting specially trained teachers into relatively small classes, by using a social worker or visiting teacher to bring the home and school into contact, and by giving the children a variety of enriching experiences which middle-class children are more likely to get in their homes, these children will get a better start in school and thus a better start in life. More recently, with funds under the Economic Opportunity Act, preschool classes have been set up for socially disadvantaged children, based on a growing conviction that these children are missing experiences in their third and fourth years that are crucial to average or good mental development.

Another group of children from working-class families achieve rather well in school, either because their families give them fairly adequate intellectual stimulation or because they have greater than average inborn intellectual capacity. For them some cities have developed "enrichment programs," which involve placing the more promising children in smaller classes, giving them special counseling and guidance, encouraging their parents to take more interest in their education, and giving them access to museums, libraries, theaters, and concerts. A widely known example is the Demonstration Guidance Project of Junior High School No. 43 and the George Washington High School of New York City.[1] This program stimulated a considerable group of boys and girls to graduate from high school and to enter college who would probably not have done so if they had not received special attention. Financial assistance for college attendance is a necessary part of such a program.

As changing technology and automation have reduced the number of juvenile jobs, there has arisen a major problem of unemployment among youth aptly called "social dynamite" by James B. Conant. The rate of unemployment among young men aged sixteen to twenty is far higher than the rate after age twenty-one. This problem has been kept down to some extent by increased attendance in high schools and colleges, which holds young people off the labor market. Still, in the early 1960s, some 40 per cent of boys and 35 per cent of girls were dropping out of school at sixteen or seventeen, without completing a high school course.

Some of these boys and girls make a fairly good adjustment to adult society by getting and keeping jobs and, in the case of girls, by getting married. But approximately 15 per cent of boys and girls were failing both in school and out of school in 1960. They were appropriately called "alienated youth," for they had no secure position in society, and they were either hostile or apathetic toward the prevailing values and expectations of the society in which they live. In slum areas the alienated reached 25 or 30 per cent of the total youth group. From this segment came the majority of delinquents in the 1960s.

1. David Schreiber, *The Higher Horizons Program: First Annual Progress Report, 1959–60* (New York, Board of Education, 1961).

Social Change and Education

While still in school these boys and girls behaved so badly that they made teaching difficult for teachers in the seventh, eighth, and ninth grades. In neighborhoods dominated by working-class youth, they made junior high school uncomfortable for academically motivated youth, and their presence in school and local community stimulated middle-class parents to move out of such areas in order to find school and recreation facilities more acceptable to their adolescent children.

Two types of educational experimentation have been tried in order to help alienated young people get into a channel of better social adjustment and of satisfactory growth toward adulthood.

Work-study programs have been established at the junior high school level, especially for boys, to give them the moral and manual training that may make them better workers and better citizens. A survey of such programs in 1961 showed a variety that were considered promising by their sponsors.[2] Less striking modifications of the academic program have been tried for boys and girls in many schools. These programs generally are geared to the low level of school achievement these young people have shown. The aim is to give them a type of instruction suitable to adolescents but not requiring more than a sixth or seventh grade level of reading and computing skills. The Economic Opportunity Act of 1964 provides substantial sums of money for work experience programs for unemployed youth aged sixteen to twenty-one, as well as for new and experimental forms of vocational training.

The deep-seated racial segregation of the South has been complemented since World War I with a system of de facto segregation in northern and western industrial cities that has resulted in extensive and pervasive segregation of Negro youth in the schools of the country. In 1960, 50 per cent of Negro children and youth lived in the South and went to segregated schools, 33 per cent lived in the North or West and went to segregated schools, and approximately one-sixth lived in the North or West and went to integrated schools. (A "segregated school" is here defined as one containing 90 per cent or more Negro pupils.)

The process of urbanization produced large slum areas usually

2. George W. Burchill, ed., *Work Study Programs for Alienated Youth* (Chicago, Science Research Associates, 1962).

Education for the Solution of Social Problems

near the centers of the large cities. By the close of World War II these areas were clearly a threat to decent living conditions not only for the people living in them but also for the people living near them.

The urban flight was not stopped. People who could afford it moved further from the center of the city and often outside the city to middle-class suburbs. Between 1945 and 1960 there was a substantial increase of economic stratification in the residential distribution of the American people. That is, a growing proportion of working-class people lived in working-class sections and a growing proportion of middle-class people in middle-class areas. This means that a growing proportion of children attended schools that were either 90 per cent or more working-class in composition or 90 per cent or more middle-class. This pattern of economic stratification was paralleled by a growing racial stratification in the northern cities since increasing proportions of the city working-class people were Negroes.

Some counter-trends were evident by 1960. Working-class people were settling in suburbs as industry became decentralized and highways were improved. At the same time, some former slum areas were reclaimed for middle-class apartment buildings, and a few mixed-class residential areas with mixed racial composition came into being.

An educational answer to the problem of economic segregation was worked out early in the century in the form of the comprehensive high school, which took pupils from all social classes and of all levels of ability and gave them a varied set of educational experiences together in a single school. This was regarded as a democratic form of school, which mixed the social classes and gave a substantial opportunity for working-class and middle-class youth to share experiences. Elementary schools were likely to have a more homogeneous social-class composition, because even in small cities there is some residential segregation that affects elementary schools.

The comprehensive high school could not have a mixed social-class composition in the big cities as they became more stratified if the school attendance were limited to a fixed geographical area, as was generally the case. By 1960 there were many high schools in the big cities with overwhelmingly working-class composition and many others on the edges of the city or in the suburbs with overwhelmingly middle-class composition. The mixed-class high school was in the minority.

One of the causes of the growing economic and racial stratification in the big cities was the composition and nature of the high school. As the working-class group increased in a given high school, the status ratio (the ratio of middle-class pupils to working-class pupils) was reduced to a critical point at which middle-class parents, with academic aspirations and middle-class social customs, found the school undesirable for their children and therefore moved away in search of middle-class schools. In order to meet this problem, many high schools in the big cities adopted "multi-track" schemes of organization, separating pupils into several different groups according to learning ability and educational performance. Since these characteristics are statistically related to socioeconomic status, the multi-track scheme tends to bring children of similar socioeconomic status and similar educational aspirations together. Thus there are generally one or more "schools within a school" which contain pupils with strong academic motivation. The children of higher social status tend to be placed in the superior group, which makes the school more tolerable for their parents. Whatever may be the value of homogeneous grouping in helping children to achieve according to the level of their intelligence (and this is repeatedly questioned by research studies), there is no doubt that teachers and parents alike favor a multi-track system in a school where the status ratio has fallen below the critical point. This is because the multi-track organization gives some assurance to middle-class parents and to working-class parents who seriously want their children to get the most out of education that their children will be given special help and special consideration.

This was the situation in the big cities about 1960. But the tendency continued for the volume of lower-class residential area to expand around the center of the city and for the middle-class suburbs to grow. Low-cost public housing was making a physical improvement in the "gray areas," but the social composition of these areas remained pretty much the same. Expressways gave suburban dwellers quicker and more comfortable access to the center of the city and to any other points they needed to reach.

There was growing talk of the need for "social urban renewal" that would restore the central city or parts of it as a good place to live for all kinds of people—rich or poor, white or colored. It was dimly realized that the schools would have to be involved in such a process of urban renewal as active agents of the needed changes, but in 1960 no one had clear ideas of what should be done, and there was no public consensus on plans or programs of social urban renewal.

The development of city-suburb combinations known as metropolitan areas has created a number of political and technological problems. The principal political problem has been that of creating orderly cooperation among a host of small local governmental units which provide such services as sewage disposal, water, fire and police protection, parks, and highways. In spite of the overwhelming tendency toward bigness in metropolitan areas, government has continued to be largely dispersed in many small township and district units. For example, in some areas an elected township board of supervisors employs a treasurer to handle township money, and at the same time and for congruent or nearly congruent territory a board of school trustees employs a treasurer to handle school money. County government is weak in most areas of the North and Central part of the country. Metropolitan areas sometimes include parts of two or more states, which complicates the problem even more.

The multiplicity of local school districts in a metropolitan area has both advantages and disadvantages. The principal advantage is that citizens are interested in their schools by having responsibility for them, with the consequence that they have supported local schools quite well and have created a kind of competition, especially among suburbs, that makes for diversity and for excellence. On the other hand, there are grave inequities of financing among districts of a metropolitan area. Often a district with factories and small population will have plenty of money for schools while a contiguous district that houses most of the factory workers will have no industrial property and very little tax money for schools.

The financial inequities have been reduced in recent years by the development of state support of public schools on a per-pupil basis, which is more or less equal for all districts and sometimes favors the poorer districts. There have also been some attempts at combining local school districts to make a larger district which can support a junior college. There is even some talk of establishing an area-wide educational authority with its own taxing power, to be responsible for such functions as purchasing, planning, and constructing school buildings, teacher certification, pensions, adult education, and the maintenance of community colleges, teachers colleges, and technical institutes. This area-wide school board or commission would be separate from the local school boards, which would continue to be responsible for the support of local elementary and secondary schools.

THE GROWTH OF BIG EDUCATION

As the United States has grown, education has grown. But education has grown faster than other elements of the society, in terms of the relative proportions of students, teachers, and resources employed. In other words, education has become more useful and more necessary. In 1900, most children went to a one-room school and quit when they reached their fourteenth birthday. Only 10 per cent of the fourteen through seventeen age-group were in school.

There have been two general types of educational response to the challenge of twentieth-century social change. One is sheer growth, and the other is change of emphasis, or of functions of education, which have just been documented. We have seen (Figs. 1 and 2) that the percentage of fourteen to seventeen year-olds in school has gone from 10 to 85 in sixty years. Enrollment in secondary schools and colleges has multiplied since 1900: high school attendance is almost as widespread in 1960 as elementary school attendance in 1900; college enrollment has increased from 4 to 28 per cent of the eighteen to twenty-one group.

Change in Size of Educational Units

Throughout the century, the individual school, the school system, and the college and university have grown bigger. This reflects the urbanization of the country, together with the conviction that a small school is not as good as a larger one.

As it was with the one-room school, so it was with the small school district. In the first nationwide survey of local school districts, the United States Office of Education found 127,244 public school districts in 1932 (see Table 2). Maryland, with its county-unit form of school organization, had only 24 districts, while Illi-

Table 2. Statistics of School Districts

	Number of public school districts†	*Number of public school systems*†	*Number of public schools*	*Number of one-teacher schools*	*Public school enrollment below college level*	*Average enrollment in systems*
931–32	127,244		270,000*	143,000	26,300,000	205
937–38	118,892			121,000		
941–42	108,579		208,000	108,000	25,500,000	235
949–50	83,614	86,000*	153,000	60,000	25,111,000	290
956–57	50,454	52,943	130,000*	31,000*	31,400,000	595
961–62	35,555	37,019	107,000	13,333	38,253,000	1,035
962–63	33,086	35,000			39,746,000	1,135
963–64	31,015	31,705			41,537,000	1,310
964–65	28,814	29,500			42,784,000	1,450

ources: Biennial Surveys of Education, U.S. Office of Education. U.S. Office of Education, *Digest of Educational Statistics*, 1964.

* Estimated on the basis of data from neighboring years.

· The term "public school system" includes two types of governmental entity with responsibility for providing public schools:

(1) those which are fiscally independent of any other government unit and are listed as "school districts" in this table;

(2) those with less autonomy, which are treated in the census as a dependent agency of some other government unit. For example, the New York City school system is one of these "dependent" systems. The number of public school districts includes a rather large number of "non-operating" districts, which are rural districts that do not operate schools but collect local taxes and pay the tuition cost of children in their district who attend school in a neighboring district. There were 6,031 non-operating districts in 1962 and 3,158 in 1964.

nois had 12,070. The Midwestern farm states all had thousands of small districts, generally with three citizens serving as school trustees. Consequently, in those days, those states had more members of school boards than school teachers. By 1940 the number of school districts was down to 117,000; 84,000 in 1950; 50,000 in 1956; and 29,000 in 1964. Of these districts in 1964, more than 3,000 were "non-operating"—that is, they did not operate schools

Social Change and Education

but collected tax funds to pay tuition for their children in neighboring district schools. Nevertheless, five farm states in 1963 still had more than 1,500 school districts each and together accounted for 33 per cent of all school systems in the country. Thirty-eight per cent of all public school pupils were transported at public expense in 1961–62.

Table 3. Statistics of Public School System Size

Number of pupils in system	Number of School Systems				
	1951–52	1956–57	1959–60	1961–62	1963–64
25,000+	58	107	121	132	143
12,000–24,999	97	175	230	266	293
6,000–11,999	265	549	623	671	774
3,000– 5,999	611	1,176	1,458	1,496	1,599
1,200– 2,999	1,600*	2,856	3,082	3,276	3,522
600– 1,199	3,000*	3,221	3,187	3,159	3,210
300– 599	4,400*	4,013	3,630	3,486	2,663
150– 299	5,047	4,127	3,429	3,081 ⎫	
50– 149	7,902	6,218	4,765	4,214 ⎬	15,559
1– 49	34,400	21,752	14,871	11,213 ⎭	
Non-operating	10,000*	8,743	7,029	6,031	3,942
Total	67,380	52,937	42,428	37,025	31,705

Number of schools per school system	1956–57	1961–62
20 or more	646	697
10–19	1,081	1,184
3– 9	6,175	5,862
2	4,596	3,474
1	31,651	19,828
Non-operating	8,743	6,031

* Estimated.
Source: U.S. Office of Education, Progress of Public Education in the United States; Annual Reports, and U.S. Bureau of the Census, 1962 Census of Governments. Public School Systems in the United States, 1961–62. Preliminary Report, No. 3, July 6, 1962.

Meanwhile the average school district increased in school attendance, with the systems of 1,200 or more pupils accounting for most of the recent increases (see Table 3). The sharp increase after 1952 results partly from the higher postwar birth rate. Many school systems passed the 1,200 mark in enrollment even though their towns or cities did not show much increase of population. The number of large school districts with 25,000 or more pupils has increased, but the most rapid growth is in systems of 1,200 to 12,000 because of the growth of small- and medium-sized cities, especially in suburban areas.

Table 4. Size of Public High Schools

Enrollment	1930	1938	1946	1952	1959
5,000+	27	41	19	5	4
2,500–4,999	134	199	150	97	181
1,000–2,499	934	1,444	1,369	1,536	2,652
500– 999	1,421	1,940	2,251	2,757	4,528
300– 499	1,478	2,271	2,386	3,106	4,009
200– 299	1,633	2,561	2,651	3,103	3,386
100– 199	4,603	6,407	5,923	6,025	5,210
75– 99	2,543	2,661	2,548	2,086	1,513
50– 74	3,521	3,051	3,119	2,311	1,478
25– 49	3,866	2,643	2,689	1,896	1,010
1– 24	2,077	1,372	1,209	824	255
Total	22,237	24,590	24,314	23,746	24,226
Average	234	297	284	324	457

Source: U.S. Office of Education, *Statistics of Education in the United States,* 1958–59 Series. Public Secondary Schools, Table 2.

The large school systems are, of course, in the large cities. They have all grown very much in enrollment during the 1950s as a result of the postwar baby boom rather than as a result of overall population growth. In fact, New York, Chicago, Detroit, Boston, St. Louis, and other large cities actually lost population between 1950 and 1960, but they all had large increases in school enrollment.

Consolidation of rural elementary schools and growing urbanization slowly increased the size of high schools from an average of 87 in 1900 to 234 in 1930, when 54 per cent of public high schools had less than 100 pupils, to 457 in 1959, when about 50 per cent had more than 300 pupils (see Table 4).

Colleges and universities grew in a more striking fashion than high schools. In 1900 the average size of 977 colleges and universi-

Social Change and Education

ties was 243 students; in 1930 it was 780; and in 1962, 2,010. During this period the number of small institutions varied considerably, but there was a steady growth in medium-sized and large institutions. In 1963, there were 85 universities with more than 10,000 degree-credit students in the autumn of the year (see Table 5).

Table 5. Sizes of Colleges and Universities

Resident college enrollment in November	N of 4-year institutions		N of junior colleges	
	1953	1963	1953	1963
1– 199	277	184	252	148
200– 499	416	257	157	183
500– 999	312	358	60	112
1,000–2,499	218	358	34	75
2,500–4,999	83	152	12	32
5,000–9,999	61	109	5	19
10,000+	33	85	1	8
Number of institutions	1,400	1,503	521	577
Enrollment in median institutions	550	930	241	420

It is difficult to predict the future of the large school systems. Certainly more cities will reach a size where they have more than 25,000 pupils—the number of such cities doubled between 1950 and 1960. There were 143 such school systems in 1963, with 27 per cent of total public school enrollment. On the other hand, the suburbs will continue to grow, and they have medium-sized school systems. Probably some sort of metropolitan area school district will develop, with a hundred thousand to a million pupils; but it is doubtful that this kind of district will operate as the big-city district does today, with one central administration. More probably there will be a decentralization of administration into districts with 10,000 to 25,000 elementary and secondary school pupils. In other words, there will be a search for the optimum size of school district, and the size will not be determined primarily by the number of people living within the limits of a city or metropolitan area.

High schools will continue for a time to grow to a larger average size, through the elimination of smaller schools. However, it is doubtful that schools with less than 500 pupils will disappear, as has been urged by James B. Conant. It requires a community of some 6,000 to 10,000 to provide pupils for a four-year high school of 500 pupils, and communities smaller than this are not likely to disappear or give up their own local high schools. Probably a number of devices for introducing outside help for the more advanced high school students will be developed, including television, teaching machines, and short-term courses of a special nature in the county seat. Regional vocational high schools will come into being to serve rural counties that do not have enough students to support a county vocational unit.

A study by Roger Barker [3] comparing a small high school with a large one challenges the recommendations made by Conant. Barker studied the actual participation of students in the various high school activities outside the curriculum and found that the average student had much more of such activity in a small school than in a big school. The average student took greater part in musical activities, dramatics, school clubs, journalism, and athletics. The large school presumably offers a number of special or advanced courses not available in a small school, and it may have a library with a wider assortment of books. But its classes may be larger and conducted in such a way that a student gets little personal contact with the teacher.

At the level of higher education the average size will no doubt increase, but not very much—for two reasons. One is the tendency for very large universities to subdivide into separate administrative and geographical units. Therefore the number of universities with many more than 10,000 students on a single campus is not likely to increase very much. Nobody seems to be in favor of the very large campus; it does not contribute to efficiency or economy. Instead, the large public universities will probably continue to subdivide into branches in different locations or into systems of coordinated institutions. Table 5 shows that the number of institutions with more than 10,000 enrollment increased from 34 in 1953 to 93 in 1963. However, the same decade saw a substantial trend toward

3. Roger Barker, et al., *Big School–Small School: Studies of the Effects of High School Size upon the Behavior and Experiences of Students* (Lawrence, University of Kansas, Department of Psychology, 1962).

subdivision of the largest universities and toward limiting the growth of individual institutions after they passed the 10,000 mark.

The other reason average size will not increase very much is that colleges with enrollments as low as 200 seem to be viable. Quite a number of liberal arts colleges of 200 to 500 students are doing very well, according to their own expectations and those of their students and alumni, and will not try to increase in size. In 1962, the 481 Protestant church-related colleges had an average enrollment of 782, and the 334 Roman Catholic colleges averaged 1,057. Many of these colleges have stable enrollments under 500. More than half the junior colleges in the country were under 500 in 1965.

On the whole, then, we do not look forward to much more *bigness* in schools and colleges, but we may expect the smaller school systems and colleges to decline in numbers, thus increasing the *average* sizes somewhat beyond 1960 levels.

National Educational Organizations

As the American educational system slowly developed during the nineteenth century, it became clear that the schools and colleges were *not* to be administered or controlled by the national government. The common schools were left to local responsibility, except for the maintenance of minimum standards by state officials and except for a few states that used state departments of education for stimulation and coordination, such as Massachusetts and New York. Higher education was largely in the hands of private groups. One could hardly speak in a positive sense of an American system of education. However, some kind of national or regional coordination was clearly necessary, and shortly after the turn of the century voluntary organizations emerged in large numbers to meet the need for coordination, mutual stimulation, and maintenance of standards of instruction (see Table 6). The great majority of these associations are national in scope, signifying a sense of national unity that came into being without any pressure or even suggestion from the national government. Moreover, most of them have set up their national offices in the nation's capital city.

The first of the voluntary organizations, and the largest of all, was founded in the nineteenth century. The National Education

Association became the organizing center of the public school interests of the country. Almost from the beginning it has concerned itself with the quality and content of teaching in the public schools.

Table 6. Emergence of National and Regional Organizations
in Education

	Date of initiation
National Education Association	1857
American Association of School Administrators	1865
National Society for the Study of Education	1895
College Entrance Examination Board	1900
Regional Accrediting Associations of Colleges and Secondary Schools	
New England Association	1886
Middle States Association	1887
North Central Association	1895
Southern Association	1895
Northwest Association	1917
Western Association	1948
Associations of Medical Schools, Engineering Schools, Dental Schools, etc.	
Association of Urban Universities	1914
American Federation of Teachers	1916
American Council on Education	1918
Association of American Colleges	
Association of American Universities	
American Association of Junior Colleges	
National Catholic Education Association	
American Association of Teachers Colleges	
American Vocational Education Association	
Progressive Education Association	1919
American Association for Adult Education	1926
Council of Chief State School Officers	
American Personnel and Guidance Associations	
Cooperative Test Service	
Educational Policies Commission	1934
Subsidiaries of the National Education Association	
National Teacher Examination Service	c.1940
National Commission on Teacher Education and Professional Standards	1946
American Association of Colleges for Teacher Education	1948
National School Boards Association	

Through a series of commissions it has made most of the major pronouncements about educational policy that have been made in this country.

Social Change and Education

Based in a loose way on state education associations, the NEA has a separate membership fee, a separate publication series, and consists more of a federation of *functional* organizations than of state organizations: the Association of Elementary School Principals; Association of Secondary School Principals; Association for Supervision and Curriculum Development; National Council of the Social Studies; National Association of Science Teachers; Association for Higher Education; Association for Childhood Education. Generally, these organizations came into existence between 1920 and 1950, sponsored and assisted by the parent body. They have offices in the handsome new building of the Association in Washington.

The National Education Association has come to be *the* spokesman for public education in the United States. It works closely with the American Association of School Administrators. The two organizations are separate in constitution, membership, and officers; but they share a building in Washington and they work closely together in the Educational Policies Commission, the major policy-forming organization for public education.

The Educational Policies Commission was created by the National Education Association and the American Association of School Administrators in 1934, at a time when the educational system was seriously threatened by the depression. Supported for its first eight years by a grant from the General Education Board of the Rockefeller Foundation, the Commission consisted of two groups of people—ex-officio members, who were officers of the NEA and the AASA, and members-at-large, who were elected by the Commission itself. Among the latter have been such men as James B. Conant, Dwight Eisenhower (then President of Columbia University), George S. Counts, Charles Beard, and superintendents of the major school systems of the country. The Commission works through a series of short, concise pronouncements on educational policy, hammered out through a system of drafts by experts in the areas to be covered and thoroughly discussed and agreed upon by the Commission, paragraph by paragraph. From the earliest report, written mainly by the historian Charles Beard and entitled *The Unique Functions of Education in American Democracy,* to the *Central Purpose of American Education,* written mainly by Executive Secretary James E. Russell and published in 1961, the pronouncements of the Commission have commanded national attention, as representative of the best leadership in the field of public education.

Parallel in its influence to the National Education Association is the American Council on Education, made up of public and private institutions and organizations. The Council does not have persons as members.

The Council was founded in 1918, at the same time that the National Research Council and the Social Science Research Council were formed, primarily to assist the government in organizing the resources of universities for the conduct of World War I. The war was over before much was accomplished, but the three councils remained in existence. The two science councils attracted support from such private foundations as the Rockefeller Foundation and the Carnegie Corporation, and came into a stable existence as representatives of scholarship on a national scale, together with the American Council of Learned Societies. But the American Council on Education did not at first attract much support from foundations or from universities.

It was not until the depression of the 1930s forced the higher institutions into a measure of national cooperation that the American Council found a function. In this it was aided materially by the General Education Board, which was to spend $8 million between 1934 and 1942 on its Program in General Education—a program for improving the care and education of youth aged twelve to twenty. After deciding not to set up their own operating organization in this field, the trustees of the General Education Board looked around for one or more representative national education organizations, and eventually decided to grant money to three of them—the National Education Association for its Educational Policies Commission; the Progressive Education Association for its Commission on the Relations of School and College, its Commission on the Study of Adolescents, and its Commission on Human Relations; and the American Council on Education for the American Youth Commission and the Commission on Teacher Education.[4]

George F. Zook was brought to Washington to head the Ameri-

4. Raymond B. Fosdick, *An Adventure in Giving: The Story of the General Education Board* (New York, Harper, 1962).

Social Change and Education

can Council on Education from the presidency at Akron University. The General Education Board made a grant for general support of the Council in addition to its grants for the commissions which worked in the field of general education. The ACE had the advantage of representing privately as well as publicly supported education. Catholic educators cooperated in the ACE, as did the representatives of Protestant churches in church-related colleges. The strongest leadership came from the larger private and state universities.

By 1940 the ACE had found a secure place in the national scene as a representative of publicly and privately supported higher education. During World War II it was useful in relating government to higher education, and after the war its influence continued to grow. The Council was able to buy a building in Washington and to build a strong though small professional staff.

In 1962 the American Council on Education received grants of $2,000,000 from the Ford Foundation and $500,000 from the Carnegie Corporation to support a program of reorganization and expansion over a five-year period. The Council is working on policy for higher education, on research in higher education, and represents colleges and universities in relations with the federal government. There are five major commissions, concerned with policies and objectives for higher education; relations with the federal government; international affairs in education; academic affairs; and administrative affairs.

We can see that the emergence of these two outstanding national organizations came in response to the society's demands for more national coordination and concentration of decision-making power. Their growing strength tended to keep the government agencies in a relatively weak policy-making position, even though these agencies were spending vast sums in education and research.

We might speak of two phases in the growth of national organizations in education. The first phase consisted of the formation of organizations by the various interest or functional groups in education and the development of internal cohesion within them. This phase was particularly concentrated in the period between 1915 and 1945. In the second, postwar phase, these organizations moved to come to grips with the enormous expansion of education and with the problems of educational policy in an emergent society.

At the present time the national educational organizations function to facilitate (a) dealing with the federal government, which has become more and more important to most educational institutions; (b) setting and maintaining standards; (c) planning for improvement and for adaptation to social change.

EDUCATION IN AN AFFLUENT SOCIETY

During the first half of the century the United States passed the invisible boundary line that separates an economy of scarcity from an economy of abundance. By 1960 the concept of an *affluent society* was generally recognized and with it the problem of finding socially valuable ways of consuming the vast production made possible by technological development.

Thus the conviction that it was good for business and industry to spend more money on research and development was fortified by the conclusion that the field of education and research was one in which greater public expenditures could be made with advantages to the health, national defense, and economic growth of the country. Therefore the flow of federal funds into education and research increased after 1950 and encountered remarkably little political resistance or substantive criticism either in Washington or among educators and scientists.

This is not the same thing as saying that the financing of education has ceased to be a problem. The federal government contributes very little to the cost of primary and secondary education —less than 5 per cent in 1962. Most communities watch their school expenditures closely, and many proposals for issuing bonds to build new schools have been defeated at local elections. Nevertheless, expenditures on primary and secondary schools have increased sharply as the national income has risen. The expenditure per pupil in public schools has quintupled, in dollars of constant purchasing power, between 1920 and 1960. Whether or not the federal government supports a larger part of the cost of elementary and secondary education, it seems that the society will maintain

Table 7. Sources of Educational and General Income, Institutions of Higher Education *
(Percentage distribution)

	1930	1953–54	1957–58	1959–60	All	1961–62 Public	Private
Student fees	29.9	23.6	25.0	24.6	24.9	12.7	40.2
Federal government (total)	4.3	17.8	19.0	22.1	25.4	22.7	28.8
Research			14.3	17.6	21.0	16.1	27.2
Other			4.7	4.5	4.4	6.6	1.6
State governments	31.2	31.7	30.4	29.5	27.7	48.4	1.9
Local governments		3.8	3.5	3.2	3.2	5.4	0.2
Endowment earnings	14.2	5.4	4.9	4.4	†	†	†
Private gifts and grants	5.4	8.2	8.7	8.1	7.4	2.9	13.1
Other educational and general income	15.0	9.5	8.5	8.1	11.4†	8.1†	15.8†
Total amount (millions)	$483	$2,357	$3,763	$4,713	$6,072	$3,397	$2,675

Source: U.S. Office of Education, *Digest of Educational Statistics*, 1964. Tables 79 and 80.
Historical Statistics of the United States, Bureau of the Census, 1957, p. 212.
* The figures exclude income from auxiliary enterprises and activities, from gifts and grants for buildings, endowment, and from student loan funds.
† Endowment earnings included in "other income" for 1961–62.

education at those levels with little questioning of the desirability of such expenditure.

The problem now is to support the expansion of higher education during the period of rapid growth from 1965 to 1970 resulting from the sharp increase of births after World War II. It is widely estimated that 1970 enrollment in colleges and universities will double that of 1960. The cost of new buildings alone is estimated at $18 billion from 1960 to 1970. The annual cost of higher education in 1969–70 has been estimated at $12 billion.[5] This compares with about $5 billion in 1960, and does not include the bill for research projects and installations managed by universities but paid for by government, industry, and private foundations.

The federal government has slowly been increasing its share of the support of higher education, from 18 per cent in 1954 to 25 per cent in 1962 (see Table 7). The Council for Financial Aid to Education, supported largely by business interests and conservative with respect to federal support of education, has estimated that half the bill for higher education in 1970 may be paid by federal, state, and local governments, a fifth by student fees, and a fifth by private grants and gifts—an increase in quantity of money provided, but not in proportion of support by government. Since private gifts and grants at present amount to less than 10 per cent of the total cost, this factor will have to increase substantially if the federal government's share does not increase. On the other hand, Professor Seymour Harris, of Harvard University, believes that the share of the total bill paid by government is likely to decrease, and he expects the proportion of the cost paid by student tuition fees to double in the next decade.[6] The issue lies here—will the federal government substantially increase its support for higher education, will private gifts be substantially and relatively increased, or will student fees carry an increased part of the load?

The American Council on Education has urged the federal government to increase its support of higher education. In a pamphlet distributed widely, the Council says: [7]

5. Kenneth A. Simon and Marie G. Fullam, *Projections of Educational Statistics to 1973–74* (Washington, D.C., U.S. Office of Education, Circular 754, 1964).

6. Seymour E. Harris, *Higher Education: Resources and Finance* (New York, McGraw-Hill, 1962), Tables 2–3.

7. "A Federal Program to Develop Higher Education as a National Resource" (Washington, D.C., American Council on Education, 1963).

The American Council on Education believes that the problems confronting higher education transcend state and local concerns, and thus have become an urgent national concern. We believe that, to maintain and develop higher education as a national resource, the Federal Government must supplement other sources of support. The Federal Government should do this, not to "aid" higher education, but to meet a national obligation to conserve and strengthen a national resource.

The Council therefore proposes a broad program of Federal action to help expand and improve American higher education.

During the first half of the century a large number of educational organizations were formed and they generally took on a national character. At times their functions and interests came into conflict with those of other organizations and there followed a time of tension.

We are just now in such a time of tension. The stronger national organizations are adjusting to the emergence of a policy-making activity within the federal government—carried on by the National Science Foundation, the National Institutes of Health, and the Office of Education. As these agencies allocate large sums of money, they are drawn inevitably into the act of making policy. However, they find that policy is already being made by educational institutions acting in voluntary associations. Thus there is a balance of power in policy-making. It would be difficult to predict how this balance will swing during the coming decades. Strong forces of tradition and ideology support the voluntary associations in the function of policy-making, and they are equipped by organization and leadership to perform this function adequately. On the other hand, the federal government's responsibility is growing greater as its expenditures grow greater, and it is bound to push for more voice in the making of policy. Thus the relation of voluntary associations to national government is being worked out in the field of education as in other fields, each side gaining strength and skill as time goes on.

The National Education Association (along with the American Council on Education the principal private organizations with power in the making of educational policy) strives to do two quite different things. It works on problems of national policy and improvement of education and, at the same time, the problems of raising the material welfare and improving working conditions of the classroom teachers. In the first area the NEA works very closely with the American Association of School Administrators, with which it shares its Washington building. But in the area of salaries and welfare the classroom teachers do not always agree with the school superintendents.

On the other hand, the American Federation of Teachers places much of its attention on teachers' salaries and welfare and has recently come into sharp rivalry with the NEA on this subject. The first strong development of teachers' unions came during the depression of the 1930s in several large cities where teachers banded together to strengthen their claims to regular pay, to avoid severe salary cuts, etc. In Chicago and New York the American Federation of Teachers became especially strong at this time and has continued to be strong ever since. There were several small local organizations of college teachers during the depression, but they faded away and left only the branches where the elementary and secondary school were predominant. The AFT was part of the American Federation of Labor and did not profit especially from the rise of the CIO during the depression.

In 1960 the membership of the AFT was some 50,000, compared with 700,000 dues-paying members of the NEA. But in Chicago and New York and a few other cities, there were actually more teacher members of the AFT than of the NEA.

The AFT stressed the raising of teachers' salaries during the postwar period, but did not gain much strength on this account since the general shortage of teachers was pushing salaries up everywhere, and the teachers' union did not seem to be essential in this respect. However, the problems of teachers' salaries, assignment of teachers, hours and conditions of work, etc. were becoming acute by 1960, and there arose a movement to provide for collective bargaining, spearheaded by the AFT. This first came to a head in New York City, where the Board of Education agreed to negotiate with a teachers' organization, and held an election in 1961 to find out what organization would represent a majority of teachers. Two organizations were on the ballot—the American Federation of Teachers local and a local teachers' organization that had the blessing of the National Education Association. When the AFT won a decisive victory, the union then announced that it would proceed to seek a similar agreement with other school boards throughout the country. This posed a problem for the NEA, which claimed to represent the economic as well as the professional interests of the teachers, but had not been active as a bargaining agent. The 1960s will resolve this problem somehow and will tell whether the American teachers generally want to join the ranks of organized labor.

CHANGING CHURCH AND CHANGING EDUCATION

The churches have undergone social change during the twentieth century, affecting their traditional interest and involvement in education. The church has supported education and has been assisted by education during this century. The proportion of students in institutions of higher education remained more or less stable at about 50 per cent in private institutions for the first fifty years of the century and then moved toward the public end of the scale. Probably the proportion in colleges and universities under church control has decreased.

The nineteenth century was a period of initiative for the Protestant churches in founding and developing colleges and universities; in fact they were responsible for most of the liberal arts colleges. In 1900 such colleges were about at their height of influence and size relative to other types of institutions. Churches played a strong part in the governing of the University of Chicago, Northwestern University, Syracuse, Colgate, Wesleyan, University of Southern California, Emory, Princeton—to name some which later became independent.

On the other hand, the Roman Catholic Church has increased its support of higher education and now maintains several universities with good graduate and professional schools. At the primary and secondary school levels there is very little control or administration of schools by Protestant churches, but the Roman Catholic Church has maintained a strong system of parish schools at the elementary level and has expanded its system of secondary schools. Yet in spite of an energetic campaign to build new parish schools, new secondary schools, and college buildings, the Roman Catholic Church does not care for as large a proportion of Catholic youth in its own schools and colleges as it did before World War II. For example, in 1960 there were about twice as many Catholic students in non-Catholic institutions of higher education as in Catholic colleges and universities. It has been estimated that this trend will continue, with three out of four Catholic students enrolled in non-Catholic institutions by 1970.

It appears that the Catholic Church and its people have become more closely integrated with the Protestants and Jews in the American society since 1900. Then a great many Catholics were recent immigrants, and they and their churches were isolated from the mainstream of American life as well as from the older Irish and German elements in the Catholic Church. Then as they lost some of their ethnic attitudes and values and as they moved up the socio-economic scale they became more like a cross-section of Americans. This is seen in the nature of the students in Catholic colleges. Before World War II a number of studies showed the existence of what was called "anti-intellectualism" in Catholic colleges. Students were less interested in the world of ideas than were students in non-Catholic colleges and were more likely to follow business careers than the professions. But since World War II Catholic students in Catholic colleges have become very similar to non-Catholic students in other colleges in their occupational aspirations and their intellectual and social interests.

Together with this evidence that students in Catholic and non-Catholic colleges are becoming more alike goes the growing emphasis within the Catholic Church on "ecumenism"—or cooperation with other Christian churches—which has been going on as a conscious policy of the Church since about 1900. The statement of St. Augustine is often quoted: "Every good and true Christian should understand that wherever he discovers truth it is the Lord's."

The increasing tendency of Catholic educators and students to find more in common with non-Catholics is seen in the developing program of the Newman clubs. Started shortly after 1900 on non-

Social Change and Education

Catholic university campuses, the Newman Club is a social and religious organization led by a Catholic chaplain. Such an organization might remain aloof from non-Catholic groups, but this has not been the case. Newman clubs cooperate with Protestant and Jewish religious organizations on the campus to promote joint action and joint study based on religious values.

Since World War II there has been a growth of church-supported elementary and secondary schools on a local or parish basis among some Protestant denominations. The Lutherans have increased their support of such schools. So also has a group of fundamentalist churches which did not exist in 1900; the Assembly of God, the Pentecostal denominations, and several fundamentalist Baptist and Calvinist groups have established parochial schools which they call Christian Schools. These operations run counter to the general trend of the society toward public-supported education of a secular kind and represent an effort by religious groups that are not satisfied with what they see in the ideological trends of the society to maintain and strengthen their own ideologies.

The major Protestant denominations and the majority of Jewish congregations have remained within the dominant ideological trend. They are international in outlook, more rational and less supra-rational in their approach to social and economic problems, and they show a strong tendency to unite and forget what they increasingly regard as minor differences of theological belief. This century has seen the merger of the Congregational and Christian churches, with active discussions of combining the Protestant Episcopal and Presbyterian, and the Methodist and Evangelical Reformed churches. In the discussion stage in 1965 is a union of Protestant Episcopal, Presbyterian, Methodist, and United Church of Christ.

These churches have committed themselves to the support of public education, though they retain an interest in certain church-supported liberal arts colleges, and they maintain their own theological schools. With respect to the teaching of religion, the churches that maintain their own schools make the teaching of religion a regular and important part of the curriculum. They work directly with the pupil as well as through his family to teach him religious beliefs and attitudes and church loyalty.

The churches that do not maintain separate schools are divided within themselves on the relation of religious education to education in the public schools. One group of church people, since about 1925, has committed itself to a program of nondenominational religious teaching during the week, on "released time"—that is, school time released by the public schools for this purpose. The procedure varies from holding classes in religion in the school building, with teachers provided by the churches supporting the program, to holding classes in the separate churches, for which children are excused from school. The U.S. Supreme Court ruled that the use of school buildings for church-supported religious teaching was unconstitutional and, in 1962, ruled that public prayers in the schools were unconstitutional. Still there are various forms of cooperation between public schools and churches that go unchallenged in states and areas where religious beliefs are fairly homogeneous. This is true of rural Kentucky, for example, where most public schools continue religious observances that probably would be ruled illegal in areas that are more cosmopolitan and heterogeneous in religious outlook.

The other group within the churches, including most Jewish groups, takes the position that the separation of church and state demands a sharp differentiation between religious instruction, to be given by the church on its own property and its own time, and secular education to be given by the public schools. This group commits itself to the task of creating an educational program within the church that is voluntary for the church family and aimed at (1) teaching the child the meaning of religion as interpreted by his church; (2) relating the child, the adolescent, and the adult to the church as a social fellowship with ethical purposes; and (3) teaching the individual the social ethics of his church.

The methods and concepts of religious education held by this group are close, in many ways, to the methods and concepts of secular education. Since about 1920 there has grown up a profession of religious education, with training centers in several universities not closely related to any one denomination—Columbia University, University of Pittsburgh, Northwestern, Chicago, Yale—as well as others with closer church ties. Leaders in the field of religious education have formed the Religious Education Association, which has a strong research department. The National Council of Churches of Christ, with headquarters in New York City, has a

Social Change and Education

Research Division and a Division of Curriculum with staff members who maintain close professional relations with social scientists and educationists in the universities and schools of education.

One example of this close association is the Workshop of Religious Education Research held under the auspices of the Religious Education Association at Cornell University in 1961, with participation of about sixty people with interests in research in the field of religious and ethical development. Director of the workshop was Professor Stuart Cook, Chairman of the Department of Psychology of New York University; members of the staff were drawn from several universities without church connection as well as from Catholic universities and from Protestant theological schools. Another example is the Character Research Project, located at Union College under the leadership of Ernest Ligon, psychologist, which applies psychological concepts to religious and character education through cooperation with a number of local churches from the more liberal Protestant denominations.

To sum up the relations of church and education at the middle of the twentieth century and to suggest future trends, we must recognize a dominant theme and perhaps several subsidiary ones. The dominant Protestant trend, illustrated in the work of the National Council of Churches and the Religious Education Association, is toward cooperation among the churches, emphasis upon a social ethic, use of the methods and concepts of secular education whenever they can be applied usefully, and an ecumenical movement that looks toward a world society in which the churches of the world unite to promote brotherhood and peace.

A subsidiary theme can be seen in the Roman Catholic Church's strong educational program, growing emphasis on secondary and higher education under Church auspices, and religious education aimed at personal religious observance as well as at a social ethic with growing international emphasis. The Catholic educators use methods and concepts of secular psychology and sociology, but with less eclecticism than the Protestant educators.

Still another subsidiary theme is the isolationism of the fundamentalist Protestant churches, in the sense of building a wall of religious dogma and social solidarity around themselves as well as in the sense of remaining aloof from international cooperation which means acceptance of other faiths as having validity in other societies. These churches make an increasing use of education to build loyalty and belief in their own religious and social mores, but they have little use for the modern methods of psychology and education.

CHANGES IN THE TEACHING PROFESSION

The corps of teachers was of course forced to grow as the educational system grew. In 1900 school and college teachers made up 1.24 per cent of the adult population aged twenty to sixty-four;

Table 8. Percentage of Population Aged 20–64 Who Are Teachers*

	Elementary and secondary school teachers	College and university teachers
1890	1.22	.04
1900	1.18	.06
1920	1.25	.08
1930	1.32	.11
1940	1.25	.14
1950	1.18	.22
1960	1.70	.31
1970 (estimated)	1.63	.38

Source: Robert J. Havighurst and Bernice Neugarten, *Society and Education*, Second Edition, Boston, Allyn and Bacon, 1962, Table 16.6.
* The total number of teachers have been compared with the general population aged 20–64. There are a few teachers under 20 and over 64.

in 1950, 1.40 per cent; and in 1960, 2.0 per cent (see Table 8). Thus the proportion of people who were teachers grew very rapidly after 1950.

Teachers had come traditionally from the farms of the country. Sons and daughters of farmers who wanted to leave the farm found that they could prepare easily for teaching, first in a one-room rural school and then later in town or city. There was a liberal sprinkling of teachers with an upper-middle-class background who had gone into teaching because they saw this kind of service as most interesting and attractive; often they were daughters or sons of teachers or clergymen. Only a relatively small fraction made a lifelong career of school teaching. The majority of women teachers married and left the profession. Many men went into college teaching after several years of school teaching. Thus the teaching profession at the beginning of the century had a changing composition quite different from the more stable professions of medicine, law, and the clergy.

By 1960 the teaching profession was becoming more stable in that the average length of service had increased, the level of educational preparation had increased substantially, and teachers were coming largely from the urban working and lower-middle classes. A new type of person entered teaching between 1900 and 1960—the teacher of vocational subjects, agriculture, commerce, or trades. This person, generally a man, was skilled in the techniques of some area of manual work but shared with other teachers a liking for the school regimen—daily, weekly, and yearly—which was different from any other calling and had its peculiar rewards and satisfactions for certain kinds of people.

Another element of the teaching force which differentiates 1960 from 1900 is the increased number of married women. This has tended to increase the average age of teachers, as married women have either remained in the profession or come back to it after their children were grown.

Among college teachers there has also been a substantial change. The small number of college teachers in 1900 were generally of middle-class background and upper-middle in orientation. Many had been reared in farm families. There has been an enormous expansion in numbers of college teachers during the twentieth century, and the profession has become a socially complex group. The earlier nonmobile upper-middle-class group was supplemented by a large number of upward-mobile urban men and women, many the children or grandchildren of immigrants. Since higher education expanded rapidly after 1920, and since there were no organized barriers to prevent or reduce upward mobility into college teaching, this became an important avenue for mobile young people who were intellectually active and aggressive. The proportions of college teachers with Jewish, Italian, Polish, and Japanese backgrounds have grown very much since 1930. The attitudes of these people toward the aims and values of college education and toward social change are probably quite different from the attitudes of college teachers born into upper-middle-class old-American families.

Thus we see that education has grown faster than the country in the twentieth century. Relatively more people are being educated and to higher levels. At the same time, the units of education—the school districts and the individual schools—have been growing larger. After World War II the federal government came into primary and secondary education, first to improve its performance and then to support some of its functions.

With the development of a large and complex educational system there was a need for the setting of standards, for coordination of effort among large numbers of various types of institutions, and for stimulation of new and improved programs. Since the national government deliberately did not involve itself in these activities, a system of voluntary national and regional organizations emerged to perform these functions.

CHAPTER THIRTEEN

Federal Involvement in Education

THE BEGINNINGS OF FEDERAL ASSISTANCE

While responsibility for the education of citizens was clearly reserved to the states when the Constitution was written, the clause permitting the federal government to act within the states on behalf of the national welfare has been used repeatedly as the basis for federal participation in educational affairs. In the middle of the last century the teaching of applied science was clearly a national need, and the national government stepped in to meet that need through the land-grant college movement, an experiment with no European model. Yale University had established a department of chemistry and Harvard had opened its Lawrence School of Science before 1850, but they were for educated persons who wanted to become scholars in the sciences. What the educational reformers developed was a new type of university to give the industrial classes—farmers, mechanics, businessmen—a scientific and practical education. They wanted a scientific agriculture, an industry based on science and technology, and a home presided over by a woman who would be both laboratory technician and housewife.

The land-grant colleges began when the Morrill Act of 1862 gave grants of land for the support of institutions concerned primarily with teaching "agriculture and the mechanic arts." In 1890 the Second Morrill Act provided annual payments to the states for support of the land-grant colleges. The Adams Act of 1906 increased the federal contribution to agricultural experiment stations and gave the Secretary of Agriculture more controls over their expenditures. The amount of support was increased in 1925, 1935, 1946, and 1955. The Smith-Lever Act of 1914 provided funds on a matching basis for the establishment of agricultural extension pro-

This chapter is by Robert J. Havighurst. See Notes on Authors.

grams. Today there are some ten thousand county agents working under this program.

Direct federal government assistance to schools below the college level began in 1917 with the Smith-Hughes Act, which provided for payments toward the cost of training youths for vocations in agriculture, industry, and business. The George-Dean Act later expanded this kind of support. Thus the federal government moved into the most locally oriented of all types of instruction—preparation of young people for occupations in their own home communities.

The federal government has slowly taken over the support of certain educational functions regarded as necessary for the national welfare. In order of appearance these functions are: the collection and dissemination of facts about education; the development of agriculture through training and research; the vocational training of youth; the welfare of youth in times of economic crisis; the conduct of research on health; the conduct of research in support of national defense; the conduct of research in support of industrial development.

A departure from traditional vocational training programs came in response to the national emergency of the 1930s. As unemployment rose during the depression decade, young people found it increasingly difficult to get work; by 1933 there were a quarter of a million homeless youths wandering from one place to another in search of a livelihood. The federal government established the Civilian Conservation Corps to provide socially useful work for boys out of school and the National Youth Administration Program to provide part-time work with sufficient pay to enable boys and girls to continue their secondary school or college education.

In 1900 the participation of the federal government in educational affairs was minimal, although it was beginning to be felt. By 1930 the principle of federal assistance to vocational education was well established, but the federal outlay in dollars was still very small. By 1960 the federal government had moved into the support of education as a major force, and the question was no longer whether there should be federal aid to education but what forms this aid should take and how much of the total educational bill should be paid by the federal government. By this time the federal government, under the Public Health Service, was supporting basic

Federal Involvement in Education

research on problems of health. Basic research, which had been considered a function of universities, became a function of government and was carried on through educational institutions or through research institutes.

Meanwhile, a new form of federal government participation in education came about through the National Defense Education Act. This law, passed in 1958, was justified as a means of national defense since the nation was still technically in a state of emergency, which gave the federal government powers it would not have in "normal" times. The National Defense Education Act was expanded by subsequent congressional acts to include support for such educational activities as the training of school librarians, teachers of geography, and teachers of preschool classes for "culturally deprived" children. More recently, with funds under the Economic Opportunity Act, preschool classes have been set up for socially disadvantaged children, based on a growing conviction that these children are missing experiences in their third and fourth years that are crucial to average or good mental development.

The racial segregation of schools in the South was ruled unconstitutional by the United States Supreme Court in 1954, which required the southern states to desegregate the schools with reasonable speed. Ten years later there was a "token" desegregation in process in most southern states, while the border states of Maryland, Kentucky, Missouri, and southern Illinois had desegregated their schools much as the northern states had, so that such school segregation as existed was almost entirely due to residential segregation. The segregation of the northern industrial cities and of the border states became a controversial issue in several cities early in the 1960s, when a number of Negro organizations began to work for integration in the schools in spite of residential segregation. They argued that schools attended by Negro children were generally older, more crowded, and staffed by inferior teachers when compared with schools attended by white children. They asked not only for better buildings, more classrooms, and better teachers for Negro children but also for measures aimed specifically at mixing Negro and white children in the same schools. They also pointed out that in a few cities the attendance districts of schools were being defined in order to maintain segregated schools. A series of far-reaching court decisions in the early 1960s generally supported the moves for integrated schools. These decisions began to require school boards to show explicit efforts to establish and maintain integrated schools even in spite of patterns of residential segregation of Negroes.

RESEARCH AND DEVELOPMENT RELATED TO EDUCATION

In any catalogue of major social changes the emergence of "research and development" must stand out as a most important phenomenon. Some industrial corporations have maintained research laboratories since the earliest decades of this century. It has been understood that industrial development and progress depend upon continuing research. But the amount of money spent on research hardly reached a billion dollars a year in 1940.

It was during World War II that the federal government began to spend large sums of money on research and development for military purposes. Since World War II, federal grants for the support of research have been part of an enormous investment by the United States public agencies and private business in the field of basic and applied research and development. These three categories are defined as follows:

Basic research: fundamental scientific investigation aimed at increasing knowledge

Applied research: knowledge applied to a practical objective

Development: designing and testing of new products and materials

In relation to the gross national product, national expenditures on research and development grew from 1.02 per cent in 1950 to 2.78 per cent in 1960, and an estimated 3.0 per cent in 1964. Table 1 shows that gross expenditures on research and development almost quadrupled during the decade from 1950 to 1960. University expenditures increased at the same rate.

Table 1 shows the trend of national expenditures on research and development since the war. The support for research and development comes preponderantly from the federal government,

Federal Involvement in Education

which subsidizes research and development in private industry and in universities. Growth of the research budget in universities has been extraordinary since 1940. It was 4 per cent of their total expenditures in 1940 and 20 per cent in 1960. This research has been done mainly in some 10 per cent of the institutions of higher education, although another 10 per cent have participated in a small way through the work of several of their professors. A few universities have received very large sums for research. In 1959–60 Harvard University received $18 million from the federal government, of which $11,860,000 was solely for research purposes. Federal funds supplied a quarter of Harvard's budget in that year and over half of

Table 1. Expenditures for Research and Development Related to Gross National Product and Federal Government Expenditures

	GNP in billions of dollars	Expenditures on R. and D. in billions of dollars	Percentage of GNP	Federal expenditures on R. and D. in billions of dollars	Federal R. and D. a percentage of total federal gov expenditure
1930	91	.17	0.19		
1940	101	.35	0.35	.07	0.8
1950	285	2.9	1.02	1.08	2.7
1955	398	6.4	1.61	3.88	6.0
1957	443	10.0	2.26		
1959	483	12.4	2.57		
1960	504	14.0	2.78	7.74	10.1
1961	520	16.0	3.08	8.79	10.8
1962	555			10.37	
1963	585			14.0	14.5
1964	610			15.3	15

Source: Adapted from *Hearings before a Subcommittee of the Committee on Appropriations*, House of Representatives, 87th Congress, Department of Health, Education and Welfare, Part 4, *Report on Manpower for Medical Research*, Appendix A, Table 1 and 2, Washington, D.C., U.S. Government Printing Office, 1962.

the budget of its medical school. Universities more specialized than Harvard received even more of their support from the government. Massachusetts Institute of Technology and California Institute of Technology received almost 80 per cent of their operating incomes from the federal government in 1958–59.

Research and Development Related to Education

The National Defense Research Committee, created in 1940 to advise the government on military research, decided to work through existing facilities in colleges and universities rather than to set up government laboratories. This policy was continued by its successor, the Office of Scientific Research and Development. During World War II twenty-eight government owned research centers were set up at eighteen universities and managed by the universities. The Office of Naval Research also supported basic and applied research in universities.

After the war the government continued to support research for military purposes at a fairly high level and expanded its program of support for research in the field of health through the National Institutes of Health. So convinced were the members of Congress of the values of federally supported research that they frequently appropriated more for the Institutes of Health than was requested by the offices of those institutes. Appropriations to the National Institutes of Health grew from $48 million in 1947 to $1,045 million in 1965. Furthermore, the Congress voted money to the Office of Education to support research on certain aspects of education to be conducted by universities. By 1960 the Congress was also providing funds for research grants administered by the Children's Bureau and by the Social Security Administration.

As the federal government's interest in supporting nonmilitary research and development became clearly defined after the war, an organization was needed to advise the President on matters of national policy affected by, or pertaining to, science and technology and to help the Congress understand and evaluate proposed legislation in this area. In 1962 Congress established the Office of Science and Technology, whose Director is a presidential assistant as well as Chairman of the President's Science Advisory Committee and the Federal Council for Science and Technology. The Science Advisory Committee has called on panels of advisors for reports on the impact of research and technology on questions of health, welfare, and education.

The $15 billion in federal funds for research and development in fiscal 1964 was broken down roughly as follows: Department of Defense, $7.7 billion; National Aeronautics and Space Administration, $4.2 billion; Atomic Energy Commission, $1.5 billion; and $1.6 billion for the Department of Health, Education and Welfare.

Federal Involvement in Education

the National Science Foundation, the Department of Agriculture, and other agencies. Private industry spent about half as much as the federal government on research and development; and universities and other nonprofit institutions provided about 3 per cent of nationwide expenditure.

In 1962 about 10 per cent of federal government research and development funds was spent in government agencies; 63 per cent was spent in private industry, 7 per cent in universities proper, and 10 per cent in nonprofit corporations and university research centers.

In the words of Jerome B. Wiesner, Director of the Office of Science and Technology in 1963–4, such figures as those given above, indicate the following:

> In the first place, they show that the Federal Government has been obliged to meet the need for major and continuing research funds that otherwise are beyond the capabilities of non-Federal institutions but on which the well-being of the nation depends. Research in many areas—such as highways, weather services, aspects of health, and water resource development—has come to be recognized as a Federal responsibility, where private institutions cannot capture sufficient or prompt returns as incentives. However, the figures also indicate that the Federal Government and industry have also developed a unique partnership, giving rise to the concept of an "R & D industry" largely supported by government, while at the same time the government itself has become heavily dependent on industrial skills and facilities for necessary work. Finally, the mutual interdependence of the universities and the government is clear, even discounting the additional flow of funds to the campus for strictly educational purposes.[1]

In 1952 federal government obligations for research in universities amounted to $295 million, of which 89 per cent was provided by the Department of Defense and the Atomic Energy Commission. In 1960 the analogous figures were $846 million and 63 per cent.

1. Statement of Jerome B. Wiesner, Director, Office of Science and Technology, at Hearings before Subcommittee on Science, Research, and Development of the House Committee on Science and Astronautics, 88th Congress, 1st Session, 1963.

This reduction in the military emphasis of government-supported research was accompanied by the expansion of research under the Department of Health, Education and Welfare, especially under the National Aeronautics and Space Administration and under the National Science Foundation.

The share of the Department of Health, Education and Welfare increased from 5 to 18 per cent, largely granted through the National Institutes of Health to research workers in universities. Total NIH appropriations for research outside of the Institutes themselves (called extramural research) grew from $8 million in 1947 to $430 million in 1962.

EFFECTS OF FEDERAL SUPPORT OF SCIENCE

A great deal of discussion has gone on among college and university educators and government officials concerning the effects of federal government programs on higher education. In a 1960 report the President's Science Advisory Committee asked how the federal government and the universities should proceed to establish and maintain the kind of environment required for scientific progress and for the making of good young scientists. "American science in the next generation must, quite literally, double and redouble in size and strength." This is a societal decision, not a decision by educators, and the government will put it into effect.

Because basic research and graduate education go together, the government provides fellowships for graduate students and research contracts with universities where graduate students can serve as apprentices. One result of this policy is an increase in the size of the graduate schools in the better universities. Graduate enrollment at the Massachusetts Institute of Technology went from 1025 students in 1954 to 2,892 in 1961, whereas undergraduate enrollment increased only from 3,481 to 3,562.

There has been a change of emphasis in some universities from undergraduate teaching to research. "The research outlook of fed-

Federal Involvement in Education

eral science agencies has conquered the major universities, pene-
trated the minor ones, and now confronts the colleges." [2]

The graduate school dean at Harvard said that in the science departments at Harvard, "Senior professors are so harassed that they
can hardly even learn the names of their section men" (graduate
assistants in laboratories). The chairman of a mathematics department in a state university says that he does not know the names of
all of his instructors. Federal-financed research tends to reduce the
frequency of contact of professors with undergraduates but increases contact with graduate students.

The report on *Harvard and the Federal Government* made under
the direction of President Pusey says:

> University and Government people alike have been slow to
> realize the significance of their new relationship. The Govern-
> ment now calls on the universities for achievements that de-
> pend on the highest qualities of creativity, but sometimes
> through purchasing procedures that could destroy the en-
> vironment in which such qualities flourish. This is not from
> any wrong intentions on the part of individual agencies; in
> general, they have bent over backward in favor of academic
> freedom, and have done a great deal to adapt government
> methods to the requirements of a university. Indeed, in the
> process of asking Congress for funds, they sometimes exag-
> gerate the potential practical achievements of the basic re-
> search they propose to support. But a relationship based on a
> short-term grant for specific purposes, which was perfectly
> sensible when such grants were only a tiny increment to an
> academic budget, may be self-defeating when the grants have
> become a major reliance of the university. At that stage, the
> donor would do well to consider the general health of the in-
> stitution which he is building up, if only in order to protect his
> investment.

> As universities recognize that there is no substitute today
> for federal support in many fields of science, they must ask the
> Government to recognize, in the way it makes its grants, that
> the university is a creative force because it is concerned with
> all fields of knowledge, and because it offers scholars the intel-

2. This and other quotations are from Harold Orlans, *The Effects of Federal Programs on Higher Education* (Washington, D.C., The Brookings Institution, 1962).

lectual independence that goes with permanent status. If they are to make this clear, universities themselves need to understand their relationships with Government and to set up proper channels through which to inform Government of their point of view on the issues which may well affect their basic character in the future.[3]

Orlans points out three ill effects of federal support of science research in the major universities. Federal stipends to graduate science students lower the quality of undergraduate laboratory instruction by taking these graduate students away from teaching as laboratory assistants. Many of these people are probably being permanently removed from teaching. An imbalance in the scientific curriculum has been created because a concentration on quantitative and "scientific" approaches leads to a gain in rigor but a frequent narrowing of perspective and understanding. The yearly income of the science faculty has been raised above that of the humanities because of federal funds for summer research work and because of increased competition among universities for good men in the sciences.

The general view among the educators who have studied the situation is that there is a danger of loss of freedom by the universities, but this danger can be avoided. In his Farewell Address President Eisenhower said, "The prospect of domination of the nation's scholars by federal employment, project allocations, and the power of money is ever present—and is gravely to be regarded."

One of the first issues arose with reference to the "disclaimer affidavit" that the National Defense Education Act required from students who borrowed money. Several of the stronger universities and colleges refused to accept federal funds that were tied to the affidavit disclaiming membership in organizations suspected of left-wing tendencies. The affidavit was later discontinued.

Another type of concern about the growth of federal support of science in the universities is stated by Alvin M. Weinberg, Director of the Oak Ridge National Laboratory, in an article entitled "Big Science: A Liability?"[4] Science grows fat and lazy with too much money, he says. It becomes easier to spend money than to spend

3. Nathan M. Pusey, *Harvard and the Federal Government* (Cambridge, Mass., Harvard University Press, 1961).

4. Alvin M. Weinberg, "Big Science: A Liability?" *Context: A University of Chicago Magazine*, 1:2 (1961), 1–5.

thought. The 1961 federal expenditure on research and development was $8.4 billion, or 10 per cent of the federal budget and 1.6 per cent of the Gross National Product (GNP). Weinberg suggests that this may be too much, especially since 80 per cent of this money is for military purposes. He proposes that some figure— perhaps something less than one per cent of the GNP—be agreed upon as the long-term expenditure for federally supported non-defense science and that this figure be maintained for a period such as fifteen years. Thus scientists could get used to the idea that science spending would increase only as fast as the GNP.

The danger of a near monopoly by the federal government of physical scientists and engineers and of concentrating them on a narrow range of problems was the subject of an editorial entitled "How Guard Our Diversity in Science" printed in *Science,* April 12, 1963, and written by Carryl P. Haskins of the Carnegie Institution of Washington:

> Recently Jerome Wiesner testified before the House Committee on Government Appropriations that the government plans to allocate for the coming fiscal year the sum of $12.3 billion for support of research and development in the nation. Although this sum represents only about 15 per cent of the overall federal budget, it amounts to well over one-third that portion not formally committed.
>
> These are awesome figures. Their positive impact is clear enough. But there are cautionary aspects that cannot be stressed too often. They were introduced by the President when he observed that federally financed activities in defense, space, and atomic energy absorb roughly two-thirds of our total supply of physical scientists and engineers. They are further emphasized by a committee headed by J. Herbert Hollooman, Assistant Secretary of Commerce for Science and Technology. Such is the stress created by this drain that we are actually falling behind Western Europe, England, and Japan in our resources of scientific talent available to industrial production.
>
> Throughout our national history we have depended on a demand mechanism to distribute human effort and resources in a pattern which, if sometimes wasteful in the short term, in the long term provided proven benefits. This approach has

served us well. But it assumed two fundamental premises, among others: that available resources of trained human talent would continue to be great enough to fill all demands, and that their commitments would continue to be highly plural in nature and, moreover, flexible. What do we do when so large a fraction of the reserve is being inflexibly committed to specific enterprises that the bottom of the barrel is visible? What do we do when—as is not yet universally recognized—it is not dollars but unbuyable human gifts that will set the limit?

One of the problems in the federal financing of research in universities is the high degree of concentration of money on a small number of institutions. Of all federal funds for research given to universities in 1959–60, 68 per cent went to twenty-five universities, 82 per cent went to fifty, and 94 per cent to one hundred.[5] Although there were 186 private liberal arts colleges and fifty-five state colleges participating in federal programs of research, their share of the federal research funds totaled 1.1 per cent.

The twenty-five major participants in federal research and development programs in 1960, with federal research income of $4,499,000 to $43,176,000 (not including funds for the operation of government-owned research centers), were:

California Institute of Technology	New York University
University of California	Ohio State University
University of Chicago	Pennsylvania State University
Columbia University	University of Pennsylvania
Cornell University	University of Pittsburgh
Duke University	Princeton University
Harvard University	Stanford University
Illinois Institute of Technology	University of Texas
University of Illinois	Washington University
Johns Hopkins University	(St. Louis)
Massachusetts Institute of Technology	University of Washington (Seattle)
University of Michigan	University of Wisconsin
University of Minnesota	Yale University

5. J. Kenneth Little, *A Survey of Federal Programs in Higher Education: Summary* (Washington, D.C., U.S. Office of Education Bulletin, No. 5, 1963).

Federal Involvement in Education

In 1960 the twenty top institutions received 89 per cent of the Atomic Energy Commission money expended through universities, 88 per cent of the NASA funds, 83 per cent of the Department of Defense university grants, 54 per cent of NSF research grants, and 54 per cent of National Institutes of Health grants.

These institutions also had the largest numbers of graduate students and awarded 52 per cent of all the doctorates in science granted in 1957–58. Moreover, they were spending the most money on research and were training the greatest numbers of graduate students in the 1930s, when federal government support was negligible. Nevertheless, it is now a policy of the government to expand the numbers of strong university centers for graduate work. The President's Science Advisory Committee in 1960 said, "Existing strong institutions cannot fully meet the nation's future needs. We must hope that where there were only a handful of generally first-rate academic centers of science a generation ago and maybe as many as fifteen or twenty today, there will be thirty or forty in another fifteen years." [6]

Since 1960 there has been a broadening of government research grants to a wider range of universities. In 1962 there were more than a hundred universities conducting research for the government at a rate of more than $1 million each annually.

Another problem is that of concentration of federal funds in certain limited areas of research. Table 2 shows the concentration in the physical and life sciences. Whereas the government paid 80 per cent of the cost of university research in the physical sciences in 1957–58, it paid only 38 per cent of the cost of social science research. At Harvard in 1960–61 federal agencies provided $3.9 million for work in the natural sciences (excluding grants to the Medical School and the School of Public Health), $0.6 million for work in the social sciences, and $0.06 million for work in the humanities. In general, the social sciences got about 5 per cent of the federal research dollar in 1960–64. Within the social sciences, psychology got about 50 per cent of government funds, economics about 45 per cent, and the remaining 5 per cent was spread over sociology, anthropology, political science, history, and so on. The

6. The President's Science Advisory Committee, *Scientific Progress, the Universities, and the Federal Government* (Washington, D.C., U.S. Government Printing Office, 1960), p. 14.

Effects of Federal Support of Science

reason generally given for the favored positions of psychology and economics is that they employ more mathematics and more "objective" methods—that is, they are the social sciences most like the physical sciences.

Table 2. Distribution of Federal Research Funds by Fields

| | | Fiscal year | |
| | 1962 | 1963 | 1964* |
		(in millions of dollars)	
Biological sciences	97.9	136.7	189.5
Medical sciences	198.0	242.8	270.7
Agricultural sciences	21.1	23.7	27.7
Psychological sciences	27.6	33.5	48.9
Social sciences	18.0	23.0	31.3
Other sciences	1.6	1.9	2.1
Physical sciences, proper	618.1	793.2	1,031.0
Mathematical sciences	22.6	29.2	42.5
Engineering sciences	80.4	111.2	138.4
Total federal funds for basic research	1,085	1,395	1,782

Source: National Science Foundation, *Federal Funds for Research, Development, and Other Scientific Activities*, Vol. XII.
* These are estimates based on the budget requests for 1964.

With such large amounts of government money going to so many different persons and institutions, the whole research activity of higher education has come to depend very largely on the government, and it is important that the procedures as well as the policies of government support be aimed at high quality work as well as at building a large and stable research program. Individual persons and institutions must be satisfied with the methods of evaluating research proposals and the methods of administering funds. They must see these procedures as objective and fair to all concerned.

The most significant postwar act of the federal government in relation to the universities was the establishment of the National Science Foundation. This was called for by Vannevar Bush, head of the wartime Office of Scientific Research and Development, in his book *Science—The Endless Frontier*. The Foundation was established by the government in 1950. It is headed by a director appointed by the president and is governed by a National Science

Board of twenty-four scientists responsible for approving the awards of research grants and fellowships. Congress directed the National Science Foundation "to strengthen basic research and education in the sciences—throughout the United States—and to avoid undue concentration of such research and education." The functions of the NSF were classified as follows: the promotion, support, and coordination of basic scientific research; the awarding of scholarships and fellowships for study in science; the fostering of international scientific cooperation; and the acquisition and dissemination of information regarding scientific and technical personnel. Here, at last, was what the scientists had been looking for—an agency with money to spend on the advancement of basic science that was not dominated by the practical aims of military defense, conquest of space, agricultural productivity, or the curing of disease. Those who favor federal support for university research generally wish to see the NSF share of the government's research dollar increased.

From the point of view of one interested in the functions of education in the emergent society, the most important event of the year 1965 may have been the introduction in the Congress of bills to establish a National Humanities Foundation or a National Arts Foundation. These bills would establish for the humanities and arts one or two government-supported foundations analogous in structure and function to the National Science Foundation. In one of the bills, the Foundation is authorized and directed:

1. To develop and encourage the pursuit of a national policy for the promotion of scholarship, education, research, and creative work and performance in the humanities and the arts;

2. To insure that suitable means (including grants, loans, and other forms of assistance) are provided for educating and developing scholars and teachers in the humanities and the arts, and artists, at any stage of their growth;

3. To assist by institutional grants, loans, and other means, public and other nonprofit organizations concerned with encouraging and developing scholars and teachers in the humanities, and artists, in order to enable each institution to develop its own program of research and instruction; and to initiate and promote by contracts, grants, and loans, programs to improve teaching in the humanities and arts;

4. To award scholarships and graduate fellowships, including postdoctoral fellowships, and grants for research and for creative work and performance in the humanities and the arts;

5. To foster the improvement of library and museum resources and services for research and for teaching at all levels in the humanities and the arts, and to foster the interchange of information in the humanities and the arts in the United States and with other countries.

The Humanities Foundation may become the source of federal government support for a vast program aimed at raising the level of culture in the United States. It may assist not only schools and colleges but also artists and others interested in the performing arts. It may move in the directions outlined by a report published by the Rockefeller Brothers Fund in 1965 on "The Performing Arts: Problems and Prospects." This report calls on the government to provide a sum between $40 and $60 million annually to subsidize:

> Fifty permanent theater companies, approximating the metropolitan areas with populations of more than 500,000, sufficiently large to support year-round resident theater.
>
> Fifty symphony orchestras, which would provide, along with full-orchestra concerts, musicians for smaller musical groups.
>
> Six regional opera companies, offering short seasons in several metropolitan areas not yet ready to support year-round performances. These would be in addition to the present four major resident companies and two permanent national touring companies.
>
> Six regional choral groups.
>
> Six regional dance companies in addition to the two major resident dance groups already established.

In an affluent society the responsibilities of education may reasonably be extended to include the quality of the use of leisure time by its citizens. Such a change may occur in the United States during the coming decades.

FEDERAL SUPPORT OF PUBLIC EDUCATION

Events of the 1950s and early 1960s brought the federal government obliquely into the position of supporting education at all age levels. Support for higher education and research in universities was demanded by the growing need of the economy and of the defense establishment for trained manpower and for research. Support for new forms of vocational education and for work experience programs was demanded by the presence of large and growing numbers of unemployed and unemployable youth. Support for elementary school and preschool education was demanded by the growing numbers of socially disadvantaged children in the slums of big cities. All these forms of support were demanded from the federal government because the state and local tax systems were not developing an ability to raise the money needed for educational and other local and state needs. The federal government had easier access to tax money. But there was still no system of direct federal support of public education. Except for the support of vocational education the federal government was in theory providing emergency support that would assist education for a short time and would help to bring about innovation. A great deal of the federal government's participation has been developed through the National Defense Education Act of 1958. Although the law was passed when the nation was technically in a state of emergency, few people expect to see the federal government withdraw from the field of education entered under this law. Almost all of the nation's two thousand colleges and universities now participate in some kind of federal program. They get low-cost long-term loans for buildings, and their students get government loans and government scholarships. The federal government's move into the field of student support with the GI Bill after World War II has in effect been continued by the NDEA provisions for graduate student fellowships and for loans to college students.

A major question raised in connection with the NDEA is whether the federal government should direct its aid to students or to institutions or to both. The National Science Foundation has also been involved quite directly in the affairs of colleges and universities through its interest in training people for scientific careers. Its Division of Scientific Personnel and Education has become a power in education. Its fellowships for graduate students and for teachers of science and mathematics started in 1951 with $1.5 million and have steadily expanded to include seven major fellowship programs in 1960 and two international fellowship programs started in that year. Funds for the support of education in the sciences grew from $1.5 million in 1952 to $70 million in 1961, most of which went into the training of people. Most of these funds have gone to people in the natural sciences and mathematics, a small amount to people in the behavioral sciences, and nothing to people in the humanities. This has understandably influenced the distribution of graduate students among the various fields of knowledge.

The newly created National Aeronautics and Space Administration moved quickly into the field of education by supporting research and the training of space scientists. And throughout the period from 1950 to 1965 the National Institutes of Health increased their support of university research and training of research scientists.

Perhaps the Russians deserve the credit for pushing the federal government into the schools. The move might have come anyway, even if Sputnik had not been launched, because the great postwar economic boom combined with the low birthrate of the 1930s depression to produce an enormous demand for well trained and able young men and women that could not easily be met. This caused people to ask why the schools were not turning out more college graduates and more young people with high scientific and mathematical achievement. The National Defense Education Act was an effort to meet this situation through training people for guidance work in secondary schools, through training more teachers of foreign language for secondary and elementary schools, and through paying for research in visual education.

While the NDEA was attacking a part of the problem, the National Science Foundation turned its attention to science and mathematics teaching in the secondary and elementary schools. Since science and mathematics teachers were in short supply because of the competition between industry and schools for the services of people trained in these areas, the NSF began giving supplemental training to high school teachers to improve their ability to teach science and mathematics. At about the same time the NSF became interested in the subject matter of school science and mathematics and began to support several major curriculum projects. Eventually the NSF started a program of identification and motivation of high school students gifted in science by providing special summer schools for them. In 1961, $1.75 million was spent on institutes for 6,400 superior high school students. From 1952 to 1961 inclusive the NSF spent $52 million on projects in science and mathematics education. It is estimated in 1960 and 1961 that NSF sponsored institutes reached between 10 and 20 per cent of the nation's high school teachers of science and mathematics. Millions of dollars were allocated to the Physical Sciences Study Committee, the School Mathematics Study Group, and the Biological Science Curriculum Study. As of 1961 the Foundation had supported more than fifteen projects in science education. Approximately 85 per cent of all program expenditures went for secondary school curriculum projects. By 1965 the National Defense Education Act was revised to include activities quite different from its original and continuing program. Money was made available to train guidance personnel for elementary schools, to train teachers for culturally deprived children, including teachers for preschool classes, and to train school librarians. In 1964 the Economic Opportunity Act put the federal government behind an extension of the primary schools downward to preschool ages and an extension of the secondary schools outward to provide educational work experience for people sixteen to twenty-one who had dropped out of school. In 1965 the Aid to Education Act provided $1.06 billion to public school systems to supplement the education of children of families at the poverty level.

THE MONEY COST OF EDUCATION

During this century there has been a great increase in the real money spent on education, even after allowance is made for shrinkage in the purchasing power of the dollar. American schools have traditionally been financed locally. Even though the states were responsible for a system of public education, they generally left it to the local community—town, township, or county. In the field of higher education the states were slow to move, though most of them were supporting a university by 1900. Public school education was supported to the extent of 75 per cent of its cost by local school districts in 1929. Then the states began to support local schools from

Table 3. Cost of Education in the United States, 1900–60
(In millions of dollars, at current prices)

School year	Elementary and secondary schools		Colleges and universities	Total	GNP* (in billions of dollars)	Per cent of GNP
1899–1900	233	19	40	292	17	1.7
1909–10	450	50	81	581	35	1.7
1919–20	967	215	184	1,366	85	1.6
1929–30	1,950	750	535	3,235	104	3.1
1939–40	1,500	1,000	740	3,240	91	3.6
1949–50	4,300	2,350	2,130	8,780	258	3.4
1955–56	8,550	4,300	3,950	16,800	397	4.2
1957–58	11,200	5,100	4,850	21,150	443	4.8
1959–60	12,590	5,435	6,616	24,641	483	5.1
1961–62	21,200		8,230	29,430	518	5.7
1963–64	24,100		9,600	33,700	585	5.8

Sources: Adapted from U.S. Office of Education, *Digest of Educational Statistics, 1964.* Table 112. Theodore W. Schultz, "Capital Formation by Education," *Journal of Political Economy*, 68:571-583, 1960.
* The Gross National Product is for the calendar year in which the school year commences.

state funds, and the federal government limited itself to assistance to vocational education. In 1962 local districts paid 55 per cent of the cost of public elementary and secondary education, the states paid 40 per cent, and the federal government paid 5 per cent. By this time the cost of higher education was being borne substantially by state and federal government.

Approximately three times as much of the Gross National Product (GNP) was spent on education in 1960 as in 1900 (see Table 3). Adjusted for the dollar's purchasing power, the resources allocated to education were multiplied twenty times between 1900

Federal Involvement in Education

and 1956. According to Schultz and other economists this was an investment in the development of human capital that paid very good profits.[7] People received more education, which made them more efficient producers, increased their own earning power, and increased the productivity of the economy in which they worked. With about 6 per cent of the GNP going into education, the United States invests relatively more in education than most countries. (At the Conference on Education and Economic development held at Santiago, Chile, in March 1962, the assembled Ministers of Education of the South American countries agreed on a goal of 4 per cent of the GNP for education in their respective countries. Most of the Latin American countries were spending 2 to 3 per cent of their GNP on education.)

If relatively more money is to be spent on education, the question concerning the expansion of federal government support will be raised more and more forcefully. In one way or another, federal support of education appears to be inevitable. A principal barrier to federal assistance for elementary and secondary schools is the unwillingness of Roman Catholic voters to see federal funds go to public schools and not to church-maintained schools. Meanwhile, in various ways the federal government has increased its support of elementary and secondary education and has taken an increasing share of the cost of both private and public higher education since World War II.

For eighty years after the federal government started to aid higher education through the Morrill Act the pace of federal advance into the support of education was deliberate and largely limited to support of vocational education. Then, after 1955, the government plunged into support of education and of research in educational institutions. By 1966 the federal government was spending some $4.5 billion on education and research, or 13 per cent of the national bill. Except for support of vocational education, none of this money was for basic support of established educational programs; it was for expansion of educational services, for improvement of education, and for support of graduate and undergraduate students.

In 1962 the National Aeronautics and Space Administration se-

7. Theodore Schultz, "Capital Formation by Education," *Journal of Political Economy, 68* (1960), 571–83.

lected ten universities to train ten graduate students each to become space scientists. Each university was given $1.5 million for a space-science laboratory and $200,000 for the cost of maintaining and teaching ten students over a four-year period. This is probably the largest investment yet made in the beginning of a twentieth-century career.

Four major centers of educational research and development were founded in the early 1960s at Harvard, the University of Pittsburgh, the University of Wisconsin, and the University of Oregon. Each of these has a budget of the order of $1 million per year, largely provided by the federal government. The Education Act of 1965 provided $100 million to give initial support to a number of regional centers for educational research and development. It is likely that thirty to forty such centers will be established by 1970 to test and demonstrate improved educational procedures and to disseminate information about them.

An example of federal financing of research and development in the field of education is given by the story of Educational Services Incorporated, a nonprofit corporation located in the Boston area and relying heavily on college and school teachers in that region for its leading ideas. Even before ESI was founded, the Physical Sciences Study Committee was started in 1956 by a group of university physicists, of whom Jerrold Zaccharias of MIT was the leading spirit. They felt that physical science teaching in the secondary schools was out of date and needed a thorough overhaul. In the first year the NSF gave them $300,000 to begin their work. They formed writing committees to prepare new teaching materials, organized groups of high school teachers to try out these materials, gave them teachers' manuals, prepared kits of simple and cheap laboratory apparatus, put demonstration lectures on film, and began writing a series of paper back books on various aspects of physical science. The PSSC became a part of Educational Services Incorporated, which developed a variety of international as well as national programs. In 1958 the NSF contributed $443,000, the Ford Foundation $500,000, and the A.P. Sloan Foundation $250,-000. Other grants followed to support projects costing an average of $1.5 million a year from 1959 through 1961. The federal government's Agency for International Development provided $3.2 million for the Kanpur-Indo American Program for 1962–65 as well

Federal Involvement in Education

as $172,500 for a program introducing the PSSC ideas to African education. After 1961 ESI went into the field of elementary science instruction with an NSF grant of $231,500.[8] The Physical Sciences Study Committee estimated that by 1963–64 approximately four thousand high school physics teachers were using its materials and methods as their principal resource—at least half of the physics teachers of the country. By 1963 ESI was working in thirteen project areas, including physical science at the elementary, secondary and college levels, mathematics in elementary and secondary schools, microbiology, engineering, semiconductor electronics, and social studies and humanities. Educational development projects were being conducted with federal government support in Africa, Afghanistan, and India.

PROBLEMS OF CONTROL AND COORDINATION

Before World War II much university research was done with support from the private foundations such as Rockefeller, Carnegie, Russell Sage, and Commonwealth. The typical foundation is governed by a board of trustees that employs a staff to evaluate proposals and requests. The staff advises the trustees concerning approval or disapproval of these proposals and requests. A staff officer is expected to be well informed in his field, a good judge of men and of research proposals, and objective or neutral in his attitudes toward institutions and people who might receive grants.

The government agencies developed a different procedure for evaluating research proposals. Their own staff members were generally not so well prepared to evaluate proposals as the typical foundation executive. However, the agencies with largest research grant programs developed a system of advisory panels consisting of research specialists, usually on university faculties, who studied proposals, sometimes made visits to get more information, and then recommended action to councils also consisting of experienced re-

8. *Progress Report, Educational Services Incorporated* (Watertown, Mass., 1962).

search persons who were not regular government employees. Thus, a researcher who made an application for funds was judged by a panel of his peers, usually people a little better informed than he about the general area of his research. This procedure was used by the National Institutes of Health, which in 1963 awarded 15,233 grants totalling $425 million, and by the National Science Foundation, which provided 2,657 grants in 1963 for a total of $112 million. However, some fifteen agencies relied entirely upon their own staff to evaluate applications.

This procedure for making government grants and other aspects of government procedure and policy were under a searching study by the House Select Committee on Government Research, chaired by representative Carl Elliott. That committee proposed to make ten studies, the first of which was completed and reported in 1964.[9] This report found that the ten universities that received 38 per cent of federal research funds had somewhat more than a third of the members of review panels on their faculties. This might lead one to suppose that the review panels were likely to support proposals from their own institutions even though an individual panel member generally withdrew from the consideration of proposals from his institution. However, the same ten universities awarded 32 per cent of the Ph.D. degrees granted in 1960–63 and clearly were the outstanding research centers. The House Committee also asked the grantee institutions to express the degree of their satisfaction or dissatisfaction with the procedures used by various government agencies in making and administering research grants. On the whole, the grantee institutions expressed a "reasonable" level of satisfaction. No doubt the Congress will continue this type of evaluation of the federal fund-granting organizations from time to time, since they are now and probably will continue to be the major supporters of research.

The principal agencies for federal aid to education are the United States Office of Education and the National Science Foundation, with the National Humanities Foundation as a strong future organization. One of the important problems of government policy

9. U.S. House of Representatives, Select Committee on Government Research, *Study Number 1, Administration of Research and Development Grants* (Washington, D.C., U.S. Government Printing Office, 1964).

Federal Involvement in Education

during the next five years is to work out an efficient division of labor and responsibility among these agencies.

For 1964–65 the National Science Foundation received $420 million, its largest budget up to that date. The bulk of this money goes to universities for the support of research and training in the sciences. However, a considerable sum goes to projects for the improvement of education in the sciences and mathematics in secondary schools. The NSF has supported the secondary school programs of the Physical Sciences Study Committee, the Biological Sciences Curriculum Study, the Chemical Education Materials Study, the Chemical Board Approach Project, and the School Mathematics Study Group.

Since 1955 the U.S. Office of Education has had the assignment of administering large funds under the National Defense Education Act of 1963, the Higher Education Facilities Act, and the Federal Aid to Education Act of 1965. In addition, the USOE administers the Cooperative Research Program, in which grants are made to universities for research on educational problems; at first they were limited to problems of mental retardation, then were expanded to cover research on gifted children, and were later extended to cover a variety of aspects of education, including international comparisons of educational methods and educational efficiency. Thus the Office of Education has become a larger source of funds for educational experimentation than such private foundations as the Ford Foundation, the Kellogg Foundation, and the Carnegie Corporation.

The Office of Education was reorganized in 1962 to take account of its emerging functions. A staff Committee on the Mission and Organization of the Office of Education reported that the Office of Education "must assume the role of a voice of conscience within the Federal Government, speaking for the long-term national interest in education, in contrast to the voices that speak of a shorter-range federal interest in the many uses to which education can be put." [10] The Committee suggested the following as the functions of the Office of Education:

1. Carrying out established Federal policy in the field of education.

10. *A Federal Education Agency for the Future* (Washington, D.C., U.S. Government Printing Office, 1961).

2. Being the Federal Government's educational auditor, to keep account of what is going on in the field of education.

3. Carrying out a developing policy in the field of international aspects of education.

4. Formulating national policy in the field of education.

There are many educators who doubt the wisdom of giving this much policy-making power to the United States Office of Education. Among them are the supporters of an expanded National Science Foundation. These two agencies are becoming rivals for the power that goes with money for research and development in the field of education.

With the responsibility of allocating large sums for educational research and development, the choices made by the National Science Foundation and the U.S. Office of Education of what to support, what to encourage, and what not to support are bound to have an influence on educational policy. In effect, since 1960 the federal government has supported two major educational policy-making bodies, neither of which had a policy-making function four years earlier. Some of the policy questions now affected by federal government action are:

1. What directions should vocational education take in the light of contemporary trends in the labor force?

2. What should educational agencies do about unemployed youth in the age range sixteen to twenty-one?

3. Should public education extend below age five for children of socially disadvantaged families?

4. How should science and mathematics be taught in the elementary and secondary schools?

5. What proportion of college-age youth should go to college?

6. Should the federal government concentrate aid for scientific research and training in a small number of leading universities, or should the government deliberately assist average universities to improve their research and training programs?

According to the report by Representative Edith Green of Oregon, "The Federal Government and Education," in 1963 there were forty-two government agencies and departments involved in educational activities. Some of these programs overlap, and some are administered with little or no knowledge of other similar government programs. Mrs. Green proposed:

Federal Involvement in Education

1. Creation within the executive branch of the government of an Interagency Council on Education to coordinate the educational activities of all federal agencies and departments.

2. Creation of a nonlegislative Joint Congressional Committee on Education to provide the Congress with an overall picture of federal educational activities and educational needs.

3. Combining the Office of Education and the National Science Foundation, the only two agencies of the federal government whose primary concern is education.

Another proposal is that the National Science Foundation should take responsibility for higher and graduate education while the Office of Education takes responsibility for elementary and secondary education.

EDUCATION AS AN INSTRUMENT OF SOCIAL CHANGE

The fact that we have spoken so often of the uses to which education is put by the society is significant of a strong tendency to use education consciously and explicitly as an agent of society for making certain changes and achieving certain purposes. We are much more clear about the instrumental character of education than we were in 1900. We have found the educational system to be an effective agent for technological development, and we have found it to be our best instrument for dealing with the perplexing social problems of the twentieth century—from assimilation of the European immigrant to assimilation of the southern rural immigrant, and for meeting problems of juvenile delinquency and unemployment.

No doubt we will continue to use education for the solution of social problems, and no doubt we will expand the educational system, with more and more use of federal government funds for national purposes.

At the same time, we will become more sophisticated in our use of education. We know that education in itself is seldom the sole agent of change. When we want to use education to reduce unemployment of young people, we do not simply pass a law requiring them to stay longer in school. We know that education must be adapted to the special characteristics and needs of youth who drop out of school early and then remain unemployed. If we want to use education for improvement of citizenship, we know that we must ask ourselves what kind of education contributes to good citizenship in the emergent society. Should we have more history and more science? Should we create new secondary school courses in world geography and world politics? Or perhaps we should emphasize in the elementary and secondary schools the habits and skills of independent learning so that our graduates may continue to study and learn in the area of citizenship all their lives.

The conscious use of education to assist in desirable social change will probably expand in two related areas. The area of social urban renewal depends on the skillful adjustment of the school system to plans for metropolitan development. At the same time, the use of schools to supplement families which are doing an inadequate job of rearing children for participation in modern society will certainly be extended when current studies with culturally deprived children indicate the best ways for doing this. Education is used by people who know what they want and who understand how it works or can be made to work. Education gives power, when skillfully used.

CHAPTER FOURTEEN

The Rise of Big Government

THE BIGGEST OF THE BIG ORGANIZATIONS

Not one of the other great hierarchies in the United States today is so complex, so extended vertically and externally, or coordinates such a great diversity of people and activities as the federal government. None shows such a high division of social labor and such infinite specialization as the complex of departments and interdependent agencies whose combined duties and activities extend to all parts of the world and to every corner of America. The elaborate social structures of the great corporations manage and directly control a highly diversified, powerful technology, yet today their great empires are less extended and powerful than the federal system. The structures of national associations and educational, and church institutions are complex and, in bigness, of a kind with the federal government, but each has a smaller and simpler structure.[1]

M. H. Stans, recently Director of the Budget, succinctly summarized this diversity and immensity:

> The United States government is the world's biggest spender, lender, borrower, employer, property owner, tenant, and insurer. The government taxes and spends more than $90 billion a year; employs 2.5 million civilians and 2.8 million

This chapter is by W. Lloyd Warner and John H. Trimm. See Notes on Authors.

1. The major portion of the evidence used in the chapters on government comes from official federal documents, most of which are listed at the end of this chapter. As an example of procedure, the charts and material used in Chapter 15 were developed from a combination of the statutory appropriations, the Congressional Directory, the Civil Service Commission Reports, and more recently the Budgets, the Organization Manuals, charts supplied by the department or agency, and departmental telephone directories. Other sources included the standard studies of some of the departments and agencies, reports on reorganization from committees and some of the more general professional treatises on the United States government.

560

military personnel; owns 767,766,434 acres of land; owns 421,620 buildings and leases 96,381,000 square feet of building space; has $15 billion in farm commodities and stockpiled strategic materials; owns $122 billion in military equipment; has lent $24 billion to veterans, home owners, business, farmers, and foreign countries. The United States government is big, any way you look at it.

As the social system of the American national community evolves and the localities and regions lose part of their autonomy and as more social, political, and economic functions move into the national sphere, most of the newly emerged activities and many of the more traditional ones come under the control of, or are strongly influenced by, the great hierarchies of the federal government. Science advances under federal funds and guidance, and new agencies, such as the National Aeronautics and Space Administration (NASA) and the Atomic Energy Commission (AEC), appear. Health, educational achievement, and the advancement of knowledge are increasingly defined as national concerns—not just as individual pursuits but as duties and goals of the whole society. The welfare and protection of the less fortunate and the dependent are no longer only a private obligation, and new and old agencies are represented in the cabinet as parts of the Department of Health, Education and Welfare.

In less than a generation the seemingly stodgy Department of Agriculture has quietly and doggedly achieved an agrarian economic and social revolution. The department and its collaborators, including the universities, transformed the land and its people by harnessing the botanical and biological sciences; their field men and agencies spread out into the farms and towns of rural America. The Agriculture Department preceded all other institutions, including corporations, as an organization of research and development men who successfully put their new scientific technology to work and revolutionized American rural life. What the Russian and Chinese Communist national systems are trying to do now has already been done in America. Our present problems are not hunger and inadequate production but surpluses, overproduction, and imbalances in distribution. As the society grows, as the national moral order takes over responsibilities—including those that will necessarily emerge

The Rise of Big Government

from an advancing technology, a changing population, and a growing society—the hierarchies of the national government will necessarily play a stronger role in the intimate lives of individual Americans and in the social, economic, and political areas of the local and national communities.

FROM THE BEGINNING

The first President began the task of fashioning a new national government after the adoption of the Constitution. Vestiges of the prior confederation were carried into the new order, but most aspects were allowed to fade. Using the concept of a cabinet, President Washington created four positions: Secretaries of State, of War, and of the Treasury, and the Attorney General. The Departments of State, of War, and of the Treasury were also created. The Post Office, which had been established under the Articles of Confederation, continued to exist with a Postmaster General but under the supervision of the Secretary of the Treasury. The President made his appointments subject to the confirmation of the Senate. The same procedure of presidential appointment and Senate confirmation was followed for several other government positions.

During President Washington's term the total number of federal government civilian employees ranged between 800 and 1,000, with 1,300 military personnel; in 1960 there were some seventy major departments, agencies, and bureaus. Table 1 indicates the number of each type—cabinet, independent agency or department, legislative department, and the executive office of the President— operating for each decade for the past 140 years. However, we are not looking at the same structures in each decade, for the continually evolving process has brought additions, dropouts, and combinations. In most cases agencies defined as temporary have not been included in the count. Although the President always had secretarial and other assistants, these positions were not formalized and other units created or added until 1939.

In 1900 there were only seventeen major departments and independent agencies of the federal government; by 1930 there were thirty-nine, primarily independent agencies. The cabinet had two additions—the Departments of Commerce and of Labor—and the legislative group added the General Accounting Office. In the period 1930–60 the number of independent agencies as well as the total number of all departments and agencies nearly doubled; de-

Table 1. Number of Independent Departments, Agencies, and Bureaus, 1820–1960

Year	Cabinet	Independent agencies and departments	Legislative departments	Executive* office (President)	Total
1960	10ᶜ	47	5	8	70ᵈ
1950	9	40	5	7	61
1940	10	29	5	5	49
1930	10	24	5	0	39
1920	10	17	4	0	31
1910	9	5	4	0	18
1900	8	5	4	0	17
1890	8	5	4	0	17
1880	7	3	4	0	14
1870	7	2	4	0	13
1860	7	1	4	0	12
1850	7	1	3	0	11
1840	6	0	3	0	9
1830	6ᵇ	0	3	0	9
1820	5ᵃ	0	3	0	8

* The President always had assistants and staff, but nothing was formalized until 1939.
a. The Cabinet consisted of the following: Secretaries of State, Treasury, War, Navy, and the Attorney General. The Justice Department was not created until 1870.
b. The Postmaster General was asked to join the Cabinet in 1829. The Post Office did not become an executive department until 1872. However, the Post Office had existed as a department prior to 1789 and was supervised by the Treasury after 1789.
c. Since 1960, the census date we use as a base line for this analysis, two departments have been added, the Department of Housing and Urban Development and the Department of Transportation. Certain independent agencies and bureaus from other departments have been transferred to them.
d. There is an additional group of 54 selected boards, committees, and commissions, primarily of a temporary or special nature. *U.S. Government Organizations Manual, 1961–62*, dated June 1, 1961. There are also international bilateral and multilateral organizations.

partments were created in what is now called the Executive Office of the President—a total of eight in 1960.

Table 2 presents by type the seventy different major departments, agencies, and bureaus that constituted the federal govern-

Table 2. Year of Establishment of Cabinet and Legislative Departments, Independent Agencies, and Executive Offices

Period of estab- lishment	Cabinet and legislative departments	Year of establishment	Independent agencies	Year of establishment	Executive offices of the President	Year of establishment
1789–99	State	1789				
	Treasury	1789				
	*War (see Defense)	1789				
	*Attorney General (see Justice)	1789				
	Architect of the Capitol	1793				
	*Navy (see Defense)	1798				
1800–49	Library of Congress	1800	Smithsonian Institution	1846		
	U.S. Botanical Gardens	1820				
	*Post Office	1829				
	Interior	1849				
1850–99	Government Printing Office	1860	District of Columbia	1878 (1790)		
	*Comm. of Agriculture (see Agriculture)	1862	Civil Service Commission	1883		
	Justice	1870	Interstate Commerce Commission	1887		
	Post Office (Cabinet status)	1872				
	Agriculture	1889				
1900–24	*Commerce and Labor (see Commerce; Labor)	1903	Commission on Fine Arts	1910		
	Commerce	1913	*The Panama Canal (see Canal Zone Government)	1912		
	Labor	1913	Federal Reserve System	1913		
	General Accounting Office	1921	Federal Trade Commission	1915		
			*Nat'l Advisory Committee for Aeronautics (see Nat'l Aeronautics & Space Administration)	1915		

1925–49

*Federal Security Agency (see Health, Education and Welfare) — 1939
*Air Force (see Defense) — 1947
Defense — 1949

American Battle Monuments Commission — 1923
*Board of Tax Appeals (see Tax Court of U.S.) — 1924
*U.S. Board of Mediation (see Nat'l. Mediation Board) — 1926
*Federal Radio Commission (see Federal Communications Commission) — 1927
Veterans Administration — 1930
Federal Deposit Insurance Corporation — 1933
Tennessee Valley Authority — 1933
*Alley Dwelling Authority (see Nat'l. Capitol Housing Authority) — 1933
National Mediation Board — 1934
Federal Communications Commission — 1934
Securities & Exchange Commission — 1934
Nat'l. Labor Relations Board — 1935
Railroad Retirement Board — 1935
Civil Aeronautics Board — 1938
*Federal Farm Board (see Farm Credit Admin.) — 1939 (1933) (1929)
Tax Court of the U.S. — 1942

Bureau of the Budget — 1939
White House Office — 1939
Council of Economic Advisers — 1946
National Security Council — 1947
Central Intelligence Agency — 1947

* Indicates units that have been superseded by, or incorporated into, later units. Reference is made to the later unit.

Table 2. Year of Establishment of Cabinet and Legislative Departments, Independent Agencies, and Executive Offices (*cont.*)

Period of establishment	Cabinet and legislative departments	Year of establishment	Independent agencies	Year of establishment	Executive offices of the President	Year of establishment
1925–49 (cont.)			Nat'l. Capitol Housing Authority	**1943**		
			*War Contracts Adjustment Board (see Renegotiation Board)	**1944**		
			Export-Import Bank of Washington	**1945** (1939) (1934)		
			Indian Claims Commission	**1946**		
			Atomic Energy Commission	**1946**		
			Federal Mediation and Conciliation Service	**1947**		
			Housing and Home Finance Agency	**1947**		
			Selective Service System	**1947**		
			*Panama Railroad Company (see Panama Canal Co.)	**1948** (1904)		
			*War Claims Commission (see Foreign Claims Settlement Commission)	**1948**		
			General Services Admin.	**1949**		
			*Virgin Islands Company (see Virgin Islands Corporation)	**1949** (1934)		
1950–60	Health, Education and Welfare	**1953**	National Science Foundation	**1950**	Advisory Committee on Government Organization	**1953**
			Subversive Activities Control Board	**1950**	National Aeronautics and Space Council	**1958**
			Renegotiation Board	**1951**		
			Panama Canal Company	**1951**		

1950–60 (cont.)

Board of Review	1952
Nat'l. Capitol Planning Commission	1952 (1926) (1924)
Farm Credit Administration	1953
Small Business Admin.	1953
U.S. Information Agency	1953
Foreign Claims Settlement Commission	1954
St. Lawrence Seaway Development Corporation	1954
District of Columbia Redevelopment Land Agency	1954 (1949) (1946)
Federal Home Loan Bank Board	1955 (1947) (1932)
Federal Aviation Agency	1958
Nat'l. Aeronautic & Space Administration	1958
Development Loan Fund	1958 (1957)
Virgin Island Corporation	1958
Nat'l. Capitol Transportation Agency	1960

* Indicates units that have been superseded by, or incorporated into, later units. Reference is made to the later unit.

The Rise of Big Government

ment in 1960–61 with their founding dates and indicates the evolution of the total structure of the federal government through time. Only those units that have persisted are listed; when pertinent, other significant dates in the life history of the unit are indicated. The classification for type of structure is the one used in the organization manuals of the federal government. The major additions during the nineteenth century were to the Cabinet, and in the twentieth century the independent agency became the main structural type.

The preponderant growth in numbers has been, first, in the independent agencies and, next, in the group immediately around the President. The agencies patterned after the original Interstate Commerce Commission have been a development of the post-Wilsonian period. The agency movement really began in the 1920s and was given great impetus by President Franklin D. Roosevelt. As a result of the emphasis on agencies forty years elapsed between the separation and creation of the Departments of Commerce and of Labor in 1913 and the establishment in 1953 of the Department of Health, Education and Welfare, previously included in the Federal Security Agency. The creation of the Defense Department caused a net decline in the total number of Cabinet departments in 1949.

As these independent entities increased in number, they have also increased in size. As each unit has become more complex in number of people employed, money spent, functions performed, and, in many cases, geographical spread, reorganization has streamlined and simplified the structure. The usual net effect, however, has been to increase the number of vertical layers and recombine the hierarchy horizontally, thus effecting more manageable form. (The evolution and elaboration of structure is the subject of the next chapter.)

The Post Office is the only department inherited from the Continental Congress and until recently was the largest employer in the federal government. It was the first major department that linked the various sections of the country through a communications network. Though primitive and slow at first, the postal system provided a necessary interconnection between the various sectors.

"By 1791, there were only 89 post offices and less than 2,000 miles of post roads; nine-tenths of the service was provided by riders on horseback and 324,000 letters were carried." [2] By 1960 there were 35,238 post offices in the United States with gross receipts of over $3 billion. The initial organization consisted of the Postmaster General, Chief Clerk, clerks, and seventy-five post offices distributed along the eastern coast of the United States. Additions and growth are indicated in Table 3. The top-level organizational structure has also been changed as increases were made. The office of the Second Assistant Postmaster General was added in 1810, the Third Assistant in 1836, and the Fourth in 1891; in 1948 they were replaced by the office of the Deputy Postmaster General and the offices of the Assistant Postmaster General for Operations, Transportation, Finance, and Facilities. The offices of Assistant Postmaster General for Personnel, of Chief Postal Inspector, and of General Counsel were established in 1952 as separate senior executive offices, and the Office of Research and Engineering was established in 1960.

Until the early 1900s the proportion of civilian workers employed by the Post Office was never less than half the total of all federal workers, but as its numbers increased enormously, so did the work force of other departments and agencies. The Defense Department rose from more than 2.0 per cent of the federal civilian work force in 1820 to about 44 per cent in 1960. All other departments and agencies held fairly steadily with 29 per cent in 1820 and 33 per cent in 1960.

A major thrust in the development of the federal government is the change from a domestically oriented nation to a dominant international power. Reflecting this transformation is the tremendous increase in the number employed by Defense, the 175,000 employees of the Veterans Administration, and the 158,000 persons employed outside the United States.

The second major thrust is the shift from a rural, agricultural society to an urban, industrial one. Although concerned with a continually declining percentage of the total population, the Department of Agriculture now employs approximately 100,000 people. Indicating the influences toward an urban, industrial, and welfare oriented society are the Department of Health, Education and Wel-

2. Chester Wright, *Economic History of the United States* (New York, McGraw-Hill, 1949), p. 219.

Table 3. Paid Civilian Employment of the Federal Government, 1820–1960

Year	Post Office		Defense		All other		Total number	
	N	%	N	%	N	%	N	%
1960	563,000	23.5	1,047,000	43.6	789,000	32.9	2,399,000	100
1950	484,679	24.7	753,149	38.4	722,880	36.9	1,960,708	100
1940	323,481	31.0	256,025	24.6	462,914	44.4	1,042,420	100
1930	297,895	49.6	108,462	18.0	194,962	32.4	601,319	100
1920	242,400	37.0	237,212	36.2	175,653	26.8	655,265	100
1910	209,005	53.8	58,320	15.0	121,383	31.2	388,708	100
1900	136,192	56.9	44,524	18.6	58,760	24.5	239,476	100
1890	95,449	60.6	20,561	13.1	41,432	26.3	157,442	100
1880	56,421	56.4	16,297	16.3	27,302	27.3	100,020	100
1870	36,696	71.9	1,183	2.3	13,141	25.8	51,020	100
1860	30,269	82.5	946	2.6	5,457	14.9	37,000	100
1850	21,391	81.4	403	1.5	4,480	17.1	26,000	100
1840	14,290	79.2	598	3.3	3,150	17.5	18,000	100
1830	8,764	76.3	377	3.3	2,350	20.4	11,500	100
1820	4,766	69.0	161	2.3	1,987	28.7	6,900	100

Sources: *Historical Statistics of the United States, Paid Civilian Employment of the Federal Government: 1816–1957*, Series Y 241–250; *1961 Annual Report, U.S. Civil Service Commission*, June 30, 1961.

fare, with approximately 70,000 employees, and the Housing and Home Finance Agency, employing about 12,000. Other departments related to this change within the society are the Departments of Commerce and of Labor (established at the turn of the twentieth century as one department and later separated) and such agencies as the Interstate Commerce Commission, which regulates, in the public interest, common carriers engaged in interstate commerce and foreign commerce as it takes place within the United States; the Federal Trade Commission, whose purpose is to maintain free competitive enterprise and prevent monopoly or deceptive trade practices; the Federal Power Commission, which regulates creation and sale of hydroelectric power in interstate commerce (including flood control in rivers and harbors) and the transportation and sale of natural gas; and the National Labor Relations Board, which prohibits certain unfair labor practices, designates appropriate units for collective bargaining, and conducts secret ballots to determine the exclusive representative of employees.

The Treasury Department, consisting of approximately 75,000 people, is another major employer. The fact that about two-thirds of the Treasury's employees are in the revenue service indicates the third major theme: the federal government has become a major collector and dispenser of funds.

The White House Group or Executive Office of the President was not given official status until the reorganization plan of 1939. However, in addition to the advisers and secretaries to the President, there are currently eight agencies and bureaus in the Executive White House Group, employing 2,880 people; over half of these are in Civil Defense Mobilization. The eight agencies and bureaus are the Bureau of the Budget, Council of Economic Advisers, National Aeronautics and Space Council, which advises the President on policies and programs in aeronautical and space activities, National Security Council, which advises the President on integration of domestic, foreign, and military policies relating to national security; Office of Civil and Defense Mobilization; President's Advisory Committee on Government Organization; the White House Office; and the Central Intelligence Agency (for which there is no count, but the number is in the thousands).

The departments and agencies responsible to the Congress and

The Rise of Big Government

known as the Legislative Group have increased in number of units by only one in the last hundred years, but each of these five organizations has grown considerably, with the total increase threefold in the last sixty years. The five units are the Architect of the Capitol, the Library of Congress, the United States Botanic Garden (all established by 1830), the Government Printing Office (1860), and the General Accounting Office (1921), which conducts an independent audit of government financial transactions and determines how well the agencies are handling their financial affairs.

The federal judiciary, consisting of the United States Supreme Court and the federal court system, has grown primarily in districts and number of judges and staff necessary to process the case load. The impact of the federal judiciary, however, cannot be measured by size and appropriations but by the range and scope of the cases accepted, the decisions rendered, and the implementation of these decisions.

Each decade since 1900 has been symbolized and sometimes dominated by certain personalities and administrations, and these are reflected in the types of emphasis given to the existing government organizations and the development of new ones: the first decade by T. Roosevelt and Taft, the second by Wilson, the third by Harding-Coolidge-Hoover, the fourth and fifth by F. D. Roosevelt and Truman, the sixth by Eisenhower, and the present by Kennedy and Johnson.

Theodore Roosevelt's interest in conservation is revealed in the development of the Bureau of Reclamation, the National Park Service, the bureau of Mines (Interior Department), the Forest Service, and the Bureau of Plant Industry (Agriculture Department). He also took a considerable interest in the renovation of the White House and established the Commission of Fine Arts. Two other significant developments were the creation of the Federal Bureau of Investigation (FBI), in the Justice Department, and the Bureau of Standards, in the Commerce Department. Roosevelt's interest in conservation, the thrust into the international political area, "trust busting" with increasingly effective government controls of economic affairs, and his "square deal" for everyone— which had welfare implications—set the stage for some of the structural–functional changes that were to take place in the federal government during the following fifty years.

Taft bridged the period between Roosevelt and Wilson. It is often said that Taft spent his four years legalizing what Roosevelt had done in the prior seven.

Among the several permanent achievements of the Wilson period, 1912 to 1920, were three major regulatory agencies—the Federal Trade Commission, the Federal Reserve System (for banking), and the Federal Power Commission. In agriculture there was the formalization of the Extension Service and the creation of the Farm Credit Administration. In labor and welfare there was the creation of the Childrens' Bureau, the Women's Bureau, the Conciliation Service, and the Employees' Compensation Commission. Recognition of our international commercial interests came with the establishment of the Bureau of Foreign and Domestic Commerce and the Tariff Commission. The National Advisory Committee for Aeronautics, established at this time, continued to function until NASA was formed in 1958.

The 1920s were a decade of strong contrasts—Harding, Coolidge, and Hoover—an era marked by a desire to return to "normalcy,"conservatism in the White House and other key places of the government, and a stock market constantly spiralling upward. The decade ended in the stock market crash and the worst depression the nation had yet experienced. Agriculture had been in a gradual economic decline during the entire decade.

Despite the espoused philosophy of limited government activities during the 1920s, increases in the federal government continued but under a policy of retrenchment from the international scene and a shoring up of the domestic economy with emphasis on efficiency in government. The Bureau of the Budget and the General Accounting Office were formed. In the area of reglation there were two major developments: the Food and Drug Administration, formalized from earlier beginnings, and the Federal Radio Commission, the forerunner of the Federal Communications Commission, were established. The Board of Tax Appeals, now known as the Tax Court of the United States, the American Battle Monuments Commission, the National Capital Park and Planning Commission, and the Mount Rushmore National Memorial Commission were created. Two research organizations were added—the Bureau of Home Economics and the Bureau of Dairy Industry. World War I led to the Veterans Administration.

THE AGENCY EXPLOSION SINCE THE 1930s

The 1930s, dominated by the great depression and the leadership of Franklin D. Roosevelt, was in sharp contrast to the prior decade. The society, in ferment and unrest, was ready to experiment with new theories and approaches to its problems. The decade is significant, not only for the new economic and social directions taken in efforts to solve the problems of internal and external economic imbalance but also because our way of life was threatened by another world war at the end of the period.

Roosevelt and his depression-solving administration were responsible for the alphabetical agency explosion of the 1930s. Beginning with the National Industrial Recovery Administration and its flying blue eagle symbol, all types of organizational units appeared with names abbreviated to initials. Many structures were of a temporary nature, but the more significant ones have persisted. Although the Federal Home Loan Bank Board and the Reconstruction Finance Corporation came at the close of the Hoover administration, because of their nature they have been identified with Roosevelt and his "New Deal."

The Federal Housing Administration and Federal Deposit Insurance Corporation were formed to aid in maintaining homes and securing savings deposits; the Securities and Exchange Commission, to prevent the issuance of fraudulent securities; the Federal Communications Commission, to police the airways; for the farmer and rural population, the Federal Crop Insurance Corporation, the Rural Electrification Administration, and the Tennessee Valley Authority; and finally for the industrial urban groups, the National Labor Relations Board and the Social Security Board. As a result of the wider range of new functions, the expanding role of the federal government in the society became that of a very energetic, active partner.

Roosevelt was retained in office in both 1940 and 1944. The society needed to be mobilized as never before to marshall and maintain the military effort. Numerous agencies and commissions were created to perform, facilitate, and coordinate all the new activities of a nation at war—raising manpower through the draft, raising money through war bond drives and increased taxation, allocation of food and materials through rationing and priorities, and the production of goods through control agencies. Of great interest during this period was a modus operandi between the government and private enterprises that made it unnecessary for the government to nationalize or own in order to control them. The willingness of all parties to cooperate creatively in exploring and establishing new ways of operating while maintaining the basic essences of the private enterprise system is very significant.

A major structural change in the 1940s was the merging of the three major military services into a Department of Defense. The Secretary of Defense is now a Cabinet officer, with the respective service secretaries subordinate to him. The Joint Chiefs of Staff was created, with a chairman appointed by the President.

A major technological development in the war was nuclear fission, and the Atomic Energy Commission was created to encourage its useful application. Also from the war came the Selective Service System and the Foreign Claims Settlement Commission of the United States, originally named the War Claims Commission.

Reflecting the internal developments of the society was the establishment of the Housing and Home Finance Agency (previously discussed); the Federal Mediation and Conciliation Service, a further extension of the federal government into labor–management relations; and the General Services Administration, an attempt to put together into one large government agency a number of housekeeping activities and functions previously performed by a variety of organizations.

In foreign affairs the United States' role in creating and actively maintaining the United Nations is in direct contrast to the withdrawal tactics and opposition to the League of Nations following World War I. In addition, the Marshall Plan—to assist foreign countries to re-establish themselves after World War II—and other aid programs were begun and a series of organizations created to administer them. The Economic Cooperation Administration, created in 1948, was absorbed by the Mutual Security Administration in 1951, which was transferred to the Foreign Operations Adminis-

The Rise of Big Government

tration in 1953 and succeeded by the International Cooperation Administration. This is the historical evolution of what is now the Agency for International Development. In addition, the Export–Import Bank, created in 1934, was given independent status in 1945, and the International Bank for Reconstruction and Development, more commonly known as the World Bank, started its operations in 1946. The United States had become a dominant power and was not able to retreat from its responsibilities after World War II.

In the 1950s, however, the country was marked by overtones of a desire to withdraw from international areas. The orientation was to maintain the basic fabric of the society and a strong economy as a means of fulfilling international and internal commitments and as an example in the international ideological battle with the Communist states. Concern was voiced that the economy might be strained because of the newly accepted international responsibilities. The development of the atomic bomb stimulated interest in the peaceful uses of atomic energy and things scientific. The National Science Foundation was created to stimulate research. Concern for the welfare of the businessman is reflected in the creation of the Small Business Administration, the St. Lawrence Seaway, and the independence of the Federal Home Loan Bank Board. The first Cabinet post to be created in forty years, but a logical extension from the last additions (departments of Commerce and of Labor), and reflecting the movement of tides within the society pertaining to industrialization, urbanization, and welfare, was the Department of Health, Education and Welfare.

The domestic issue of civil rights was sparked by the Supreme Court decision on school segregation in 1954. President Eisenhower followed the decision with enforcement actions and the creation of the Civil Rights Commission to support investigation into, and action on, the problem. With domestic reaction to international events came the Subversive Activities Control Board, the U.S. Information Agency, and the Development Loan Fund.

Advances in air travel and acceptance of it as a means of transportation that required governmental regulation brought about the creation of the Federal Aviation Agency. But the act that confirmed the fact that the 1950s introduced the air-space era was the Russians' successful launching of Sputnik I. This action significantly shook those in the society who were trying to retreat and relax. The creation of the National Aeronautics and Space Administration followed, and the American society began to take up the challenge and to stress the search for new knowledge and new ways of doing things.

FUNCTIONS ADOPTED BY THE
FEDERAL GOVERNMENT

In describing the functions of government, the Tenth Amendment to the Constitution reads:

> The powers not delegated to the United States by the Constitution, nor prohibited by it to the states, are reserved to the states respectively, or to the people.

Initially a distinction was made between the functions to be performed at the national level, state-local level, and those not to be performed by government at all but left to the people. When analyzing the functions of government and making comparisons among the three levels, these distinctions must be kept in mind; the federal government was delegated functions that no other level of government or the public was allowed to perform. But the federal government was also denied the right to perform certain functions.

How many of the functions currently being performed at the federal level were previously carried out at the state and (or) local level? If the function was previously performed at either the state and (or) local level, when did it shift to the federal level? Did the function continue to be performed in part or cooperatively with either one or both of the other levels? (The same function could be performed at all three levels simultaneously or at only one or two.)

How many of the functions currently being performed at the federal level were previously in the private sector (those functions that became public as the result of being taken over by the federal government rather than by a state or local government)?

The second case is not an example of transfer of function from

The Rise of Big Government

the local to the federal level but of a change in the role of the federal government within the greater society.

In the following tables 112 functions [3] of the federal government are compared. The statements of the functions are generalized to be appropriate for all levels of government—federal, state, or local. However, the functions are based on those performed by the federal government in 1960, thus leaving open the possibility that we are missing those that no longer exist but did exist in the early or middle period and those performed only at the state and local but not at the federal level. Thus, it may be misleading to make comparisons among the three levels without factoring out some functions or adding others.

In Tables 4 and 5 it is apparent that many, but not all, of the functions counted are performed by all levels of government. It is obvious that there has been an increase in government functions; it is very important to note that this is true at all government levels, contrary to the tendency to assume that it is only the federal government that has been increasing its range of functions. However, the tables show that, by our classification, the federal government has tended historically to perform more functions than the others. The reason is in part inherent in the structure, since only the fed-

3. The functions and activities performed by each department, agency, or bureau of the federal government were systematically examined. These were then listed and classified. All of these functions and activities were then generalized and classified apart from the government department etc. that might perform them. Just as any one department or agency might perform a number of functions and activities, so any particular function or activity might be performed by one or any number of departments, bureaus, and agencies.

Classification of departments, agencies, and bureaus listed as Foreign and Domestic—and within the Domestic—is on the basis of title and major orientation or individual specific.

To save space, we list here only ten of the eighteen broader functions and activities and a few examples of the 118 detailed ones. Under the major category, Protection of Rights (one of the eighteen), are five subcategories, among them civil rights, granting and protecting patents and copyrights, and Indian services and protection. Under Law Enforcement are sixteen, including liquor control, immigration and maritime controls, and operation of penal institutions. Health and Medical Protection services include inspection of food and drug products. Housing covers the operation and promotion of low-rent housing and four other subcategories. Education includes aid to education, school lunches, and four others; Social Services has eleven; Regulation of Business, such items as regulation of securities and exchange, regulation of competitive practices, and seven others; Conservation, nine activities; National Defense (air, navy, army, etc.) has eight; and Foreign Relations, six. Intergovernmental Services has six housekeeping and other functions.

eral government can coin money, conduct foreign relations, wage war, and so forth.

Other functions too may be performed at all three levels of government. Table 5 indicates that in the early period the federal government performed 73 per cent of the 37 government functions; the local level was next with 54 per cent. By the middle period the fed-

Table 4. Number of Functions Performed and Percentage of
Total Number of Functions Performed Today (112)

	Early (1790–1830)		Middle (1830–1900)		Recent (1900–1960)	
	N	%	N	%	N	%
Federal	27	24	46	41	112	100
State	13	12	17	15	58	52
Local	20	18	21	19	36	32

eral level handled 90 per cent of the functions, whereas the local had dropped from 54 per cent to 41 per cent. The local level is actually performing one more function, but relative to the overall increase in the number of functions performed by all government levels, there is a percentage decline. The implications of the data

Table 5. Number of Functions Performed and Percentage of Total
Number of Functions Performed during Each Period

	Early (1790–1830)		Middle (1830–1900)		Recent (1900–1960)	
	N	%	N	%	N	%
Federal	27	73	46	90	112	100
State	13	35	17	33	58	52
Local	20	54	21	41	36	32
Total number of functions for period	37	100	51	100	112	100

are that the process has involved not so much a transfer of functions from local to federal government as a delegation to the federal level of new functions as they are required by social and technological development.

For the society to survive, its functions and activities must be

The Rise of Big Government

related to its basic needs; they will be colored by each particular period. Factors in each period influence both the range of functions and activities and who or what body performs them. The evolution of the structures reflects the transition from a rural, agriculturally oriented to an urban and highly industrialized society and the emergence of the United States as one of the great world powers.

Welfare and Civil Rights Functions

In the colonial period and early days of the United States responsibility for what later became government functions, particularly what is known as welfare activities today, was with the family on an extended kin basis. For the needy who could not obtain help from family or private philanthropy, the public facilities were meager if not completely lacking. As the society's focus moved from agriculture to mercantilism and industrialization and as people gradually began to shift from rural to urban centers, the political "spoils system" was developing—first at the national level, with Jackson, and then at the state and, particularly, the local level, as a means of "taking care" of people. Not a private but a quasipublic system of welfare began to evolve, particularly in the urban areas.

Muckrakers, some of the early novelists, and others like Lincoln Steffens told eloquently how public monies were diverted by political office holders not only for their own enrichment but also to "look after" their constituents. Even today the number of municipal employees per unit of population is greater in the older major cities, those with long established city departments; the employee-population ratio is perhaps as much as double that of younger but equally large cities. Many reasons might be given for these differences, but it would seem that it is a legacy of the earlier patronage systems, which have for the most part been replaced by the systematization of many welfare functions.

The spoils system was the product of a transitional phase. The need for employing other means at the national level finally became apparent, and the U.S. Civil Service Commission was one of the first steps. With urbanization family size tended to decline; greater geographical and social mobility tended to reduce extended kinship ties; it thus became more difficult for the family to continue its welfare functions. These factors, together with the moral constraints aimed against the "corruption" associated with the political machines of the large urban areas, continued to force many of these functions into the public arena. To assure equal benefits to all the citizenry, wherever they might originate or elect to go, required that federal attention be given to those problems, although they might be handled locally.

More and more functions gradually became the concern of the many and were formally rationalized into the national system. Statements concerning civil rights appear in the Constitution, amendments to the Constitution, legislative acts, executive acts and policies, and departmental acts and policies. These documents and practices have generated directives charging existing departments with the responsibility for pertinent activities or functions, and new agencies have been created for their execution. The Department of Justice and the Attorney General have traditionally been charged with the major responsibility in the field of civil rights. However, the initial functions have been differentiated and elaborated over time to the point that in 1957 the Division of Civil Rights was established within the Justice Department. The filtration into other departments and agencies is demonstrated by the hiring policies reflected in the Civil Service Commission and appointments at higher levels. Also closely related is the President's Committee on Equal Employment Opportunity, which was formed by combining the President's Committees on Government Contracts and Government Employment to enforce and eliminate discriminatory practices in hiring. In addition, another agency was created, the Commission on Civil Rights, to investigate and report on cases involving civil rights. Originally intended to be a temporary two-year organization, this commission has been given extensions and, it appears, might achieve permanent status.

The term "civil rights" now has a very specific and rather narrow meaning, which is a product of the times. But the responsibilities of the Civil Rights Division of the Justice Department revive the breadth of the term; they include the "enforcement of all Federal statutes affecting civil rights, such as the Federal election laws, the Corrupt Practices Act, and the Hatch Act; and the laws relating to illegal deprivation of rights of citizens; obstruction of justice; peonage and slavery; illegal use of search warrants; custody, es-

The Rise of Big Government

cape, and sentence of Federal prisoners; and the protection of merchant seamen." [4]

In the earlier periods there was much concern about illegal search, extended detention without hearing or trial, and other points enumerated in the first ten amendments to the Constitution, the "Bill of Rights." The original concern and subsequent enforcement of the legislative acts protecting civil rights were not limited to minority or racially distinct groups but to the existing citizenry as a whole. Had this not been true, then these explicit statements would not have appeared in the Constitution.

Conservation and Loan Functions

Conservation covers a range of functions often thought to have a long history because the creation of the Interior Department dates back to 1849. Although it originally included the General Land Office, "the role of the Department of the Interior changed in the more than one hundred years of its existence from that of general housekeeper for the Federal Government to that of custodian of the nation's natural resources." [5]

Some legislative acts during the nineteenth century concerned conservation, but not until the close of the century was there an apparent awareness of what was happening to the country's natural resources. Under Theodore Roosevelt's administration came the first major accomplishments: the Bureau of Reclamation (1902), the Bureau of Plant Industry (1902), the Forest Service (1905), and the National Park Service (1906). The Bureau of Mines (1910), the Grazing Service (1934), and the Soil Conservation Service (1935) have been added.

The Fish and Wildlife Service is an example of how a diverse range of functions is eventually put together structurally. In 1871 a Commissioner of Fish and Fisheries was appointed to head the Fish Commission. In 1903, when the Department of Commerce and Labor was established, the Fish Commission became a section of the new department. When the Department of Commerce and Labor was separated in 1913, the Bureau of Fisheries remained

4. *U.S. Government Organization Manual*, 1961–62, p. 216.
5. Ibid., p. 236.

with the Commerce Department. It was transferred to the Interior Department in 1939. The Bureau of Biological Survey was established in 1905 as a part of the Division of Entomology in the Department of Agriculture, was transferred to the Interior Department in 1939, and was combined with the Bureau of Fisheries in 1940 to form the U.S. Fish and Wildlife Service.

While consolidation of older functions went on, elaboration of newer functions continued; the Federal Power Commission (1920), the Tennessee Valley Authority (1933), the Atomic Energy Commission (1946), the Outdoor Recreation Resources Review Commission (1958), and the St. Lawrence Seaway Development Corporation (1954) are examples of these newer independent conservation agencies. Whether by intent or otherwise, the conservation label has been a convenient device to use when the federal government felt it necessary to assert authority and control in a particular situation. Much that is done in the name of conservation is complex and designed to serve multiple ends.

Other subdivisions in the Interior Department are the Bonneville Power Administration, the Southeastern Power Administration, and the Southwestern Power Administration—for flood control, water power, and electric power. The Agriculture Department's Soil Conservation Service has its own program for soil and water control, which became particularly important in the 1950s in the Great Plains conservation program. The range of programs under the conservation label clearly illustrates that the resources to be conserved and the goals of conservation are subject to change and definition.

Another growing activity of the federal government is the lending of money. The recipients of government loans seem to break into at least the following four groups: (1) urban individuals who are lent money primarily for home purchase or improvement, (2) large and small business firms, (3) farmers, for home purchase and improvement and loans (and payments) for crops, soil conservation, storage, etc., and (4) war veterans.

The first major effort of the federal government in the lending business was the 1916 Federal Farm Loan Act. Although three years earlier the federal government had been instrumental in liberalizing credit terms to farmers in the Federal Reserve Act, the farmers' long-standing problem of not being able to obtain mort-

The Rise of Big Government

gages and other types of loans was not rectified. Other programs, administered through the Federal Land Banks, Federal Intermediate Credit Banks, the Production Credit Corporation, and Banks for Cooperatives, were instituted to assist the farmers and their organizations with financial problems.

Government lending on a grand scale was initiated in 1932 with the creation of the Reconstruction Finance Corporation (RFC), whose stated purposes were to aid in financing agriculture, commerce, and industry, to encourage small business, to help maintain the economic stability of the country, and to assist in promoting maximum employment and production. Although instituted during the Hoover administration as an antidepression measure, the agency was continued, expanded, and generally identified with the Roosevelt administration. Jesse Jones, then Chairman of the RFC, reported in 1939 that the Corporation had twenty different categories of loans reaching into almost every aspect of the economy.[6]

The Corporation persisted through World War II, undergoing several transfers and changes. Liquidation was started in 1954, and the Corporation was abolished in 1957; its remaining functions were transferred to the Housing and Home Finance Agency, General Services Administration, Treasury Department, and the Small Business Administration.

The Small Business Administration (1953), the first peacetime agency devoted to small business, was organized not only to counsel but also to make loans to businesses that qualified.

In the 1930s the federal government also began to insure or guarantee loans to individuals for purchase or improvement of homes, in order to facilitate the expansion of credit to persons who might otherwise be unable to obtain a loan. These functions, together with others from the RFC and Area Redevelopment, are now lodged in the Housing and Home Finance Agency.

Protection of civil rights, conservation of natural resources, and lending of money are examples of the emergence onto the national scene of activities that have been defined and redefined to meet the needs of the society. With the Constitution setting the guidelines of

6. *Reconstruction Finance Corporation—Seven Year Report to the President and the Congress, Feb. 2, 1932–Feb. 2, 1939,* Jesse H. Jones, Chairman (Washington, D.C., U.S. Government Printing Office, 1939).

principle in the broadest sense, the people of each era have taken their accumulated heritage and defined it in terms meaningful and useful to them. As the American society has moved from a rural to an urban collectivity, problems that were at one time defined as local and private are now national and public.

As sectionalism in America declines and a national collectivity emerges, the federal government as arbitrator, interpreter, and reflector of the values and beliefs of the society takes on new significance. The ambivalence of the American people toward these new powers continues, as is reflected in recent public opinion polls. "While the polls turned up considerable suspicion of big business' power, this feeling was not translated into a broad demand for extreme action. . . . Public opinion has apparently become increasingly hospitable to government intervention, the Princeton pollsters found." [7]

A good current example of the heightened ambivalence around federal–local relations is Urban Renewal or Area Redevelopment. Many older cities have had to face the reality that their cores have been abandoned by both people and business. This process is not new, as much evidence indicates; but since World War II, particularly during the 1950s, it has moved with considerable vigor. Panicked by the problems of a blighted center and an ever-expanding periphery, the administrators and citizenry of these communities looked for help. The questions of who is to do the job and how it is to be done largely determine whether anything will be accomplished.

In some instances a leading family or families have assumed the initiative, such as the Rockefellers in New York City or the Mellons in Pittsburgh. Local public and private interests have been able to work together in other cities. Because of the scope and complexity of the problems, however, federal aid has also been sought. In these instances employment and other variables were important, for in some cases industry had left the area altogether. More was needed than tearing down and erecting buildings; new life had to be injected into the community. As Congress appropriated funds and

7. "Opinion Poll Reveals More Public Support for Antitrust Goals," *Wall Street Journal*, August 2, 1962.

established programs, many communities have rushed to take advantage of the opportunities. A new cabinet post for urban affairs has just been established, and the first Secretary has been appointed.

Two major programs provide aid to urban areas. First, the Urban Planning Assistance Program, started in 1954, functions as a section of the Urban Renewal Administration, a constituent unit of the Housing and Home Finance Agency. Recent figures indicate some 765 approved projects, covering 2,360 areas and localities, plus some thirty state-wide projects.[8] The Urban Renewal Administration is responsible for the administration of the program of slum clearance and urban renewal, the urban planning assistance program, and the demonstration program. Field operations are carried on through the seven regional offices of the Housing and Home Finance Agency.

The other major program was established in 1961 under the direction of the Area Redevelopment Administration of the Department of Commerce. The legislation authorized certain federal aids for those areas designated by the administration as "redevelopment areas"—loans for industrial or commercial facilities, technical assistance, etc. The ARA exercises program control and provides policy direction for these activities with the assistance and cooperation of other federal agencies. A staff of field representatives provides direct assistance to state and local agencies concerned with economic development. Where possible, accelerated public works programs are used and integrated into the plan.

In the first annual report of ARA, 930 areas in the states and possessions were designated eligible for assistance. Programs were prepared and submitted for 621 areas, and provisional approval was given to 544 areas for their Overall Economic Development Program (OEDP).[9] Programs are set up for annual review, and an area's designation as eligible can be reconsidered at any time.

8. *Urban Planning Assistance Programs Project Directory*, Urban Renewal Administration, Housing and Home Finance Agency, March 31, 1962.
9. *Annual Report on the Area Redevelopment Administration of the U.S. Department of Commerce, 1962.*

FEDERALIZATION OF STATE FUNCTIONS

Despite the continued cry about encroachment of the federal government, numerous candidates for offices at all levels of government and from both political parties campaign on the grounds that they can get more federal aid for their constituencies than their opponents can. The attitude toward the federalization of state functions in this statement is typical:

> While many people are generally in favor of cutting down federal activities, they found it a little harder to specify just which activities should be cut down. States whose officials talked the loudest about states rights often didn't follow through. Southern lawmakers, for example, found their constituents were getting more Federal payments for vocational education, library services, and other programs than they were paying in taxes to the Federal Government, and opposed any cutback in those programs. Southerners were among the leaders in the fight against Eisenhower Administration plans to cut down Federal aid for school districts around Federal military installations.[10]

School integration has particularly aggravated the ambivalence, since federal funds are to be used only for integrated schools.

While elsewhere

> larger cities—and frequently governors of big Northern and Western states—opposed any turnback, too. Many cities found their efforts to increase property taxes fought locally, their pleas for larger state aid rejected by legislatures dominated in large part by rural representatives. So they have turned more and more to Federal Government, where their voice is larger.

> Some political observers argue state governments may be

10. Allan L. Otter, "Governors Agree Trend to Federalization of State Functions is Continuing to Grow," *Wall Street Journal,* June 30, 1961.

The Rise of Big Government

> slowly withering—their role preempted more and more by expanding cities at one end and an expanding Federal Government at the other. Ultimately, these observers suggest, states may be becoming little more than conduits for Federal funds earmarked for the cities.[11]

The role of state governments is going through change; they appear certain to remain, but the transformation of their role and functions appears equally certain.

Government at all levels—federal, state, and local—has gone into business or has supported or facilitated private interests to accomplish public improvements. Whether the problem is urban or rural, appropriate actions are eventually stimulated in both the public and private sector to achieve certain ends by creative means. The Aerospace Corporation, RAND Corporation, System Development Corporation, and the Mitre Corporation are examples of the government-sponsored private, incorporated, nonprofit type of enterprise. The Aerospace Corporation was established to eliminate conflict and criticism but apparently has not been particularly successful in accomplishing either objective. The situation seems to be summarized in the following statement:

> The increasing reliance of government agencies on nonprofit companies already has raised such howls of anguish from industrialists that President Kennedy last July instructed Budget Director David E. Bell to look into the whole matter.[12]

Another criticism is typical (the agencies referred to are the Area Redevelopment Agency and the Rural Electrification Agency):

> Among other things, the agencies have provided financing for an Illinois ski resort, a Tennessee nightgown factory, and a Massachusetts study of sea scallops and flounder.[13]

These are examples of how, with one objective in mind—assisting urban and rural areas—the net effect may turn out to be something quite different.

11. Ibid.
12. R. F. Roper, "Aerospace Corporation Stirs Criticism of Pentagon's Use of Non-Profit Firms," *Wall Street Journal*, Dec. 4, 1961.
13. "Two Federal Agencies Push Government Deeper into Field of Business Financing," *Wall Street Journal*, April 6, 1962.

Other organizational frameworks that have been used for this purpose are the Tennessee Valley Authority, as previously discussed, and the Federal Reserve System. Member banks own the stock of the Reserve banks, but the President appoints, with Senate confirmation, the seven governors who are the senior policy-making body. All national banks are required to belong to the system; for state-chartered banks it is optional.

REDEFINITION OF PRIVATE PROPERTY AND RESPONSIBILITY

Through the years of change and federal growth, one of the most significant developments has concerned the definition of private property. As distances have dwarfed and more people are packed into the greater urban complexities, the mutual interrelatedness of individuals becomes more apparent. Coupled with this has been the emergence of the great corporations with hundreds of thousands of stockholders, employees, and customers, all with vested interests, and a managerial elite whose power far exceeds their degree of ownership. These organizations, although chartered in only one state, generally reach out into most, if not all, of the fifty states of the Union and around the world.

What is true of the business corporations is also true of all other large-scale institutions utilizing the corporate form of organization. The large state universities provide another kind of example; many have branches throughout their own state and also own properties, which have been donated or purchased, in other states for research, income, and other purposes. Cooperative research efforts between the state and private universities have sometimes been formalized into new corporate bodies to carry out their respective tasks. These same state-supported schools are linked internationally, assisting in the establishment of campuses throughout the world. The states in which these schools were spawned no longer bound their activities or interests. The social responsibility of ownership is emphasized, replacing the concept of arbitrary and independent use of property.

The Rise of Big Government

The fear and anxiety felt in some quarters over the nationalization of the educational system and the limitations placed on the Federal Office of Education have not prevented certain federal developments from taking place. Those favoring federal aid to education often cite the land-grant colleges as examples of federal aid without federal control.[14] However, some educators are questioning whether the great flood of governmental funds for research and development is not "distorting the entire spirit and purpose of U.S. universities. . . . In 1958–59, for example, the United States supplied 67.2 per cent of Johns Hopkins' operating income, 78.2 per cent of M.I.T.'s, and 83.6 per cent of Caltech's."[15] All three of these institutions are technically private, but under these circumstances some university men wonder whether the traditional definitions of public and private still hold, or whether not only these three but also a good many of our other leading universities are becoming "agencies of the government."

Although defense and space projects account for much of what is being spent on research, other departments, agencies, and divisions of the federal government are also awarding substantial research grants. Some universities and academicians have become expert in acquiring these funds. However, this does not mean that the projects developed from these research funds are not supported by university funds also. In some cases the 15 per cent of direct costs allowed for overhead is only about half the actual cost, and thus the universities must devote their resources to those projects for which they can get research grants. The overall balance of the university can thus become distorted, with some departments and programs heavily supported in relation to the rest.

A problem in education at the elementary level is the "Impacted Area" school.[16] The program was started in 1950 to help school systems overtaxed by the influx of families into the area because of the opening up of federal military or civilian installations. The federal government has been in the vexing position of having either to award funds to the affected communities, which sometimes have

14. "U.S. School Aid without Controls Cited by President," *Chicago Sun Times,* Nov. 13, 1961.
15. "The University and Federal Money: Impoverishment by Riches," *Time,* Aug. 24, 1962.
16. Jonathan Spirah, " 'Impacted Area' Schools: Their Integration is Proving Costly, Wasteful and Vexing," *Wall Street Journal,* Sept. 3, 1963.

segregated schools, or to construct and operate schools on federal property with or without local cooperation. Although the administration has been trying to cut back the impacted area aid program and Congress has allowed some portions of the program to expire, the expectation is that it will be extended. Southern congressmen have been particularly interested in its continuation.

Agricultural "surplus," one of the most burdensome and perplexing problems of the past several administrations, is a paradox in a world where many people are continually facing starvation. This abundance is the unanticipated result of one of the most intensively and successfully implemented programs of agricultural research and application any society has ever attempted. The program coupled the efforts of land-grant colleges, the Department of Agriculture, experiment stations, and extension services to the initiative and enterprise of the independent farm owners.

To some the surplus problem seems to stem from imperfections within the market economy added to inappropriate control measures that together have augmented the problem rather than ameliorated it. Many aspects of the problem relate to the transformations taking place in agriculture. Farming, ranching, and dairying are becoming big-business operations. Mechanization linked with large-scale operations is squeezing out the small marginal farmers. With encroaching urbanization and industrialization, along with improved transportation, many small farmers are subsidizing their own marginal farm operation—and adding to the surpluses—by working in neighboring factories. In the dairy industry research is constantly increasing the yield of milk per cow, forcing the government to raise price supports to protect the dairymen while a "fat" and cost-conscious society are buying fewer dairy products.[17]

The ambivalence of the farmer between having controls or being subjected to the forces of the free market is only "logically" perplexing. Some of the problem revolves around size, for it is just as difficult to draw legislation that is equally applicable to the large and small farmer as it is for large and small business. For farm groups to seek government help in the solution of their problems is not new; agricultural interests have been lobbying at the state and national levels of government during the past hundred years. That

17. Joe Western, "Milk Deluge: Federal Farm Officials Consider New Drastic Curbs to Trim Surplus," *Wall Street Journal,* Dec. 13, 1961.

this type of activity will be continued seems certain, for there appears to be just as much reaction against a Secretary of Agriculture who suggests that the government should get out of the agricultural business as against the Secretary who suggests more controls. The problem, of course, is for the leaders of farmers' organizations to coalesce the divergent economic and regional views of the farm population and make them effective politically.

The dominant industrial side of the society characterized increasingly by a welfare philosophy is also increasingly subject to federal control. Beginning in 1912 with the establishment of the Children's Bureau (now in the Department of Health, Education and Welfare) and followed in 1918 by the Women's Bureau (in the Department of Labor), legislation of a welfare nature has been on the increase. The last thirty years, particularly, have seen the extension of aid to the aged, dependent children, underprivileged individuals of all kinds, and the disabled. This same period has seen the commitment of the federal government to programs of "fair employment" and other assistance for those suffering economic loss from the operations of the economic system. Minimum-wage legislation has also been used to try to raise the standard of living of our poorest citizens.

The shift in responsibility for welfare from local sources, administered by the political boss and private facilities, to public institutions at the local, state, and federal levels continues. Professionals in welfare administration are taking over the operation of various public agencies, and often the simultaneous developments in private welfare are not taken into account by them. Private welfare has also become a big business administered by professionals; the United Community Fund campaign and the Red Feather services have become an institutionalized part of society. In addition, private welfare—some required by law—is also provided by business enterprises in the various "fringe benefit" programs for health insurance, unemployment compensation, life insurance, pensions. These various fringe programs are generally coordinated with other private and public plans. The design of many pension plans is to combine federal Social Security benefits with the private provisions to give a certain minimum amount to the participants.

The proposals to link health insurance (including Medicare) with the Social Security program were feared as a further "encroach-

Redefinition of Private Property and Responsibility

ment" in an area still regarded by many, despite the numerous quasi-public health plans, as private.

The continuing movement of the federal government to formulate additional compulsory programs is viewed with alarm by some, but by others it is seen as a means of reducing hardship. What may be interpreted as an opportunity for the highly talented may be overpowering to the less talented. The society is continually plagued by the problem of providing opportunity and freedom without exploitation and license. The welfare programs are an attempt to distribute the economic benefits of our society so that individual effort will be rewarded, but everyone will have a basic security against economic hardship with a minimum of controls.

Although expressly committed to the separation of government and business and to a policy that the government that governs least governs best, we see in the elaboration and expansion of federal structure an implicit denial of this. The various segments of society have consistently sought government action whenever it was felt necessary to achieve desired ends, regardless of philosophy or ideals. The representatives of the heterogeneous elements of our highly complex society are able to gather under a wide range of governmental superstructures that project their respective interests. The decisions made in these bodies tend to rest on a broad base of acceptance, which provides the homogeneity that holds the society together, allows for actions that have wide support, and provides for ongoing accomplishment.

As if to emphasize that the rapidly developing federal structure continues to reflect and reinforce the ongoing emergent character of the society, in the brief period since 1960 (the basic census date for this research) two new departments, Housing and Urban Development and the Department of Transportation have been added. Each of them put together and reorganized older agencies and bureaus and thus reduced structural diversities. Although the elevation to cabinet level emphasizes the increasing importance of their activities, the inclusion of two or three more grades at the top, an under secretary and assistant secretaries, expands the vertical extension of the two hierarchies. Separate diversities have thus been considerably reduced, but the new reorganizations have increased the distance from the bottom to the top of each organization.

MEN AND MONEY: MEASURES OF EXPANSION

The enormous expansion of the federal structure can be partly measured by the increases in men employed and tax money collected and spent. The disproportionate growth of the federal forces in relation to the growth of the society can be observed by comparing the civilian work force of the federal government with the increases in the population and in the American civilian labor force; the increasing power of the federal government can be observed by comparing federal tax collections with those of local communities and the states.

There are several kinds of important questions about the getting and spending of taxes that have to do with the expansion of the federal government and the steady attrition of that power away from local and state communities. How much have our tax monies increased in total dollars since the beginning of the century? How much in proportion to the increasing Gross National Product? What proportions of the taxes in 1900 and at intervening periods, as well as today, were taken by the three levels of government—local, state, and federal? How much did the take of each rise or fall in this period? From what parts and elements of the society did the money come for each of the three levels at each period of time? The answers to the first few questions give us a rough measure of the expansion of the several kinds of government. The last one asks about basic changes in the economic relations our several governments have had with the American people.

We will begin with the increase in all tax revenues and the changes in the proportions taken by the local, state, and federal governments since 1902 (see Table 6). In 1902 the total taxes of all governments was 1.4 billion dollars; in 1957 they had risen to 98.6 billion, an increase of 141 times in fifty-five years.

In 1902 the local governments got 52 per cent of the total revenues; today their proportion has dropped to 14 per cent, that of the federal government has risen from 37 per cent to 71 per cent, and that of the states from 11 to 15 per cent.

Men and Money: Measures of Expansion

While all large societies have always had the problem of assessing and collecting taxes, the American people have only gradually learned to accept the necessity for increasing taxes; but what to tax, how the tax is to be collected, and for what purpose still are questions that plague us. All types and kinds of things have been taxed,

Table 6. Percentage of Total Taxes by Local, State, and Federal Government

	1902	1932	1942	1957
Total (in billions)	$1.4	$8.0	$20.8	$98.6
Federal	37%	23%	59%	71%
State	11	24	19	15
Local	52	53	22	14

including people, property, goods, services, transactions, gifts, inheritance, and income. A combination has been formed into the complex maze that now constitutes our tax structure. Since all three levels of government are involved, continual redefinition of the rights and relationships of the various levels is required.

Table 7. Percentage of Total Tax Income by Source

Taxes	1902 %	1932 %	1942 %	1957 %
Individual income	0	6	17	38
Corporation income	0	8	24	22
Sales*	38	19	28	21
Property	51	56	22	13
Subtotal	89	89	91	94
Death, gift, and inheritance	0	3	3	2
Motor vehicle and operator's license	0	4	2	1
Other	11	4	4	3
Total	100	100	100	100

Source: *Historical Statistics of the U. S., Colonial Times to 1957*, pp. 723–24, 726, and 729.
* Includes customs duties, general sales, motor fuel, alcoholic beverages, tobacco products, etc.

The Rise of Big Government

Indirect taxes appear to have been as popular in 1789 as they are among many in 1960. The federal government's first attempt to raise funds through taxation was customs duties; the first act of the new Congress was the Tariff of 1789.[18] While levies were imposed on certain domestic goods and a direct tax was tried, the principal source of revenue until after the turn of the twentieth century continued to be customs duties, an unfortunate choice because of the great fluctuations in imports and thus in revenue. More recently, however, indirect taxes have yielded relatively rich returns on such domestic products as tobacco, alcoholic beverages, and motor fuel.

Taxation of personal income was started at the federal level during the Civil War. The tax was imposed in 1862, raised in 1865, and allowed to expire in 1872. The next attempt, a 2 per cent proportional income tax, was found unconstitutional in 1894. The personal income tax became constitutional in 1913 with the adoption of the Sixteenth Amendment to the Constitution.

Federal taxation of corporations was tried briefly during the Civil War, then ceased, and was not imposed again until 1909. In 1913, with the adoption of the Sixteenth Amendment, corporation and individual income taxes were combined for several years as a withholding tax on corporation stockholders. After World War I the tax was regarded as a levy on the corporate entity. The corporation income tax rate has gradually risen from 10 per cent in 1920 to 52 per cent in 1952.

The first death taxes were imposed by the federal government in 1798 but were not permanent until the Federal Estate Tax law of 1916 was passed. Federal excise taxes have been collected on entertainment, luggage, jewelry, cosmetics, and other so-called "luxury" items.

Since the beginning of the century approximately 90 per cent of all taxes have derived from four major sources—individual income, corporate income, sales, and property—and another 5 per cent from death, gift, and inheritance taxes and motor vehicle and operators' licenses fees. A summary is given in Table 7 of percentages of all government taxes by the source of the tax from 1902 to 1957. In 1902 the principal tax source was property, and the other major source, listed under the general heading of sales, was customs duties.

18. Chester Wright, *Economic History of the United States*.

Men and Money: Measures of Expansion

The thirty years between 1902 and 1932 reflect major changes in the source of taxes; taxation of income of both individuals and corporations began to show up, while, in percentage, the sales source was reduced by almost half. In the sales tax category the largest contribution was from tobacco products, followed by customs. Then death, gift, and inheritance taxes began, as well as taxes on motor vehicle and operators' licenses, stemming from the widespread introduction of the automobile.

Between 1932 and 1942 the property tax withered by well over half while sales increased 9 per cent, with alcoholic beverages the largest category, followed by tobacco products and motor fuel, just ahead of customs taxes.

Table 8. Federal Taxes, in Percentage

Taxes	1902 %	1932 %	1942 %	1957 %
Individual income	0	22	26	51
Corporation income	0	33	39	30
Sales*	95	40	28	16
Property	0	0	0	0
Other	5	5	7	3
Total	100	100	100	100

Source: *Historical Statistics of the U. S., Colonial Times to 1957*, pp. 723–24.
* Includes customs duties, general sales, motor fuel, alcoholic beverages, tobacco products, etc.

By 1942 income taxes, both corporate and individual were contributing over 40 per cent to the total tax collections, as opposed to 14 per cent just ten years earlier. The actual volume in most categories increased, but the relative changes are reflected in the percentage shifts. By 1957 the income taxes were contributing 50 per cent of an ever-increasing total tax collection (Table 7).

Table 8, which shows the federal tax structure, reflects the change from an emphasis on customs and excise duties, in the sales category, to the income taxes. The table also indicates that the federal government has not looked to the property tax as a source of revenue; the other levels of government have been the recipients of the property tax revenues. At the federal level the sales category de-

The Rise of Big Government

clines from 95 per cent to 16 per cent in the fifty-five year period shown, while the combined income taxes moved from zero to 81 per cent in the same period. Within the sales category would be the change from customs duties to excise duties on alcoholic beverages, tobacco products, fuel oil, etc.

At the state level, as shown in Table 9, the major sources of

Table 9. State Taxes, in Percentage

Taxes	1902 %	1932 %	1942 %	1957 %
Individual income	0	4	6	11
Corporation income	0	4	7	7
Sales	18	38	57	58
Property	53	17	7	3
Subtotal	71	63	77	79
Death, gift, and inheritance	0	10	3	2
Motor vehicle and operator's license	0	18	11	9
Other	29	9	9	10
Total	100	100	100	100

Source: *Historical Statistics of the U. S., Colonial Times to 1957*, p. 726.

revenue in 1902 were the property tax, miscellaneous taxes, and the sales tax. In the fifty-five year period the sales tax category increased from 18 per cent to 58 per cent, while the property tax declined from 53 per cent to 3 per cent. The increased usage in many states of a general sales tax levied as a percentage of each dollar of purchase and covering most items is the major source of the increase in this category. Death, gift, and inheritance taxes, along with motor vehicle and operator's license taxes, rose from zero in 1902 to high points in 1932 and have been on the relative decline since. Income taxes, both individual and corporate, have gradually increased.

At the local level the property tax continues to be the major source of revenue. While the property tax percentage has declined relatively since 1932 in terms of all tax dollars collected, in actual dollars property tax revenues have increased and are primarily used for local expenditures. Almost 90 per cent of all local taxes were

Men and Money: Measures of Expansion

from property in 1902 and 1957. Sales taxes increased from one per cent in 1932 to 7 per cent in 1957; all others were one per cent or less.

There has been a movement at the local level to employ sales and income taxes, which have hitherto been typically assessed at the state and federal levels. One controversy today relating to the core cities of major metropolitan areas is whether the city should tax individuals who are employed in the city but who live in suburban areas outside the city limits. These cities, having felt the decline in income caused by the exodus to the suburbs, have gradually been resorting to sales and income taxes.

Table 10. Gross National Product and Federal Expenditures, 1870–1960

Year	Federal expenditures as per cent of GNP in actual dollars	Federal expenditures as per cent of GNP in 1929 dollars
1960	15.17	n.a.
1955	16.24	16.27
1950	13.91	12.31
1940	8.95	8.96
1930	3.73	3.72
1920	8.47	8.48
1910	2.20	2.21
1900	2.65	2.63
1890	2.27	2.33
1880	2.79	2.79
1870	5.63	5.61

The federal government has grown proportionately even more than the rapidly expanding society. By examining the percentage of the Gross National Product taken for federal expenditures, we can learn whether there has been a disproportionate increase in the money value of the nation's goods and services used by the federal government. The GNP grew from $6,710 million in 1870 to $17,300 million in 1900, $106,000 million in 1940, and $504,400 million in 1960. Meanwhile, the federal expenditures started at 5.6 per cent of the GNP in 1870 and rose to 15.17 per cent of the value of all goods and services of the American society in 1960 (see Table 10). Although our economic productivity grew many times, the

The Rise of Big Government

proportion taken by the federal government grew even more—it increased over three times.[19]

The relationship between the GNP and federal expenditures is shown in Table 10. Each of the war periods again stands out as federal expenditures take a significantly larger proportion of a larger GNP. Typically, war periods have seen the expansion of federal expenditures, increased taxes, and a larger GNP. The years 1870, 1900 (less than the others), 1920, 1940, and 1955 reflect the increases around the Civil War, the Spanish American War, World War I, World War II, and the Korean conflict.

In 1960 the Defense Department received half of the federal budget; the Department of Health, Education and Welfare and the Department of Agriculture each received 6 per cent; NASA (space) and the Veterans Administration each was allotted 5 per cent. The interest on the national debt amounted to 11 per cent and foreign aid to 4.5 per cent. Expenditures for all other purposes, including all other agencies and departments, amounted to 12.5 per cent.

In 1930 the percentage for defense was about half that of 1960; the Veterans Administration was about the same. Interest on the national debt was not quite twice in percentage what it was in 1960. All other categories took the remaining half. At the turn of the century, defense took 37 per cent, veterans affairs 27 per cent, interest on the national debt 8 per cent, and all other categories 28 per cent. The disbursal of the funds is strongly influenced by how recently a war has taken place.

The United States government started off in debt in 1789 and, with the exception of the mid-1830s,[20] has had a national debt to be serviced ever since. As we look back 30 and 60 years, we see that both defense expenditures and veterans affairs have substantially large percentages. There have been periodic slowdowns, as in the 1920s, but the general trend in military and allied expenditures since the Civil War has been upward, reflecting in part the progression of the United States to the position of one of the world's great powers.

19. *Historical Statistics of the U.S., Colonial Times to 1957*, p. 139. M. Slade Kendrich, *A Century and a Half of Federal Expenditure* (National Bureau of Economic Research, Inc., 1955). This publication uses 1926 as the base period.

20. *Historical Statistics of the U.S., Colonial Times to 1957*, p. 718.

Most Americans know that the federal government does not itself spend all it collects but by various arrangements passes a substantial part, through what is called intergovernmental payments, to
the states and local communities. The total amount spent in 1960–
61 was in excess of $7 billion. Since federal officials and agencies

Table 11. Direct Federal Aid Payments to States under
Cooperative Arrangements, 1960–61

States	Amount of aid (millions of dollars)	Per cent of total aid	Per cent of total population 1960
California	$ 633	8.9	8.8
New York	461	6.5	9.4
Texas	361	5.1	5.4
Illinois	353	5.0	5.6
Pennsylvania	311	4.4	6.3
Ohio	305	4.3	5.4
Michigan	245	3.4	4.4
Louisiana	200	2.8	1.8
Missouri	198	2.8	2.4
Georgia	183	2.6	2.2
Florida	175	2.5	2.8
Tennessee	173	2.4	2.0
Alabama	172	2.4	1.8
Massachusetts	172	2.4	2.9
Oklahoma	168	2.4	1.3
North Carolina	146	2.1	2.5
Minnesota	142	2.0	1.9
Indiana	141	2.0	2.6
Kentucky	136	1.9	1.7
Virginia	132	1.8	2.2
Subtotal	4,807	67.7	73.4
Other 30 states	2,295	32.3	26.6
Total	$7,102	100.0	100.0

Source: *Intergovernmental Relations.* Table by Subcommittee on Intergovernmental Relations, Committee on Government Operations, U. S. Senate, April 1,
1963.

determine which activities of which states and localities get how
much, as well as when, the recipients of these funds are likely to be
in a dependent and at times subordinate position. Moreover, they
and the communities they represent necessarily feel the homo-

The Rise of Big Government

geneous pressure of the central authority of the total society. Table 11 presents a summary of aid payments made in 1960–61 to the top twenty states, each of which received over $130 million. This 40 per cent of the states receives slightly over two-thirds of the funds: they have almost three-fourths of the nation's population and include most of the heavily populated states as well as some of the less populated states. Many of the densely populated states appear to receive less than would be expected from their population percentage.

The sums involved are large enough to warrant the recipients' spending considerable time and attention to obtain them. Were these funds not available, there would be great financial pressure on state and local governments; governors, states legislators, mayors, and councilmen look anxiously toward Washington.

The increasing role of the federal government as a major employer is displayed in Table 12. The figures in the table are for American civilian employees only and do not include the military and certain alien civilian employees.

The United States population increased by nineteen times between 1820 and 1960, and the civilian labor force went up by about twenty-two times; the civilian federal employees rose from 0.2 to 3.7 per cent of the total civilian work force, approximately nineteen times. It is easily seen that the increase in the American population and number of workers has been greatly exceeded by the expansion of the federal government. Federal structural expansion is closely related to numbers of men and women employed.

While the total number of federal civilian employees increased by 348 times between 1820 and 1960, from 6,900 to 2,400,000, the number of civilian employees working in Washington, D. C., increased 400 times. However, the percentage of all government employees working in Washington increased by less than 2 per cent during the same period. Attesting to the growth and development of the federal government is the rise of the capital city of Washington itself. Set in the marshy wilderness of Virginia with but "109 habitable brick houses and 263 wooden" [21] in 1800, today Washington is the ninth largest city and the tenth largest standard metropolitan

21. C. M. Green, *Washington: Village and Capital, 1800–1878* (Princeton, Princeton University Press, 1962), p. 4.

Men and Money: Measures of Expansion

statistical area in the nation, according to the 1960 census. There are 240,000 federal civilian employees at work there.

With the development of regional, district, and state offices of the federal government, other major cities and metropolitan areas have become focal points of federal activities. The competition for these

Table 12. Total Population, Work Force, and Number of
Federal Civilian Employees

	Total population	*Civilian labor force (employed)*	*Civilian employees in federal government*	*Per cent of work force employed by federal gov't*
1960	179,323,000	64,267,000[a]	2,399,000[d]	3.7
1950	150,697,000	59,748,000[a]	1,961,000[c]	3.3
1940	131,669,000	47,520,000[a]	1,043,000[c]	2.2
1930	122,775,000	45,480,000[a]	601,000[c]	1.3
1920	105,711,000	42,434,000[b]	655,000[c]	1.5
1910	91,972,000	37,371,000[b]	389,000[c]	1.0
1901	75,995,000	29,073,000[b]	239,000[c]	0.8
1891	62,948,000	23,318,000[b]	158,000[c]	0.7
1881	50,156,000	17,392,000[b]	100,000[c]	0.6
1871	38,558,000	12,925,000[b]	51,000[c]	0.4
1861	31,443,000	10,533,000[b]	37,000[c]	0.4
1851	23,192,000	7,697,000[b]	26,000[c]	0.3
1841	17,069,000	5,420,000[b]	18,000[c]	0.3
1831	12,866,000	3,932,000[b]	11,500[c]	0.3
1821	9,638,000	2,881,000[b]	6,900[c]	0.2

Source: Population from 1820–1950: *Historical Statistics of the United States, Colonial Times to 1957*. Population for 1960: *U. S. Census 1960*, Department of Commerce.

a. Civilian labor force (employed) 14 years and over: *Statistical Abstracts of U. S., 1960*, p. 205.

b. Gainful workers or experienced civilian labor force, persons 10 years old and over: *Statistical Abstracts of U. S., 1960*, p. 204.

c. Figures are given for the years 1901, 1891, 1881, 1871, etc. and not for decades: *Historical Statistics of the United States, Colonial Times to 1957*, p. 710.

d. *1961 Annual Report*, U. S. Civil Service Commission, June 30, 1961.

branch offices is very great because of the employment opportunities. They are placed typically in or adjacent to other major metropolitan areas, with certain cities appearing especially favored for regional offices. A mutually supporting effect results as leaders who occupy high positions in the large hierarchical structures gather and

The Rise of Big Government

move about in the great megalopolitan areas. Key decisions are continually being made in these major centers, with leaders in Washington or New York often acting as the final arbiters.

Concomitant with the emergence of the nation from a minor to a major world power, from a rural to an urban, from an agrarian to an industrial, and from a locally oriented to a nationally oriented society, it has been necessary for the federal government to expand its range and scope of functions, which are reflected in its greater degree of responsibility and revealed in its increased activities.

As the society has been emerging into a great collectivity, the structural evolution of this great organism is of major concern and will be discussed in the next chapter.

Sources

Publications of the United States Government (Washington, D.C., U.S. Government Printing Office):

Budgets of the U.S. Government (1921–1963).

Century of Service, The First 100 Years of the United States Department of Agriculture (1963).

Challenge and Change, A Brief History of the United States Department of Labor 1913–1963 (1963).

Congressional Directory (1866–1960).

Data on Research and Development, No. 33, National Science Foundation (April 1962).

Federal Funds for Science X, National Science Foundation 61–82 (1962).

Historical Statistics of the U.S., Colonial Times to 1957 (1960).

Historical Summary of Governmental Finances in the United States, 1957 Census of Governments.

Handbook on Programs of the U.S. Department of Health, Education, and Welfare (1960–1963).

Interstate Commerce Commission Activities, 1887–1937 (1937).

Interstate Commerce Commission Activities, 1937–1962, Supplement to the 75th Annual Report (1962).

Journal of the Continental Congress (1775–1786).

New Directions in Health, Education, and Welfare, Tenth Anniversary (1963).

Official Register of the United States (1816–1962).

Reconstruction Finance Corporation, Seven Year Report 1932 to 1939.

Review of Data of Research and Development No. 16, National Science Foundation (1959).

Reports of the Congressional Committees and Sub-Committees both annual and special.

Statistical Abstract of the United States (1878–1963).

Tennessee Valley Authority, 1958, 25th Anniversary Year (1959).

The Anvil and the Plow, U.S. Department of Labor, 1913–1963 (1963).

United States Government Organization Manual (1935–1963).

United States Civil Service Commission, Annual Report (1887–1963).

United States Civil Service Commission, Diamond Anniversary, History of Federal Civil Service (1959).

United States Statutes at Large (1789–1963).

Urban Planning Assistance Programs Project Directory, Urban Renewal Administration, Housing, and Home Finance Agency (1962).

Non-government sources:

Cochran, Thomas C. and William Miller, *The Age of Enterprise, A Social History of Industrial America,* New York, Macmillan, 1942.

Dewhurst, J. Frederick and Associates, *America's Needs and Resources,* New York, The 20th Century Fund, 1955.

Encyclopaedia Britannica, Chicago, 1960.

Fabricant, Solomon, *The Trend of Government Activity in the U.S. Since 1900,* New York, National Bureau of Economic Research, Inc., No. 56, 1952.

Green, Constance M., *Washington, Village and Capital, 1800–1878,* Princeton, Princeton University Press, 1962.

Kendrich, M. Slade, *A Century and a Half of Federal Expenditures,* New York, National Bureau of Economic Research, Inc., 1955.

Mason, Edward S. (ed.), *The Corporation in Modern Society,* Cambridge, Mass., Harvard University Press, 1960.

Price, Don K., *Government and Science, Their Dynamic Relation in American Democracy,* New York, New York University Press, 1954.

Smith, Darrell H., *The Bureau of Education: Its History, Activities, and Organization,* Institute for Government Research, Monograph No. 14, Baltimore, The Johns Hopkins Press, 1923.

The Book of the States, Chicago: The Council of State Governments, 1958–59 and 1962–63.

Weber, Max, *Theory of Social and Economic Organization,* trans. Henderson and Parsons, Glencoe, Ill., The Free Press, 1957.

Wooddy, Carroll H., *The Growth of the Federal Government, 1915–1932,* New York, McGraw-Hill, 1934.

Wright, C. W., *Economic History of the United States,* New York, McGraw-Hill, 1949.

Journals

Hicks, H. G. and B. B. Graves, "Is There an Organizational Multiplier?"
Journal of the Academy of Management (March 1963).
The Chicago Sun Times
The New York Times
The Reader's Guide
Time
Wall Street Journal

CHAPTER FIFTEEN

The Evolving Federal Structure

SIX ILLUSTRATIVE AGENCIES

The processes of growth and expansion by which small structures have evolved into large-scale independent federal agencies and departments can be illustrated by describing six federal structures, thus providing a cross section.

The Department of Agriculture is used as a major structural model for a number of reasons. Agriculture was long the dominant occupation and way of life in the American society. The department began as a dependent subsection of the Patent Office, then became a part of the State Department, was eventually given independent status at less than cabinet rank, and was finally given cabinet status. The growth and development of the department can be considered typical of large-scale organizations that are allowed and encouraged to add new functions and to elaborate and diversify these functions. The resulting proliferation of positions becomes visible in the structure and will be described in detail.

The Treasury, as the original department to handle money matters, early acquired a diverse range of functions and activities. Since it handled domestic as well as international affairs, Treasury served as housekeeper, health and welfare agent, and financier for the federal government until new departments were added to the Cabinet.

The Office of Education is given special treatment because it has had a varied career because of the controversies regarding the role of federal government in education. Local control of education has been highly valued. However, the increasing role of education in the society calls for careful examination of these conceptions and relationships.

This chapter is by W. Lloyd Warner and John H. Trimm. See Notes on Authors.

The Evolving Federal Structure

The creation of the Department of Health, Education and Welfare in 1953 is of interest from an organizational standpoint in that it was the first addition to the Cabinet in forty years. Many of its constituent parts have long histories and had functioned as parts of other departments prior to their amalgamation in 1939 as the Federal Security Agency. The evolution of the department is quite different from those with much smaller beginnings and reflects the next extension from industrialization and urbanization to social welfare.

The Housing and Home Finance Agency (HHFA) is a combination of federal units closely identified with the problems of urbanization. It was established in 1947, but some of its components have much longer histories. From the standpoint of creation and structure, the HHFA is comparable to the Federal Security Agency. (It has very recently become a department.)

The Interstate Commerce Commission (ICC) serves as the prototype for the numerous independent agencies that have arisen since its inception in 1887. The Civil Service Commission was established in 1883 to serve the government itself, whereas the ICC was intended to regulate an aspect of the domestic economy. The establishment of these agencies was a departure from the procedure of creating departments.

The development of the independent agency with a supervisory board or commission was a device to distribute power. The agency is technically independent, but the responsibility for the appointment of the commissioners and directors is shared by the President and the Congress. It is an example of adaptation in answer to certain needs of the overall structure of the federal government. In earlier government documents the agencies tended to be identified with the executive branch. Recently this identification has been under serious attack and Congress is making an attempt to clarify the position of the agency and to strengthen its independence by emphasizing that it is not a part of the executive branch and is as much responsible to Congress as to the President.

The Interstate Commerce Commission, the Federal Security Agency (as the nucleus for the Department of Health, Education and Welfare), and the Housing and Home Finance Agency reflect the movement of the society from an agrarian to a highly industrialized orientation. The Office of Education has played a dual role;

now located in a welfare-oriented department, it is also linked to research and the current directions of science together with the National Science Foundation, the Department of Defense, the Atomic Energy Commission, and the National Aeronautics and Space Administration.

These functions and their related activities are examples of the increasing position of the federal government as the major collector and dispenser of funds and regulator of the moral order.

THE DEPARTMENT OF AGRICULTURE

The Agriculture Department is probably the most effective example of a systematic effort on the part of the federal government to influence a large segment of the society to accept and utilize scientific discovery and improved technology as soon as it has been developed. The government has initiated and underwritten research through the Agriculture Department, and through the system of extension specialists related to the land-grant colleges it has relayed the information directly to the farmer.

With agriculture as the major economic activity of the country, in his last annual message to Congress President Washington proposed that a Board of Agriculture be established. But when President Madison was later confronted with the idea, he rejected it on the grounds that he thought it would be unconstitutional.

Proposals and counterproposals were made until 1837, when the Commissioner of Patents, a former Commissioner for Indian Affairs who had taken a particular interest in agriculture, recommended that a public depository be established for collecting and distributing seeds and plants. Appropriations—intermittent but sufficient for the Patent Office to carry on agricultural activities—began in 1839. The Patent Commissioner distributed seeds without appropriations from 1837 to 1839. The Agricultural Section of the Patent Office grew slowly while suggestions and proposals were being made for establishing an independent department or bureau. The Patent Office, originally in the State Department, was moved in

The Evolving Federal Structure

1849 to the new Department of the Interior, where it continued its agricultural activities.

An agricultural clerkship was proposed in 1842 but not created until 1852.

The position of Superintendent of Agriculture was then created under the Commissioner of Patents, and the structure in Chart 1 operated until the Department of Agriculture, with a Commissioner at its head, was established in 1862.

Chart 1. U.S. Department of Agriculture, 1859–62

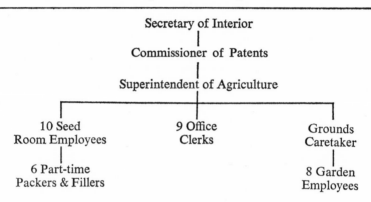

Employees:	Regular	11
	Temporary and Part-time	24
	Total Employees:	35

The immediate effect on structure of the creation of the Department of Agriculture in 1862 as an independent entity but with less than cabinet status is seen in Chart 2. Emphasis is on the statistical gathering and dispersing function, typical of a number of government departments, and on continuing to procure and distribute new seeds and plants. The introduction of chemists and a librarian marks the beginning of research activities.

The structure at this point remains relatively simple, but as sections begin to form, the organization moves from a rather informal to a more formal structure with supervisor-subordinate relationships.

In 1862 two major pieces of legislation underscored much of the thinking and feeling of the time. The Morrill Act provided for the donation of public lands to the several states and territories to establish colleges for the benefit of agriculture and mechanical arts. The Homestead Act provided widespread distribution of land at low cost; this act had been under discussion for about forty years, and with the secession of the South and the commitment of the new Republican Party to the idea, it was passed.

The next significant year for agriculture was 1889, when it was fully recognized as an executive department under the Secretary of Agriculture, a member of the Cabinet.

Chart 2. U.S. Department of Agriculture, 1862

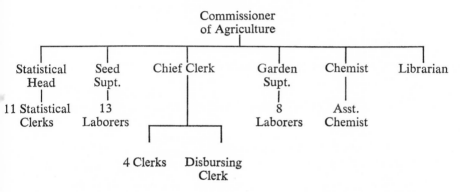

Total Employees: 45

Chart 3, for 1889, shows the increase from three to five levels by the addition of an Assistant Secretary and assistants to the heads of what are now divisions and bureaus (previously the sections of the former department). Some fifteen individuals, mostly heads of divisions and bureaus, report to the Secretary and Assistant Secretary; six reported to the Commissioner in 1862.

Between 1862 and 1889 various new specialized divisions and bureaus were created: the Bureau of Animal Husbandry and the Divisions of Forestry, Ornithology and Mammalogy, Entomology, Chemistry, Botany, Pomology, and Microscopy. In 1889 the Department was performing a far wider range of functions and activities; this is apparent in the eclipse of the original sections, excepting the Statistical Division and the administrative Chief Clerk. From the standpoint of structural development, of particular interest is

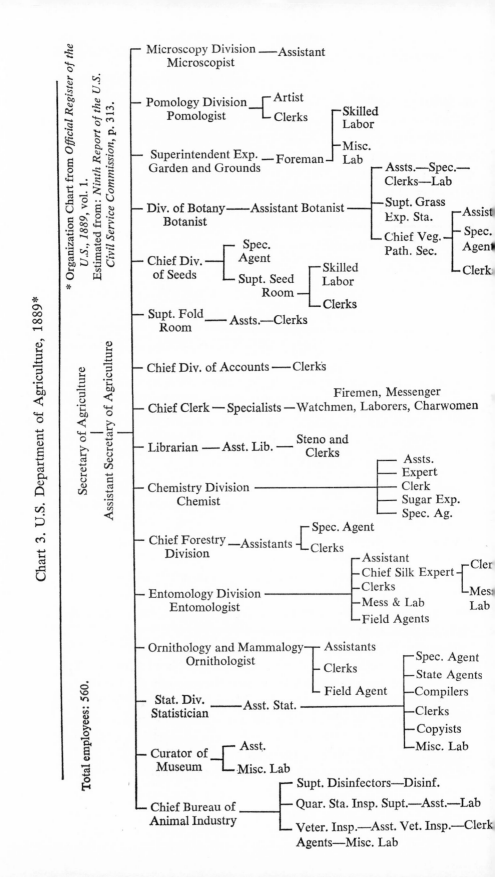

Chart 3. U.S. Department of Agriculture, 1889*

* Organization Chart from *Official Register of the U.S., 1889*, vol. 1.
Estimated from: *Ninth Report of the U.S. Civil Service Commission*, p. 313.

Total employees: 560.

Secretary of Agriculture

Assistant Secretary of Agriculture

Microscopy Division
Microscopist —— Assistant

Pomology Division
Pomologist —— Artist / Clerks

Superintendent Exp.
Garden and Grounds —— Foreman —— Skilled Labor / Misc. Lab

Div. of Botany
Botanist —— Assistant Botanist —— Assts.—Spec. Clerks—Lab / Supt. Grass Exp. Sta. / Chief Veg. Path. Sec. —— Assist / Spec. Agent / Clerk

Chief Div. of Seeds —— Spec. Agent / Supt. Seed Room —— Skilled Labor / Clerks

Supt. Fold Room —— Assts.—Clerks

Chief Div. of Accounts —— Clerks

Chief Clerk — Specialists — Firemen, Messenger Watchmen, Laborers, Charwomen

Librarian —— Asst. Lib. —— Steno and Clerks

Chemistry Division
Chemist —— Assts. / Expert / Clerk / Sugar Exp. / Spec. Ag.

Chief Forestry Division —— Assistants —— Spec. Agent / Clerks

Entomology Division
Entomologist —— Assistant / Chief Silk Expert —— Cler / Mess Lab / Clerks / Mess & Lab / Field Agents

Ornithology and Mammalogy
Ornithologist —— Assistants / Clerks / Field Agent

Stat. Div.
Statistician —— Asst. Stat. —— Spec. Agent / State Agents / Compilers / Clerks / Copyists / Misc. Lab

Curator of Museum —— Asst. / Misc. Lab

Chief Bureau of Animal Industry —— Supt. Disinfectors—Disinf. / Quar. Sta. Insp. Supt.—Asst.—Lab / Veter. Insp.—Asst. Vet. Insp.—Clerk Agents—Misc. Lab the Office of the Secretary and the Administration section. Starting with the position of Chief Clerk, who was initially assistant to the Commissioner or Secretary and in charge of administration, numerous positions have been created to service the needs of the organization as it grows and develops.

The department increased in size by approximately thirteen times during this twenty-seven-year period—from 45 to 560 total employees.[1] The reorganization the department experienced in the period following is typical of many departments and agencies. The number of employees more than doubled from 1889 to 1900 (from 1,500 to 3,300), and the number of major units reporting to the Secretary and Assistant Secretary was reduced from eighteen to fourteen by eliminating five units and adding the Bureau of Plant Industry. The sections eliminated were the divisions of Experimental Garden and Grounds, Ornithology and Mammalogy, Pomology, Botany, and Vegetable Pathology and Physiology. Their duties were reassigned. The Weather Bureau, previously a part of the Signal Corps of the Department of the Army, was transferred to the department in 1890.

Extraordinary growth requires that periodic review be made of the organization structure to determine necessary modifications in order to curtail the growing complexity that stems from increased numbers of positions and people and range of functions and activities. During the thirty-year period from 1900 to 1930 the number of major sections of the Department of Agriculture increased from fourteen to eighteen units plus the Solicitor and the Legal Staff. However, these figures mask the fact that only nine of the prior fourteen titles were observable in 1930: Weather Bureau, Library, Forestry Service, and Bureaus of Biological Survey, Entomology, Animal Industry, Plant Industry, and Chemistry and Soils; and these last two were combined into one bureau. Also, the Forestry Division of Agriculture had added to it the Forestry Service of the Interior Department, making one combined service for the federal government in the Agriculture Department.

The new titles include the Director of Personnel and Business Administration, the Solicitor and the legal staff, Office of Informa-

1. This figure represents a close approximation for, as is indicated in the Annual Report of the Civil Service Commission, the unclassified service of the Department of Agriculture away from Washington was not available.

tion, Office of Experiment Station, the Extension Service, Plant Quarantine and Control Administration, the Food, Drug, and Insecticide Administration, the Bureau of Agricultural Economics, the Bureau of Home Economics, the Bureau of Dairy Industry, and the Bureau of Public Roads. As indicated in Chart 5, these changes are the results of new combinations and additions to facilitate the functions and activities added. The number of personnel increased by approximately eight times in this thirty-year period—from 3,300 to 25,000. The number of levels increased to seven and eight from the five and six at the turn of the century. The proliferation of positions resulting from specialization creates horizontal expansion, and the hierarchical extension creates vertical expansion. The titles of the major subsections of the department continue to be indicative of the kind of work or problems assigned there.

For purposes of clarity and because of the limitations of space, sections of the department have been picked to illustrate the type and kind of expansion that went on between 1900 and 1930. The sections—chosen for range and diversity—are the Office of the Solicitor, the Director of Information, the Director of Personnel and Business Administration, and the Extension Service.

In Chart 6 four sections of the Department of Agriculture illustrate the increase in the number of levels between the Secretary and operative level for 1930: the Solicitor's Office, the Extension Service, the Personnel and Business Administration Division, and the Office of Information.

The Division of Personnel and Business Administration is the earlier position of Chief Clerk expanded through the process of differentiation and specialization to service a department of about 25,000 employees. The Office of Information developed from the department's efforts to publish and disseminate information. By 1930 the Director of Information was responsible not only for publications emanating from the department but also for releases to the press and the new medium of radio. The Office of the Solicitor represents the need in government departments for legal assistance in the performance of duties; it is also recognition of the growth of the legal profession and the dependence of any formal organization on its services.

The Extension Service links the department to the various states, directly relating the land-grant colleges and state extension services

Chart 4. U.S. Department of Agriculture, 1900 and 1901 Reorganization in 1901

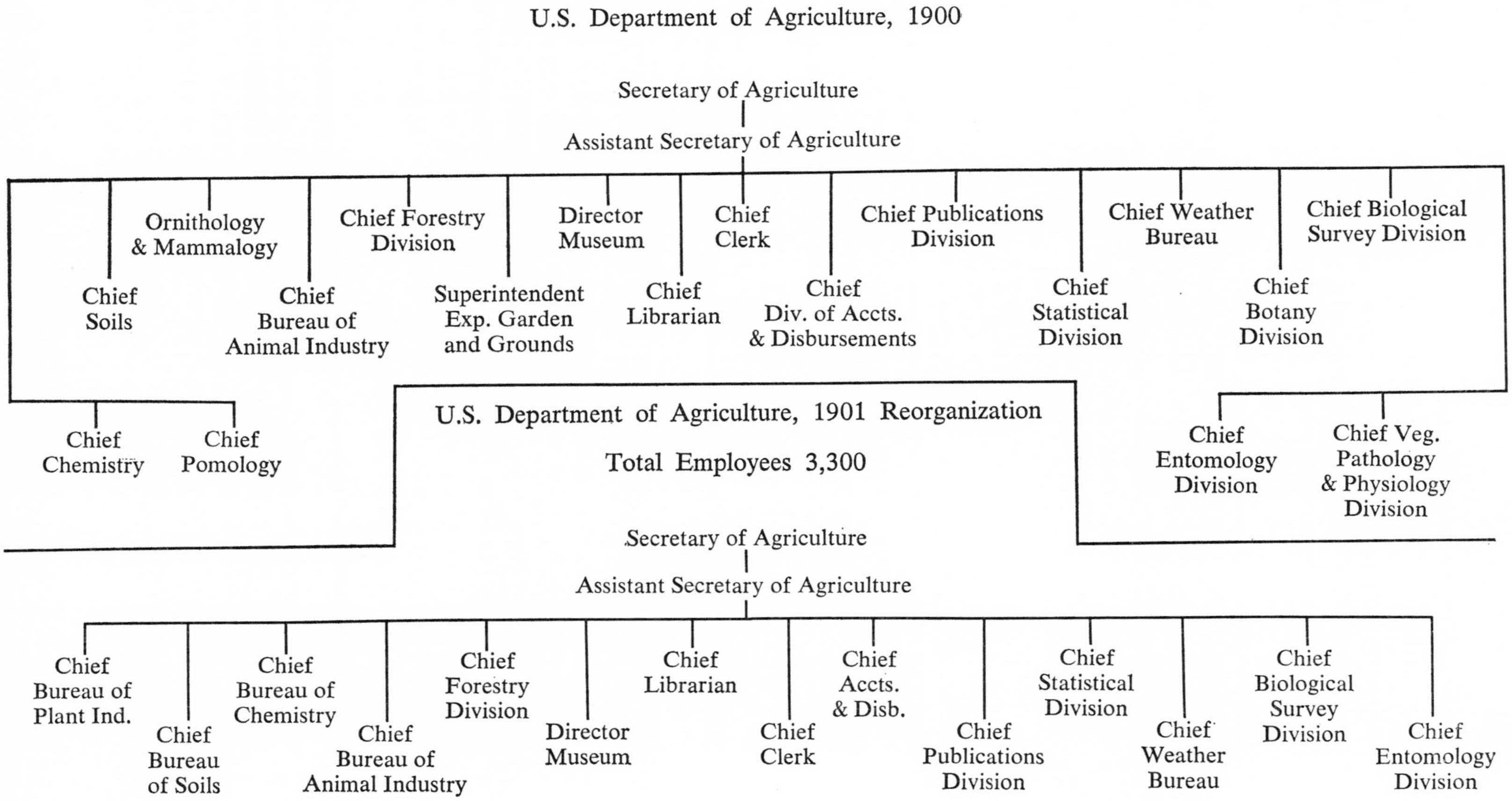

U.S. Department of Agriculture, 1900

Secretary of Agriculture

Assistant Secretary of Agriculture

- Chief Soils
- Ornithology & Mammalogy
- Chief Bureau of Animal Industry
- Chief Forestry Division
- Superintendent Exp. Garden and Grounds
- Director Museum
- Chief Librarian
- Chief Clerk
- Chief Div. of Accts. & Disbursements
- Chief Publications Division
- Chief Statistical Division
- Chief Weather Bureau
- Chief Biological Survey Division
- Chief Botany Division
- Chief Entomology Division
- Chief Veg. Pathology & Physiology Division
- Chief Chemistry
- Chief Pomology

U.S. Department of Agriculture, 1901 Reorganization

Total Employees 3,300

Secretary of Agriculture

Assistant Secretary of Agriculture

- Chief Bureau of Plant Ind.
- Chief Bureau of Soils
- Chief Bureau of Chemistry
- Chief Bureau of Animal Industry
- Chief Forestry Division
- Director Museum
- Chief Librarian
- Chief Clerk
- Chief Accts. & Disb.
- Chief Publications Division
- Chief Statistical Division
- Chief Weather Bureau
- Chief Biological Survey Division
- Chief Entomology Division

Chart 5. U.S. Department of Agriculture, 1930*

Total Personnel—25,000

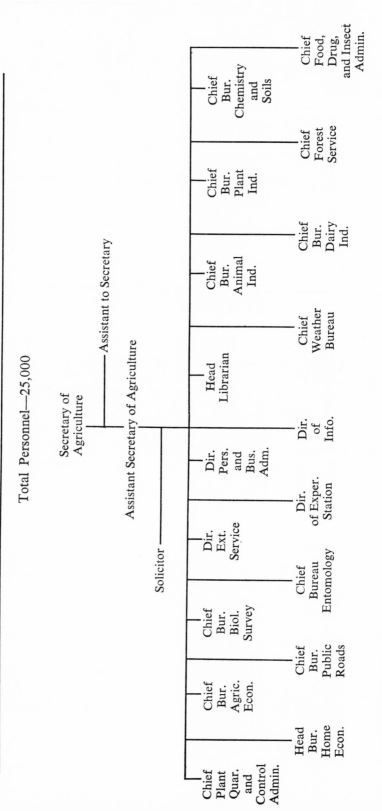

* Charts based upon *Official Register of U.S., 1930.*

Chart 6. Selected Illustrative Sections, U.S. Department of Agriculture, 1930

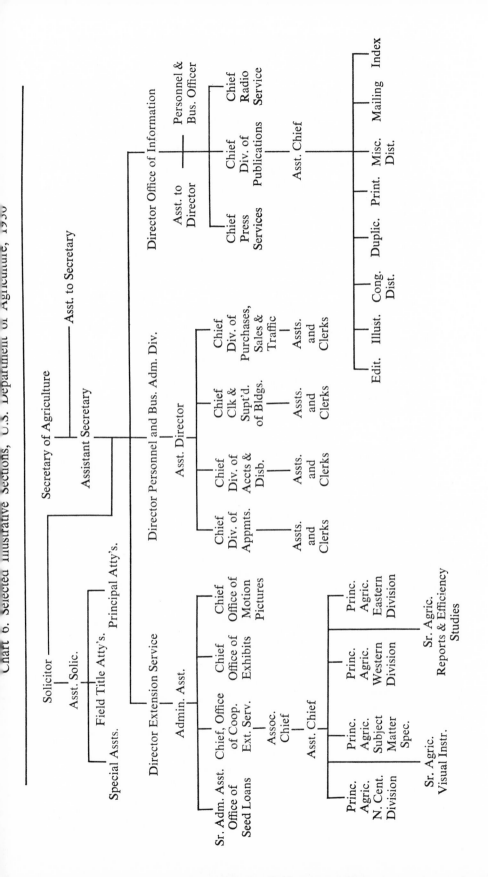

The Evolving Federal Structure

and coordinating efforts at the federal, state, and local level. Advances in relevant knowledge can be channeled directly through the Extension Service to farmers in all parts of the country. As shown in the chart, the nation has been divided into three major areas with a Principal Agriculturalist in charge of each. The organizational link that places the vast educational and research facilities of the federal government at the disposal of any local farmer is the Extension Service of the Agriculture Department. The county extension specialist is the state-sponsored direct contact with the farmer. Thus the formal structure provides links from the local level, to the state level, and on to the federal level, directly connecting the farmer and the federal government.

The services provided include research findings, statistical information, technological advances. To prevent the spread of disease among plants and animals requires control of imports, elimination of the diseased, and other preventive measures such as inoculations. These functions were greatly increased between 1900 and 1930 as emphasis was placed on the improvement of animals and seeds.

As markets became nationwide and impersonal because of the distances between producer and consumer, opportunities for deception in products developed, and government reacted by challenging the concept of *caveat emptor* and imposing restrictions and controls. The Food, Drug, and Insecticide Administration was formally constituted in 1930, but some of its law enforcement functions began in 1906–07.

The Bureau of Public Roads was created as the Office of Road Inquiry in the Department of Agriculture in 1894, but, the major need for roads did not come until the automobile. Not until 1916, with the Federal Aid Road Act, were federal funds initiated for highways; they were administered by the Department of Agriculture through the Office of Public Roads and Rural Engineering. In 1918 the Bureau of Public Roads, which we see in Chart 5, was established.

Discussion aimed at having the Agriculture Department become more interested and active in marketing efforts began in the 1890s. In 1913 the Office of Markets was established for a variety of activities, including problems of transportation and distribution costs, cooperative marketing, establishment of grades and standards of produce, and advice on more efficient operations.

During the post-World War I period, with expanding agriculture in a relatively contracting market, a change of approach was required. The system that had been so well established and implemented in the extension service was beginning to pay off. Agriculture was in a depressed state during most of the 1920s despite the high-level prosperity of other industries and the economy as a whole. Agricultural surpluses started then and have required attention and regulatory action ever since.

In the 1930s the entire economy, not just agriculture, was in its worst depression, and the desire and need for action were expressed everywhere. To the new Secretary of Agriculture, Henry A. Wallace, son of the man who had died in the office just nine years before, fell the task of trying to solve agriculture's problems.

Some of the agencies of the Agriculture Department that date from the 1930s are the Commodity Credit Corporation, 1933; Commodity Exchange Authority (1923), 1936; Marketing Agreements Acts, 1937; Rural Electrification, 1935; Soil and Water Conservation, 1937; Federal Surplus Commodities Corporation, 1935; and the Federal Crop Insurance Corporation, 1938. With the outbreak of World War II, however, came a different set of problems; the United States became the arsenal of democracy, supplying not only guns but butter.

After the war the old problems returned, and new programs and new agencies were created to deal with surpluses: the Farmers Home Administration, 1946; the expanded Agricultural Marketing Service, which now includes the school lunch program, 1946, and the milk program, 1954; the Commodity Stabilization Service, 1953; and the Foreign Agricultural Service, 1954.

This brief sketch of some of the developments during the period from 1930 to 1960 is concluded with Chart 7, which summarizes and presents structurally the Department of Agriculture as it appeared in 1960. A new level has been created, for the department now has an Undersecretary with four assistant secretaries—for Administration, Federal–State Relations, Agricultural Stabilization, and Marketing and Foreign Agriculture. Also functioning at this level is the Director of Agricultural Credit Service and the General Counsel and his legal staff. To these six major administrators the heads of all other units, large and small, report directly or indirectly.

Chart 7. U.S. Department of Agriculture, 1960

Total Personnel 98,000

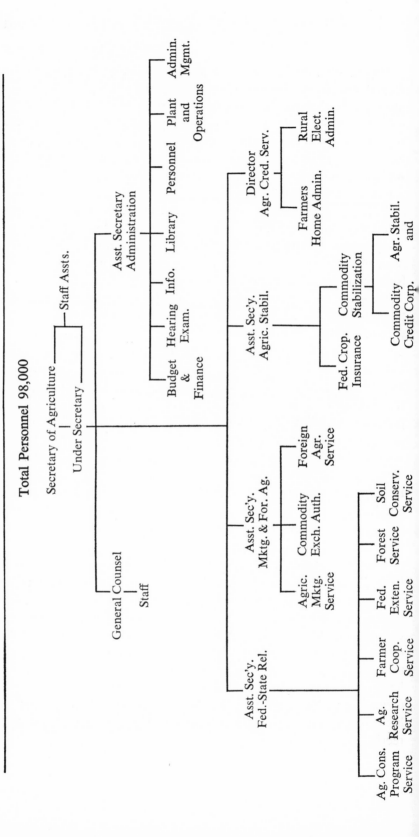

The titles of the six major administrators are so general that one has to move down to the fourth or fifth level in the structure to pick up many of the titles previously at the third level. To demonstrate the structural development, Charts 8 and 9 have been drawn in detail. The Secretary and Undersecretary, as indicated in Chart 7, have the six major administrators plus their ten staff assistants. The twenty-three major units, then, are reporting to the six senior administrators. These charts are intended to show how the structure has grown and how differentiation has taken place both vertically and horizontally. In Charts 8 and 9 the Office of the Assistant Secretary for Federal–State Relations is shown in detail for illustrative purposes. Because of space limitations, only selected portions of this section of the department are presented.

The emphasis in Chart 8 is only on the position of Assistant Secretary for Federal–State Relations. From the major units reporting to the Assistant Secretary, the Agricultural Research Service has been selected. Of the units reporting to the Administrator for Agricultural Research Service, the Farm Research unit was selected. There are seven divisions within the Farm Research unit, of which only the Animal Disease and Parasite Research Division has been used. Counting vertically at this point, there are eight levels within the hierarchy, considering the Under Secretary as a level and the Associate Administrator as a level. While the emphasis at present is on the vertical direction, it is also possible to sense the horizontal spread taking place at each of the levels. Space does not permit demonstrating this differentiation completely.

Chart 9 is a continuation of Chart 8. The additional detail begins with the Deputy Administrator for Farm Research through his Assistant Deputy to the Director for Animal Disease and Parasite Research Division. This represents eight levels in the hierarchy. The analysis at this point indicates that there is a minimum of two or more levels before the operative group of individuals is reached. First-line supervision or group leaders can be used beyond the last two levels of Assistant Director and Assistant to the Director. The vertical extension of the department has increased in a hundred years from three levels to approximately eleven or twelve levels, lateral spread of lines of authority and activity from six to twenty-three, and the total number of employees from 45 to 98,000, an increase of approximately 2,200 times.

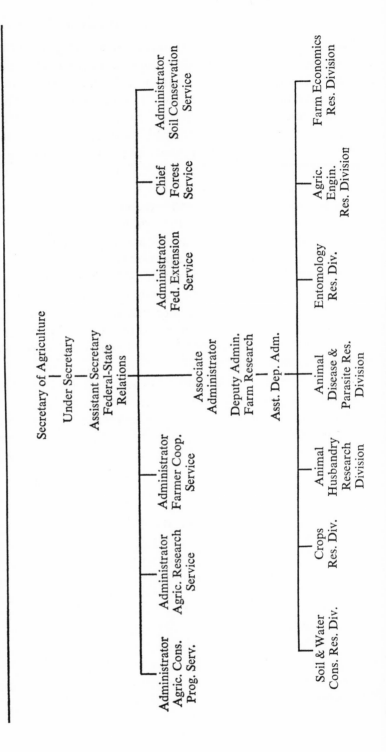

Chart 8. U.S. Department of Agriculture, 1960 (Partial Detail of Chart 7)

The transfer of three major units from the department in 1939–40 reduced the diversity of functions in certain directions. The Weather Bureau and the Bureau of Roads were transferred to the Commerce Department, and the Food, Drug and Insecticide Administration to the newly formed Federal Security Administra-

Chart 9. U.S. Department of Agriculture, 1960 (Partial Detail of Chart 8)

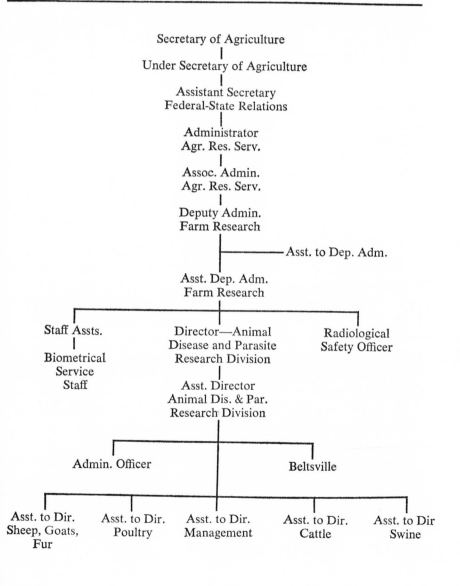

tion as one of its initial units. The transfer of these three units had little effect on the growth of the department.

Thus, for many reasons, which have changed through the hundred-year period, the Department of Agriculture has been accepted and has grown and developed. Agriculture as the dominant industry and way of life required assistance to improve both scientifically and technologically. As the fruits of the extended and elaborated system began to be harvested, other problems surrounding surpluses required coordination, regulation, and control measures. However, advances in the body of knowledge are no less important today than previously to the farmer while he is trying to solve the problems resulting from these improvements. During the hundred years functions and activities have been developed, added, and transferred out of the department, but the basic ones and those required by the contemporary period remain.

THE TREASURY DEPARTMENT

The Treasury is of considerable interest not only because of its great age but also because it was the original financial institution and a department to which internal affairs could be added. Over the years it has been assigned a wide range of tasks; many remain, while others have been transferred elsewhere.

The Treasury had a strong start with Alexander Hamilton at its head. The staff of approximately fifty people multiplied sixfold in the first ten years so that by 1800 it numbered around 300. The original structure consisted of the Secretary, an Assistant Secretary, a Comptroller, an Auditor, a Register, and the Treasurer as the key officers.

The Post Office, carried over from the Continental Congress, was maintained as a separate department of the Treasury until 1829, when President Jackson asked the Postmaster General to join the Cabinet. The supervisory link to the Treasury Department occurred through the revenue yielded to the federal government by the creation and use of stamps.

The Mint of the United States was started in 1792 as a unit of the Treasury Department, in 1799 was given independent status reporting directly to the President, and in 1873 was returned to the Treasury and became the Bureau of the Mint.

The Public Health Service began as a unit of the Treasury Department in 1798. The original Collections of Customs assessed fees on the masters or owners of sailing vessels for the care and treatment of American seamen. The Marine Hospital Service, parent organization of what eventually became the Public Health Service, was developed from these fees.

The Coast Guard also originated in the Treasury in 1790 as the Revenue Cutter Service; it was later combined with other small units—the Lifesaving Service, the Lighthouse Service, and the Bureau of Marine Inspection and Navigation—to form the Coast Guard. Since 1915 the Coast Guard has operated during wartime as a service in the navy and is part of the Armed Forces, but during peacetime it still operates as a service in the Treasury Department.

Other early changes involved the Assistant to the Secretary of the Treasury, whose title was changed to Commissioner of the Revenue in 1792. In 1812 the General Land Office was added. These two changes created new units in the department on a par with those already in existence. When the Department of the Interior was formed in 1849, the General Land Office was transferred to it. The housekeeping duties of the federal government as well as functions related to land and other internal affairs were also assigned to the Interior Department.

The next major period of activity for the Treasury Department was the 1860s. The department had altered its structure to include an Assistant Secretary, thus creating a new level in the hierarchy. Employees at this time numbered approximately 3,000,[2] distributed among fourteen bureaus and divisions.

Significant additions to the Treasury's functions and activities came in 1862 with the Bureau of Engraving and Printing and the Secret Service, created to suppress counterfeiting and forgery (protecting the Chief Executive and his family was not added to their duties until after the assassination of President McKinley).

The Internal Revenue Service, which now has approximately two-

2. This includes all employees of the Custom, Lighthouse, and Revenue Cutter Service (*Official Register of the U.S., 1857–58*).

The Evolving Federal Structure

thirds of the department's employees, was also added in 1862. Some of its functions were previously performed by other sections of the department. Formal organization of the Revenue Service became necessary in the 1860s in part because of the imposition and collection of taxes at the federal level to help finance the Civil War.

The functions of the Comptroller were originally to keep the Treasury Seal and affix it to all accounts and vouchers payable to the United States government. In 1863 the Office of the Comptroller of the Currency was created by congressional act as a part of the national banking system to supervise the organization, operation, and liquidation of national banks. Charters for operating a bank could be obtained from any of the various state governments or from the federal government and were now subject to the Comptroller. The accounting functions of the Comptroller were transferred to what is now known as the General Accounting Office, since 1921 a legislative agency controlled by Congress.

At the turn of the twentieth century the Treasury Department, with approximately 28,000 employees, was composed of the following divisions and bureaus, all of which had approximately the same status: [3]

United States Treasury Department—1900

1. Secretary of the Treasury
2. Three Assistant Secretaries of the Treasury
3. Office of the Secretary (including all staff personnel for Secretary and Assistant Secretaries)
4. Office of the Chief Clerk and Superintendent
5. Secret Service Division
6. Office of the Comptroller of the Treasury
7. Office of the Comptroller of the Currency
8. Office of the Six Auditors
9. Office of the Treasurer of the United States
10. Office of the Register of the Treasury
11. Office of the Commissioner of Internal Revenue
12. Bureau of Navigation

3. Detailed organization charts of the functions of the three assistant secretaries are not available. Source: *Official Register of the U.S., 1901*, vol. 1.

13. Bureau of Statistics
14. Bureau of Engraving and Printing
15. Office of the Supervising Architect
16. United States Coast and Geodetic Survey
17. Bureau of the Mint
18. United States Assay Officer
19. United States Shipping Commissioners
20. Steamboat Inspection Services
21. Bureau of Immigration
22. National Bureau of Standards
23. Customs Service
24. Revenue Cutter Service
25. Internal Revenue Service
26. Marine Hospital Service
27. Office of the Life-Saving Service
28. Lighthouse Service

The Bureau of Standards was transferred to the Department of Commerce and Labor, organized in 1903.

The reformulation of legislation in regard to budgetary accounting and control was accomplished in 1921 with the creation of the General Accounting Office, reporting directly to Congress, and the Bureau of the Budget, which was in the Treasury Department but under the immediate direction of the President until 1939, when it was included in the units composing the Executive Office of the President.

The Bureau of Customs was established in 1927 to bring all the Treasury's functions in this area into a major unit in the department. Another addition, and with an interesting range of activities, was the Bureau of Narcotics, created in 1930. Since many illegal narcotics are smuggled in through the ports, it was appropriate to include narcotics with Treasury's functions of Coast Guard, Customs, and related activities.

In 1930 the Treasury Department organization consisted of the Secretary, the Undersecretary, three assistant secretaries, and fourteen bureaus and divisions with an approximate total of 53,000 employees.[4]

4. Does not include the enlisted personnel of the U.S. Coast Guard.

The Evolving Federal Structure

During the last thirty years the activities of the Treasury Department have expanded in three major areas—international monetary plans, increased national debt, and increased revenue resulting from high-level spending in both war and peacetime. The last point is related to sale of government securities and enforcement of the tax laws. Examples of this development were the creation of the Bureau of the Public Debt in 1940, the United States Savings Bond Division in 1945, and the Office of Defense Lending in 1957. The Office of International Finance was created in 1947 to coordinate the enlarging range of functions and activities caused by our emergence as an international power.

In 1960 the Treasury Department was composed of the Secretary, two deputy secretaries, five assistant secretaries, a general counsel, special assistants and assistants to the Secretary, twenty-seven bureau and division heads, and approximately 76,000 employees.[5] It is a classic example of the evolution of an old and major department of the federal government.

OFFICE OF EDUCATION

The Office of Education has had a varied career because of public fear that a powerful federal office of education would eventually destroy local autonomy. Structurally, this Office is significant, for it was one of the several older units put together to form the Federal Security Agency. The demands of a welfare-oriented society required cabinet status for this Agency, and it was given the name of Health, Education and Welfare.

After more than twenty years of discussion the Department of Education was established in 1867 with the following mandate:

> That there shall be established, at the city of Washington, a department of education, for the purpose of collecting such statistics and facts as shall show the condition and progress of education in the several states and territories, and of diffusing

5. Does not include the approximately 30,000 military employees of the U.S. Coast Guard.

such information respecting the organization and management of schools and school systems, and methods of teaching, as shall aid the people of the United States in the establishment and maintenance of efficient school systems, and otherwise promote the cause of education throughout the country.

That it shall be the duty of the Commissioner of Education to present annually to Congress a report embodying the results of his investigations and labors, together with a statement of such facts and recommendations as will, in his judgement, subserve the purpose for which this department is established. In the first report made by the commissioner of education under this act, there shall be presented a statement of the several grants of land made by Congress to promote education, and the manner in which these several trusts have been managed, the amount of funds arising therefrom, and the annual proceeds of the same, as far as the same can be determined.[6]

The original budget of $9,400 provided for a commissioner and three clerks. However, fears continued over the founding of a national education department. In the appropriation bill of the following year, the salary of the commissioner was reduced by $1,000, and the Department of Education became the Bureau of Education within the Department of Interior. The Office nonetheless grew and expanded; placing it in the Interior Department did not hinder its development.

In 1884 the duty of providing for the education of the children of Alaska was given to the Secretary of the Interior, who assigned it to the Commissioner of Education. From this initial assignment two more sets of activities developed. While making his inspection of Alaska in 1890, the commissioner was impressed by the limited food supply of the natives. Investigations of the problem indicated that the introduction of the domesticated Siberian reindeer would relieve the food shortage, add to the clothing supply, and provide a remunerative industry. A plan was devised to introduce the reindeer and give instruction in their care so that eventually the natives could become self-supporting and independent. The success of the program is indicated by the fact that from the 143 deer introduced in 1892 there were an estimated 180,000 in 1920.

6. *U.S. Statutes, 1867* (Washington, D.C., U.S. Government Printing Office).

The Evolving Federal Structure

The second set of activities in Alaska involved the medical aid program that resulted from the purely local and sporadic first aid given by teachers in cases of destitution and sudden illness. The burdens of such work steadily increased. To meet the lack of professional care, teachers were given medical supplies and elementary instruction in emergency aid. By 1909 contractual arrangements had been made with physicians and hospitals to serve the natives, and in 1910 a hospital was built. In 1911, at the request of the Commissioner of Education, a liaison between Education and the Public Health Service was established, and an officer was assigned to Education to aid in the supervision and instruction in medical relief and sanitation. The work of medical relief continued under the Bureau of Education even though separate funds were now granted for the work.

Although the first Morrill Act for establishing land-grant colleges was passed in 1862, it was not until the second Morrill Act of 1890 that permanent annual grants of federal funds for endowment and support of land-grant colleges were authorized. The funds were to be administered by the Secretary of the Interior, who assigned these duties to the Commissioner of Education, and in 1895 a special clerk for land-grant college statistics was approved. Funds for land-grant colleges were increased by the Nelson Amendment (1907) and the Bankhead-Jones Act (1935). The amount of money involved increased from $750,000 in 1890 to $5,052,000 in 1960. The functions performed, which were first assigned to one person, were merged into the Collegiate–Professional Section between 1900 and 1930, when the personnel numbered approximately twenty. Between 1930 and 1960 the Higher Education Division was formed and administered by an Assistant Commissioner; it absorbed the functions of the Collegiate–Professional section, and the division had a total personnel of 199 in 1960.

Federal aid to the states for vocational education below the college level was started in 1917 with the Smith-Hughes Act and administered by a Federal Board for Vocational Education. The Commissioner of Education was a member of the Board, but the functions and activities were separate from the Office of Education. In 1933 the organizational arrangement was changed, however, by Executive Order, which transferred the functions of the Federal Board for Vocational Education to the Department of the Interior, assigned to the Commissioner of Education. The Board was continued in an advisory capacity and abolished in 1946. Just prior to these additions to the Office of Education all functions relating to Alaska were taken away. The supervision of the reindeer industry was transferred to the Governor of Alaska (late 1929), and the supervision of education and medical aid for the natives of Alaska was transferred to the Office of Indian Affairs in 1931.

During World War II Student War Loans were made, and the Office of Education was authorized to collect payment on these loans.

Immediately after World War II impetus was given to international education with the passage of the Fulbright Act, which established the Board of Foreign Scholarships administered by the State Department. Legislation authorized the interchange of persons, knowledge, and skill, the rendering of technical and other services, and the interchange of developments in the field of education, arts, and science "to promote the better understanding of the United States among the peoples of the world and to strengthen cooperative international relations." [7] The Office of Education was to aid in the various programs and assist in recruitment.

Two other closely related functions were added. At the request of the Administrator of the Veterans Administration the Office was to review programs of study for veterans overseas and approve the institution of higher learning. The Attorney General was directed to consult with the Office of Education on the approval of schools for nonimmigrant aliens studying here under student visas.

Vocational education below college level was given a boost with the George-Borden Act of 1946. The act provided funds for vocational education in distributive occupations and for vocational education in agriculture, home economics, trades, and industry. It also provided that funds might be used for administration, supervision, teacher training, and vocational guidance, and for equipment and supplies for vocational instruction. Closely allied to these activities is the authorization in the federal charter of the Future Farmers of America (1950) for the Office of Education to provide facilities and personnel to assist in the administration of FFA activities. These activities would be carried on by the vocational educational

7. *Handbook on Programs of the U.S. Department of Health, Education and Welfare, 1961,* p. 180.

staff related to agriculture, which numbered fifteen people in 1960.

The Administrator of the Veterans Administration was required to use the services of the Office of Education in developing a range of cooperative educational and training programs for veterans, and the Commissioner of Education was named an *ex officio* member of the Vocational Rehabilitation and Advisory Committee to the Administrator of Veterans Administration. The Administrator of the Housing and Home Finance Agency may consult with, and secure the advice of, the Office of Education about applications for college housing loans.

Research has always been considered a part of the Bureau's activities. However, it was not until 1954 that substantially large amounts were authorized for the Commissioner to enter into contracts or jointly financed cooperative agreements with universities and colleges and state educational agencies for the conduct of research, surveys, and demonstrations in education. The coordinated impact of the research sponsored by all units of the federal government will be discussed later.

From the start library and library services have received some attention and appropriation of funds, but the greatest impetus came in 1956 with an annual appropriation of $7,500,000 for a program to extend public library services to rural areas.

The international aspects of the educational program were given further emphasis in the Mutual Security Act of 1954:

> The Office acts as agent for the Department of State in the recruitment of American educators for overseas education missions, for providing professional services on request to education missions, and for the training of foreign educators in the U.S. under the technical assistance program.[8]

The Agricultural Trade Development and Assistance Act of the same year provides for the sale of surplus agricultural commodities for foreign currencies, which may be used for international educational exchange activities authorized under the Fulbright Act and for financing programs for the interchange of persons under the Smith-Mundt Act.

8. Ibid., p. 180.

Returning to the domestic scene, a program involving large sums is the school assistance program to federally affected areas (1950-60).[9] The laws give assistance for both construction and maintenance of schools in areas affected by federal activities for children of persons who reside and work on federal property. The program was made permanent in 1958; it is referred to elsewhere, but a few comments will be made here. A total of $226,430,000 was spent by 159 people in 1960. The range of activities to assist local areas overburdened by the need to provide schools rapidly for large num-

Chart 10. Federal Security Agency, 1939

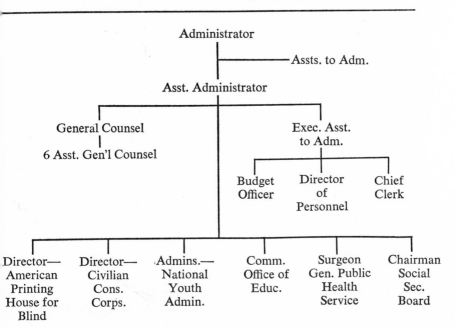

bers of children of government personnel is not an unmixed blessing. Many areas and their respective congressmen have openly sought and fought to obtain these funds; a few have recognized that they have invited the federal government into the local school system only to regret it later.

The National Defense Education Act of 1958 authorized programs in the following areas: (1) college and university student

9. Ibid., p. 184.

loan funds; (2) grants to states and loans to nonprofit private schools for purchase of equipment and improvement of state supervision to strengthen elementary and secondary school instruction in science, mathematics, and modern foreign languages; (3) fellowships for graduate study; (4) grants to states and contractual arrangements with institutions of higher learning to strengthen guidance, counseling, and testing in secondary schools and to establish institutes for secondary school guidance and counseling personnel; (5) modern foreign language institutes; (6) research and experimentation in more effective use of modern communications media for educational purposes; (7) grants to states for development of area vocational education programs in scientific or technical fields; and (8) grants to states to improve statistical services of state educational agencies.

The two major structural changes affecting the Office of Education, which were passed over earlier, will now be discussed. They are related to the increasing impact of education in the society as it shifts toward an urban, industrialized, and welfare-oriented society.

The creation of the Federal Security Agency (FSA) in 1939 (Chart 10) with the Office of Education as one of the constituent units was the most significant structural change since the early placement of the Office in the Interior Department. The purpose was to group those agencies of the government having to do with the social and economic security, educational opportunity, and health of the citizens of the nation. The reasons for regrouping them were to reduce expenditures, increase efficiency, and eliminate overlapping and duplication of effort.

In addition to the Office of Education the FSA included the Civilian Conservation Corps (CCC), the National Youth Administration (NYA), the Public Health Service, the Social Security Board, which included the U.S. Employment Service, and the American Printing House for the Blind. The Food and Drug Administration and Saint Elizabeth's Hospital were added to FSA in 1940, and the Office of Vocational Rehabilitation was added in 1943. From its inception it was structurally more like a Cabinet department than an agency. Legislation continued to add responsibilities and funds for the Office of Education to administer.

DEPARTMENT OF HEALTH, EDUCATION AND WELFARE

The other major structural change was the actual creation of the Department of Health, Education and Welfare from the Federal Security Agency in 1953, the first new Cabinet department in forty years (Chart 11). The movement for the department had bipartisan support and was not affected by the change in administration and political party in 1953. The reasons and purposes for creating the department were almost identical with those for the formation of FSA.

In the new department the oldest component part is the Public Health Service, which began in 1798 with the authorization of marine hospitals to care for merchant seamen. Saint Elizabeth's Hospital, established in 1855 in the Interior Department as the Government Hospital for the Insane, was transferred in 1940 to the Federal Security Agency. The hospital received its present name in 1916.

Three federally aided corporations that are now a part of HEW date back to 1857. Gallaudet College, created in 1857 was originally known as the Columbia Institution for the Instruction of the Deaf and the Dumb and the Blind. It was functionally related to the Interior Department until 1939, when it was transferred to the Federal Security Agency. The American Printing House for the Blind, incorporated by the Kentucky Legislature in 1858 and adopted by the Congress in 1879, is now functionally related to HEW. Howard University, established in 1867, admits students of both sexes of every race, creed, color, and national origin, but it accepts and discharges a special responsibility for the admission and training of Negro students. Originally related to the Interior Department, the functions were transferred to the Federal Security Agency in 1939.

The Food and Drug Act of 1906 provided for law enforcement functions to be carried on by different organizational groups of the Department of Agriculture. They were the functional antecedents of what was officially named the Food and Drug Administration in 1930. The administration was transferred to the Federal Security Agency in 1940.

The Children's Bureau was created in 1912 and placed in the Department of Labor in 1913. The bureau cooperates with national, state, and local organizations and agencies, both public and private, in planning for the development and extension of services for children and youth. The bureau was transferred to the Federal Security Agency and made a part of the Social Security Administration in 1946.

Legislation on Vocational Rehabilitation dates from 1920. The functions were assigned to the independent Federal Board for Vocational Education, created in 1917. The Board was transferred in 1933 to the Interior Department and assigned to the Office of Education. The Office of Vocational Rehabilitation was created in 1943 to administer the expanded program of state–federal vocational rehabilitation provided by legislation in that year.

The Social Security Administration dates from legislation starting in 1935. The original Social Security Board was transferred to the Federal Security Agency in 1939. The Social Security Administration as it is now constituted was established in 1946. The administration is composed of four bureaus: the Bureau of Old-Age and Survivors Insurance, with more than 580 district offices; the Bureau of Public Assistance; the Children's Bureau; and the Bureau of Federal Credit Unions.

In summary, the predecessor of the Department of Health, Education and Welfare, the FSA, combined several of the agencies created in the 1930s by the Franklin D. Roosevelt administration. These new agencies, together with several older units, reflected the needs of the society to better coordinate these functions and activities at the national level.

The organization structure at both the crucial points in the development of the Department of Health, Education and Welfare are shown in Charts 10 and 11. The elaborations, consolidations, and additions can be observed. Administratively the diagram for 1953 reflects the elevation of the agency to a cabinet department. The structure remained relatively the same in 1960 with approximately 70,000 employees in HEW, 1,100 of whom are in the Office of Education.

Chart 11. Health, Education, and Welfare, 1953

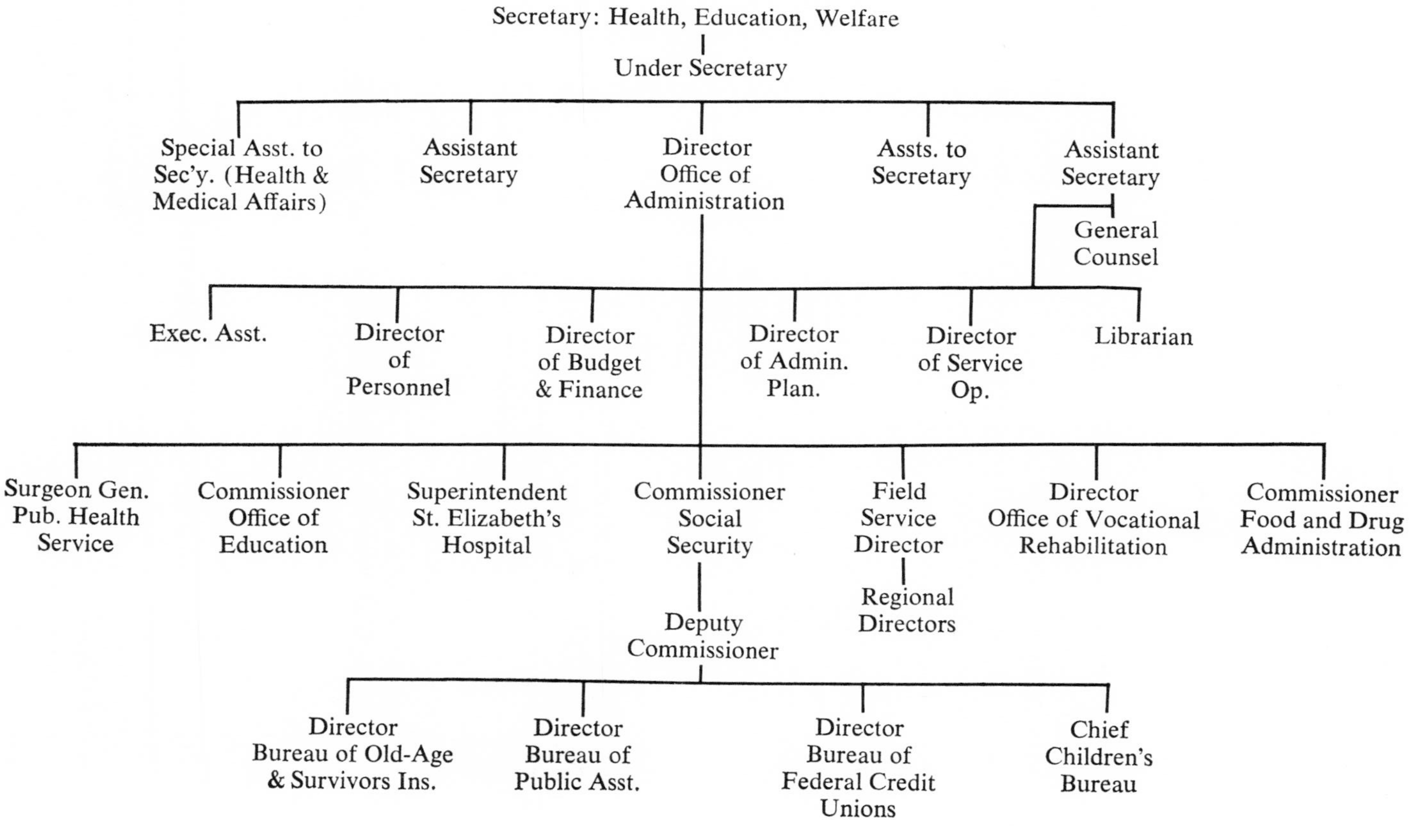

Secretary: Health, Education, Welfare

Under Secretary

Special Asst. to Sec'y. (Health & Medical Affairs)

Assistant Secretary

Assts. to Secretary

Assistant Secretary

General Counsel

Librarian

Director Office of Administration

Director of Personnel

Director of Budget & Finance

Director of Admin. Plan.

Director of Service Op.

Field Service Director

Regional Directors

Director Office of Vocational Rehabilitation

Commissioner Food and Drug Administration

Exec. Asst.

Surgeon Gen. Pub. Health Service

Commissioner Office of Education

Superintendent St. Elizabeth's Hospital

Commissioner Social Security

Deputy Commissioner

Director Bureau of Old-Age & Survivors Ins.

Director Bureau of Public Asst.

Director Bureau of Federal Credit Unions

Chief Children's Bureau

THE HOUSING AND HOME FINANCE AGENCY

The creation of the Housing and Home Finance Agency (HHFA) in 1947 is another step reflecting the degree of industrialization and urbanization of the American society. The HHFA is a collection of several other agencies that had been created to deal with various problems as they developed in prior years. Some functions and activities started in the 1930s as a result of the great depression, when the federal government moved to aid home owners through various types of loan assistance.

The development of the great urban complexes cutting across state lines in some cases and stretching in endless links caused other problems, which gave rise to further agencies and constituent units. They have all been combined into HHFA. The organization consists of five major units; two constituent units, the Community Facilities Administration and the Urban Renewal Administration, and three constituent agencies, the Federal Housing Administration, the Public Housing Administration, and the Federal National Mortgage Association.

The Federal Housing Administration was established in 1934 and has an office in each state plus the District of Columbia and Puerto Rico. When HHFA was created in 1947, FHA was one of the constituent units.

The Federal National Mortgage Association was originally chartered in 1938 and rechartered as a unit of HHFA in 1954. The association operates five area offices serving the major geographical divisions of the United States.

The Public Housing Administration was established as a unit of HHFA in 1947. It is a successor to two other agencies, the Federal Public Housing Authority and the United States Housing Authority. The FPHA was created in 1942 and assumed the duties of the USHA, which had been established in 1937.

In 1954 both the Urban Renewal Administration and the Voluntary Home Mortgage Credit Program were established. The former has a threefold program related to slum clearance, urban planning, and techniques for slum elimination. The functions of the Voluntary Home Mortgage Credit Program's national committee and seven regional committees is to help obtain private mortgage credit for FHA-insured and Veterans Administration-guaranteed loans in areas and communities where there may be inadequate facilities for such loans.

The Federal Home Loan Bank Board is the successor to organizations dating back to legislation in 1932, 1933, and 1934. Originally a part of HHFA it was made an independent agency in 1955 and assumed the functions of the boards of the Home Loan Bank Board and the Home Owners Loan Corporation.

The organization of the Housing and Home Finance Agency consisted of the Administrator, Deputy Administrator, the heads of the five major units, and between 11,000 and 12,000 employees (1960). At the founding of the Agency in 1947 the number of employees was approximately 14,000 and has tended to decline. HHFA is similar in structure to the former Federal Security Agency in resembling a Cabinet department (it recently was incorporated into a new Cabinet department) rather than a typical agency.

THE INTERSTATE COMMERCE COMMISSION

The Interstate Commerce Commission (ICC), created in 1887, is the first regulatory agency. Although the U.S. Civil Service Commission, created in 1883, was the first organization of the federal government using the agency form of structure, the ICC was the first federal agency to be used for regulatory purposes. Our shift in emphasis at this point is to highlight the introduction of a new structural form. A gradual transformation in the value and belief system of the society was necessary to allow the federal government to develop and exercise these regulatory functions over the affairs of business. The extension of these activities has paralleled the industrialization and urbanization of the society.

The Evolving Federal Structure

It is of interest that the stimulation for the ICC came from farmers and rural groups. Railroads had been developing for over thirty years when in the post-Civil War period, spurred by the Grange movement, railway regulation proposals began receiving the attention of Congress. More than 150 bills and resolutions touching on various phases of railway control were introduced by Senators and Representatives during the years 1868 to 1886. Finally, in 1887, much to the surprise and opposition of many, the compromise act to regulate commerce and establish the Interstate Commerce Commission was passed and signed by the President. Although fraught with all the problems inherent in the establishment of any new and exploratory organization, the Commission rapidly gained respect and prestige. The initial organization was composed of five commissioners, a secretary as chief administrative officer, three divisions, and a total of thirty-two employees.

Despite the later efforts of the Commission, the law was so written that recourse to the courts was necessary. Conflicts in interpretation after ten years left the Commission with little regulatory power. Some additional legislation helped strengthen it, and in 1906 the Hepburn Act gave the Commission definite if limited regulatory authority. The Commission was also increased from five to seven members. In 1911 the organization consisted of seven commissioners, a secretary, seven major divisions each reporting to its respective commissioner, and more than 500 employees.

In 1917 the number of commissioners and the number of major divisions were increased to nine. A general secretary with now approximately 1,550 employees continued to function along with the commissioners.

The Transportation Act of 1920 increased the commissioners' duties and responsibilities. Commissioners were increased to the present number, eleven. The railways were on the whole fairly prosperous when the depression set in despite the increase in competiton for other means of transportation. By 1930 the Commission had a peak of around 2,300 employees organized in thirteen bureaus.

Legislation of the 1930s brought changes to the ICC for most areas of activity. Most important was the Motor Carrier Act of 1935. The commission was now exercising complete or partial authority over railroads, motor carriers, water lines, express companies, pipelines, sleeping car companies, private transportation facilities when in the service of common carriers subject to its jurisdiction, and airmail carriers. The regulation of airmail rates was transferred to the Civil Aeronautics Authority in 1938. The Transportation Act of 1940 extended the Commission's authority over water carriers, transferring some authority from the Maritime Commission.

The numbers of employees of the Commission has varied considerably over the past thirty years. Low points in employment were 1936 (1,600), 1945 (1,900), and 1954 (1,800). The Commission is now organized with a Chairman, a Vice Chairman, the Secretary, the managing director (a recent addition), the general counsel, ten bureaus, thirteen regions with eighty-eight offices, plus an office in Alaska, and approximately 2,400 employees.

The ICC has persisted in spite of the variety of opinion about the role it should play. Further, it has been the prototype for other regulatory agencies such as the Federal Reserve System, Federal Trade Commission, Federal Power Commission, Federal Communications Commission, Securities and Exchange Commission, National Labor Relations Board, Civil Aeronautics Board, and Federal Aviation Agency. As technology has advanced and changes in the social order have occurred, additional areas of business activity have been brought under the purview of the federal government and appropriate agencies created as overseers.

THE FUNCTION–STRUCTURE RELATIONSHIP

Structurally speaking, the classic evolutionary phases that these examples demonstrate are the movement from individuals, to sections, to divisions, to bureaus, and potential or actual independent departments. A series of statuses or positions is created around a series of functions and activities to be performed. Some of these positions and their functions are specialized to the activities for which

The Evolving Federal Structure

the department or agency was created. Others, common to all functioning organizations, are related to its maintenance, perpetuation, growth, and development and are necessary to its success. For growth and proliferation to take place the functions of each status or position are initially segmented and specialized, and new ones are added as required by growth or the addition of new activities.

In the examples, the Department of Agriculture in particular, it is shown through time in the various charts that the original Chief Clerk is now known as the Assistant Secretary for Administration and has an elaborated hierarchical set of positions supporting him. This elaboration of structure resulted from specialization necessitated by the increased size and complexity of the structure as well as by technological advances in methods. The Agriculture Department has grown from one person to approximately 100,000 persons in slightly over one hundred years. During this period the advances in budgeting, cost accounting, personnel techniques, and administrative practices and procedures have all led to the elaborate administrative structure. Structure, size, money handled, number of employees, and range of functions are all highly interrelated and mutually influence and interact as variables to shape the individual organizational units and the entire federal government structure.

Before concluding this chapter it is necessary to shift attention to an analysis of functions and weld structure and function together. One way of analyzing functions for any given organization in order to gain better insight into how they grow and develop is the following classification.

1. Assigned: Those functions and activities specifically stated in legislative or executive acts and thereby delegated to the department, agency, or bureau. These are the functions we have been discussing above.

2. Auxiliary: Those functions and activities an organization must perform in order to carry out its assigned functions but for which no explicit assignment will ever be made.

3. Administrative-Bureaucratic: Those functions related to the rationalized defining and ordering of functions into positions structured hierarchically and considered necessary for efficient operation as the organization ages and develops.

This classification is sufficiently general to apply to any organization whether it be a business, a government department, or an association.

As examples of assigned functions the first cabinet post (State) and one of the most recent cabinet posts (Health, Education and Welfare) will be used.

> Be it enacted . . . that there shall be an Executive Department, to be denominated the Department of Foreign Affairs and that there shall be a principal office . . . to be called the Secretary for the department of Foreign Affairs, who shall perform and execute such duties as shall from time to time be enjoined on or intrusted to him by the President of the U. S., agreeable to the Constitution, relative to correspondences, commissions or instructions to or with public ministers from foreign states or princes, or to memorials or other applications from foreign public ministers or other foreigners, or to such other matters respecting foreign affairs, as the President of the U. S. shall assign to the said department; add furthermore, that the said principal officer shall conduct the business of the said department in such manner as the President of the U. S. shall from time to time order or instruct.[10]

In contrast to this elaborate statement, the Department of Health, Education and Welfare was created by Executive Order of the President "for the purpose of improving the administration of those agencies of the government the major responsibilities of which are to promote the general welfare in the fields of health, education, and social security." [11]

The mandate examples given, as well as most others, stake out an area of activity; however, the specifics relating to the accomplishment of the major purpose are not stated. The assumption is that those administering the organization will within prudent limits perform all those functions and activities for the successful operation of the organization.

The other two types of functions and activities are necessary and

10. *U.S. Statutes,* Session I (Washington, D.C., U.S. Government Printing Office), Chapter 4, July 31, 1789.
11. *U.S. Government Organization Manual,* 1959–60.

can be anticipated in general. However, the actual structural form in which they will be revealed is related to the evolution and the needs of the organization as they change through time.

The auxiliary functions tend to be those that are partially unique to the organization in that no two organizations necessarily perform these functions nor need they be performed in the same way. However, most organizations have to perform some of them, which denies some of the uniqueness. Many of these functions tend to relate the organization to its environment and to other organizations and elements of the greater society. In brief, the auxiliary functions include the external as opposed to internal functions but are not limited exclusively to these aspects of the organization.

In almost all cases the department, agency, or bureau must set up a group to perform liaison activities with the Congress. Another equally important area in many cases is the public information section, which relates the organization to the greater society. Another series of important relationships is establishing lines of communications and operating procedures between the organization and the Executive Group at the White House as well as the other necessary government organizations. The office of a legal general counsel is found almost consistently throughout the major departments, agencies, and bureaus. More specific examples may be given. The earlier references to the Office of Education, which became involved in raising reindeer and administering the medical program in Alaska, are illustrative. In its annual *Handbook on Programs* the Department of Health, Education and Welfare lists by section the associations most closely related to the interests and activities of that particular division of the department. The attitudes and opinions of the financial community, large investors, and the general public are of concern to the Treasury Department in the marketing of all types of government securities. The Department of Agriculture has complex sets of relationships with the land-grant colleges, extension programs, farm associations for the adult and youth, and agricultural education in the secondary schools.

The administrative–bureaucratic functions are readily apparent and tend to elaborate and grow parallel with the growth of the organization. These functions and activities are generally found under the direction of an administrative assistant secretary or director of administrative services. In some cases there may be some more careful delineation and separation of functions. However, the following divisions will be found in some form: budget and finance, management, security, audit and comptroller, and others that will be specific to the particular department or agency.

These administrative functions develop with size and are a function of size. With specialization, rationalization of procedures, and the elaboration of hierarchies, these administrative functions become necessary and facilitating. The more rationalized the system becomes, the closer in many ways it approximates the Weberian model.[12] However, as current research indicates, there are dysfunctional effects of bureaucratization, as well as functional, because of the human element. Humanity appears to be incapable of functioning as the "ideal model" would propose. Thus the bureaucratic process to rationalize systems for efficient organization to achieve group ends becomes the end in itself, and the initial ends are lost in the process.

Observance of the above phenomenon has led to the question, "Is there an organizational multiplier?"[13] The question involves the relationship of the three types of functions as revealed in terms of numbers of people. The problem is perhaps most clearly seen in a military example—how many men are needed behind the lines or in the various rear echelons to keep one fighting man going? Industry as well as government is faced with and concerned with this problem.

The federal government taken as a whole continues to add functions and to administer existing functions to larger numbers of people and in a more complete way, all of which requires more employees.

However, the various departments and agencies examined earlier in the chapter did not show the same growth patterns. The oldest of the departments, Treasury, has had a long, continuously increasing growth. Some of Treasury's functions are such that growth will probably continue.

The Agriculture Department, like Treasury, has had a very decided growth and increase from the beginning. However, because

12. Max Weber, *Theory of Social and Economic Organization,* trans. Henderson and Parsons (Glencoe, Illinois, Free Press, 1957).

13. H. G. Hicks and B. B. Graves, "Is There an Organizational Multiplier?" *Academy of Management Journal* (March 1963), p. 70.

The Evolving Federal Structure

the agricultural programs have been so successful, the percentage of the population engaged in farming has been steadily declining. The apparent paradox, then, is that we have a case of more people administering to relatively fewer people. Some reasons for the paradox relate to the "surplus" program and the various aid, marketing, and conservation programs devised to cope with it.

Health, Education and Welfare is another type. Originally, several well established units were combined to form the new independent Federal Security Agency, which always resembled a cabinet department more than an agency. After functioning as an agency for fourteen years it was renamed and made an addition to the Cabinet. The administration of many of the functions and activities of this department would not appear to be on the decline. Continued growth in terms of number of employees and money seems certain.

The Office of Education has experienced considerable growth by some definitions but not relative to the growth pattern and size of some of the other government departments and agencies. Perhaps this stems from the strongly ambivalent feelings that have always surrounded it that if the department became too strong, education would become nationalized. The right to control education at the local level has always been jealously guarded, although technically speaking the function is the states' responsibility and is delegated to the local community. Although the Office of Education administers ever increasing sums of money, its relative strength appears weak.

The first regulatory agency, the Interstate Commerce Commission, has experienced a slow, gradual growth. As the case load has increased with additional types of carriers to be scrutinized, increases in personnel and budget have been necessary. A continuance of this growth pattern appears certain unless unusual functions and activities are added to the Commission's responsibilities.

An agency recently groomed for and now in the Cabinet is the Housing and Home Finance Agency. Like Health, Education and Welfare, it was formed from several existing units which gave it a ready-made appearance. With the loss of the Home Loan Bank Board in 1955 the total number of employees declined by several thousand. The agency's lowest employment was in 1957, when there was also a decline in the number of employees in the Public Housing Administration. Since this low point, however, there has been a slow but gradual increase that will probably continue as urbanization is accepted as the way of life.

These departments and agencies merely give examples of the processes that have been going on in all of the constituent units of the federal government. The study of the individual units reveals the process of gradual elaboration, reorganization to simplify into a smaller number of larger units reporting to the top, and usual increase in the number of layers and horizontal divisions in the hierarchy. The evolution and emergence of a vast federal hierarchy administering an increasing range of functions and activities is concomitant with the emergence of the national society.

Index

JUNE M. COLLINS, Associate Professor of Social Anthropology, Southern Illinois University, is a social anthropologist and sociologist. She has done extensive research in the United States and Mexico and has published on modern American life and Indian culture.

GEORGE D. DOWNING, Chairman of the Department of Marketing, Arizona State University, and formerly an executive at General Electric, is a specialist on business organization and a consultant on the problems of corporate enterprise.

ROBERT J. HAVIGHURST, Professor of Education, University of Chicago, has done many years of research on American education, on its institutions, and on American life. He is author or coauthor of numerous books, including *Society and Education, The Public Schools of Chicago, Growing Up In River City,* and *American Higher Education in the 1960's.*

WILLIAM E. HENRY, Professor of Psychology and Human Development, University of Chicago, has done extensive research on the personalities of executives in business and in government. He is the author of many professional publications, among them *The Analysis of Fantasy.*

DESMOND D. MARTIN, Assistant Professor of Management, University of Cincinnati, is at present continuing research on the structure and functions of trade associations.

FRANK C. NALL II, Assistant Professor of Sociology, Southern Illinois University, is coauthor of "Service, Professional, and other Civic Clubs," in *Rural Social Systems and Adult Education.* He has acted as research consultant to a variety of national associations.

JOHN H. TRIMM, Assistant Professor of Management, University of Arizona, has done research on American corporations and governmental organizations and contributed to the research for *The American Federal Executive.*

DARAB B. UNWALLA, Associate Professor of Management, Michigan State University, is the author or coauthor of *The Enterprising Man, Human Relations in Industry: Textile Technocracy,* and *Automation: Rationalization and Human Relations in the Textile Industry.*

W. LLOYD WARNER, University Professor of Social Research, Michigan State University, has done extensive research on American society. He is the author or coauthor of several books, including *Yankee City Series, Big Business Leaders in America, The American Federal Executive,* and *Social Class in America.*

GIBSON WINTER, Professor in the Divinity School, University of Chicago, is the author of many articles and several books, including *The Suburban Captivity of the Churches, Love and Conflict, New Patterns in Family Life,* and *The New Creation as Metropolis.*